THE ECLIPSE OF
A GREAT POWER

Modern Britain 1870–1992

Foundations of modern Britain

General editor: *Geoffrey Holmes*

THE TRANSFORMATION OF MEDIEVAL ENGLAND
1370–1529
John A. F. Thomson

THE EMERGENCE OF A NATION STATE
The commonwealth of England 1529–1660
Alan G. R. Smith

THE MAKING OF A GREAT POWER
Late Stuart and Early Georgian Britain
1660–1722
Geoffrey Holmes

THE AGE OF OLIGARCHY
Pre-Industrial Britain 1722–1783
Geoffrey Holmes and Daniel Szechi

THE FORGING OF THE MODERN STATE
Early industrial Britain 1783–1870
Eric J. Evans

THE ECLIPSE OF A GREAT POWER
Modern Britain 1870–1992. Second Edition
Keith Robbins

THE ECLIPSE OF A GREAT POWER
Modern Britain 1870–1992

SECOND EDITION

Keith Robbins

LONGMAN
LONDON AND NEW YORK

Longman Group Limited
Longman House, Burnt Mill, Harlow
Essex CM20 2JE, England
and Associated Companies throughout the world.

Published in the United States of America
by Longman Publishing, New York

© Keith Robbins 1983, 1994

First published 1983
Seventh impression 1993
Second edition 1994

British Library Cataloguing-in-Publication Data
A catalogue record for this book is
available from the British Library.

ISBN 0 582 09612X CSD
     0 582 096111 PPR

Library of Congress Cataloguing-in-Publication Data

Robbins, Keith
    The eclipse of a great power: modern Britain, 1870–1992/Keith Robbins. — 2nd ed.
       p.   cm. — (Foundations of modern Britain)
    Includes index.
    ISBN 0–582–09612–X (cased). — ISBN 0–582–09611–1 (paper)
    1. Great Britain—History—Victoria, 1837–1901. 2. Great Britain—History—20th century.
I. Title. II. Series.
    DA560.R53   1994
    941.081—dc20
                                                                                    94–841
                                                                                    CIP

Produced by Longman Singapore Publishers Pte Ltd
Printed in Singapore

Contents

Contents

Editor's foreword

So prodigious has been the output of specialised work on British history during the past twenty years, and so rich its diversity, that scholars and students thirst continually after fresh syntheses. Even those who read for the pure pleasure of informing themselves about the past have become quite reconciled to the fact that little can now be taken for granted. An absorbing interest in local situations, as a way to understanding more general ones; a concern with those processes of social change which accompany economic, educational and cultural development, and which often condition political activity too: these and many other strong currents of modern historiography have washed away some of our more comfortable orthodoxies. Even when we know *what* happened, there is endless scope for debate about *why* things happened and with what consequences.

In such circumstances a new series of general textbooks on British history would not seem to call for elaborate justification. However, the six volumes constituting *Foundations of Modern Britain* do have a distinct rationale and they embody some novel features. For one thing, they make a serious attempt to present a history of Britain from the point at which 'Britain' became first a recognisable entity and then a Great Power, and to trace the foundations of this state in the history of pre-eighteenth-century England. The fact that five of the six authors either have taught or are teaching in Scottish universities, while one has held a chair in the University of Wales, should at least help to remind them that one aim of the series is to avoid excessive Anglo-centricity. The first two volumes, spanning the years 1370–1660, will certainly concentrate primarily on the history of England, emphasising those developments which first prepared the way for, and later confirmed her emergence as an independent 'Commonwealth', free from Continental trammels whether territorial or ecclesiastical. But the reader should also be aware, as he reads them, of England's ultimate role as the heart of a wider island kingdom in which men of three nations came to be associated. During the period covered by volumes 3, 4 and 5, 1660–1870, this 'United Kingdom of Great Britain' became not only a domestic reality but the centre of an Empire and the possessor of world-wide influence. Space will allow only limited treatment of Ireland and of Anglo-Irish relations until after the Union of 1801. It is appropriate, however, that in the final volume of the series reasserted nationalism should figure almost as strongly as the erosion of imperial status in the story of Britain's slide down the slippery slope from palmy greatness to anxious mediocrity. The terminal date of volume 6, 1975, is deliberately chosen: the year in which

Britain, tortured once again by her Irish inheritance and facing demands for Scottish devolution, or even independence, belatedly recognised that the days of complacent self-sufficiency as regards Europe, too, were past.

As well as paying more than mere lip-service to its own title, the present series adopts an irreverent attitude to time-honoured chronological divisions. Those lines of demarcation between volumes which dominated virtually every English history series conceived before 1960 (and, with a few exceptions, have displayed a remarkable capacity for survival subsequently) are seen as a quite unnecessary obstacle to readers' understanding of the way modern historiography has reshaped whole vistas of our island's history in the past forty years. Years such as 1485, 1603, 1689, 1714, 1760 or 1815 established themselves in textbook lore at a time when they accurately reflected the heavily political and constitutional emphasis of traditional history teaching. Even on those terms they have become of limited utility. But equally seriously, the conventions which such divisions perpetuate often make it extremely difficult for authors to accommodate fundamental aspects of social and economic development within their allotted compass. The brutal slicing off of 'Tawney's century' (1540–1640) at 1603 is perhaps the worst of these atrocities; but it is not the only one.

All dates are to some extent arbitrary as lines of division, and all present their own difficulties. It is hoped, none the less, that those selected in this series to enclose periods which are in any case a good deal longer than average, may prove less inhibiting and confusing than some of their predecessors and much more adaptable to the needs of British history courses in universities and colleges.

In one further important respect the authors have kept in mind the practical requirements of students and teachers. Their approach eschews lengthy narrative wherever possible and concentrates, within chapters short enough to be rapidly absorbed, on the development of themes and the discussion of problems. Yet at the same time they attempt to satisfy their readers' need for basic information in two ways: by providing, at appropriate stages, skeletal 'frameworks' of events, chronologically ordered, within which the subsequent analysis and interplay of argument can be set; and by placing at the end of each volume a 'compendium' of factual data, including statistics, on a scale much greater than that of normal textbook appendices.

These compendia are essential companions to the texts and are designed for ready and constant use. The frequent references to them which punctuate so many chapters in this series will be found within square brackets, for example thus [B]. They should be easily distinguishable from the numerous arabic numbers within round brackets inserted in each text, e.g. (117). These refer readers to the Bibliography, in which most items are thematically arranged and serially numbered. Superior numerals are for the references which appear at the end of the relevant chapter.

Geoffrey Holmes

Preface to the First Edition

The mass of material which confronts the historian of this period is daunting. Despite the scope of this volume its coverage cannot be comprehensive. However, within its four-part structure, central themes (with variations) are pursued from the beginning to the end. Each part is preceded by a chronology setting out for each year some of the most important political, social and cultural developments. The bibliography has been compiled on a thematic basis. Specific reference notes have been kept to a minimum. They indicate, to a degree, the range of the author's indebtedness to other scholars, but all such help cannot be acknowledged in a work of this kind as comprehensively as might otherwise have been possible. The writer's chief personal debt is to the general editor of this series, Professor Geoffrey Holmes, who has guided and criticized with exemplary thoroughness. The discussion of cricket is only one of a number of topics to benefit from his Yorkshire shrewdness. Dr E. J. Evans, who is writing the preceding volume, has also been helpful.

My family has tolerated this book with a properly diminishing degree of patience, for which I am grateful.

Llanfairfechan/Glasgow
May 1981

Preface to the Second Edition

The second edition of this book has enabled me to add a select number of suggestions for further reading to the existing bibliography. The final part of this volume, taking the account down to 1993, is entirely new. The treatment is broadly comparable to that adopted in the four parts of the original book. The writing of contemporary history is a hazardous business and the assessment attempted here makes no claim that its stopping point coincides with an epoch-making transition. There were, however, some years in which it was at least claimed that Britain was 'great' again. Talk of 'decline' or even, more circumspectly, of the 'eclipse of a great power' seemed to more optimistic writers redolent of that sense of crisis in the late 1970s when the book was originally composed. It will be for the reader to decide how far developments discussed in the new part have indeed made its title inappropriate. This second edition was completed as news was received of the death of Professor Geoffrey Holmes, the general editor of the series of which it is a part. His poor health precluded the possibility that this volume could benefit from his meticulous attention. It is appropriate, however, to pay tribute to his original inspiration in shaping the foundations. All the contributors are glad that the success of the series gave him quiet satisfaction and rejoice in its completion with the appearance of his own volumes.

University of Wales
Lampeter
November 1993

List of Maps

To the memory of
Edith Carpenter (née Tuckfield), 1887–1978
Henry James Carpenter, 1888–1975
Edith Ellen Robbins (née Williams), 1884–1967
A historian was probably not what they expected their grandson to become, but they enriched his early years and, incidentally, taught him much about their century.
Gilbert Robbins, 1881–1941
A German bomb (p. 186) destroyed his shop and his spirit, but the only grandson he knew salutes his achievement.

PART ONE

1870–1901

FRAMEWORK OF EVENTS 1870–1901

1870   Order in Council reforms Civil Service (except Foreign Office): War Office Act –
        Commander-in-Chief subordinated to Secretary of State: Franco-Prussian War
        (July–Sept), followed by siege of Paris: Irish Land Act: W. E. Forster's Educa-
        tion Act: Married Women's Property Act.
            Papal infallibility decree: W. G. Grace and his brothers found Gloucestershire
        Cricket Club.

1871   Paris capitulates and armistice with Prussia signed (Jan): London conference
        abrogates Black Sea clauses of 1856 treaty: Trade Union Act and Criminal Law
        Amendment Act – trade unions legalized and their funds protected as Friendly
        Societies, picketing again illegal: 'Parliamentary committee' of TUC formed.
            University Tests Act – allows students to enter Oxford and Cambridge without
        religious tests: Abolition of 'purchase' in British Army (July): English FA Cup
        competition established: Bank holidays introduced in England and Wales.

1872   National Agricultural Labourers Union (May): Ballot Act – voting by secret bal-
        lot and abolition of public nomination (July): Geneva arbitration verdict on the
        Alabama case: Murder of Lord Mayo, Viceroy of India.

1873   Gladstone resigns after defeat of Irish University Bill (Mar) – resumes office when
        Disraeli refuses to form a minority administration: Judicature Act brings together
        (England and Wales) the Courts of Common Law, Chancery, Admiralty, Probate
        and the Divorce Court into one Supreme Court of Judicature, divided into the
        High Court of Justice and the Court of Appeal: Ashanti War – expedition from
        coastal settlements against Kumasi.
            Foundation of Girton College Cambridge.

1874   Kumasi falls (Feb) and first Ashanti War ends: Fiji islands annexed (Oct): Gener-
        al Election (Feb): New Cons. gvt appoints Royal Commission on the labour laws:
        Factory Act reduces working week to 56½ hours (Aug).
            Public Worship Act attempts to curb ritualism in the Church of England.

1875   Gladstone resigns Liberal leadership in the Commons (Jan) – Lord Hartington re-
        places him (Feb): Public Health Act – brings order and comprehensiveness to the
        duties of local authorities in sanitation and public health generally: Artisans'
        Dwellings Act: Food and Drugs Act: Plimsoll's Merchant Shipping Act: Conspira-
        cy and Protection of Property Act – legalizes peaceful picketing: Employers and
        Workmen Act – penalty for breach of contract limited to payment of civil dam-
        ages: Gvt purchase of Suez Canal Co. shares.
            Trial by Jury begins Gilbert and Sullivan partnership.

1876   Queen Victoria becomes Empress of India: Gladstone's pamphlet on *The Bulga-
        rian Horrors* . . .: Disraeli becomes earl of Beaconsfield.
            Hans Richter conducts concerts in London: Alexander Graham Bell invents
        telephone.

1877   Failure of Constantinople conference on reforming Ottoman Empire (Jan): Lon-
        don protocol on Turkish reforms (Mar) – Sultan rejects (Apr): Russia declares
        war on Ottoman Turkey (Apr): Annexation of Transvaal (Apr): Prisons Act – all
        local prisons brought under control of the Home Office: National Liberal Federa-
        tion formed (Apr).
            All-England Lawn Tennis Championship first played at Wimbledon.

1878   Fleet sent to Constantinople. Derby (Foreign Secretary) resigns but later with-
        draws when fleet is recalled: Treaty of San Stefano between Russia and Turkey
        (Mar) – British gvt calls out reserves and sends Indian troops to Malta. Derby

3

resigns and is succeeded by Salisbury (Apr): Britain administers Cyprus – Congress and Treaty of Berlin (June–July): Afghan War (Nov–May 1879).

W. Booth founds Salvation Army: Roman Catholic hierarchy restored in Scotland: Convention for formation of a Universal Postal Union: Gilchrist and Thomas perfect their process for steel manufacture: Swan's carbon filament lamp.

1879   Zulu War – British defeat at Isandhlwana (Jan) – peace (Sept): Further fighting in Afghanistan (Sept–Oct): Austro-German Dual Alliance signed: Irish Land League formed: Gladstone's electoral campaign in Midlothian (Nov–Dec): Transvaal republic proclaimed (Dec).

Edison perfects electric light.

1880   General Election (April) – Liberal victory: The Bradlaugh affair (May–June): Employers Liability Act – compensation for workmen if negligence by employer established for industrial injuries: 'Boycotting' begins in Ireland: Transvaal declares independence – war (Oct).

First test match between England and Australia.

1881   British defeats at Laing's Nek and Majuba Hill (Jan–Feb), Pretoria Convention (Apr) concedes independence to the two Afrikaner states subject to the suzerainty of the British Crown: Irish MPS obstruct Commons business (Jan–Feb), Habeas Corpus suspended in Ireland: Irish Land Act (Aug): imprisonment of Parnell (Oct): Beaconsfield dies (Apr), Salisbury leads Tories in Lords and Northcote in Commons: Rising of Arabi Pasha in Egypt (Sept).

Revised version of the New Testament published.

1882   'Kilmainham treaty' – agreement between Gladstone and Parnell – and murders in Phoenix Park, Dublin (May): Arabi Pasha leads anti-foreign riots in Alexandria (June) – navy bombards Alexandria (July) – Bright resigns from Cabinet – Egyptians defeated at Tel-el-Kebir (Sept) – followed by occupation of Egypt and Sudan – Arabi Pasha banished: Married Women's Property Act gives married women in England and Wales rights to separate ownership of property (Aug).

1883   Corrupt and Illegal Practices Act reduces election expenditure and increases penalties for corrupt practices (Aug): Mahdi rebellion leads to evacuation of the Sudan: Social Democratic Federation consolidated.

Boys' Brigade founded in Glasgow: J. Seeley's *Expansion of England*.

1884   London convention on the Transvaal (Feb): Gordon sent to the Sudan – The Mahdi takes Omdurman: Imperial Federation League founded: Fabian Society formed: Royal Commission on the housing of the working classes appointed: Third Reform Act (Dec).

Parsons produces first practical steam-engine for making electricity.

1885   The Mahdi takes Khartoum, General Gordon dies (Jan): Russian occupation of Penjdeh, Afghanistan, provokes Anglo-Russian crisis (Mar): Compromise settlement over Afghanistan frontier (Sept): Redistribution Act establishes modern pattern of constituencies (June): Convention regarding Egyptian finances: Gladstone resigns following hostile amendment to the budget – Salisbury PM (June): Scottish Secretaryship established: General Election (Nov): Gold discovered in the Transvaal: Third Burmese War begins (Oct).

1886   Annexation of Upper Burma (Jan): Salisbury resigns, being defeated in the Commons – Gladstone becomes PM: Irish Home Rule Bill introduced (Apr): Liberal party splits – gvt defeated (June): General Election – Cons. victory (Jul): Indian National Congress formed (Dec).

Severn Tunnel opened: Royal Commission on the Scottish Highlands: First Amateur Golf Championship: *English Historical Review* commences.

1887 First Colonial Conference held (Apr): Queen Victoria's Golden Jubilee: Mediterranean and Near Eastern agreements with Italy and Austria (Feb, March, Dec): 'Bloody Sunday' demonstrations in Trafalgar Square (Nov): Cymru Fydd group in Welsh politics.

1888 Local Government Act establishes county councils in England and Wales (Aug): Strike of women match workers employed by Bryant and May.
Dunlop invents pneumatic tyre.

1889 London dock strike (Aug–Sept): Naval Defence Act: Formation of the London County Council.
C. Booth, *Life and Labour of the People in London* (first vol.)

1890 Britain exchanges Heligoland for Zanzibar and Pemba: Housing of the Working Classes Act: Parnell resigns as leader of the Irish Nationalists (Dec).
Failure of Baring's Bank: Free elementary education in England: Forth bridge completed: H. M. Stanley, *In Darkest Africa*.

1891 Hartington becomes duke of Devonshire – J. Chamberlain succeeds him as Liberal Unionist leader in Commons: 'Newcastle programme' adopted by National Liberal Federation and 'endorsed' by Gladstone – encourages allotments, local option (drink), church disestablishment in Scotland and Wales and various electoral reforms: Death of Parnell (Oct).
W. Morris, *News from Nowhere*: Conan Doyle, *Sherlock Holmes*: Free primary education.

1892 General Election (July): Gladstone succeeds Salisbury as PM.

1893 First meeting of the Independent Labour party – in Bradford – under Keir Hardie: National Free Labour Association formed: Second Irish Home Rule Bill – rejected in the Lords (Sept): Matabele rising in S. Rhodesia (July): Franco-Russian alliance: Franco-British agreement on Siam.

1894 Gladstone resigns as PM – succeeded by Rosebery (Mar): Harcourt's budget introduces death duties (Apr): Parish councils established in England: Spencer's naval building programme: Uganda annexed.

1895 Rosebery gvt defeated in Commons, General Election, Salisbury PM, J. Chamberlain becomes Colonial Secretary: Jameson Raid (S. Africa) (Dec).
London School of Economics and Political Science founded: National Trust formed.

1896 Jameson surrenders, Rhodes resigns as PM of Cape Colony (Jan): Further rising in Matabeleland (Mar–Oct): Rosebery resigns Liberal leadership (Oct).
National Portrait Gallery opened; *Daily Mail* first published: Sunday opening of Museums.

1897 Queen Victoria's Diamond Jubilee: Second Colonial Conference: Workmen's Compensation Act (Aug): Formation of the Scottish TUC.
Tate Gallery opened.

1898 Kitchener defeats Mahdist forces at Omdurman (Sept): 'Fashoda crisis' between Britain and France follows: Irish Local Government Act follows the English pattern.

1899 Campbell-Bannerman succeeds Harcourt as Liberal leader (Jan): Bloemfontein Conference between Britain and the S. African republics (Mar–July): Settlement of British Guiana/Venezuela boundary dispute: Establishment of the Board of Education: Boer War begins (Oct), British forces sustain early defeats at Magersfontein and Colenso (Dec), Roberts and Kitchener appointed Commander-in-Chief and Chief of Staff respectively.

1900 Formation of the Labour Representation Committee to organize 'Labour' parliamentary candidatures (Feb): Capture of Bloemfontein (Mar), Relief of Mafeking (May) and annexation of Orange Free State: Boxer Rising in China (May): General Election (Oct) – Cons. victory.

First issue of *Daily Express*.

1901   Inauguration of the Commonwealth of Australia (Jan): Death of Queen Victoria (Jan): PM's confidential memorandum on Britain's 'isolation' (May): J. Chamberlain speaks on British–German relations at Edinburgh (Oct): Hay–Pauncefote treaty with the United States: Taff Vale judgement confirms that trade unions can be sued for damages for actions taken by their agents.

Formation of the British Academy: B. S. Rowntree, *Poverty*.

Prologue

Strange though it may seem, in 1870 a small group of islands off the mainland of Europe dominated a large part of the world. The 'British' were established in Newfoundland and New Zealand, Cape Colony and Calcutta, Nova Scotia and New South Wales, to name but a few. Their influence was ubiquitous. A century later, with a few small exceptions, the British were confined to their islands. No other people in the modern world has experienced such a dramatic change. Yet, even in 1870, the vast area of the globe shaded red was deceptive, masking an infinite variety of control. While in a sense the empire was something which 'belonged' to the British Crown, and the British had settled in Canada, New Zealand, 'Australia' and 'South Africa', it did not constitute a homogeneous whole. The areas of settlement were substantially self-governing. Canadians, however, to take but one example, were not 'foreigners' and English-speaking Canadians considered themselves in some sense British. The citizens of Durban, Sydney, Toronto or Birmingham might all be accommodated within a framework of imperial unity. From the very outset, therefore, an ambiguity surrounded the British and a simple antithesis between exuberant self-confidence in 1870 and dismal self-doubt a century later is unsatisfactory. So is a contrast between an imperial state and a European state, or between cohesion and confusion in culture and religion. If such a view contains some truth, the full picture is more blurred. The eclipse of a Great Power is a complex process, operating at many different levels. Thus, this is not merely a history of England, with a few pious gestures to the periphery, but of the experience of the United Kingdom as a whole. Its social, cultural, political, economic and religious complexity is considered in a framework not normally attempted. It reflects a conviction that the conflicting conceptions the British had of themselves had, in turn, a subtle bearing on their place in the world.

CHAPTER 1

The nature of the United Kingdom

'It certainly does look', wrote the Home Secretary, Matthews, to Lord Salisbury in 1887, 'as though the spirit of nationality, which has united Germany and Italy, were operating to disintegrate this country.'(122) Such private gloom contrasts strongly with the public celebrations which were to honour Queen Victoria's Jubilee. It was a recognition that the United Kingdom, the heart of the empire, was a multinational state which could be divided in a number of ways. It could become a federation, or England, Ireland, Scotland and Wales could become sovereign states, or Ireland could separate from Great Britain. Such developments could happen, but most late Victorians believed that the United Kingdom could accommodate differences of culture, language and religion.

ENGLAND

England dominated the United Kingdom, much as Prussia dominated imperial Germany. The various acts of union which had produced the constitutional structure as it existed in 1870 reflected England's strength. The disparity in power and population, evident enough in 1707 and 1801, had become even more marked in the nineteenth century. England was by far the most populous element in the United Kingdom and its population continued to grow at a proportionally faster rate [A]. England had a remarkable history as a centralized state. Even if regional differences of speech, custom and diet between, say, Yorkshire and Devon, were striking, English identity was not in doubt. England could absorb the steady trickle of immigrants from the European mainland and from Ireland, Scotland and Wales. Some of these settlers mingled solely with their compatriots in church, club or pub and kept alive their consciousness of difference. The compact and distinctive pattern of non-English British settlement was particularly evident in a city like Liverpool, but it was repeated in other major English cities. A Scotsman even penetrated to Thomas Hardy's 'Casterbridge'.

Racial stereotypes were quite common in late-Victorian England – jokes and songs about the Irish were common, often made by the Irish themselves – but, while it would be unusual to find no friction in areas where the Irish settled extensively, communal violence was exceptional(123). It was not difficult for non-English Britons to rise to positions of the highest importance in business, administration and government in England, both locally and centrally. The English assumed, usually correctly, that everybody was in the process of becoming English; or, putting it differently, that the amalgam of 'Britishness' being formed in

England would become the norm for the rest of the British Isles. These circumstances made it difficult for the English to worry about a specifically English nationality distinct from British nationality. The United Kingdom Parliament sat in England and the British Museum was situated in London. London was the capital both of the United Kingdom and of England and there was no need to show excessive devotion to St George.

IRELAND

In contrast, national identity was of great importance in Ireland, though it divided rather than united Irishmen(126). Such concern arose from the complex pattern of conquest and settlement in Ireland. Roughly two-thirds of the inhabitants of Ireland were Catholic and one-third Protestant, but not evenly distributed in these proportions throughout the country. Ireland had suffered badly during the mid-century famine, though not all parts equally. Death and emigration had halved the island's population. Some economic historians have divided Ireland into a basically subsistence economy in the West and a money economy in the East. The Irish language was rapidly losing ground and Irish speakers were increasingly located in the West where living standards were lowest. Some Irishmen, particularly among the section of the Protestants who could be called 'Anglo-Irish', saw Ireland's future as 'West Britain', a distinct but not detached part of the United Kingdom(147). Others saw this future as separate from that of the English-dominated world: an independent Gaelic state. Some blamed the London government for Irish economic difficulties and believed that improvement could only come when the Irish economy was controlled from Dublin. There were others, however, who were not interested in anglicized Dublin – the real struggle was to get Irish land into Irish hands(124). From the North, the Protestants of thrusting, expanding Belfast looked askance at southern pretensions. Even the Protestants did not constitute a solid front. Presbyterians and Methodists resented Anglican exclusiveness almost as much as they feared Catholic supremacy. These political, cultural, religious and economic rifts in Irish society meant that when the 'spirit of nationality' spread it evoked conflicting responses.

For their part, London governments had never been sure whether to treat Ireland as a quasi-colonial dependency or simply another part of the United Kingdom. The government of Ireland still retained special features. There was a Lord Lieutenant who represented the Crown, a separate administration presided over by the Chief Secretary for Ireland (a member of the United Kingdom government, though unlikely to be an Irishman), and separate courts (though they operated on the principles of English law). In other respects, however, Ireland was represented at Westminster as a constituent part of the United Kingdom; indeed, in terms of population, over-represented [D]. Nevertheless, violence was never far below the surface, particularly in the Irish countryside. When Gladstone came to power in 1868, the memory of Fenian activities in Chester, Manchester and London was still fresh in England. The Prime Minister declared that it was his mission to pacify (not to 'liberate') Ireland. Irish grievances, he supposed, could be met by settling the religious question and tackling the problem of land, not by tampering with the union between Britain and Ireland(124).

The minority Anglican Church in Ireland was disestablished in 1869, though it received adequate financial compensation(131). The same legislation withdrew grants previously paid to Roman Catholics and Presbyterians. Most Irish churchmen were prepared to accept the solution, but Gladstone's opponents were worried about its implications for the Anglican Church in England and Wales. The land settlement produced similar fears. Gladstone's Land Act (1870) attempted to compensate any tenant 'unjustly' evicted and to ensure that he received payment for improvements he had made. Legislation was difficult to fashion because different cultural attitudes towards land-ownership were involved. The 'Bright clauses' were designed to help tenants buy land, though some Liberals doubted whether it was their government's business to establish Irish peasants on smallholdings. Some of Gladstone's landed friends were afraid that any revision of the relationship between landlord and tenant might, in due course, apply outside Ireland. His Irish legislation, however, gained Gladstone little credit with the Irish Catholic hierarchy, as was demonstrated by the failure of his offer to set up a University of Dublin which both Catholics and Protestants could attend on equal terms – such a desirable symbiosis being made possible by the exclusion of modern history and theology from its curriculum. The hierarchy wanted a Roman Catholic university and in the wake of Gladstone's failure his government tottered to an electoral defeat in 1874.

Disraeli, Gladstone's successor, had attacked the Liberals for bowing before the threat of violence in Ireland. He believed that the best way to govern Ireland was not to have a special Irish policy. Such a principle was not easy to apply after 1874. This election produced a majority of Irish MPs, led by Isaac Butt, who declared themselves Home Rulers (though it was not very clear what 'Home Rule' meant). Such a party, distinct from the Conservatives and Liberals, made Irish politics increasingly different from that of the rest of the United Kingdom. Butt, whose annual motion in the Commons in favour of Home Rule attracted only his own supporters, was replaced as leader by Charles Stewart Parnell in 1878, a stronger figure who was to bring order to his party and disorder to the Commons. In Ireland itself, landlord–tenant relations deteriorated as the fall in agricultural prices made it difficult for tenants to pay their rents. Parnell was a paradox – a Protestant leader of Catholics, an Anglo-Irish gentleman who claimed to speak for Ireland, a landlord inspiring a revolt of tenants and a Cambridge-educated hater of England. 'We will never gain anything from England unless we tread upon her toes', was his message in 1877, 'we will never gain a single pennyworth from her by conciliation'.(124, 125) This sort of language enabled him to maintain ambiguous connections with the Fenians. In 1879, Michael Davitt's Irish National Land League emerged, pledged to protect tenants in their holdings and ultimately make them owners of their farms. Parnell was persuaded to accept its presidency and thus link the rural agitation with the parliamentary campaign. Although a self-contained coldness about Parnell makes analysis of his objectives uncertain he talked in the United States in 1880 of Irishmen not being satisfied 'until we have destroyed the last link which keeps Ireland bound to England'.

Gladstone returned to the task of governing Ireland in 1880, determined to tackle the land problem. For his part, Parnell urged 'boycotting' as a sure way of maintaining pressure on the government. The new Chief Secretary, W. E. Forster, successfully argued that the restoration of law and order in the countryside should precede a new land bill. A bill designed to protect persons and property led to angry scenes and Parnell was ejected from the Commons. Feeling in Ireland ran so high that a rural insurrection could easily have occurred, but Parnell had no intention of forsaking his parliamentary role. A bill moved in 1881 substantially satisfied the old demands for fair rents, fixity of tenure and free sale, though it was to prove difficult to operate. Parnell's attitude was more than usually ambivalent. Gladstone lost patience and had him arrested. Six months later, in April 1882, after a 'treaty', Parnell was released, agreeing to commend the Land Act in return for certain amendments to it. Coercion was to be dropped. The subsequent assassination of the new Chief Secretary in Phoenix Park, Dublin, although criticized by Parnell, confirmed British prejudices about Irish behaviour. Surprisingly, a relatively calm period then ensued, with Parnell playing the parliamentary card.

In 1885 this emphasis apparently paid off. The trebling of the franchise in Ireland led to the complete domination – outside eastern Ulster – of Parnell's party. It had eighty-six MPs, just the margin of Gladstone's majority over the Conservatives, and its voting discipline was good [C, D]. For months previously, when the Conservatives had been in power, some arcane manoeuvring had gone on to see whether they might introduce Home Rule, but it had come to nothing. Even so, Parnell advised Irishmen in Britain to vote Tory. In the confused period that followed there was some talk of an 'agreed measure' before, in obscure circumstances, Gladstone's conversion to Home Rule became known. Many factors were involved in his decision – and it certainly must be seen in the context of 'high politics' – but in the end Gladstone seems to have concluded that some form of self-government for Ireland was inevitable. Since the Whigs in his party were hostile, as was the House of Lords, it was not clear how this was to be achieved. The bill provided for a two-tier legislature in Ireland, to which an executive would be responsible. The supremacy of Westminster was to be retained in matters relating to the Crown, peace and war, defence, foreign and colonial policy, customs and excise, trade and navigation, the post office, coinage and legal tender – not inconsiderable safeguards. It was difficult, however, to reconcile the stress placed upon the limited powers of the proposed legislature with the idea that Irish representation at Westminster should cease. If Ireland remained a full part of the United Kingdom such exclusion seemed strange. There were other objections from within the Liberal party. Joseph Chamberlain, from the radical wing, had earlier been prepared to support a scheme for an Irish 'central board' to which would be devolved certain legislative powers over education and communications. He now argued that Gladstone's proposal was the first step on a road which would lead to complete separation – an unacceptable course.

11

Was it a first step towards secession or was it a measure which, if it had pass-ed, would have avoided the subsequent break-up of the United Kingdom? The evidence is conflicting. Parnell did say that he would accept Gladstone's bill as 'a final settlement of our national question', although the previous year he had de-clared that no man had the right to set a boundary to the onward march of a na-tion. In the event, Parnell had to pay the penalty, if that is the word, for the ambiguity which was the essence of his political style. Murder and intimidation turned even a lifelong supporter of Irish aspirations, like John Bright(82), against Home Rule. On the other hand, the strongest aspect of Gladstone's case was that the manifest wish of Irishmen for some form of self-government could not be denied indefinitely. But it was not an unanswerable case. The consent of the British people as a whole was required before the wishes of a majority in Ire-land could be granted; the relevant framework was the United Kingdom. If, in reply, Irish Home Rulers did not accept this point and insisted that Ireland itself was the only test, opponents of Home Rule, concentrated in Ulster, could say that the province of Ulster had the right to make its own decision. The emerg-ence of the 'Orange card', which Lord Randolph Churchill thought was the one to play, was an aspect which Gladstone seems to have underestimated. In attempting to grant Home Rule to Ireland it was revealed that Ireland was almost as diverse as Britain itself. In the event, the bill was defeated in June 1886 by 341 votes to 311 – Bright, Chamberlain and Hartington being the most prominent of the 93 Liberals who voted against the government and ensured its defeat. The Conservatives and Liberal Unionists gained a majority in the en-suing election, though the Irish party held its ground in Ireland. Six years later, Gladstone was back in office and tried again, but although a Home Rule bill pass-ed through all its stages in the Commons (this time allowing Ireland eighty Westminster MPs who could vote only on imperial issues or on anything relating to Ireland) it was rejected in the Lords. Gladstone's colleagues did not want a constitutional crisis over Ireland.

Unionist governments, from 1886 until the end of the century, had a different approach. They concentrated on further land reform, granting tenants a high percentage advance towards purchasing their holdings and setting up a central office to deal with questions relating to Irish land. The Prime Minister, Salisbury and his Chief Secretary, Balfour, argued that Home Rule had little relevance to Ireland's real needs. If land tenure could be settled and agriculture modernized then the emotion would go out of Irish politics. 'Killing Home Rule by kind-ness', however, was accompanied by a vigorous security policy. Balfour would not be intimidated and accepted the epithet 'bloody' with equanimity. Inevit-ably, there were cries of 'police violence', but Balfour survived. By the century's end, the Conservatives could argue that Ireland was both a less violent and more prosperous country(136). Their policies had, however, been helped by a series of unpredictable events which destroyed the unity of the Irish Home Rulers. Parnell had survived attempts to link him with the Phoenix Park murders, but he could not surmount the storm, both in Ireland and Britain, caused by the revela-tion in 1890 that he had been living with the wife of a former Irish MP and had children by her. His career was destroyed and by the end of 1891 he was dead.

His party split into opposing factions and there was no longer an Irish Prime Minister simply waiting in the wings.

In the 1890s, therefore, a combination of circumstances removed Home Rule from practical politics, but those who thought it could be forgotten altogether were wrong. The Irish question was not simply a matter of land – what was at issue was the identity of a nation. Ultimately, cultural questions could not be divorced from politics. Douglas Hyde, son of a Protestant clergyman, learnt the Irish language and urged on his fellow countrymen the 'necessity for de-Anglicizing Ireland', but they did not all share his view(124). Indeed, while the sixth Earl of Longford took the unusual step of writing plays in Irish, the mass of Irishmen seemed largely indifferent to the Celtic bliss which was apparently theirs. Observers detected in the Irish a disposition to hate the English and to imitate them as fast as possible. The promotion of a Gaelic revival only emphasized how different was the perspective of Belfast. Northern Presbyterians found the southern anguish over Anglicization quite irrelevant. Their Scots–Irish culture was not English but, in their view, was an inheritance quite compatible with remaining British.

SCOTLAND

The 'Celtic Fringe' was a phrase used by lazy writers to link Ireland, Scotland and Wales, and to distinguish them from 'Anglo-Saxon' England. Scotland as a whole, however, could not be described as a 'Celtic' society(129). Its regions, from the Highlands and Islands to Berwickshire, from Aberdeenshire to Galloway, continued to show great diversity. In addition, over the previous fifty years, the dramatic expansion of Glasgow and the towns of Lanarkshire had created a new phenomenon – a major city on a world scale. Edinburgh remained very conscious of its status as the capital of Scotland. In such a context, a movement akin to the Irish Land League was unlikely. Yet, while differences of outlook and interest remained, improvements in transport were bringing more Scotsmen into easier contact with each other than ever before. It was only in 1880 that the railway reached Oban on the west coast, but it made travel through the Highlands much easier. Steamships performed the same service for the Islands.

Scottish nationhood was a puzzling phenomenon in the 1870s(128). No Scotsman forgot that Scotland had been an independent kingdom, but the prevailing view, expressed in press and pulpit, was that the 1707 Union had proved beneficial and should stand. Under that settlement, Scotland had retained a separate legal, ecclesiastical and educational system. Within this framework, most Scots felt able to express their identity adequately. Nevertheless, there were various indications of a more self-conscious Scottish nationalism(127). The erection of the Wallace monument at Stirling was one sign. Determined efforts were made to stop 'England' being used as a synonym for 'Britain'. 'Scotch', when not referring to drink, was steadily banished. Some enthusiasts insisted that Scotland should have its due weight in heraldic matters. Edinburgh prided itself, though with less justification than formerly, on being an intellectual centre of European significance. The Royal Scottish Museum and the National Gallery of Scotland added to the capital's attractions. Much effort was expended in describing Scotland as more 'democratic' and literate than England. This 'Scottishness' did not exclude 'Britishness', indeed, as newspapers, hotels and headed notepaper still testified, Scotland was 'North Britain'.

Even so, Scotland's political role within the United Kingdom was becoming more contentious. In mid-century, despite the birth of vigorous contested politics in Scotland after 1832, there was still no Scottish political class. Scotland was represented in Parliament either by its aristocracy, which had been substantially Anglicized, at least to the extent of being educated in England, or by lawyers whose ultimate ambitions lay in the legal sphere in Edinburgh. After the Second Reform Act, however, MPs were increasingly drawn from and responsible to a wider section of Scottish society. A Scotch Education Department (1872) superintended the school boards and in 1884 Gladstone set up a Scottish Office and appointed a Secretary for Scotland. This department was to have responsibility in Scotland for public health, the Poor Law, roads, bridges, fisheries and other matters. This step was supported both by Whig magnates like Argyll and Rosebery and by the Convention of Royal Burghs. It was a measure of administrative devolution within the political establishment rather than a concession to a popular campaign. In 1892 the Scottish Secretary became a member of the United Kingdom Cabinet.

Home Rule for Scotland had little support before 1886, but it was a notion Gladstone himself encouraged. He was, after all, a Scot by descent. A Scottish Home Rule Association was formed in Edinburgh in 1886 and, within ten years, the Scottish Liberal Association felt that 'the true solution of the question may be found in granting Home Rule legislatures on a federal basis to Scotland, England, Ireland and Wales', though Ireland had priority(127). The British Liberal leadership never took the idea further. Gladstone had enough on his hands in Ireland, and Rosebery was as much opposed to political nationalism as he favoured administrative devolution. Home Rule for Scotland remained a matter of spasmodic interest, frequently among Scottish exiles in London. At the end of the century, therefore, Scotland adhered firmly to the British party system. Its allegiance to Liberalism was marked – there was always a Liberal majority in Scotland whatever the United Kingdom result.

The only example of 'deviance' was in the Highlands and Islands where conditions resembled the west of Ireland. In both regions, economic and cultural/linguistic crisis coincided. The 'clearances' dominated one set of well-trained memories and the famine the other. However, by the 1880s, it was rare for a crofter to be ejected from home and land. Economic conditions in the Highlands were slowly improving. Such agitation as did develop was often – and rightly – attributed to the influence of Irish emissaries, though the decline of sheep-farming did cause distress. In 1885, Crofter candidates had defeated the official Liberals in a number of Highland seats and the Highland Land Reform Association was active. A Crofters' Commission was set up in 1886 after a Royal Commission had investigated the Highlands. In these years, rehearsing his later role in Ireland, Balfour applied a mixture of coercion and conciliation to keep the

Highlands quiet. If Balfour offended, he offended his fellow Scots. The position of the Gaelic language was likewise largely a matter for the Scots themselves. The 1891 census disclosed that only 6 per cent of Scots spoke Gaelic, chiefly in the Highlands and Islands where the proportion was therefore much higher. The considerable number of Highlanders who migrated to Glasgow did not sustain their language on any scale. Like Irish, but unlike Welsh, a Celtic language did not gain an industrial base. Thus, Scottish Gaelic was a regional rather than a national question. Lowland Scots did not consider Gaelic to be their language; indeed it was more frequently considered to be an alien irrelevance. The Scottish business and professional classes were more interested in the world overseas. It was a Scottish conceit to believe that Scotland ran the British Empire. Caledonian societies were scattered across the globe – a testimony to the activity of Scottish firms. During the years of agricultural depression in England, many farms were purchased by Scotsmen conspicuously 'on the make'. It was a Scotsman in England who could claim credit, early in the new century, for the formation of the National Farmers Union. In 1893, the Canadian Liberal leader, Sir Wilfrid Laurier, declared that if he were not French he would have chosen to be 'Scotch' – a remark which went down well in Scotland. After all, with Scotsmen prominent, if not dominant, in the leadership of the United Kingdom political parties at this time, Scotsmen were not anxious to be restricted to Scotland.

WALES

In 1870, Wales was often regarded as little more than the Highlands of England. Thirty years later, that mistake was less often made. Legally, politically, statistically, administratively and ecclesiastically the concept of 'England and Wales' seemed firmly established. Since 'West Britain' (Ireland) already existed, perhaps Wales was the British mid-West! Despite the paucity of distinctive institutions and the fact that it lacked a capital city, Wales possessed a strong cultural, religious and linguistic identity(135). Although the smallest country in the United Kingdom in area and population, it managed to retain a high percentage of its natural increase, reaching over 2 million by 1901(139). Unlike Irishmen, Scotsmen and Englishmen in this period, Welshmen did not flock to the United States. This absorptive capacity of the Welsh economy had important consequences for the cultural life of Wales. There was a steady drift from the rural counties into the southern mining valleys and the northern coastal towns. As a result, while the English language gained the ascendancy in these areas it did not do so totally. Welsh-speakers, for the most part, were migrants within Wales rather than exiles in Boston or Nova Scotia. It has been argued that the Welsh language was saved rather than destroyed by industrialism. If industry had not developed, the substantially Welsh-speaking rural population would have migrated in large numbers. By the end of the century, per 1,000 of the Welsh population, 498 spoke English only, 151 spoke Welsh only and the remainder spoke both languages.

The language played a considerable part in the political life of Wales. The

1846 Commission of Inquiry into Welsh education had called it a 'disastrous barrier to all moral improvement and popular progress in Wales'. In the following decades, the emphasis in schools was placed upon developing fluency in English – the language of 'modernity'. There was, however, a flourishing periodical press which gave fresh currency to written Welsh. Few in Wales believed that the English language could or should be kept out. The crucial question was whether English-learners would retain their Welsh. Pessimists believed that they would not. A small group of Welsh-speakers had set sail from Liverpool in 1865 to found a colony in Patagonia where Welsh would survive. Despite the growing accessibility of England made possible by railways and road improvements – communications in Wales ran from east to west rather than from north to south – it seemed too dramatic to talk of the death of the Welsh language. Besides, in the last couple of decades in the century the educational climate was changing. The 1880 Aberdare Report deplored 'narrowness' whether Welsh or English. Education in Wales could improve 'without destroying the Welsh type of character or converting the people of Wales into Englishmen'. Since the Welsh possessed 'a distinct nationality' there should be educational provision to safeguard the Welsh heritage. At its highest level, it was felt that Wales should no longer endure the indignity of being the sole region of the United Kingdom without a university. Hitherto, Welshmen had gone to England or Scotland for university education, but university colleges were started at Aberystwyth (1872), Cardiff (1883) and Bangor (1884) and they formed the federal University of Wales in 1893. Lord Rosebery took the view that the university embodied 'the spirit of nationality in its best form'. Some Welshmen did not agree. They wanted that spirit to take a political form.

The period after the 1868 election was one of unchallengeable Liberal superiority in Wales. Gladstone in turn carefully cultivated the Principality, looking for support during the Home Rule crisis and, on the whole, finding it. He also urged that 'subject to the claims of imperial patriotism', Welshmen ought to consider what the 'fair claims' of Wales might be. In the same year, 1887, Cymru Fydd (the coming Wales) was founded, with Tom Ellis, newly elected Liberal MP for Merionethshire as president. Ellis, who also described himself as a Welsh Nationalist, urged the establishment of a Welsh Parliament with its own executive. The idea was much discussed in the 1890s, but failed to generate great enthusiasm. By becoming Chief Whip in Rosebery's government, Ellis appeared to believe that Wales could best be served at Westminster. This putative leader of a 'Welsh party' died in 1899 when he was only forty. His place was taken by another young Welsh-speaking Welshman, David Lloyd George, who also advocated domestic self-government for Wales, though he had no wish 'to advance one single step along the road to separation'. In South Wales, however, there was little desire for 'self-government', even with this rider(141).

Although Welsh political battles were fought between Liberals, Liberal Unionists and Tories, the ethos, atmosphere and even the issues were not exactly the same as in England. The attack on the established Church and its characterization as *Eglwys Saesneg* (the English Church) had nationalist aspects(149). The campaign for disestablishment placed the Anglican Gladstone in a quandary from which not even his Welsh wife or North Wales home could save him. In 1891, to his displeasure, the 'Newcastle programme' did commit the Liberal party to Welsh disestablishment. Such an assurance, though it did not satisfy all nonconformists, did cement the relationship between Liberalism in Wales and England. This link survived the animosities of the Welsh 'tithe war' when the Tories, the landlords and the English sometimes became indistinguishable targets of popular hostility. By the end of the century, in any case, the Welsh land question was not quite so contentious. One experienced politician noted that there were too few Welsh farmers to 'play the Irish game'. They were not united enough and were too close to the forces of law and order(122).

Thus, despite the anxieties noted at the beginning of this chapter, the United Kingdom had survived and its internal problems had not hindered the expansion of the empire or incapacitated the country in its international dealings.

CHAPTER 2

Crown Imperial

In 1898, the Canadian government issued a special postage stamp to celebrate the advent of imperial penny postage. Its motto was: 'We hold a vaster Empire than has been.' Certainly, the contrast in its extent, even as compared with 1870, was striking. Yet, paradoxically, the late-Victorian expansion in Africa and Asia was an indication that the decades of informal control and unchallenged supremacy across the globe were over. Other European states, joined at the close by Japan and the United States, were extremely active too. In 1898, Lord Salisbury divided the nations of the world into the 'living' and 'dying. Although he was not specific, the Ottoman and Chinese Empires seemed ripe for 'death'. While some had felt in 1870 that the British Empire was already large enough, it seemed necessary to expand in order to protect what had already been acquired. The old world of influence, of commerce without direct control, was preferable, but it was no longer on offer(37). It was a case of expand or perish. John Ruskin was one of those who talked of planting colonies as if he were a gardener in spring. Sir John Seeley, author of *The Expansion of England* (1883), predicted a future in which the United States and Russia would dwarf France and Germany – and England too, unless the Empire could be consolidated(32).

AFRICA

It was the 'scramble for Africa' which caught the late-Victorian imagination(31). The activities of explorers in the 1850s and 1860s, culminating in Stanley's east–west crossing of the continent between 1874 and 1877, were avidly followed. The Livingstonian formula of 'Christianity and Commerce' would transform African society to the mutual benefit of Africans and Europeans. This upsurge of interest – a confused mixture of idealism, scientific enquiry and desire for profit – did not at first have clear political connotations. As late as 1865, for example, a Commons Select Committee on West Africa thought that the British stations on the coast, with the possible exception of Sierra Leone, should be given up. The expense of maintaining them could not be justified – a bizarre prelude to thirty years of expansion. Such a transformation has led historians to seek general explanations, though no single reason seems satisfying. There was no 'master plan' followed by successive governments; on the whole, indeed, governments tried to avoid direct involvement, preferring to work through trading companies or individuals. Gladstonian governments, supposedly devoted to economy, involved themselves in expensive wars. Conservative governments, on occasion, could be sceptical about the imperial enterprise. Once begun, however, it seemed that the process could not stop until all Africa had been partitioned(36).

In West Africa, British control gradually extended inland from those supposedly redundant coastal bases, but it was only in the 1890s, when trade might have been threatened by French penetration that the London government acted. The boundaries of 'Nigeria' were finally drawn in 1898, though even then it was not administered as one territory. The frontiers of the Gold Coast (Ghana), Gambia and Sierra Leone had also been settled by this stage. It took time, however, for British rule to make a deep impact in the hinterland. The commercial possibilities of these regions seemed good, though they were not suitable for European settlement.

In North Africa, Gladstone's 'temporary' occupation of Egypt in 1882 showed every sign of becoming permanent. Lord Cromer's administration of the country was sometimes admired even by those who opposed occupation. Was not Egypt better governed than Persia? Even those few, like Wilfrid Scawen Blunt, who believed in 'Egypt for the Egyptians' could not quite answer the point that if Britain did leave another European state would step in. The Suez Canal, opened in 1869, had become the artery of empire, the major route to India and beyond; its security could not be jeopardized. It then became necessary to conquer the Sudan in order to safeguard Egypt. Gladstone mishandled this task disastrously. His failure to send a relief expedition in time led many to hold him personally responsible for the death of General Gordon in 1885. Subsequent governments were more circumspect and, so long as no other European country tried to meddle, they felt that the Mahdi and his followers in the Sudan could be left alone. The possibility that they would divert the Nile and starve Egypt was usually thought to be remote. However, French interest in the Upper Nile became alarming and in 1898 Kitchener reconquered the Sudan, technically on behalf of Egypt.

The Upper Nile had also been secured from the south. In East Africa, British merchants and companies had made terms with the Arab Sultan of Zanzibar, whose authority extended to the mainland. His position was waning, however, and there was anxiety about German intervention. In 1890, Britain concluded an agreement with Germany by which she gained predominance in the area in contention, giving up Heligoland (a North Sea island) in return. The British East Africa Company was already trading in the vicinity. In 1894, not without opposition from his colleagues, Rosebery declared Uganda a British protectorate. An East African protectorate (the later Kenya) was also formed and a railway planned between Mombasa and Lake Victoria. The Upper Nile was safe.

Despite occasional friction with France and Germany, the African 'auction' might be said to have gone well. There was even some levity as statesmen in faraway capitals, who had never visited these new territories, sometimes wondered whether they actually existed. Southern Africa was a source of more serious interest. In the first place, the gold and diamonds of South Africa had been discovered in sufficient quantities by the 1870s to make it apparent that the region had enormous mineral wealth. Secondly, there were two Afrikaner republics, the Transvaal and the Orange Free State, which were determined to maintain their independence. No other European colonial power in Africa had to reckon with another European community in the way that the British did in South Africa. Thirdly, the military power of the Zulus was not negligible. The British did not subdue them until 1879, having been previously humiliated at the Battle of Isandhlwana. Fourthly, the automatic acquiescence of the English-speakers of the Cape could not be altogether guaranteed.

A solution for South Africa appeared to be federation on the model of Canada. Lord Carnarvon, Disraeli's Colonial Secretary, annexed the Transvaal in April 1877 when that republic's finances were precarious. In February 1881, when Gladstone was in office, the Afrikaners rebelled and defeated a British army at Majuba. Gladstone conceded the Transvaal its independence, though Britain continued to claim 'suzerainty'. Later, gold discoveries on the Witwatersrand sustained the Transvaalers and they developed their own outlet to the sea at Delagoa Bay in Portuguese Mozambique. The British in turn annexed the remaining coastal strip of Zululand and moved into Bechuanaland (Botswana). Finally, to the north, Cecil Rhodes's British South Africa Company was given a charter to administer Matabeleland and Mashonaland (Zimbabwe). The cause of the British Empire was paramount for Rhodes and making money took second place. He became Prime Minister of Cape Colony in 1890, but was less successful in politics. In 1895, an invading force under Dr Jameson moved into Transvaal claiming to be acting on behalf of the Uitlanders (the non-Afrikaners who had flooded into the Rand), but it was easily defeated. President Kruger's position was strengthened and he used his country's wealth to buy arms. The Orange Free State made an alliance with him in 1897. Rhodes also had considerable problems to the north where both the Matabele and Mashona peoples rebelled, for a time endangering the settlement there. In these circumstances the future development of South Africa was very uncertain, and it was very likely that it would be decided by the use of force.

The relative ease with which a large part of Africa had been 'acquired' in the last decades of the century can be exaggerated. Administration and government presented more problems than conquest. Rebellion could still occur, though large military garrisons were not normally required. The paramountcy of the British Crown could often be fitted into existing structures of authority(33). Having taken such trouble, the British had no doubt that their rule would last for a long time. It was inconceivable that Africans could develop along the path towards 'responsible' government in the foreseeable future. Commercially, the immediate gains for Britain were not great, but the continent of Africa could be viewed, in Joseph Chamberlain's words, as an 'undeveloped estate'.

INDIA

Before the 'scramble for Africa', India had been the unchallenged centre of the British Empire for many decades. The 1857 Mutiny had come as an unpleasant shock, but even those who thought that Britain should not be in India believed that it ought to be suppressed. The British government did then assume direct responsibility for the government of India; there was a Secretary of State in London and a Viceroy in Calcutta. Although another mutiny could not be ruled out, external dangers were thought to pose a more serious threat to British rule in India. The expansion of the Russian Empire across central Asia caused considerable worry in London. India looked vulnerable. Even so, following the failure of a British expedition into Afghanistan in the 1830s there was a reluctance to advocate a 'forward' policy. After 1874, however, the Conservatives made much of India. Disraeli persuaded Queen Victoria to take the style 'Empress of India' – a gesture aimed at the British public as much as the Indian. In 1878, the government of India did find itself involved in an expensive and ultimately ineffective campaign in Afghanistan. Gladstone called it 'frivolous' and certainly its failure did not help the Conservatives. Lord Ripon, appointed Viceroy by Gladstone in 1880, did extricate himself from direct rule in Afghanistan, though he retained some forward positions and still attempted to control its foreign policy. In the early 1890s there were further developments on this troubled frontier – the small town of Chitral being seen by successive viceroys as a vital symbolic British presence to deter the Russians from invading. This 'great game' remained a source of anxiety at the end of the century, although historians disagree about the extent to which there really was a Russian threat. On the edge of India it was difficult to know where to draw the line – in the east the problem was similar. Britain already controlled Lower Burma and after a military campaign in 1885–86 Upper Burma was also annexed. Quite apart from strategic considerations, the government of India acted with an eye to opinion elsewhere in India. If the periphery could not be held, then the core might crumble too. The British were in India as conquerors – a dangerous fact to forget(34).

Even so, the British in India also saw themselves as a people with a mission. They did not believe that Indians would govern themselves. There were so many conflicting religions, languages and peoples that only a strong alien presence held the structure together. Government could be decentralized and Indians associated with it, but British control should not be jeopardized. Universities in Bombay, Calcutta and Madras extended higher education to Indians and the lawyers among them were not excluded from the High Courts of Judicature when these were established in 1861. The proposal that Indian magistrates should be granted criminal jurisdiction over Europeans in India was very contentious. So was the entry of Indians into the Indian Civil Service. They had to travel to England to seek entry under the competitive system and by the mid 1870s only a handful had been successful.

The fundamental issue, however, was not the administration of justice or the Civil Service but politics. The general view was that radical change was undesirable. Ripon, as Viceroy, attempted to give British rule a more liberal tone. He introduced a scheme of local self-government which he wanted to be an 'instrument of political and popular education'. However, neither Ripon nor his immediate successors were prepared to go much further. Some Indian opinion was becoming impatient and discontented. The Indian National Congress, formed in 1885, initially concentrated upon such questions as the size of legislative councils and the Civil Service examinations, but more far-reaching objectives then appeared. Naoroji, elected a British Liberal MP in 1892, had published *The Poverty of India* fourteen years earlier. He suggested that most of India's poverty could ultimately be laid at the door of Britain. Curzon, a future Viceroy, thought such criticism quite unrepresentative, arguing in the Commons in 1892 that Congress only stood for a 'minute and almost microscopic minority of the total population of India'. Defenders of British rule pointed to the building of railways, roads and ports. Indians replied that the British had benefited from these developments more than they had. This debate became more strident as the century drew to a close(35).

In cultural terms, the contact between Britain and India was not one-sided. Since the eighteenth century, British scholars had interested themselves in Indian religious and philosophical ideas. A section of the British intelligentsia, using Muller's translations, increasingly sought 'Light from the East'. India loomed large in the experience of an intelligent and influential section of the British middle class. Kipling brilliantly explored these Anglo-Indian worlds and made the continent come alive for many readers who remained at home. When service in the Indian army is also taken into account, the cumulative impact of India on British life was certainly greater than that of any one European country. A love of India, however, by no means implied that India should be 'free'. Intellectuals like Fitzjames Stephens and Henry Maine were by no means contemptuous of Indian society, but the more they studied it the more convinced they were that the British would have to bear the burden of rule.

COLONIES OF SETTLEMENT

'Dear, happy England seems already like the land of shadow, beautiful and beloved, but abandoned for ever', wrote the daughter of an English vicarage as she sailed for Western Australia. Once there, she worked hard to establish a garden 'productive in all English vegetables' and, as for her house, 'English was written on it and on every foot of ground around it.'[1] Her story illustrates the paradox of British overseas settlement – besides India and Africa the third major facet of the British imperial experience. The emigrants from the British Isles were going to new homes in distant places, but in many cases they still cherished the old. Between 1861 and 1900, 7½ million people left the United Kingdom, over 1 million to Australia and New Zealand, some 800,000 to Canada, but only a few hundred thousand to South Africa. For many supporters of empire the settlement of 'surplus' population overseas was of vital importance. Canada, Australia, New Zealand and even South Africa were thought to be 'vacant' territories. Into the 1890s and beyond, Rhodes was among those who thought that the United Kingdom could not support a population above 40 millions without a grave risk of civil war and internal chaos. The proper solution was for the British race to establish a number of overseas 'branches'. It was disappointing for such enthusiasts that over 5 million emigrants went to the United States and were thus 'lost'. There was little doubt, however, that the colonies would develop as viable places for settlement. Australia, for example, was ceasing to be thought of as a mere 'camping-ground for money-making purposes'.

The ultimate future of these territories was a matter for speculation. Although fast clippers, and then steamers, reduced the time taken to reach the Antipodes, the distance was still vast. What is impressive, none the less, is the effort to maintain contacts. Public schools and universities in England and Scotland remained the goal of prosperous colonists. George Lansbury and Tom Mann, British labour leaders, had both experienced life in Australia. The Anglican Church in Australia stocked its episcopate from England. Presbyterians from New Zealand came to Edinburgh. Imperial penny postage, celebrated by the Canadian government, was largely due to the efforts of Henniker-Heaton, a Conservative MP who had spent some years in Australia. *The Times* commented that his success 'rendered vocal innumerable chords which have long been dumb, and acclaimed the unity of the Empire by the responsive chorus of myriads of gladdened hearts'.[2]

The pattern of government and administration in the colonies differed in detail but not in principle from that of Britain, though the politics of New Zealand and Australia were generally more radical in such matters as the franchise, the secret ballot, payment for MPs and votes for women. Trade reinforced the sentimental connection, though some colonies were already talking about 'safeguarding' their industrial development. Improvements in transport and refrigeration meant that New Zealand dairy products could reach the British market. New Zealand looked to the London money market to finance her ambitious development programme. No British government after 1870 attempted direct control over the internal affairs of these colonies. London was reluctant to provide for even a kind of imperial military reserve. British troops, for example, had recently been withdrawn from New Zealand, with the clear implication that Maoris and settlers had to work out their own *modus vivendi*. The Colonial Laws Validity Act, 1865, with its doctrine of 'repugnancy' – that colonial legislation which conflicted with Westminster legislation was invalid – was rarely invoked. Among all the countries of settlement it was Canada which led the way and seemed to offer the model for future colonial development. Although federation was urged elsewhere, it was the turn of the century before the Commonwealth of Australia emerged. By 1890, however, when Natal and Western Australia received self-government, there was no part of the settled empire which did not order its own affairs.

In theory, however, the British Empire was still a unity, both legally and diplomatically, though care was taken, particularly in the case of Canada, to take note of colonial opinion in negotiations which affected them. A Canadian High Commissioner was appointed to London in 1880 and it was widely assumed that Canada would assert itself in other ways – as would all the colonies in time. Even so, the monarchy still seemed solidly entrenched as a symbol of British unity. It was argued that Canada would maintain the close link with Britain in order to counteract the influence, and possibly the ambitions, of the United States. Self-interest and sentiment would keep the British Empire together. From the mid 1870s onwards, however, this bland confidence was disturbed as 'imperialism' became a creed rather than simply a fact. There was increasing enthusiasm, at least in Britain itself, for the idea of 'imperial federation', though schemes for it varied in detail. The Imperial Federation League (1884) stressed the need for some common council to strengthen the bonds of sentiment. It was a vision which caught the younger generation, men like Lord Rosebery who knew the colonies at first hand. Lord Jersey, reporting on an inter-colonial conference at Ottawa in 1894, argued that Britain could 'settle the direction of their trade and the current of their sentiments for, it may be, generations. Such an opportunity may not soon recur, as the sands of time run down quickly.'[3]

Even in the 1870s however, a close reading of such a supposed imperialist as Disraeli reveals that he had already dismissed the idea of imperial federation. Some kind of 'federal' structure might have been established at the time when the colonies were given self-government, but that moment had passed. It seemed from overseas that imperial federation, especially when accompanied by talk of a customs union, was a device to reassert Britain's authority. By the end of the century it looked as though a colonial empire of 'loose ties' would evolve. In this respect, the longevity of Queen Victoria was constitutionally helpful. The colonial premiers could not do other than come to London to celebrate her jubilees in 1887 and 1897. While in the imperial capital, they held informal discussions with British ministers. It was doubtful, however, whether the Queen could provide jubilees indefinitely, and the collaboration between the different parts of the greatest empire the world had ever seen might require a more substantial basis. In the longer term, the survival of the British Empire and, indeed, of the United Kingdom itself, would rest on the subtle interrelationship between the successful functioning of the political system, the continued expansion of the economy and the capacity to deter potential opponents from waging war. These linkages will be explored subsequently, but before they are considered one unpleasant fact has to be remembered. Although many contemporaries would have liked to ignore it, the United Kingdom, the mother of the British Empire, was also a European power.

---

1. W. K. Hancock, *Politics in Pitcairn* (1947) p. 51
2. Mrs A. Porter, *Life and letters of Sir John Henniker-Heaton* (1916)
3. Cited in I. M. Cumpston, *The growth of the British Commonwealth, 1880–1932* (1973), p. 216

CHAPTER 3

The imperial island and the European mainland

'Bismarck sticks in my throat', wrote the Dean of St Paul's as he heard of the Prussian successes in the war against France in 1870. It was all very alarming, he added, 'when one reflects that our own turn may come.'[1] Despite the attention devoted to empire, contemporaries realized that the United Kingdom could be directly threatened from the mainland of Europe. There was general agreement that complete detachment and indifference was impossible, but how far, and in what manner, British influence could be exercised was a matter of controversy. Britain's insular position, at a time when that still had great military and naval significance, inevitably produced a mental outlook which set the United Kingdom apart from its neighbours. Their extraordinary expansion, the apparent stability of their political institutions, their peculiar belief in freedom, their dislike of bureaucracy and their colonial preoccupations had all helped to create, or reinforce, among the British a sense of self-sufficiency, not to say smugness. Slowly but discernibly after 1870 that confidence was eroded, though not destroyed. It was ceasing to be axiomatic that British methods in commerce and industry, education and even government necessarily led the field.

The Franco-Prussian War was a warning that the peaceful evolution of the Continent could not be guaranteed(1). General war in Europe was a possibility on a number of occasions over the next three decades – in 1875, for example. War was not an illegal act and all European statesmen were prepared to resort to it if there seemed a sufficiently clear balance of advantage. Yet there was an awareness that while the Franco-Prussian War had seemed a tolerably swift and efficient affair future wars might be more lengthy and destructive. During these decades the British continued to fight many small wars – in Burma, Afghanistan, West and South Africa – but they had no desire to fight on the mainland of Europe. They were apprehensive that any conflict might spread into a major conflagration – which, in the end, might draw them in. The prospect of supremacy in Europe by any single state or alliance of states was, however, equally distasteful. British foreign policy, therefore, had to steer a course which avoided both dangers(2).

The British people could not be said to influence the making of foreign policy in any direct fashion. The initiative remained firmly with the Prime Minister or the Foreign Secretary – the latter normally sitting in the House of Lords. Yet, as the electorate expanded, the 'political nation' was increasingly anxious to trespass into the arcane and hitherto largely aristocratic area of foreign affairs. University teachers and clergymen felt bound to express their horror at the behaviour of foreign powers. The storm which accompanied the revelation of Turkish atrocities against Bulgarians (1876) and Armenians (1894) had no parallel elsewhere in Europe(3). Politicians had at least to take note of this public concern, though they may have derived comfort from the fact that this high-mindedness was not always shared lower down the social scale. Britannia calls for sympathy, wrote a contemporary working-class rhymer (the author's great-grandfather):

> Bulgaria is the sound
> Our purse is always needed
> When foreign folks go wrong
> But better would she look at home
> Where help is needed most
> And stop the want and misery
> Around our native coast.

At least in comparison with many European states, however, information about British diplomatic negotiations was available in the form of 'blue books', though admittedly they were published after the event. The government could be subjected to informed criticism by MPs, and disagreement about foreign policy was thought normal and acceptable rather than, as in some European countries, inadmissible or unpatriotic. By the same token, however, foreign policy debate was essentially an aspect of the constant party struggle(8).

Foreign policy was implemented by a small bureaucracy which consisted of the Foreign Office (in London) and the Diplomatic and Consular Services (abroad)(4). Ambassadors and ministers were often men of influence, still possessing considerable latitude in the exercise of their judgement. They did not, however, 'make' policy; they only advised. How much weight was attached to their advice depended on many things – the personality of the Foreign Secretary, his standing in the Cabinet, and the views of Parliament. Five policy-makers – Gladstone, Disraeli, Salisbury, Rosebery and Joseph Chamberlain – merit special mention though, of course, they all had to operate within economic and military constraints which make it difficult to determine the importance of personal influence [B]. Gladstone had a European not an insular mind, being profoundly conscious of Europe's classical and Christian inheritance. He held that while all European states inevitably had their individual interests, they should not act unilaterally. The 'Concert of Europe' should not be a mere phrase, but a working system of co-operation. Disraeli brought a different approach. He accused Gladstone of being more concerned with abstract principles than with British interests. Nevertheless, as he told an audience in Manchester in 1872, while he counselled 'firmness and decision at the right moment', he did not favour turbulent and aggressive diplomacy. Britain should exhibit a proud reserve in its dealings with Europe since Britain's power had never been so great nor her resources so vast and inexhaustible. Salisbury was altogether less flamboyant and more pessimistic. 'English policy', he had written in 1877, with fine aristocratic exaggeration, 'is to float lazily down stream, occasionally putting out a diplomatic boat-hook to avoid collisions.'[2] In practice, however, during his long tenure of office, British foreign policy amounted to rather more than messing about in boats. Rosebery was different again both in temperament and capacity. He was young, ambitious and intelligent but, in the end, not destined to guide Britain into the twentieth century. He had to rest content with winning the Derby. Joseph Chamberlain, unlike the others, was neither a Prime Minister nor a Foreign Secretary in these decades, but as Colonial Secretary after 1895 he was not notably reticent in his opinions and his colleagues could not ignore them. He was particularly aware of the connection between imperial and European policy. Can one speak, however, of a clear distinction between Liberal and Conservative foreign policy? Taking the rhetoric of Gladstone and Disraeli at face value, one would certainly believe so, but reality had a habit of restricting both men's freedom of action. Rosebery did not even pretend that continuity of foreign policy between governments of different colours constituted a crime(81). Conservatives, however, never doubted that the defence of the 'national interest' was an absolute priority, while Liberals urged that a higher morality did have a place in international affairs. This difference of approach (if not always of policy) can be seen in the reactions to one of the most intransigent problems of the period – the fate of the Ottoman Empire.

It was generally agreed throughout Europe that the days of Ottoman rule were numbered. The 'Christian' peoples of the Balkans – Serbs, Bulgars and 'Macedonians' in particular – were perpetually on the brink of revolt against Turkish domination and the Sultan's effective authority in North Africa was waning. But, if 'Turkey-in-Europe' collapsed, what was to happen to the remainder of the empire? Vienna and St Petersburg both felt that the fate of the Balkans was too serious a business to be left to the Balkan peoples. The Russians were believed to have designs on Constantinople and it was this possibility which chiefly concerned successive British governments. It is not, therefore, surprising that this 'Eastern Question' loomed large and often dominated Britain's relationship with other European powers.

WESTERN EUROPE

In 1870, however, it was the war between France and Prussia which was uppermost in men's minds. It was only four years since Prussia had overwhelmed Austria in the Battle of Sadowa and settled power-relationships in central Europe. It was a surprise to find Prussia so swiftly embroiled with the France of Napoleon III, and there was considerable alarm. The general opinion, however, was that the United Kingdom should not support one side or the other, even though the outcome might determine the course of international relations for decades. The Liberal government rightly held that Britain had no treaty obligations to either party to the war, and only if neutral Belgium had been violated might the Cabinet have changed its mind. In the event, since France and Prussia agreed new safeguards for Belgium, London simply watched and waited. The Prussian success, most conspicuously at the battle of Sedan in September 1870, made it apparent that a formidable power had arrived. A new German Empire was proclaimed in January 1871 embracing all the German states except Austria. John Morley, later a Cabinet minister but then a mere journalist, thought that within twenty years fear of Germany would bring Russia and France together – and he was only a few years out in his forecast. He also predicted that Germany and Britain 'by geographical position, by slow Teutonic ponderosity, by common sense and true scientific training' would be allies against such a combination – and in this he was quite wrong.[3] But the fact that Morley could even speculate about possible 'allies' was significant. It meant that he accepted that Britain might have to offer herself in the shifting market of European alliances and alignments. For the moment, however, there was a reluctance to discuss the 'balance of power' too explicitly. It seemed an awesomely mechanical concept at a time when popular sentiment aspired to friendship between nations or conceived an affinity between particular peoples.

British sympathies during the Franco-Prussian War had fluctuated, but there was no general support for France or approval of Napoleon III. Despite his fear of Bismarck, the Dean of St Paul's felt that the 'spirit of falsehood' had led to France's downfall. Frederic Harrison and J. M. Ludlow, two other intellectuals, were very distressed, seeing France as the embodiment of enlightenment – and one considered himself a Positivist thinker and the other a Christian Socialist. French was the most widely learnt modern language in Britain and the proximity of France meant that Parisian fashions speedily reached London, though they were not always approved. French impressionist painting, for example, as mediated in the late 1870s by Whistler, received a distinctly chilly reception for many years. The British, in turn, most easily visited France and they established little colonies on the Mediterranean coast. Yet, to visit France – either during these decades or subsequently – was not necessarily to comprehend or sympathize with the country. The British tended to consider the French frivolous, inefficient and untrustworthy; the French considered the British pompous, smug and hypocritical. Beneath Franco-British civility there was real acerbity.

The realities of international relations did not seem conducive to greater intimacy. The military defeat of 1870 inevitably weakened France diplomatically and her virtually static population raised doubts about re-establishing her military might. From a British standpoint, in any case, the revival of French strength would be distinctly double-edged. In May 1875, France appealed to Britain and Russia for support against the possibility of a renewed German attack. Quite what Bismarck intended during this 'war in sight' crisis is still rather a mystery, but the French alarm was genuine. Disraeli expressed his concern, but fortunately for him was not called upon to define his attitude more precisely since the crisis faded away. There was general disapproval of the German incorporation of Alsace-Lorraine in 1871, but no disposition to assist in regaining the provinces or, indeed, to underwrite France(1). Lord Derby, Disraeli's Foreign Secretary, took comfort from the fact that British policy had involved no risk and cost no trouble, while giving the impression of doing more than had in fact been done. Certainly, Britain wished France to survive, but even the appearance there of the spirit of revenge – as, for example, during the Boulanger episode of 1887 – caused almost as much alarm in London as it did in Berlin. On the other hand, there was concern lest France should become too weak.

The paradox was that a French recovery (if only of prestige) could only take place outside Europe in parts of the world where a clash with Britain was most likely. Bismarck well understood this fact. Ever since 1830, when Algeria had been annexed, France had been turning its attention to North Africa. By the 1870s, the most contentious areas were Tunis and Egypt. In 1875, Disraeli authorized the purchase of the Khedive of Egypt's Suez Canal shares – the ruler had gone bankrupt. He wished to prevent the newly completed canal coming exclusively under French influence – which would jeopardize the vital imperial route to India. Three years later, however, Salisbury worked with France to impose financial advisers and a constitution upon the Khedive and this augured well for future collaboration. When Gladstone returned to office in 1880 he opposed further French expansion in North Africa (the occupation of Tunis in 1881, for example) and relations between Paris and London deteriorated. Unfortunately for Gladstone, there was also discontent within Egypt at the role of Europeans and the operation of Franco-British financial control. In 1882, some Europeans were killed and the British and French fleets appeared off Alexandria. The British fleet bombarded its forts in July and by September a British military force had defeated Arabi Pasha, the dissident leader. The French, who had not taken part in the bombardment or military operations, now found the British installed in Egypt on a temporary but indefinite basis(31).

The British occupation of Egypt (technically it still remained Ottoman territory) hindered Franco-British co-operation for the remainder of the century. It was a situation which Bismarck was easily able to exploit – over the next few years, for example, when he abandoned his prejudice against colonies, the Franco-British split helped him both in Africa and the Pacific. Berlin sided with France during the West Africa Conference (1884–85). In 1887, Salisbury did initiate a negotiation with the Sultan of Turkey which resulted in an undertaking to leave Egypt within three years, but then the Sultan pulled back under pressure from France and Russia. Although Salisbury believed that only improved relations with France could restore flexibility to British diplomacy he was not prepared to offer Turkey better terms. He was prepared to accept that relations with France could not be improved. As Morley had predicted, Paris and St Petersburg grew closer, culminating in an exchange of notes in January 1894 pledging mutual aid in the event of a German attack.

In the early 1890s, Rosebery was no more successful in achieving a reconciliation with France than Salisbury had been. Both countries did agree in 1893 that Siam should remain independent and not be annexed by either, but the Nile valley remained very contentious. Both countries manoeuvred for position in the Upper Nile and in March 1895 Sir Edward Grey publicly warned France that intervention in the area would be considered an 'unfriendly act'. Nevertheless, in June 1896 the French government ordered a Captain Marchand to proceed there from West Africa. Meanwhile, the British government had embarked on the reconquest of the Sudan from Egypt. It was in mid-September 1898, after some interesting battles on the way, that Kitchener arrived in the obscure village of Fashoda to find Marchand already installed. For a time it seemed that conflict could not be avoided. Salisbury would not give way. At length, lacking support from Russia, the French ordered Marchand to withdraw and, in March 1899, withdrew their claim to a place on the Nile. The relations between the two countries had reached a nadir and perhaps could only improve in the future.

CENTRAL, SOUTHERN AND EASTERN EUROPE

The new German Empire – the King of Prussia had been proclaimed Emperor at Versailles in 1871 – evoked conflicting feelings in Britain. Many believed that German unification was both desirable and inevitable. Nevertheless, there were qualms about the power and size of the new state. It could so easily dominate Europe. Even so, there were many aspects of British life where German influence and connections were strong. There were close, if unstable, links between the royal families and German philosophical and theological ideas were fashionable. James Bryce and R. B. Haldane were among those who studied in German universities and expressed a devotion to German *Kultur*. Protestantism, too, was supposed to link the two countries – hymnody certainly did. The British musical world was dominated by German music and musicians. The music of Wagner was brought to London by Hans Richter in 1877 and a period of study in Leipzig often gave a young British composer an 'established reputation'. Although Edward Elgar was not so privileged, he did come up specially from Worcester for the first British performance of the *Siegfried Idyll*, returning in the middle of the night by the 'fish and milk' train. On the other hand, there was apprehension, by the 1890s, about the growth of German industry and uncertainty about Germany's internal political development. No doubt it was fascinating (so some historians believed) that the origins of Anglo-Saxon representative institutions could be located deep in the Black Forest, but such a discovery did not still contemporary anxieties. The notion of a common heritage, however, was not devoid of political or diplomatic significance. Joseph Chamberlain was only one of a number of politicians to talk about a 'natural affinity' between Britain and Germany.

Bismarck dominated German policy for twenty years until his dismissal in 1890 and there was no one to match him on the British side for shrewdness, foresight or ruthlessness. Initially he had been willing to humour Gladstone. When the Russians announced that they were no longer going to honour the clauses of the Treaty of Paris (1856) which neutralized the Black Sea, Bismarck persuaded them to agree to a conference in London in March 1871. Thus, Gladstone was able to believe that the Concert of Europe had sanctioned the abrogation. Unfortunately for the Prime Minister, this modest display of solidarity was not the prelude to easy and intimate relations with Germany. In the following years, Bismarck consolidated the *Dreikaiserbund* (a league which linked St Petersburg, Vienna and Berlin) which, with France weak, left Britain no leverage in Europe. Disraeli liked to think that he would not be hemmed in, but while the three empires accepted the status quo in the Balkans there was little he could do. However, when the Sultan failed to suppress a rising in Bosnia and Hercegovina with his normal care, it looked as if the future of Turkey in Europe was again in doubt. Fearing that the imperial powers would exploit Balkan unrest for their own purposes, Disraeli publicly expressed Britain's concern, though he assented to the reform programme proposed to Constantinople by Andrássy, the Austro-Hungarian Foreign Minister. But by May 1876 it was clear that the *Dreikaiserbund* was not satisfied with the Turkish reaction to its proposals. A new 'Berlin Memorandum' hinted at the possibility of coercion, but this time Disraeli would not give support. British ships were sent to the vicinity of the Straits as a deterrent. Some puzzling approaches from Bismarck earlier in the year had led Disraeli to believe that the *Dreikaiserbund* might break up.

Meanwhile, the Turks had recovered the initiative in the Balkans, defeating Serbian, Montenegrin and Bulgarian forces. This victory, however, was to be their undoing, for subsequent atrocities upset the conscience of Christian Britain. Gladstone (who had retired from politics after his election defeat in 1874) turned aside from pondering 'future retribution' to write a pamphlet on *The Bulgarian Horrors and the Question of the East*(3). It was apparent that Disraeli (now Lord Beaconsfield) had dismissed the early reports of atrocities too flippantly, but he was unrepentant. He calculated that, once the British people had expressed their revulsion, the old anxieties about Russian intentions would reappear. This feeling of suspicion went back at least to the Crimean War. Russia was seen as a powerful if backward state with inordinate territorial ambitions in south-eastern Europe and central Asia, threatening British interests in both places. Actual knowledge of Russia was limited. It was a rare Englishman, like W. J. Birkbeck, who made himself an authority on the Russian Orthodox Church.

When a conference on the position opened at Constantinople in December 1876 Disraeli was still hoping that this latent anti-Russian feeling would surface and strengthen his hand. He was at loggerheads with Lord Derby and Lord Salisbury (the British representative) and refused to put pressure on Turkey – which Salisbury believed necessary to achieve a settlement. The conference broke up, with the Turks agreeing to further reforms and the British Ambassador in Constantinople ready, as always, to vouch for their sincerity. The Russians, who had been bracing themselves to intervene for months finally managed to go to war in April 1877. They were warned against taking any action which would threaten British interests at Constantinople and the Straits. The Russians made hard work of the war and, as the months passed, voices in British music-halls sang that they did not want to fight but, by jingo, they had the men, the ships and the money to stop the Russians from taking Constantinople. After an armistice in January 1878, the Russians signed the Treaty of San Stefano with the Turks in March. Russian gains in Asia Minor, and a possible bilateral settlement of the Straits question were unacceptable in London. Disraeli transferred a few Indian troops to Malta as a warning that Britain's views could not be ignored. Derby resigned from the Foreign Office in protest at so momentous a step. Since he, or his wife, had thoughtfully been passing Cabinet secrets to the Russians for some time, Disraeli was unperturbed.

Bismarck now intervened. Vienna, as well as London, had been angered by the San Stefano agreement and the Russians conceded that he should be the 'honest broker' at a congress to be held in Berlin. Disraeli traded compliments with Bismarck at this conference and returned to Britain in July 1878 with the news that he had achieved 'peace with honour'. Russia had been persuaded to give up the 'Big' Bulgaria that had been earlier proposed, although she was allowed to retain Batum. Cyprus came under British occupation and administration. Quite apart from the bases it would provide, perhaps the Sultan would be inspired by a shining example of administration so close at hand. Disraeli liked to believe that he had once again made Britain's opinions 'count' in Europe. In 1879, he described his foreign policy as 'not to be neutral and non-interfering but to act and to act with allies'. In fact, the appearance of a restored Concert of Europe was deceptive and the allies with whom Britain could act were not very conspicuous. Bismarck had no wish to draw close to Britain(5). While Gladstone floundered in Egypt, the Transvaal and Afghanistan, he could dominate European politics and even develop a modest colonial empire. Not that Europe was tranquil. In 1879, Bismarck committed himself to a Dual Alliance with Austria-Hungary and the Russians were included in the *Dreikaiserbündnis* of 1881, but he was aware that Balkan developments, in particular, would possibly compel him to choose between his two allies. On expiry in 1884, the agreement was renewed for a further three years. In addition, in 1882, he had concluded an alliance with Italy, basically to safeguard Austria-Hungary should the Central Powers find themselves in a war against Russia. If it was Bismarck's objective, as he delicately put it, to 'squash Gladstone against the wall, so that he can yap no more', he largely succeeded. His further speculation, that Gladstone would die in a madhouse, is believed to have proved inaccurate(2).

When Salisbury returned to office in 1886 he realized that the only way to restore the position of Britain in Europe was to bargain with Bismarck, though he had no wish to be a mere appendage of the Bismarckian system. The Liberals, he commented sardonically, had indeed achieved their long-desired Concert of Europe – they had united the Continent against England. Salisbury therefore allowed it to be suggested to Berlin that a close union between the greatest military power and the greatest naval power would be highly advantageous, but his overture made no progress. The Balkans were again in turmoil. The Bulgarians had shown themselves during their brief independence less than wholly grateful to their Russian benefactor. When, therefore, the adjoining province of Eastern Roumelia declared in favour of union with Bulgaria, the diplomatic roles formerly played by the powers were reversed. While the Russians wanted the Berlin settlement – which banned the union – upheld, Salisbury suggested that the solution lay in a personal union between the Bulgarian ruler and the province. He had come to consider Bulgarian nationalism a more effective barrier against the spread of Russian influence in the Balkans than any treaty. The eventual settlement followed the suggestion made by Salisbury but the episode increased tension between France and Germany and between Russia and Austria-Hungary. Salisbury needed German support over Egypt, but had no wish to be pushed into conflict with France or Russia. It was in this circumstance that he concluded the rather vague Mediterranean Agreement (February 1887) with Italy and Austria-Hungary. It was designed to preserve the status quo in the Eastern Mediterranean.

In his Midlothian campaign in 1879, Gladstone had referred to Austria-Hungary as 'the unflinching foe of freedom in every country in Europe', but Salisbury felt no embarrassment at reaching agreement with such a power(2). Goodwill towards Italy, on the other hand, was general. Italian colonial ambitions worried France more than Britain. Because of Austria-Hungary's alliance with Germany this new (and secret) agreement gave Britain, at one stage removed, a connection with Berlin. A few months later, Bismarck concluded a 'Reinsurance' treaty with Russia, but it did not give him a free hand against France and he also had to acquiesce in the future possible Russian control of the Straits and Constantinople. Ignorant of this treaty and having been rebuffed by the Sultan of Turkey over Egypt, Salisbury concluded a second secret Mediterranean Agreement with Italy and Austria-Hungary in December 1887. This new arrangement extended to Asia Minor as well as the Balkans and was made in anticipation of a Russian assault. London had also noted the closer relations between Russia and France. It seemed that Britain had come very close to a Continental commitment. In fact, its seriousness was not put to the test since Russia did not move into the Balkans. Nevertheless, in 1889 Bismarck did make an approach to Salisbury about an alliance, which was rejected on constitutional grounds, though it is difficult to believe that it could have proved politically acceptable. As it happened, Bismarck's career was drawing to an end (he was dismissed by the new emperor, Wilhelm II, in 1890) and the 'Reinsurance' treaty between Germany and Russia was allowed to lapse after his departure. Salisbury wished to remain on good terms with the Triple Alliance, but not to become part of that grouping(5).

In the post-Bismarckian era, relations between Britain and Germany seemed cordial. In July 1890 the Germans agreed to give up large claims in East Africa in return for Heligoland. They seem still to have hoped that a quadruple alliance would prove possible so as to restrain France and Russia, but Salisbury would not be drawn. When he left office in August 1892 he could claim that he had very considerably enhanced Britain's European status. Rosebery, both as Foreign Secretary and Prime Minister, was also convinced that limited co-operation with the Triple Alliance was the best policy. But, over the next few years, a host of difficulties suddenly erupted – from Afghanistan to Egypt, Siam and Uganda – and showed that Salisbury's achievement was at best precarious. Naval building was characteristic of all the major powers and increased tension was evident – Gladstone resigned in 1894 rather than approve the British programme. Franco-Russian naval co-operation was a feature of the early 1890s and it is not surprising that Rosebery found it difficult to decide which of the many issues confronting him was of greatest importance. Was it the Far East, where Japan's strength was shown for the first time in the defeat of China in 1894? Was it the revived dispute with Russia concerning India's northern frontiers, the Pamirs question? Was it the Near East, where Turkish massacres of Armenians in 1894 revived all the old emotions of the Eastern Question? From Siam to Samoa to South Africa the problems multiplied, making it apparent how difficult it was for Britain to be thought of as a European power in a complete sense. Yet these same disputes, which did involve the major European powers, also demonstrated that the chance of solving them also lay in Europe. British interests had become so ubiquitous, as Rosebery noted, that scarcely any question could arise anywhere which did not involve them. When Salisbury returned to office in 1895 he declared that he wished to remain good friends with Germany as he had been in 1892; leaning to the Triple Alliance without belonging to it, as he put it. He was to find in the last years of the century that the world had become harsher for Britain. Salisbury concluded in October 1897 that Britain had to strengthen her position on the Nile 'and to withdraw as much as possible from all responsibilities at Constantinople'(2).

THE ZENITH OF EUROPE

If the end of the obsession with the Straits terminated one British preoccupation, there were fresh anxieties in the 1890s which placed all European problems in a wider context. In 1895, there was a sudden crisis in relations with the United States when President Cleveland declared that he would fix Venezuela's disputed boundary with British Guiana and compel Britain to accept it. The Foreign Office did not like being talked to in that manner. The dispute blew over, but it was an uncomfortable indication of growing American influence and potential if not actual power(7). The Treaty of Shimonoseki, imposed by Japan on China in 1895, caused great concern in Europe, although Britain did not join with Russia, France and Germany in compelling Japan to revise its terms. It was in this global context that there was increasing talk of British isolation, 'splendid' or otherwise. The Mediterranean Agreements were not renewed in 1896 and the connection, at a remove, with Berlin thus ended. Nothing took their place. In his famous 'dying nations' speech in May 1898 Salisbury reaffirmed his belief that Britain would maintain 'against all-comers that which we possess, and we know, in spite of the jargon about isolation, that we are competent to do so'.[4] Chamberlain, interested in a possible alliance with Germany, took a different line. Declaring later in the same month that all the powerful states of Europe had made alliances, he suggested that Britain was envied by all and was liable to be confronted by so powerful a combination that not even the most extreme and most hotheaded politician could contemplate it without uneasiness. Salisbury, who was not hotheaded, did not believe that Britain would be simultaneously threatened in all parts of the globe by all the major powers and refused to change policy. By the end of 1898 Chamberlain accepted temporary defeat. The following year, the war in South Africa against the Afrikaners gave the Cabinet ample chance to assess just how viable was Britain's detached European status.

---

1. Miss Mozley, ed., *The letters of the Rev. J. B. Mozley* (1885) pp. 313–14
2. Lady G. Cecil, *Life of Robert, Marquis of Salisbury*, ii (1921), p. 130
3. F. W. Hirst, ed., *Early life and letters of John Morley* (1927), l, pp. 178–9
4. Cited in J. Joll, ed., *Britain and Europe* (1967), p. 192

CHAPTER 4

The defence of the realm

In September 1899, on the eve of the South African War, General Sir Redvers Buller expressed the hope that there would be some period when the military men and the diplomatic and political forces were brought into line(51). He was not the first soldier, nor the last, to desire such perfection. Few armed services have ever been called upon to perform the multiplicity of tasks expected of the British Army with such limited resources. The provision of an adequate institutional framework for the co-ordination of military and political objectives was never easy to achieve. In part, this failure reflected an ambiguity in late-Victorian society about the role of an army(53). Soldiers should be seen, though not too often, but there was a reluctance to give them too much of a hearing. Most late Victorians contrived to go through life without coming into direct contact with the military machine – an innocence which distinguished them from their European contemporaries. The role of the army in maintaining internal law and order had been much reduced by the development of the police force. The government of India, it was generally agreed, required its quota of men and the Indian Army usually attracted able but not particularly well-connected young men. In 1869, there were some 65,000 British troops and 120,000 native troops, a ratio which remained, although the size of the garrison had increased slightly by the end of the century. Recruiting such a force was never easy, but any reduction might precipitate another mutiny(57).

India apart, what was the purpose of the army? Lord Stanhope, Secretary for War in Salisbury's second Cabinet, wrote an important memorandum in 1891 arguing that home defence required two corps of regular troops and one composed partly of regulars and partly of militia. If these requirements were met, it would be desirable to be able to send two corps abroad. He added that the likelihood of any deployment in Europe was sufficiently improbable to make the defence of the United Kingdom the pressing duty of the military authorities. His view was not widely contested. Stanhope's conclusion was more an underlying assumption than a conscious decision. It was better for British diplomacy to deal ineffectively with the other major European powers who possessed large armies than for Britain to expand her own army. 'Militarism' was a Continental disease of no relevance to an island race. If the safety of the realm could be secured at sea then the army could remain relatively insignificant. Since the maintenance of naval supremacy was expensive enough, the army would have to take second place.

Nevertheless, within this financial constraint the army did change, though not as thoroughly as the Cardwell reforms after 1868 had led some observers to expect. It became more 'humane' with the abolition of flogging and the reduction

to twelve years from twenty-one of the period of enlistment. Even more conten-
tiously, Cardwell abolished the purchase of commissions, thereby opening the
path of promotion to 'merit' – though this was a criterion easier to enunciate
than implement. He augmented the home reserve by withdrawing British troops
from the self-governing colonies and introduced the concept of the 'linked battalion' – each regiment had, in theory, one battalion at home and one abroad. He
territorialized the infantry regiments of the line, developing strong local connections as an aid to recruitment. These reforms, it has been observed, acquired an
almost legendary reputation(57). In practice, successive governments sent an
increasing proportion of battalions abroad and the home-based battalions were
little more than training units. Officers complained about the poor quality of
recruits from urban England and traditional recruiting grounds in Scotland and
Ireland. The royal Commander-in-Chief, the Duke of Cambridge, remained in
office for decades, only grudgingly accepting the principle of promotion by
merit. While subsequent field-marshals like Kitchener, Robertson and Wilson
could steadily make their way despite modest sócial backgrounds, the composition of the officer class had not greatly changed. Officers gallantly had no wish to
undermine the army's sense of honour by the excessive use of the 'confidential
report'. Manliness and horsemanship were still thought to be as reliable indicators of future capacity as passing the Staff College course. Attempts had been
made at the mid-century to improve the standard of instruction both at Wool-
wich and Sandhurst but, by Continental standards, the curriculum remained conservative. The army, it was said, was not just another profession. The inconclu-
siveness of successive enquiries into army education suggested to the cynical that
the subject did not much matter.

Politicians, often approaching these problems from opposite standpoints,
sometimes came to the same conclusion. It was one thing to reduce privilege and
utter incompetence, another to encourage a professionalism which might lead
soldiers to think that they could make policy. An argument against the abolition
of purchase was that it would reduce the military presence in the highest political
and social circles. *The Brain of an Army* (1890) by Spenser Wilkinson was one of
a number of works to advocate a general staff on the Continental model(52).
Campbell-Bannerman, Secretary for War after 1892, saw no need for a small
group of senior officers to be set apart specifically to ruminate on general planning questions freed from all executive functions. The Duke of Cambridge was
finally persuaded to resign as Commander-in-Chief in 1894, but his departure
did not resolve the problem of 'professionalism' in the army. His successor,
Wolseley, once the dashing Sir Garnet but now a rather sick man, proved less
effective as a reformer than some had anticipated. It just seemed a matter of restoring the balance between the battalions at home and abroad and increasing the
enlistments. Lord Lansdowne, Secretary for War, could argue in 1897 that the
establishment was stronger by 30,000 men than it had been in 1870 and there
was a reserve of 78,000 men. A little tinkering with the Cardwell system was all
that was needed. Finance was the major constraint on a more searching policy of
expansion, but a small army was also thought politically desirable. Wolseley
abhorred men of Mr Gladstone's stamp who were churchwardens and parish

vestry men more than Englishmen. He wished that it had been his lot to have been cast in an era when a new Cromwell would clear the country of such frothing talkers and let the soldiers rule. Such sentiments could not be expected to appeal to Liberals(57).

In a speech in Edinburgh in 1897 Lansdowne complacently noted that since 1870 Britain had engaged in military operations in different parts of the world which had been got through 'not only without disgrace, but with considerable credit to the forces concerned'(57). Little wars had created big men, brimful of irrelevant experience(54). The army had been active on the Indian north-west frontier on several occasions, in the Ashanti campaign of 1873–74 against the Boers in 1880–81, in Burma, Egypt and the Sudan. In these campaigns the terrain sometimes constituted a bigger obstacle than the enemy. The British were normally successful against opponents who were frequently more numerous but were less well equipped than themselves. Defeats at the hands of the Zulus at Isandhlwana in 1879 and the Boers at Majuba Hill in 1881 caused momentary anguish but not fundamental disquiet. The triumph of Kitchener's victory at Omdurman in 1898 was fresh in the public mind. Episodes such as these, reported with skill and bravery by correspondents who sometimes were wounded or even killed, confirmed the impression that individual character and courage could still matter supremely in warfare. The private soldier, still frequently (and not without justice) regarded as a licentious and drunken brute who merited the attention of a Christian evangelist, became a hero when he was far away.

Such campaigns, however, only gave commanders the experience of dealing with relatively small forces. They did not have to wrestle with the logistical problems of putting a major army into the field, supplying it and co-ordinating its activities in battle. They grew unreasonably confident in the superiority of their arms and ammunition. The smokeless magazine rifle, an innovation of the 1890s, seemed to the Inspector-General of Cavalry to be likely to enhance the moral effect of a cavalry charge. It would never do to seek protection from the enemy's fire. Napier's use of elephants in Abyssinia was masterly, but the utility of the animal elsewhere might be limited; plans to emulate Hannibal, it must be admitted, have not come to light. Judged by the yardstick of imperial success – and that seemed to be all that mattered – the British Army performed adequately. Campbell-Bannerman was still arguing in the 1890s that foreign policy did not envisage military interference in Europe; there was no need to consider two army corps for possible service in such a remote region.

The British Empire was so conspicuously the product of naval supremacy that there was little dispute about the need to preserve naval strength. In the 1870s, that mastery did not seem in jeopardy; the United States was recovering from the Civil War, an imperial German navy did not exist and French naval expenditure declined after the Franco-Prussian War. This lack of competition suited the sailors and the politicians for, with the coming of the ironclad, the size of the British fleet meant that the cost of new building or re-equipment was formidable. There was also some complacency among designers and engineers in the United Kingdom – there was more innovation and inventiveness in France. There was a sentimental reluctance to deprive ships completely of their sails.

Gunnery improvements, both in range and reliability, were probably handicapped by the fact that it was not until the mid 1880s that the navy had control over its own ordnance. Before then, army and navy had been compelled to try to work together. In the early 1880s, however, mounted breech-loaders had been developed. The invention of the torpedo necessitated, among other things, the elaborate division of ships into watertight compartments. In 1881, the *Inflexible* was launched, weighing an unprecedented 11,800 tons. Even though small by later standards, it indicated the steadily accelerating requirements of naval building(55).

Rapid technological change approximately coincided with the end of unchallenged naval supremacy. By the middle 1880s, the French possessed nearly the same number of first-class battleships as the British. The first naval scare was initiated by W. T. Stead in his *Pall Mall Gazette*. Even Gladstone was forced to make a substantial increase in the estimates both for shipbuilding and ordnance. Continuing friction with France seemed to admit of no relaxation in this programme. When Russia, too, emerged as a naval power, British strategists feared Franco-Russian naval co-operation and the grave threat which it would pose to the British position in the Mediterranean. An official report in 1888 even doubted whether the navy was maintaining the two-power standard – something which the Naval Defence Act, 1889, tried to remedy. It was clear, however, that improvements in design, particularly in armour and gunnery, necessitated the building of a new class of ships – the Royal Sovereign class – rather than simply adding extra vessels. Within a few years, the situation repeated itself. In 1893–94 the rapid development of cordite-firing guns led to a fresh programme of building, causing considerable problems for the Liberal conscience. The subject became one of abiding press and public interest. Even if marginal to the economy as a whole, naval construction meant jobs for particular areas and produced a significant conjuncture of interests between capitalists and workers. By 1900, the mild panic seemed to be passing. Few supposed that technical improvements would suddenly stop, but confidence was derived from the fact that the French Navy (and the Russian) remained quiet during the Fashoda crisis.

Even so, the responsibilities of the navy across the world remained formidable. Its experience of actual fighting was restricted to minor engagements against distant opponents. A situation could arise in which the navy simply could not cope with the protection of the British merchant marine – which was larger than that of all other nations combined. Supplies of foodstuffs and raw materials from all over the globe were vital to Britain. The American A. T. Mahan's book *The Influence of Sea Power upon History* (1890) with its stress upon the vital part played by a battle fleet in maintaining commercial and imperial greatness had a great impact – though the ability to read English was not confined to the United Kingdom. The new German Minister of Marine, Tirpitz, admired Mahan and the expansion of the imperial German navy began in the late 1890s. Both the United States and Japan started building major fleets for the first time. This growth of navies was a world-wide phenomenon; even the Argentine, Chilean and Brazilian navies could not be dismissed. Such universal expansion was unprecedented. At the time, however, the popular mind was more impressed by the display of British naval might assembled at Spithead to celebrate the Diamond Jubilee in 1897. It was so regrettable that other powers seemed more inclined to emulate this display than to be overawed by it. In any case, an uncomfortable few shared the knowledge that submarines and mines might be able to blow that magnificent assembly out of the sea. There was also some irony in the fact that the rapid improvements in transport and communications within Europe and the United States were shifting the balance of advantage back in favour of land power. On both counts, therefore, there were grounds for supposing that the *Pax Britannica* was coming to an end. Too many potential challenges were appearing simultaneously in different parts of the globe to sustain the naval predominance which had come to seem normal. If there remained a gap between reality and appearance it could not be maintained for long.

CHAPTER 5

The approach of democracy

The capacity of the British political system to change yet to appear the same was a source of puzzlement to late-nineteenth-century foreign observers. The new wine and the old bottles were not easily distinguishable. The approach of democracy evoked both apprehension and excitement, though what it precisely involved was still a matter for speculation. The velvet-jacketed Sheffield seer Edward Carpenter urged his readers to start on the journey *Towards Democracy* (1883). On the other hand, as Gladstone noted, Britain was becoming responsible for settling the affairs of a quarter of the human race although she only possessed a population less than that of any major European power. Empire was ultimately based upon the ability to use force and subdue populations. In a sense, therefore, the United Kingdom was becoming an 'imperial democracy', though there was an inherent tension in the concept. The two processes were taking place simultaneously but, in a longer perspective, they might not be reconcilable.

INSTITUTIONS AND CONVENTIONS

The fact that Queen, Lords and Commons guided the country into the twentieth century suggested a stress upon continuity in a period of rapid change. The monarchy was unchallengeable and republicanism never more than a fickle and insignificant force. The jubilees of Queen Victoria in 1887 and 1897 were splendid public occasions. All the world, it almost seemed, came to London to do homage. The Queen's personal power and influence had, however, been declining and not simply due to her increasing age. Successive Prime Ministers, preoccupied by party management and aware of 'public opinion' steadily asserted their own authority. Royal views on certain military and ecclesiastical matters were still important, but they could not invariably carry the day. Empress of India she might be, but her imperial cousins in Berlin, Vienna and St Petersburg all had more power. On the other hand, Victoria was not, and was not disposed to become, a 'democratic queen'.

The survival of the House of Lords, with its powers formally uncurtailed at the end of the century was remarkable. Hereditary peers – some 500 were entitled to attend – assembled in unpredictable numbers to scrutinize bills sent up from the Commons and, if they saw fit, to amend them. The peerage was predominantly Conservative, the more so as Gladstonian Liberalism upset many Whig aristocrats. It was such a House that rejected Gladstone's Second Irish Home Rule Bill in 1893. Radicals had been attacking the Upper House for decades, but Gladstone could not persuade his colleagues to tackle its constitutional position even in this instance. Most Liberals considered the power of veto incompatible with the transition to democratic government and found the subordination of the Commons intolerable. Defenders of the House pointed out that no government possessed electoral endorsement for all its measures and a second chamber might safeguard the views of the people on a particular issue. Despite its importance, however, the constitutional position of the House of Lords never moved to the centre of political controversy. Beaconsfield, Rosebery and Salisbury found it an agreeable political home, satisfyingly immune from direct electoral pressure. Only Gladstone of the Prime Ministers in these decades stayed in the Commons.

The Lower House changed in character, composition and procedure, but not drastically. Members of Parliament still had to be men of means, if not wealth, for they were not paid. Although the property qualification had been abandoned, few MPs lacked property. After the Oaths Act, 1888, which followed the stand taken by Charles Bradlaugh, the celebrated secularist, they could be of any religious persuasion or none. They were expected to attend the Commons, but this did not need to be too onerous an obligation. The House normally functioned only between February and July and recesses were jealously guarded. No MP attended each day during the session. Obstruction by Irish MPs in the 1880s at last forced some restriction on debating time. Liberty of speech, Gladstone declared, could not reach a point at which it would 'inflict upon the House of Commons an incapacity for the discharge of its duties'.[1] It was somewhat galling for the Mother of Parliaments to resort to the French device of the 'closure'. Men still jibbed, however, at the notion that they were professional politicians. They were still suspicious of any improvements in their facilities which might compromise their independence. The hours of the House reflected the fact that MPs had other business to attend to. Even so, back-benchers had increasingly to accept that the government dominated parliamentary business. Those solid country gentlemen who began to find politics too demanding had to look for another club. Those who remained found their parliamentary lives guided by the Whips. The independence and authority of the Speaker received additional recognition(78).

These changes largely arose because the Reform Acts of 1867 and 1884 substantially extended the franchise and in turn led to the strengthening of party discipline(77). After 1886, two in three of the adult male population in England and Wales were entitled to vote and three in five in Scotland[C]. By no means all those entitled to vote did vote, since registration procedures and residence requirements remained complicated. The 1867 Act had not, in itself, eliminated former electoral practices and expectations(79). Some great landlords, for example, still expected to receive the votes of their tenants and penalized them, in one way or another, if they did not oblige. It continued to be a common assumption in the counties that landed families were necessarily best qualified to represent such constituencies. But, despite the strength of such attitudes, the 'party' rather than the 'interest' became electorally significant. The Ballot Act, 1872, which made voting secret, profoundly changed the character of elections, though 'influence' did not disappear overnight. The constituency associations in the counties were often run by men who had previously managed elections without their aid. The 1880 Election disclosed the continuing existence of various corrupt practices, but an Act of 1883 substantially eliminated them. The large urban constituencies, though not so susceptible to 'influence', were also still affected by their previous traditions. Before 1867, for example, 40 per cent of the Leicester electorate might be termed working class, compared with only 7 per cent in Leeds.[2] There was considerable variation in the sophistication of the methods used to get people to the polls. In general, however, while great diversity still existed within and between urban constituencies, the fact that there were regular contests for town councils made town-dwellers more party conscious and less inhibited in expressing opinions than countrymen.

Important organizational changes took place within both major parties. A National Union of Conservative and Constitution Associations was formed in 1867 and, after a shaky start, took an active role in propaganda. The Tories also established their 'Central Office'. Their Chief Whip at Westminster maintained close connections with both bodies. At a local level, Conservative clubs were successfully set up in many working-class districts. Initiative in organizational matters was not restricted to activity in London. It was in Birmingham that the Liberals set up an elaborate network of ward organizations, both for municipal and general election purposes – though eighteenth-century precedents for this 'novel' structure can be found. In 1877, the National Liberal Association was formed in Birmingham, with Joseph Chamberlain as its first president and the 'caucus' in the city gained some notoriety for its tactics and methods. While these organizational changes can be exaggerated, they did help to implant party loyalties among the new electorate.

It was generally assumed that party competition would remain the basis of the British political system, though there was always a minority, which included Sir Henry Maine in his *Popular Government*, which was puzzled by the admiration expressed for the raucous rituals of party strife. It was not clear, however, in the new electoral circumstances, that the appeal of the two parties would be so nearly equal that there would be regular alternation in government. The party leaderships were on uncertain ground here and had to feel their way. From their standpoint, the increasing participation of the electorate was an ambiguous development. National political 'decisions' had long been taken by a small, fairly homogeneous, political and social élite. It was not easy to tell how the world of 'high politics' would react to burgeoning bourgeois aspirations, not to mention those of the working class. In fact, no one party did capture the allegiance of the enlarged electorate. Liberals, who had believed that the future must rest with the 'popular' party, gloomily saw the Conservatives dominating the last decade of the century(81, 83). Strictly speaking, there were more than two parties for, the Irish apart, there were Liberal Unionists and even, for a short time, a 'Fourth party' of skirmishing Tories. The Liberal Unionists, who had separated because of their opposition to Home Rule for Ireland, were scarcely a 'third force' and worked closely with the Conservatives.

The Cabinets of both parties were still drawn predominantly from the aristocracy or from established political families. There were, of course, exceptions – new men who reached high office without such advantages. The most conspicuous example in Gladstone's first Cabinet (1868) was John Bright, the first religious dissenter to reach such a position. Bright's performance in office, however, was disappointing and did not match his reputation in the country(82). In the 1880s, Joseph Chamberlain, a Midlands industrialist of Unitarian stock and a reforming mayor of Birmingham before entering Parliament, sprang into national prominence and might have become Gladstone's successor. Instead, he split the Liberal party (over Home Rule) and found a place in a Conservative Cabinet. Gladstone's 1892 Cabinet included such 'unconnected' figures as Asquith, Morley, Fowler and Bryce – all of non-Anglican background. Such infiltration, however, was not confined to Liberal administrations. Disraeli and Salisbury both appointed W. H. Smith, the newsagent, to their Cabinets and Rosebery's administration in 1894–95 was more 'landed' in character than Salisbury's last Cabinet.

It was in Parliament that ministers made or marred their reputations, although an increasingly heavy burden of explanation and exhortation was required outside its walls. Bright had shown that speaking before large audiences was a vital part of a politician's equipment. Others were compelled to follow him on to the platform. Gladstone came to relish this mission to the people – so long as the people did not attempt to dictate to him. Even so, Gladstone's Midlothian campaign in 1880 seemed irresponsible demagoguery to his critics. Paradoxically, his election there depended a good deal upon the deference shown by Lord Rosebery's tenants to their landlord's candidate. Lord Hartington had to trundle round North-east Lancashire in 1880 making speeches. On the other hand, Disraeli's speeches outside Parliament only occasionally assumed political significance. Salisbury did set himself the task of becoming a platform orator – with some success. These big speeches, invariably fully reported in local and national papers, could turn the shyest of aristocrats into a master of rhetoric.

POLITICAL PARTIES [B, C, D]

The 'essence' of the political parties and the reasons for their success on particular occasions cannot easily be defined. In asking what men voted for, or what parties stood for, one is, as always, confronted by a complex fusion of personality and policy. Neither main party was compact and homogeneous; each had elements tugging in opposing directions. They both accepted the evolving system with apparent equanimity – the measures of 1884–85 caused far less alarm and excitement than the reform of 1867 [C]. Neither party could afford to be exclusively identified with one social class. Each, and in more than theory, appealed with some chance of success to all sections of the electorate. Despite the efforts of Bright and others in the mid-century, a specifically middle-class party had not emerged. The Liberal party in these decades was a combination of Whig aristocrats, business and professional men, and some working-class elements. From the

1870s onwards, 'Lib-Lab' MPs appeared in a number of constituencies. Gladstone appointed Broadhurst, a former stonemason, to a junior ministry in 1886. The Conservatives in Parliament were not quite so diverse socially, but their electoral support was. Voting behaviour reflected a subtle blend of class identification, status aspiration, occupation and religious affiliation; sometimes these indicators could all point in one direction, but they could also conflict. The successful party would be the one which could most accurately judge the weight to be attached to these factors at any given moment. Of course, the full electoral strength of the working classes had not yet been displayed, but there was little sign of a massive or fundamental alienation from the political system. Given the nature of their support, however, it is not surprising that both major parties were a little apprehensive about the future.

Liberalism was avowedly more 'ideological' than Conservatism. Most Liberal voters did not, even so, spend hours brooding over Mill's *On Liberty*, but they frequently expressed a desire to advance the cause of individual freedom and remove the obstacles in the path of the talented. This assault on 'privilege' characterized Gladstone's first government, though it should not be mistaken for egalitarianism. An example of this concern was the University Tests Act, 1871, which abolished such religious subscriptions as still existed at the old English universities. In 1870, an Order in Council carried forward the changes in the recruitment to the Civil Service which had begun after the Northcote–Trevelyan Report of 1853. The Judicature Act, 1873, was another illustration of the Liberal desire to reform the structure of the State. These achievements pleased, but also satisfied, many Liberal supporters. The scope for this kind of change was not endless. *Laissez-faire* has been variously interpreted, but most Liberals did not want the State to take a controlling role in economic or social policy. They were apprehensive about an expanding bureaucracy. On the other hand, in the 1890s, younger Liberals felt that Liberalism could not be satisfied with the removal of formal impediments to equal citizenship. They argued that 'open competition' had no practical significance for millions. There was a clear tension between stressing the merits of individual freedom and the urge to 'improve'. How far should central or local government intervene in housing, health and education, if necessary displacing voluntary agencies? If, of course, the role of the State was extended, increased taxation would be required. Should such taxation fall upon consumption or income? Many Liberals wished to abolish income tax, but it showed remarkable resilience. In 1894, however, it was a Liberal Chancellor, Harcourt, who wished to raise it by a further penny to 8d. in the pound. He had toyed with the idea of introducing a graduated tax, but instead reserved the application of this principle to a new estates duty. Rosebery, the Prime Minister, a large landowner himself, was not enthusiastic. He cast a lamenting look on the 'variety and richness of intellectual forces' which were passing away and feared the 'cleavage of classes'. Harcourt answered that the 'horizontal division of parties' was an inevitable result of household suffrage. The dilemma for the Liberals was that if they did take an 'advanced' line on taxation and other matters, they might still fail to satisfy working-class aspirations, while losing substantial middle-class support.

The Conservatives well understood the position in which their opponents were placed and had begun to make progress at their expense. In the 1890s, it did appear as if the two parties were beginning to have different social bases. British Conservatism, however, had shown itself to be a remarkably malleable political outlook – far less rigid than its European equivalents and more success-ful. Sentiment centred on throne and altar, on the empire and on a strong for-eign policy, but policy could be pragmatic. Conservatives were untroubled by a vision of an ideal society. They started with the existing reality and adjusted judiciously, so they believed, in the light of past experience. In this light, the role of the State posed fewer intellectual problems for them than it did for Liberals. The Conservatives in the 1870s may not have had a comprehensive programme of social reform – Disraeli did not believe in comprehensive prog-rammes – but their legislative record was important. The Public Health Act, 1875, for example, brought some order to a mass of sanitary legislation. Cross's Artisans' Dwelling Act of the same year allowed, but did not direct, local au-thorities to demolish slums. It would be wrong, however, to think in terms of a Conservative housing policy. Housing was still a matter for private individuals and voluntary agencies. *Omnia Sanitas* notwithstanding, the lowest levels of society, the 'submerged tenth' were as likely to resist cleanliness with as much vigour as they resisted godliness(84).

Disraeli's government showed some flexibility in its legislation on industrial relations. It set up a Royal Commission on the labour laws, though the commis-sioners were handicapped by a trade union boycott. Picketing was one of the most contentious issues, as it was to be a century later. The 'Sheffield outrages' of 1867, when trade-unionists had taken violent action against non-unionists, were fresh in public memory. Gladstone's Criminal Law Amendment Act, 1871, had set very severe limitations on picketing, though an accompanying Act had reinforced the legal status of trade unions. In 1875, the Conservatives passed the Employers and Workmen Act and the Conspiracy and Protection of Property Act. The former, which replaced the terms 'master' and 'servant', limited the penalty for breach of contract arising out of a dispute to payment of civil dam-ages. The latter stressed that peaceful picketing was legal, though severe limita-tions on the extent of interference with essential services remained. The Tories could not be said to have established a 'special relationship' with the trade union movement, but their attitudes were not rigid. Although there were occasional references to the Tory devotion to 'One Nation', Salisbury's domestic policy was prosaically pragmatic. There were, it is true, attempts by Lord Randolph Chur-chill and others to give a positive content to the term 'Tory Democracy' but, by a combination of luck and good judgement, Salisbury was able to resist their challenges.

Ultimately, therefore, it was the party leaders who defined what 'Liberalism' or 'Conservatism' really meant. In the 1870s the competition was between Glad-stone and Disraeli. The very diversity of Gladstone's ideas and background helped to fuse together Whig, Liberal and Radical elements. He was 'provincial' by virtue of his Liverpool origins, yet 'metropolitan' by habit. He was Scots by descent, found himself (through marriage) with his home in Wales, but was strongly linked to the English governing class through Eton and Oxford. His devotion to classical culture was not at the expense of financial acumen. He was strongly Anglican in religion, but his moral zeal appealed to dissenters. When such a vigorous man straddled such frequently separated worlds, he apparently left little scope for an opponent. Disraeli did not try to match him on his own ground. His success lay in his very unrepresentativeness. Here was a baptized Jew, a proto-Zionist, a novelist, a man of uncertain financial status, the possessor of a 'Continental' mind, at the head of a very British party. It seemed that such an outsider could reconcile cleavages and conflicts with less difficulty than a more conventional figure might have experienced.

Their parties found it hard to replace Gladstone and Disraeli. Gladstone, of course, outlived Disraeli by many years and his active old age complicated the question of the succession. Rosebery, who seemed an odd choice to superintend the transition to democracy, had very brilliant personal qualities but was unstable. Harcourt could provide no greater cohesion. It was left to an apparently undistinguished Scot, Campbell-Bannerman, to guide a party which was seemingly anxious for leadership but also reluctant to accept it. After Disraeli's death in 1881, the Conservatives also experienced difficulties in choosing a new leader. Salisbury and Northcote shared the task in their respective Houses, and Lord Randolph hovered in the wings. In 1885, Queen Victoria invited Salisbury to form the first Conservative government after Disraeli's death. During his years in office (until 1900) Salisbury was also Foreign Secretary and his main interest lay in this sphere. His conduct of domestic business can be seen as a rather gloomy holding operation. Government 'by the people' was not only undesirable, it was impossible. Nevertheless, the age seemed to demand it and all that could be done to mitigate the damage that popular government would cause was attempted.

Babies born in the 1890s, unlike their predecessors in the 1870s, would not automatically grow up to be Liberals or Conservatives. Until then, the degree to which the established parties and old political families maintained 'business as usual' is perhaps surprising. Even so, the political parties were aware of 'pressure from without', the Liberals especially(80). Various temperance bodies drew attention to the evils of drink and some of them pressed for legislation to ban or restrict its sale, or to introduce 'local option' in the matter. Peace societies urged the merits of proposals to make international disputes become subject to arbitration procedures. Women, children and animals all had their advocates. Some of these associations were explicitly and specifically political, trying to put pressure on the parties to move in their direction. The Liberals were subject to most attention, and some of their politicians saw the party disintegrating from the activities of 'faddists'. In fact, the strength of these groups was not as great as their numbers or zeal might suggest. In part, this was because some of these groups cancelled each other out and because they were often divided internally between members who were anxious simply to educate the public and those who desired legislation, between 'sanctionists' and 'moral suasionists'. Should men be compelled to abstain from alcohol as they were now being compelled to be vaccinated? An archbishop of York declared a personal preference for England free rather than England sober – but he was an Irishman.

There remained one large unanswered question at the turn of the century; how did the world of labour stand in relation to the political system? Differences of outlook and aspiration between skilled and unskilled, between trade and trade, between 'respectable' and 'unrespectable' were manifold; nevertheless, there was a labour movement. Trade unions were, by definition, working-class bodies. At the beginning of the 1870s, they remained predominantly craft associations whose membership was only a small proportion of the working population. Once legal issues had been resolved (as we have seen they were for a time in the mid-1870s) trade-unionists could carry on with their fundamental function of negotiating with the employers about conditions and terms of labour. But this simple picture was changing. The Trades Union Congress, which attempted to co-ordinate (for it could not control) the work of the individual unions is generally held to have begun in 1868. Over the next thirty years, many more industries were unionized, among the most prominent being mining and the railways. Joseph Arch brought about a rapid advance among agricultural workers in the 1870s. By the last two decades of the century, there was a much more general atmosphere of industrial tension and militancy. The period from 1889 is often taken to see the development of the 'new unionism', particularly in the London area. Some strikes were conspicuously successful both in London and the provinces, compelling employers to improve wages, reduce working hours, modify the shift system and improve working conditions. The most dramatic, though not the most successful, was the London dock strike of 1889.

Unions mushroomed, charging low subscriptions and enrolling many workers who had never joined before. Membership of trade unions topped the 2 million mark at the end of the century, but the situation was very unstable. Some unions collapsed as quickly as they were formed. They were very anxious to claim to be 'national', but this style often had little relationship to reality. It still remained the case that most workers were not members of trade unions. Trade union leaders experienced industrial defeats as well as victories. Employers increased contacts among themselves and a National Free Labour Association was formed to assist in the breaking of strikes. The presence of 'blacklegs' at many disputes once again focused attention on the problem of picketing. The *Lyons* v. *Wilkins* case (1897–98) placed a very restrictive interpretation on what had been thought to be the law. Such a decision in the Courts, combined with victory of the engineering employers in a major strike over the same period, suggested that the unions needed to think afresh about their legal, political and industrial position(85).

The political role of trade unions, if indeed they should have one, was far from clear among unionists themselves. The leaders of the second Reform Act era, like George Howell (1833–1910), often campaigned for an extension of the franchise, but disclaimed any wish 'to turn our trades societies into political organizations'. The small number of trade-unionists who entered the Commons in the 1870s – Alexander McDonald and Thomas Burt being the best known – did so as Liberals. There was a rich vein of self-help among many 'aristocrats of labour' and a firm commitment to Liberalism. Some constituency associations were prepared to accept working men. By the time of the 'new unionism', however, the 'Lib-Lab' solution was increasingly decried. Working men did need separate and independent 'Labour' representation if their interests in such fields as housing, health, education and employment were to be adequately represented. In 1892, Keir Hardie, Havelock Wilson and John Burns all won parliamentary seats on such a platform.

But did 'labour representation' imply a distinct political party or involve a commitment to Socialism? A Social Democratic Federation (SDF), devoted in principle to the spread of Marxism, had been formed in 1883. It was guided by H. M. Hyndman, an Etonian who had little patience with trade-unionism as it then existed, seeing it as too securely embedded within the bosom of capitalism. Working-class SDF members were, nevertheless, active in trade-unionism, particularly in London. Socialism was slowly ceasing to be something exotically European. William Morris, poet, designer and craftsman, left the SDF in 1884 to found his own Socialist League. He contrasted useful work with useless toil (1885), founded the Hammersmith Socialist League (1890) and published his Utopian novel *News from Nowhere* (1891). The Fabian Society, formed with the objective of reconstructing society 'in accordance with the highest moral possibilities' evolved between 1884 and 1889. The *Essays*, published in the former year, revealed that the time was approaching when capital could be made public property. Karl Marx brooded in London until his death in 1883. The Independent Labour party (ILP) was formed in Bradford in 1893 with Keir Hardie in the chair. It quickly spread in the industrial areas of the north of England. 'Labour' remained in its title, but 'Socialism' was implied. Sophisticated metropolitan Fabians thought the ILP somewhat provincial, wondering whether any good thing could come out of Bradford. The Fabians held out little hope for a third party unless the electoral system was changed and a second ballot permitted. The poor showing of independent labour candidates in the 1895 General Election – Hardie lost his seat – seemed to confirm their scepticism. They thought there was more to be gained from trying to spread collectivist ideas among rising Liberal politicians.

In the later 1890s, therefore, it was not clear what this ferment of ideas would lead to. There were talks and proposals to try to link up the various Socialist societies with the trade unions and co-operative movement, but the outcome was still uncertain. Each union contained pro- and anti-ILP factions. 'Militancy' did have its advocates, but the kind of disorder which had accompanied the SDF's meeting in Trafalgar Square in 1886 seemed to other trade-unionists to jeopardize what could be obtained under existing political conditions. They were not anxious to become deeply involved in party politics on behalf of a Socialism whose form and content was still inchoate. It did seem that the two parties which had presided over the transition to democracy might yet flourish under an even wider franchise in a new century.

---

1. Cited in W. D. Handcock, ed., *English historical documents*, xii(2) (1977), p. 93
2. D. Fraser, *Urban politics in Victorian England* (Leicester, 1976)

CHAPTER 6

The mature economy

In 1870, British businessmen could look back on decades of sustained economic expansion. Industrial growth had been averaging 3 to 4 per cent per annum for most of the nineteenth century. The United Kingdom remained the most highly industrialized country in the world; still an example for others to emulate or envy. Free Trade had firmly established itself as the basis of British commercial policy and it could still be thought that other industrializing countries would adopt the same principle. But, despite the evidence of achievement, there was a developing awareness, which had a political dimension, that economic growth was more precarious than it had become customary to assume. The failure of the Overend Gurney bank (1866) showed that disaster could still strike the world of banking and finance. In a different sphere, the American Civil War had recently caused serious problems of supply for the Lancashire cotton industry and showed that it could be dislocated by events beyond its control.

Such experiences, if causing disquiet, were not normally thought to presage disaster; booms and slumps had to be enjoyed and endured, though economists wrestled, without entire success, to understand the causes of these enigmatic cyclical fluctuations. By any standards, the British export performance in engineering machinery, textiles, iron and steel and coal, looked formidable – and was still rising. The renewed boom of 1872–73 temporarily set at rest the doubts of some industrialists and economists who thought they saw signs of complacency rather than maturity. Imports of food and raw materials were rising at a faster rate than exports, both by volume and value – but that could be considered as simply an aspect of the international division of effort which free trade assumed. The United Kingdom continued to show a healthy surplus on its balance of payments, thanks in good measure to the country's 'invisible' earnings derived from shipping, insurance, brokerage and income from overseas investment. The importance of this income was a reflection of the growing significance of the 'City'. By the 1870s, there was a greater concentration of financial expertise in London than anywhere else in the world. Governments could not do better than to bring their funding requirements to Britain.

Could economic growth last indefinitely? Could political stability be maintained without it? It was recognized that a distinctive set of circumstances had produced an industrial revolution in Britain – but it could occur elsewhere. Techniques of production could be mastered by foreigners and there was no reason why they could not improve upon British inventions. They might well have access to better and cheaper supplies of raw materials. They might well locate factories more advantageously, in changing circumstances, than they were located in Britain. They could all learn from Britain's experience, and there were signs that this was already happening on a considerable scale. While cottons continued to be exported, British manufacturers found it steadily more difficult to penetrate European or American markets, and had to look increasingly to Asia. How much longer could such predominance in a particular commodity last? Cheap food was a great boon, but was it really wise to permit such a drastic drop in the scale of British agriculture?

Such questions gained fresh urgency in the wake of the 'Great Depression' which allegedly began in 1873 and did not end until 1896. This phenomenon, sometimes called a 'myth', has been extensively considered by economic historians. The consensus seems to be that as a comprehensive description of this period the notion is seriously misleading. The rate of industrial growth did fall, but the process was probably under way before 1873 – certainly growing foreign competition was apparent before that date – and there was no sharp and sustained upturn after 1896. In the 1880s, the growth rate fell below 2 per cent; significantly below that of Germany and the United States. Saul argues that the 'terms of trade' changed significantly in the middle of this period – a movement which continued well after 1895(175). Profits were low until 1895. He also suggests that the downward trend in prices – traditionally the dominant feature of the 'Great Depression' – may have begun as early as the mid-1860s and, in several respects, come to an end in the mid-1880s. Part of the difficulty in dealing with the problem of a depression lies in terminology. If we mean by it a failure to sustain previous rates of growth then the description is accurate, but there was no general decline. If unemployment did rise, for those still in work the fall in prices and the growth in real wages produced a continuing sensation of improvement. The absence of comprehensive 'unemployment statistics' and the incompleteness of statistical information on production during these decades should engender caution. It is worth noting, too, that at the time economists and commentators were not unanimous in their interpretation of the data. However, the appointment of Royal Commissions to consider the agricultural depression and also trade and industry bears witness to contemporary disquiet about the state of the economy.

Anxiety also stemmed from an awareness of the changes taking place in fundamental industrial processes. The quality and efficiency of steel-making, to take but one example, improved most dramatically in these decades. In 1879, British steelmakers produced 1 million tons, outstripping the combined European total. In the next decades, though, producers elsewhere in Europe made more effective use of the new Gilchrist Thomas process. German production rapidly expanded and surpassed the British total in 1893. The United States had outstripped Britain seven years earlier. Even so, British production did not register a decline, and so long as world trade expanded, this dethronement from the top position did not seem too serious(176). After all, was it not unreasonable to expect Britain to be supreme in every industrial process for ever? Perhaps, for a change, Britain might be able to learn from the mistakes made by pioneers.

If this reflection was consoling, anxiety about the quality of British entrepreneurship was still apparent. Some historians have discerned a disconcerting tendency for the sons of successful businessmen to be diverted into the patronage of art or the cultivation of country gardens. But, while it is not difficult to produce examples of such conspicuous degeneracy, it is also not difficult to find a second or third generation in a family business who disdained such pursuits and devoted themselves to business with relentless energy. Put in a general form, the argument about management in these decades is inconclusive and, ultimately, becomes a matter of words. Just what do we mean by 'entrepreneurial enterprise'? What is a 'capacity to innovate'? Economic historians, skilled in discerning dynamic qualities by long years of selecting students for their courses, have offered the fruits of their reflections. Some American scholars have obligingly pronounced the late-Victorian entrepreneur on the way to redemption, but the path to salvation is not yet secure. Business histories, expanding in an era of business contraction, have made it plain that a great multiplicity of factors entered into the success or failure of particular companies. Failure could be due to shortcomings in product design, in marketing, in financing, or in management structure, but no ranking of these factors is universally applicable. It also becomes evident that the ability to adapt and refine an existing business structure may be even more important than the capacity to innovate. And 'success' and 'failure' are not as easy to measure as might appear at first sight. A given enterprise may score differently if the comparison is with its international competitors, if the criterion is the rapidity with which it digests technological change or if the yardstick is the rate of return on capital(177). That in turn raises questions about the definition of a sector within a national economy within which comparisons may legitimately be made and also whether international contrasts are helpful, given that so many additional 'variables' then complicate the picture. Contemporary industrialists were well aware that a successful company needed a combination of skills and talents. W. H. Lever, the soap manufacturer, thought he needed orderly executives, inventive engineers and imaginative advertisers. He also needed Scotsmen to bargain on price because they had no imagination.

Lever's own business steadily expanded, but it is sometimes suggested that there were too many small firms during these decades all trying to produce a wide range of products. They thus failed to benefit from economies of scale. The response of industrialists to legislation in the mid-century designed to facilitate the creation of joint-stock companies was limited. Payne notes that as late as 1885 limited companies only constituted between 5 and 10 per cent of the total number of important businesses, though the proportion was higher in shipping, iron and steel, and cotton(177). Thus, most manufacturing firms remained as family enterprises and there was no substantial divorce of ownership from control. By the end of the century, however, the air was full of talk about possible business mergers. The Imperial Tobacco Company, formed in 1901, became the largest company in the United Kingdom. Its largest constituent component was the Bristol firm of Wills, widely identified with the famous *Woodbine* cigarette. The purpose of the merger was to enable British manufacturers to resist the American tobacco challenge. Even so, the heads of the merging family businesses retained as much power as they could in their own hands. The Calico Printers Association, formed two years earlier from the merger of many more companies in the calico-printing industry, and the fifth largest United Kingdom company, was another example of this process of consolidation and concentration. This particular company soon ran into serious difficulties with its management structure and, although they were eventually overcome, it was evident that relatively small companies were not invariably handicapped by their size. Large companies usually only operated successfully if there was a sufficiently large and fairly stable market for their particular products. If the market was not big enough or was highly volatile they could experience financial problems more quickly than small companies with less productive capacity. On the other hand, the criticism that British companies did persist in producing a larger range of goods than their overseas competitors may have more validity. Specialization did reduce production costs and British firms often saw themselves as generalists. Yet, paradoxically, British industry during this period is also accused of being insufficiently sensitive to the individual requirements of customers, offering standard lines on a 'take it or leave it' basis. It is difficult to see how both of these criticisms can be equally true. And if there was a lack of innovation, it was not invariably the fault of the supplier. Customer conservatism could restrain inventiveness – this was certainly the experience of some British locomotive builders. Clients were only too satisfied with what they knew. The relationship between continuity and change, in short, is as complex in the world of commerce as in any other sphere(178).

If there was concern about cotton and, to some extent, about iron and steel, coal presented a different picture and so did shipbuilding, at least during some years. Total United Kingdom coal output rose steadily from 110 million tons in 1870 to 225 million in 1900, and the proportion exported increased from 13.4 to 25.9 per cent. A doubling of the tonnage is impressive – though in the thirty years before 1870 the increase was nearly fourfold. By value, however, the figures were less reassuring, showing considerable fluctuation. In 1900, however, net coal output formed some 6 per cent of the national income. But, although it looked secure, coal-mining could be quite suddenly hit by changes in overseas demand and a drop in the requirements of any power-using industry. In such circumstances, the considerable variation in productivity, type of coal mined and profitability, could become of considerable importance. Some regions were more vulnerable than others. On the whole, the increased tonnage was raised by traditional means and, with output soaring and markets apparently available, there was little incentive to innovate. The prosperity of coal naturally also brought success to the ports and railways of South Wales and North-east England which expanded with the export trade.

The age of the sailing-ship was coming to an end, though only in the 1870s did new steamship tonnages begin to overtake new sailing-ship tonnages. The advent of the steamship benefited both the coal industry and the steel industry – and shipbuilding too. Deane and Cole place the peak of shipbuilding's relative importance in the British economy during the decade 1875–84. The average size of steamships built in British yards rose to 1,600 tons in the 1890s – still small by later standards, but an increasingly expensive item for companies to finance. It became vitally important to match supply and demand. Britain's own merchant marine was a formidable size, though perhaps too large for the cargo it could profitably carry. By the end of the century, the advent of turbines and oil-fired vessels indicated a new age in sea-transport(179).

On land, while the traffic receipts and operating profits of most of the railway companies steadily grew, the number of new lines constructed dropped sharply. There was, after all, a limit to the number of small seaside towns which could be equipped with a railway for, in effect, two months of the year. The Great Central Railway, establishing a direct Manchester and Sheffield route to London terminating at Marylebone, was the last major railway and the return on the investment was poor. However, the construction of the Forth Bridge and the Severn Tunnel in the 1880s, did bring major improvements to the railway system. Some brave spirits wanted even more expansion but more sombre railwaymen, conscious of the internal combustion engine, feared that their industry was at its peak by the end of the century.

THE SECOND PHASE

Despite the strength of the 'staple' industries, it was becoming evident that continued growth could only be achieved by moving people from established industries to new ones. It was in this 'second phase' that economic historians have seen shortcomings in the British performance(180). They have noted the number of inventions made and developed in the United States from the mid-century onwards, such as the Singer sewing machine, the Yale lock, the typewriter and an impressive array of machine tools. The Americans also pioneered the systematic organization of mass production – being pushed in this direction by labour shortages. British interest in 'scientific management' was limited, but there were exciting developments in electrical, chemical and transport engineering which run counter to the impression of sturdy conservatism. It is, of course, misleading to think of any major industrial development during this period as exclusive to one country – Germans, Russians, Americans and finally an Englishman all played their part, for example, in the development of the electric light bulb. British inventors were certainly active in the electrical industry, although it is true that the industry expanded more rapidly in the United States. The continuing cheapness and ready availability of coal and steam power in Britain helps to explain why electricity supply did not expand more swiftly. The story is not very different in the chemical industry. Although some pioneering work continued in the United Kingdom, the lead, both in invention and production, passed to the United States and Germany. Of course, the 'chemical industry' covered a great many specialisms and subdivisions and some were in a much healthier state than others. The general picture, however, is one of sluggish growth (by international standards), though such a pattern is not easy to explain. Ritual reference to the number of chemistry graduates in Germany as compared with Britain only provides part of the answer. Other industries disclose a similar pattern. In cycle and motor-car production, for example, although there were ingenious British engineers and inventors at work, the lead in the 1890s rested with France and Germany. Again, it may well be the very comprehensiveness of the British railway network which inhibited rapid development. The legal restrictions on road vehicles (often imposed under the pressure of horse and railway interests) were more far-reaching than on the Continent. It was only in 1896 that the requirement that a vehicle should be preceded by a man with a red flag was repealed. British motor cars were made in small workshops in small numbers, with scarcely a whiff of an 'assembly line'. The age of the mass motor car still lay in the future. Cycling, however, made steady progress. In 1895, for example, A. J. Balfour wrote excitedly to Lady Elcho to reveal that he had just ventured out into the London traffic on a cycle – judiciously choosing a Sunday afternoon to make his début. The industry did export successfully but the scale of operations remained small. In general, in all these industries, British businessmen hovered uneasily on the edge of the modern mass-production era, perhaps more doubtful than they should have been about their future markets both at home and abroad(184).

There is another paradox about these decades. At the height of the 'Great Depression', striking changes took place in the distributive trades. The 1880s and 1890s witnessed a 'consumer revolution', drawing into the market social groups which had previously not had money to spare. The number and membership of Co-operative societies jumped dramatically and their percentage of total retail sales doubled in the late century. 'Marks and Spencer's Penny Bazaar' became a well-known slogan in the north of England. The partners set up their headquarters in Manchester in 1897 and were on the threshold of yet greater commercial achievements. Department stores like Marshall and Snelgrove, Barkers and Harrods were becoming an essential aspect of middle-class life. Specialized multiple grocers like Liptons or Home and Colonial, shoe shops like Freeman Hardy and Willis, chemists like Boots (with 150 shops by 1900), tailors like Hepworths, newspaper and book stores like W. H. Smith, and scores of others, transformed the retail scene. The products ranged from cocoa and chocolates made by Frys, Cadburys and Rowntrees, to Cherry Blossom Boot Polish and Beecham's Pills(181).

The advertiser came into his own, making good use of the expanding newspaper and magazine industry. Brand names – Bovril, Colman's Mustard or Pears' Soap – were implanted in the public mind by skilful jingles and pictures. W. H. Lever saw to it that his soap and sunlight became synonymous. Every level of business joined in the verbal excitement. 'Let us improve your understanding' was the punning contribution of the author's grandfather, a Bristol shoe repairer. His enthusiasm for novel window displays was subsequently to earn him the obituary accolade 'pioneer of advertising'. Lever – who insisted that the bath at his Hampstead house had specially fitted enormous taps so that he would not waste time waiting for it to fill – would have approved of this zeal for publicity.

The 1881 census identified 12,000 different occupations in the United Kingdom – a figure which had risen to 15,000 in 1901 – and clearly they cannot all be described. However, noteworthy at the close of the century were the numbers employed in coal-mining, building, and food and drink – which all showed considerable growth. For the first time, over a million men were engaged in conveying people, goods and messages, though drivers of horse-drawn vehicles still outnumbered those of motor cars by two hundred to one. 'Commercial occupations' showed a notable rise. The three-quarters of a million 'professional people' possessed the highest social status, if not necessarily the highest incomes, among the middle classes. 'Professional men' embraced the clergy, the law, medicine, education and the arts. The Royal College of Surgeons, the Law Society and other self-regulating professional bodies had been chartered earlier in the century. The Institute of Chartered Accountants was established in London in 1880 (charters having been given to associations in Scotland some decades earlier). The Institute of Electrical Engineers, which adopted that title in 1888, is one example of another tendency – specialization within what had hitherto been a general profession. Among the professional associations to be chartered during this period were those for librarians, surveyors, chemists and company secretaries. As qualifications proliferated, there was less room for men who, earlier in the century, would not have troubled unduly whether they were described as architects, surveyors or engineers. If this was restrictive, the benefit was that standards of practice did improve and it was less easy for quacks and fraudulent operators to function. Even the clergy of all denominations were increasingly given 'professional' preparation in pastoral care and the delivery of sermons(182).

INVESTMENT

One other striking feature of this period was the continued growth of British overseas investment. The precise volume of capital exports is a matter of difficult calculation and economists produce different figures. More than half of the capital exports went to the temperate regions of recent settlement. Lending tended to involve a relatively small number of borrowers at any one time. The main receiving areas during the 1880s were Argentina, Australia and the United States. One recent author contends, however, that despite political developments, after the early 1870s there was no shift of investment either to the established empire or to newly acquired colonies(183). The imperial share of investment reached a peak of 67 per cent in 1885 but dropped to 25 per cent during the 1890s. Private investors, domestic banks and insurance companies were strongly influenced by the decline in yields on consols and mortgages in Britain and took advantage of improved communications, the simplification of currencies and the steady acceptance of gold as the world monetary standard, to seek financial rewards abroad. Both in the United States and Argentina, a large share of British investment went into railways. There was, of course, always an element of risk. Baring Brothers, deeply involved in Latin American finance, over-reached themselves in the late 1880s and had to be rescued by the Bank of England. Various other international factors led to a slackening of overseas investment in the 1890s.

Whether lending overseas on this scale was desirable from the general standpoint of the British economy continues to be debated. The most advantageous mixture of home and foreign investment (and how the one interacts with the other) is a matter of great complexity. So is the relationship between foreign investment and the export of goods. In general, despite some suggestions to the contrary, it seems unlikely that it was any bias towards overseas investment which starved industry within Britain of the investment it required, although housing may be an exception. In this period, most British businessmen disliked raising capital from the market in any case. Throughout the United Kingdom, banks are sometimes held to have been culpably aloof from the requirements of industry, but the exploration of the relationship between businessmen and their bankers is only in its infancy. Some evidence from Ulster and Clydeside suggests, contrary to some received opinion, that banks were very willing to support their customers in particular projects. Naturally, bankers had to make their own assessment of the risks in the knowledge that if a bank failed – as happened to the City of Glasgow Bank in 1878 – the repercussions for a community could be extremely serious.

The scale of overseas investment will still cause controversy, as will the role of the banks, but in this period it was not judged to be the business of government to interfere in these matters 'in the national interest'. No government could decide whether or not a given firm should expand or diversify. Overseas, it was the duty of British diplomatic and consular officials to try to ensure fair competition for British businessmen, not to become businessmen themselves. One historian suggests that Victorians were so devoted to Free Trade that the direct interests of British trade were often sacrificed to an ideal.[1] To a few contemporaries, this devotion was perverse. It seemed obvious that the world was not following Britain's Free Trade example. Germany introduced a measure of protectionism in 1879, France in 1882 and the United States in 1883 and 1890. This last, the McKinley tariff, had certain very obvious consequences in Britain, crippling, at least for a time, the exports of the South Wales tinplate industry. But there was no British retaliation. Even so, during the last decade of the century, both in Parliament and outside, the dogma of Free Trade was being questioned. So, too, was the assumption that a major obligation of government was to keep public expenditure low. Peacock and Wiseman discern, from the 1880s, the replacement of the doctrine of retrenchment as the effective curb on government expenditure by the notion of 'taxable capacity'.[2] With the outbreak of the Boer War, with increased levels of expenditure and taxation, the way was open for new concepts of the proper relationship between government and society and between economics and politics.

---

1. D. C. M. Platt, *Finance, trade and politics in British foreign policy 1815–1914* (Oxford, 1968), pp. 182–3
2. A. T. Peacock and J. Wiseman, *The growth of public expenditure in the United Kingdom* (Princeton, 1967), p. 66

CHAPTER 7

Town and country

The 1901 census reports revealed that almost 77 per cent of the population of England, Scotland and Wales lived in 'urban districts' – some 25 million people. And, in general, the rate of population growth was higher in the more populous urban districts. After the mid-century, the rate of rural population growth failed to keep pace with the urban and, in many instances, rural population actually declined(152). By the end of the century, however, this absolute decline changed in certain parts of Britain as population began to spread outside town boundaries into the 'suburbs'. Such a movement cannot exactly be described as a rural renaissance. It was, rather, a blurring of the border between 'town' and 'country', though that distinction had not been obliterated.

In the late nineteenth century, Great Britain boasted a cluster of great cities. In 1890, five of them – London, Manchester, Glasgow, Liverpool and Birmingham – had the distinction of being among the world's top thirty in population: a feat never to be repeated(153). England was unusual in Europe in not being a country with a 'primate' city. 'London' – precise statistics are difficult because the definition of the metropolis was constantly shifting – contained in the 1890s some 20 per cent of the total population of England and Wales. However, despite the capital's major position, the aggregate population of the next sixteen cities had grown more rapidly than London over every census decade since 1871. By 1901, about thirty cities in England and Wales had populations of over 100,000, containing a quarter of the total population. The position of Glasgow in relation to Scotland conformed more to the Continental pattern. In 1891, it contained some 20 per cent of the country's population and outnumbered the aggregate of the seven next largest cities in Scotland. In Wales, only Cardiff could be compared in size with the major English provincial cities and it was still quite small. In Ireland, within the territory of the eventual republic, the towns could not retain their own natural increase let alone absorb migrants from the countryside. Dublin grew only slowly. In what was to be Northern Ireland, Belfast was growing, with a population virtually equal to that of Dublin, while small towns like Ballymena and Londonderry also expanded(161).

Urbanization on this scale within the United Kingdom produced a baffling mixture of responses. The supposed connection between the 'city' and 'degeneracy' had deep roots in English literary culture(156). Pessimistic observers felt gloomy about the swelling 'masses' who inhabited the cities and felt that the link between 'urban' and 'urbanity', the 'city' and 'civilization' was about to dissolve. These laments often have a despairing tinge since the process seemed irreversible. Optimistic observers, however, found the dynamic life of the city irresistible. It was not change and decay they saw around them but change and improvement(155). The size of cities permitted a range of social and cultural activities which were impossible in the countryside. Moreover, it was claimed that the industrial cities, unlike earlier cities, were not parasitic upon the countryside. They provided work and employment on an ever-expanding scale. To condemn cities simply because, in their rapid development, housing and sanitation were inadequate, was short-sighted. Such defects could be overcome with energy and initiative. To an extent, this debate was political. Tory critics tended to idealize the virtues of an integrated rural hierarchy in which there were reciprocal obligations. Liberal critics, on the other hand, saw such relationships as stifling and restrictive. They praised cities as places where men could make their way unfettered by deference. Later, Socialists were critical of such self-made men and the patronage they exercised as 'city fathers'. The social divisions of cities, they suggested, expressed a hierarchy as rigid as anything which existed in the countryside.

Although the situation was changing quite rapidly, it remained true at the end of the century that life expectancy was still lowest in great cities. The Registrar-General calculated, for example, that a Manchester-born man living in Manchester might expect to live just over half as long as his country cousin(153). Not all cities were equally unhealthy; Bristol and Leicester were much better than Manchester, Liverpool or Newcastle. The crude death-rate was made particularly grim by the high level of infant mortality – the figures being again worst in the northern industrial cities. Contemporaries had little doubt that bad housing and inadequate health care were largely responsible for this poor record. Housing associations, under various auspices, endeavoured to increase the supply of houses and improve standards but the task was beyond them. Housing was particularly bad in Scotland(154). While in England and Wales in 1901 there was 8.2 per cent overcrowding (i.e. more than two persons per room) the figure for Scotland was 50.6 per cent(134). There had been little improvement since 1871. Considerably more than half of all Scottish families lived in 'houses' of not more than two rooms. In Dundee, Glasgow and Edinburgh in particular, the characteristic tenement blocks were invariably crowded and epidemic diseases were frequent(167). Thousands of people lived in 'single ends', making 'room and kitchen' seem luxury. The 'common closes' frequently became dumping grounds and squalor and disease marched hand in hand. Across the Irish Sea, there was a significant reduction in overcrowding in Belfast, but it remained at some 40 per cent in Dublin. It has been noted, however, that the downward trend in death-rates was less noticeable in Ireland than in Britain and the slums of Dublin were probably the worst in the British Isles. As in Glasgow, improvements in public drainage did not necessarily improve the sanitary conditions in tenements.

Whatever the conditions in Dublin, Glasgow or Newcastle, it was London itself which attracted most comment(157). The capital of the United Kingdom was still by far the largest city, with its population spilling over into such areas as Leyton, Tottenham, East and West Ham, Willesden, Croydon, Hornsey and Walthamstow; these were the fastest-growing communities in England. Visitors to London were invariably struck by the contrast between the East and the West End. The nonconformist minister Andrew Mearns in his *The Bitter Cry of Out-*

cast London (1883) described the 'pestilential human rookeries' he encountered. The Liverpool shipowner, Charles Booth, organized and financed a great investigation into the *Life and Labour of the London Poor*. His findings were embodied in seventeen volumes which appeared between 1889 and 1902. In bold terms, he found that some 30 per cent of the population lived in varying degrees of poverty. Booth was not simply a statistician. He believed that the very poor could be taken out of the 'daily struggle for existence' and advocated a 'Socialism to preserve individualism'. His 'very poor' class would come under State regulation for the Socialistic side of life already included hospitals, poor-houses and prisons. The remaining groups, he suggested, could be liberated to pursue their own betterment in a properly individualistic fashion. While saddened by many of his discoveries, Booth was not depressed by them. London could conquer its problems. He later advocated an old-age pension, considering that 'an endowment for all old people paid for out of taxation would, if the amount granted be small, have no adverse but rather a favourable influence on private accumulation, and that the spirit of independence would not suffer'.[1] Like many late Victorians, he saw the need for a greater role for the State, but trembled before the possibly debilitating consequences if that role should become too extensive.

In 1901, Seebohm Rowntree published his *Poverty. A Study of Town Life* based on enquiries carried out a couple of years earlier. The town in question was the ancient northern cathedral city of York where he was a chocolate manufacturer. To romantic southerners it seemed from a distance the antithesis of the metropolitan 'Great Wen'. This study distinguished between 'primary' and 'secondary' poverty. Fecklessness and intemperance could lead individuals and families into a poverty which they could avoid. The full application of existing statutes in the field of public health could help to prevent some poverty. Even so, he argued that 'nearly 30 per cent of the population are living in poverty and are ill-housed, ill-clothed, and under-fed'. His careful investigation had shown that a 'typical provincial town' contained the same amount of poverty as London. Rowntree's dietary studies made his point very vividly, but it was not clear what 'this land of abounding wealth' would do about the problem he had identified.[2]

Some visionaries would not wait for the working out of social and economic improvements over a long period. Ebenezer Howard, for example, deplored the fact that men still flooded into any city, whether York, London or Glasgow. Neither what he called the 'town magnet' nor the 'country magnet' represented 'the full plan and purpose of nature'. What was needed was a 'garden city' – a comprehensive plan which would be acceptable to Socialists and Individualists. He conceded that the 'time for the complete reconstruction of London' had not yet come, but once a small garden city had been established and been shown to be feasible that reconstruction would inevitably follow.[3] Pending such a development, however, suburban expansion perhaps offered the way forward. The Bristol Tramway Company, for example, extended electric tramways into the suburbs and working men and women could be carried for 4 miles and over for 1d. They could shop in the city but live, and sometimes work, outside it. The factory inspectors concluded in 1899 that such tramways might well become an important factor in the solution of the 'overcrowding problem'.

However attractive was the prospect of the garden city, most town councils had to tackle their enormous problems more prosaically. The last decades of the century saw a great growth in civic pride. In Birmingham, for example, reaching its climax when Joseph Chamberlain was mayor (1873–76), the leading citizens of the city tried to create a late-Victorian Florence. Chamberlain was not unique in retiring from business in 1874 to devote himself to municipal affairs. He persuaded his colleagues to tackle three 'big measures' – the municipalization of gas and water, and a city improvement scheme. He urged businessmen to devote their talents to municipal enterprise. The members of a city council should consider themselves 'the directors of this great business'.[4] Within eight years, as the result of the efforts of the newly appointed Medical Officer of Health for Birmingham more than 3,000 wells, used by 60,000 people, were condemned. Although the city improvement scheme was not without its critics, who said that the Corporation Street project was using resources which should have been devoted to working-class housing, Birmingham laid claim to being 'the best-governed city in the world'. What was more, it had two football clubs, Aston Villa and Birmingham City, and Warwickshire County Cricket Club, an art gallery and a fine public library. It had Bournville which George Cadbury, the cocoa and chocolate manufacturer, developed in open country to the south. Josiah Mason had provided money to establish a scientific college with courses designed to meet 'the practical, mechanical and artistic requirements of the Midland district . . . to the exclusion of mere literary education and instruction'(219). In the 1870s, it evolved into a university college, with Chamberlain as its president shortly afterwards. At the end of the century it received an independent charter as the University of Birmingham. By that stage, it permitted a modicum of 'mere literary education'. Despite the vital role played by religious nonconformists in its civic life – men like Dale, Dawson and Chamberlain himself – there were those who felt that all Birmingham needed was a bishop. The first one did not arrive until 1905.

Bristol was another city with its dissenting élite of energetic citizens and once again the cocoa bean contributed potently to civic welfare aided, in this case, by the popularity of the tobacco leaf. The Fry and Wills families figured prominently in city life – Sir William Henry Wills gave an art gallery 'to his fellow citizens' in 1904. Bristol, too, had its university college trembling on the brink of independent status. Alfred Marshall, the economist, had told its citizens in 1877 that the new university college would help their city into the new age. A Bristol businessman 'with the light of science guiding him on his path' would 'go boldly and vigorously on, trying that which had not been done before, overcoming new difficulties, pioneering new paths'(219). In many cities, local historians were active in celebrating and chronicling the civic past – an activity encouraged by a vigorous local press.

In retrospect, these decades witnessed the zenith of municipal pride and civic achievement. In 1903, the Austrian observer Redlich, commented that nothing could be more disquieting to an average Englishman than the thought that he had to follow the orders of a London Office 'as if they were so many provisions of the law', but it was not long before this robust localism came to seem rather antiquated.[5] Back in 1885, when the large cities were subdivided into separate constituencies rather than provided with additional seats on a city-wide basis, commentators in Birmingham and Manchester wrote that it would prove a significant step along the route to the emasculation of the political power of the cities. They were being proved right. Of course, there were other factors in this decline – notably the fact that the uniformity of provision seemed to entail centralization of control.

THE COUNTRY

On Boxing Day 1899, Cecil Sharp chanced to see the Headington Morris Men in action. His enjoyment of their performance led him to a general interest in the music and songs of the English countryside. His work in preserving on paper this heritage was invaluable, but the self-sufficient and enclosed rural society which had produced the songs he admired could not be preserved. The countryside, it seemed, had to surrender before the inexorable advance of urban attitudes and values. Country cousins became ever more conscious of the inferiority of their 'facilities' and entertainment. Education certainly came into the villages, but it was not always well received. School attendance figures throughout the United Kingdom were lower in the rural areas than in the towns. In Scotland, for example, this school log-book told a familiar story: 'The attendance is yet small as is generally the case till after the Martinmas term, when the children engaged in herding cattle, etc., come home for the winter.' In this context, particular occasions for absence were lambing and potato-planting (April–May), turnip-thinning (June–July), sheep-shearing (July), harvest (August–September) and potato-lifting (October)(218). These were co-operative and communal enterprises requiring whole families; school was a tiresome interruption. Besides, the curriculum of the village school was normally conceived by urban minds. It was assumed, too, that the able child who might aspire to secondary education could only do so in the nearest town. In education, and in other respects, advancement and urban life became virtually synonymous(172).

The advantages of 'modern life' could not be denied. Mains water from a tap removed the necessity for a trip to the well – and a social occasion as well. It had to be admitted that a water-closet had advantages over an earth-closet. Candles had their limitations as sources of illumination; gas mantles seemed a great advance. Better lighting, though by no means universally available, began to upset the traditional rhythms of waking and sleeping. Differences between the pattern of activity (or inactivity) in the four seasons became slowly less striking. But although there was change, to an extent, in these respects, the climate was not susceptible to control. Farming was still a physically very demanding occupation – shifting heavy weights of milk, hay, straw, roots, feeding-stuffs, manure and water. Mowers, reapers and self-binding reapers did help with the harvest, but milking was still universally done by hand. It was only at the end of the century that there were experiments with milking machines. In field work, the productivity of farms depended largely on the speed and strength of the horses – there were about 1½ million of them in Britain in 1901(158).

In 1851 about a quarter of the occupied British males were employed in agriculture, a figure which dropped to about 17 per cent in 1881 and 12 per cent in 1901. It was this dramatic decline which made Britain so different from practically every other country in the world.(159). During these decades, between a third and a half of the labour force in the United States, France, Germany, Denmark, Sweden and Italy were still on the farm(162). Within the United Kingdom, this same decline accentuated the broad difference between Britain and Ireland. The number of tenant farmers did not decline so rapidly, but most farms had to make do with fewer labourers and this was a spur to mechanization. Taking the United Kingdom as a whole, the contribution of agriculture to national output, estimated at about one-sixth in 1870, fell to about one-twelfth by the end of the century. By this time, British farmers supplied about a quarter of the wheat consumed in Britain, less than half the butter, cheese and pigmeat, and about three-fifths of the beef, mutton and lamb. The acreage in Britain devoted to wheat had halved by the end of the century from what it had been in 1871, though the acreage devoted to oats slightly increased(160).

The cumulative effect of these changes in British agriculture was enormous. No part of the country remained immune. Nevertheless, scholars have stressed that the depression did have different consequences in different areas. There were prosperous new developments, like the emergence of market gardening in such areas as the Vale of Evesham and parts of the Thames valley. Milk producers could aim to supply the growing London market from as far away as West Wales. But, though growth points can be identified, when wheat slumped from an average price of 55 s. a quarter in 1870–74 to 28 s. in 1895–99, British farming could never be the same; bankruptcies and untenanted farms were common. The livestock producer suffered a collapse in prices too, though not quite of such magnitude. The first cargo of frozen mutton left New Zealand for the United Kingdom in 1882. A million carcasses a year were exported by the end of the decade. The British urban population demanded cheap food and came to assume that it was a right to which it was entitled(162).

Not surprisingly, Royal Commissions to investigate the state of agriculture were appointed in the early 1880s and again in the mid-1890s. The former seemed to become very obsessed in its deliberations by the British weather – there had indeed been wet summers in 1875, 1877, 1878 and, above all, in 1879 – but it could propose no remedy. More helpfully, the Agricultural Holdings Act, 1883, gave to farmers a statutory right of compensation for improvements they made to their farms, although the government resisted the idea of setting up machinery to fix 'fair' rents. It was in these circumstances that the smallholder suddenly became the favourite of politicians. Jesse Collings, Birmingham businessman and politician, but a son of rural Devon, advocated a system of peasant proprietorship with the slogan: 'Three Acres and a Cow.' He and others took up the cause of 'allotments' but were disappointed at their slow progress. The second Royal Commission produced a number of weighty reports, but skirted the issue of protection and made modest recommendations concerning tenure, tithes and agricultural education. New university colleges, like those at Bangor and Reading, had agricultural courses and Wye College was established in 1894. As far as government was concerned, Salisbury set up the Board of Agriculture in 1889 and, although the post was initially thought suitable for country squires like Chaplin and Long, it stimulated and disseminated much agricultural research. Help was also given to farmers in such matters as the preparation of their accounts. The future of the industry was still a matter of debate and anxiety – there was no guidance to be had from anywhere else in the world. The general impact of the changes was that farming was becoming a business to be managed rather than a way of life or a symbol of status.

The structure of power in the countryside was also changing, though not quite as rapidly as economic developments might have led one to expect. It had long been a feature of landowning in Britain that many great landowners were not completely dependent upon their rents from farming to sustain their standard of living. And while some estates, both great and small, were under pressure, land could still be managed profitably. Sir Frederic Knight even succeeded in reclaiming large areas of the Royal Forest of Exmoor during this period of agricultural decline. The social hierarchy in the countryside was thus still very evident even though the structure of local government was becoming more democratic. County councils, established in 1888, gradually whittled away the powers which the gentry and aristocracy had been accustomed to exercise for centuries. Rural district and parish councils, set up in 1894, brought representative government into the villages. For the most part, however, no rural revolution took place; the squire and the vicar still had their place. Rural squires still found a place at the Cabinet table. Henry Chaplin, first President of the Board of Agriculture, must have been one of the last ministers to specialize in drawing horses during Cabinet meetings. He obligingly left them on the table as presents for his colleagues. But, symbolically and actually, all over the United Kingdom fires were going out that had reputedly been kept going for centuries. In Ireland, legend had it that when a fire went out the soul departed from the householders; whether this was also happening it is not easy to judge.

The countryside was increasingly coming to be seen as an 'amenity'. James Bryce, a politician who had once scaled Mount Ararat, regularly but unsuccessfully proposed bills in Parliament, from the mid-1880s onwards, designed to increase access to mountains and moorlands. A Commons Preservation Society had been founded in 1865 which, although chiefly concerned with the preservation of open spaces in towns, also took up the battle in the countryside. An 1882 Act enabled owners to place a monument in the care of the State and many did so. In 1901, however, the owner of Stonehenge enclosed it in a barbed-wire fence and charged an admission fee – to the great annoyance of the Commons Preservation Society. In 1895, the National Trust for Places of Historic Interest and Natural Beauty was formed – its twin concerns being reflected in its title(173). It was chiefly cyclists – there were some 60,000 members of the Cyclists' Touring Club in 1900 – who could penetrate to such places, but they did so in increasing numbers. Walkers, who formed 'rambling clubs', also ventured deeper into the countryside after reaching their starting-point by rail. Railway companies promoted 'excursions' to cater for a somewhat different market. Many town-dwellers flocked to the seaside in summer and there were resorts for all tastes and classes from Scarborough to Scunthorpe and Blackpool to Bournemouth. The 'masses' tended to go on 'excursions' and the 'classes' on 'vacations'. Even Mr Gladstone took to going regularly to Penmaenmawr in North Wales to enjoy the mountains and the sea, although he was careful to take adequate reading matter with him. There could be no more satisfying fusion of work, recreation and education, of town and country, than to read Homer beside the seaside in September.

---

1. Handcock, op. cit., p. 177
2. B. S. Rowntree, *Poverty* (1901)
3. Sir Ebenezer Howard, *Tomorrow* (1898)
4. A. Briggs, *History of Birmingham*, ii (1952), pp. 70–4
5. Cited in D. Read, *The English provinces* (1964), p. 239.

CHAPTER 8

Recreation and education

In the late nineteenth century, leisure became a serious business. An astonishing variety of games and pastimes were codified and given a nationwide competitive structure. Pre-industrial recreations, such as cock-fighting and bull-baiting, still survived, though sports involving cruelty to animals were increasingly abhorred, certainly by the middle class. The passion of some aristocrats and working men for boxing and the turf upset the sensible and prudent. Certainly, the more brutal public spectacles were coming to an end. There were few successors to the famous prize-fight of 1860 between the English champion, Sayers, and his American opponent Heenan, which lasted for two hours and twenty minutes. At the end of the 1860s, the marquis of Queensberry lent his name to a set of rules for boxing with gloves. To the disappointment of some spectators, the regulations eliminated 'spiking, biting, gouging, strangling, butting... scratching with the nails, kicking, falling on an antagonist with the knees...'(247). But it took decades for the boxing public to become reconciled to classified weights and timed rounds.

It was, perhaps, urbanization which contributed to the decline in the popularity and acceptability of sports involving what came to be considered as cruelty to animals. In place of what had been essentially rural sports came a wide variety of ball games, many of considerable antiquity but now simplified and codified. Football emerged as the dominant winter game of the British Isles. The Football Association had been formed in 1863 and its initial major task was to get agreement on a set of rules. The FA Cup competition, established in 1871, speeded up uniformity of practice and added a framework within which the game could develop. Until 1882, when Blackburn Rovers defeated the Old Etonians, the gentlemen amateurs of southern England set the standards. Through the 1870s, however, new teams were being formed in the North and Midlands which were to challenge the dominance of the public schools. Initially, they were frequently connected with churches or chapels but quickly turned into independent organizations. They flourished chiefly in industrial areas where a Saturday afternoon holiday had become normal. By the mid-1880s, professional players were permitted, though tightly bound to the club that signed them. Although players could be transferred from one club to another, teams frequently remained predominantly local in composition and were powerful expressions of community sentiment.

Gradually, the style of the game took its modern shape. One little refinement was the introduction of the goal-net in 1891! An English Football League was established in 1888, but it cannot be described as truly national, consisting as it did only of clubs from Lancashire and the Midlands. Clubs from London and the

South remained outside when a second division was formed in the 1892/93 season. It was in the South that resistance to professionalism had been strongest and when the Royal Arsenal club turned professional in 1891 it was an outcast among London clubs. There was a Southern League, formed in the 1894/95 season, which steadily expanded, but clubs from the South did not play against those from the Midlands and the North – except in the FA Cup. Tottenham Hotspur's victory in the final of that competition in 1901 was the first significant success of a southern professional club. Over 110,000 people watched this match at the Crystal Palace, contrasting with some 2,000 who had watched the first final played at the Oval thirty years earlier. Football inevitably reflected certain social realities. Amateur sides like the Corinthian Casuals could still be fitter and stronger than working-class professional teams and beat them(248).

Football spread quickly throughout the rest of the British Isles. The Queen's Park club in Glasgow, formed in 1867, remained the premier Scottish club for several decades and appeared south of the border. The Scottish Football Association was formed in 1873 and a league followed twenty years later. After much resistance, professionalism was legalized in Scotland in 1893. Within Glasgow, Rangers was founded in 1873 and Celtic in 1888 – a rivalry which was more than a mere clash of footballing skills. A Welsh Football Association emerged in 1876 and an Irish (in Belfast) in 1880. For the first decade of its Irish existence, football stayed in Ulster, then it spread insidiously in the South. International matches between England and Scotland started in 1872, though they had no regular venue. Wales played Scotland for the first time in 1876 and England three years later. Ireland made its international début in 1882, losing 0–13 to England. By the mid-1880s a United Kingdom four-country championship had been established, but as yet no games took place against national or club sides elsewhere in Europe – where the game was spreading, largely under British influence.

Although football became the most popular winter game, rugby also made substantial progress, though there were disputes about the rules until the mid-1880s. The number of clubs rose from 31 in 1872 to 481 in 1893. This expansion led to suggestions that players might at least be compensated for loss of wages if not actually receive pay. A rift appeared between the essentially middle-class clubs of southern England and those of Yorkshire and Lancashire where the game had spread among the working class. The Northern Rugby Football Union, established in Huddersfield in 1895, permitted part-time professionalism and, in due course, a different code emerged – to be known later as Rugby League. Its Challenge Cup was launched in 1896. Rugby League remained confined for the moment to northern England, but the strongly amateur Rugby Union spread throughout the British Isles. In Scotland, the game was firmly established in the endowed schools and the clubs of their 'former pupils'. It became the popular winter game in the Scottish Borders – whence came the variant of seven-a-side rugby. It was chiefly in the bigger towns that rugby advanced in Ireland; in the countryside, Gaelic football and hurling were in the ascendancy. The Gaelic Football Association, which controlled these games, banned its members from indulging in 'foreign' sports. Rugby came late to Wales, but spread rapidly in the southern industrial areas. The Welsh quickly showed a flair for the game and did a great deal to establish the playing positions which are now used. As in the case of football, international matches within the British Isles soon followed. Partly because of the dissension in England caused by the issue of professionalism, Wales emerged as the dominant rugby nation: in the South, it became the popular game, pushing football into a poor second place. International matches, both in football and rugby, established a form of popular nationalism within the United Kingdom for which there was no previous parallel.

The summer scene was rather different. Cricket was largely confined to England where the centre of attention (after 1873) was the county championship. Initially, seven sides (composed of amateurs and professionals) took part, to be joined by a further six. Social distinctions were particularly evident in cricket – in northern England some professionals employed by clubs bowled in their clogs. In the northern counties, in particular, cricket excited deep passions and gambling on the outcome of matches was not unknown. In 1895, the forty-seven-year-old Dr W. G. Grace scored 1,000 runs in May. He also showed formidable skill on the bowling green. In these decades, too, lawn tennis emerged in its modern form. The first Wimbledon Championship was competed for in 1877. As in other games, it took some time for the players and officials to agree on the rules and styles of play, but by the 1880s men at least were using an overarm service and the game speeded up. Initially, spectator interest had been solely centred on individual performance, but international team competitions emerged and by the end of the century moves were being made to start what became the Davis Cup competition.

The mania for sports and games was normally thought to be a healthy sign and there was a belief that physical activity on this scale was beneficial. The increasingly high standards of play had important repercussions on dress for both sexes. Gradually, small areas of flesh were exposed to the eyes of spectators. Future generations, encumbered by leisure and the abolition of work, may yet regard the contribution made by the United Kingdom to the world of sport during these decades as one of its most important legacies. In the short term, the spread of the major British games throughout the empire was another sign of its unity. Cricket, Rugby Union and golf spread most rapidly. Cricket and rugby tours to Australia, New Zealand and South Africa were regularly undertaken shortly after rules had been agreed within the United Kingdom. Cricket broke through barriers of religion and colour in India. One of the stars of the English cricket scene was Ranjitsinhji, the maharajah of Nawanagar, who became (in 1899) the first batsman to score 3,000 runs in a summer. The Royal Calcutta and the Royal Bombay golf clubs were the oldest in the world outside the British Isles. In contrast, and a significant aspect of cultural history, there was very little sporting contact with the Continent, although British businessmen brought rugby to France and the first visit there by a British rugby club took place in 1893. There were no international football matches with mainland nations. In the summer, only the Dutch and the Danes, for some unfathomable reason, displayed any interest in cricket.

EDUCATION

Educational provision throughout the United Kingdom was as varied as its games, dialects and eating habits(214). The 1870 Education Act was designed to provide school accommodation for children in districts where there was insufficient provision for their elementary education. In such instances, the responsibility would fall upon school boards, whose schools would not teach any denominational formulary. Fees (not to excede 9d) were still charged, but could be remitted in certain circumstances. Alongside the 'public elementary schools', the voluntary system survived, indeed flourished, particularly since school boards could pay the fees of children attending these, mainly church, schools. All ratepayers, including women, could vote and stand for these school boards. By the end of the century, there were some 2,500 in England and Wales, with responsibility for nearly 5,700 schools and 2 million pupils. The number of voluntary schools rose from nearly 9,000 to over 14,000, with two and a half times more pupils than in board schools. The number of Roman Catholic schools more than doubled, to become a significant sector for the first time. In 1880, education was made compulsory up to the age of thirteen – though with the possibility of earlier exemption. In 1891, education effectively became free for both board and voluntary school pupils.

Elementary education was a self-contained system. Its basic task was to inculcate the 'three Rs' but, during the 1870s, grants were allowed to schools for children who were successfully examined in certain subjects. Indeed, it became sufficient to establish that a class was proficient in such subjects for payments to be made. In general, however, payment by results declined, though the thinking behind such a system did not disappear. Was not the performance of the pupils the only reliable indication of the teacher's ability and diligence? The curriculum itself was certainly broader at the end of the century than it had been thirty years earlier. Depending on local circumstances, there could be provision for English, geography, science and domestic subjects. History was little regarded. The number of elementary teachers in all schools rapidly expanded, from some 12,000 in 1870 to nearly five times that number in 1900, with the proportion of women rising from a half to two-thirds. The number of pupil teachers and ancillary assistants increased steadily. Most teachers came from denominational training colleges, although this situation was beginning to change. The quality of the basic instruction given over this period is not to be despised, but both the elementary teachers and their pupils formed a distinct social category. The education given and received was for a caste and, even if supplemented by evening classes and 'adult schools' (as was increasingly possible in many areas) it was not expected or desired that pupils should have unrealistic expectations. Nevertheless, some avenues of advance were opened up. In urban areas, 'higher-grade' schools were established, particularly in the 1890s, which were in effect secondary schools. They offered systematic courses and were particularly strong in scientific and practical subjects. They were especially attractive to parents from the skilled working class. Some of these schools, indeed, offered better facilities and better teaching than some grammar schools. On the whole, however, the grammar schools were being reformed – many of their endowments had been in a chaotic state – and they could offer some scholarships which enabled working-class children to receive an 'arts' and a 'science' education. Even so, the proportion of children who could avail themselves of such a ladder was small. The conclusion to the 1895 Royal Commission on Secondary Education argued that the educational opportunities offered in most towns and in all country districts were 'still far behind the requirements of our time'(215).

The Clarendon Commission (1861) and the Taunton Commission (1864) had conducted investigations into secondary education. The former had concerned itself with the nine great public schools of England, and the latter with a wider range of schools(223). The teaching of the classics continued to occupy a central place, but there was an increasing emphasis on modern languages, mathematics and science. The Headmasters' Conference was formed in 1869 and, in time, membership of that body became vital for any independent school with serious academic aspirations. Even so, considerable variation remained in the independent sector and the inspection of schools was minimal. But examinations did provide another yardstick of performance, and the importance of paper qualifications for entry into various professions became one of the features of the age. In England, however, it was not a government department which organized and supervised a system of public examinations. The initiative was taken by the Oxford and Cambridge Board in 1874.

The 1895 Bryce Commission admitted that the disadvantages suffered by young Englishmen in industry and commerce owing to the 'superior preparation' of their Continental competitors were considerable.[1] The Royal Commission on Technical Instruction had made the same point even more strongly in 1884. An Act five years later enabled local authorities to give support to technical education from the rates. Private initiatives were not lacking. The City and Guilds of London Institute was created in 1880 and its examinations stimulated the teaching of practical subjects. Quintin Hogg's Regent Street Polytechnic spawned similar institutions throughout London. By the end of the century, they were educating some 40,000 students, standing 'like forts in the sea of London temptations to youthful dissipation, ignorance and idleness'.[2] Such an enterprise was a typical example of the fusion of private and public funds for educational purposes.

Speaking in 1876, Mark Pattison calculated that there were some 228,500 young persons in England and Wales between the ages of 18 and 21, of whom approximately half were males. Of this 114,000 'educable material', only some 5,000 were to be found in universities. Making the inevitable comparison with Germany, he considered this condition to be 'nothing less than a state of national destitution'(219). Partly in response to such criticism, higher education was transformed in the last quarter of the century. A rash of new university colleges emerged, though not by any deliberate act of central government. Not until 1889 was a very modest grant made by the Treasury to assist these colleges in provincial cities. It was then decreed that a body of men well versed in academic questions was to 'elaborate a plan for the distribution of the grant'. By 1900, over 1,000 students graduated at Manchester, Liverpool, Birmingham, Leeds,

Nottingham, Newcastle, Bristol and Sheffield.[3] The total was modest, but a structure for further expansion had been set up.

These new colleges provoked an extended debate about the purpose of a university. What was the relationship between a 'useful' or 'technical' education on the one hand and a 'liberal' or 'humane' education on the other. Did specifically vocational studies have a place in the curriculum? The response could have produced a complete cleavage between these new university colleges and Oxford and Cambridge, but it did not. The new colleges did not become completely technical institutions and Oxford and Cambridge were reformed, both in their financial arrangements and courses. The Universities' Tests Act, 1871, removed any requirement upon undergraduates to attend any religious service or conform to any creed as a condition of taking a degree – except in divinity. The statutes of the universities and the colleges were extensively revised with the general intention of increasing university rather than college revenues. This money was used to establish scientific laboratories – the Clarendon and the Cavendish – and to permit specialization within the arts and applied sciences – law and history, for example, both became respectable disciplines in their own right. Additional chairs were established, but the college system substantially survived the attempt to turn the ancient universities into research institutions in which the emphasis would fall upon 'subjects'. After 1878, dons could marry without thereby losing their posts, and many of them became family men and men of the world, or at least of the rather distinct worlds of North Oxford or Newnham.

The Scottish educational system remained distinct from that south of the border. In 1870, literacy was significantly higher in Scotland than in England or Wales, and there was a thoroughly national school system in existence. The 1872 Scottish Education Act set up school boards throughout the country. Accommodation occupied a great deal of their time since, in the next thirty years, the number of pupils rose from nearly 300,000 to nearly a million. The system of payment by results came later to Scotland and stayed longer. The Act guaranteed the teaching of religion in schools according to Presbyterian tenets and in consequence, within a few years, some 80 per cent of the schools run by the Presbyterian churches were closed. Roman Catholic and Episcopalian schools continued to exist, but by the end of the century out of 3,104 elementary schools in Scotland, 2,744 were public. During this period, more effort was put into the expansion of elementary provision rather than into developing secondary schools – attendance at the latter even dropped. Private schools like Loretto, Glenalmond and Merchiston Castle, modelled on English public schools, together with the endowed schools in the cities, made the running. A complex but quite extensive provision of bursaries did provide a ladder for poor but talented children. There were more children in the private than in the public sector – a situation which only changed with the establishment of higher grade schools in the twentieth century. Perhaps because of the all-pervasive presence of that source of inspiration, the First Book of Discipline, the atmosphere of Scottish education was more formal than in England(225).

The existence of four ancient universities in Scotland meant that a higher proportion of the relevant age group went to university in Scotland than anywhere else in the United Kingdom. There were vocal doubts, however, about the structure of Scottish university education. Was the Scottish system of Ordinary degrees, followed by Honours for a smaller number, still satisfactory? Did the broad curriculum which was obligatory allow sufficient specialization? The system of lecturing to large classes did permit the cost of education to remain low and allow many poor students to follow courses, but the relatively poor performance of Scottish competitors in the various public examinations organized on a United Kingdom basis raised questions about standards. While the best Honours graduates were on a par with the best graduates of English universities, Ordinary graduates fared badly. The late-Victorian debate about the curriculum and the purpose of a university took the same general form as in England, but the merits, or otherwise, of the Scottish system were often not considered dispassionately. They became part of a wider discussion of 'Anglicization'. St Andrews apart, residence was not a feature of Scottish university education. The bulk of the student body tended to be locally recruited, so that the Scottish university ethos was different from Oxford, Cambridge or Durham. In such a context, student representative bodies were formed in Scotland at a time when they were unknown in England. It should be added that there was something rather awesome about a Scottish professor. Distinguished scholars like Richard Jebb or Gilbert Murray came north of the border, perhaps as much attracted by the long vacations as by the admiration of Glaswegians. In return, there were those who suspected that the university colleges of England and Wales were being expanded to provide employment for Scottish graduates in philosophy(217).

When Pattison, who was rector of Lincoln College, Oxford, addressed the Social Science Association in 1876, he took no account of that portion of the age-group he was considering that was female. Such indifference could not be sustained at the end of the century. The education of women was becoming an increasingly contentious matter, involving, as it inevitably did more general questions about their status. At the end of the century, elementary education was all that working-class girls could expect to receive. For upper-middle-class girls, however, the provision was changing, and the Bryce Commission in 1895 singled out the increased availability of secondary education for them as perhaps the single most important educational development since the Taunton Commission. Founded in 1872, the Girls' Public Day School Trust had established thirty-six schools by 1894. Their curricula differed little from that provided in comparable schools for boys. Such expansion took place throughout the United Kingdom. Alexandra College (1866) and the Dominican Convent (1882) provided undenominational and Catholic higher education for girls in Dublin. In Scotland, perhaps the most notable private foundation was St Leonard's, started at St Andrews in 1877. Days schools appeared in Glasgow and Edinburgh at about the same time. The first headmistress of St Leonard's was one of the first three women to pass the Cambridge Tripos. Girton and Newnham Colleges at Cambridge and Somerville and Lady Margaret Hall at Oxford were in existence by the end of the 1870s. Queen Margaret College in Glasgow was the creation of the 'Association for the Higher Education of Women in Glasgow and the West of Scotland'. London University admitted women to both membership and degrees. The Scottish universities had done the same by 1892, but Oxford and Cambridge showed no desire to be pushed into acting precipitately in the awarding of degrees. However, although men still far outnumbered women, it could no longer be assumed higher education need only cater for males.[4]

---

1. Handcock, op. cit., p. 520
2. E. M. Hogg, *Quintin Hogg* (1904), p. 227
3. W. H. G. Armytage, *Civic universities* (1955)
4. J. Kamm, *Hope deferred: Girls' education in English history* (1965)

CHAPTER 9

Creeds and cultures

Although Christian assumptions continued to pervade late-Victorian institutional and social life, church leaders knew that the status of Christianity was becoming more uncertain. In the final decades of the century the proportion of the United Kingdom population not in church membership grew – although church membership is not easy to define. But if the proportion fell, almost all denominations continued to expand and the churches occupied a prominent place in community life(230).

No other country in Europe was as ecclesiastically complex as the United Kingdom [G]. The 'Anglican' Church of England, in England and Wales, and the 'Presbyterian' Church of Scotland, in Scotland, were the 'established churches', though the nature and form of this establishment differed. The sister-churches, the Episcopal Church in Scotland and the Presbyterian Church in England, were not 'established'. Nonconformists (sometimes still called dissenters) objected to the principle of a State Church and increasingly came to call themselves 'Free Churchmen'. Baptists and Congregationalists and various Methodist bodies were the strongest Free Churches in England and Wales, although not all Methodists were happy with the 'Free Church' label. These denominations were much weaker in Scotland and Ireland. In Scotland, the largest non-established churches were unique to Scotland – the Free Church of Scotland and the United Presbyterians. After 1871, there was no established church in Ireland. In all four countries, the Roman Catholic Church belonged in the non-established category; only in Ireland did it embrace the majority of the population. Britain (though not Ireland) can thus be described as a Protestant State in so far as recognition was extended to Anglican or Presbyterian churches. The different position of the Crown north and south of the border sometimes troubled delicate ecclesiastical consciences, though it did not alarm Queen Victoria(227).

The divisions between the churches sometimes centred on points of theology, at others on church government or forms of worship. There was still vigour and sometimes venom in these issues. Nevertheless, the tendency was for churches to unite rather than split further. The spectacular divisions in the Church of Scotland and within Methodism during the 1840s were not to be repeated. Despite continuing differences of emphasis between them, the free churches had formed a national council by the 1890s. It had no power over its constituent elements but it appeared to indicate a general willingness to co-operate. Despite alarm at the spread of 'ritualism' in the Church of England, there were even informal talks between Anglican bishops and leading nonconformists – held in the safety of neutral Switzerland. There was no likelihood that institutional unity would emerge; the best that could be hoped for was greater understanding and mutual sympathy. By the end of the century, it seemed that the church structure of the British Isles had settled into five segments – Roman Catholic, Anglican, Presbyterian and Baptist/Congregational and Methodist. Each church remained convinced, with varying degrees of intensity, that it held to the true gospel.

Although these five ecclesiastical families were all active in the United Kingdom, their relative numerical strength varied widely between country and country, region and region. For this reason, it is not very helpful to consider church membership on a United Kingdom basis. Complex historical reasons had ensured that churches of the same family were very conscious of their regional or national identity within the United Kingdom. This was particularly true of Welsh-speaking free churches in Wales. In Ireland, too, the Catholic, Anglican, Presbyterian and Methodist traditions encapsulated, preserved and even promoted differing notions of Irish cultural and national identity. In England, for example, the Bible Christians (a variant of Methodism) were virtually confined to the west country. In Scotland, the Episcopalians were particularly strong in the Grampian region. The Church of England saw itself as the Church of the English people. The coherence of England would be lost if its link with the State were to be weakened. It would appear, however, speaking generally, that religious commitment was weaker in England than elsewhere in the United Kingdom. While a peculiar deficiency in English character may provide the explanation, it may also be that in Ireland, Scotland and Wales religious allegiance was a means of reinforcing national or cultural identity. The same pressures did not exist within England. It is likely that the growth-rate of the English churches owed much to migrants from elsewhere in the United Kingdom. This was most conspicuously true of the Roman Catholic Church in respect of Irish immigration. Even in the most international of churches, Irish and English congregations did not easily mix. Finally, the number of Welsh and Scottish preachers ministering to the recalcitrant English is noteworthy. A. C. Tait (1868–82) began the Scottish occupation of the see of Canterbury.

United Kingdom churches did not have very close contacts with European churches. The Church of England's charm, in the eyes of many of its adherents, lay in its English character; it elevated and sanctified English virtues. Its hybrid nature meant that it did not easily relate either to Continental Calvinism or Lutheranism. The last attempts at some measure of unity between Anglicans and German Lutherans had been in the early eighteenth century. High Churchmen or Anglo-Catholics, growing in numbers and influence, did not regard the Church of England as a Protestant church and wished to distance themselves from the Reformation and its spiritual descendants. Charles Kingsley, novelist and 'Broad Churchman', invariably took an independent line. He hoped that the Germans, an exemplary race, could become members of the Church of England, but this suggestion seems to have had no consequence. In Scotland, where the ecclesiastical pattern was more directly comparable with some parts of Europe, the kirk did have connections with the Continent. The growth of Roman Catholicism focused more attention on Rome, but many converts, not least Cardinal Newman himself, were not anxious to become Italianate Englishmen. British Baptists and Methodists did encourage small missions in Europe, but their European counterparts could not compare with them in numbers or status. They looked more frequently across the Atlantic and their preachers collected honorary degrees from American institutions. In general, British religious links were with the United States and the empire rather than with Europe(228).

Ecclesiastical diversity reflected class as well as regional or national divisions, though not according to a neat sociological pattern. No one church drew its membership exclusively from one section of society, though some small bodies like the Society of Friends (Quakers) came near to doing so. Nevertheless, the cleavage between 'church' and 'chapel' was far more than merely an ecclesiastical or theological division. It corresponded to a deep difference in social status and ethos. The established churches, both locally and nationally, were linked to a wider social establishment. No one, it has been said, became a nonconformist for fun. Nonconformists were thinly represented in the higher levels of the professions and armed services, though they were more prominent in business. Church life was very different from chapel life: a chapel minister was not the same as a church clergyman: a chapel building did not, normally, look like a parish church. These differences reflected not only contrasting attitudes to the role of the laity but also the educational and social inclinations of the membership. Of course, within nonconformity there were gradations of wealth and status between Wesleyan and Primitive Methodist, between Congregationalist and Baptist, and between different congregations of the same denomination in one city. Contemporaries recognized these gradations and, by and large, accepted them.

Some sections of the working class were involved in the organization and activity of the churches. Even so, it was apparent by the end of the century that the 'masses' had no deep connection with organized religion. It was often supposed, wrongly, that this alienation was of recent origin and could be overcome by the erection of Methodist Central Halls in the cities, or the establishment of 'settlements' under Anglican or Free Church auspices in poor areas – such as Toynbee Hall, or by the vigorous campaigns of the newly established Salvation Army. William Booth, a former travelling evangelist with the Methodist New Connexion wrote *How to Reach the Masses with the Gospel* (1872). A few years later the constitution of the Army was consolidated with Booth as General. With the paper *The War Cry*, the brass bands, the military uniform, their 'articles of war', the new recruits battled for conversions with uninhibited zeal. But it was only in the decade after 1890, when Booth published *In Darkest England and the Way Out*, that the General was held in polite society to have reached a more mature understanding of the 'whole' man. Before he was finally promoted to glory, Booth received advance notice of approbation in the shape of an honorary degree from the University of Oxford(227).

The glorious vulgarity of the Salvation Army brought it to the attention of both police and public, but it did not succeed in converting the masses *en bloc*. It did, however, compel other churches to take a fresh look at their organization and methods. One solution might be to create more bishops – the first suffragans were created in 1870. Not only that, but there was an increase in the number of dioceses in the 1880s including Liverpool and Newcastle upon Tyne. It was hoped that the new diocese of Truro would show the flag among Methodist miners and fishermen. And the bishops were not only more numerous, they were more assiduous than their mid-century predecessors and they had to be more fit. The bishop of Ripon, Chadwick notes, delivered about 190 sermons and addresses, travelled about 13,000 miles and wrote about 5,000 letters each year in the 1890s. There was much to be done in opening new churches and finding clergy to staff them(227).

The Church of England was not easy to manage. The three late-Victorian archbishops all had to struggle to maintain its unity in the face of contending parties and factions. The Evangelicals were not averse to detecting plots to subvert what they considered to be its essentially Protestant character. Anglo-Catholics were reluctant to allow their experiments in worship to be restricted by episcopal authority (in which they otherwise placed great store) or custom and convention. Broad Churchmen displayed an obtrusive indifference. Religious ritual occasioned the greatest controversy. Colour and elaboration in worship, it was alleged, had a great attraction for the urban working class. Music and art stimulated religious sensibilities in a way which preaching and reading could not hope to emulate. Whether it was indeed the vestments they wore rather than the devotion they displayed which accounted for the popularity of 'slum priests' cannot be determined.

Some contemporary churchmen believed that the churches could never regain their position among the working classes unless they declared their abhorrence of poverty and deprivation. And that involved an identification with Socialism, hitherto frequently equated with atheism. There was much discussion of an ancient problem; whether sin caused poverty or poverty caused sin. Clerical inspiration produced the Guild of St Matthew (1877) and the Christian Social Union (1889) and in the following decade practically every denomination had a Socialist society, though the numbers involved should not be exaggerated. It scarcely needs to be said that most clergy and laity were not Socialists (of whatever hue) and some were strong critics of Socialist tendencies. Supporters of direct political action were allegedly in danger of neglecting the inescapable transcendental dimension of Christianity(233).

The pursuit of salvation, however that was understood, remained at the heart of religion. Many thinking contemporaries, however, found the traditional emphases and doctrines of Christianity either incredible or morally unacceptable. 'Doubt' continued to spread. The Darwinian theory of evolution seemed to many to undermine the biblical account of the role of God the creator. The continuing studies of biblical scholars in Germany and Britain also upset belief in the authority of the Bible as that had often been conceived. When men asked whether the Bible was 'true', it was difficult to give a clear answer. In addition, hell seemed an unworthy destination for serious Victorians and heaven scarcely better. Moral dignity was increasingly offended by notions of 'redemption' or 'atonement'. It is difficult to quantify the drift away from Christianity since those who ceased to believe did not, for the most part, join organizations which preached ethical values without any religious basis. Societies of avowed rationalists and secularists only had small memberships. Perhaps this reflects the fact that many who ceased to worship, or who stopped calling themselves Christians, continued to admire what they still called 'Christian values'. They had withdrawn wistfully from Christianity rather than with a triumphal sense of release from falsehood. They were frequently agnostics rather than atheists. Alternative world-views were canvassed, from Schopenhauer and Nietzsche on the one hand to the Hindu sacred writings on the other, but the adherents of anti-Christian philosophies or other religions were few. In the 1890s, however, there was an aggressive hedonism and conscientious Bohemianism which allowed the decade to merit the 'naughty' label. It remained the case, however, that most of those who abandoned Christianity continued to behave as though it were still true(224).

CULTURE

There were those for whom the pursuit of 'culture' offered an alternative purpose in life. Matthew Arnold used the term in 1869 to mean 'the study of perfection'. He thought he could distil appropriate elements of 'sweetness and light' which could suffuse the entire nation. No groups or classes would escape from the impress of Hellenism. This culture was to be as all-embracing as his father's conception of the Church of England had aspired to be a generation earlier. He therefore bravely launched his assault on 'narrowness, one-sidedness and incompleteness'. Thomas Arnold of Rugby had found it intolerable that differences of dogma or organization prevented Englishmen from belonging to a national church. His son, convinced that the sea of faith was ebbing, believed that religion could no longer hold society together. It was necessary to establish a culture which met man's deepest needs but did not depend upon any religious validation. Its totality was to be contrasted with the provinciality which he found so distressingly prevalent.

Such a programme was misconceived. Culture could not replace religion as the cement of British society because religion had not been the cement of that society since the seventeenth century. A classically based culture, launched by a temporary Professor of Poetry at Oxford would undoubtedly have its appeal, but it would be unlikely to be a universal one. Arnold aimed to bring 'all our fellow men, in the East of London and elsewhere' along with him in the 'progress towards perfection', but he did not succeed. His new secular pilgrimage was as subject to tensions of class and nationality as had been the Christian pilgrimage of grace. The perception of perfection was not likely to be the same in Poplar as it was in Oxford. No creed, it appeared, was likely to find universal acceptance and no culture would be ubiquitous. Arnold might contemplate the ebbing of faith from his vantage point on Dover beach but, ironically, fishing communities were among the most faithful in the United Kingdom.

HIGH CULTURE

The term 'culture' also came to be used to refer to the general body of the arts – the 'high culture' of music, painting and literature. In this sphere, British achievement was patchy and, on the whole, not very distinguished. In painting, Pre-Raphaelite influences predominated in the early period. Burne-Jones had the greatest appeal to contemporaries who considered themselves to have taste. Increasingly, however, the question which dominated critical circles was the status of representational art as a whole. Perhaps the emergence of photography had fatally undermined the artist's function as a recorder of likeness. That photography itself could be a form of art had still to be fully appreciated. No British artist, however, appears to have responded to the general challenge. British paintings, at least in comparison with French, remained conservative in form and composition. Even so, Victorian art has been treated with more critical respect in recent years. The official voice of painting remained the Royal Academy in London but, as usual, it was not unchallenged. While the commissioning and purchase of painting remained in relatively few hands, a notable feature of the period was the growth of the provincial art gallery – as, for example, in Bristol or Liverpool. Painting in Scotland remained distinct both in its expression and organization. There was little painting in Wales and what there was had little merit. There were attempts to develop an 'Irish School', but particularly Celtic qualities were, on the whole, lacking.

The differing status of the visual arts in different parts of the United Kingdom reflected the social structure. Aristocratic patronage was only patchily available and in its absence how was art to survive? Wealthy industrialists might not be willing to become patrons, or if they did, might only pay for what they liked. That the State should pay artists was out of the question. William Morris tackled the place which art should occupy in society from another perspective. Until his death in 1896, he stressed the merits of individual craftsmanship – from wallpapers to woven fabrics – in an age increasingly dominated by the machine. His influence on interior design was profound, though substantially limited to the upper classes. With the exception of Morris, who became a very individual Socialist, most British painters did not find themselves alienated from society or antagonistic to it. Sir Edward Burne-Jones went shooting in the Highlands with the best of men. Aesthetic criticism remained a recondite activity, but reproductions of contemporary paintings did appear in artisan houses. The deeper questions of the place of art and artists in society remained unanswered.

MUSIC

While not exactly a 'land without music', the musical life of the British Isles was certainly a restricted one by Continental standards. There was not one single permanent opera-house in the United Kingdom; a brief season at Covent Garden, with alien performers, satisfied the aristocracy during the Season. In 1894, *The Times* complained that Verdi's *Falstaff* contained no dull moments and therefore limited the opportunity for 'comfortable conversation during the music'. The Wagnerians – and Bernard Shaw as a music critic – gradually brought about a change in the outlook of the opera-going public. The serious upper middle class moved into the seats vacated by the frivolous aristocracy. British composers of opera were not conspicuous, though to Joseph Parry falls the honour due for the writing of the first Welsh-language opera, *Hywel a Blodwen*. The combination of Gilbert and Sullivan, however, at its best, achieved both a wide appeal and artistic distinction. Sullivan's independent orchestral compositions are rarely played. Choral singing flourished. Choirs often had their popular repertoire, but also wished to be judged on their capacity to sing *The Messiah* or *Elijah* – to which they frequently added the contemporary *Crucifixion* by Stainer.

No English composer could escape from this pervasive zeal for oratorio but, at the close of the century, Elgar's *Dream of Gerontius* gave fresh life to an established tradition. His *Enigma Variations* displayed his mastery of orchestral writing. By the end of the century, thanks to the concerts in the Queen's Hall, orchestral music could regularly be heard in London, though foreign conductors and soloists seemed, almost by definition, superior to native performers. Orchestral music in the north of England and the midlands owed much to the Anglicized Hallé, who based himself in Manchester. There was no professional orchestra in Wales, Scotland or Ireland. Music-making, throughout large areas of the country, was an amateur activity, sometimes transcending social barriers. Specifically working-class choirs, however, were common in industrial areas. Published music had become much cheaper and was not beyond the reach of artisan pockets. The piano, similarly, had reached many humble homes; moreover, it was played. Brass bands were formed in many factories.[1] They did not play while you worked but, as in the case of the Wills band in Bristol, they saw you off on the annual outing.

By 1900, however, there were signs of change. Arnold's despised nonconformist businessmen who in the city of Bristol had built its Colston Hall for concert purposes were disappointed by the apparent waning in the popularity of music festivals. The music critic of the *Western Daily Press* noted that 'high-class concerts' were not drawing crowds while 'ballad-type programmes' were.[2] It seemed that this semi-serious, semi-popular musical tradition was in crisis, perhaps to be replaced by the higher technical standards emanating from the Royal College of Music on the one hand and an audience simply seeking pleasure and entertainment on the other. The music-hall was fast losing its licentious and socially disreputable character; George Robey, who began his career in the 1890s, was on the road to respectability, though not too far along it.

LITERATURE

The 1860s had seen a good deal of concern about the uncivilized nature of the secondary schoolchild. The Taunton Commission considered that 'it would be a most valuable result if anything like a real interest in English literature could be made general in England'. A more humble task was to instruct the population to read and write. The percentage of male literacy in England and Wales moved up from 80.6 in 1871 to 97.2 in 1900, and female literacy from 73.2 to 96.8. Such figures, however, are not very illuminating, since they only refer to that segment of the population which married in those particular years and could sign the marriage register. There was a long way to go before millions could read effectively, let alone take a 'real interest' in the classics of English literature. However, the Bible and the works of Shakespeare, Dickens and Scott could often be found in the homes both of artisan and aristocrat – appropriate distinctions being maintained by the quality of the editions which were on the shelves. It was difficult, however, for any late-Victorian author to have such a wide appeal. The general growth of literacy was eroding the middle ground. Authors, books and newspaper publishers responded by producing works for a highly differentiated reading public. Mrs Henry Wood's *East Lynne* sold 430,000 copies between 1861 and 1898 and her publishers claimed that the total sales of all her novels amounted to over 2½ million copies.[3] Hall Caine and Marie Corelli were her equivalents later in the century. Thomas Hardy, Henry James or George Meredith did not approach such popular success and had to rest content with critical approval. R. L. Stevenson's *Treasure Island* and *Kidnapped* did sell well, but not his other works. By 1900, the formidable talent of Kipling had emerged, though critics did not find it easy to 'place' him.

The focus of literary society was London – the themes of Mrs Humphrey Ward and Henry James had no regional basis. The exception was Hardy, who brooded over change and decay in rural Wessex. Writers in Wales and Scotland also took local themes, but their fame rarely penetrated to England. The strength of Scottish publishing allowed the Scottish writer to find a domestic market for his work, whereas the Welsh writer in English had no substantial publisher in Wales. Writing in Welsh, both prose and poetry, was vigorous and expanding but had little resonance outside the Principality. Irish writers like Oscar Wilde, Bernard Shaw and W. B. Yeats did have an impact in England and their work was often more acceptable there than in Ireland.

The distinctive patterns of culture, class and region can be seen in other literary fields. The theatre revived. More attention was given to the play as a whole rather than to the virtuoso performances of leading actors and actresses. Theatre, however, was probably outside the experience of the bulk of the population. There was no regular theatre in Wales and in Ireland only in Dublin – though some touring companies did perform elsewhere in these countries from time to time. The situation was the same in Scotland, outside the two major cities. Theatres were much more common in England, where they not only existed in major cities but also in Bath or York.

Newspapers still had a predominantly middle-class readership. Such new productions as *Tit-Bits* (1880) and *Pearson's Weekly* (1890) did little to change the pattern and even the *Daily Mail* (1896) did not reach the working class. Serious papers like *The Times* had to survive on small circulations, and so did the host of literary-cum-news magazines.

A common literary culture thus still seemed far away. Only about 8 per cent of the population availed themselves of the greatly increased provision of public libraries. It was in his last great novel, *Jude the Obscure* (1895) that Hardy portrayed the tragedy of a man trapped between his cultural aspirations and the social realities of Oxford. Jude was not the only man to find himself lost in the cultural confusions of late-Victorian Britain.

---

1. J. F. Russell and J. H. Elliott, *The brass band movement* (1936)
2. H. Meller, *Leisure and the changing city, 1870–1914* (1976), p. 222
3. R. D. Altick, *The English common reader* (Chicago, 1957), p. 171

PART TWO

1901–1931

PART TWO
1900–1902

1902   Alliance with Japan (Jan): Colonial Conference (June–Aug): Balfour succeeds Salisbury as PM (July): Education Act: Treaty of Vereeniging (June) ends South African War.

        J. A. Hobson, *Imperialism*.

1903   Wyndham's Act: Royal Commission on the S. African War reports: J. Chamberlain launches his campaign for tariff reform: Committee of Imperial Defence established: Emmeline Pankhurst forms the Women's Social and Political Union.

1904   Franco-British *entente* signed (Apr): Russo-Japanese War (Feb).

        J. M. Barrie, *Peter Pan*.

1905   Foundation of Sinn Féin and of the Ulster Unionist Council: Balfour resigns as PM, Campbell-Bannerman forms Liberal gvt (Dec): Franco-German crisis over Morocco (Dec): Start of suffragette agitation: Royal Commission on the Poor Law.

1906   General Election (Jan) – Liberal victory: *Dreadnought* launched: Transvaal granted responsible government: All-India Moslem League formed: Trade Disputes Act reverses implications of Taff Vale judgment.

        Galsworthy, *Forsyte Saga*: F. G. Hopkins discovers vitamins.

1907   Entente with Russia signed (Aug): Haldane's military reforms lead to creation of an Expeditionary Force and a Territorial Army: New Zealand becomes a Dominion.

        United Methodist Church formed: Hampstead Garden Suburb blossoms.

1908   Asquith succeeds Campbell-Bannerman as PM (Mar): Old Age Pensions Act: Crisis over Austrian action in Bosnia.

        Olympic Games held in London: Baden-Powell forms Boy Scout mvt:

1909   Lloyd George's controversial budget is rejected by the Lords: Town Planning Act: British–German naval rivalry at its height: Morley–Minto reforms in India.

        Blériot flies the Channel: Imperial Cricket Conference formed.

1910   General Election (Jan) – Liberal gvt depends on Labour and Irish support: Constitutional crisis concerning the powers of the House of Lords: Death of King Edward VII (May): General Election (Dec) – retains political balance: Labour exchanges set up: Union of S. Africa formed.

        B. Russell and A. N. Whitehead, *Principia Mathematica*: N. Angell, *The Great Illusion*: World Missionary Conference in Edinburgh.

1911   Parliament Act restricts Lords' power of veto: Payment of MPs: National Insurance Act introduces sickness and unemployment provision: Second crisis over the future of Morocco (Agadir): Bonar Law replaces Balfour as Cons. leader: Widespread strikes and industrial discontent: First Imperial (as opposed to Colonial) Conference.

1912   Third Irish Home Rule Bill introduced: Welsh Church Disestablishment Bill introduced: Further industrial disputes – strikes in mines and London docks: Campaign for 'Votes for women' takes militant turn: Ulster covenant signed (Sept).

        Daily Herald first published: R. F. Scott at South Pole.

1913   Home Rule Bill twice passed by Commons and twice rejected by Lords.

1914   Buckingham Palace Conference on future of Ireland (July):
        First World War

        4 August, UK declares war on Germany – 10 August, on Austria-Hungary: British Expeditionary Force departs for France: Retreat from Mons (Aug): First Battle of Ypres (Oct).

1915   Second Battle of Ypres (Apr): British troops land at Gallipoli (Apr): Formation of coalition gvt (May): Reinforcements sent to Gallipoli: British attack at Loos (Sept): Haig replaces French as British commander in France:

1916   First Conscription Bill (Jan): Evacuation of Gallipoli completed (Jan): Second Conscription Bill (Apr): Battle of Jutland (May): Battle of the Somme begins (July): Lloyd George gives 'knock-out blow' interview: Lloyd George becomes PM in a new coalition gvt (Dec): Easter rising in Dublin proclaims Irish Republic, but it is suppressed.

1917   United States enters the war (Apr): Shipping losses raise serious food problems: Battle of Passchendaele (Oct–Nov): Russia asks for peace from Germany (Nov): British forces capture Jerusalem (Dec): Lansdowne publishes letter in the *Daily Telegraph* advocating a negotiated peace: Balfour (Foreign Secretary) supports idea of a Jewish National Home in Palestine.

1918   Lloyd George makes 'War Aims' speech at the TUC (Jan): German spring offensive (March) – last attack (July): Successful British tank attack (Aug): Allies break Hindenburg Line (Sept): Turkey signs armistice (Oct): Austria-Hungary signs armistice (3 Nov): Germany signs armistice (11 Nov):

General Election (Dec) – Victory for Lloyd George coalition: Fisher's Education Act: Representation of the People Act.

1919   Peace settlement – treaties of Versailles (June), St-Germain (Sept), Neuilly (Nov): German fleet scuttled at Scapa Flow (June): Guerrilla war breaks out in Ireland – Sinn Féin congress declares Irish independence: Government of India Act: Massacre at Amritsar: British forces in N. Russia – withdrawn from Murmansk (Oct): Report of Coal Commission under Sankey (June): Lady Astor becomes first British woman MP to take her seat.

Severe influenza epidemic (Mar): Enabling Act permits establishment of the Assembly of the Church of England: Alcock and Brown achieve first direct flight across the Atlantic (June).

1920   Treaty of Trianon between Allies and Hungary (June): 'Council of Action' threatens general strike if Britain goes to war against the Soviet Union: Government of Ireland Act (Dec): British Communist party formed (Aug).

Welwyn Garden City launched: British Board of Film Censors set up: Lambeth conference of churches of the Anglican Communion: (Royal) Institute of International Affairs formed.

1921   Safeguarding of Industries Act (July): Labour party conference rejects affiliation with Communists (June): Parliament of Northern Ireland opens: Articles of agreement for a treaty bring to an end to hostilities between British gvt and Irish irregular forces (Dec): Washington Four-Power treaty concerning the Pacific (Dec): India given fiscal and tariff autonomy.

Foundation of the Institute of Historical Research in London: Eliot, *The Waste Land*.

1922   Washington Nine-Power treaty concerning China and Five-Power treaty concerning naval ratios (Feb): Kingdom of Egypt formally receives independence – Britain and Egypt share sovereignty over the Sudan: Chanak crisis in the Near East: Civil war in the Irish Free State – last British troops leave the Free State: Carlton Club meeting of Cons. MPs (19 Oct) leads to fall of Lloyd George coalition: General Election (Nov) – Cons. victory: S. Rhodesia votes against joining S. Africa.

British Broadcasting Company formed: Austin Seven meets demand for a small car for the domestic market.

1923   French troops occupy the Ruhr – British disapproval plain (Jan): Responsible gvt in Southern Rhodesia: Matrimonial Causes Act gives women equality in divorce suits (July): General Election (Dec).

         Establishment of Royal Fine Art Commission: First English FA Cup Final played at Wembley Stadium.

1924   First Labour gvt formed (Jan): Britain recognizes the Soviet Union (Feb) Dawes Plan accepted by London conference – Ruhr evacuation agreed (Aug): 'Zinoviev letter' coincides with General Election campaign (Oct).

         British Empire Exhibition at Wembley.

1925   Return to fixed gold parity – £1 = \$4.86 (Apr): Lloyd George succeeds Asquith as Liberal leader: Dominions Office established: Locarno Pact (Oct): Plaid Cymru founded.

         Dearmer edits *Songs of Praise*.

1926   General Strike (3–12 May): Imperial Conference – considers report of the Inter-imperial Relations Committee chaired by Balfour (Oct–Nov): Simon Commission appointed to consider working of the 1919 Government of India Act.

         Council for the Preservation of Rural England founded: Central Electricity Board set up.

1927   Rupture of diplomatic relations with the Soviet Union (May): Trade Disputes Act.

         British Broadcasting Corporation established: First sound film.

1928   Revised Church of England Prayer Book rejected in Commons: Women enfranchised on the same basis as men (Oct): Kellogg–Briand pact.

1929   Local Government Act (England and Wales): General Election (May) – Mac Donald forms minority Labour gvt: US stock market collapses (Oct).

         Most Presbyterian churches in Scotland unite to form the Church of Scotland.

1930   London naval treaty (April): Rhineland evacuation completed: Independence of Iraq recognized: Civil disobedience campaign in India: Simon Report on India published: Wei-Hai-Wei evacuated (Oct): Passfield White Paper on Palestine advocates halt to Jewish immigration (Oct): First Round Table Conference on Indian self-government (Nov).

         Daily Worker first published: *Daily News* and *Daily Chronicle* merge as the *News Chronicle*: Youth Hostels Association founded: R101 destroyed on first flight to India.

1931   Mosley forms the New party (Feb): Report of Macmillan committee on finance and industry (June): Report of May committee on national expenditure (July): Formation of National gvt (Sept): Gold standard suspended (Sept): General Election (Oct) – large National majority: Japan occupies Manchuria (Sept): Gandhi attends second Round Table Conference in London (Sept–Dec): Statute of Westminster defines inter-imperial relations (Dec).

CHAPTER 10

Goodbye to all that: war and peace

In the late 1920s, in a series of novels, plays and autobiographies, celebrated writers waved their farewell to arms(59). A decade had elapsed before some of them had felt able to come to terms with their experiences between 1914 and 1918. Ironically, the books were published at a time when there was disquiet on the international front. Wars and rumours of wars dominated the experience of men born in the 1880s. They shattered the hopes and expectations of individuals. They exposed the precariousness and fragility of British power. Although there were feverish attempts to return to 'normality' – politically, economically, socially, culturally and even militarily – the position of the United Kingdom in the world and the domestic circumstances of its people could never be the same again(60).

The century began with British forces fighting a frustrating and unsatisfactory war in South Africa(61). In theory, it should not have been a difficult task to defeat the armed might of Afrikanerdom, even if the initiative rested with the Boers. It proved to be a more demanding struggle than anyone had anticipated. Eventually, nearly half a million men served on the imperial side, about half of whom were British regulars. Some 20,000 men died, either in battle or from various diseases, and a slightly higher figure were wounded. The war itself went through various phases, revealing, in its earlier and more conventional stages, inadequacies and shortcomings in British strategy and weaponry. Even so, by 1901, many observers thought that a British victory was in sight. However, the guerrilla tactics employed by the Afrikaners ensured that this was far from being the case. Their knowledge of the country, strong tactical sense and skilled horsemanship, forced Kitchener to devise new methods in order to defeat them. Blockhouses, originally built alongside the railways, were extended and the areas they enclosed systematically 'swept'. The British also developed a system of 'concentration camps' – denuding areas of the countryside by collecting women and children together. This policy attracted a good deal of criticism from Campbell-Bannerman, Leader of the Opposition, who talked of the government employing 'methods of barbarism'. Steps were belatedly taken to improve conditions in the camps. Cumulatively, these measures wore down Afrikaner resistance, despite many brilliant counter-thrusts. A peace treaty was signed on 31 May 1902[E].

The war had ended in victory, but scarcely in triumph. It was not encouraging that the mighty British Empire had taken so long to subdue two small states. Inevitably, a Royal Commission was appointed. Reporting in the summer of 1903, it came to the disturbing conclusion (having asked some 22,000 questions) that the British had never possessed a plan of campaign. Shortcomings in training were also disclosed and there was criticism of the casual attitude adopted towards the gathering of intelligence. Some were inclined to believe that the love of polo was the root of all evil. It was easy to highlight such matters in retrospect, but the problems of 'planning', the structure of command and the relationship between generals and politicians could not be easily remedied. A rather grandly named Committee of Imperial Defence, subsequently to be chaired by successive Prime Ministers, began work in 1903. Attended by politicians, sailors and soldiers, the agenda for its meetings ranged widely, considering both general issues and the detailed problems of particular regions in the empire, but it did not become an executive body, or one which laid down defence policy. The War Office and the Admiralty continued on their separate ways. At this point, Lord Esher, confidant of the King and dissenting member of the Royal Commission, chaired a committee charged with reorganizing the War Office. Fresh from his masterly organization of Queen Victoria's funeral, Esher proposed both a general staff and sweeping changes of personnel, but had to admit defeat. Arnold-Forster, the new War Minister, pressed to promote efficiency and find economies, was not very successful in either respect. The government was in difficulties over other questions and army reform collapsed.

The proposals Arnold-Forster did consider reflected his belief in the navy as a defence against invasion. Because of this shield there was no need to maintain large auxiliary forces for home defence. As matters stood, the United Kingdom was clearly not in the same military league as the other major powers in Europe. Should it seek to compete with them? There were indeed some advocates of compulsory military service, including Lord Roberts, the hero, if there was one, of the South African War. Their campaign, however, had little impact on the politicians. Coming into office at the end of 1905, the Liberals remained very firmly opposed to conscription. Instead, Haldane, the eminently philosophical War Minister, embarked on a wide-ranging programme of army reform during the period up to 1912. In consequence, the army was at last equipped with a general staff. While leaving untouched the 'linked battalion' principle, he organized an Expeditionary Force of six infantry divisions and one cavalry division, with appropriate logistical support. The yeomanry and volunteers (non-regulars) were organized into a territorial force which could amount to fourteen divisions and fourteen mounted brigades. This was at least presented as a programme of reorganization rather than expansion, because sections of the Liberal party remained intensely critical of military expenditure. Officers' training corps proliferated in schools and universities. Despite Haldane's vigorous efforts, Spiers points out that the territorial force fell far short of its target and the attendance at annual camp was less than perfect. He notes that by September 1913 only 1,090 officers and 17,788 non-commissioned officers and men had volunteered to serve abroad on mobilization(57).

If the mentality of 'home defence' still prevailed, the expeditionary force was devised for some purpose. Was it in fact going to be sent overseas and to what end? Staff talks with the French Army were approved by the incoming Foreign Secretary, Grey, at the end of 1905, confronted as he was by a deteriorating international situation. These talks continued spasmodically over the next few years, but there was no firm plan on the British side, as the next Moroccan crisis, in 1911, revealed. Leading government ministers were prepared to see the bulk, though not all of the Expeditionary Force serve on the Continent – if circumstances justified it. What those circumstances would be could only be conjectured and there was no commitment to military intervention. The Cabinet retained the final decision, even if a certain intimacy with the French created a climate of expectation. It would be too ambitious to suppose that Haldane foresaw the situation which occurred in 1914 and planned accordingly. What he did was to make intervention a possibility(56).

The navy viewed the army reforms with some apprehension. Fisher, who became First Sea Lord in 1904, had already made his mark as a reformer in the sphere of naval education. His major initiative was to redistribute the main naval forces, establishing a 'Home Fleet'. The purpose of his changes was to permit the use of the big battleships of the Atlantic, Channel and Home Fleets against Germany. But rearrangement of existing resources was not enough. In 1906 the *Dreadnought* was completed. Contemporaries admired its size (17,900 tons), the number and range of its guns and its speed (it was turbine-engined). Technological innovation was not a British preserve, indeed it transpired that the Germans were to show superiority in the range and accuracy of their guns and in the quality of their shells and mines. Serious alarm about German naval construction manifested itself in 1908. An Admiralty request for six further ships in the 1909 estimates met opposition from some Cabinet ministers who wanted four. Eventually, the 'compromise' of eight (but over a longer period) was reached. It was in this connection that the famous cry, 'We want eight and we won't wait', was raised. This expansion, and further orders over the next few years, not only produced financial strain for the exchequer but also posed serious difficulties in recruitment and training. Oil supplies began to be a matter of great concern. There was already apprehension that the submarine (whose design and performance was changing rapidly) might make a major difference to war at sea. Public opinion, however, seemed convinced that superiority at sea was still essential for the survival of the United Kingdom and the British Empire. Fisher, busily feuding with Lord Charles Beresford, remained at the Admiralty until 1910. He opposed the plans to send an Expeditionary Force to France, and his successor, Wilson, took the same line in 1911 – even threatening to refuse to transport it. The navy still liked to think in 'blue water' terms: it could and would defend the United Kingdom. Resources should not be squandered trying to make Britain a military power(55). To an extent, these opposed viewpoints were being resolved, though the Committee of Imperial Defence did not gain the authority over the Admiralty or the War Office that some considered essential. Despite the alarms and crises, undertaking comprehensive planning for a European war was not something a Liberal government could quite bring itself to do.

There was one further unknown – the use of the air. The Frenchman, Blériot, flew the Channel in 1909 and H. G. Wells was not alone in predicting that the aircraft or the airship might play a large part in a future war. On the eve of 1914 that still looked unlikely. Like other European powers, Britain possessed a small motley collection of aircraft and a few men who liked to think of themselves as pilots. Since parachutes did not exist, they tended to have short lives. King George watched a young naval lieutenant fly a biplane from a wooden platform on the foredeck of the *Hibernia* in Weymouth Bay in 1913. What was even more amazing was that the ship was steaming at 10½ knots at the time. Sceptics remained unconvinced by such antics.

THE WAR

War had been feared, desired, threatened and avoided for so long that its actual outbreak in 1914 was something of a surprise(61). There was a widespread, though not universal, expectation that it would not last long. Admiral Beatty's initial reaction was one of relief that it had come in the summer months 'and before the dark nights of winter are on us it ought to be all over'. Poets and preachers wrote and spoke in honour of the men who marched away. The archbishop of York, conscious that this was the first major war since Britain had become a democracy, was not alone in wondering how the nation would stand the strain. In the event, only Morley and Burns resigned from the Cabinet. 'Business as usual' was the first irrelevant watchword. The Cabinet struggled to show itself efficient. The Prime Minister hastily appointed Kitchener Secretary of State for War in the mistaken assumption that a soldier would know how to organize it.

The British Expeditionary Force (BEF) did get away to the Continent within a fortnight. When it fitted snugly alongside the superior Belgian and French forces it was only a couple of divisions short – a feat of organization. It soon found itself in action in Belgium against the advancing Germans and soon found itself in retreat. But in the First Battle of Ypres, from mid-October to mid-November, it played its part in stabilizing the line – at a heavy price. Half of the men who had arrived in August were casualties. The 'wastage' far exceeded expectations. British marksmanship was excellent, but there was a serious shortage of machine-guns. The hazard of mud was already evident. Churchill's sudden dash to assist the Belgians at Antwerp had no effect on the outcome. By November 1914, the front line had been established, stretching from the Belgian coast to Switzerland. It was already clear that, at least for the time being, the Germans were better equipped to prepare for trench warfare. The failure of the German advance was, of course, only relative. The Germans controlled all but a small portion of Belgium, and northern France. The French had lost almost all their coal and iron – so vital for heavy industry in wartime. As both sides consolidated their positions, London began to appreciate that the war would not be over by Christmas. To play its part, the United Kingdom would have to raise a new army.

Some hoped for success at sea, either as a result of major naval engagements or of the policy of blockade. Initially, however, there were few contacts in home waters. Both navies seemed more afraid of being defeated than anxious to gain victory. British communications across the Channel to France were not harassed. Battles in the Indian, Pacific and South Atlantic Oceans were exciting, but remote. It was becoming clear that mines and submarines would present a great danger to surface vessels. Much was expected from the policy of blockade, and British vessels boldly searched neutral ships for vital 'contraband' which might assist the German war effort.

Kitchener announced that millions of extra soldiers would be needed – a whole New Army. In response to Kitchener's famous exhortation – 'Your country needs YOU' – over a million men had volunteered by Christmas 1914. The problem was to give these raw recruits training, barracks and equipment. Mobilization on this scale stretched the administrative resources of the War Office. At the same time, the acute shortage of shells was gradually making it clear to people and government alike that the home front was as important as the front line.

Supposing that this New Army could be trained and equipped, where should it be sent? Some ministers were unwilling to believe that Britain's duty was simply to slot into place beside the French on the Western Front. The idea of amphibious expeditions – almost anywhere – had great attraction. Eventually, towards the end of 1914, attention was fixed on forcing the Dardanelles. Such a success would, among other things, give encouragement to the Russians, who needed it. The respective roles of navy and army in this enterprise were never clear from the start, and subsequently individuals were anxious to fudge their responsibility. The naval bombardment of the Turkish forts in March 1915 came near to success – a fact of which the navy was not aware. The engagement was broken off. The troops withdrew to Egypt and regrouped. It was mistakenly decided, the following month, to redeem the failure by landing at Gallipoli. This improvised offensive proved a disaster, though not one which was to be admitted for many months.

The French had never been very enthusiastic about this diversion of effort and pressed for more British help on the Western Front. In the spring of 1915 British troops fought in the Battle of Neuve Chapelle, and again in April and May – the Second Battle of Ypres. In this latter encounter, gas was used for the first time. Nothing decisive emerged from these spring battles. Casualties inexorably mounted, but the generals did not know how to make progress against the fortified German lines. Haig replaced French as British commander in France after his handling of the Battle of Loos and at the end of 1915 Robertson was appointed Chief of the Imperial General Staff, but it was doubtful whether new faces would make much difference. Only when such fundamental problems as the shortage of shells had been overcome would there be a chance of a breakthrough. Lloyd George, Minister of Munitions in the coalition government formed in May 1915, put his quick brain to this task. There was also increasing pressure for the introduction of conscription, and by the end of 1915 the Prime Minister was no longer able to resist it. In January 1916, voluntary recruitment came to an end, and all bachelors between eighteen and forty-one were liable to be called up – a provision extended to married men in April.

Despite the increased manpower that would be available, the position of the British army in France was awkward and anomalous. It was usually impossible for the British commander to stand up to his French counterpart in a war which was being fought on French soil. As it happened, the epic struggle waged around the French fortress at Verdun was almost entirely Franco-German in character. The British did mount small counter-offensives in their sector to try to ease the pressure on the French, but their total impact was slight. The French held out, though at heavy cost, not least to their morale. They felt it was the turn of the British to bear the brunt of the fighting and British opinion also desired greater action. It was against this background that the Franco-British offensive on the Somme was launched in June 1916. The British army took a bigger share than on any previous occasion and on 1 July, the first day of actual battle, it sustained some 60,000 casualties. The artillery assembled to bombard the enemy looked more formidable than it actually was. Politicians and public were to be again disappointed. Some blamed the generals, some the shells, but the engagement went on until mid-November, causing some half a million British casualties. The Germans were pushed back about 5 miles.

Failure on the Somme produced the first sustained meditation on British war aims. Politicians and public alike began to wonder whether continued bloody slaughter was the only way out(62). Victory was still desirable, but the cost in human life and in social and economic disruption was beginning to seem excessive. Some Liberal and Labour opinion began to press for 'peace by negotiation'. They pressed for clarification of what Britain was fighting for. The Union of Democratic Control, a body formed soon after the outbreak of war, began to gain in numbers and influence, particularly among trade-unionists. Questioning, however, was not confined to the Left. Conservatives feared that prolongation of the war might lead to social breakdown.

It was not only the military situation which caused gloom. The Battle of Jutland had taken place in May 1916 – the only significant encounter between the opposing surface fleets in northern waters during the war. The battle itself was a strange affair. The expectation that the British Grand Fleet would inflict a comprehensive defeat on the Germans – if an encounter ever took place – was proved wrong. On this occasion, British losses were heavier than the German. However, the German fleet retired to its bases and that was some consolation. Less comforting was the fact that Berlin concentrated thereafter on submarine construction. The British did not know what to do next, oppressed by the knowledge that while the navy could not win the war, it might still lose it. A few days later the sea claimed another victim – Kitchener was shipwrecked and drowned on his way to Russia. His replacement as Secretary for War was Lloyd George.

Lloyd George had little time for talk of peace by negotiation, whether suggested by MPs or by President Wilson. He told the press in September that he expected to deliver a 'knock-out blow' – it would mean harnessing the full economic and industrial potential of Britain and France. Three months later he became Prime Minister, heading a new coalition. He remained determined to fight to the finish, but nevertheless had to persuade both his own public and President Wilson that British war aims were both liberal and achievable. It was vital not to alienate the United States because its power and influence might yet be the factor that determined the outcome of the war. What Lloyd George most needed, however, was the scent of victory. He advocated a unified command in France and pinned his faith in the new French commander, Nivelle, who promised an amazing breakthrough, at little cost. This attack, in mid-April 1917, was not a complete failure but it was also not the decisive victory he had promised. Nivelle was dismissed the following month. Haig and Robertson, who had disliked being subordinated to a Frenchman, were not too displeased at the Prime Minister's embarrassment.

In January 1917, after much argument, the German government had renewed unrestricted submarine warfare; and this step, together with the offer to Mexico of an offensive alliance (discovered by British Intelligence) brought the United States into the war in April 1917. By this time, British merchant losses had soared, and supplies of food and raw materials were in grave jeopardy. It was only Lloyd George's imposition of the convoy system upon a reluctant Admiralty that reduced losses and avoided disaster. It gradually became clear that the German attempt to cripple the United Kingdom before American aid became effective had failed.

Perhaps the time was ripe for another major land offensive in Europe. Lloyd George allowed himself to be persuaded of the merits of breaking out of the Ypres salient and attacking the German Army from the rear. The battle began on 31 July, but there was no break-out. Three months later, having advanced 4 miles and lost some 300,000 men, the engagement was called off. To enter the village of Passchendaele, British soldiers had struggled on through seas of mud and a landscape incredibly disfigured by the intensive artillery bombardment. In November, a tank attack at Cambrai gained in a few days as much ground as had been won at Passchendaele in months. Until this point, the tank had proved rather a disappointment, its mechanical unreliability crippled its effectiveness in other respects. No one quite knew what to do next after the success at Cambrai, and the Germans soon regained the ground won by the tanks.

In the meantime, the overall position of the Allies had worsened. Initially, the abdication of the Tsar of Russia in March 1917 had been welcomed in London. The new Russian government headed by Kerensky was pledged to fight on, and there was hope that it would do so with increased vigour. By the summer, however, it was becoming clear that continued Russian participation could not be guaranteed. If Russia dropped out, then in due course the balance of forces on the Western Front would become ominous. Much would then depend on the United States. Although there was still resentment at some of Wilson's early statements about the responsibility for the war, American assistance was now generally welcomed.

There were additional complications. The March Revolution in Russia was part symptom and part cause of an unrest which spread through all the belligerent countries and from which Britain was not exempt. Labour discontent grew and might be directed into wider political objectives. A large convention in Leeds in June 1917 exuberantly welcomed the Russian Revolution and set about organizing, not very effectively, British 'soviets'. Opponents of war were less unpopular than formerly. An impending Socialist conference in Sweden seemed to challenge the authority of the existing governments. Henderson, the leading Labour minister, resigned from the Cabinet after failing to persuade Lloyd George that a British Labour delegation should be allowed to attend. After this incident, the division in the Labour party between 'pro-war' and 'anti-war' factions became less important, and attention focused on war aims. While neither Henderson nor MacDonald were Marxists, the Bolshevik Revolution was a further confirmation that the war had released long pent-up pressures for change in Europe.

There was, however, one military success to report. In December 1917 British troops entered Jerusalem – but this event made little impact on the Germans. In the early months of 1918 Lloyd George occupied himself in persuading public opinion of the righteousness of the British cause and in skirmishing with his own generals. He sought that elusive united command which would give coherence to Anglo-French military strategy. In the East, the Bolshevik Revolution and the withdrawal of Russia from the war gave the Germans their final chance in the West. In March, having reinforced their armies, the Germans launched a major offensive. The British and French were driven back and divided. Their communications were cut and the Germans showed that a trench line could be broken. Over the next three months, they gained more ground than the British had done at Cambrai. This emergency at last led to the appointment of a supreme commander – Foch. In effect, however, all he could do was to hope that, sooner or later, the Germans would be unable to sustain their advance. President Wilson's willingness to commit American troops to the fighting would also prove to be vital. By July, it became clear that the Germans had not been able to turn the flank of either the British or French armies. Moreover, their lines were now extended and reserves had already been committed in substantial numbers.

Even so, there were few who anticipated that the war would be over by the end of the year. Haig and Foch began their counter-attacks, using tanks effectively with infantry for the first time, but although the Germans were steadily pushed back, they were not routed. After so many years, it was gratifying to see the Allied divisions advancing. By early October, with progress maintained, it looked as if the Germans could not keep up their position in France. While a stand might be made in the Rhineland, military morale was cracking and revolution threatened. Was it not better to seek an armistice? In the Balkans, too, things were going badly for the Central Powers. At the end of September, Bulgaria surrendered unconditionally. The combination of these circumstances led the Germans to abandon the struggle, and Ottoman Turkey and Austria-Hungary did likewise. The war came to an end at 11 a.m. on 11 November 1918, almost as suddenly as it had begun [E].

In August 1914, Admiral Beatty had surmised that there would not be enough money in the world to allow a gigantic struggle to be continued for any great length of time. He had been proved wrong, but the strain had enormous repercussions which are explored in subsequent chapters. Although that impression was sometimes conveyed, the British had not won the war on their own. By any standards, however, the formation of a mass army had been a major achievement. There will always be a temptation to believe that more imaginative leadership or a different strategy would have brought earlier success. That can never be proved. What was clear was that most recruits wished to leave the army as soon as possible. Bond notes that at the close of the war there were over 3½ million troops paid for by the United Kingdom government. A year later that figure had dropped to about 800,000 and by November 1920 it was down to 370,000(63). But the signature of the armistice did not mean that the world was at peace. Contingents of troops were operating in Russia, various places in the Middle East and in Ireland. Some of these commitments were short-lived, but there seemed little doubt that it was in the sphere of imperial defence that the much-reduced army would be required to serve. And there were those who feared that the failure to restore order in Ireland would not be lost on the inhabitants of Egypt or India. Wherever the general staff looked in 1920 it saw 'our garrisons beset by potential dangers which may far exceed their strength'; Afghanistan, Palestine, Shanghai and Iraq all illustrated the point. Even though the general staff could note in 1925 that Britain's true strategic frontier was the Rhine, there was a tendency to regard the war against Germany as 'abnormal' if not an aberration. Other aspects of that war could also seem exceptional. Defenders of cavalry suggested that the dramatic development of the tank had been due to the unexpected trench stalemate. There was, in any case, apparently no money to be spent on the systematic development of the tank. It was left to angular enthusiasts to praise its potential(63).

Although the army saw itself as the Cinderella service, financial cuts also hit the navy. Having seen the removal of the German Navy as a major challenge, a new contest with the United States was a real possibility in the immediate post-war period. However, successive governments would not countenance heavy naval expenditure. The Washington Naval Treaty of 1921–22 was seen as a first step in a general programme of naval disarmament. Some kind of navy was indeed indispensable, but what was it for? There was no unambiguous enemy in sight. It is not surprising that in these circumstances there was considerable delay in implementing the Admiralty's plans for the construction of aircraft carriers, to take but one example. Since there were a number of technical uncertainties to be resolved such delay was probably fortuitous(65).

In March 1918, during the German spring offensive, the Royal Air Force was formed. It was a controversial testimony to the very rapid development in the use of aircraft during the war. The reconnaissance role, though still important, developed into direct aerial combat and, finally, into bombing. A great deal of glamour attached to the fighter pilots – perhaps some compensation for the very high casualty rate. During March 1918, for example, the British lost over 1,000 of the 1,250 machines they had available in France. Mechanically, a great deal could, and did, go wrong. Even so, at the end of the war, there was little doubt that aircraft had great potential – although some theorists lost all touch with reality. Use of air power in a colonial context – in Iraq or Somaliland – enabled successive governments to keep down occupation costs. The RAF survived as an independent arm, but only just(64). Lacking a war, the other services fought hard to eliminate this upstart but failed. The Admiralty Board then began a protracted campaign to get back the Royal Naval Air Service. If there is something pathetic about these jurisdictional squabbles, they illustrate the fact that few yet appreciated the extent of the co-ordination between traditionally distinct services which twentieth-century warfare would demand. Just after the war Churchill floated the idea of a Ministry of Defence for just this purpose, but received little support. And, after all, whether there would ever be another major war was only a matter of speculation. A great many people still believed that the Great War had been the war to end war. In 1919, in somewhat mysterious circumstances, the Cabinet had decreed that the service departments were to formulate their estimates on the assumption that no great war was to be anticipated for ten years. A decade later that 'rule' was still intact and Cabinet and novelists appeared to be united in waving goodbye to all that.

CHAPTER 11

Into Europe – and back again

Fortunately for the United Kingdom, the other European states did not take advantage of her South African War. The rivalry between France and Russia, on the one hand, and Germany and Austria-Hungary on the other, prevented co-operation. Nevertheless, there was considerable unease about Britain's relationship with Europe. Even if 'splendid isolation' was an exaggerated description of Britain's international position, it was correct to say that the United Kingdom did not belong to either of the existing alliances in Europe. Lord Salisbury continued to believe that this detachment was entirely right. He asked whether Britain had ever in practice felt in danger because of her 'isolation' and remained convinced that the answer was negative. Some of his younger colleagues were less sure. They felt that Salisbury's confidence belonged to the nineteenth century; the new century looked altogether more complicated and dangerous, not least in Europe(9).

THE APPROACH OF WAR

Two men bear the responsibility for the conduct of British foreign policy between 1902 and 1914, though we can only speculate on the importance of their individual contribution to the course of events – Lord Lansdowne (1902–05) and Sir Edward Grey (1905–16) [B]. The war, whose course and conclusion has just been discussed, inevitably conditions our consideration of their diplomacy. We know that they failed and are tempted, at each turn, to discover a way in which war might have been avoided. There can be little doubt that they did seek to avoid it. Both would have agreed that Britain had two basic interests; that the rival alliance systems should remain antagonistic but they should not go to war. The 'balance of power' would prevent any state or group of states from dominating Europe. It was to be hoped that Britain would not have to contribute directly to its maintenance by a positive alignment with one side. War in Europe would be disastrous because Britain might have to join the conflict, with incalculable consequences for her world position. The pursuit of peace conveniently linked self-interest and morality, though not all contemporaries would have accepted the proposition that peace was ethically superior to war. There was a struggle for survival between states as much as there was between individuals. War was the ultimate arbiter, with the beneficial side-effect that patriotic fervour diminished domestic social tension. Neither Lansdowne nor Grey subscribed to the view that war was inevitable or desirable, though they did not believe that it was illegal.

Lansdowne, an urbane, conservative, thoughtful Anglo-Irish aristocrat, remained in office when Balfour became Prime Minister in 1902. There was some alarm in the Cabinet at the steady growth of Germany but, outside Europe, it was Russia, France's ally, which gave cause for concern. It was this anxiety which led him to seek an alliance with Japan, which he concluded in January 1902. It provided for British neutrality in the event of a war between Japan and a single power (i.e. Russia) or British belligerency if Japan went to war with two hostile powers (i.e. Russia and France). The treaty was generally welcomed, although there was anxiety that Britain might be drawn into war. Speaking from the Opposition benches, Grey was even prepared to call Japan Britain's 'partner'. Fortunately, when Russia and Japan did go to war in December 1903, no other state was involved. Because it did reduce the supposed Russian threat to India, her unexpected defeat was generally welcomed in London, though Russian naval losses in the Far East focused fresh attention on German naval strength. France, too, was concerned about the consequences in Europe of the Russian defeat. It was in this context that negotiations with Britain were begun, or at least accelerated.

The Franco-British *entente* (for it was not a formal alliance) was concluded, not without difficulty, in April 1904. The bargaining had centred on colonial questions. In the event, the French agreed to accept the British position in Egypt and, in effect, the British withdrew opposition to French designs on Morocco. Other lesser colonial matters were also resolved. Lansdowne's primary objective was to improve relations with France. He had no wish to exacerbate relations with Germany. Nevertheless, there was acrimony and suspicion between London and Berlin and the new agreement did nothing to lessen this tension. There was in theory no reason why it should not be supplemented by a comparable agreement with Germany. It would be wrong, therefore, to see Britain at this stage siding firmly with France. Parisian observers rightly detected an ambivalent love/hate quality in the relationship between Britain and Germany. British musical, literary, commercial and church contacts were stronger with Germany than they were with France. Animosity towards Britain, from at least the time of the Fashoda crisis, did not completely disappear in France. European relationships were still fluid. The 'Bully of the Boers' was not greatly loved anywhere in Europe so that, despite the emotional barrier of Alsace-Lorraine, a *rapprochement* between Germany and France could not be ruled out, even if it entailed a subordinate status for France. Paris knew that it still could not rely upon London for help if pressure came from Berlin.

These ambiguities in the new relationship were not resolved, even though the French pressed for clarification of the British position. There was, of course, a change of government and Foreign Secretary at the end of 1905. Sir Edward Grey's diffidence masked great determination(11). Despite the fact that Rosebery, his erstwhile mentor, had been a critic of the French agreement, Grey was resolved to uphold it. Writing a few months before assuming office he declared his determination not to be dragged back into the German net. He adhered to what he believed to be continuity in foreign policy and had no desire to conduct a specifically Liberal foreign policy, supposing he had known what it was. Nevertheless, some Liberal MPs did not want Liberalism to stop at Dover and tried to remind him of their concern. He remained largely unmoved. It was significant, however, that in the following years he was subject to criticism on these grounds. Liberal intellectuals wanted foreign policy to be less secret. They were suspicious of the limited social segment from which the Foreign Office and Diplomatic Service were drawn. Unfortunately, when the Foreign Office was made more efficient, they then suspected that officials were having an undue influence on policy(10).

Grey faced a major international crisis over Morocco immediately on coming into office. In the months that followed he gave strong support to France and the *entente* emerged stronger from the crisis. He tried to maintain the position that Britain would not fight to give France Morocco, but she would fight to save the *entente*. He authorized military conversations but claimed not to know their outcome. He found German diplomacy short-sighted. Berlin did not seem to realize that Britain invariably drifted into opposition to any power which attempted to establish a hegemony in Europe. Time and again he returned to what he regarded as German bullying. Only when Berlin appreciated that the *entente* could not be shaken would he be prepared to talk. If Grey himself claimed that he was not, in principle, 'anti-German', others were less reticent. A Foreign Office clerk, Eyre Crowe drew up a memorandum in 1907 of such a thorough character that it was a tribute to his German upbringing. He painted a sombre picture of German intentions. Some of his colleagues took the view that the German desire for a 'place in the sun' was not unreasonable. The difficulty was that German aspirations seemed so cloudy that the basis for a specific negotiation scarcely existed. From time to time over the next few years, greater co-operation was achieved between London and Berlin, but suspicion was never far below the surface(15).

In 1911, Morocco was again the occasion for an international storm. Germany took offence at French penetration of the country and dispatched a gunboat to Agadir to make this displeasure apparent. Grey had never liked the extent to which the initiative in Morocco rested with France and made it clear that Britain would not fight to prevent some stake for Germany or alternative compensation. But it was Lloyd George, with the Foreign Secretary's blessing, who declared in a speech at the Mansion House on 21 July that Britain would not be treated as if she were of no account in the Cabinet of Nations. In the autumn, a Franco-German compromise was reached and the *entente* remained intact. Critics on the left of the Liberal party attacked Grey's response to the crisis and there was disquiet in the Cabinet when the Franco-British military conversations became generally known. For a time, Grey had to submit to an unusual degree of scrutiny and Haldane disappeared to Germany to see if he could resolve the naval race. Grey resolutely opposed any notion that such an agreement could be obtained by a declaration of British neutrality. That would give the Germans a free hand in Europe. On the other hand, he saw no merit in a formal treaty between Britain and France which spelt out the details of their relationship so that each side knew precisely where it stood. His policy over the next few years oscillated between these two points(13).

The Foreign Secretary was still prepared to consider an agreement with Germany, possibly involving colonial concessions at the expense of others, because of his anxiety about Russia. In 1907, he had been prepared to take what seemed to him to be the logical step of reaching an agreement with St Petersburg. This arrangement, too, chiefly centred on a colonial question – Persia. Both countries accepted 'spheres of influence' and Grey defended this division on the grounds that it safeguarded the security of India. Critics pointed out that there was no reason to suppose that the agreement would be honoured. Although he did not say so, Grey shared such suspicions, but felt that in any case Britain did not have the power to resist a Russian advance in the area. Although it was not emphasized, there was a wider European dimension to the agreement. Britain was now on more intimate terms with France's ally. It was in these circumstances that the term 'Triple Entente' was accepted, though there were elements in the Liberal Cabinet opposed to its use. Many back-bench Liberal MPs did not like an agreement with autocratic Russia and their antagonism grew when they observed her in action in Persia. While not opposed to naval conversations with Russia, Grey resisted the notion that the time was ripe to conclude an alliance.

The Balkans had long been considered the most unstable area of Europe. Grey had gained considerable prestige from his success in persuading the ambassadors of the Great Powers to meet in London to consider some of the wider issues arising out of the Balkan Wars of 1912–13. Even so, the assassination of the heir to the Austrian throne at Sarajevo on 28 June 1914 caused a great shock. There was a good deal of sympathy in London for the Habsburgs and scant support for Serbia. Even though it was difficult to see how the Serbian government could be held responsible for the incident, a short and sharp shock administered promptly by Vienna might have been acceptable. There seems to have been little general awareness in the Press or elsewhere of the possibility of complications. Talking to the German Ambassador on 9 July Grey stressed that England wished to preserve an absolutely free hand.

On 4 August the Cabinet heard that German troops had violated Belgian territory. The ultimatum which Grey was then authorized to send received no reply. Britain was at war. Ever since, there has been debate about the wisdom of Grey's 'absolutely free hand'. For some, he displayed a fatal early partiality for France and Russia; for others, he remained too remote throughout late July and missed an opportunity to act as a conciliator. Refinements of these positions can be made when the detailed diplomacy is considered. In retrospect, Grey himself did not believe that he could have prevented a major European conflict. He could, however, have prevented British involvement if he had wished. Until the very last moment, there was strong opposition to intervention in the Cabinet. It was the invasion of Belgium that tipped the balance. Grey himself saw no conflict between what he termed an 'obligation of honour' to France and national self-interest. Britain could only stay out if she was prepared to accept the German domination of Europe(12).

THE DIPLOMACY OF WAR

Committed to the war though he was, Grey had little doubt that it meant the end of British and European civilization as he knew it. Although depressed and despondent, he remained in office and tried to fashion a new foreign policy in wartime. He did not believe he had much scope. War was something best left to the soldiers and only military success could give him freedom of manoeuvre. He deprecated the tone of much of the propaganda that speedily poured from the presses and looked askance at that which the government itself sponsored. Tired and increasingly worried about his sight, the Foreign Secretary was not the man to explain to the country what the war was about. Asquith and Lloyd George did their best, though they did not go into details about the government's objectives. The Prime Minister chose Dublin as the place to explain that the restoration of Belgium would be the test of the ability of all small nations to live in peace untroubled by a powerful neighbour. Given the desperate fighting to prevent the collapse of France, it seemed otiose to issue a more elaborate statement. The only binding step was the agreement with France and Russia that no power would make a separate peace with Germany(16).

Although British opinion swung round to supporting the war, the gallant Russian ally was a source of concern to both Left and Right. A Russian victory in eastern Europe was naturally desired, but it seemed inevitable that the consequence would be a major extension of Russian power into central Europe. That was almost as undesirable as a German victory. Sir John Clapham, the economic historian, was only one of a number of distinguished people who felt it necessary to reveal that they were Teutons not Slavs. Visions of the Russians in Constantinople sprang readily to mind. Old India hands quickly saw the danger. But it was another matter to say how the Russian ally could be deterred. In fact, it was soon apparent that the Russians were not going to be hammering at the gates of Vienna or even of Prague and in many ways the Russian contribution to the war could not have turned out better. The Germans and Austrians were kept busy, but the Russians never looked like winning.

The status quo on the Western Front was an effective deterrent to peace by negotiation. The British and French insisted that there could be no discussion until the Germans withdrew from the Belgian and French territory they illegally occupied. The Germans insisted that it was only reasonable for talks to begin on the basis of the actual status quo. Neither side was prepared to talk when it thought it was losing ground and neither side was prepared to talk when it thought it was gaining ground.

The diplomacy of the war had, therefore, to concentrate on the perimeter. Italy was an obvious target since it was believed that the Italian army would be a positive factor. Despite her links with the Central Powers, Italy declared herself neutral in August 1914. A mixed bag of territorial goodies in Asia Minor and on the other side of the Adriatic brought Italy into the war in support of Britain and France in April 1915. Over the next couple of years it proved to be the kind of support which required the constant dispatch of financial and mechanical assistance. In south-eastern Europe British diplomacy did not have such success.

Ottoman Turkey joined the Central Powers in October 1914 and an attempt to entice Bulgaria into the war on the Allied side was a conspicuous failure. Bulgaria joined the Central Powers in the late autumn of 1915. This naturally disposed the Romanians to stress their Latin culture and, disastrously, to assist the Allies in August 1916.

Although there was a certain thrill to be gained from trying to bid for the Bulgarian corn harvest, the central issue soon became the future of Austria-Hungary. It had been no part of Britain's original intention in going to war to destroy the Habsburg Empire. Liberals did talk about the 'suppressed nationalities' – the Czechs or the Croats – but 'autonomy' was a suitably vague word to use to describe their future. In the first couple of years of the war, the more promising path seemed to be to try detaching Austria-Hungary from Germany. It was not a very promising enticement to open separate negotiations – involving a complex chain of European princes – to propose dissolution. In the last two years of the war, however, when it became clear that Vienna could not be detached from Berlin, Lloyd George permitted rather generous gestures of encouragement to political exiles. It would do British Liberals no harm to realize, at a time when the cost of war weighed heavily with them, that they were on a mission of liberation.

At the end of 1917, with the Bolshevik Revolution fresh in conservative minds, Lloyd George faced renewed advocacy of peace by negotiations. Lansdowne made one such plea in a famous letter in the *Daily Telegraph*. If talks did not begin, he foresaw that Britain and Europe would be plunged into poverty, chaos and revolution. In response, Lloyd George declared in January 1918 that Britain was not fighting an aggressive war against the German people, although the 'great wrong' of 1871 (Alsace-Lorraine) would have to be righted. He added that Austria-Hungary would have to be reconstituted, though not necessarily destroyed, and Poland would be reborn. Above all, he advocated an international organization which would offer an alternative to war as a means of settling disputes. He proposed a 'League of Nations', though it was not clear precisely what this term entailed. Such aspirations satisfied his immediate audience, the TUC, and he hoped it would satisfy President Wilson(17).

The problem to which Grey did continue to give a great deal of attention before he left office in 1916 was American neutrality. Grey could not be expected to agree with the even-handedness of the initial American assessment of responsibility for the war, but he did feel it important to keep emotion under control. Subtle British propaganda in the United States created a climate of sympathy in many quarters. It was vital not to forfeit goodwill by a too vigorous application of blockade policy, bearing in mind American feeling about the 'freedom of the seas'. The Foreign Secretary was very polite to Colonel House when he arrived, on President Wilson's behalf, to see whether there might be common ground between the belligerents. The British reaped their reward when the United States did join the war in April 1917. Yet even then, America was an 'associated power' not an ally. She had joined the war because she believed her own interests to be threatened, not out of goodwill towards Britain or France. Nevertheless, it was important to keep as much in tune with American thinking about the post-war world as possible. The accident of war had taken Britain into Europe, but it was not clear that she would stay there.

THE AFTERMATH

It has been apparent that before 1914 British Foreign Secretaries had increasingly to concentrate on European issues, though no clear or universally acceptable conception of Britain's European role emerged. The war did not settle that question either. If it was still generally agreed that Britain made the right decision in 1914, the scale of the bloodshed made both politicians and public recoil from the prospect of a new war. Yet, European problems would not go away, and successive governments adopted a stance towards them which was not markedly different from that of their pre-war predecessors. Britain was still not considered by her leaders to be one European state among many. She remained, in their judgement, an outsider, capable, on occasion, of helping the 'Europeans' to resolve their obsessive differences. It seemed inevitable that this should be so. The relationship with the empire, shortly to be considered, remained of paramount importance. That in turn put relations with the United States on a different basis from relations with France or Germany. Even if they disagreed with one another, as they not infrequently did, the British and the Americans normally understood each other. Even if the 'special relationship' contained elements of fantasy, it was not altogether fanciful. The idea of the League of Nations, for example, was one which had a fatal attraction for a particular type of Anglo-American mind and little resonance in Europe. It was this continuing attachment, notwithstanding naval rivalry and the refusal of the American Senate to ratify the Treaty of Versailles, which helped to make adjustment to Europe seem unattractive.

The conduct of foreign policy after 1919 was more complicated that it had been before 1914. The failure of diplomacy to prevent war inevitably meant that politicians and diplomats had forfeited their claim to possess an arcane expertise. Others were not unwilling to step into their place. The League of Nations Union was one post-war body which felt fully entitled to match its wisdom against that of the government of the day, particularly if it was a Conservative government. It became the most vocal and organized pressure group on foreign affairs the country had ever known. Its pamphlets, public meetings and petitions were more significant than any mere reform of the Foreign Office – though that did take place.

No Foreign Secretary after him approached Grey's length of service and standing. During the war, there were demands for the 'democratic control' of foreign policy, though there was little agreement about how it might be effected. Lloyd George never showed much liking for any attempts to control him. Unlike Grey, who never went anywhere if he could avoid it (and he usually did avoid it), Lloyd George distinctly believed in the efficacious consequences of his presence. Curzon, who became Foreign Secretary in the post-war coalition, did not enjoy basking in the reflected glory of his master and deplored his penchant for conference diplomacy in the immediate post-war years. Curzon also served in the two brief Conservative governments that followed but was never able to do justice to his talents. In 1924, MacDonald was so confident of his that he emulated Salisbury and became his own Foreign Secretary for the brief life of the Labour government. Austen Chamberlain (1924–29) was highly esteemed in his own lifetime and maintained the authority of his office at every opportunity. In 1929, Arthur Henderson was allowed the prize which MacDonald declined to award him in 1924. MacDonald and Henderson were the first Labour Foreign Secretaries, but a 'Socialist foreign policy' was only faintly discernible. The Foreign Office conducted its business as usual. Even so, the perspective of Mac-Donald and Henderson (differing from each other though they did) was not that of their public school and university-educated predecessors. Both men had extensive contacts with the European Labour movement and attached some importance to them. Austen Chamberlain knew his way around a different kind of Europe, having an unusually good command of French and German. Whatever his policy, he came nearest among Foreign Secretaries in this period to possessing a receptiveness to European ideas and aspirations. Unlike his Prime Minister, he did not believe that Aix-les-Bains summed up all Europe had to offer.

Since much of central and eastern Europe was still in turmoil, it was somewhat deceptive in 1918 to talk of 'peace'. British opinion disliked the reality of continuing conflict. Public notions of justice and the necessity for reparations, fashioned in the emotion of war, could not be abandoned as easily as they had been engendered. Only the prospect of a quick peace settlement seemed likely to restore stability. To this end, Lloyd George spent most of the first six months of 1919 in Paris.

Sadly, the timorous Franco-British partnership of pre-1914 had not been turned into a deep alliance and understanding by the war. Bearing the biggest military burden, the French discounted the significance of the British blockade of Germany and of the war at sea in general. They looked askance at British expansion outside Europe. French commentators argued that Britain would gain the greatest advantage from the war. Pétain would have liked 'a brilliant, clearly French, victory over Germany'. And indeed, at the peace conference, Lloyd George tried to minimize German territorial losses. He ensured that a plebiscite was held in Silesia to determine the boundary between Germany and the new Poland, that Danzig was made a Free City and that the Rhineland was demilitarized, but not separated from Germany. He thought that too severe a peace would drive the Germans to Bolshevism as their only salvation; the actual amount of German reparations should be settled at a later date.

At the time, the Treaty of Versailles was broadly acceptable to British opinion, though some critics on the Right wished that Germany had been dismembered. Such a step would, of course, have required the occupation of Germany. Labour and Liberal commentators usually disliked what they termed the one-sided application of self-determination. What about the Germans of Austria and Czechoslovakia? They argued that a new Germany equipped with a democratic government should not be treated as though it was the old imperial Germany. The economist Keynes, in a brilliant polemic, argued that Germany could not possibly pay for the reparations which were planned. Critics of the settlement found little consolation in the new League of Nations and regretted the exclusion of Germany from membership. Within a few years, influential sections of British opinion were persuading themselves that a revision of the treaty was urgently needed if a lasting peace was to be established in Europe.

In general, the settlement revealed the continuing ambiguity of British European policy. The British military guarantee to France, for example, was made conditional on American participation. Some Frenchmen saw the entire peace settlement as 'la paix des Anglo-Saxonnes' – an alien imposition from outside Europe. In the event, the British guarantee to France lapsed when President Wilson failed to carry Congress. It seemed that in measure as the United States isolated itself from the rest of the world so the British retreated from western Europe. In the early 1920s, Franco-British relations were extremely fragile and even the prospect of war could not be ruled out. The French insisted on the reparations payments to which they were entitled and were ready, as their occupation of the Ruhr in 1923 showed, to take vigorous action to secure them. The British regarded this zeal as excessive and legalistic. They argued that Germany was alienated rather than integrated by such conduct. French treaties with the new states of East Central Europe were not warmly regarded in London either. London liked to see itself as the detached arbiter of European affairs and felt that Paris was becoming too assertive. In August 1924, however, the Dawes Plan, agreed at a conference in London, seemed to offer a way out of the reparations impasse by drawing up a new schedule of payments. The French agreed to withdraw from the Ruhr. MacDonald's good offices in this matter meant that the incoming Conservative government might be able to make further progress in achieving Franco-German reconciliation.

It was perhaps only in 1925 that Europeans began to feel that a start towards a real peace was being made. Stresemann in Germany and Briand in France showed a welcome willingness to make a fresh start and Chamberlain wanted to assist. His efforts culminated in the Locarno Conference where, on 16 October 1925, a famous pact was signed. Britain, France and Germany undertook to settle any disputes between themselves by arbitration. France, Germany and Belgium mutually guaranteed each other's frontiers – an undertaking underwritten by Britain and Italy. Germany undertook to settle any dispute with Poland or Czechoslovakia by arbitration. France, but not Britain, guaranteed Poland and Czechoslovakia against German aggression. *The Times* took pride in the part Britain had played in getting the Europeans to sort out their problems.

The pact did not denote any fundamental change in British policy. Indeed, both inside and outside the Cabinet, there were those who saw Locarno as a way of very strictly limiting Britain's Continental commitments. Austen Chamberlain himself told the Committee of Imperial Defence that the treaty reduced rather than extended British liabilities. Even if this were true, the Dominions made it clear at the Imperial Conference in 1926 that they did not hold themselves bound by it. It was noted, too, that Britain had extended no guarantee to Germany's eastern frontiers. Not that there was much difference between a British guarantee and its absence. The Chiefs of Staff in 1926 felt that the armed services could only 'take note' of Continental commitments. Dispatch of small expeditionary forces across the Channel could never be more than a pledge of readiness to fulfil the guarantees. They could not actually fulfil them. The hope was that the continent of Europe could become self-regulating, allowing Britain to concentrate on the world beyond. In the meantime, the Big Three at Geneva enjoyed their regular meetings. Germany joined the League of Nations in 1926 and she continued to make regular payments under the Dawes Plan. There was some suspicion of illicit German rearmament, but it was not pursued. However, Stresemann died in 1929 and the future of Germany looked more uncertain. In this context, in May 1930, the French government put flesh on a proposal made by Briand the previous September; the European nations should establish a federal link, primarily economic in character.

The British reaction, relayed by Arthur Henderson, was distinctly frosty. Britain could not help to create any economic or political group which might be thought hostile to the American, or indeed any other continent. Since one of MacDonald's first actions on returning to office in 1929 had been to visit the United States – where he received a warm welcome – he was in no mood to encourage a European bloc. It was also feared that such an association might weaken political co-operation within the world-wide British Empire. The final objection was that such a scheme might damage the League of Nations. Henderson was an enthusiast for the League in a way no other Foreign Secretary had been. He was undeterred by suggestions that 'collective security' – which underlay the League – could not possibly work. MacDonald and the Conservatives, for rather different reasons, were sceptical about the League's claim to universal authority. Yet, such was the general support in the country for the League that politicians were reluctant to give a public airing to the practical difficulties of which they were conscious. A dangerous cleavage developed between the working assumptions of governments and popular expectations.

By 1931, therefore, British policy towards Europe showed a strong resemblance to what it had been before 1914. Federalism had been emphatically rejected. The League of Nations was considered an awkward auxiliary to policy and not a substitute for it. There was no vital British interest in eastern Europe. The continuing task seemed to be to promote an amicable balance between France and Germany without being committed to either(18).

One novelty, however, was the existence of the Soviet Union. It was like and yet unlike other states in that it purported to be the agent of international revolution. The Comintern, established in Moscow, was an agency for potential subversion. Its existence raised the possibility that future conflict in Europe might be as much about ideology as about boundaries. Immediately after the close of the Great War there had been talk, led by Churchill, of crushing Bolshevism by force. There were Allied forces in Russia and in contact with anti-Bolshevik elements. The possibility of smothering Bolshevism in its cradle was alluring but the task of administering Russia was not. A major war in Russia would have caused great complications at home and the weight of Cabinet opinion was against it. When the Bolshevik regime established itself, diplomatic relations were opened, but only the first Labour government tried, abortively, to extend them by concluding a commercial treaty. The 'Zinoviev' letter, which purported to come from Moscow and urged the Communist party of Great Britain to work for the proposed treaty because of the opportunities for subversion which it would provide, played a part in Labour's 1924 Election defeat. The Conservatives broke off diplomatic relations with the Soviet Union in 1927 in rather muddled circumstances arising out of a raid on the Soviet trading agency in London. Henderson subsequently restored contacts, but no intimacy developed. Even Labour governments were content to see the Soviet Union remain on the periphery of Europe.

The ideological dimension in foreign policy was not confined to the Soviet Union. Mussolini took power in Italy in 1922 and unveiled the brave new world of Fascism. Except on the Left, hostility to Mussolini was not great. His Italy was an acceptable partner in the Locarno Pact and Fascism appeared to cause no problems, except, possibly, for the Italians. As for other 'Fascist' movements elsewhere in Europe, their emphasis on nationalism seemed to make them less of a danger than Communism. A 'Fascist International' might be a contradiction in terms. In the later 1920s, therefore, Europe seemed poised to take unpredictable political paths but Britain, to the distress of some, seemed still attached to familiar and unexciting ways.

CHAPTER 12

British Empire to British Commonwealth

During the South African War, Canadians, Australians and other imperial troops fought alongside men from the British Isles. Beneath this appearance of unity, however, there were disconcerting tendencies. Imperial volunteers in South Africa experienced a heightened national rather than imperial consciousness. It was generally becoming evident that the status of the 'Dominions' required clarification. After the war, the Colonial Secretary, Joseph Chamberlain, pressed for imperial consolidation and at the 1902 Colonial Conference (which coincided with Edward VII's coronation) again proposed a federal council. This time, not even New Zealand supported the idea. His pleas for free trade within the empire and a greater sharing of the burden of imperial defence also fell on unreceptive ears. It was, however, agreed that colonial conferences should be held regularly – every four years – rather than depend upon the incidence of a royal jubilee or coronation. Their organization remained the responsibility of the Colonial Office – a separate secretariat being rejected. In 1911, the 'Colonial' Conference became the 'Imperial' Conference. The term 'dominion' was still rather unsatisfactory, but at least represented an advance on 'self-governing colony'. The term 'commonwealth' was also surfacing as an alternative to 'empire', though its proponents did not wish it to imply any relaxation of imperial ties; quite the contrary. They believed that the empire had to federate or disintegrate – but most politicians rejected that stark choice(32).

The Dominions could not be described as states in a full sense because they lacked, among other things, control over their own foreign policy. Britain acted on their behalf. It was the defence burden to sustain this responsibility that London found increasingly onerous. The Dominions replied that they did not play their full part because they were not invited to play a full part. In 1911, however, Grey did treat the visiting Prime Ministers to a confidential address on foreign affairs. He painted a broad picture of the dangers facing the British Empire. He knew that Britain's treaty with Japan had not been popular – the Australian Defence Minister reported that his countrymen felt that 'to a certain extent it degraded the position of the empire to go into a treaty with an Asiatic country' – but said that it was vital. So ended the first lesson in foreign affairs. Empire policy had to be to safeguard the United Kingdom and, although no machinery for consultation on foreign policy was created, more information did trickle through.

The decision to commit the British Empire to war in 1914 was taken by the United Kingdom Cabinet alone, though it was confident of Dominion approval. On the whole, such confidence was justified. Andrew Fisher of Australia committed his country 'to the last man and the last shilling', though some Labour supporters lamented an imperial connection which involved Australia in the deeds of the 'British ruling class'. There was also some Afrikaner and French Canadian opposition. Nevertheless, on the whole, the way in which the British Empire went to war in 1914 seemed most impressive. The fact that Australia, New Zealand and South Africa all had their eyes on neighbouring German colonies did help. Their support gave London confidence that in a 'long haul' the resources of men and materials in the empire could tip the balance.

The Dominion leaders did not expect to play a passive role. W. M. Hughes, the new Australian Prime Minister, came to London in 1916 armed with support from other Dominion leaders and demanded consultation. Lloyd George responded to his fellow Welshman by establishing a rather grandiloquent Imperial War Cabinet. The spring of 1917 saw Dominion leaders in conference in London and similar sessions took place in the summer of 1918. They welcomed this development as a forum for consultation but did not want it to become a permanent executive. The Dominion leaders were primarily responsible to their own people and any politician who lingered too long in London might be in difficulties at home. The only man to stay in London was Smuts of South Africa, his country's Defence Minister. In 1917, it was agreed that the readjustment of the constitutional relations of the component parts of the empire was too important and intricate a subject to be dealt with during the war, but should be tackled at a special post-war conference. It was evident that the Dominions wanted equality. One manifestation of this was their insistence on being individually named for League of Nations purposes and not lumped together anonymously under the heading of British Empire. Foreign states found the situation quite bewildering. The Americans, in particular, suspected the British of sharp practice, though they soon found that the Australians were no mere lackeys of London.

Imperial conferences took place in 1921, 1923 and 1926. At the first, Smuts had a plan for the 'Constitution of the British Commonwealth', but there was a general feeling that a 'family' did not need a rule book and it was not discussed. One immediate problem was the Japanese alliance, which was due for renewal. The delegates adjourned *en bloc* for Washington where, after American and Dominion pressure, the British agreed not to renew it. Two other incidents illustrate the prevailing tendency. The Dominion response to the Chanak crisis (1922) – when it seemed, for a time, that Britain might go to war with Turkey – showed that Lloyd George could not expect automatic endorsement(38). The diplomatic unity of the British Empire was a fiction. Less dramatically, Canada signed a halibut fishery agreement with the United States in March 1923 without the aid of the British Embassy in Washington. Its treaty-making power was endorsed at the subsequent Imperial Conference. Although Australia and New Zealand were not very interested, the way was now open for the Dominions to establish their own diplomatic missions abroad. In turn, the British government established a Dominions Office which was separate from the Colonial Office, although, initially, the Colonial Secretary doubled as Dominions Secretary.

At the 1926 conference, Baldwin referred in his opening remarks to the task of reconciling 'the principle of self-government in external as well as domestic affairs with the necessity for a policy in foreign affairs of general Imperial concern which will commend itself to a number of different Governments and Parliaments'. Lord Balfour chaired a committee which emerged with a formula which became classic. Great Britain and the Dominions were 'autonomous communities within the British Empire, equal in status, in no way subordinate one to another in any aspect of their domestic or external affairs, though united by a common allegiance to the Crown'. Awkward words like 'sovereignty' or 'independence' were eschewed. The terms 'empire' and 'commonwealth' both appeared, and the 'communities' were found to be simultaneously 'within' the empire and 'members' of the Commonwealth. The members were equal in 'status', though manifestly not in other respects. Diplomatic dealings between governments would henceforth proceed through high commissioners and the governor-general would represent the Crown alone. Dominion legislation could not in future be found 'repugnant' under the 1865 Colonial Laws Validity Act. These points and kindred matters were embodied in the 1931 Statute of Westminster. At that date, the old white empire formally came to an end, though Australia did not adopt the legislation until 1942 and New Zealand not until 1947. Newfoundland, trembling on the brink of bankruptcy, never did. The Irish Free State, on the other hand, pressed ahead with further steps to eradicate the British link. On the whole, however, great store was still set upon the Crown as the continuing symbol of a British Commonwealth(39).

Although the process of constitutional definition might seem negative, it was still thought important that British emigrants should go to the colonies rather than to 'foreign' countries. Between 1922 and 1931, when the natural increase in the United Kingdom population was nearly 2¾ million, emigration removed 25 per cent of this increase. Two-thirds went to Canada, Australia and New Zealand, and almost all the remainder to the United States. Fewer than 20,000 went to Kenya, Rhodesia and South Africa. The Dominion governments used the London money market for their borrowing requirements and a high proportion of United Kingdom overseas investment went to the empire. The great British Empire Exhibition at Wembley in 1924 had to be extended into 1925, and was visited by over 17 million people. The Empire Marketing Board conducted a vigorous advertising campaign to persuade people to buy empire products. Empire Free Trade, at least in the eyes of Lord Beaverbrook, seemed to offer a solution to all problems(197).

The Statute of Westminster was presented as a 'family' arrangement, without implications for the remainder of the empire. Even so, it had long been recognized that India constituted a special case. Agitation and unrest had been apparent there before 1914. Japan's defeat of Russia in 1905 showed that European states were not invincible. Yet it would be premature to speak of a strong Indian national consciousness. Religious animosities were not going to disappear. The All-India Moslem League was founded in 1906, and strong Hindu movements were also apparent. Morley, the incoming Secretary of State for India in 1905, had been prepared to listen to 'moderates' like Gokhale, though not to men of violence. The 1909 Government of India Act extended the principle of representative government by providing for non-official majorities in the central and provincial legislative councils. The Indian electorates were very small (and communal), but an important change had been made. Even so, Morley shared the prevailing view that 'responsible' government could not be envisaged in India. It did not seem unreasonable to believe that British rule alone kept India together. The splendid Delhi durbar of 1911, attended by the King-Emperor, showed the confidence of the British. They were asserting their position as successors to the Moghul emperors by moving India's capital from Calcutta. British rule also depended on Indian co-operation and, on the eve of war in 1914, that still seemed forthcoming(35).

There was some opposition to Indian involvement in the war, but not as much as some officials feared. Indian princes contributed financially on a princely scale. Even M. K. Gandhi, champion of the Indians in South Africa, came to London and set about organizing an Indian ambulance unit. On the other hand, the 'humiliation' suffered by India in 1914 brought greater unity both within the Congress movement and between it and the Moslem League. They agreed on proposals for extending the principle of elected representation. The wartime viceroys were not unsympathetic and action proceded on two levels. Indian representatives were invited to attend the Imperial War Conference and proposals for a system of 'half-responsible' government within India were considered. In London in August 1917 it was announced that the British government intended to promote the 'increasing association of Indians in every branch of the administration and the gradual development of self-governing institutions with a view to the progressive realisation of responsible government in India as an integral part of the British Empire'. The 1919 Government of India Act established 'dyarchy' in the provinces – responsibility for some matters was transferred to Indian ministers while the governor retained full control over others.

Even so, India in the early 1920s was far from peaceful. There were Moslem protests and resentment arising from the massacre at Amritsar in 1919 when the local army commander was responsible for heavy loss of life when he used machine-guns to disperse a mob. Some Indians would not take part in the provincial governments in protest. Gandhi sprang into prominence, launching his campaigns of civil disobedience. British rule was under increasing pressure, though not yet seriously threatened. A review of the 1919 Act was brought forward, but the Commission of Enquiry under Sir John Simon was resented because it did not contain a single Indian. Congress drew up its own plans for the future 'Commonwealth of India' at the end of 1928. It was agreed that civil disobedience would begin again if the British did not accept them within a year. The British could not allow their enquiry to be swept aside and waited until the Simon Commission's Report was published in June 1930. In the meantime, civil disobedience was widespread and Gandhi and thousands of others were detained in May 1930. Simon's Report rejected independence and envisaged continuing British control over central government, though it suggested that full responsible government was possible at the provincial level. The princely states might be drawn into a federation. It was proposed to hold a series of Round Table conferences in London and their outcome would be important, not only for India but also for Burma and Ceylon, and indeed for the entire dependent empire(40).

Outside India, however, immediate change was unlikely. In Africa before

1914, the boundaries and administrative structures were only in process of consolidation, leading to such new creations as 'Nigeria' and 'Kenya'. The war
brought the final phase of British imperial expansion with the assumption of
mandates in the Middle East over Palestine and Iraq (from the former Ottoman
Empire) and in Africa where German East Africa became Tanganyika. There
was, however, some significance in the fact that these were 'mandates' rather
than direct acquisitions. Britain explicitly undertook a responsibility to govern in
the interests of the governed, with the assumption that self-government would
follow after an appropriate period of guidance and development. Such a 'trusteeship', although unenforceable, also had implications for other colonies. In
Kenya, for example, it was finally asserted after the war that African interests
were paramount and white settlers could not expect to advance to Dominion status. In Southern Rhodesia, on the other hand, white settlers were given very
substantial powers of internal self-government in 1923. In West Africa, where
white settlement did not complicate matters, the somewhat pretentious notion of
the 'Dual Mandate' was evolved. Great stress was placed upon the role of 'native authorities' in local administration. Lack of white manpower made such reliance almost inevitable in any case. What most stands out, however, throughout
the entire dependent empire, is the variety of contexts in which British rule
operated. Although the Colonial Office in London 'controlled' everything, the
maintenance of imperial authority depended on many factors beyond its
control(33).

Talk of trusteeship did not mean that imperial rule would shortly cease: a certain timelessness pervades the colonial administration of the 1920s. It was remarkable how little British rule rested on the overt use of force. However, political activity among Africans was not unknown. In 1920, petitioners claiming to
represent the intelligentsia of British West Africa reminded their monarch in
London of the principle that taxation went with effective representation. The
connection with the British Empire should remain 'inviolate,' but should not
preclude self-government. A congress which purported to embrace Nigeria, the
Gold Coast, Gambia and Sierra Leone was necessarily difficult to organize, and
the British knew that at this stage there was no mass movement behind this coastal élite. It was only on the Mediterranean littoral that any formal change took
place. In 1922, Egypt was declared 'independent', but British troops and influence remained. In 1930, the mandate in Iraq also came to an end, on similar
conditions. British influence throughout the Middle East had never been higher.
Yet it was already clear that in Palestine at least the responsibility of administration might prove onerous. In 1917, Balfour had declared his support for a Jewish
national home in Palestine and the Jewish element in the population began to
build up. Arab hostility increased and a major crisis was in the making.

Looking back over thirty years to the South African War, it is possible to detect a certain ebbing of imperial authority and enthusiasm(41). That tendency
was neither dramatic nor universal. In 1916, for example, the Viceroy of India
gaily considered Mesopotamia an area ripe for British or Indian settlement – a
'second Egypt'. After the war, such confidence is more difficult to find. Ever
since J. A. Hobson's book *Imperialism* (1902), some elements on the Left were

critical of the whole imperial enterprise. It was easier, however, to deplore the existence of the empire than to know what to do with it. Sidney Webb (Lord Passfield), who became Colonial Secretary in 1929, showed no disposition to put himself out of business. Rather, it was Labour's task to see that trusteeship was honoured; though it was Ramsay MacDonald in this same government who wrote to the Viceroy of India urging him in strong terms to stand firm before the agitation which he faced. Liberal opinion deplored such events as the Amritsar massacres, but felt that the *Pax Britannica* also prevented massacres both in India and elsewhere. It was an ambivalence towards the empire which permeated many levels of British society.

CHAPTER 13

Reshaping the United Kingdom: Britain and Ireland

The map of Europe changed radically in the first quarter of the twentieth century. After 1919, the principle of national self-determination was supposed to inaugurate a new and peaceful era. It did not do so. There were innumerable problems involving boundaries and minorities. The United Kingdom was not immune from these problems. In December 1922 it, too, was divided, after years of bloodshed, bitterness and confusion. The Union of Great Britain and Ireland ceased – though in the process Ireland was itself divided.

Twenty years earlier, when the condition of Ireland was more than usually paradoxical, few would have predicted such an outcome(124). At the turn of the century, a Conservative government could reject even the notion of Home Rule with equanimity and continue on a course designed to give Ireland equality of status within the United Kingdom. An Irish Local Government Act, 1898 gave Ireland a structure of county councils, and urban and rural district councils, little different from that operating across the Irish Sea. The 1903 Land Act (Wyndham's Act) greatly increased the funds available for land purchase and, with the help of further legislation, there was substantial transfer of land to tenants: almost two-thirds by 1917. Sir Horace Plunket and Father Finlay encouraged the development of co-operative creameries, in an attempt to modernize the Irish dairy industry – Irish butter faced severe competition from Denmark and New Zealand. Irish agricultural wages were still below the British level, but they were rising and greater rural prosperity was reflected in the spread of shops in the country districts. Industry, too, was recovering strongly, thanks to the vigorous development of export markets in the three main areas of linen-weaving and spinning, brewing, distilling and mineral waters, and shipbuilding and engineering. In all of these respects, Ireland seemed to be growing closer to Britain rather than moving away.

However, this relative prosperity developed in an atmosphere of political confusion. The great days of the Anglo-Irish literary movement generated a fresh sense of pride and national self-confidence, although the riots which accompanied the staging of Synge's drama *Playboy of the Western World* in 1907 showed how dangerous it could be if a writer looked too closely at the reality beneath nationalist myth. The Gaelic language enthusiasts continued to strive against 'Anglicization', though they could draw little comfort from the 1911 census which showed that only 18 per cent of the population had any Irish. The theme of self-reliance was developed by Arthur Griffith, founder in 1905 of Sinn Féin ('Ourselves'). It was axiomatic that Ireland was 'a distinct nation', whose independence should be re-established; though that might not mean total separation. Rejecting a destiny as 'the fruitful mother of flocks and herds', the

Irish people should manufacture their own goods, if necessary behind a tariff barrier. In his view, the union with Britain did not allow Ireland the freedom to develop in such a fashion. Even though Sinn Féin remained a small group, there was an obvious attraction in its deceptively simple theme.

Concern about Irish economic development was not confined to critics of the British connection. Many Unionists uncritically accepted an 1896 Report on Ireland's financial position in the United Kingdom which purported to show that Ireland was overtaxed – a conclusion made possible by neglecting the amount of public expenditure by the United Kingdom government in Ireland(133). Indeed, in 1904–05, it had briefly seemed as though some further administrative 'devolution' might be slipped through which would prove acceptable to both Unionists and moderate Home Rulers. In the end, attitudes towards the proposed central council hardened on traditional lines and the plan was abandoned. There was, however, one lasting legacy in the shape of the Ulster Unionist Council which was formed to rally northern opinion against any 'back door schemes' which might lead to Home Rule. The strength of Unionism in the North-east was solidly grounded in the cultural inheritance of the majority, but it was the economic aspect which came to the fore. While Sinn Féin talked of the industrialization which might develop behind a protective tariff, the Belfast businessman feared the potential loss of the Free Trade area of the United Kingdom. The Belfast region, it has been noted, was responsible for some 90 per cent of Irish non-food manufactured exports.

If, even so, Home Rule were still to come it looked as though it would be achieved through Parliament. The two wings of the Irish party at Westminster, split since the Parnell scandal, had just come together under the leadership of John Redmond. The 1906 Liberal victory raised fresh hopes for Redmond and his followers, even though the new government did not need their support in the lobbies. But, under Campbell-Bannerman, 'step by step' seemed the order of the day. The Irish Council Bill of 1907 was quite unacceptable to the Home Rulers even as a first step and had to be withdrawn. Redmond was then under some pressure not to take part in Westminster politics (which he rather enjoyed) but he was determined to stay. The Liberals persisted with housing, land and education legislation for Ireland, but they did not touch the 'great matter'.

It was the clash between the Liberal government and the House of Lords in 1909 which transformed Irish prospects. If the Liberals did amend the power of the Upper Chamber that would remove one obstacle to Home Rule. In these circumstances Asquith began to talk of a possible system of full self-government in regard to 'purely Irish affairs' which would also be consistent with the supremacy of the imperial Parliament. He knew that 'Irish' votes in Lancashire and Scotland might be of crucial importance in the January 1910 Election. The Liberals did emerge as the largest single party, but the Irish and Labour held the balance, as they did again in December 1910. The prospects for Home Rule were decisively changed, particularly since the House of Lords had lost its power of veto under the 1911 Parliament Act and could now only delay measures for two years(140).

At the same time, the constitutional structure of the United Kingdom as a whole came under fresh scrutiny. If there had to be some 'Home Rule' for Ireland, it might make more sense in a context of 'Home Rule All-Round'. The United Kingdom, it was argued, might be transformed into a federal state, with each of the four constituent 'nations' becoming responsible for their own internal affairs while the 'imperial Parliament' at Westminster managed external matters, defence and the economy. The Canadian federation seemed a success and Australia had just been created on a comparable basis. The idea was briefly considered at the abortive Buckingham Palace Conference of 1910. Its attraction for imperially minded Conservatives was that it would relieve the pressure of domestic business at Westminster and enable it to function, they fondly hoped, as the true Parliament of the empire. However, to most Conservatives it seemed too radical a remedy to adopt simply as a way of dealing with the Irish difficulty. They did not think there was much enthusiasm for such a step in Scotland or Wales, quite apart from England.

Home Rule never ceased to be Liberal policy in Scotland throughout this period, as the Scottish Liberal Association reminded the Westminster government from time to time. Yet there was never any serious suggestion that Scottish Liberal MPs should embarrass their southern colleagues on the matter. Even an enthusiastic group of 'Young Scots' accepted the slogan 'Scotland for Liberalism' rather than create a separate Scottish party. It had been legislation specifically for Scotland which had early fallen foul of the House of Lords, and this treatment encouraged general Scottish loyalty to the government in the constitutional crisis. *The Scotsman* bluntly told Unionists that feeling against the House of Lords was so strong in Scotland that it was not worth their while even contesting a Highland seat. Indeed, in January 1910 the anti-Unionists won more Scottish seats than in any year since 1885. Back-benchers did introduce a few Scottish Home Rule bills before 1914, but their unsuccessful proposals did stress that the supremacy of Westminster was to remain unaffected. Critics of Home Rule did not see how this could be. It was Balfour, himself a Scot, who made the most incisive comments on this point. But, speaking generally, it is probably correct to suggest that about half of the Scottish electorate and at least half of the Scottish MPs, professed to support some kind of Home Rule. Scottish Unionists, on the other hand, tended to be more vehement in their opposition to it than were their English colleagues. Whatever the justice of the complaint that Scottish problems did not receive adequate attention at Westminster, Englishmen might complain about the excessive Scottish presence in British government – a third of Campbell-Bannerman's Cabinet were Scotsmen(127).

The Welsh grasp upon the highest offices of State was not yet comparable, though Lloyd George became the first Welsh-speaking Welshman to serve in a Cabinet when he was appointed in 1905. The 1906 Election – not a single Conservative MP was returned in Wales – showed the general nature of Welsh political feeling, but it was education rather than Home Rule which excited most comment in Wales. The most extensive 'passive resistance' to the 1902 Education Act took place in Wales, with Lloyd George at its head. This campaign was closely linked with the continuing agitation against the 'English Church' in Wales. Welsh Liberals expected action on these matters. They were mollified by the revised Education Act and were heartened by the announcement in January 1910 that the government intended to 'free Wales from its alien church'. A Royal Commission investigated the ecclesiastical situation in Wales and a measure to disestablish the Welsh Church began its course in the Commons in 1912. The degree of compensation and the extent of disendowment caused great controversy both inside and outside Parliament. In the end, MPs accepted that this was essentially a Welsh question, to be considered without reference to the position in England. Church legislation was on a par with the apparent need both of the Welsh and Scots to take special measures to protect their compatriots from excessive bibulousness(131).

Despite the attention given to disestablishment, the issue of Home Rule for Wales was never completely dormant. The Welsh Liberal Council declared for it in August 1911, though when the first bill was introduced into the Commons in March 1914 it made no progress. Keir Hardie, the Scot who sat as Labour MP for Merthyr Tydfil, was more enthusiastic for the idea than were most Welshmen. There was no sense of Pan-Celtic solidarity which required Wales to emulate Ireland. At this juncture, Irish Catholics in Wales were unpopular because of their support for the 1902 Education Act. Indeed, if there was solidarity in this decade, it was sectional rather than national in character. Welsh and English Free Churchmen stood together against Anglican pretensions and the language of working-class loyalty was beginning to have a strong appeal – an appeal which transcended Wales and even the United Kingdom(132).

Even if there had been greater pressure from Scotland and Wales for constitutional change, the question of England would have proved difficult to settle. Some believed that England should have its own Parliament too. Churchill was not among them. In a paper for the Cabinet in February 1911 he suggested that an English Parliament and executive could not exist alongside an imperial Parliament and executive. 'The external sphere', he wrote, 'touches the internal at almost every point. The fortunes of the country abroad and at home are interdependent and indissoluble.' England itself was substantially more populous and more wealthy than the other three units in a possible federation. One answer to this difficulty might be to 'regionalize' England – but there was no sign that the English wanted to be 'regionalized', though observers like J. A. Spender, the journalist, and Beatrice Webb noted after the January 1910 Election that it was only in England that the Conservatives had a majority of seats and then only south of a line from the Humber to the Dee. If the United Kingdom could be divided into a 'core' and a 'periphery' so could England itself(91) [D].

Although there was an increased awareness of a Scottish and Welsh 'dimension', it was, in the end, only the Irish question which was tackled. The Irish had political muscle and were not disposed to wait. The Irish Home Rule Bill was introduced in May 1912 and a subsequent back-bench attempt to exclude the counties of Antrim, Armagh, Down and Londonderry from its scope was defeated. The government was committed, at this stage, to the view that Ireland was not two nations but one, as Asquith put it in Dublin. Meanwhile, emotions were steadily rising in Ulster. At a huge meeting in Belfast, Sir Edward Carson, a Dublin lawyer, led a quarter of a million men in signing a solemn covenant enshrining their belief that Home Rule would be disastrous to the material well-being of Ulster and, indeed, the whole of Ireland. If a Parliament were forced on Ireland, they would not recognize its authority. Drilling was already taking place, and in January 1913 the Ulster Volunteer Force was set up by the Ulster Unionist Council. Bonar Law, the new Opposition leader, had already publicly declared that he could 'imagine no length of resistance to which Ulster will go, which I shall not be ready to support, and in which they will not be supported by the overwhelming majority of the British people'.[1] Bonar Law's action in pledging 'a great English party to follow a small Irish faction' has been frequently criticized but, whatever its strength in England, the Unionist party was not simply an English party and Bonar Law's perspective was not that of southern England.[2] Educated and in business in Glasgow, he had been born in Canada, the son of Ulster–Scots parents. Here was a personal seamless web which Home Rule threatened to break. He could not believe that Home Rule would offer more than a temporary resting place for Irish aspirations. He was British and, if strong language could not sabotage Home Rule altogether, it could assist those in Ulster who wished to remain British.

What was at issue, once again, was the appropriate political framework. Were the wishes of the majority of Irishmen sufficient to alter the political structure of the British Isles? What if the wishes of a substantial minority of Irishmen coincided with the views of a majority of their fellow citizens in the United Kingdom? The situation had reached total impasse. In Dublin, feelings grew steadily stronger and private armies, as in Ulster, made their appearance. Seeing tension increase, Asquith tried to negotiate with the Opposition and with the Irish leaders, Redmond and Carson, hoping that some formula could be found. The King became increasingly anxious and sought an elusive middle course. The prospect of civil war in Ireland seemed more likely with every month that passed. In March 1914, moving the Home Rule Bill for the third time (it had already been twice rejected in the Lords) Asquith announced a plan whereby, if a majority of the electors in any Irish county so desired, they could be excluded from the provision of the Act for six years. This compromise pleased few and the stage seemed set for armed confrontation. There were doubts, too, about the extent to which United Kingdom troops stationed in Dublin would allow themselves to be used to force a change in their status within the United Kingdom on a reluctant Ulster population. That 'Curragh mutiny' raised grave constitutional questions and was poorly handled. The Prime Minister himself had to take over direct control of military matters in order to restore the authority of the government(140).

In Ireland itself, the situation continued to deteriorate. In April 1914, the Ulster Volunteers landed a formidable quantity of arms and ammunition, exposing in the process the wavering allegiances of the northern guardians of law and order. In July, the police and army intercepted gun-runners for the southern National Volunteers, with some loss of life. There was at least an appearance of partiality in these two incidents. In London, the government now floated the suggestion that after a plebiscite any area might exclude itself from Home Rule *sine die*. In return, it was hoped that Bonar Law and Carson would acquiesce in

Home Rule for the rest of Ireland. However, negotiations failed, ostensibly on the area which could be excluded. The day before that conference broke up, news reached London of the Austrian ultimatum to Serbia. The reconstruction of the United Kingdom had to make way for the war. The Act was placed on the statute-book, though it was not to come into effect until the close of the war and until special provision had been made for Ulster. This compromise enabled the United Kingdom to go to war maintaining an appearance of national unity.

John Redmond pledged Ireland's support for the war – in which his own brother was subsequently to be killed. Many Irishmen volunteered and saw service abroad, though the formation of an Ulster division was a reminder of political issues. When the coalition government was formed both Carson and Redmond were offered posts, though only Carson accepted. However, other Irishmen saw the European conflict as Ireland's chance to gain freedom. Never again would London be so preoccupied elsewhere. Irish Volunteers and Sinn Féiners began to consider an armed insurrection. Sir Roger Casement, renouncing the Crown from which he had received a knighthood, gave his allegiance to the Ireland that was yet to be and entered into treasonable relations with Germany. The rising was timed for Easter 1916, but when Casement landed from a German submarine off the Irish coast on Good Friday he brought no secular good news with him. At first, it seemed as if the rising would be cancelled, but on Easter Monday some Volunteers went ahead, proclaimed an Irish Republic and seized the General Post Office. Four days, and over 500 deaths later, the provisional government surrendered.

While bitterly fought, the rebellion was largely confined to Dublin. It was also the case that many more Irish volunteers were fighting in France for the United Kingdom than National Volunteers were fighting in Ireland for Ireland. In the circumstances of war, severe punishments were thought justified but, if comprehensible, the subsequent executions of Casement, Connolly and other leaders were probably fatal to the continuance of the United Kingdom. If the majority of Irishmen in the South had been at most lukewarm towards the rebellion, the manner of its suppression led the participants to appear as heroes. Asquith asked Lloyd George to try to bring all the Irish parties together, but he could achieve little. Power in Ireland was passing from Redmond and his colleagues. The Irish Convention, set up in the latter years of the war, proved little more than a holding operation. It proved impossible to impose conscription on Ireland.

The return of peace saw two rival bodies in Ireland, both claiming authority. The United Kingdom government was supposed to be continuing as before, with administration centred on Dublin Castle. At the same time, the Dáil (Parliament) of the Irish Republic, with de Valera as president, operated an administration. Sinn Féin did not take up its seats at Westminster though its candidates had won in every constituency outside Ulster in the 1918 Election. The Irish Republican Army (IRA) (by no means under the complete control of the Dáil) was formed in January 1919 and launched a campaign of terror against the Royal Irish Constabulary and the United Kingdom Army. Although the IRA was outnumbered, its guerrilla tactics meant that it could not easily be defeated. Lloyd George authorized the recruitment of the 'Black and Tans' (irregular contingents of demobilized soldiers) whose reprisal tactics disgraced Britain's good name in the world in the eyes of the Prime Minister's critics. Unabashed, the Prime Minister declared that he would not yield to the 'murder gang' in the South. He was convinced that a completely independent and republican Ireland would endanger Britain's security.[3]

The 1920 Government of Ireland Act tried to square the Irish circle. Under its provisions, the United Kingdom would be maintained, because a small number of Irish MPs would continue to sit at Westminster. But there would also be Home Rule, though for two Irelands, not one(138). There would be subordinate Parliaments both in Dublin and Belfast. A 'Council of Ireland' was to link these two bodies and thus consecrate a unity that was not discernible. Protestant Ulstermen, recognizing that some form of devolution in Ireland was inevitable, accepted the subordinate Parliament in Belfast which they had never sought. King George opened its first session in June 1921. It had extensive powers over domestic affairs and operated in the same manner as the Westminster Parliament, though with a Senate rather than a House of Lords. The leader of the majority party became Prime Minister and he chose his Cabinet from his party colleagues. Unlike anywhere else in the United Kingdom, however, the fulcrum of political activity in the 'province' was the issue of national allegiance. Unionists outnumbered their opponents by roughly two to one in the area (not co-extensive with the historic province of Ulster) which became Northern Ireland. It was, therefore, inevitable that this Unionist majority would dominate political life. From the outset, the new government had to operate in the knowledge that about a third of the population did not acknowledge the existence of 'Northern Ireland'. The Belfast government became a more effective administration than some thought likely, even though gerrymandering and coercion played some part in maintaining Unionist control. Schooled in Edinburgh, the dominant figure of Sir James Craig had none of his asperities softened by exposure to the compromises of English life(137).

The Government of Ireland Act failed in the South. Sinn Féin refused to play any part in the proposed Dublin Parliament and even the four members touchingly elected by Dublin University could not give it a fully representative character. The violent struggle went on. By the early summer of 1921, however, Lloyd George came to have second thoughts; coercion was not only offensive, it was unsuccessful, and King George was alarmed. United Kingdom authority could be asserted in Ireland, but only by means that would make it impossible subsequently to govern by consent. A cease-fire was agreed in July – at a time when the IRA was distinctly hard-pressed. In this coincidence, however, lay the possibility of an agreement. On 5 December 1921, it was reached. From the Irish side, Collins and Griffith agreed to the demise of the Irish Republic while the United Kingdom government was prepared to negotiate 'articles of agreement for a treaty' with subjects of the Crown. What emerged from this bizarre situation was the Irish Free State, accorded Dominion status on an analogy with Canada and still, though with infinite reluctance, recognizing the position of the Crown. The Irish Dáil approved the settlement, but only by a small majority. De Valera resigned in protest and Griffith formed a new government to which Westminster formally transferred power in March 1922. In June, pro-treaty groups gained nearly three-quarters of the seats in the first election for the Free

State Parliament. Nevertheless, civil war began and the destruction that followed, both of life and property, exceeded that sustained during the previous 'troubles'. The United Kingdom government did not intervene.

Although the United Kingdom of Great Britain and Ireland had thus come to an end, the complete dissolution of the Union was less easy. Members of the Dáil, somewhat enigmatically, had agreed to recognize the 'common citizenship of Ireland with Great Britain'. The Royal Navy retained access to port facilities in three harbours in the Free State. Citizens of the Irish Free State could, and did, vote in United Kingdom elections. At the same time, in the Free State, anti-British sentiment remained strong, particularly after the Boundary Commission confirmed the frontier between the two countries. The Council of Ireland, which had never worked, was abolished in 1925. The settlement was broadly acceptable in the rest of the United Kingdom. There was general relief that the army would no longer be involved in Ireland. With the formation of the Northern Ireland Parliament, Ulstermen were substantially left on their own.

This solution of the Irish question largely ended discussion of possible 'Home Rule All-Round'(142). There was some pressure from Wales and Scotland but it was not strong. The divided and decaying Liberal party was no longer in a position to deliver what it had once professed to desire. In Scotland, and to an extent in Wales, it was the rising Labour party which favoured home Rule, though it could not deliver either. Ramsay MacDonald, Scot though he was, needed to establish Labour throughout Britain. Devolution might only come when that had been achieved. In the wake of Lloyd George, Welshmen were closer to the centre of British politics than they had ever been and Lloyd George himself began to lose interest in the Principality. However, both in Wales and Scotland, national parties were formed in the post-war period. Plaid Cymru (the party of Wales) was founded in 1925 with a radical social and economic programme for a 'self-governing' Wales. Its leaders, particularly the writer Saunders Lewis, were intensely concerned about the language and culture of Wales, where the proportion of Welsh-speakers was to fall to 37 per cent in 1931. It remained to be seen whether a party dominated by cultural concern could have any impact at a time when economic problems were mounting(132). In Scotland, a National party was formed in June 1928 with the objective of 'self-government for Scotland with independent national status within the British group of nations'(127). Despite a good deal of publicity, the electoral impact of the party seemed unlikely to extend very far beyond the absorbing world of Scottish university politics. English politicians at Westminster took little notice. Any notion of an English National party would have seemed an absurdity. England was indeed not the same as Britain, but it absorbed outside elements in such a way that to distinguish them could seem quite superfluous. If the kingdom had been partially dismembered, its surviving elements seemed securely bound together(143).

---

1. Cited in A. C. Hepburn, *The conflict of nationality in modern Ireland* (1980), p. 75
2. N. Mansergh, *The Irish question, 1840–1921* (1965), p. 195
3. C. Townsend, *The British campaign in Ireland, 1919–21* (Oxford, 1975)

CHAPTER 14

Democratic participation and the parties

As far back as 1852, Karl Marx argued that universal suffrage would ensure the political supremacy of the working class in England. The franchise reforms of 1867 and 1884 appear, in retrospect, to be steps along the road to this goal, even if that was not the intention of their authors. The problem of 'the democracy' puzzled the leaders of both major parties. Some prominent Liberals believed that only a further extension of the franchise would enable them to become a party of government once again. Others were depressed by the outcome of the 1900 'Khaki' Election. Their experience seemed to suggest that if the franchise had been wider it would have resulted in an even bigger Conservative majority such was the 'unthinking' sentiment of the masses. Some historians find contemporary opinion on this point misleading and suggest that the imperial war did not arouse much enthusiasm among the working classes. And, of course, when the Liberals did win the 1906 Election handsomely there seemed no great urgency about franchise reform. The government's supporters expected it to get on with more important matters. There might be time to turn to it before the next election – which would be seven years away. The governments of Edwardian and Georgian Britain were placed in office by what was still a relatively small electorate – scarcely 8 million in 1914 of whom some half a million had plural votes. But the events of these years suggested that this system could not last much longer[C].

The Conservative party appeared to be in the greatest difficulty. Balfour, who succeeded his uncle as Prime Minister in July 1902, puzzled both his contemporaries and recent biographers. Intelligent, cynical, religious, languid – all these adjectives are appropriate. Despite his great gifts, he seemed incapable of committing himself passionately to any political cause and inspiring enthusiasm among his supporters. His three years in office were marked by increasing difficulties within the party and government. He abandoned office in December 1905 while he still had a parliamentary majority – possibly in the hope that the difficulties within the Liberal party might be as great as he experienced and prevent Campbell-Bannerman from forming a government. Despite some achievements in foreign affairs, defence and education, the central problem on which unity could not be maintained was tariff reform. Disappointed by the colonial response to his ideas for imperial preference, Chamberlain decided to put his ideas before the British people. He resigned from the Cabinet in September 1903 and tried to persuade his party and the country that the Free Trade era was at an end. He made some converts among those convinced that British industry did now need protection, but a band of Unionist Free Traders remained adamant. Balfour himself vacillated and at times advanced a policy that only he

123

could understand. The issue was of great importance, but the political conflict went wider. The initiative was a final effort by the ageing ex-Liberal – he was to be incapacitated by a stroke in 1906 – to give the Conservative party a positive programme. Most contemporaries believed that Chamberlain lost the argument, but in any case the struggle did the party no good. Balfour remained as party leader after the defeat of 1906 but was not very successful. The dilemma was clear. Was the Conservative party simply to carry out a rearguard defence of the established social order, probably with diminishing success, or could it adapt and become a major party in a democratic era? Balfour did not seem to know the answer. It was clear that there were issues on which a stand might be made. The Conservatives were to succeed in winning back support and they made a respectable showing in both elections of 1910(86).

Soon after his defeat in 1906 Balfour publicly affirmed his belief that it was the duty of the House of Lords to protect the country from laws which would be the products of one hasty and passionate election. The battle over the constitution was already joined. Naturally, basking in success, the Liberals took a different view of their government's authority. The House of Lords, being non-elected and possessing a Conservative majority, had no business to interfere with the legislation of a government with such a 'mandate'. Campbell-Bannerman, affable and elderly, had no patience with 'foolery' from the Opposition benches. But the House of Lords did in fact interfere with Liberal education, liquor licensing and Scottish proposals and Campbell-Bannerman did nothing. By the time ill-health forced him to make way for Asquith in April 1908 it began to look as though his administration had been 'ploughing the sands'. The unease in the Liberal ranks centred on fundamental matters of principle and strategy. It seems likely that success in 1906 did not come from a massive endorsement of a 'social reform' programme – for no such programme had been offered. Nonconformists (heavily represented on the Liberal back benches) felt strongly about education and the drink question and at least an attempt had been made to satisfy them. But what next?

Asquith's arrival in office coincided with, though was not caused by, renewed interest in the 'social question'. Articulate and conceited, a classical blending of nonconformist ancestry, Balliol brilliance and social aspiration, Asquith would not take the initiative but he might give his colleagues their head. Liberal philosophers, social theorists and journalists had been busy formulating a doctrine of 'positive liberty', a 'New Liberalism' which united a concern for the freedom of the individual with a willingness to use the power of the State to give the masses a 'real' rather than a merely theoretical liberty(88,89,90). In the Cabinet, Churchill and Lloyd George (free though they were of any taint of university philosophy) saw their chance to identify the Liberals as the party of social progress. Keen to eradicate his Conservative past, Churchill thrust schemes before his colleagues. Asquith himself, in the budget he had prepared for 1908, introduced an old-age pension as of right. The idea had been in the air for a decade, but the Liberals naturally took the credit. Also in 1908 came an eight-hour working day for miners and the establishment of labour exchanges, whose purpose was to match the requirements of employers and workmen. Beveridge and others began to undertake enquiries into the nature of unemployment(87). If, in sum, these measures were modest, they appeared to indicate a new direction. Well aware of a potential challenge from the Labour party, Churchill and Lloyd George toured the country making attractive speeches about Liberalism and social reform. Their problem, however, was that the simultaneously increasing naval expenditure brought budgetary difficulties. It was in this context that Lloyd George framed his famous 1909 budget(92).

He envisaged increases in the tax yield from tobacco and drink, increases in death duties and income tax, and certain land taxes. Landed wealth seemed to be his major target – one which would cause least difficulty for the party. Although still a matter of controversy, he probably did not intend to provoke the Lords into rejecting his proposals, but was neither surprised nor disappointed when they did so. Conservative peers swiftly argued that this budget had too much 'tacked on' for it to be regarded simply as a finance bill (which they traditionally left alone). They had a right to defeat it. There was nothing Lloyd George liked better than a duke in his sights and throughout the summer he whipped up feeling against the landed aristocracy. Having heard Asquith declare publicly that the power of veto held by the Lords would have to be curbed, Liberals assumed that he had royal backing for the creation of extra peerages, should that prove necessary. But, although he asked for a dissolution of Parliament he had neither asked for nor received any such guarantee from King Edward(91).

The outcome of the January 1910 Election left both major parties able to claim success and general political confusion, compounded by the inconvenient death of the King in May. Since the peers remained obdurate, King George tried to coax the party leaders into a solution which would avoid the need for a further election, but even his nautical knowledge failed to steady the ship of State. The December election confirmed the party position but did enable the government to act. The previously introduced Parliament Bill now went up to the Lords. It decreed that the peers would have no power over money bills (to be so certified by the Speaker) and could only veto other measures for a period of two years. It also reduced the maximum interval between general elections to five years. The Lords had been prepared to interpret the January election as a verdict on the budget and had passed it. Would they accept this limitation of their power? Although a considerable number of peers saw beauty in death at the last ditch, the Conservative leadership saved the King embarrassment and deprived 249 good and true men of the peerages which might otherwise have been theirs in a special creation. The Parliament Act did not destroy the political power of the aristocracy but it did severely restrict it. It represented another historic adjustment of the ancient constitution in the face of democracy – or so Liberals believed. Conservatives were bitterly angry because they realized that there was now no obstacle which could prevent Irish Home Rule. And they argued, not without justice, that there was no popular 'mandate' for such a step. They even floated the notion of a referendum on specific major issues so that 'the people' could speak directly, rather than have party machines purport to speak on their behalf. Although nothing came of this idea, Bonar Law (who succeeded Balfour in 1911) was, in his own word, 'vicious' in his pursuit of the government on the Irish issue over the next few years. He was confident that on this matter (if on nothing else) he could win an election. Asquith denied him the opportunity.

There were other matters besides the House of Lords which raised questions about the constitution, Parliament, parties and pressure groups.

When Miss Emily Davison was trampled to death by oncoming racehorses at the 1913 Derby her action was not consonant with the notion that reasoned debate would produce votes for women. It was an issue which divided, embarrassed and vexed the Liberal Cabinet and to which no solution was found. The return of the Liberals revived a matter which had become dormant, though much debated in the 1870s. The National Union of Women's Suffrage Societies brought together a number of bodies in 1897, and by 1914 it claimed 53,000 members and 480 branches. Mrs Fawcett and other respectable, professional middle-class ladies demurely desired the vote for women 'as it is, and may be given to men' – not adult female suffrage. Liberal by inclination, they were prepared to 'wait and see', but it became clear that Asquith was inclined to wait a long time. He saw that there were admirable reasons for resisting the storm. To give the vote to all women (supposing it were also given to all men) would mean that women would preponderate in the electorate. Could issues of war and peace be determined by women who would not fight? To give the vote to propertied women would be a 'progressive' gesture which would benefit the Tories. Eminent medical men drew attention to the fact that the mind of a woman was always threatened with danger from the 'reverberations of her physiological emergencies'. And working men, accustomed to having their boots blacked by their wives, were more likely to associate themselves with Mr Gladstone's view that a political role trespassed upon the delicacy and refinement of women than they were with the passionate advocacy of a Bertrand Russell. It was, in other words, not merely a matter of 'votes' but touched deeply on the domestic and social roles of men and women, and parties, communities and families were all divided in their reactions. Women committed to a belief in 'separate spheres' organized themselves effectively to demonstrate their belief that women could not organize themselves effectively. At the opposite extreme, the Women's Social and Political Union (1903), galvanized by the Pankhursts, embarked on a campaign of militancy which, among other things, led to attacks on post-boxes but brought them no nearer the ballot box(93).

When miners rioted wildly in Tonypandy in November 1910, when infantry and cavalry patrolled the Rhondda valley, when striking railwaymen were shot dead by troops in West Wales during the long, hot, bitter summer of 1911, it did not seem consonant with the notion that reasoned debate would produce industrial and social harmony. In area after area – Manchester, Hull, London, South Wales – and in industry after industry – the docks, the coal-mines, the railways – there were strikes on a scale and intensity beyond the experience of the Cabinet. It found it hard to judge whether an almost apocalyptic insurrection was imminent or whether the strikes had an economic cause and could have an economic solution. Syndicalism, the notion that workers should control and operate their own industries, was widely discussed and feared. It had the advantage of seeming foreign in origin. Anarchists were thought to be active in every coalfield. There were strong reasons why the government should do something, not least the alarming international situation. Significantly, Grey was brought into the discussions already being held by Asquith, Lloyd George and Buxton (President of the Board of Trade). He had no doubt that, important though the grievances about wages or non-recognition of unions in particular industries were, the government was being told that labour intended to have a bigger share and had demonstrated its power. He himself saw no reason why men employed in a big business should not have as great an interest in it as the proprietors or shareholders. His assessment of the coal strike of 1912 was that the bulk of the miners had more to lose than gain by revolution and so had the bulk of the people. In such circumstances, there ought not to be one. He was right in his assessment. But the government did find itself drawn directly into wage negotiation in a new way and one which by no means all its supporters welcomed. Liberal businessmen pointed out that members of the government were singularly lacking in industrial or commercial experience. The dilemma was clear but, although support could be lost to Right or Left, the Cabinet could feel with justice that its middle course had minimized its political losses.

The Labour party did not make as much progress as its supporters had hoped. It was still a party only in parliamentary terms and it was not very harmonious there either. Personal rivalries between Hardie, MacDonald, Henderson and Snowden were partly merely normal and partly fundamental. How was the 'leader' or 'chairman' to be chosen and what was to be the scope of his authority? What was the relationship between MPs and the trade unions and between Liberal and Labour? MacDonald had negotiated a secret agreement with the Liberal Chief Whip in 1903 under which the two parties gave each other a clear run in certain constituencies. Both had benefited in 1906, but other elements in the movement resented being 'lackeys of Liberalism'. Every so often a 'clean Socialist' would demand that both 'capitalist' parties should be treated impartially. MacDonald was unimpressed by the 'wild ravings' of Syndicalists or Marxists and wrote, endlessly, about 'organic transformation'. Chairman of the party again in 1911, his most difficult task was to manage relations with the government. It depended on his support (and that of the Irish), but it retained the initiative and knew that Labour had no wish to see a Conservative government. The Liberals included payment of MPs in their legislative programme and in return MacDonald supported Lloyd George's 1911 National Insurance Bill, the centrepiece of his post-budget legislation. The essence of the scheme was that a worker could pay a regular contribution through an 'approved society', which could be a trade union, in return for which he would receive sick benefit and could call on the services of an insurance panel doctor. MacDonald declared in Parliament that he favoured the insurance principle rather than the 'free gift'. A minority of his colleagues felt that such a statement was a betrayal of Socialism. Such disagreements made collaboration at the next election unlikely. Viewed as competing parties, both sides could take comfort; the Liberals showed that they could win back seats from Labour at by-elections, but Labour looked likely to be able to field more candidates than ever before. Ideologically, it was an open question whether the New Liberals were wresting the initiative from Socialists or vice versa(89,94).

The trade unions, or at least their officials, were still primarily concerned about their legal status and the position of their funds. The Taff Vale judgment by the House of Lords in July 1901 caused great confusion because it affirmed, in this particular dispute, that the funds of a union could be drawn upon if its officials were found liable in an action brought for damages. Sustained pressure on the Liberals in opposition to reverse this interpretation of the law brought its reward in the 1906 Trades Disputes Act which restored the immunities which had been thought to apply before the 1901 judgment. The Liberal Cabinet, stiff with lawyers, seems not to have lingered unduly over its decision. Interestingly, too, the Conservative peers made no amendment in the Lords. Lansdowne felt that excessive privileges were being conferred, 'dangerous privileges on one class and on one class only', but felt that opposition to it was useless. Supporters of the measure argued that it helped to redress the balance between employers and workers at a time when that still rested with employers. In addition, it would prevent the alienation of organized labour from Parliament and the law. The Osborne judgment (1909) raised a cognate question. The Lords declared that a trade union could not make its members pay a levy for the upkeep of Labour MPs – something on which the party had heavily depended. Once again, though not until 1913 and to the dismay of some of their supporters, the Liberals came to the rescue. The Trade Union Act allowed trade unions to keep a separate 'political' fund. Members who did not wish to contribute to it could opt out. Opponents of the measure, fearing intimidation, would have preferred to require those who wished to contribute to contract in. Against the background of militancy it was again felt best not to appear provocative. So, by courtesy of the Liberals, Labour and the trade unions were able to consolidate their co-operation. Trade union membership and confidence grew steadily, but it would be wrong to exaggerate its political or economic unity(85) [F].

The circumstance of war raised fresh questions about the role of the parties and the participation of the people. In 1910, Lloyd George had privately mooted the idea of a coalition government with an agreed programme to tackle defence, social policy and Ireland. The radical tribune suggested, in effect, that sterile party polemics was against the national interest but no agreed programme proved possible. Initially, in 1914, Asquith saw no reason why a Liberal government should not prosecute the war on its own, but his problems mounted as the dimensions of the conflict became clear. In May 1915, although the Liberals retained their parliamentary majority, Asquith agreed to Bonar Law's suggestion that his government should be reconstituted. From the Prime Minister's standpoint, potentially embarrassing criticism was defused by associating Conservatives with the administration. Some back-benchers in both parties were unhappy, though for contrary reasons. Liberals saw their party's integrity being threatened; Conservatives, finding it difficult to believe that Liberals could win a war, wished to wait for a more comprehensive crumbling of their morale. The Liberals did hold most of the important posts but they were joined by Bonar Law, Lansdowne and Curzon from the Conservatives. Arthur Henderson became the first Labour member of a Cabinet, thus rounding off the impression of national unity. It was hoped that his trade union contacts would be of great value.

This first coalition proved a disappointment. Individuals performed well, but as the war dragged on it appeared to lack drive and determination. By the end of 1916, there was a widespread conviction in political circles that Asquith was too dilatory. A small war committee charged solely with the direction of the war would be the answer. At first, Asquith did not seem to object, but then suspected that he would only have a position of honour. At this stage, Bonar Law and Lloyd George did not want him to resign, but press comment stimulated the desire for a 'smash'. Asquith stiffened his terms, but overestimated his support. The Conservative ministers resigned, as did Asquith himself on 6 December. When Bonar Law declined the royal invitation, Lloyd George was the man of the hour. He formed an administration with all-party support and set up a five-man War Cabinet of himself, Curzon, Bonar Law, Henderson and Milner.

The two coalition governments, formed with scarcely a reference to Parliament or people, were to destroy the pre-war structure of British politics, though that was not their intention. In theory, when peace returned, the followers of Asquith and Lloyd George would fight as one. In reality, this already seemed unlikely and there would never again be a Liberal government. Such a curious demise of a Liberal administration, so full of individual talent, has provoked endless speculation. If a choice has to be made from among the rich array of alternatives, ranging from Asquith's bibulousness to the inevitability of Socialism, it must be the unpredictable pressures of war. The Liberals went into war with no desire to see State regulation extend to all aspects of commercial and industrial life. Liberty was at the heart of British Liberalism and freedom would be lost if the State ultimately assumed responsibility for everything. When the war came, first the Defence of the Realm Act and then military conscription seemed to many Liberals to represent unjustified intrusions on the liberty of the individual. In fighting for liberty, liberty would itself be extinguished and Britain would become 'Prussianized'. As one step seemed inexorably to lead to another, Liberals lost heart.

If the party system was fractured by the war, a return to pre-1914 patterns was made impossible by the 1918 Representation of the People Act. The most salient fact was that it virtually tripled the electorate, a substantial portion of that increase being 'mature' women over thirty. All adult males over twenty-one had the vote. Important changes were also made in the conduct of elections and the size of constituencies. The political supremacy of the working class was indeed now possible and all parties knew it and some feared it [C].

Lloyd George's future was the most intriguing political question at the close of the war. Would he use his press contacts to launch a new party? Would he wrest control of the Liberal party organization from the Asquithites? Would he preside over a fusion of the Liberals and Conservatives to defeat Labour? Perhaps he might even lead Labour? In December 1918, his continuance as Prime Minister was assured when the Conservatives and Coalition Liberals gained a large majority. It was a result which reflected a mood of victory and perhaps of revenge. Among the first electoral victims of the extension of democracy were Asquith and the Labour leaders, MacDonald, Henderson and Snowden. For the moment, Lloyd George had enormous personal prestige, but the time might come when the Conservative majority in the coalition felt that he was no longer needed at the helm [D].

The domestic programme of the administration was far from clear. It was uncertain whether Free Trade would survive or how 'Homes fit for heroes', which Lloyd George promised, would blend with Conservative doctrine. After Lloyd George returned from the Paris Peace Conference, he urged the desirability of 'fusion' upon his colleagues. Although opposition to this proposal might have been chiefly expected from the Conservatives, it was the Coalition Liberals who, in March 1920, vetoed the proposal. They would not abandon the possibility of Liberal reunion. Lloyd George was dismayed, arguing that his administration was Liberal in tone even if it might be thought to be Conservative in complexion. It was not accidental, however, that Asquith's return to the Commons the previous month gave a fresh boost to the notion of independent Liberalism. Fortunately for the Prime Minister, Austen Chamberlain, who became the Conservative leader after Bonar Law's retirement in March 1921, was loyal – though the same could not be said of all his party(95).

Coalition leaders talked of returning to 'normality', but the concept had little meaning. With Ireland in rebellion, Europe still far from peaceful and armoured cars assisting the preservation of law and order in George Square, Glasgow, 'class war' seemed imminent. Among all its other problems, the relationship with organized labour was paramount. Lloyd George still had a reputation for radicalism, but it was now combined with a concern for social order. His government's record in this sphere has recently been vigorously defended. The establishment of a Ministry of Health (1919) was accompanied by a requirement that local authorities should provide housing for the needy, and many of them hastily began to erect the so-called 'Addison' houses. The Education Act, 1918, had long-term implications. The second part of the 1911 National Insurance Act was extended to all industrial workers. A new bill brought some 12 million workers into the scheme, and in 1921 'uncovenanted benefits', beyond the amount covered by insurance, were offered. Such provision was threatened, however, by the scale of unemployment as the post-war boom petered out.

If these, and other measures, were conciliatory, Lloyd George would not yield the authority of government to trade union power. The war had strengthened the position of organized labour. During its final phase, most workers had enjoyed a rise in real wages. Many trade union leaders had a status and bargaining position which they had never had before and they were determined not to slip back. In early 1919 the Miners' Federation demanded shorter hours, 30 per cent higher wages and the nationalization of the coal-mines. The appointment of a Royal Commission under Lord Sankey gained Lloyd George time. A majority of its members favoured nationalization, though not without reservations. The Prime Minister, to the fury of the miners, used these doubts as a reason for rejecting nationalization. Railwaymen were another group of workers to bring their claims to the fore. There were attempts to reconstitute the 'triple alliance' of miners, railwaymen and transport workers which had seemed so potent on the eve of the First World War. 'Direct action' by London dockers in the summer of 1920 when they refused to load a ship bound for Poland with munitions seemed successful. They believed they had deterred Lloyd George from taking any further anti-Bolshevik action.

A trial of strength seemed inevitable and in the spring of 1921 a General Strike appeared possible. Decontrol in the coal industry was brought forward and wage cuts were threatened. The miners countered with demands for a national board and a national pool. They received promises of support from the transport workers and railwaymen. The government took emergency measures which would involve the use of troops. However, there were divisions in the miners' executive and, also on 15 April, 'Black Friday', the other two unions refused to strike in sympathy. The miners went ahead on their own but had to accept a comprehensive defeat at the end of June. They were bitter about their 'betrayal', but there was a good deal of latent resentment among other unions at the extent to which miners regarded themselves as a special case. That problem was shortly to reappear. Industrial–political militancy had stumbled because of the precariousness of that class solidarity on which its supporters set such store. Trade union leaders, however, still found that they had a ready access to Downing Street(95).

It was, perhaps, the success of the government in this matter which contributed to its downfall. Conservative MPs began to believe that Lloyd George was not indispensable. His style of government, not least his zeal in distributing peerages in return for contributions to his 'political fund', offended their sense of propriety. It also offended the Conservative Central Office which would have liked a bigger share of the proceeds. The handling of the Chanak crisis caused further disquiet (p. 110). On 19 October 1922, a majority of Conservative MPs voted at a meeting at the Carlton Club to withdraw from the coalition before, allegedly, the Prime Minister destroyed their party as he had done the Liberals. The following day, Lloyd George resigned – never to return. He had tried to reconcile his radical instincts with the need to preserve the institutions of the country and national unity. He had been modestly successful. But there was a widely felt desire for a return to 'straightforward' government by a single political party. The men who led this movement have been stigmatized as 'second-class brains'; politicians who were to rule the country until 1940 and fritter away Britain's power in the world. On the other hand, it could be said that these 'pygmies' did try unheroically to restore political stability after the tantrums of personality. Political leaders were, indeed, increasingly 'ordinary' men, or had to contrive to appear so, not scions of a traditional political class. The transition, already apparent in the mixed social composition of the pre-1914 Liberal governments, was not from the reign of 'great men' to 'little men', but to a form of politics where a new low-key leadership was what democracy seemed to require.

Certainly, Bonar Law was not a 'dynamic force' – the reproach levelled against Lloyd George by the hitherto inconspicuous Baldwin. Some leading Conservatives, Austen Chamberlain, Birkenhead and Balfour among them, would not join Bonar Law's Cabinet, still professing loyalty to the defunct coalition. They said that they would not indulge in factious opposition and almost kept their promise. In the November 1922 election, the Conservatives gained a clear majority [D]. However, Bonar Law was a sick man and remained in office for only six months. His successor was the modest Stanley Baldwin whose swift rise to the top had been so immodest. That two successive Conservative leaders in these years were ironmasters was a symbol that the party represented business rather than land. But Baldwin knew that the Conservatives could not survive if they simply appeared to be defending entrenched interests. The creation of wealth, not its redistribution, was the vital task, but that was easier said than done. Both employers and workers excelled in supposing that their particular industry had a right to exist at a particular size and in a particular place. That would take a long time to change.

Suddenly, in a speech in late October 1923, Baldwin revealed that day and night his thoughts had been filled with the problem of rising unemployment. The only way it could be fought, he declared, was by protecting the home market. Having come to that conclusion, he added, the only thing to do 'as the leader of a democratic party' was to tell the people and invite their endorsement. While the dissident, ex-coalition Conservatives rallied to his side during the ensuing election, the Liberal factions came together to defend Free Trade. Baldwin was disappointed by the outcome. The Conservatives remained the largest party, but had no majority over the combined strength of Labour and the Liberals. Baldwin was defeated in the Commons in January 1924 and the King took the constitutionally correct course of calling upon Ramsay MacDonald, the leader of Labour, the next largest party, to form a government [D].

Labour's post-war progress had been rapid. Although its leaders had suffered defeats in 1918, it fielded nearly five times as many candidates as its previous maximum. Its vote rose substantially and as early as 1919 the party was showing an ability to win by-elections. Late in the war, Henderson and Sidney Webb had drawn up a new constitution for the party, one effect of which was to make possible individual membership of a local Labour party. If Labour therefore seemed to be evolving into just the same kind of party as its opponents, its executive was in practice to be dominated by the block vote of trade unions. The Socialist nature of the party was made explicit by the insistence in clause four that producers 'by hand and brain' should be secured the full fruits of their industry 'upon the basis of the common ownership of the means of production and the best obtainable system of popular administration and control of each industry or service'. A policy statement, *Labour and the New Social Order*, elaborated this commitment in terms of a 'National minimum' and 'Democratic control of industry'(94).

Even so, in 1918, few would have forecast the appearance of a Labour government within five years and some Labour supporters believed that success had come too quickly. They wanted to see a Labour government with an overall majority so that Socialism could be introduced at once. It was disconcerting that the parties of 'bourgeois capitalism' should have made way for Labour so soon. MacDonald, elected leader in 1922 (and the first real 'leader'), disagreed, believing that Labour had to show that it could become a party of government. He

132

dominated his Cabinet and party, though it was difficult to keep 'intellectuals' and trade-unionists together. Labour, in his view, should certainly represent working-class aspirations, but it should also be more. The party should encourage that flow of middle-class, ex-Liberal support which had already begun(97).

In office, MacDonald behaved traditionally, to the dismay of those who expected instant change at home and abroad. The Civil Service, the armed forces and industry all continued as before. His parliamentary position left him with little alternative and he respected Parliament. Wheatley's Housing Act, extending to forty years the subsidy given by central government for houses built for rent at controlled prices, was the government's best-known measure. Conservative spokesmen were quick to point out that a Labour government had not, in itself, brought about a sharp fall in unemployment. Nor was there evidence that industrial strife had come to an end. Bevin, leader of the Transport and General Workers Union (TGWU), argued that governments came and governments went, but the fight of the workers remained constant. A succession of strikes proved his point.

The brief government came to an end in October – defeated in a vote of censure over its handling of a prosecution involving the Communist *Workers Weekly*. For the third time in three years, the country went to the polls and this time returned an overall Conservative majority. It looked as though a two-party system was returning, though with Labour in the position formerly occupied by the Liberals. Baldwin had his second chance.

Although Neville Chamberlain, the energetic Health Minister, was determined that the Conservatives would leave their mark as 'social reformers' and, over the next few years, could point to achievements in the sphere of health, housing and pensions, culminating in the local government reform of 1929, industrial questions overshadowed the life of this administration. In June 1925, the mineowners gave a month's notice of their intention to terminate existing wage agreements. Reduction in wages, they claimed, was the only way to reduce prices and maintain competitiveness. Trade union leaders, representing about a million miners, accused the owners of inefficiency. The mood of industrial workers was again militant. Their leaders promised them imminent release from the shackles of wage slavery. This confrontation placed the government in a dilemma. Baldwin was disposed to be conciliatory towards the trade unions in his public statements, but he could not go too far. Many of his back-benchers, not to mention some of his Cabinet colleagues, believed that a trial of strength was again unavoidable. There were indications, once more, that other unions would support the miners and a General Strike was a real prospect. Baldwin initially tried to argue that the issue was simply between the miners and their employers. The government did not have the authority or the power to coerce either party. The mining industry would be left to market forces and, in the process, some owners would go to the wall and many miners would have to leave the industry. Eventually, supply and demand would be matched. However, even Conservative governments were increasingly expected to 'control' the economy and to be judged by their success in doing so.

Baldwin gained time by setting up another Royal Commission on the mining industry and subsidizing it in the interval. On 6 August, however, he warned the Commons that a minority could not be expected to coerce the whole community; if it tried to do so, the government would act. The Home Office began to plan accordingly, and did so more effectively than the trade unions. The Royal Commission, which reported in March 1926, rejected nationalization (except of royalties), accepted the need for reduced wages, but saw no need for longer working hours, placing its faith in pit amalgamations. It suggested that conditions in all mines should be improved when general prosperity returned. On 1 May, the miners went on strike, but the TUC, to whom the 'conduct of the dispute' was left, tried unsuccessfully to find a formula. On 3 May, at midnight, the General Strike began. The government declared that it had to be called off absolutely and without reserve. It lasted for nine days. Both sides had reason to be proud of the response. The solidarity of trade-unionists was magnificent; equally magnificent was the reaction of non-trade-unionists. Social relations between the two sides remained relatively good-humoured. Baldwin repeatedly stressed that in his view there were two distinct issues – the stoppage in the coal industry and the General Strike. The latter was an attempt 'presumably to try to force Parliament and the community to bend to its will'. It soon became clear to the TUC, especially to those who had never wanted a strike, that political revolution could lie at the end of the road they had taken. After an attempt at unofficial mediation by Samuel, chairman of the Royal Commission, had failed, the TUC broke loose and, in effect, surrendered unconditionally. No promises concerning victimization were given by the government, though Baldwin was at his solemn best. The owners were in no mood for concessions and eventually, in December 1926, the miners went sullenly back to work – for longer hours and lower wages(96,100).

Subsequently, Baldwin was under considerable pressure to put the trade unions in their place and he acceded in two respects. The 1927 Trade Disputes Act made illegal sympathetic strikes designed to coerce the government. It was a symbolic measure and never subsequently invoked. His other action simply made trade-unionists contract in to pay the political levy to the Labour party. Balwin could have gone further but judged it wiser not to do so. Beyond this he had no solution to the cleavage in the nation. He saw a mining industry locked in the solidarity of inefficiency, with both owners and miners resisting mechanization and pit amalgamations. The crisis had sapped his limited capacity to make new proposals. By 1928, however, there were a few contacts between leading employers and trade-unionists though nothing dramatic emerged. The trade union movement was in a sober mood, having lost about a third of its accumulated financial reserves during the strike and a half a million members in the following twelve months(98,99).

By the later 1920s, the two opposition parties seemed to be making the running and the Cabinet was not sanguine about the outcome of the next election. After Asquith's death in 1926, Lloyd George reigned supreme. What was more – a subject of intense internal party controversy – he had a substantial political fund at his disposal. The Liberals ambitiously declared that they could conquer unemployment, unveiling plans for a far-reaching programme of public works which could, apparently, be financed without additional taxation. Part of the reason for Liberal optimism lay in the supposedly unhappy condition of Labour. Its leadership had been distinctly uneasy during the General Strike. MacDonald had been anxious not to tarnish the parliamentary party's respectability. He made a virtue of the fact that he was not himself a trade-unionist. Very strict steps were taken to prevent Communist infiltration into the Labour party – not that relations had ever been intimate in the half a dozen years of the Communist party's existence. MacDonald kept the advocates of a national minimum wage at a distance and would not endorse their manifesto, *Socialism in Our Time*. Significantly, *Labour and the Nation* was the title of the manifesto approved at the party's annual conference in 1928. The idea of workers' control found little support, though there was some strong language in the document; Labour would end 'the capitalist dictatorship in which democracy finds everywhere its most insidious and most relentless foe'.

MacDonald soon had the opportunity to tackle capitalist dictatorship. In the 1929 Election, the Conservatives gained most votes, Labour most seats and the Liberals insufficient of either. He formed another government without an overall majority. Unemployment, which was made the special responsibility of J. H. Thomas, was recognized as a major problem, though few appreciated that the world was on the brink of a major crisis that would exacerbate it. In early 1930, an energetic junior minister and Socialist convert from an old county family, Sir Oswald Mosley, presented his solution in a memorandum to the Cabinet. He advocated increased pensions, earlier retirement, tariff protection for industry, expansion of British agriculture and planned foreign trade. The Cabinet was not impressed. Mosley resigned, but failed in his efforts to rally party rank and file against the leadership. Unemployment steadily mounted. The government increased the Treasury Grants to the Unemployment Fund and augmented the allowances for the wife of an unemployed man, but these steps were palliatives not cures. By 1931, unemployment had climbed to 2¼ million. The European money markets were in turmoil after the collapse of the Vienna Credit Anstalt in May. British banks had lent generously and profitably in Germany and central Europe in earlier years but now they could not get their money back. The Bank of England informed the Prime Minister in August that a loan from New York was imperative and would not be forthcoming unless economies were made. The Cabinet's discussion centred on the possibility of a 10 per cent cut in unemployment benefit. Since MacDonald only gained a small majority at the meeting on 23 August Labour could not carry on as an effective government. MacDonald told his colleagues that the King would call a meeting of all three party leaders. He himself subsequently yielded to entreaties that he should remain in office and on 24 August it was announced that Britain had a new government, a National government, in order to save the country from disaster.

'Democracy has arrived at a gallop in England', Baldwin had written to Halifax in 1928, 'and I feel all the time that it is a race for life; can we educate them before the crash comes?'[1] Despite the peaks of conflict, democratic participation and the old political order had blended without that sustained friction which some had anticipated (and desired). When moving a government bill in 1928 to

give women the vote on the same terms as men (and thus make them a majority
in the 1929 electorate) the Home Secretary could confidently ask whether there
was any MP 'who fears the consequences of the democratic vote as we established it in 1918'(93). Even so, Labour's collapse in 1931 threatened the renewed
alienation of its working-class support from the parliamentary system and raised
the possibility that the 'crash' might yet come(102).

---

1. H. van Thal, ed., *The Prime Ministers*, ii (1975), p. 269

CHAPTER 15

The end of the Free Trade era

Landmarks, turning-points, watersheds and even steep and sharp waterfalls figure prominently in the imagery of historians. In the history of the economy, the nineteenth century is often thought to end in 1914. The Great War, it is suggested, inaugurated a new age which lasted until 1945. There is, however, no real reason why the nineteenth century should not be allowed to end in 1899. From then onwards, the debate about Free Trade sharpened, as concern about Britain's industrial base deepened. Certainly, the war produced new policies in Britain, and disrupted the international economic order, but there was no disposition to start in a new direction in 1919. The majority view was that the old order ought to be restored. While 1920–45 can be seen as an extension of the nineteenth century, it was in 1931 that the attempted return to normal had to be abandoned. The decision in that year to go off the Gold Standard was, for many contemporaries, both a sign of national humiliation and the end of an era. Arnold Toynbee's contemporary assessment was that 1931 was unlike any year 'pre-war' or 'post-war' in that men all over the world 'were seriously contemplating and frankly discussing the possibility that the Western system of Society might break down and cease to work'.[1] All 'periods' have their limitations, but the one we have adopted has less than many.

The century opened with contradictory forecasts – calamity and steady progress. It was becoming accepted that Britain could not 'dominate' world trade; her share in manufacturing goods had fallen to 28.4 per cent in 1900, though it was to rise again to 29.9 per cent in 1913. Such figures, even if reliable, mask the fluctuations and 1913 was the peak of a boom. By 1913, the German share had risen to 26.5 per cent and the American to 12.6 per cent. Britain was finding it increasingly difficult to compete with Germany in eastern European and Latin American markets(185). E. E. Williams, author of *Made in Germany* (1896) continued to draw attention to the German 'threat'. Articles in *The Times* in 1902 analysed the 'crisis of industry'. Yet British exports, by volume, were still rising and to have achieved annual growth-rates of around 2 per cent since the turn of the century was a steady performance for a 'mature' economy(186). The staple trades seemed still to be holding their own. The continuing expansion of the coal industry was notable; from 223 million tons at the turn of the century to 236 million in 1905 and a peak of 287 million in 1913. More than one-third of this last figure was exported. World demand for coal steadily rose and, despite American and German production, the future seemed bright. Germany herself was importing in 1913 nearly twice as much coal as she had done fifteen years earlier. In Latin American markets, in that year, Britain was still exporting fifteen times as much coal as the United States. Nevertheless, British labour productivity was falling, which raised mining costs. Was it wise, in these circumstances, to have over one million men committed to the industry? Britain seemed to be falling behind other countries in mechanizing pits and, compared with the integrated coal industry of the Ruhr, there were too many small mines – or so it was said(186).

The cotton industry seemed to be recovering from its stagnation in the 1890s, with total output and exports increasing, and some improvements in machinery and organization. Even so, those in the industry were well aware that mills were being set up in such countries as India, Japan, Brazil and China. More and more countries were supplying an increasing proportion of their own needs. In 1913, however, cottons still accounted for nearly a quarter of Britain's exports.

In the same year, according to Payne, Britain was supplying less than one-third of the international market in iron and steel and was importing an amount equivalent to 45 per cent of her exports. Even so, output was still rising. Between 1900 and 1913, the index of iron and steel products rose from 71.3 to 100(186). In shipbuilding, the United Kingdom still constructed some 60 per cent of the world's mercantile tonnage (1900–14) and naval building accelerated. This general industrial boom turned down in 1913; among the causes may have been a reaction in North America after feverish trading, the diversion of European energies into the training of armies and a partial monsoon failure in India. If we accept such explanations, they indicate Britain's vulnerability to events overseas which she could not control(187).

Imports of manufactured goods, foodstuffs, textile and other raw materials rose more rapidly than exports, although if the years 1896–1900 are compared with 1911–13, the balance of trade gap narrowed. Thanks to the rise in invisible earnings, there was a considerable balance of payments surplus. Overseas investment resumed its spectacular growth after the slack 1890s. Sayers puts the figure at over £100 million per annum, with Britain devoting one-sixth of its income to increasing its capital, the greater part of which financed development in other countries. The country was, as he puts it, 'gearing itself more each year to dependence on the outside world'(187). Critics, both at the time and since, have noted that this lending suited the needs of a *rentier* class seeking a steady if modest income. Cain notes that between 1909 and 1913 only 14 per cent of British overseas loans went directly into mining and manufacturing industry where bigger loans were possible.[2] Lewis argues that the way in which Britain balanced its payments in this period could not have been maintained indefinitely, even if there had been no world war. Other countries would develop their own shipping and similar services, just as they were developing their own manufactures(188).

Even if the export base of the economy was dangerously inflexible, the general pre-war picture was not one of despondency, though Free Trade moved to the fore in economic and political debate. In economic terms, it is difficult to believe that protection would at this point have solved the problems of industrial obsolescence which afflicted Britain. While a protective tariff might have encouraged innovation by securing a home market, it would have been more likely to have preserved inefficiency. On the other hand, less reverence for Free Trade as a dogma and a willingness to use tariffs as retaliatory weapons might have led to international tariff reductions – though at the risk of disrupting trade(189).

It was unfortunate that opposition to Free Trade was so closely linked to enthusiasm for empire. Some advocates of imperial preference still supposed that Britain would remain the British Empire's manufacturing centre. However, while the United Kingdom was supplying half of Canada's imports in 1870, it supplied only 24 per cent in 1900 (the Americans supplied 60 per cent). It would not be long, it seemed, before the United States 'took over' Canada. 'No man can be absolutely sure that a preferential system will secure the unity of the empire', wrote the contemporary economist W. J. Ashley, 'but to me, at any rate, it presents itself as the only direction in which there is a fighting chance.'[3] Such statements reveal the emotion behind technical arguments. One defence of Free Trade was that British imports from European countries and the United States in turn gave those countries surpluses with which to import from primary-producing countries. Thus, they did not need to compete with Britain in these markets. Empire was a source of wealth for Britain, one French economic historian argues, but only as an open system integrated into the main current of the international economy and not as a defensive mechanism to shelter Britain from foreign competition.[4] Whatever the balance of the argument, Free Trade did survive before 1914, perhaps as much for psychological as economic reasons.

The City found being the world's banker agreeable. By 1900, most countries had made gold the basis of their currencies. The Bank of England could keep sterling convertible into gold and internationally acceptable as a means of payment. This Gold Standard proved an efficient system, though it had not come about by conscious planning. It was argued that countries with trading deficits would have to release gold to pay for their extra imports. Their domestic money supply would contract, leading to higher interest rates and lower prices. Thus, competitiveness would be restored, though in the interval the level of domestic demand and, in turn, the volume of imports would be reduced. That is a 'simple' picture, but if matters did not invariably work like that, on the whole the system did work. As the country's central bank (though it was not nationalized) the Bank of England concerned itself very largely with the foreign exchanges. It demonstrated its expertise in 1907 when there was a brief financial crisis. The South African and Alaskan goldfields seemed able to ensure a sufficient supply to cover the expansion of world trade. The Bank's international role was made easier by the soundness of the British domestic banking system. The amalgamation of private banks and the expansion of branches went on simultaneously. The Scottish banks retained their own note issue, but this practice was dying out in England. The cheque system became general and the number and size of deposits increased. There were more than 2 million depositors in Trustee Savings Banks for the first time in 1916. Accounts opened with the Post Office Savings Bank rose from over 8 million to over 10 million in 1916. Building societies remained largely local, though some of the bigger societies were extending their coverage.

THE WAR AND THE GOLD STANDARD

The outbreak of war shattered the international economy. The Gold Standard was suspended, though the the major currencies were pegged at fixed parities for the duration of the conflict. It was assumed that there would be a return to the Gold Standard when circumstances permitted. During the war, Britain turned increasingly to the United States for vital machinery and the pound came under pressure. Despite the sale of securities and payment by bullion, British borrowing began on an ever-increasing scale. By 1918, the United Kingdom had incurred very large short- and long-term debts; a reversal of the nineteenth-century relationship with the United States. The war also accelerated other changes in trading patterns and debtor/creditor relationships(190). The new role of government was no less striking. In one area after another, government departments took on responsibilities which were unthinkable before 1914. The railways were taken over and vital commodities like wheat and sugar safeguarded. The resistance of ministers committed to Free Trade and *laissez-faire* principles crumbled. No one had anticipated the scale of military requirements. Lloyd George, the first Munitions Minister in May 1915, exercised wide control from the outset. This ministry was employing, directly or indirectly, over 3 million men at the close of the war. The 1917 shipping crisis, caused by the German submarine campaign, likewise resulted in far-reaching intervention, ranging from the requisition of liners to the standardization of ship design. The Ministry of Food, another newcomer, had an ever-expanding appetite; by the end of 1917, the main categories of food were price-controlled and the ministry bought up something like 85 per cent of imported foodstuffs. Many other instances could be given. Government became responsible for spending over half the national income. In 1915, so-called 'safeguarding' duties were placed by McKenna on a number of luxuries like motor cars, motor cycles and musical instruments; the sacred principle of Free Trade had been breached.

Were such developments to be merely wartime expedients? Economic policy-making from 1919 to 1931 has been found confused, frustrating and unsuccessful, with politicians and civil servants only gradually recognizing that traditional economic institutions and policies could not cope with post-war problems.[5] The Cunliffe Committee, set up to consider post-war currency questions, advocated both in 1918 and in 1919 a return to the Gold Standard as soon as it became practicable. The virtues of the system were rehearsed, though no detailed studies of its operations were made. If this was a 'banker's policy', there was little opposition in the business world. Industrialists were, in any case initially preoccupied with trying to judge prices and volumes for their products. Internationally, currencies floated freely, and sometimes wildly, and most advanced countries sought to restore the pre-war monetary standard.

The depreciation of the German mark in 1923 gave fresh encouragement to the view that gold alone could provide security. However Keynes, whose criticisms of the economic aspects of the peace settlement had brought him into public prominence, voiced disquiet at the prospect of Britain showing the way back to gold. He argued that gold was not in fact 'neutral' but was subject to the policies of the most important central banks. It was better, in his view, to seek two managed currencies, sterling and the dollar, rather than seek a spurious metallic automatism. However, in April 1925, Churchill, the Chancellor of the Exchequer in the new Conservative government, announced the return to gold at the old parity of $4.86 to the pound sterling. Claiming that sterling was thereby overvalued by some 10 per cent, Keynes denounced Churchill and his advisers in *The Economic Consequences of Mr Churchill*.

Most, though not all, subsequent comment on this important decision has sided with Keynes. Pollard sees the move as a 'not wholly rational attempt' to regain the power and the glory lost since the war. In fact, the desire to return to gold was not a peculiarly British madness. Many economic historians argue that the distortion of currency relationships, the movement away from economic liberalism, the creation of new European states determined often to be self-sufficient, all combined to render the restoration of the Gold Standard system impossible. The British error lay in failing to grasp the new position of London in world financial markets. New York and Paris now competed energetically for funds and no single centre could control their flow in the way London had done before 1914. And in these new circumstances there was insufficient co-operation between the central banks.

It is normally suggested that the overvalued pound discouraged exports, encouraged imports and placed pressure upon the balance of payments – which in turn necessitated restrictive and deflationary policies to prevent an outflow of gold and a collapse of sterling. Other economists argue that the Bank of England took effective steps, in the wake of the return to gold, to keep down the bank rate until the very eve of the 1931 crisis. It also allowed commercial banks a relatively free hand in dispensing credit. Churchill himself argued that his decision had saved the nation from 'hectic inflation' – a view that seemed ludicrous to Keynesian economists, at least before 'hectic inflation' did afflict the British nation(191).

The underlying issue in these complex matters was one of control and decision-making. Montagu Norman, Governor of the Bank of England, thought it quite wrong that merchants, manufacturers or workmen should be consulted about the return to gold, though it was quite proper to consider its impact on them. He assumed that this was a technical matter best left to the professionals. Indeed, for many bankers, the beauty of the Gold Standard was that it took the currency 'out of politics'. Some economists and industrialists, on the other hand, did not share the Bank's confidence in its own detached judgement. These issues surfaced after 1925, but were not resolved. Different circumstances, in any case, lead to different assessments of the merits or otherwise of 'independent' central banking. In the 1920s, what Brittan was later to call 'the lack of a budget constraint among voters' was not a problem.[6] Then, it was the detachment of financial mechanisms from the political process which worried critics of the government's policy and the role of the Bank of England.

In practice, the return to gold required a good deal of discretionary management by the Bank. Internationally, from 1928 onwards, many debtors suffered a steady drain of their gold reserves – some Latin American and Commonwealth countries devalued and abandoned gold in 1930. And in September 1931 the United Kingdom, too, abandoned the Gold Standard. A rise in the Bank of England's discount rate early in 1931 might have preserved funds in London, but the move would probably have been insufficient. It was the National government, so committed at its formation to the beauty of gold, which took the decision but a short while later to bid farewell to the restoration of the pre-1914 world.

INDUSTRY AFTER THE WAR

The performance of British industry in the 1920s has aroused much scholarly debate. Traditionally, the problems of the 'staple' industries were stressed, accompanied by a lament that the 'new' industries did not grow fast enough. This picture has been modified (199). Writers point out that between 1920 and 1927 Britain sustained a higher rate of growth in industrial output than in any comparable period since 1860 – though, as always, much depends on the precise dates used(192). It may also be that we have better information on the twentieth century. Once again, industrial 'success' or 'failure' can lie in the eye of the beholder. On the other side, it is noted that British industrial output did not regain its 1913 level until 1924.

There is little dispute about the difficulties experienced by the staple industries. Coal exports fell from 94 million tons in 1913 to 77 million in 1929. Four main reasons have been advanced for this decline: productivity was increasing much faster elsewhere (and a penalty was now being paid for the failure to mechanize before 1914, however unnecessary it then appeared); new mines were opened in Spain, The Netherlands and the Far East; the war stimulated greater economies in fuel utilization; and finally coal now began to suffer intense competition from other fuels. World consumption of coal was static, while consumption of petroleum trebled. Hydroelectric generation made a substantial contribution both in Europe and in the United States and further squeezed the market for coal(200) .

It is not surprising, therefore, that the problems of coal had such major repercussions on the politics of the 1920s. Although the owners have invariably been criticized, Buxton argues that they had little room for manoeuvre in response to depressed markets. Only 'central action' could have produced the necessary structural adjustment(193).

The cotton industry also suffered a dramatic relative decline, although domestic consumption increased. It was difficult to see how Asian markets could be recaptured from the Indian and Japanese cotton industries. Total production of British cotton piece goods fell from 8 million square yards in 1912 to 3.3 million in 1930. The United Kingdom's share in world cotton exports dropped from 68 per cent to 44 per cent. Initially, the industry's response was traditional – short-time working – while it tried to distinguish between cyclical fluctuation and long-term decline. Bankruptcy did remove some of the excess capacity, but in 1930 the number of spindles and looms showed only a slight reduction from what it had been in 1919. The Lancashire Cotton Corporation Ltd was formed in 1929 (with Bank of England support) by amalgamating some 200 mills. Even so, a

Labour government committee reported in 1930 that until further major improvements were introduced there was no chance that Lancashire would be able to arrest the decline of its export trade(193).

The iron and steel industries, and shipbuilding, were also in trouble. In certain specialized areas of steel-making, British firms could reach very high standards, but the industry had too many poorly located firms and plants using obsolete equipment at less than optimum capacity. One South Wales producer who was confident in 1920 that he was on the point of making the cheapest steel in the world was in the United States nine years later trying to find out how to make steel at a profit. One biting comment was that the British industry was making steel as a by-product, its main product being self-pity. Shipbuilding, too, was paying the price of over-capacity. It peaked at 2 million tons in 1920, not exceeding 1.5 million in any year over the next decade. But if the British output was only 79 per cent of pre-war level, foreign shipbuilders increased their production by 19 per cent. The Italians, French, Germans and Norwegians, in particular, used shipbuilding to protect and develop their own merchant marine. In 1930, when an even more bleak slump in orders was in prospect, the National Shipbuilders Security Ltd was formed (again with Bank of England support) to purchase redundant shipyards and to make sure that shipbuilding did not take place in them. The British merchant marine, too, began to experience keen competition, though in 1929 it still carried just under half of the world's entire seaborne trade(193).

Sir Arthur Balfour, an industrialist, was asked by the 1924 Labour government to enquire into the conditions and prospects of British industry, with special reference to exports. His committee produced a number of detailed reports and a final one in 1929. In that year, the Macmillan Committee on Banking, Finance and Credit was asked to make recommendations which would enable these agencies 'to promote the development of trade and commerce and the employment of labour'. This task reflected anxiety that Britain might be developing a *rentier* economy. The deficit on imports/exports during the 1920s was roughly double what it had been in 1913, and an overall balance was only obtained by shipping receipts and overseas investment income. But, although there was some new overseas investment, it was not on the scale achieved before 1914; a cause of dismay in some circles and relief in others. On the other hand, although British manufacturing industry suffered from this development in the long term, the import prices of primary products fell during the 1920s and thus a smaller volume of exports bought a larger volume of imports. This trend helped to mitigate the consequences of Britain's failure to share, to the same extent, in the exporting progress of other European nations. However, the terms of trade could swing the other way and a diversified and strengthened industrial base was vital for future prosperity.

The Balfour Committee drew attention to the 'new' industries and their progress has also been singled out by recent historians. Certainly, there were very important developments in such products as rayon, motor-car manufacture and various aspects of electrical engineering. However, significant though they were, Buxton notes that their total weight in the economy was still small both in terms of output and employment. Glyn and Oxborrow point out that growth was not restricted to 'new' industries; there was rapid change in building, tobacco, furniture, food, paper, printing, utilities, footwear and hosiery. Productivity in shipbuilding improved at a rate above the national average; in chemicals at a rate below. It was normal, however, to think of shipbuilding as in decline and chemicals as growing. By 1929, the output of rayon filament yarn was seven times what it had been in 1913 – though it is noteworthy that it was the American term 'rayon' rather than the British 'artificial silk' which established itself. One German calculation (though it has been challenged) suggested that the United States, and to a lesser extent Germany, had a much larger share of the market in those manufactured items which were growing most rapidly in world trade(192).

In such a context, fresh arguments were heard about the optimum size and organization of industry. The 1920s saw more mergers and more large companies. Whereas in 1907 there had been only seven British companies capitalized at over £8 million, there were twenty-five by 1924 and the number continued to rise. The most spectacular was the formation of Imperial Chemical Industries in 1926, bringing together Nobel Industries, Brunner Mond, the British Dyestuffs Corporation and United Alkali. In every respect – capital, employment, geographical spread and diversity of product – it was large. The founders declared that they had chosen their title 'of deliberate purpose'. Their conviction was that only an undertaking on such a scale could either compete or reach world trading agreements with such giants as the American Du Pont or the German IG Farben companies. One other dramatic and somewhat bizarre combination was the formation of Unilever in 1929 from Lever Brothers and the Dutch companies of Jurgens and van den Berghs. Guest Keen and Nettlefolds was the result of another merger. In some instances the resultant company structures were strongly centralized, in others they were loose and 'federal' – both solutions had their advocates. The English banks also merged again; the 'Big Five' of the Midland, Westminster, Lloyds, Barclays and the National Provincial were now dominant. Many more examples of consolidation could be given. The process called into question classical views of the virtue of competition. At what point did monopoly or oligopoly harm the public interest? This, in turn, raised once more the question of the role of government, both in relation to domestic industry and international trade(128,189,201).

Within a year of the return to peace, most of the wartime regulations on industry were removed, though some import restrictions and price controls remained. Such 'precipitate' action caused some contemporary and much subsequent criticism. Even so, despite the return to 'freedom', government expenditure did not return to what it had been in 1914 and taxpayers were apparently conditioned to higher rates. Some industries never returned to their pre-war condition. The 1921 Railways Act reduced the number of companies to four regional undertakings – the London and North Eastern, the London Midland and Scottish, the Great Western and the Southern – with as judicious a mixture of profit-making and loss-making lines as could be arranged. They could not be said to compete with one another. The civil aviation industry was subsidized in 1921: Imperial Airways was formed in 1924 with an annual, though diminishing, subsidy. The nascent aircraft industry looked to the government for orders. As a result, the Air Ministry supported a large aircraft industry whose size it, rather than market forces determined. The Department of Scientific and Industrial Research, set up in 1916, continued to receive government money. Apart from a short period in 1924, the 1915 McKenna duties were retained. Not very successfully, both during and after the war, the government involved itself closely with the dyestuffs business, and arranged some protection for it. Although further 'safeguarding' was extended to rayon and motor cars, no comprehensive policy of intervention or protection evolved. Treasury civil servants continued to dislike 'experts' who had never occupied position of executive responsibility; Keynes criticized the many British businessmen who had risen not on their own legs but on the shoulders of their fathers and grandfathers – though he was hardly 'self-made' himself; bankers thought the best thing the State could do for industry was to practise strict economy in public spending since any attempt on its part to finance enterprises other than ordinary public services would retard the restoration of a healthy national economy. It was an open question which view, or which blending of views, would triumph in the new circumstances after 1931.

THE BALANCE SHEET

England's Crisis (1931) was only one of a number of books which tried to understand what was happening to the country. Its author, the French Protestant André Siegfried, painted a gloomy picture of a country in decline. Her nineteenth-century success had led to complacency, smugness, idleness and conceit – in all social classes. Such sweeping impressions do not take account of the innovations and improvements detected in this chapter, but there was indeed a crisis and perhaps a deep-seated psychological one. The statistics of the decline of great industries show a general picture; they do not reveal the harrowing suffering as whole communities were under threat. The strongest emotion was to cling on to what was known and understood; to blame the war and hope that things would recover; to limit the size of the family (the bishops of the Church of England grudgingly blessed contraceptives in 1930); to smoke solidly and drink regularly (though to get drunk less frequently). Only in the 1930s did it become clear that it was no mere passing cloud that hung over the country's economic and industrial future.

---

1. Arnold Toynbee in *Survey of International Affairs, 1931* (1932) p. 1
2. P. Cain, 'Political economy in Edwardian England' in A. O'Day, ed., *The Edwardian Age: Conflict and stability, 1900–1914* (1979), p. 46
3. W. J. Ashley, *The tariff problem* (1911), pp. 262–3
4. F. Crouzet, 'Trade and empire: the British experience from the establishment of free trade until the First World War' in B. M. Ratcliffe ed., *Great Britain and her world, 1750–1914* (Manchester, 1975) pp. 226–7
5. D. Winch, *Economics and policy* (1969), p. 67
6. S. Brittan, 'The economic contradictions of democracy', *British Journal of Political Science*, v (2) (1975), p. 139

CHAPTER 16

Town and country

In 1917, walking down Piccadilly, the President of the Board of Agriculture became entangled with a puppy. Its female owner apologized and helpfully added, 'I promise that next time it shall be a pig.' He then realized that his message to the public to 'walk a pig instead of a puppy' had struck home.[1] Unfortunately, his scheme had later to be abandoned because of the cereal shortage. However, vegetables did take the place of flowers in the gardens of Buckingham and Lambeth palaces. The royal family eagerly inspected the produce of skilled allotment holders in unexpected parts of the capital. These were, of course, extraordinary measures, designed to increase food production in wartime; they did not obliterate the distinction between town and country.

'Country' still retained a powerful emotional appeal. An 'acre of land between the shore and the hills' was an ideal held out by the Georgian poets. In Herefordshire, where some of them settled, could still be found 'the slow experienced labourers, whose knowledge had come to them as the acorns come to the oaks'. Here was a deep 'naturalness', though there was a fear that the 'countryman' was dying out and that to urban England his voice was 'more foreign than French'(156). There was certainly another side to this idyllic portrait, but farming at least made men more robust – for this reason two-thirds of the London police force was recruited from farm-workers. Yet, could the country survive? The 1908 Smallholdings Act was an attempt to keep people on the land by turning them into small-scale farmers, but it was not very successful. In the 1920s, there were under 30,000 smallholders and some 650,000 agricultural labourers.[2] But both before and after the war the Liberal party continued to believe that in 'placing and retaining more families on the land lies the effective remedy for much of our unemployment', but still the drift from the land continued.[3] Countrywomen, in particular, seemed to look upon the town as a 'kind of Eden'. There were smart things to be looked at, if not purchased, in shop windows and there were no pigs to be fed. Women had no doubt that cottages were much more difficult to keep clean than were town houses.

The fortunes of the farming industry fluctuated. No one seriously supposed that it would play a major part in the economy, although the problem of feeding the country in time of war did cause occasional alarm. Assuming a period of peace, then the United Kingdom could continue to import food from all over the world. The scale of North American farming meant that its wheat would continue to supply the British market while a Free Trade economy remained. It seemed sensible, indeed, to use corn as a feeding-stuff and oil seeds were also imported on an increasing scale in the decade before 1914. Beef production expanded and sheep now frequently grazed on the poor pasture the cattle vacated. There was little room for sentiment in pre-war farming and shewdness was required for survival. There were a few signs of developments to come; experimental tractors made their first appearance on a small number of farms around the turn of the century.

The national need for food during the war, which became grave during the 1917 U-boat campaign, naturally brought changes. There was a considerable increase in the arable acreage – reaching a peak of 12.4 million acres in 1918. There had been nearly 15 million acres in 1870, but until the war that figure had dropped inexorably. To work this area, it was the horse that still remained vital – and bullock teams pulling wooden ploughs could still be seen on the Sussex Downs during the war. The wartime increase in arable acreage was most apparent in the West and North, where both temporary and permanent grass was ploughed up. In Scotland, the acreage under grain crops was 1,174,000 in 1914 but 1,494,000 in 1918. The Welsh counties were very successful in attaining their target acreages for ploughing in 1918. The 1917 Corn Production Act gave farmers guaranteed minimum prices for wheat and oats and ensured a minimum wage for farm-workers. The war also speeded up the application of scientific discoveries to farming. In Scotland, for example, there was a particular improvement in the quality of seed potatoes, with general benefit to crops throughout the United Kingdom.

Farming made the transition to peace in seemingly good heart. Then, in 1921, the Corn Production Act was repealed and once again farmers were left to their own devices. Between 1920 and 1922, the price of wheat fell from about 84s. to 44s. and, with record North American harvests, it was to go on falling. Farmers throughout the United Kingdom rushed to get out of arable farming. By 1931, the acreage of grain and root crops in Scotland was lower than it had been in 1914, in some areas dramatically so. The waning of the *Farmer's Glory* was at hand, as the farmer-author A. G. Street explained. By 1925, his financial position was serious and bankruptcy faced many of those who had borrowed in the immediate post-war years to purchase or stock their farms. Street moved out of corn into dairying and then, prompted by the Sugar Subsidy Act of 1925, into sugar-beet. Such dodging about was expensive, he admitted, but with corn-growing a hopeless proposition, the painful process of finding an alternative system had to be undertaken. By the late 1920s, there were some better signs; some agricultural de-rating had been permitted and an Agricultural Mortgage Corporation (1928) gave farmers some financial assistance. There was increased benefit from research into animal nutrition and chemical fertilizers. The Agricultural Research Council was set up in 1930. The Land Drainage Act, 1930, set up catchment boards to regulate rivers and streams and improve the quality of low-lying land. The number of oil and petrol engines on English and Welsh farms increased tenfold between 1913 and 1931 to reach the modest total of 65,000. There were some 30,000 tractors in 1931. It did seem, however, that only a war, or the prospect of war, could lead to a serious reconsideration of the place of agriculture in the national economy. Under Free Trade, the British farming industry could not compete; perhaps the story would be different after 1931.

The woodlands of the United Kingdom in 1914 totalled some 3.2 million acres, some 97 per cent of which was in private hands. The war led to the felling of some 450,000 acres, chiefly of conifer, and there was official concern about future stocks and resources. The Acland Committee – which led to the formation of the post-war Forestry Commission – suggested that by the year 2000 there ought to be a further 1.5 million acres above the 1914 figure, to be chiefly afforestation (the planting of land which had not carried trees in the recent past). The Commission began its work energetically and in the 1920s planted the basis of the State forests which were to transform the landscape in parts of upland England, Scotland and Wales. In the private sector, however, there was a net loss of acreage. Felling exceeded replanting and even the pre-war acreage was not restored(163).

The first Town Planning Act, 1909, did not extend effective statutory control over the use of rural land. The agricultural crisis of the 1920s meant that land was cheap and was snapped up for housing and industrial development. Anxiety on this score led to the formation of the Council for the Preservation of Rural England (CPRE) in 1926. Its purpose was primarily educational, but it also acted as a pressure group when it judged the environment to be in danger. The Society for the Protection of Birds was given royal patronage in 1904 and, at county level, various bodies urged the establishment of 'nature reserves'. The CPRE embarked on a campaign for the establishment of 'National Parks', and was encouraged by the attitude of the 1929 Labour government. The National Trust steadily increased the number of properties under its care – houses, mountains and moorlands, forests and coastline. But was such activity simply a defence of country privilege against the urban masses? There was public disquiet about the total ignorance of country life often displayed by town children. Young people, it was suggested, ought to be able to move about the country cheaply. The historian G. M. Trevelyan, a great walker, became president of the Youth Hostels Association which started in 1930. Its purpose was to help the young 'to a greater knowledge, care and love of the countryside' and a network of suitable hostels was speedily established.

According to the novelist D. H. Lawrence, the tragedy of England lay in the fact that the country was so lovely but man-made England was so vile. He conceded, however, that: 'We live in towns from choice, when we subscribe to our great civilized form. The nostalgia for the country is not *so* important. What is important is that our towns are false towns – every street a blow, every corner a stab.'(156) He dismissed Nottingham as an 'amorphous agglomeration' and had a comprehensive solution. He wanted to pull everything down, plan a nucleus, fix the focus and then erect big handsome buildings sweeping to a civic centre. It was a vision worthy of another destructive part-time architect – Adolf Hitler.

However, on a limited scale, the ideas formulated by Ebenezer Howard at the turn of the century were put into effect. In 1903, the First Garden City Ltd set about developing a town inspired by his notions on 3,000 acres in Hertfordshire. It was a gamble from the outset, with the investor risking his capital and knowing that he could expect a maximum return of 5 per cent. There were some 8,000 settlers at Letchworth within a decade. Their only amenities were fresh air and a cottage with a garden. The pioneers had to make their own activities and even get to know each other. Letchworth survived and, just after the war, another company set about developing Welwyn Garden City on basically similar principles. In both instances, great attention was paid to design and landscaping(165). In Scotland, Patrick Geddes was as fertile with new town schemes as he was with neologisms. The most original scheme was at Rosyth under the unexpected patronage of the Admiralty. After the war, a Glasgow solicitor envisaged a community of 40,000 people to the north of the city who would believe that 'intensive manual cultivation of the land is suited to our circumstances'. The development never took place(154).

Interesting though these schemes were, they scarcely affected the main structure of urban living. In the major cities, the drift away from their central core accelerated. Developments in transport, as predicted, assisted this process. In Leeds, for example, horse-trams were eliminated by 1901 and steam-trams by 1902. Electrification brought with it reduced fares and speedier journeys. It is in this period that the masses used urban transport on a large scale. The railways in a city like Leeds were not likely to play the major role in passenger movement that they did in London, but bus services developed rapidly after 1920, with vigorous competition between rival undertakings; bus and rail competed too. Miles of 'bus-route-side' land then became ripe for development and 'semis' mushroomed(166). The motor car had not yet contributed to this dispersal, though private ownership was beginning to rise steadily in the 1920s. Attractive areas in the neighbourhood of large cities were doomed. 'It cannot be long' wrote one geographer in 1927, 'before the extensions from Liverpool and its satellites in the north, Ellesmere Port in the east, and Chester on the south, spread over what remain the most delightful rural townships in all Wirrall.'(164) In 1901, indeed, H. G. Wells forecast a continuous urban belt stretching from south of the Scottish Highlands to the English Channel. Manchester purchased a substantial area of rural Cheshire in 1926 on which to build the Wythenshawe estate. Such areas had to accept their 'suburban destiny'. In most northern cities, however, this was usually a process of redistributing an existing population. Speaking generally, the North was in decline, a reflection of its industrial crisis. The Manchester conurbation reached its maximum population of nearly 2½ million in 1931.[4] Towns like Bolton, Bury, Rochdale and Ashton declined in the 1920s while Oldham and four neighbouring districts had reached their peak in 1911. In the West Midlands, however, population continued to increase, adding further pressure on the housing stock. The appearance of Bournville stood in striking contrast to other areas of Birmingham. There, as elsewhere, the prosperous citizens moved further and further out and the large suburban villas of earlier decades became almost inner-city flats and tenements.

Above all, population in and around London continued to grow. Inner London peaked at 4.536 million in 1901 and dropped to 4.397 million in 1931. Outer London grew from 2.050 million to 3.819 million and the population of neighbouring counties increased by a further million.[5] Metropolitan communications were improved by the electrification of the Southern Railway in the 1920s and the extensions, north of the river, to the Northern and Bakerloo lines. Bus services greatly expanded during this decade too. Not all workers, of course, travelled directly into the heart of London, since some new industry had a suburban location. New main roads became increasingly important; Western Avenue and the North Circular Road were both built in the early 1920s. The transport needs of London led to suggestions for a co-ordinating body though it was not until 1933 that the London Passenger Transport Board was set up.

The growth of London and the South-east on this scale came as a surprise, and its significance was not fully apprehended. Before 1914 London had suffered serious unemployment but now it was South Wales, the North-east, the North-west, Scotland and Northern Ireland which suffered. What many had assumed to be an almost eternal pattern of industrial specialization throughout the United Kingdom was coming to an end. Geographers noted that the crisis in the staple industries generated unusual population flows. Unlike in earlier periods, they were not mainly from country areas to industrial towns, but shifts between existing industrialized urban areas(168). In the English North-east, for example, a net outflow of 33,000 in the decade before 1914 rose to 141,000 up to 1921 and more than 190,000 between 1921 and 1931.[6] What could, or should, be done about this drift was not something which received very serious consideration; it might, after all, reverse itself.

Planning might be the answer. However, if local authorities were to control development they needed more power than the 1909 Act supplied. The 1919 Housing and Town Planning Act made it compulsory for some of the larger authorities to prepare planning schemes and encouraged consultation between neighbouring authorities. In 1927, Neville Chamberlain, who then had ministerial responsibility for such matters, created the Greater London Regional Planning Committee, one of whose first steps was to commission a study of the feasibility of separating London from its satellite areas by a girdle of agricultural land. Thus the 'green belt' made its official début. Chamberlain, one of the few national politicians to have personal local government experience, grasped that its entire overhaul was due. The old Poor Law Unions and their guardians were abolished and in their place came public assistance committees under the aegis of county and county borough councils. The councils received additional power over roads, planning and public health in general. The urban and rural district councils were also reorganized, though they were kept separate. This kind of local government, however, was not genuinely local in the sense of being financially independent. Revenue from rates required supplementation in the form of block grants from central government. Despite its importance, the Act did not grapple fundamentally with the problems of urban sprawl and the erosion of old boundaries. It would be an exaggeration, however, to believe that H. G. Wells' vision, or nightmare, had yet materialized. Urban overspill had not yet eradicated the differences of ethos and outlook between town and country(169).

---

1. Lord Ernle, *Whippingham to Westminster* (1938), p. 307
2. G. E. Mingay, *Rural life in Victorian England* (1977), p. 105
3. *Liberal Land Report* (1925), p. 421
4. C. F. Carter ed., *Manchester and its region* (Manchester, 1962), p. 57
5. J. T. Coppock and H. C. Prince, eds., *Greater London* (1964), p. 34
6. J. W. House, *The North East* (Newton Abbot, 1969), p. 45

CHAPTER 17

Battles of the mind and body

EDUCATION

In 1902, the Commons debated the government's new Education Bill on the day the South African War ended. It was an apt coincidence. Prophets used the new century as an occasion to consider the 'breakers' ahead and were not very confident. Prince George and others urged the country to 'wake up'. Asquith noted that the 'undisputed hegemony' in trade had come to an end. The country was handicapped in the struggle for commercial survival by what Rosebery described as 'the badness of our educational system'.[1] Sadler, a civil servant with knowledge of the American and German educational systems, thought that the survival of empire depended upon 'sea power and school power'. In 1899, a Board of Education had replaced the former Education Committee of the Privy Council, but the government had jibbed at granting it 'control' over education(215).

The two separate categories of elementary school and the three of secondary school remained untouched. The county councils, though not uniformly, had risen to the challenge of developing technical education. By 1902, some 450,000 students were attending technical schools or evening classes – a threefold increase over a decade. Some school boards, however, saw this development as an 'outflanking policy' which threatened their future. They were anxious to extend their post-primary role. Sidney Webb and the civil servants at the Board, among others, were determined to stop them. Pressure for a 'single authority' to replace the many boards, committees and *ad hoc* authorities developed from many 'expert' quarters, though their defenders saw them as bastions of educational democracy. It was in this context that Balfour decided to act boldly, calculating that if he offended Chamberlain and the Opposition the Liberals themselves would not be of one mind about education. Asquith rightly feared that a 'single authority' would cause 'infinite confusion and division' in his party.[2]

The 1902 Act laid educational responsibilities upon county, county borough and borough councils with populations of over 10,000 and urban district councils with more than 20,000. The Board of Education would deal with 318 local education authorities instead of several thousand school boards and the managers of even more voluntary schools. The councils were obliged to take over the functions of school boards. The most contentious aspect was the financial security given to Anglican and Roman Catholic schools in return for a degree of public control. Lloyd George, whose initial private reaction was favourable, soon saw that he had to accept the nonconformist view that education would be 'the tool of the Church, the servant of the Treasury, and the slave of the capitalist' under such proposals.[3] Haldane and other 'Liberal imperialists' felt that any shortcomings in the measure were balanced by its merits. When they returned to office, the Liberals did not find it easy to meet nonconformist grievances.

Although it was the political battle which held the headlines, in the long run the Act was a notable educational reform. The views of Morant, Permanent Secretary of the Board after 1903 were dominant. His former experience as a tutor to the crown prince of Siam helped immeasurably in defining the purpose of a 'secondary' school. The 1904 regulations stated that it should provide a general education 'of wider scope and more advanced degree' than the elementary schools for scholars up to and beyond the age of sixteen. Although Morant can be defended against charges of hostility to scientific or technical knowledge, his approach, as a Wykehamist, was 'humane'. He wished to spread as much as possible of the ethos of the endowed grammer and public schools.

The majority of secondary schoolchildren left at sixteen or earlier and doubts still remained about the suitability of the education they received as a preparation for industry and commerce. The secondary schools run by voluntary bodies could obtain a grant from both the local authority and the Board of Education (after 1919 they had to make a choice). The number of secondary schools increased and the existing ones grew steadily in size. Even so, by 1930, some 56 per cent of public expenditure on education went into the elementary sector and only 19 per cent into the secondary. Standards were monitored by the creation of a secondary branch of the inspectorate. Until 1917, when the School Certificate and Higher School Certificate were introduced, the structure of examinations was confused and complex. Variety, however, remained characteristic of the school system. In 1910, for example, 'central' schools were introduced in London designed to give a fuller opportunity to those children who had just failed to obtain scholarships or free places at secondary schools. By 1931, there were over eighty of them with either a 'commercial' or a 'technical' bias. Central schools then spread more generally throughout England and Wales. In 1914, about 1 child in 40 from a public elementary school obtained a free secondary education at the age of eleven, in 1921, 1 in 20, and in 1929, 1 in 13(215).

Some of these changes stemmed from the Education Act of 1918, the work of the historian H. A. L. Fisher. Its philosophy was enshrined in the statement that children were not to be debarred from any form of education, for which they were equipped, through inability to pay fees. The school-leaving age was fixed at fourteen and the 'half-time' system was phased out. Fees for elementary schools were abolished. Legal restrictions were placed on the employment of school-age children. Fisher also envisaged a system of 'continuation schools' for those who left school at fourteen. However, these and the nursery schools were largely stillborn in post-war economic circumstances. The Burnham Committee, established in 1919, with trade union and local authority representation, made some progress in trying to raise the status and pay of teachers(216).

The shape of future educational policy was much discussed in the 1920s. *Secondary Education for All*, edited by R. H. Tawney and published by the Labour party in 1922, advocated a universal system extending from the ages of eleven to sixteen. In 1926, the Hadow Report on the Education of the Adolescent accepted that secondary education should not be for a 'selected few' but for all. The age of eleven should be the the point of transition between 'primary' (a term it wished to see replace 'elementary') and secondary education. The school-leaving age should rise to fifteen. A period of reorganization followed, though not uniformly throughout the country since much still depended on local initiative. Writing in 1931, an author commented that in London there were 557 council schools and 359 'non-provided' schools. Of these, 295 council and 35 'non-provided' had either been, or were being, reorganized. In consequence, not for the first or last time, many schools were 'in a somewhat fluid condition'![4] The benefits from these changes were not thought to be merely scholastic. 'The classification of our schools', Baldwin wrote in 1929, 'has been on the lines of social rather than educational distinction; a youth's school badge has been his social label. The interests of social unity demand the removal of this source of class prejudice and the drastic remodelling of the national structure to form a coherent whole.' If that was the view of a Conservative Prime Minister, writers on the Left saw even greater scope for educational and hence social change(215).

The drastic remodelling of which Baldwin spoke did not apply to his old school, Harrow. The public schools were generally thriving, though the period of continuous expansion was over and a few had to close. In the new circumstances after 1902, a sharper definition of 'public school' became possible by excluding schools in receipt of public funds. A public school increasingly came to be thought of as a boarding school. Products of the major public schools normally occupied prominent positions in public life. Within the Board of Education itself, for example, of the 92 higher officials in 1910, only 19 had been to schools not represented on the Headmasters' Conference and 28 had come from Eton, Harrow and Winchester. In the Foreign Service, 65 per cent of recuits entering between 1923 and 1928 attended one or other of the eleven leading public schools. Before 1914 a number of 'progressive' schools were founded, whose headmasters deliberately broke with the prevailing public school ethos – Bedales and Abbotsholme were the most conspicuous examples. After the war, new schools were founded, the most well known being Bryanston and Stowe. Their new emphasis attempted to meet criticism of public schools in such books as Alec Waugh's *The Loom of Youth*. In 1924, one landmark was reached – a Cabinet was formed which lacked any Etonian representation. It is little wonder that it had such a short life(223).

In 1901 there were 20,000 full-time university students – a figure which had more than doubled by 1931. The federal university of London, with splendid new buildings in Bloomsbury, was the largest in the country. New university colleges were founded in the 1920s at Exeter, Hull and Leicester, while Swansea became an additional college of the federal University of Wales. The Scottish universities grew steadily in size. Women were admitted to degrees at Oxford in 1920 though at Cambridge they were only allowed 'titular' degrees. In discussing the educational system, Haldane argued in 1907 that for the production 'of that limited body of men and women whose calling requires high talent, the university or its equivalent alone suffices'. The large universities were now able to offer an impressive range of courses. In London, a School of Oriental Studies and a School of Slavonic and East European Studies extended the range of regional research. In 1921, Oxford showed its zeal for keeping abreast of the times by establishing a new School of Politics, Philosophy and Economics. At Cambridge, a separate English Tripos was smuggled in during the war. A small number of 'State scholarships' assisted the admission of students from working-class backgrounds to universities. The proportion of students to population was roughly three times greater in Scotland than in England, with Wales in between. Students tended to go to their 'local' university, but the universities as a whole came increasingly to be part of a system. The University Grants Committee (UGC) was set up in 1919 and was made responsible to the Treasury not the Board of Education. In this period, however, parliamentary grants provided only about 35 per cent of the income of the universities taken as a whole.[5]

Various facilities for 'continued education' also existed. The 'adult schools', often under Quaker sponsorship flourished in many cities, though peak attendances were reached before 1914. Ruskin College, Oxford was founded in 1899 with trade union backing. Local authorities, universities and the Workers' Educational Association co-operated in organizing classes for adults, particularly in economics and social studies. Coleg Harlech, founded in North Wales in 1927, was another example of a residential college specifically designed to give students a 'second chance'. A sense of the past was also increasingly cultivated throughout the educational system. History teachers became familiar figures in schools for the first time. The Historical Association (1906) and its journal *History* (1916) attempted to spread in schools and among the general public 'a sense of the profound and increasing importance of history in national life'. The Wiltshire Education Committee was only one of a number of authorities to suggest that every child should realize 'what he inherits from the past, and what duties he owes as a patriot and a citizen'.

It had taken two wars to give legislative impetus to educational reform but great confusion remained, both in organization and objective. Vocational training, technical instruction, humane scholarship, character-building, basic literacy and social engineering all co-existed in an educational system which outsiders found very unsystematic. And perhaps it was as well that they did.

RELIGION

One of the inheritances from the past which the Wiltshire schoolchild assimilated was the Christian religion, but according to R. J. Campbell, a leading Free Church minister, there was no blinking the fact that 'if the churches represent Christianity, then Christianity is rapidly losing its hold in this professedly religious country, as well as in every other country of the civilized world'.[6] A few years earlier, between November 1902 and November 1903, the *Daily News* investigated the religious life of London and concluded that out of a population of 6¼ million there were 1¼ million regular churchgoers, drawn largely from the lower middle class. Analysis in detail confirmed that 'Sunday after Sunday the doors of places of worship are thrown open, but the people do not enter. Churches have simply no attraction for them. Thousands are either hostile or indifferent to every kind of religious communion.'[7] An investigation in Liverpool in 1911 found many people anxious to be identified as 'Church of England', with the explanation: 'We don't go anywhere, but don't want to be looked upon as heathens.' Very few described themselves as secularists, atheists or spiritualists. Sunday-schools still attracted large attendances and did not lose ground until after 1918. It would be misleading, too, to suggest that 'non-church-going' became the accepted convention in all parts of the United Kingdom at the same time. Dramatic 'revivals' of religion were still possible, though they did not seem to occur in England any more. During 1904–05, some 100,000 people were reputed to have joined the various nonconformist denominations in Wales. This was 'popular' religion, largely without ministerial guidance. In 1911 it was argued that public opinion in Scotland was still 'on the side of church-going', at any rate once every Sunday. Anyone staying at home had to think of a reason for doing so.[8]

Explanations for this 'non-church-going' varied. Thanks to '"week-ends", Society functions, Sunday trains, motor cars, etc. the day of rest has been turned into a saturnalia in which the idle rich and the rowdy poor vie with each other in bidding defiance to all things sacred'; so wrote the author of *Scotland's Battles for Spiritual Independence*. Other authors saw the craze for excitement and entertainment leaving the churches stranded and the solution lay in placing leisure pursuits in a Christian framework. At least one minister of the Gospel felt obliged publicly to express 'his great gratitude to the athletes for the good they were doing'. But there were limits. 'What preacher', wrote a Methodist minister in 1906, 'in the calm possession of his senses, ever does want to compete with the theatre any more than he wants to kick a ball about his church by way of competing with the football field?[9]

The appeal of Mammon, however, was not exactly new and could not be the only explanation. Could the traditional creeds still be adhered to? There was, according to R. J. Campbell, a need for a new theology which would present the Christian faith clearly and simply, stripping it of the irrelevancies of ecclesiasticism. His own writings and sermons aroused a great deal of interest, perhaps confirming a common view that: 'The religion of Christ is bigger and wider than the ritual of the churches . . . .'[10] Traditional theologians found such presentations insipid and meretricious and did not hesitate to say so. The solution to the difficulties of Christian belief could not be found simply by removing the difficulties. Neville Figgis, Cambridge don and Anglican priest, attacked those who supposed that 'if we only gave up our rather absurd attachment to the "tinsel of miracle", or our antiquated and non-modern notion of marriage, or a fanatical and unhealthy doctrine of sin . . . then all would be well . . .'. The attack on Christianity came not from the 'melancholy unfaith' of those who would honour but could not adore, not from the 'languid refusal of some diletante agnostic too much bored to decide' but from those who proclaimed that 'this world is all' and were determined to crush the contemptible Christian churches.[11]

Some churchmen now believed that the time had come to close ranks. Relationships between different denominations were certainly improving. When one leading preacher moved from one branch of Methodism in the nineteenth century another preacher fraternally remarked: 'They say this dog barks well – but he comes from a dirty kennel.'[12] In telling this tale in 1910, a prominent Wesleyan Methodist used it to make the point that such language would no longer be acceptable. In 1907, the Bible Christians, the Methodist New Connexion and the United Methodist Free Church came together as the United Methodist Church. After the war, further negotiations took place and in 1932 a single Methodist Church was formed from a union of the Primitive Methodists, United Methodists and Wesleyan Methodists. In Scotland, the United Free Church was formed in 1900 from a union of the United Presbyterians and a majority of the Free Church. In 1929, the United Free Church rejoined the Church of Scotland. The Church of England, too, began to discuss its attitude to the non-episcopal churches, particularly at the 1920 Lambeth Conference, although no common mind emerged.

The Roman Catholic Church in Britain, steadily growing in numbers, took no part in such deliberations. Anglican 'orders' had been declared invalid by the Pope in 1896 and Cardinal Vaughan expressed the view that the reunion of the churches was 'a snare of the Evil One'. Notwithstanding this insight, a curious set of conversations took place in the mid-1920s between some leading Anglicans, urged on by Lord Halifax, and a Belgian cardinal. They led nowhere(232).

The improvement in relations, at least between the non-Roman Catholic churches, was in part made possible by a weakening of the social rift between 'church' and 'chapel', though it had by no means disappeared. One leading Free Churchmen expressed the view in 1897 that the decay of the disabilities from which they had once suffered made it more difficult to dissent in the present. That judgement became even more true in succeeding decades. 'I care nothing about denominations', wrote one brilliant young Free Churchman from 'somewhere in France' during the war, and he spoke for many.[13]

Other soldiers went further. Could slaughter on the Somme be fitted into a Christian explanation of the world? Many concluded that it could not, and remnants of belief drained away in the suffering. The ready identification of the war as 'just' by leading clergymen came, subsequently at least, to appear too glib. The small sect of Quakers maintained a pacifist witness — though not without internal division. Clergy and laity from other denominations formed the Fellowship of Reconciliation as an expression of their abhorrence of war. Other Christians saw in the evil of war a vindication of the Gospel in so far as what was happening discredited widely held notions of 'progress' or of the essential goodness of man. Even if such an argument was convincing, church leaders had to recognize that not even a visit from the bishop of London to the front, or the poetry of 'Woodbine Willie', could comfort many distressed combatants(62).

After the war, 'relevance' became the watchword. Alderman Sheppard, first Labour lord mayor of Bristol, told a conference on religion in the Labour movement that some of the finest Christian workers he knew 'rarely attended church or chapel' and many churchmen appeared to endorse such a view.[14] Vast discussions took place on Christian attitudes to politics, economics and citizenship. William Temple, bishop of Manchester, led the Church of England deep into the thickets of social policy. It appeared that the articulate spokesmen of the churches moved to the Left; whether they took their congregations with them is another matter. Ironically, the mixed allegiances of MPs deliberated upon the revised Prayer Book, presented for their consideration by the Church of England. They found it not to their taste. In general, therefore, Christianity and the churches occupied a puzzling position. Few either inside or outside the Church of England wished to see it disestablished. 'Positivists, agnostics, idealists, pessimists, optimists, sceptics, theists, atheists jostle one another and nobody knows what his next-door neighbour thinks', was how Figgis described the position before 1914, and that pluralism widened even further afterwards(233).[15]

SPORT

'Sport to be considered an essential element in Art' was the rather unlikely observation in the manifesto issued in 1914 by the Futurist group of *avant-garde* aesthetic critics. There is no evidence that they practised what they preached. Other contemporaries placed sport more demurely in the context of 'physical education' or worried about its relationship to religion. Sport had to be taken seriously, though its replacement by real war in 1914 was a setback. Some cricketers still asserted the supremacy of their martial art, to be rebuked by the secretary of the MCC who urged cricketers everywhere to find their heroes 'on the great field of battle'. Others used the same kind of analogy. 'You have played well with one another and against one another for the Cup', said Lord Derby in presenting the FA Cup in April 1915, 'play with one another for England now.' The Football Association took due note and the professional game was abandoned for the duration of the war. Racegoers had largely to restrict their interest in horses to the (limited) adventures of the British cavalry on foreign soil. Ducal owners of racehorses gracefully withdrew them to unobtrusive stables. Pigeon-fanciers, normally a harmless breed, found themselves singled out in a special Defence of the Realm regulation which banned the unauthorized keeping and release of racing pigeons. These birds were, of course, in demand elsewhere. There was some relaxation in these austerities before the end of the war, but organized sport was still generally considered a dangerous distraction (247,248).

Whatever its bearing on the war effort, this attitude towards sport was testimony to its significance in the lives of millions. In the pre-war decade, physical fitness had been stressed – in part prompted by shortcomings apparent among volunteers for the South African War – but the needs of the spectator were not neglected. Football grounds, though still far from luxurious, became both more capacious and more protected against the elements. In 1907, the English Rugby Football Union bought a site of some 10 acres at Twickenham – a step which some considered too ambitious. It was gratifying to be able to record a victory over Wales in the first international played on the ground in 1910. Cricket was enjoying what many considered to be its golden age, with the tone frequently being set by the free-hitting, free-scoring activities of the amateur clubs. In the county championship, Yorkshire, captained by Lord Hawke from 1883 to 1910, only fell below fourth place twice in the years 1895–1914. Increasingly, however, finance came to be a major consideration, though it was still the case, in both cricket and football, that local teams were local.

In 1908, London was host to the fourth Olympic Games of the modern era. Athletes from nineteen nations engaged in swimming, fencing, gymnastics, and track and field athletics. In the marathon, the race leader collapsed at the finishing line and was illicitly helped over it by officials. He was naturally disqualified, but Queen Alexandra, who happened to be on hand, awarded the disconsolate Italian a special gold cup. The revived Olympic movement was supposed to contribute to international harmony and her gesture no doubt helped.

The internationalization of all sport was proceeding apace. In 1909 the Imperial Cricket Conference was formed, consisting of the MCC, Australia and South

Africa – the leading nations. In 1912 a triangular tournament was held between this trio in England, but it was not a success – chiefly because the organizers showed no capacity to hold off the rain. Backed by princely purses, cricket made great progress in India. The first Indian representative side came to England in 1911 – the same year in which the King-Emperor was reciprocating the entertainment by mounting elephants in India. A combined West Indies team made its first visit, though it was not accorded 'first-class' status. In Rugby Union, tours of teams from the British Isles to New Zealand and South Africa became firmly established and after 1910 France joined the competition between the home countries.

After the hiatus of war, all sports resumed their vigorous activity and the grazing animals were forced to depart from Twickenham. When the home rugby championship was resumed, England emerged as the best team in the early 1920s followed a little later by Scotland. The French achieved their first victory over England in 1927 and over Wales in 1928. The Irish Rugby Union survived political partition and the Irish rugby team was composed of players from North and South. The British Lions (as they were known after 1924) continued to tour overseas. Rugby's strength remained in the middle classes, the public schools and the ancient universities; its amateurism was jealously guarded. The social life of a rugby club almost rivalled the golf course as a place for the promotion of business.

Football, on the other hand, 'tainted' by professionalism, came even more clearly to be the game of the masses, though distinguished amateur teams, like the Corinthian Casuals, still survived. After the war, the English Football League became truly national for the first time. Divisions One and Two were expanded and a Third Division formed, split into north and south. The 'English' League also included a few Welsh sides – Cardiff City being elected to Division Two in 1920–21. The FA Cup Final rapidly approached the status of a hallowed occasion, particularly when it was transferred to Wembley Stadium in 1923. Spectators were obligingly informed in the official programme that the ground area was equal to that of the biblical city of Jerusalem. It may have been a desire to test this proposition which led the scholars in the crowd to spill over on to the pitch in great numbers. Only the gallant action of a policeman on a white horse made play possible. A tradition was also established that it was the monarch who presented the Cup to the winners. In 1929, the Rugby League Challenge Cup Final was played at Wembley – an exotic northern ritual oddly out of place in the capital city.

International football after 1919 was bedevilled by political problems. The Fédération Internationale de Football Association (FIFA) had been formed in Europe in 1904, but relations with the superior Football Associations of the United Kingdom were difficult from the start. After the war, the British Associations patriotically declared that they would not play ball with ex-enemy or neutral countries. There was a complete rupture with FIFA, complicated by disputes over the place of football in the Olympic Games and the question of professionalism. Attempts to establish a European football championship went ahead without British teams. Relationships improved slowly, but in the 1920s, only England of the home countries made occasional forays into Europe. England's first defeat by a foreign country was sustained in Madrid in 1929. It indicated that the arrogance of football's founding country was ceasing to be justified.

Between the home countries, the matches between England and Scotland held pride of place. There were 129,810 spectators at Hampden Park, Glasgow – then a world record – for the match against England in 1931. Wales and Ireland were the poor relations of the British soccer world. Unlike rugby, Irish football was seriously complicated by politics. An Irish Free State FA was established alongside the existing Irish FA, and the Irish Free State competed internationally. Taking advantage of the desire of talented players to leave depressed regions, English clubs increasingly turned their attention to Scotland and Northern Ireland. At the club level, English football was increasingly a microcosm of the football of the British Isles.

Cricket remained essentially an English game, although Glamorgan became the last county to join the championship – usually near the bottom. It was believed that the Scottish summer was so short that players never had time to get padded up. Test cricket involved 'England' against visiting teams, though the Englishness of the side did not require the exclusion of the occasional Scot or Indian. Australia remained the prime opponent and, with only two short intervals, established apparently effortless superiority. Donald Bradman proved very difficult to get out. In 1919, as an experiment, county cricket matches lasted for two days, with extended play in the evenings, but an 'afterwork' crowd did not materialize – confirming that watching cricket, except in northern regions, was a habit of the leisured and elderly. Professional cricketers formed the core of a county side, but they were normally captained by an amateur. 'Star' professionals had their fame playing (as did the Trinidadian Learie Constantine) in the Lancashire League. Fame came to many cricketers, and other sportsmen, but fortune did not normally accompany it. That was a stage in the evolution of sport which was still to come.

---

1. H. C. G. Matthew, *The Liberal Imperialists* (Oxford, 1973), pp. 224–5
2. Matthew, op. cit., p. 232
3. J. Grigg, *Lloyd George: The people's champion* (1978), pp. 52–3
4. A. C. Ford, *Education in London in 1931* (1931), p. 7
5. A. H. Halsey, *Trends in British society* (1972), p. 207
6. R. J. Campbell, *Christianity and the social order* (1907), p. 8
7. R. Mudie Smith, ed., *The religious life of London* (1904)
8. W. F. Gray, *Non-church going* (Edinburgh, 1911), p. 6
9. Cited in S. Yeo, *Religion and voluntary organizations in crisis* (1976), p. 313
10. R. J. Campbell, *The New Theology* (1907); K. G. Robbins, 'The spiritual pilgrimage of the Rev. R. J. Campbell', *Journal of Ecclesiastical History*. Apr. 1979
11. J. N. Figgis, *Antichrist and other sermons* (1913), pp. 11–14
12. C. H. Kelly, *Memories* (1910), p. 190
13. J. H. Shakespeare, *The churches at the cross-roads* (1918), p. 208
14. *The religion in the Labour movement* (1919), p. 43
15. J. N. Figgis, *Civilisation at the cross roads* (1912), p. 36

CHAPTER 18

Waltzing through the Waste Land

A. J. Penty, a social theorist, writing in 1919, welcomed signs of discontent and revolt against 'authority', but feared that it would be accompanied by an attack on 'culture'. Any healthy social system depended on living traditions, 'though a false culture like the academic one of today tends to separate people by dividing them in classes and groups and finally isolating them as individuals'. He desired a 'true' culture. He was not alone, but equally not alone in his unwillingness to say what it was. Conservative writers feared that the onrush of democracy would trample beneath it the fairest flowers of civilization, and some were convinced that 'only through oligarchy does civilized democracy know itself'. The part played by 'the few' in the world of the arts was so important that without them the mass of the citizens would be 'unlettered, superstitious and half-brutal barbarians'.[1] J. A. Hobson, the economist and social critic, would have none of this. 'The low tastes and character of the mass of the workers', he argued in 1902, 'are directly imposed upon them by the very class which taunts them with possessing them.' The workers did not offer a worse natural soil 'than the class which at present lives upon their degradation'.[2] Once the people had an ample margin of energy and leisure, they would recognize the claims of literature, art and science.

LITERATURE

In 1923, I. A. Richards and C. K. Ogden wrote a book on the meaning of meaning and they also worried about the principles of literary criticism. In posing such questions, post-war writers saw themselves in revolt against the self-indulgence of Romanticism. They asked afresh what a writer was trying to achieve and how his efforts could be best assessed. Perennial problems were posed with a classical novelty.

It would be mistaken to see this concern as simply a product of the war, for the literary scene was in turmoil before 1914. Orage's *New Age* was only one of a number of 'little magazines' which stood in striking contrast to the placid world of Georgian poetry. T. E. Hulme rediscovered Original Sin, but died in 1917 before he was able to exploit the fact. T. S. Eliot reached England from the United States in 1915. The war did bring a change of mood if the work of Rupert Brooke is compared with that of Wilfred Owen, but the revolution in style in Eliot's *Waste Land* (1922) cannot be directly attributed to it.

Some contemporaries found Eliot incomprehensible, but he saw himself as resurrecting a tradition. Grierson's critical edition of Donne (1912) presaged a revived interest in metaphysical poetry. Bridges's edition of Gerard Manley Hopkins (1918) presaged a revived interest in an 'alternative' Victorian. That interest was not very wide. A critical journal like the *Criterion* (1922) had a small circulation. On the other hand, men like W. H. Davies, de la Mare, Masefield and Drinkwater continued to publish, regardless of critical disdain, and found eager readers. Of the poets who had established reputations before 1914, perhaps only W. B. Yeats was both widely read and critically esteemed.

Novels were still widely read and widely published. Authors to join Kipling and Conrad in general esteem were Wells, Bennett and Galsworthy in the pre-war period. Wells was fascinated by the world of science and by social mobility, not least his own. From novels, he was to turn to the history of the world and other matters. Galsworthy wrote steadily from the beginning of the century until his death in 1933. He chronicled the Forsytes and moved sure-footedly with them through the complexities of Edwardian society. Bennett moved to France, fame and fortune on the success of his novels set in his native Potteries. His entry into the middle class 'by the help of God and strict attention to business' gave him satisfaction, but contrasts strongly with James Joyce's alienation. His work was considered obscene and banned. The 'stream of consciousness' did not only flow among exiled Irishmen. After the war, Virginia Woolf tried to escape the tyranny of narrative. D. H. Lawrence, prolific in a variety of forms, met notoriety with the banned *Lady Chatterley's Lover*. Eliot thought Lawrence lacked social and intellectual training and there had long been surprise that anything good could come out of Nottingham. The critic Leavis felt that a man from Missouri was in no position to throw stones. After his post-war *Passage to India*, E. M. Forster had no more novels about his intellectual upper-middle-class world to offer. P. G. Wodehouse, in contrast, wrote a novel every year after 1902. Dorothy Sayers wrote her first detective story in 1923 and dons and poets rushed to emulate her. John Buchan continued to write best-selling stories in the intervals between helping to run the British Empire. T. E. Lawrence wrote about himself. Evelyn Waugh burst upon the public with his scintillating accounts of the dreary Bright Young Things.

Writing novels and poetry was not confined to the south of England, though that is where English writers tended to live, when they lived in England at all. In Scotland, 'Hugh MacDiarmid' delivered himself extensively on the experiences of a drunk man looking at the thistle. Those most active in Scottish literary circles talked about a Scottish literary renaissance. More congenial to the Scottish reading public were writers of the 'Kailyard' school of homely fiction – Annie S. Swan and 'Ian Maclaren'. They also provided English readers with their image of Scottish life. Gaelic literature, chiefly poetry, remained as detached from the experience of most Scots as it did from the English. On stage, J. M. Barrie's *Peter Pan* (1904) appealed north and south of the border. The Welsh industrial novel in English was slow to develop – partly because novel-writing was not a particularly Welsh genre. By the later 1920s, however, Welsh poets and short-story writers, brooding on their industrial wounds, were creating an awareness of Wales beyond the Principality. T. S. Eliot approved of Idris Davies, although he too lacked social and intellectual training. Writing in Welsh showed great vitality in traditional forms and largely reflected the different tensions of rural Wales.

Historians long to find in literature evidence of social trends, but writers do not write for their benefit. The richness and variety of literature does mean, however, that we can find social vignettes of every kind, whether of a Nottinghamshire mining village or Magdalen College, Oxford. Whether, in turn, that is what D. H. Lawrence and Compton Mackenzie try to provide is a matter to be referred back to Richards and Ogden.

MUSIC

British music was restored to life in the early twentieth century by a composer who looked like a cavalry officer, walked his dogs and loved the races – Edward Elgar. His first symphony received over 100 performances in its first year – an unparalleled achievement. Everybody could sing '*Land of Hope and Glory*' to his tune. He was a familiar figure at those musical festivals up and down the country which achieved new heights of esteem and performance. If there were relatively few professional musicians, the solid middle class sang and played solidly. It is tempting to think of Elgar in terms of grandiloquent imperialism – the musician of the empire *par excellence* – but beneath an element of bombast lay a melancholic awareness of the impermanence of all human institutions.

English composers even tried to write operas – Delius, Ethel Smyth and Rutland Boughton. The latter tried to create an English Bayreuth at Glastonbury in Somerset. At Cambridge, Edward Dent began translating and producing Mozart's operas.

The part-Welsh Vaughan Williams and the part-Swedish Holst wrote rather self-consciously English music, going back to English sixteenth- and seventeenth-century composers and to folk-songs. This interest in folk-songs was common throughout the British Isles. One English composer, Bax, even immersed himself in the 'Celtic Twilight' in search of inspiration.

Elgar expressed a willingness to 'write a popular tune occasionally', but the 'classical' world remained largely self-contained. In the home, the piano continued to dominate and the army of piano teachers expanded. Brass bands became even more popular and were paraded on the slightest pretext. Working class though they largely were, the bands were becoming musically 'respectable'. Elgar, at the close of his career, bridged a social and cultural gap by writing a special suite for brass. A blending of musical offerings also emerged from the seaside orchestras at resorts like Bournemouth and Scarborough. Music could be provided for all occasions to suit every ear. Glamour surrounded the stars of the music-hall. Popular songs of the pre-1914 era have survived to the present and still encourage us to keep right on to the end of the road. The halls flourished in the big cities and there was a vast network of concert parties touring the country.

Outside influences on the British popular music scene were still few, but they were increasing and they came from across the Atlantic rather than from

Europe. The wild craze for the cakewalk and ragtime reached London in 1906. The Viennese waltz was in competition with Scott Joplin, though it held its own in the 1920s. After the war, American influences became even more pronounced. Jazz came to England in 1919, brought by the (white) Original Dixieland Jazz Band direct to the Hammersmith Palais. Louis Armstrong, Duke Ellington and Paul Whiteman soon became well known. All sorts of people began to sing the 'blues'. Musicals by Jerome Kern or George Gershwin were the rage in the later 1920s. One could execute a shimmy, Charleston or tango, for this was the Jazz Age. The unjazzy Gracie Fields from Rochdale put up 'Sally, Pride of our Alley' to compete with 'dear old Swannee'. It also became apparent, as one would expect, that a Lancashire lass excelled at 'Singing in the Rain'.

'Serious' composing did not cease with Elgar (whose last major composition was in 1919). A Lancashire lad, William Walton, shocked and dazzled post-war salons, but also breathed new life into the venerable English oratorio. Other young composers of the 1920s, Arthur Bliss and Constant Lambert experimented with jazz rhythms in some works and also broke new ground by writing ballet music – a further indication of widening musical horizons.

PAINTING AND SCULPTURE

British painting remained self-contained at the beginning of the century. A Gauguin, Matisse or Kandinsky only impinged on an insular public after two exhibitions of Post-Impressionist paintings organized in London by Roger Fry in 1910 and 1912. Augustus John, Wyndham Lewis, Stanley Spencer and Paul Nash all assimilated these revelations to some degree. John spent the four years before the war camping with gypsies, more anxious to preserve his fame as a Bohemian than as a painter. Conflicts between individuals and schools of thought abounded. Some resented Fry's attempt to set aesthetic rules, while acknowledging his services in promoting an awareness of European developments. Wyndham Lewis, perhaps because he was born on a yacht off Nova Scotia, was invariably quarrelling and forming Rebel Art Centres. Jacob Epstein's nude figures executed on a London building in 1908 caused outrage. After the war, the Southern Rhodesian government happened to take over the building and began actively to assist the weather in destroying the offending figures.

The war had a deep effect on Epstein and other painters and sculptors. A number of his post-war works have been interpreted as a revulsion against the horrors of war. Many British artists saw active service and the 'War Artist Scheme' sent Nash, Lewis, John and others to the front to paint. Nash in particular mingled the monstrous and the magical in powerful combination. After the war, the tone was initially set by the 'Bloomsbury' influences of Fry, Duncan Grant and Vanessa Bell. Fry struck a profound note when he observed that artists were increasingly constrained by 'the exiguity of modern apartments'. Stanley Spencer's unique, if increasingly predictable vision, attracted much attention. There was one exciting figure, the Glasgow architect, designer and painter Charles Rennie Mackintosh, but at the time he was more respected in

Germany and even Russia than in Britain. Art deco flowered briefly in the wake of the 1925 Paris Exhibition. The building of cinemas allowed some scope for decorative extravagance. Epstein's post-war work for London Transport at St James's Park station led to him not receiving another commission for twenty years from a public body. Reliefs by Gill, Moore and others for the same building caused less excitement, probably because they could scarcely be seen. Moore and Barbara Hepworth, who had spent substantial periods in France and Italy respectively, gave their first public exhibitions in London in 1928. There was nothing insular about their outlook(238).

In general, the British public was not greatly concerned about the country's standing in the world of the fine arts. Even so, the augmentation of existing collections in London, Glasgow and elsewhere did allow more people to see a greater range of paintings than ever before. Private benefactors brought a fine group of pictures to Hull and Cardiff, places not hitherto thought of in terms of painting. The National Art-Collections Fund, set up in 1903, did its inadequate best to prevent masterpieces from British collections being sold to foreign buyers. Few artists starved and some became very wealthy. The possibility of interesting a wider section of the population in art now existed on a wider scale, certainly outside London, than had ever existed before; it still remained to be exploited.

RADIO

'I still believe', wrote John Reith in his diary in October 1922, 'there is some great work for me to do in the world.'[3] A few months later he became general manager of the new British Broadcasting Company. The public first became aware of broadcasting in 1920 when the *Daily Mail* sponsored a recital by Dame Nellie Melba transmitted by the Marconi Company. The effect was so stunning that there was no repetition for about eighteen months. Pressure then mounted from various firms wishing to market receivers and this new company received an official licence to transmit and, in effect, a monopoly. Reith, a sturdy Scot, believed that the new broadcasters had a duty to uplift as well as entertain the listeners. American broadcasting dismayed him and he wanted a 'high moral tone' in Britain. A 1925 government committee concluded that it would be quite improper for any broadcasting company to make a profit. It would also be wrong to set aside wavelengths for groups of listeners, however large, who pressed for 'trite and commonplace performances'.

The Company became the Corporation in 1926, with a Board of Governors appointed by the Crown on the advice of the Prime Minister. Reith introduced public figures to the new medium. The archbishop of Canterbury, recovering swiftly from his justified amazement that it was possible to listen to a wireless with the window open, conducted a studio service at the end of 1923. King George was first heard over the air at the opening of the Wembley Exhibition in 1924. Political leaders first submitted during the 1924 General Election, though only the canny Baldwin took the trouble to learn the tricks of the trade – and he had his reward. Daventry, then the biggest transmitting station in the world, opened in July 1925, ensuring that 94 per cent of Britain could receive the National programme and benefit from 'the amenities of Metropolitan culture'. Well over 2 million untrite listeners had licences in 1927. But even before radio had fully established itself, a competitor was in the wings; complex talks were already afoot with another Scottish son of the manse – J. L. Baird. A 'televisor' was installed at 10 Downing Street to allow Ramsay MacDonald and his family to see Gracie Fields. No one could grasp what the impact of radio and television would be on the culture of the country, but it was clearly an exciting development(250).

THE FILM

At the Regent Street Polytechnic in London on 20 February 1896 the first commercial film show in Britain was staged. In the following years, new apparatus followed new apparatus and in 1904 the Daily Bioscope offered patrons regular shows in a converted shop in Billingsgate. The first films were usually newsreels – a cameraman went with the explorer Scott to the Antarctic in 1910. The colour process was discovered in 1906. King George and Queen Mary were staggered by the colour pictures of the Delhi durbar. The leading theatres in London gingerly allowed a film a weekly showing. The Shepherd's Bush studios were opened in 1914 and films became more ambitious, or at least lasted longer. Stars of music-hall and stage offered themselves to the new medium. Picture palaces sprang up all over the country and a new form of popular entertainment had become established in about a decade.

But was it an art form? Not in Britain, seems to be the critical verdict. The close links between writers, painters and film, evident in Europe, did not exist in Britain. Only with the founding of the London Film Society in 1925 could professional film-makers and film-goers see regularly the best foreign films. Whatever the quality, however, the film had come to stay and its uses multiplied. The film of the Battle of the Somme gave people at home at least some idea of what things were like at the front. Perhaps as many as 20 million people were going to 'the pictures' every week by 1917. The idea of the 'newsreel' was an early development, though not yet a very sophisticated one. Fierce commercial battles for cinema chains caught the headlines. The British film industry could not compete with the glamour and panache of Hollywood and by 1926 British films only constituted 5 per cent of what were shown on British screens. The 1927 Cinematograph Act tried to reverse this situation by introducing a quota system and banning the 'blind' booking of American films. One talented director emerged – Alfred Hitchcock – but his films in the mid-1920s were made in Germany. Even so, as the 'silent' era in the cinema ended in the late 1920s there was more optimism among British producers that they would be able to flourish in the age of the 'talkies'.

Thirty years after Hobson and others speculated on the subject of culture in an age of democracy, it might be said that neither the worst fears nor the best hopes had been realized. Pessimists who feared that the 'swinish multitude' would obliterate the cultural achievement of the inspired few in music, painting or literature were wrong. Optimists who dreamed of a core of 'true' culture released from restrictions of class or region were disappointed. Although critics hesitated about the appropriate terms, 'high', 'middle' and 'low' culture, all flourished. Aesthetic and sociological categories were closely related, but not in a simple fashion. Regional cultures complicated the critical assumptions of London, Oxford, Cambridge or Edinburgh. Education, broadcasting and the press might in time establish a 'central tradition' transcending class and region, but it had not yet appeared. The BBC was to be forced to develop a regional network. The provincial papers of Leeds, Manchester, Birmingham or Glasgow retained a powerful local appeal, but the relentless penetration of the London-based dailies even into Wales and Scotland did contribute to a degree of nationally shared information almost without parallel elsewhere in Europe. Newspaper circulations continued to rise, though radio might well affect their further advance. The invention of the crossword proved a major boon, although its cultural status was uncertain.

---

1. Cited in R. Williams, *Culture and society* (1961) Pelican edn., pp. 166–9 and pp. 187–190
2. J. A. Hobson, *The social problem* (1902) pp. 127–9
3. J. C. W. Reith, *Into the wind* (1949), p. 81

PART THREE

1931–1956

FRAMEWORK OF EVENTS 1932-1955

1932   World Disarmament Conference opens (Feb): Import Duties Act: Ottawa agreements on imperial preference – Free Trade Liberals resign: Lytton report on Manchuria (Oct): Mosley founds British Union of Fascists (Dec).

    Reunification of the Methodist churches in Britain: Shakespeare Memorial Theatre opens at Stratford-upon-Avon: Rutherford, Cockcroft and Chadwick split the atom.

1933   Hitler becomes *Reichskanzler* (Jan): World Economic Conference in London (June): Special Areas (Development and Improvement) Act (Dec): Oxford Union debate, 'King and Country'.

    London Passenger Transport Board formed: British Film Institute founded: Odeon cinema circuit.

1934   Mosley speaks at Olympia (June): London Naval Disarmament Conference ends without agreement (Oct–Dec).

    British Iron and Steel Federation formed: Peace Pledge Union founded: *Queen Mary* launched: J. B. Priestley, *English Journey*.

1935   Stresa Conference between Britain, France and Italy (Apr): British–German naval agreement (June): Publication of the Peace Ballot organized by the League of Nations Union (June): Riots in Belfast: Government of India Act (Aug): Italy invades Abyssinia (Oct): General Election (Nov): Hoare–Laval proposals (Dec) – Hoare resigns.

    British Council founded: Left Book Club starts: Jubilee of King George V: Watson-Watt invents radar: Eliot, *Murder in the Cathedral*.

1936   London naval treaty (Mar): Germany reoccupies Rhineland demilitarized zone: Franco rebellion in Spain (July): Anglo-Egyptian treaty (Aug): Abdication of Edward VIII (Dec) and accession of his brother George VI.

    Allen Lane starts Penguin Books: J. M. Keynes, *General Theory*.

1937   'Gentleman's agreements' with Italy (Jan): Britain and France release Belgium from Locarno obligations (April): Indian Constitution comes into operation (Apr): Chamberlain succeeds Baldwin as PM (May): Royal Commission on Palestine recommends end of mandate and establishment of Jewish and Arab states (July): Nyon Conference (Sept): Halifax visits Hitler (Nov): Irish Free State removes oath to the Crown. (Dec).

    Billy Butlin's first holiday camp at Skegness: Oxford Conference on Church, Community and State.

1938   Eden resigns as Foreign Secretary (Feb): German troops enter Austria – Anschluss proclaimed (Mar): Pact with Italy recognizes Italian sovereignty over Ethiopia (Apr): 'May crisis' over Czechoslovakia: Runciman mission to Czechoslovakia (July): Chamberlain visits Hitler at Berchtesgaden and Godesberg (15 and 27 Sept): Munich agreement (29 Sept).

    Lord Amulree's committee recommends a week's holiday with pay as the national standard: *Queen Elizabeth* launched: Spens Report on secondary education: Women's Voluntary Service founded: Empire Exhibition in Glasgow.

1939   Britain recognizes Franco gvt. in Spain (Feb): Guarantee to Poland (Mar): German troops enter Czechoslovakia (Mar): Italy occupies Albania (Apr): British guarantee to Romania and Greece (Apr): Germany invades Poland (1 Sept).
Second World War:
    Britain and France declare war on Germany (3 Sept): *Royal Oak* sunk in Sca-

pa Flow (Oct): Soviet Union invades Finland (Nov): Battle of the River Plate (Dec).

1940　Finland signs peace treaty with Soviet Union (Mar): Germany invades Norway and Denmark (Apr): Germany invades Belgium and The Netherlands (May): Churchill replaces Chamberlain as PM (May): British forces evacuate from Dunkirk (May–June): France capitulates (June): Royal Navy sinks French fleet (July): Italy declares war on Britain (July): Battle of Britain (Aug–Sept).

1941　British forces active in North and East Africa (Jan–Feb): US Lend-Lease Bill signed (Mar): Standard rate of income tax reaches 50 per cent (Apr): House of Commons destroyed (May): Germany invades Soviet Union (June): British occupy Syria (July): British–American 'Atlantic Charter' (Aug): Civil Defence organized: 'Russian tank week' (Sept): Second British Libyan offensive (Nov): Japan attacks Pearl Harbor – Britain declares war on Japan (Dec): Sinking of *Prince of Wales* and *Repulse* in Far East.

1942　Japanese capture Singapore (Feb) and Rangoon (Mar): British–Soviet treaty of friendship (May): Indian Congress rejects self-gvt terms offered by Cripps (Apr): Dieppe raid (Aug): British victory at El Alamein (Nov): Allied landings in N. Africa (Nov).

1943　Churchill and Roosevelt confer at Casablanca – 'unconditional surrender' proclaimed (Jan): British troops enter Tripoli (Jan): Axis surrender in North Africa (May): Allies invade Sicily (July): Allies invade Italy (Sept): Churchill, Roosevelt and Stalin meet at Teheran (Nov–Dec): Battle of the Atlantic.

1944　Allied landing at Anzio (Jan): Allies take Rome (June): D-day landing in Normandy (June): VI bombardment of Britain begins: Allies enter Paris (Aug): Churchill and Roosevelt confer at Quebec (Sept): Churchill visits Moscow (Oct): Bretton Woods agreement on post-war economic world order (July)

1945　Yalta agreement (Feb): British troops reach the Rhine (Feb) and cross (Mar): VE day – final German surrender (May): United Nations Charter promulgated (June): Potsdam Conference and agreement (July–Aug): General Election – Labour victory (July): Atomic bombs dropped on Hiroshima and Nagasaki (Aug) – VJ day (14 Aug): Beveridge Report (1942): White Paper on employment policy after the war (1944): Butler Education Act (1944). All-India Congress rejects British proposals for self-gvt (Sept): British gvt takes emergency powers following ending of Lend-Lease (Oct): United States offers loan to Britain (Dec).

　　　Perfection of polythene (1939): Greene, *The Power and the Glory* (1940). Penicillin made effective by Florey (1940): Temple, *Christianity and Social Order* (1942).

1946　Trade Disputes Act repealed: Bank of England nationalized: National Health Act (Nov): Churchill's 'Iron Curtain' speech in the United States (Mar).

　　　First British landplane service with New York opened (July): Reith Committee on New Towns reports: Arts Council founded.

1947　Peace treaties with Italy, Hungary, Romania, Bulgaria and Finland (Feb): Fuel crisis (Feb): General Marshall's speech leads to dvlpt of Marshall Aid programme (June): Sterling made convertible (July), but convertibility suspended (Aug): Attlee states that power would be transferred to India not later than June 1948. Transfer of power in fact takes place on 24 August: Budget leak – Cripps replaces Dalton at the Exchequer (Nov).

　　　First Edinburgh International Festival (Aug): School-leaving age raised to 15 (Apr): Dominions Office change to Commonwealth Relations Office (July).

1948　British Railways formed (Jan): Last British troops leave India (Feb) – Burma becomes independent and leaves Commonwealth: Brussels Treaty Organization formed (Mar): Electricity industry nationalized (Apr): Wage 'freeze' and dividend restraint (Feb): Formation of OEEC (Apr): Churchill speaks at The Hague Conference on European unity (May): Marshall Aid agreement (July): Berlin airlift (July): Formation of the Monopolies Commission (July): British withdrawal from Palestine completed (Aug): Republic of Ireland Act passed in Dublin Parliament (Dec): National Health Service inaugurated.

1949   North Atlantic Treaty Organization formed (Apr): Republic of Ireland fully inaugurated (leaves the Commonwealth) (Apr): Commonwealth PMs accept India's wish to remain a member as a republic (Apr): First meeting of Council of Europe (May): Devaluation of sterling, £1 = $2.80 (Sept).

Orwell, *1984*: Clothes rationing ends (March).

1950   British recognizes Communist China (Jan): General Election – narrow Labour victory (Feb): End of UK petrol rationing (May): Renewed fighting in Malaya: North Korea invades South Korea (June) – British troops in action (Sept): Schuman plan announced (May): European Payments Union established (Sept): Gaitskell replaces Cripps at the Exchequer (Oct): Marshall Aid suspended (Dec): Stone of Scone removed from Westminster Abbey (Dec).

1951   Major rearmament programme (Jan): Morrison replaces Bevin as Foreign Secretary (May): Burgess and Maclean flee to the Soviet Union (June): Peace treaty with Japan (Sept): Iranian gvt nationalizes its oil industry: London foreign exchange market reopens (Dec): General Election – Cons. victory (Oct).

Festival of Britain (July–Sept): Stone of Scone returns to Westminster Abbey (Aug): General Certificate of Education introduced in England and Wales.

1952   Death of George VI (Feb) – Elizabeth II succeeds: British atomic bomb exploded off Australia (Oct): Abolition of British identity cards (Feb): State of emergency declared in Kenya (Oct).

Comet makes first passenger jet aircraft flights.

1953   Coronation of Elizabeth II – televised for the first time (June): Korean armistice signed (July): Federal Constitution for the Rhodesias and Nyasaland implemented (Oct).

Hillary climbs Everest (May): Sweet (Feb) and sugar (Sept) rationing ends.

1954   Agreements on Indo-China at Geneva – UK co-chairing the conference with the Soviet Union (July): European Defence Community plan finally abandoned (Aug): Formation of South-East Asia Treaty Organization (Sept): London 9-power agreement on European security: Western European Union formed (Oct): Nasser becomes Head of State in Egypt (UK having evacuated the Suez base) (Nov): UK becomes associate of the European Coal and Steel Community (formed in April 1951) (Dec).

Formation of the UK Atomic Energy Authority and the Independent Television Authority: Crusade by the American evangelist Billy Graham: Disasters to the Comet aircraft: Amis, *Lucky Jim*: End of rationing: Bannister runs 4-minute mile.

1955   UK joins Baghdad Pact (Apr): Eden succeeds Churchill (May) and consolidates party position in General Election (May): Austrian State treaty (May): Messina conference of the European Six (June): Simonstown naval base returned to S. Africa – though still available for British use (July): State of emergency in Cyprus (Nov): Gaitskell succeeds Attlee as Labour leader (Dec).

Commercial television begins (Sept): City of London becomes a 'smokeless zone'.

CHAPTER 19

Europe: snare or opportunity?

During the Second World War, it was the BBC's custom to broadcast a strange set of national anthems – those of the Allied nations. At this time, central London housed political and military leaders from Norway, Poland, France, The Netherlands, Czechoslovakia, Yugoslavia and elsewhere(250). British politicians did not find these excitable exiles easy to understand, possessed as they were by a preoccupation with their own national futures. But the presence of so many exiled governments had one remarkable consequence: London became, in effect, the capital of free Europe. Perhaps the United Kingdom had a unique opportunity to determine the Continent's future – if she could resolve her own deep-seated uncertainties about the European connection.

Between 1931 and 1939, Britain had again found itself deeply involved in the struggle for supremacy among the European states. While particular circumstances obviously differed, the choices were similar to those which had existed before 1914. If one state dominated Europe, Britain's survival was at risk, but to go to war itself entailed great risks. The problem was global, for there were also dangers in the Near and Far East. Military planners saw a frightening prospect of a war on two or three fronts against opponents whose combined strength would be superior: Germany, Italy and Japan. It would be foolish to regard war as anything other than a last resort.

There was much public speculation about the character of such a war; in particular about the devastating consequences which might occur at its outset from aerial bombing. Books stressed that war would be worse than that of 1914–18 and could not be regulated to 'avoid or reduce its horrors and cruelties'. Lord Cecil and a number of well-known writers issued their *Challenge to Death* in 1934. 'For the British Empire', he declared, 'peace is essential not only for its prosperity but for its very existence, and peace means peace in all the civilised world, for once war begins, there is no certainty that its extent can be limited'.[1](66)

The other European states were not convinced that peace was desirable in order to ensure the existence of the British Empire. Even before Hitler's accession to power in January 1933 the Versailles settlement looked shaky. The Disarmament Conference, on which many in Britain placed great store, made no progress. The new states of central Europe were dismayed. The attitude of the Soviet Union was uncertain. Informed circles in Britain watched the rise of the Nazis with alarm coupled with an uncertainty about the nature of the phenomenon, but no one believed that Britain could or should go to war at this juncture. Some Left-wing writers believed that Germany's frenzy stemmed from the reprehensible attempt in 1919 to 'reduce a great nation to economic and political servitude'.[2] Germany was a 'have-not' nation surrounded by 'haves' – an analysis bitterly criticized in other sections of the British press. But criticism of Versailles had become so general that it was difficult to find anyone, even in the Foreign Office, who upheld its provisions *in toto*. The National government took note of suggestions that Germany should be 'appeased' in order to 'lance the boil' before it burst. Judicious concessions, perhaps in the colonial field, would calm the German fever.

Suggestions along these lines were put forward in various quarters – the subject of Germany having become one of exceptional public interest. 'Appeasement' was not to be equated with 'capitulation', but with a reasonable attempt to identify grievances and respond to them sensibly before they led to war. One alternative, to strengthen ties with Germany's neighbours, including the Soviet Union, seemed to most contemporaries merely a repetition of the balance of power policy that had allegedly caused the Great War. Other writers, and a large section of the public, still placed their hopes in the League of Nations and a policy of sanctions, economic or even military, against an aggressor. But the League had no power and whatever effectiveness it might possess could only depend upon the willingness of its important members to co-ordinate their policies. That presupposed a common commitment to the world status quo in the mid-1930s which was conspicuously lacking. Japan had already invaded Manchuria in 1931 and it had proved impossible (and perhaps undesirable) for 'the League' to take any action. That was even more likely to be the case in Europe and on its periphery. But in Britain supporters of the League organized a 'Peace Ballot' whose results were published in June 1935. Millions of decent Britons seemed to suppose that the League could be made to work by an act of will. The three Foreign Secretaries in this period – Reading, Simon and Hoare – did not share this conviction but had nothing very convincing, during their short terms of office, to put in its place. Pressure also came from another quarter. A disaffected back-bencher, Churchill growled and grumbled about many things. One of them happened to be Nazi Germany, though neither his analysis nor his prescription had the perspicacity later achieved on the subject in his war memoirs(19).

The burden of these pressures fell upon Hoare over Abyssinia and broke him. The Italian invasion of Abyssinia in October 1935 angered League supporters and seemed to threaten the communications of the empire through the Suez Canal. On the other hand, in the spring, Britain, France and Italy had reached accord at Stresa and to alienate Italy might throw her into the arms of Germany. In these circumstances, ineffective sanctions were applied, but in December Hoare and the French Foreign Minister, Laval, reached an understanding which would, literally, have left Emperor Haile Selassie high and dry on a patch of his territory but which would otherwise satisfy the Italians. There was a public outcry when these proposals became known and Hoare had to resign. Eventually, Mussolini did conquer all Abyssinia and the Emperor had to start a new life at Bath in Somerset. The Duce also interested himself in the western Mediterranean. Intrepid Italian troops were sent to assist France when the Spanish generals staged the revolt in mid-1936 which led to the Spanish Civil War. Spain caused great indignation. Some intellectuals and workers went off to fight for the republic in what they claimed to be the cause of liberty and anti-Fascism, though they had some surprises when they arrived. The National government saw virtue in a policy of non-intervention in Spain, though it proved difficult to execute (20).

At this stage, the British Left saw 'international Fascism'; the National government saw Germany. In June 1935, the government reached a naval agreement with Germany under which Berlin agreed to restrict her navy to the ratio of 35 per cent of the British. It made sense, so it appeared, to reach a freely agreed settlement on an issue which had caused such friction before 1914. There was, thus, an implicit recognition and acceptance of the fact that Germany was rearming. In March 1936, Hitler took a carefully calculated risk and reoccupied the Rhineland demilitarized zone, confronting Eden, Hoare's successor, with his first major test. A military response seemed out of the question and there was a widespread notion in Britain that Hitler was merely marching into his own back garden. Indeed, the irony of the situation was that Hitler had forestalled plans in the Foreign Office to negotiate over the Rhineland in the hope of gaining some quid pro quo. That card could clearly now not be played, but there was still a willingness, amidst suspicion, to pursue Hitler's offer of negotiations which might lead to a new pact; the Versailles system was tottering, if it had not already collapsed(21).

Hitler was unpleasant, possibly evil, but he was clever. The government and the Foreign Office could not decide what he really wanted. It seemed plausible to believe that he wanted to include all Germans in one state and complete the process only imperfectly achieved by Bismarck. He was an Austrian and his next desire might well be the unification of his homeland with the Reich. Independent Austria had largely been preserved by a benevolent Mussolini, who was no longer benevolent. The government could not prevent such a step, nor could the defence of Austria be achieved by the threat of a general war. The British Left hated the Austrian government anyway – young Hugh Gaitskell was the Scarlet Pimpernel of Vienna, spiriting Socialists away from its evil clutches. Lord Halifax, terror of foxes on his home ground, was dispatched to a hunting exhibition in Germany in November 1937 and took the opportunity to explain to Hitler that if there should be any change in the status of Danzig, Austria or Czechoslovakia, the British government desired that it should come about through 'peaceful evolution'. And in March 1938, if the German invasion of Austria was not exactly peaceful, there was at least no fighting. It seemed that Hitler only moved when he was very sure of his ground.

If Hitler had a list, Czechoslovakia seemed likely to be next upon it. A multinational state embodying Czech national sentiment, it contained a substantial German minority, the so-called Sudetens. Particularly in the wake of what had happened to Austria, many of them clamoured to go 'home' to a Reich to which they had never belonged. Except formally under the League of Nations, Britain had no treaty obligations to Czechoslovakia, although the country excited a good deal of sympathy. But France did have such obligations, even if it was not clear how they could be carried out, and Franco-British relations held the key to central Europe. They were not good. To go back simply to 1935, London had given Paris no advance notice of the naval agreement with Germany. There was no common view about the handling of the Abyssinian crisis. The Franco-Soviet Pact, signed in May 1935 but not ratified until the following spring, was not warmly welcomed in London. But, despite the friction, there was at bottom an awareness that the two countries would be driven by events, if nothing else, into greater co-operation.

Successive British governments had resisted the idea that Britain could accept commitments in eastern Europe. To maintain such an attitude in 1938 might well mean that countries there would lose their independence – but was that a threat to British security? Arguments on this issue went on both within the Cabinet and between the government and its critics. Chamberlain, Prime Minister since June 1937, had taken a firm personal interest in foreign policy. In February 1938 Eden had resigned in a disagreement that was partly personal and partly concerned differences in the handling of relations with the United States and Italy. Halifax, his successor, was normally content to accept Chamberlain's direction. In September 1938, when there seemed a real possibility that Hitler would act to 'liberate' the Sudeten Germans, the Prime Minister took what was then the dramatic step of flying to Germany on two occasions for talks with Hitler to resolve the crisis. The agreement reached at Munich at the end of the month involved the detachment of 'Sudeten' territory from Czechoslovakia and other territorial adjustments by Prague. Hitler also pledged that the 'method of consultation' would be used in dealing with any other questions between Britain and Germany. At least for a moment, Chamberlain was exultant; general appeasement alone could save the world from chaos. Churchill, on the other hand, talked of an unmitigated defeat and a shameful betrayal of the Czechs. The argument has continued ever since(22).

The government, its unity only slightly impaired, was prepared to guarantee the rump of Czechoslovakia, but when German troops marched into Prague in March 1939 it held that the circumstances were such that the guarantee was inoperable. Relations between Czechs and Slovaks were bad. Thus the way now seemed open for further German expansion in eastern Europe. Initially, it was in this context that a guarantee to Poland – a major departure from tradition – was discussed. But, although it was difficult to see how Britain could help the Poles, opinion in Parliament and the country was now prepared to accept such a proposal – the German 'protectorate' over Bohemia and Moravia showed that Nazi ambitions were not limited to bringing all Germans into one state. By this juncture, British opinion (and, importantly, opinion in the Dominions) was coming to the view that enough latitude had been shown towards Germany. If Hitler ignored further ignored further warnings and attacked Poland then it would mean general war; still not an agreeable prospect. There was little enthusiasm in the government (though there was from Labour and Churchill) for an alliance with the Soviet Union. Rather strange negotiations took place, but they proved abortive. The Nazi–Soviet Pact was signed in August 1939. Whether greater zeal on the part of the Cabinet could have prevented that agreement remains contentious. Certainly, Chamberlain and his colleagues were not anxious to become entangled with Moscow, taking the view that the Soviet Union did not epitomize a new civilization.

When Germany invaded Poland in September 1939, Britain did go to war, even though little could be done to help Poland herself. There was rather less doubt about the justice and wisdom of this step than there had been in 1914. There was agreement, however, among Labour supporters and dissident Conservatives that a different foreign policy could have avoided war – though agreement did not go much beyond this point. But no amount of executive brilliance could alter the fact that Britain was again playing a major role in European politics while lacking the power to do so effectively. For most of what was now the 'inter-war' period Britain's imperial commitments had been deemed to preclude the possibility of fighting in Europe, and only in the last few years before 1939 was that assumption revised. It was in this unsatisfactory position of semi-involvement and semi-detachment that Britain approached the Second (and last) European War.

Poland was swiftly defeated and partitioned between Germany and the Soviet Union and then, over the winter, nothing much happened. Britain and France watched and waited, occasionally frightening the enemy by dropping pamphlets from the skies. The military débâcle in the spring of 1940 and its domestic political consequences – the rise of Churchill – are discussed subsequently. In foreign policy, the results were equally momentous. In a frantic, last-minute, gesture as France collapsed, Churchill made the suggestion of an Act of Union between the two countries. If nobly meant, it must have seemed like an attempt by Britain to gain control of France's colonies and navy. The proposal came to nothing and France signed an armistice in June. The Vichy regime was established in southern France and Germany directly controlled the North. The fall of France left Britain on her own. King George was not the only man to find some consolation in no longer having to deal with foreigners. It was a battle for survival. Victory in the skies in the Battle of Britain in the late summer of 1940 enhanced this mood of self-reliance. More sober spirits who, in gloomy moments, privately wondered whether Britain might not have to negotiate with Hitler also realized that it was difficult to see how the German domination of mainland Europe could be reversed by Britain alone. The Soviet Union had made its own arrangements with Hitler and they seemed to be still firm. The United States had not come into the war, nor was it likely to. Churchill did his best to enter into a chummy naval relationship with the American President, but Roosevelt was unable to be more than 'well-disposed'(23).

The German invasion of the Soviet Union in June 1941 changed one of these conditions. Churchill at once offered the Russians what little assistance he could spare. This commitment was formalized in July 1941. The Nazi–Soviet pact was buried and Communists everywhere rallied round to face the new enemy. The initial German successes in the East seemed to confirm the wisdom of the Italian decision to help Berlin by intervening after the fall of France. The Italians soon ran into difficulties in the Balkans when an attack on Greece failed to yield quick results.

The entry of the United States into the war following the Japanese attack on

Pearl Harbor in December 1941 completely changed the nature of the war, especially since Germany and Italy gratuitously declared war on the United States a few days later. Churchill was confident that, although there would be many hazards and setbacks ahead, the United States, the Soviet Union and the British Empire would win. It was also very likely that his two new allies would determine the general pattern of the peace settlement, at whatever date that might be. The alliance of the 'Big Three' was basically to defeat Germany and their interests thereafter might diverge sharply. Churchill worked on the ties of language and shared political values with the United States and an almost unparalleled period of intimacy and collaboration did ensue. To some extent, Churchill was the intermediary. Stalin never travelled far, leaving Churchill to visit Moscow – as in August 1942. The British Prime Minister went to the United States and Canada quite frequently. Roosevelt never came to London. When Roosevelt and Churchill met on 'neutral' ground as at Casablanca in January 1943, it was clear that the American was the senior partner. Churchill had little alternative but to accept the view that Germany should surrender unconditionally. Even so, Churchill could get his way in some matters, notably on the invasion of Italy and the timing of a landing in France. After the collapse of Mussolini's regime in July 1943, the Big Three, a little prematurely, were poised to arrange the future of the world. At the Teheran Conference in November 1943 Churchill had his first substantial experience of American–Soviet agreement (against his beloved Balkan operations) at his expense, though amity remained on the surface. In the last phase of the war, 1944–45, it became steadily more apparent that Britain was the weakest of the three states. Differences between Britain and the United States were apparent at the Yalta Conference in February 1945, particularly about France, Italy and, implicitly, future East–West relations. Such differences should not be exaggerated, but they did exist.

Planning for the post-war world went on at a number of levels. Globally, the British had signed the Declaration of the United Nations in January 1942 and thereafter took part in the lengthy discussions which came to a head at San Francisco in the late spring of 1945 to form a new body to replace the defunct League of Nations. Its Charter was ratified in October 1945. Great hopes may have been placed in this new body, but Britain's relationship with Europe presented the most immediately pressing problem. During the war, 'federalism' was in the air and Churchill espoused the idea of some kind of Council of Europe in 1943. In 1944, for example, the exiled governments of Belgium, The Netherlands and Luxembourg agreed to attempt a post-war economic union. Britain had two major difficulties, one psychological, the other political. The United Kingdom was robustly proud of the fact that she had neither been invaded nor defeated; she lacked the incentive to make a new start. Then the future of France and Germany raised enormous difficulties. De Gaulle had spent a good deal of the war in London claiming to be the embodiment of French resistance. Churchill had been more sympathetic to his susceptibilities than the Americans, but friction was not far away. De Gaulle was determined to see France fully restored as a Great Power but it was not clear that he was the man who would lead this struggle. He had chosen France, not the other way round. Likewise, Germany was to present great problems, but Britain was only one of the Allies occupying Germany and its future would be decided by the interaction of all their interests.

The Labour government in 1945, with Ernest Bevin as Foreign Secretary, tried to be optimistic. Great hope was placed on the United Nations. In Europe, the United Kingdom was extensively (and expensively) committed to running its occupation zone of Germany, but that was not seen by the government as a prelude to wider political integration. From the Potsdam Conference (July 1945) emerged the *de facto* extension of Russian influence in eastern Europe – perhaps an inevitable corollary of the war. The ultimate future of a disarmed and demilitarized Germany was still uncertain. Even so, Bevin hoped that the consolidation of Europe into two opposing blocs could be avoided. He recognized the Soviet Union's need for security, but hoped that free elections and political pluralism might be preserved in eastern Europe. There remained a vague notion that a Labour government might be able to influence the Soviet Union. After all, certain elements in the party were critical of the United States and the designs of capitalism. The Left accused him of capitulating to a Conservative and Foreign Office view of the world. However, uncertain of American intentions (they were supposed to be going to withdraw their forces), Bevin at times feared a tacit understanding between Washington and Moscow whereby all Europe, not just the East, would come within the Russian sphere(26).

Moreover, it was becoming increasingly clear that Britain did not have sufficient resources to sustain an independent role in Europe. Britain had liberated Greece, but was then caught up in a bitter civil war between pro- and anti-Communist factions. The success of the former was largely presented by the presence of British troops. In February 1947 the Labour government announced that it could not bear this burden. The following month, President Truman announced his 'Doctrine' – that free peoples everywhere should be assisted in preventing subjugation by armed minorities or outside pressure – and announced immediate aid for Greece and Turkey. In addition, in June 1947, Secretary of State Marshall announced American willingness to aid European recovery as a whole. Bevin set about organizing his European colleagues to make speedy use of this promise. Under Franco-British auspices, the Committee for European Economic Co-operation was set up in July. Whether intentionally or not, Marshall Aid in effect established the contours of American and Russian influence in Europe. The Russians would not participate and ensured that Czechoslovakia did not do so either. Most British people now felt increasingly worried about Soviet intentions. It was, therefore, reassuring to find that the United States now seemed prepared to uphold the security of western Europe. The Americans had come to the conclusion that they could not afford to see it collapse. In economic terms, Britain had little alternative but to grasp gratefully at what was being offered, though there was also a keen awareness of the extent to which American actions in restoring a capitalist economy in Europe corresponded also with American interests. There was a general, if controlled, resentment at Britain's increasingly subordinate status; the Big Three era was fading fast.

Bevin did not have much difficulty in accepting the political logic of the Truman Doctrine and the Marshall Plan. Events in Europe, particularly the Communist *coup d'état* in Czechoslovakia in 1948, were a severe blow to those Labour intellectuals who thought that a European half-way house between Soviet communism and American capitalism might be possible. The Berlin blockade, from June 1948 to May 1949, again placed the Soviet Union in an unattractive light. It was in this atmosphere that, in January 1948, Bevin announced plans for the 'consolidation of western Europe'. In March 1947, he had already signed a fifty year treaty of alliance with France – symbolically, at Dunkirk – but a revived Germany was still the putative enemy. Franco-British relations were in quite good order (de Gaulle had retired to the country and Communist influence was waning) and in March 1948 the two countries joined the Benelux states in the Treaty of Brussels. While the German danger was mentioned, the countries were concerned about the Soviet Union and pledged mutual and collective military aid in the event of aggression. Even so, in such an eventuality, the American attitude would be crucial and German rearmament also came into the picture. The Euro-American link was strengthened with the formation of the North Atlantic Treaty Organization (NATO) in April 1949.

A month later, the Council of Europe came into existence. The Labour government approached its formation very gingerly, partly because of Churchill's activities. The Conservative leader still saw himself as a roving world statesman and made a number of famous speeches. At Zurich in 1946, for example, he appeared to support the idea of a United States of Europe – though the text makes it clear that Britain, which already belonged to the British Commonwealth of Nations, could not join. Even so, Churchill turned up at the prestigious meeting of the Congress of the European Movement held at The Hague in 1948 – out of which the Council in part sprang. The Labour government declined even to be represented at The Hague. After extensive discussions, it was agreed that the new Council should consist of a Committee of Ministers and an Assembly of parliamentarians drawn from the member countries. They were to meet regularly to discuss matters of common interest, but their function remained consultative, not executive. The French and Belgians were upset by such an anodyne outcome. Supported by the Scandinavian countries, Britain had blocked the possibility that the Council might develop any independent strength. Even its limited functions gave Bevin some anxiety. The British sense of priorities in these matters was indicated by the fact that the first British delegation to the Assembly in August 1949 publicly argued about its expense allowances. Aloofness, if not hostility, to 'Europeanism' was not confined to the government. While Churchill dabbled, somewhat ambiguously, in European matters, the bulk of the Conservative party and public opinion as a whole remained largely indifferent(25).

The events of the summer of 1950 confirm this impression. The freshly confirmed Labour government was confronted in May with a momentous decision. The Federal Republic of Germany had been set up in 1949 – the division of Germany having taken place *de facto*. The Christian Democrat government was anxious to strengthen its ties with France. Binding the two economies together would be a sign of amity; the pooling of coal and steel production, to be run by a supranational High Authority, would be the first step. Schuman, the French Foreign Minister expressed his support. Would the British participate? The invitation found the Cabinet dispersed and the issue not judged to be important enough to warrant its recall. The acting Prime Minister, Morrison, felt confident that he could react coldly. He declared that the Durham miners would not tolerate the plan – a devastating objection. In mid-June, Attlee confirmed that the interests and constitution of the United Kingdom were such that membership could not be contemplated. This time, however, the strange Europeans were not to be frightened by British hostility into abandoning their plans and the European Coal and Steel Community (ECSC) came into existence. The Conservatives criticized the government's decision, but their own reservations about the wisdom of any economic integration were apparent. Both parties looked on with imperial equanimity as the initiative in western Europe slipped steadily away from London.

The return of the Conservatives in 1951 did not produce a marked change. In the last few months of Labour rule, hostility towards western European developments had become rampant. Bevin, and his successor Morrison, both talked in private about 'standing up' to the pretensions of the Strasbourg Assembly, and even of withdrawing altogether from the Council of Europe. The idea that West German rearmament should take place within a European framework had little appeal; many Labour MPs were hostile to German rearmament under any auspices. The Conservative government showed no greater sympathy for any form of integration. Eden, the new Foreign Secretary, told an American audience that the British people knew in their bones that they could not join a European federation. The mooted European Defence Community was also a plan where British bones registered resistance, although in the end it was the French Assembly which voted against it in August 1954. In the following months, Eden took the initiative, touring the western Europe capitals, advocating instead the adherence of Federal Germany to the Brussels treaty and its membership of NATO on equal terms. Eventually, substantially this solution was reached. To make this agreement possible, Eden went further than any previous Foreign Secretary had done in peace: British forces in Europe would remain at their existing levels and not be withdrawn against the wishes of a majority of the Brussels treaty states – except in a grave overseas or financial crisis. All of this was worth while, from the prevailing British view, because it seemed to stave off the threat of 'federalism'. To their dismay, the British were shortly to discover that this was not the case(24).

At the end of his career, Churchill was determined to prove that his country was still rather special. After the death of Stalin in March 1953, he tried to arrange *détente* with the new men in Moscow. He also wanted the Americans to take part in a summit. Although a meeting was arranged in January 1954 (at Foreign Minister level), which led to the Geneva Conference on the Indo-China War, Churchill was disappointed. He conceived the idea of a personal visit to Moscow – a dramatic repetition of his wartime travels. By the spring of 1955, he reluctantly accepted that neither he nor his country could end the Cold War. He resigned in April 1955.

Eden, his successor, had never served in government outside departments dealing with international affairs. There was, therefore, an expectation that his newly endorsed government would excel in this area. Such hopes were soon shattered. As far as Europe was concerned, Eden had no wish to change course, but European politicians and officials still showed a distressing tendency to pursue the idea of closer co-operation in western Europe. After months of lobbying, Monnet, the retiring president of the ECSC High Authority, announced in October 1955 the formation of an 'Action Committee for the United States of Europe'. The conference at Messina in June, when the ECSC countries had discussed further common action, had encouraged him. A working committee was set up under the Belgian Foreign Minister, Spaak, to further these discussions. The British had not totally ignored these proceedings – a middle-rank official from the Board of Trade had been sent to Messina and, initially, there was British representation on the Spaak Committee before it was withdrawn in November 1955. Planning went ahead without the British. Eden smelt insidious supranationalism at work and the attitude in London varied between open scepticism about the European efforts and frank hostility to them.

A major reason for this detachment was that British ministers persisted in seeing the United Kingdom as one of the Big Three, automatically entitled to a leading role in any international conference. Britain retained its permanent seat on the Security Council of the United Nations. Eden played a prominent part in the July 1955 Geneva meeting which aspired to reduce tension in Europe. Even though there was little specific agreement, the 'Geneva spirit' did seem to have an effect on the new Soviet leaders, Khrushchev and Bulganin. The Foreign Ministers met again in November and, despite deep divisions on Germany and European security in general, the atmosphere seemed better. The Soviet leaders paid a visit to Britain in April 1956. There was a promise of greatly expanded trade between the two countries. But in the autumn the Hungarian rebellion broke out and was crushed by determined Soviet action. There was sympathy for the Hungarians, but nothing could be done to help them. It became clear that the map of Europe now possessed an ominously fixed character. The Soviet Union was not going to relinquish its hegemony in eastern Europe. In turn, in western Europe the Six pressed on towards the establishment of a Common Market. The British remained outside – at a time when the Suez Crisis disclosed their country's inability to act independently outside Europe. Until 1956 it was still possible to think that Britain's relations with Europe and the world had not fundamentally changed. It was not an illusion that could be maintained for much longer(27).

---

1. Lord Cecil et al., *Challenge to death* (1934), p. xii
2. C. R. Buxton, *The alternative to war* (1936), p. 30

CHAPTER 20

The last great British war

'We cannot foresee the time', wrote the Chiefs of Staff in December 1937, 'when our defence forces will be strong enough to safeguard our trade, territory and vital interests against Germany, Italy and Japan at the same time. . . .'(68) The government would have to reduce the number of potential enemies and also gain some allies. International developments made it plain that their assessment was not academic. The British Empire's vulnerability was apparent, but it was not easy to see how its defence could be made more secure in a short time. The public was only slowly appreciating the great danger in which the country was placed. Six years earlier, debate and discussion had centred upon disarmament. At the Geneva Conference in 1932 the British government urged that armaments should be reduced 'to the lowest point consistent with national safety'. Britain had already accepted some naval reductions and any further drop would have to be 'part of an international agreement'. In the months that followed, the world's naval powers naturally sought to retain what advantages they possessed and to safeguard their special needs. Experts spent a lot of time trying to define the distinction between 'offensive' and 'defensive' weapons. The desire to restrict or abolish the possibility of bombing came against the difficulty that facilities for civil aircraft construction could apparently be diverted for military purposes fairly easily. Even if there was a political will to find a solution, the technical problems of disarmament were very great.

Pending world-wide disarmament, it was the imperial position in the Far East which caused most alarm. Hong Kong and Singapore were practically indefensible and India was vulnerable if Japanese expansion in Manchuria should be followed by any further adventures. Military chiefs had no wish to be involved in a war against Japan, whatever the League of Nations Union might advocate. There was pressure on the Cabinet to abolish the 'ten-year rule' which had been introduced at the close of the Great War (p. 97). There is some doubt about when, precisely, that decision was taken, but in practice the assumption that there would not be another war for ten years did not survive Hitler's advent to power. Even so, the Treasury argued that Britain was 'no more in a position financially and economically to engage in a major war in the Far East than we are militarily'. The nation clearly wished to avoid heavy expenditure on armaments. Aware of this fact, MacDonald tried to put fresh life into the Disarmament Conference, but it effectively came to an end when Hitler gave notice, in October 1933, that Germany would withdraw from it and from the League of Nations. Not only had the proceedings displayed the very different approaches of Britain and France to security questions, they had also allowed German rearmament to gain momentum. The British public drew such a conclusion only very reluctantly. The Oxford Union passed a motion in February 1933 that the house refused in any circumstances to fight for King and Country. The views of undergraduates should not be taken too seriously, but they received some support outside university circles. Quite apart from financial factors, therefore, the government did not feel politically able to initiate a major increase in defence spending(66).

By the time Chamberlain became Prime Minister in June 1937 there had been some increased expenditure and some improvements, but large gaps still remained. The completion of the Singapore naval base was in sight, but even so, Japanese capacity was underestimated. Australia and New Zealand made their concern clear and noises were made in their direction, but was it really wise to commit the United Kingdom to sending capital ships to the Far East? There was the new problem presented by Italy in the Mediterranean. It was not until 1935 that the navy considered Italy a potential enemy. Before that date, the Admiralty had assumed that it could practically denude the Mediterranean in a Far Eastern emergency. Now the Chiefs of Staff warned that even a victorious war in the Mediterranean would possibly impair the navy's ability to carry out its wider responsibilities. There was an element of exaggeration here, but it was not until 1936–37 that the warship construction programme really accelerated. To decide to increase the estimates was one thing, to collect together again skilled men who had left the apparently declining shipbuilding industry was another. And even when the ships were built, they were not the fastest and best armed in the world. It is understandable that the 1935 naval agreement with Germany was thought desirable. The Chiefs of Staff had privately reached the conclusion that they could only send the fleet to the East if Europe seemed sufficiently settled. Of course, a good deal of thought was being given to the possible developments in submarine warfare, but the Admiralty continued to think of the submarine in the context of the battle fleet rather than as an independent operator. The limitations of this belief were to be sharply exposed in the war.

'When you think of the defence of England', Baldwin told the Commons in July 1934, 'you no longer think of the chalk cliffs of Dover; you think of the Rhine. That is where our frontier lies.'[1] He had promised a few months earlier that Britain would not be weaker in the air than any country within striking distance of her shores. In the following years, expenditure on the RAF increased, but dissatisfaction with its management remained. 'For some years now', wrote the Permanent Secretary to the Treasury, 'we have had from the Air Ministry soothing-syrup and incompetence in equal measure'(67). That was as late as February 1928. On the other hand, although after alarmingly little experiment, great faith was placed in the part strategic bombing would play in a future war. For a time bomber expenditure swept all before it, though before war did break out there was increased spending on fighter aircraft. The two principal British fighters of the Second World War, the Hurricane and the Spitfire, were now in production. This programme, together with the discovery and successful application of radar was to prove of vital significance in 1940. But before 1939 it was not clear whether the RAF was to help defend France in the event of an invasion or whether its mission was solely to defend Britain(64).

The army was in a similar predicament. It remained the poor relation of the services in fairly general estimation. The Report of the Defence Requirements Committee, for example, led Chamberlain to argue in May 1934 that 'our experience in the last war indicated that we ought to put our major resources into our Navy and our Air Force . . .'. He did not think the army would be used in Europe. The Chiefs of Staff argued in vain that without land forces capable of early intervention in Europe, Britain's inevitable lack of influence would encourage potential enemies and demoralize potential allies. At this juncture, Chamberlain was not persuaded. Subsequently, it was agreed to establish a 'Field Force', but even this was not initially to be equipped for Continental intervention. There was an 'almost instinctive aversion' in the country to such a prospect(63,68).

After he became Prime Minister, Chamberlain still believed that to expand the army on a sufficient scale for it to intervene on the Continent and to undertake its overseas obligations would mean a ruinous drain on resources. Sir Thomas Inskip was made Minister for the Co-ordination of Defence in December 1937 in a context where the different services pressed even harder than usual for a bigger share of a relatively small cake. The Cabinet still shared the view of the Army Minister, Hore-Belisha, that 'it was right to put the Continental commitment last'(68).

Against such a background, it is not surprising that in the autumn of 1938, at the time of Munich, the military view was that Britain was not yet in a position to fight. By the spring of 1939, in the rapidly changing diplomatic circumstances, there was more talk of the need to stand by France, and at the end of March the prospective size of the Territorial Army was doubled. Despite Labour opposition, there was even talk of military conscription – a step finally taken in August 1939. There was at length a readiness to accept that other dangers might be even more alarming than the financial risks. Nevertheless, from MacDonald's comment in 1934 that in respect to defence preparations 'we could not run the risk of a financial smash' to Simon's comment in 1939 that he feared the Air Ministry's programme could not be financed beyond 1939–40 'without the gravest danger to the country's stability', there was deep anxiety about the financial future(67). The difficulty was that no one could be sure when, where or how war would break out, and in what parts of the world Britain would be engaged. The only real test of the adequacy of preparations would be the actual war – but the outlook was not very encouraging.

The second war against Germany was not greeted with either astonished surprise or exuberant enthusiasm. Whatever disagreements there had been on defence and foreign policy, few doubted that Britain had to fight. Most, no doubt, still fought positively for King and Country – even Oxford undergraduates – but Left-wing commitment to the war was assisted by a loathing of Nazism. It was generally agreed that Germany would have to be 'purged' of Nazism and even be dismembered. Such desires seemed premature as Hitler's aircraft and armour swept through Poland in the first demonstration of *Blitzkrieg*. Then the lull of the 'phoney' war ensued. The British believed that they were making more efficient preparation than had been made in 1914.

Ministries of Shipping, Information, Food and Economic Warfare appeared without much delay. Chamberlain immediately formed a new small War Cabinet, mostly relying on his old associates, but making Churchill First Lord of the Admiralty. Fortunately, there was some action at sea. The pursuit of the *Graf Spee* was exciting and gratifyingly distant(71).

There was just one little war in progress in Europe. Having declined to offer the Soviet Union facilities on their soil, the Finns were invaded by the Red Army. They appealed for help and the British government agreed to send ammunition, rifles and 2,000 tons of peas. The Finns put up a brave fight, and for some months there seemed a danger that the British government would add to its burdens by fighting the Soviet Union as well, but the Finns accepted terms in March 1940.

On 4 April 1940, Chamberlain told a party meeting that Hitler had 'missed the bus'. On the night of 8 April, the German assault on Scandinavia began. The Royal Navy did not distinguish itself in the confused fighting that took place off the coast of Norway. 'We cannot go on as we are' was the feeling expressed in the House of Commons and, when confronted in the lobbies by loss of support, Chamberlain resigned. Churchill, not Halifax, was his successor. Chamberlain stayed on until his death later in the same year. Bringing Attlee and some of his Labour colleagues into the Cabinet, the Prime Minister formed his alliance to win the war. All he had to offer was 'blood, toil, tears and sweat'.

During the night before his appointment, the Germans invaded The Netherlands and Belgium. Under Lord Gort, the BEF in North-west France had gradually built up to ten divisions by May. The British and French intended to advance into Belgium if the Germans attacked, but only ten days after their offensive began the German Panzers had reached the sea at the mouth of the Somme. The British and French armies were cut off from the French armies to the south. Attacks on the vulnerable German corridor were urged from London, but they proved impracticable. The commanders on the spot considered that retreat to the sea and evacuation was the only answer. Churchill went over to Paris dreaming still of offensives – without effect. The evacuation from Dunkirk began on 27 May. This operation, in which almost the entire BEF was saved, was a masterpiece of improvisation. Over 300,000 men – more than a third being French – were brought out by 3 June. After a fashion, the French fought on until the armistice on 22 June.

The 'deliverance' of Dunkirk reinforced the British conception of themselves as an essentially island people, splendid in their sea-girt paradise. Churchill exhorted the people to conduct themselves so that men would say that 'this was their finest hour'. Men and women worked hard and long in the vital industries. It became a virtue to innovate and improvise. A million men joined the Home Guard. Mastery of the air would prove crucial and Lord Beaverbrook, as the relevant minister, gave absolute priority to fighter production. In retrospect, the British position was less precarious than contemporaries imagined. In a sense, Hitler had been too successful – he had not anticipated having to move against Britain so quickly and was not ready. He was, in any case, thinking about the East. He went through the motions of preparing an invasion force, while at the same time postponing the final decision. Since the German navy had been weakened during the Norwegian campaign, his shipping resources were seriously stretched. Everything hinged upon the encounter between the Luftwaffe and the RAF.

The Battle of Britain had no formal beginning and no formal end, but it lasted roughly from mid-July to mid-September. By the latter month, Hitler abandoned the possibility of invasion. The conflict in the air had taken place largely over London and southern England. The Germans were gravely handicapped by the limited range of their fighters and by the fact that, unlike the British, their aircraft and pilots were not recoverable. But the biggest blunder was the decision to bomb London at a time when the RAF had already taken heavy punishment and might yet have been crippled. At first this new thrust was successful, but the German losses mounted to an unacceptable level. Hitler turned to more interesting projects in the East.

Churchill looked to the United States, stressing that the whole world, including mighty America, might sink into the abyss of a new dark age if Hitler were not defeated. Lord Lothian, the British Ambassador, gave Washington a message which must then have appeared both frank and novel: 'Britain's broke; it's your money we want.' It was sadly true that London did not really want the Americans themselves. Roosevelt affably expressed the wish to get rid of the 'silly, foolish old dollar-sign' in transatlantic transactions, but 'Lend-Lease', approved in March 1941, was not simple generosity; it was a deal. Churchill talked optimistically about being given the tools and then being left to finish this job, but that was unlikely. The reality at home was the Blitz; Bristol received six full blitzes between 24 November 1940 and 11 April 1941 causing loss of life and heavy damage to property. That is but one example. The damage was not confined to the relatively near southern ports – Clydeside was another area to be heavily pounded. At sea, there were heavy shipping losses, threatening food and other supplies. Convoying and more effective marrying of naval and air patrols reduced, but did not eliminate, the danger.

Economists frequently made helpful and inaccurate predictions that the German economy would collapse, but this was a slim reed on which to rely for survival. The British wanted to do something, and bombing and subversion seemed the only answer. Bombing brought an obvious satisfaction to a nation which was itself being bombed on a comprehensive scale. Families huddled in air-raid shelters night after night felt some kind of satisfaction that something similar was happening in Germany too. Moral reservations slid away. Bomber Command promised devastating attacks on Germany, but through 1941 it, and not the enemy, was being crippled. The bomber offensives probably led to the death of more RAF pilots than German civilians. There was some surprise that Germans could take what the British took, but in November the air offensive was called off. The only other way to strike at the enemy on the Continent was through the Special Operations Executive. Highly trained individuals were sent across the Channel to indulge in sabotage and inspire subversion – though it would take more than a cloak and dagger to remove the German grip.

The only land fighting which took place was in North Africa where British forces were outnumbered by the Italians, who also had more aircraft. At the height of the Battle of Britain, the Italians advanced across the Egyptian frontier and then stopped. In December 1940, Wavell mounted a 'raid in force', advancing 500 miles along the coast and capturing large numbers of Italians and their equipment. The British were also successful in Italian East Africa. In May, Emperor Haile Selassie departed from Bath to Addis Ababa. The triumph in North Africa was shortlived. Rommel and the German Afrika Korps arrived in Libya and, Tobruk apart, the British were forced out of Cyrenaica. The situation in the Balkans was even worse. Hitler overran Yugoslavia. The British made a foolish, if valiant, attempt to save Greece, but by April 1941 they had to evacuate their forces. The Germans finished the campaign with a spectacular parachute landing on Crete. Churchill replaced Wavell by Auchinleck; not for the last time, he had an excessive faith in a new face(69).

Changing generals in North Africa did not hold the headlines for long. The following day, 22 June 1941, Hitler attacked the Soviet Union. Churchill drew a lyrical picture of Russian soldiers guarding fields which their fathers had tilled from time immemorial. Communist shop stewards in engineering factories eagerly helped their comrade, Lord Beaverbrook, now Minister of Supply, in promoting a 'Tanks for Russia' week. People began to itch for the 'Second Front'.

The United Kingdom declared war on Japan immediately after Pearl Harbor and within days Japanese bombers successfully attacked the British ships which had left Singapore and were on the high seas: the *Prince of Wales* and the *Repulse* were sunk. British naval prestige was shattered, though what made the ships so vulnerable was the lack of British fighter aircraft in the area. On 15 February 1942, the British commander at Singapore surrendered, with 60,000 British and Commonwealth troops. The Japanese attacked Burma next and India appeared to be in danger. If the situation in Asia was bad, it was no better in the North Atlantic and North Africa in the summer of 1942. At sea, the U-boat campaigns met with great success and Allied losses were running at over 4 million tons. The significance of the shipping losses was shielded from the public, but the loss of Tobruk, which Churchill had set great store on retaining, could not be disguised. Public opinion polls – a new enthusiasm – demonstrated that the government as a whole had lost support. Churchill's success rating came down to 78 per cent – for what it is worth, his lowest rating during the war. Even so, there was no one to replace him. Restrictions and rationing just had to be endured. Sweets and chocolates were rationed, to general benefit, if not applause. There was no petrol for private motoring.

Eventually, in November 1942, there was a British victory to report. Montgomery defeated Rommel at El Alamein. A few months later, the British and the Americans pledged themselves to demand the 'unconditional surrender' of their opponents. Churchill persuaded the reluctant Americans to permit the invasion of Italy. In the meantime, the planning of Operation Overlord, the landing in France, began. It was timed for the spring of 1944. However, after early successes in Sicily in the summer of 1943, the Allies faced increasing difficulties from the Germans in Italy. More generally, the British were forced to accept that Eisenhower would be the supreme commander of Overlord, though Montgomery was to make sure that his own role was not insignificant. There was a certain irony in the fact that it was the Americans who captured Rome on 4 June 1944.

The Normandy landings took place two days later, after delay and disappointment. Their success gave British morale a much-needed uplift. By the end of 1943, Britain had probably reached the pinnacle of its productive capacity. The rate of innovation could not be sustained indefinitely and the number of employable men and women was finite. Output from the land could not go on rising. Industry had to function largely with an ageing and tiring workforce. The mass of the population was beginning to find the ordinary inconveniences of life irksome. They had been borne bravely and cheerfully during the time of greatest danger, but as the pressure began to ease, so did the level of tolerance. It is not surprising, therefore, that industrial relations began to deteriorate and the number of working days lost from strikes increased dramatically. It was therefore fortunate that the Normandy landings were successful. Meticulously and ingeniously planned, they involved the greatest mixed invasion force the world had ever seen.

Paris was reached on 25 August, Brussels on 2 September and Antwerp on 4 September. What next? Much to his dismay, the decision was no longer Montgomery's. As had been arranged beforehand, he made way for Eisenhower once American troops in the field outnumbered British. Montgomery, attracted by a drive across the North German plain, wanted to capture the crossings of the Dutch rivers, but the British parachute drop at Arnhem was a disaster. Hitler's counter-attack in the Ardennes in December 1944 further delayed the Allies. The British people, however, had no doubt that victory would come. This was just as well for, since June 1944, they had their last experience of war on British soil. Flying bombs rained over England, causing relatively high casualties and reviving a phase of the war which the civilian population believed had ended. The V1 was then the most frightening weapon in existence. It showed that in a future war a formal invasion across the Channel might be redundant. After a little while, the Allied troops advanced in Europe on a wide front, as decreed by Eisenhower, and Germans forces were harassed. On 30 April 1945 Hitler shot himself and two days earlier Mussolini had been shot by Italian partisans. Henceforth, 8 May was celebrated as VE day.

British forces had played a considerable part in that victory, however much they had been overshadowed latterly by the contribution of others. The three services had combined to bring success. By the middle of the war, the Admiralty had come to see the vital importance of the aircraft-carrier and to set in hand more orders than could be completed. The engagement between the *Duke of York* and the *Scharnhorst* in December 1943, when the latter was sunk, was the last battleship engagement in European waters. No aircraft were involved. But, apart from the *Vanguard*, no further British battleships were built. The war also showed that the expectations placed on a naval blockade of Germany were too optimistic. Britain herself, however, had been shown to be very vulnerable to the depradations of the U-boat. It was, however, the American Mustang long-range fighter which helped gain mastery of the air and give British bombers their chance. Britain came a poor fourth behind the United States, the Soviet Union and Germany in aircraft production. The greatly expanded British army did, in the event, play an important Continental role in the final stages, but it was only a curious British perspective which placed the North African campaigns on a par with the German–Soviet struggle. Outside Europe, it was only rather grudgingly that the Americans admitted that British and Commonwealth forces could play a role in the final defeat of Japan.

It was the atomic bombs dropped on Hiroshima and Nagasaki which made Japan surrender. A completely new era had emerged, casting doubt on the future of mankind itself. The bombs were American, but Britain could be in a position to develop her own atomic weapons. Such a project had been under consideration since 1940 when Churchill attached great importance to it. 'It would be unforgivable', Lord Cherwell, his scientific adviser told him, 'if we let the Germans develop a process ahead of us by means of which they could defeat us in war, or reverse the verdict after they had been defeated.' Approaches were made from Washington in 1941 and in the summer of 1942 work was transferred to the United States for reasons of economy and security. Collaboration, however, was not straightforward nor without mutual suspicions. The British were tempted to resume work on their own, feeling that the Americans were trying to elbow them out, but, while the scientific base was available in Britain, the technology would require the diversion of men and materials urgently needed elsewhere. An agreement of a kind was reached between Britain and the United States at Quebec in 1943, but it was unclear at crucial points. By this stage, it had become evident that the European war would end before a British production plant could be built. However, Sir John Anderson was one minister who took the view that Britain could not afford to face the future without such a weapon 'and rely entirely on America should Russia or some other power develop it'. In November 1945, Britain, the United States and Canada affirmed their desire to promote full and effective co-operation in the field of atomic energy, but the American McMahon Act, 1946, forbade the disclosure of nuclear information to other states. Those privy to these discussions felt somewhat cheated, but not altogether surprised(70).

After the war, the incoming Prime Minister, Attlee, was determined to press ahead with a British atomic programme, partly for commercial reasons, partly because of doubt about American intentions, but most importantly because it reaffirmed Britain's position as a Great Power. Work began immediately after the war and the decision actually to make atomic bombs was taken by the Cabinet's Defence Sub-Committee in early January 1947, without public discussion or internal Whitehall debate. Progress was steady but not speedy. The first successful test was held in October 1952 on the Monte Bello islands off Australia. Defence thinking over the next few years focused increasingly on the deterrent value of the bomb. 'The discharge of our many overseas commitments in cold war conditions', the 1955 Defence White Paper declared, 'must continue to absorb a large share of the resources which we can make available for defence. For the rest, we must, in our allocation of resources, assign even higher priority to the primary deterrent, that is to say to the production of nuclear weapons and their means of delivery.'(73,74)

At the close of the war, the 'overseas commitments' remained formidable. There were armies in Germany, Austria and Greece and lesser forces in Palestine. 'So long as she remains a world power', wrote one contemporary author, close to Labour's thinking, 'Britain cannot but be interested in varying degrees in the future of Turkey, Persia, Iraq, Syria, Lebanon, Palestine, Ethiopia, Eritrea and the Somalilands.'(75) And that was just a beginning. A Communist insurgency in Malaya led to a state of emergency being declared there in 1948. Within a few years, some 50,000 British troops were in action in the peninsula. Imaginative leadership provided by General Templer after 1952 brought the situation under control, though substantial forces were still needed. In June 1950, the Korean War broke out when the Communist North invaded the South. The United States was able to organize 'United Nations' action against this aggression. The Labour government offered naval and air assistance and, more reluctantly, a military contribution. This formed part of a Commonwealth Brigade – a hangover from wartime habits rather than an omen of future military joint activity. The record of the 'Glorious Gloucesters' was good for British self-esteem. The Cabinet agreed, amid some party dissent, to nearly double the 1951 defence provision, to run over three years, compared with what had been agreed at the beginning of 1950. The economic strain was recognized, but so was the gravity of the international situation. It was the United States which bore the brunt of the fighting and, although Attlee did express concern about the possible use of the atomic bomb and ambitions of General MacArthur, Britain could only hope to influence Washington. Despite the termination of the Palestine mandate in 1948 – in circumstances of confusion and recrimination – Labour did not cease to think of a global military role. It seemed quite plausible for a soldier, Sir Ian Jacob, to write in 1950 that Britain required a 'peaceful, contented, and prosperous Africa' and in order to meet this 'requirement' Britain had to be ready to fight in the Middle East. In April 1955, Britain joined with Turkey, Iran, Pakistan and Iraq in the Baghdad Pact and, for a short time as it turned out, the RAF had access to bases in Iraq. It also seemed quite proper to exempt Malta and Cyprus from whatever self-government might occur elsewhere in the empire. Their military importance was too great. These mental attitudes only received a severe jolt after the fiasco of Suez.(75).

---

1. K. Middlemas and J. Barnes, *Baldwin* (1969), p. 775

CHAPTER 21

The British Commonwealth and the road to Suez

The British Commonwealth and Empire, declared the 1955 Conservative manifesto was 'the greatest force for peace and progress in the world today'. This hyperbole was an expression of confidence in the idea of the Commonwealth and its continued importance to Britain and the world. As far as the White Dominions were concerned, the 1931 statute still appeared to satisfy their political and constitutional requirements. They made their own decisions in 1939 but, with the exception of the Irish Free State, all came to Britain's aid. Of course, complete unanimity was not to be expected, but co-operation had survived the stresses of war. The only possible exception was South Africa where the historically anti-British Nationalist party came to power in 1948. The remaining old members still liked to belong to the British Commonwealth. Even though Australia and New Zealand were compelled to look to the United States for their defence, the British connection remained a way of warding off excessive American influence. Canada was in a similar position.

The major question was not whether old loyalties would survive, if in less strident form, but whether new loyalties to the Commonwealth idea could be implanted. And it did initially appear as if the great challenge presented by the Indian subcontinent after 1945 had been successfully met. From the time of their independence in 1947 and 1948 India, Pakistan and Ceylon (Sri Lanka) seemed to take almost as much pride in their membership as the 'old' Dominions. India did indeed quickly decide to become a republic which produced a new constitutional position. It was decided that a member state could become a republic and remain in membership if it was prepared to pay the exiguous price of recognizing the British monarch as Head of the Commonwealth. Thus, the 'British' Commonwealth was being transformed into the Commonwealth. Relations between the old and new members were good and the Labour government took special pride in the peaceful transfer of power and the enduring connection. Britain's apparent success was contrasted with the post-war armed struggles in Indo-China and the East Indies which the French and Dutch appeared likely to lose. The Commonwealth was described as a unique experiment, without precedent in history and full of promise. As a bonus, it might have the incidental benefit of preserving Britain's status in the world(48).

Even so, some countries departed. The Irish Free State left in 1949 when it became the Republic of Ireland. Burma declined to join on becoming independent in 1948. Both countries felt that membership entailed an unacceptable lingering element of subordination to the United Kingdom. It soon became clear, however, that the 'new' countries were not going to be dependent in their foreign policy. Nehru tried to disengage India from the Cold War and embark on a policy of 'non-aligment'. When a Commonwealth Division was formed in 1949 to fight in the Korean War it was composed of British, Australian, Canadian and New Zealand units (with a South African air squadron), but India would only send an ambulance team. Such latitude was quite compatible with Commonwealth membership and was accepted by the Conservatives after 1951. Churchill happily chaired the conferences of Prime Ministers (no longer 'Imperial') of 1953 and 1955 in much the same fashion as Attlee had chaired those of 1949 and 1951. The membership was the same on each occasion – Southern Rhodesia had 'observer' status – and London was the meeting place. The arrangements were in the hands of British officials. It was all very much like old times and not the outcome of the transfer of power which some predicted.

It was curious to see Churchill preside over such gatherings for their aimiable atmosphere vindicated the National government's policies towards India which he had bitterly opposed. In September 1931, it had inherited a Round Table Conference to discuss the future of the subcontinent, this time graced by Gandhi's presence in London. He had called off his civil disobedience campaign on the basis of a private understanding with the Viceroy, Lord Irwin (the later Lord Halifax). The National government would not make changes at the pace Gandhi demanded and at the expense of Indian interests he did not represent, yet it was not intransigent. The complexities of devolving power had become unnervingly apparent. Proposals for further self-government, though stopping short of Dominion status, were extensively discussed over the next few years. Hoare, then Secretary of State for India, supported by MacDonald and Baldwin, successfully carried the enormous Government of India Bill. Receiving the royal assent in August 1935, it in essence gave full self-government to the provinces of India and proposed a new federal assembly at the centre.

Some Conservatives in both Houses bitterly attacked the measure. Restless and frustrated, Churchill chose India as the cause for which to mount the funeral pyre. He painted a horrifying picture of what might happen if the British left India. His rhetoric was blistering, but his implication that Britain should stay indefinitely was unconvincing to most members of his own party. The die-hard imperialists were out manoeuvred. Yet, in a deeper sense, Churchill was right to remind his parliamentary colleagues of the facts of power. If Britain lacked the will to rule, as many Indians already sensed, then in time the entire colonial empire would also be lost. Then the United Kingdom would not be a Great Power.

The advent of war in 1939 meant that the Government of India Act had to be operated in very different circumstances from those envisaged in 1935. Britain took India into the war and, although there were protests, British authority was not in jeopardy. The replacement of the British by the Nazis held little attraction for most Indians. The war with Japan, however, had very different consequences. The naval disasters and the surrender of Singapore in February 1942 were shattering blows to British prestige. Even though the Japanese did not actually plan an advance into India, there was no certainty at the time about Japanese objectives and their presence in Burma was ominous. Churchill was under pressure both from his Labour colleagues and from President Roosevelt to gain the support of Indian politicians. Cripps, the nearest British approach to Gandhi, was sent out to intimate that full self-government would be granted immediately the war was over if a duly elected constituent assembly so desired. In the meantime, Britain would retain control of Indian defence. Despite his well-known sympathy for Indian aspirations, Cripps made no impression either on the Congress or the Moslem League. If self-government had been conceded at once, Nehru (though not Gandhi) would have supported the war against Japan. Congress decided on a civil disobedience campaign to make the British 'Quit India'. The government promptly imprisoned Nehru and Gandhi for the remainder of the war. When riots followed, British troops found themselves carrying out internal security duties and order was gradually restored. Of critical significance, the Indian army remained loyal to the British and the celebrated Gurkhas fanatically so.

Flushed with success after the Battle of El Alamein in November 1942, Churchill banged the British drum. 'We mean to hold our own', he declared, 'I have not become the King's First Minister in order to preside over the liquidation of the British Empire.' When, in the interval between hymn-singing and watching cartoon films, Churchill and Roosevelt had signed the portentous Atlantic Charter in August 1941, Churchill claimed that the references it contained to self-determination for all peoples did not apply to the British Empire. However, he was under increasing American pressure to end the British colonial era in Asia – a pressure which was not entirely disinterested. The retiring Viceroy, Lord Linlithgow, wrote that 'American uneasiness lest we should move over into the Russian camp' would be a useful bargaining counter in dealing with such suggestions (43). Some Americans, like Stimson, did indeed feel that the war would be won by the 'virile, energetic, initiative-loving, inventive Americans' whom he contrasted with the increasingly decadent British – 'a magnificent people, but they have lost their initiative'. After 1945, Labour politicians had no more wish to be thought decadent than did the Conservatives; they would dispose of their empire in their own way at their own pace. They had no qualms about returning to Asia after the war and the Americans would just have to put up with their obstinacy(44).

But the war had dented the image of British authority beyond repair. In India itself, there was little doubt that the incoming Labour government would transfer power. In 1946, Cripps again headed a British mission to try to reconcile the conflicting aspirations of the Congress and of the Moslem League. Britain had no wish to be caught up in large-scale communal conflict. Alarmed less further delay should be thought a desire to stay, Attlee announced in February 1947 that power would be transferred into responsible Indian hands by June 1948 and the British would then leave. The idea of partition was one of the solutions to be considered by the new Viceroy, Lord Mountbatten, and he soon came to the conclusion that it was inevitable. Reluctantly, Nehru accepted that the loss of life which might well accompany partition would be even greater if an attempt was made to preserve Indian unity by force. He insisted, however, that the British should make the final division of territory. Acting with great style and authority, Mountbatten successfully urged that the final date for handing over power should be brought forward to August 1947. The allegiance of the princely states remained a difficult problem but in the end, when the two states of India and Pakistan emerged, only the allegiance of Kashmir remained a source of tension. In the upheavals that accompanied independence, there was massive loss of life but, if saddened, the British were no longer responsible(47).

By 1948, Britain was not responsible for Palestine either. Its future was another source of British–American friction after 1945. Under Zionist pressure, President Truman in effect voted the British 'Morrison Plan' of July 1946 which had envisaged a federal Palestine, with Jewish and Arab provinces, under a British High Commissioner. American Jews continued to take a hostile view of British policy and to deem it pro-Arab. To Arabs, it still seemed too favourable to the Jews. As Jewish terrorism increased, and no agreed solution seemed in sight, British opinion came to favour renouncing the burden of the mandate. The two sides in Palestine were left to fight it out; both had their British supporters, though the division was not on party lines.

Party differences about the remainder of Britain's 'informal empire' in the Middle East were slight. In the summer of 1951, Morrison, Bevin's successor as Foreign Secretary, had to cope with the Iranian nationalization of the Anglo-Iranian Oil Company. The Foreign Office judged that the Iranians did not possess either the tanker fleet or marketing facilities to enable them to sell their oil abroad. It was best to let the experiment collapse – as it eventually did. Despite being a conscientious objector in the First World War, Morrison was impressively jingoistic. He toyed with the notion of sending troops to capture the Abadan refinery. Foreign policy, he thought, would be O.K. except for the bloody foreigners.

When the Egyptians also tried to twist the elderly imperial lion's tail, the Foreign Secretary reacted in a similarly fossilized fashion. 'Independent' since 1936, Egypt had nevertheless witnessed British troops installed as though they were in the Home Counties. After the war, Egyptian nationalism became more assertive. Negotiations for the withdrawal of British troops from the Canal Zone became deadlocked because the Egyptians would not, in return, co-ordinate their future defence policy with Britain. King Farouk proclaimed himself King of the Sudan and the British press savagely attacked this amorous and rotund monarch for his presumption. By 1953, when the Shah's authority had been restored in Iran and British oil interests seemed more secure, the Conservative government was prepared to be conciliatory. Churchill had condemned Labour's supposed policy of 'scuttle', but came to accept that British forces would have to withdraw from the Suez Canal Zone. The overthrow of Farouk and his eventual replacement by Nasser increased the pressure on the British to leave. In 1954, a phased withdrawal was agreed – greatly to the consternation of the 'Suez group' of Conservative MPs who believed that it would undermine Britain's standing throughout the Middle East. Future events were to prove them right – not that their own position was realistic. Britain now relied on the Hashemite Kings of Iraq and Jordan and in April 1955 signed the Baghdad Pact, a defence arrangement which also involved Turkey, Iran, Iraq and Pakistan. It was supposed to act as a deterrent against Soviet penetration. Nasser denounced it as nothing more than a device to prop up western interests and urged all Arabs to unite against it.

On 26 July 1956, President Nasser of Egypt announced the nationalization of the Suez Canal Company which was French-owned and operated the canal. Shareholders were to receive some compensation. The revenues would be used to help build a dam at Aswan on the Nile for irrigation and hydroelectricity. In London, the Egyptian action was seen as a monstrous violation of international law, confirming already deep suspicions about Nasser's ambitions. Egypt's sterling assets were at once frozen. The Labour leader, Hugh Gaitskell, declared that Cairo's action was high-handed and totally unjustifiable. Right-wing Conservatives shared Julian Amery's view that it was time to re-establish British influence 'on firm and permanent foundations'. Labour and Liberal spokesmen did not go so far, but they all deplored a unilateral disruption of international order and a possible threat to a vital sea route by a demagogic dictator. However inappropriate, lessons were drawn from the failure of 'appeasement' in the 1930s. Nasser had to be taught to obey the rules(45).

But who was going to wield the cane? The government was not anxious to use force, but would not rule it out. A possible solution was the formation of an international board representing maritime countries which would manage the canal jointly with Egypt. Menzies, the Australian Prime Minister, unsuccessfully took a proposal on these lines to Nasser in early September. British strategy then seemed to be to seek support at the United Nations Security Council. At this point, Dulles, the United States Secretary of State, took an initiative. Fearful that if the Soviet Union used its veto at the Council the British and French might feel justified in using force, he proposed an association of canal users, though American ships were not to be compelled to pay their dues to this body. The question did reach the United Nations in the first half of October and the Russians vetoed the 'Six Principles' on which the Security Council had agreed. Meanwhile, the British and French governments were in touch with the Israeli government. The Israeli attack on Egypt on 25 October did not surprise them, but on 30 October, with a fine show of impartiality, London and Paris called upon the belligerents to withdraw 10 miles east and 10 miles west of the canal. Israel complied, but the Egyptians refused. A Franco-British air bombardment began, followed by a parachute drop on Port Said, but on 6 November the British government ordered a cease-fire.

During the preceding week, the United Kingdom had been pilloried internationally in an unprecedented fashion. On 2 November, the United Nations General Assembly unanimously condemned the Franco-British action – a verdict which did not easily match the British contention that they were acting as policemen on behalf of the world body. On 5 November, the Soviet Union threatened that Russian rockets would supplement the fireworks and rockets normally seen in British skies on that day. Such unfriendliness was not surprising, but the reaction of Washington caused anger in London. While not expecting endorsement, Eden did not anticipate obstruction. The United States voted against Britain, France and Israel at the United Nations. When the

Americans put pressure on Britain's gold and dollar reserves the Prime Minister felt that he had been double-crossed by Dulles. As for the Commonwealth, the cosy cohesion of nearly a decade was shattered. Canada was openly critical and it was only Menzies who stood by Britain in a traditional way. The Indians were enthusiastically hostile and even Pakistan, which might therefore have been expected to be pro-British, declared itself moved by feelings of Moslem solidarity. Suddenly, glib assumptions about the Commonwealth came to be questioned. British politicians were forced to see that it was not susceptible to British guidance and, moreover, that the process of decolonization was still by no means complete(46).

The Suez affair disclosed that the British government did not now have the power, militarily or economically, to mount an overseas expedition if the United States disapproved. Leaving aside questions of morality, therefore, what had happened was a gross miscalculation of Britain's power and capacity. Even if the actual invasion force had been mounted more swiftly and effectively, the political ramifications had not been properly assessed. Nasser was not Arabi Pasha; the year was not 1882. The Egyptian leader was not some kind of moral recidivist but a man representative of his generation and region with whom, on new terms, a settlement might be reached. Even if it could not, there might be better ways of preserving British interests than by invading Egypt. Such a process of adjustment would not be easy. The props and assumptions of post-war policy had all proved unhelpful. Britain could no longer suppose that the United Nations would invariably find British policy congenial; the United States would, in the last resort, always look after its own interests; the Commonwealth was not likely to expand its ranks yet maintain the similarity of outlook and interest which had hitherto characterized it. After 1956, apprehensively, uncomfortably and uncertainly, the United Kingdom began to enter the post-colonial world(49).

CHAPTER 22

Party politics

When the National government was formed in August 1931, it was supposed to be a short-term expedient to deal with the economic crisis which had brought about the collapse of the Labour administration. Once the emergency was over, its work would be finished and the political parties would return to their ordinary position. What was being formed was apparently not even a coalition 'in the ordinary sense of the term' but rather the co-operation of individuals. Even so, the idea of an enduring 'National' government was not without attraction in some quarters. The post-war party governments had not been conspicuously successful. They had all been formed without a majority of the popular vote and for this reason their claim to possess a 'mandate' had its limitations. A 'National' government might more accurately represent the wishes of the electorate. The economic and financial position seemed to require that governments should possess the widest possible support. It was, perhaps, no accident that other countries in Europe seemed on the verge of creating single-party states. National governments in the United Kingdom would not destroy political parties but, by ensuring that the Cabinet included members of different parties in proportion to their elected strength, would make governments more representative.

Such a structure, however, had to reckon without Labour. While Snowden, Thomas and Sankey stayed with MacDonald, the great bulk of the Labour party opposed the new ministry. MacDonald himself was often reviled as a traitor and he was formally expelled from the party. Personal feelings ran high on all sides. MacDonald's small band could hardly be said to represent Labour as a whole in a National government. Inevitably, it depended upon the Conservatives and (divided) Liberals. Neither Parliament nor the electorate had been consulted about the wisdom of these arrangements but, apart from among Labour supporters, there was goodwill towards the experiment. Even Lloyd George backed it. Snowden's first step as Chancellor of the Exchequer was to raise income tax and cut public sector salaries in order to reduce the prospective deficit. However, he failed to check the financial speculation which had resumed within a few days of the government's formation. The American credits were running out. News of trouble in Scotland, where naval crews were refusing to work in protest against their reduced pay, further contributed to uncertainty, though the matter was soon settled. The drain on funds accelerated. On 19 September, the Bank of England advised the government to relieve it of its obligation to sell gold at a fixed price. Two days later, a short bill to this effect was rushed through Parliament. After all, the Gold Standard had not been preserved. There was some unexpected relief that this step had been taken, chiefly, no doubt, because of the belief that further severe deflation would not be necessary. Nevertheless, with the international financial situation so uncertain, it hardly seemed the moment for the political parties to resume their ordinary business.

Many Conservatives, however, had already decided that it was time for them to take power. They believed that an election would enable them, at last, to introduce a policy of protection. Churchill, the erstwhile Free Trader, put this point strongly in a public speech on 8 September 1931. The Conservative party was in an awkward mood. The previous year, Baldwin had had to fight to retain its leadership against attempts to remove him. Lord Beaverbrook, whose *Daily Express* circulated widely among all income groups, was the most vociferous critic. Showing courage and skill, Baldwin had survived the press assault, but he could not afford to ignore the mood on the back benches indefinitely. Naturally, the Labour and Liberal members of the Cabinet had no desire for an election at this point. It could only result in Conservative gains at their expense. On the other hand, a situation in which the Conservatives were in a minority in a Cabinet which depended on them, could not be expected to continue. MacDonald, Snowden and the Liberals were eventually persuaded that an election was inevitable. That raised the question of whether the three elements in the government should fight on a common programme; in the end, they submitted separate manifestos to the electorate. It was agreed that MacDonald would still be Prime Minister and the other parties agreed to serve under him if he succeeded in gaining a 'doctor's mandate', but the crucial issue was that of tariffs. The government professed to have an open mind on the matter, but in reality most Conservatives made little secret of their desire for protection. The Liberals tried to claim that they were adamantly opposed to it, but they were split among themselves and in financial difficulties. It was in this context that Lloyd George, a sick man at the time, declared that he had no faith in doctors or their mandates(101).

The National government gained a staggering triumph at the polls [D]. All the leading Labour figures were defeated, leaving only Attlee, Cripps and Lansbury with even minor ministerial experience. In a sorry state organizationally and financially, with the national and provincial press solidly against it, with the fear of inflation rampant, the Labour rout came as no surprise. Clement Attlee, a modest public school man who liked to use his military title, was elected leader of Labour because, for the moment, nothing better could be found. It was a grim task when the government's majority was nearly 500. The fall in the Labour vote was not quite as sharp as the drop in the number of Labour seats, but there was no doubting the verdict. However, from a National government standpoint the overwhelming victory had its drawbacks. Some degree of parity between its constituent elements would have been desirable, but the Conservatives were dominant and some Tory back-benchers were disinclined to defer to a non-Tory Prime Minister. They pressed strongly for protection, and if the Liberal and National Labour ministers could not stomach it, then they could depart. Baldwin's problem was that he had to control a huge parliamentary party without direct control over appointments and patronage. Even with a single-party government, he would not have found it possible to satisfy everybody, but when nine out of twenty posts in the new Cabinet were not filled by Conservatives, the difficulty was acute. The only consolation was that the scarcity of posts made it possible to exclude Churchill who had been associated with the recent press campaign against him. More generally, the National government protected Baldwin from elements on the Right of the party which found him too conciliatory. It was this circumstance that made a working relationship with MacDonald possible. The Prime Minister had no independent base but, initially at least, he still had a mind of his own. Later, he was a despondent and increasingly sick man before finally making way for Baldwin in June 1935. Despite the shock of a compliment from Churchill on his leadership of the party, Baldwin stayed calm and carried the National government through to another comfortable election victory [D].

When it was believed that there was a quick and easy answer to Britain's problems, the leading figures of this era – MacDonald, Baldwin, Chamberlain, Simon, Runciman, Hoare and Hailsham – were not highly regarded. They either could not see the solution or refused to implement it. Now, their record, if patchy and undistinguished, does not look abnormally so. They worked hard within an institutional structure which they had inherited and to which they remained committed. Sir Oswald Mosley with a New party in 1931 and the British Union of Fascists clearly thought the conventions of parliamentary government no longer adequate to the needs of the age. His national impact was slight, although his 'blackshirts' attracted a great deal of attention and a Public Order Act, 1936, was hurriedly introduced. Fascism never endangered the constitution nor was it threatened from the Communist party which likewise made no national impact although 'little Moscows' were located in some of the depressed areas of the country.

It is not surprising that the National government was re-elected in 1935 – and with an increased Conservative presence in its ranks. Unemployment, the major topic of political debate, was at its highest, at just under 3 million, from August 1931 to January 1933. By the next summer, it had fallen to around 2½ million and by June 1935 it had fallen to nearly 2 million. Production in that year was ten points higher than it had been in 1929. National supporters naturally observed that the corner had been turned, though they were not sure how or why (Ch. 23). It was extremely gratifying that this was all being done without 'New Deals' and 'Five-Year Plans' and such like. Newsreels, watched faithfully by millions, largely presented images of a society working together to solve its problems. The idea of a national consensus was a standard theme in the largely, sometimes stridently, pro-government press. And the government was abreast of the times. The benign Baldwin was better both on film and radio than the anxious Attlee. In the 1935 Election campaign, the National government sportingly sent seventeen cinema vans round the country and they were well received, even in Glasgow(103).

The problem for Labour was that while depression was general, severe depression was local and in areas where its support never wilted. The distribution of unemployment, therefore, reduced Labour's national impact as the party of the working class. In turn, the parliamentary impotence of Labour helps to explain the flirtation with alternative routes to Socialism. Such short-cuts, or 'coming struggles for power' seemed to have a particular appeal to some middle-class members of the party. At the 1932 conference, for example, Charles Trevelyan successfully moved the motion that the next Labour government 'either with or without power' should immediately promulgate 'definite Socialist legislation'. Labour managed a little rally in 1935 – it sent two cinema vans round the country – but the next Labour government was still only a dream. Leading members of the party could not decide how far to identify themselves with the protest marches of the unemployed. Many of them could not shake themselves free of the feeling that it was an unconstructive activity. High figures in the TUC had similar doubts, particularly about those under the auspices of the National Unemployed Workers Movement – a body under Communist control. Their view was that the unemployed worker was the responsibility of the union to which he had once belonged – but that began to be impractical. Slowly, however, the trade union movement began to recover from 1926. The General Secretary of the TUC, Walter Citrine steered a moderate course, trying to reduce inter-union rivalry and showing a willingness to be drawn into the implementation of the running down of some of the staple industries. He received a knighthood from MacDonald and criticism from the Left, for his pains(102).

Chamberlain, Chancellor of the Exchequer, was clearly Baldwin's political heir. He was brisk, efficient and determined – a man not greatly concerned with his own popularity once convinced of the rightness of his judgement. In domestic politics he was intellectually agile, but not one to be swept along by fads, among which he listed deficit financing. His position in the Conservative party was unchallengeable – both its organization and research section owed a good deal to his leadership. Yet, by the later 1930s, it was not easy to define what Conservatism had come to mean, wrapped as it was in National clothing – as Prime Minister Chamberlain sometimes talked of 'you Conservatives' rather than 'we Conservatives'(86). He was himself of nonconformist and commercial stock, Liberal in origin and with strong provincial roots. He was not a university man and his Cabinet contained only a faint tinge of the aristocracy. It is not unlikely that Chamberlain's essentially administrative brand of Conservatism would have gained a majority had there been an election in the ordinary way. There is one final paradox – he was not conservative in method. The mutual antipathy between Lloyd George and Chamberlain is well known, but in their dealings with civil servants and colleagues they were not dissimilar.

Whatever Chamberlain's virtues, he was not a war leader and his reputation plummeted as swiftly as it had risen. He could not project vigour and vision into a struggle he had sought to avoid. Parliamentary criticism mounted in the spring of 1940, though it may not have been shared in the country. Critics in the Commons, drawn from all parties, acted after the failure of the Norwegian campaign. 'In the name of God, go', was Leo Amery's advice during the debate on 8 May. The government's majority slumped from its usual figure of over 200 to 81. Chamberlain was not anxious to resign, partly because he did not wish Churchill to succeed him, but he had no alternative. The choice of successor lay between

Halifax and Churchill and, in circumstances that are still a little puzzling, the King chose Churchill. Ironically, he became Prime Minister because of the mismanaged Norwegian campaign, a failure in which, as First Lord of the Admiralty, he played a part. There was little inevitable about Churchill's emergence. His record over the decades led him to be regarded with suspicion by elements in all political parties, but at this juncture his ebullience and determination outweighed all other considerations. Right from the start he caught and kept the confidence of the public. He was an orator, cigar-smoker, boiler-suit wearer and above all a historian who also knew that he was making history. He never knew what it was like to travel on the London Underground, but thousands who slept there had reason to be grateful to him. Chamberlain remained leader of the Conservative party until his death in October 1940, giving Churchill loyal support in the Cabinet as well. Churchill then became leader of the Conservative party, but from the outset sought the support of all parties (105).

On the whole, the wartime coalition functioned effectively and, at least in the early stages, party differences were transcended in the common struggle(104). It was a more genuinely 'National' government than its predecessors since it contained, besides Attlee as Churchill's deputy, Morrison, Bevin and Alexander from Labour and the Liberal, Sinclair. Eden came back too, initially as War Minister and there were also former civil servants like Anderson. Over everything brooded the unpredictable genius of the Prime Minister, at last in his element. Even Churchill could not do everything and he inevitably concentrated on the major strategic and diplomatic issues. As Defence Minister (though without a ministry), all the Services received the benefit of his attention, in detail, though it was not always welcomed. Since both major parties kept an electoral truce, the Commons remained strongly Conservative, but even so there was greater consensus than during peacetime. The 1944 Education Act was a bipartisan measure. The treatment of the 1942 Beveridge Report on Social Insurance, however, was more complicated. Beveridge, with a distinguished academic reputation, had been asked to investigate this complex matter by a Labour minister. Social welfare would be a post-war priority whatever government was in power. Beveridge proposed a single insurance stamp which would cover people against all sources of poverty. His proposals excited an interest that was not confined to the Labour benches, but Churchill himself had doubts and, despite the report's fame, no legislation was brought forward. Labour's standing in the opinion polls was rising, perhaps largely because Labour ministers were in departments where the running could be made on social issues. Churchill's procrastination in this sphere and apparent total preoccupation with winning the war probably counted against him in 1945(106).

Inevitably, as the war drew to a close, there was speculation about the future of the coalition. Strictly speaking, government by one party had not existed in Britain for nearly fifteen years. Was it time to return to a system in which a single party governed? The answer was not quite as clear-cut as might appear. Conservatives were not indifferent to the need for change, whatever their opponents might say, and in the inevitably difficult post-war years an agreed programme had much to be said for it. Labour politicians, however, mindful of their increased stature in the public eye, saw a chance to show that a Labour government, with a majority, could work. The problem was Churchill. Faint hearts in the Labour ranks still believed that he could ensure a Conservative victory; a proposition which he was himself inclined to believe. But Labour doubts were overcome and the party won a famous victory. Churchill misjudged the mood of an electorate which failed to be frightened by his view that Socialism was 'inseparably interwoven with totalitarianism'. The largest single factor was a desire that the 1930s should not return again and Churchill himself could scarcely defend the record of governments he had strongly attacked at the time. No doubt, too, at a subsidiary level, the unusual shortcomings in the Conservative electoral organization played a part in what was still, for many observers, a surprising defeat. What was not a surprise was the complete eclipse of the Liberals, except outside England. The party now seemed to have no future, though there were still several millions in the country who thought of themselves as Liberals [B, D].

The astonishing extent of the Labour victory quickly gave rise to further established truths. Having at last mobilized its 'social potential', Labour would be in power for a generation. 'We are the masters now', Sir Hartley Shawcross was believed to have said – such a sentiment shows an odd sense of timing in a product of Dulwich College(107). It is true that Labour did not exclusively appeal to working-class voters. Many professional people considered themselves fortunate in that dawn to be alive. The war had seen a steady rise in the power of the State and it was not surprising that many believed that civil servants in government departments could solve social and economic problems. If the problems were mounting, so too should the number of civil servants. To an extent, such an outlook cut across party lines. The authority and scope of wartime government had been enjoyed by all politicians. For years, the men who now faced each other across the Commons had been colleagues in office. It was difficult for Conservatives to express enthusiasm for unguided free enterprise, though they tried sometimes. In addition, further contributing to expanded government activity, the war had blurred the line between civil servants and politicians, a line arguably somewhat indistinct. After 1945, the politicians generally regained their sway (though an appreciable number had been wartime civil servants themselves) but there seemed a greater need for 'expertise'. Dons, drafted into the Civil Service, often stayed on or were called in. These subtle changes did not make the headlines and officially there was a strong desire to claim that government and administration continued as before. The rebuilding of the war-damaged House of Commons in its old form (a very inconvenient building for its members) was a symbolic assertion that parliamentary government had come through the war unscathed. The supposed efficiency of Nazi dictatorship had been defeated by the inefficient Mother of Parliaments. Labour inherited this pride and it sat uneasily with its commitment to change.

Nationalization had appeared in Labour policy statements for years as the panacea for all ills, to be justified on grounds both of morality and efficiency. It came as a surprise, therefore, to learn that the new government had no blueprint. Morrison, who chaired a committee on the socialization of industries, successfully urged that nationalized industries should be managed by public corporations. The relevant minister would appoint the members of a board and they were to be ultimately responsible to him, but the ordinary business of running the industry was to be left in their hands. This arrangement would ensure that the employees would not be civil servants and the management would not be at the mercy of continuous detailed parliamentary scrutiny. It was yet another happy British compromise. Private ownership of key sectors in the economy was to end, but the State kept out of management. Nationalization did proceed broadly on this basis – the Bank of England and Civil Aviation (1946), the National Coal Board (1947), the British Transport Commission (with separate boards responsible for docks and canals, railways, London transport, road haulage and some road passenger transport), the British Electricity Authority and the Gas Council (1948). These and other lesser measures meant that some 20 per cent of the economy had been taken out of private hands. Some Labour critics began to argue that only industries with enormous difficulties were being taken over. They also wanted to know what was happening to the workers under the new arrangements. The new managers seemed even more remote than the old and 'public' ownership did not seem to involve the public(108).

The other major domestic change was the creation of a 'free' National Health Service (NHS) (1948) which offered hospital and specialist services, as well as the care of a local doctor and dentist, without charge. As Minister of Health, Aneurin Bevan bulldozed his way through the British medical profession to create a system of medical care which he believed was unequalled in the world. It was an unusual achievement for a country apparently on the verge of bankruptcy. Its expense did soon outrun the estimates and in the wake of the 1949 sterling devaluation Attlee announced a small charge for NHS prescriptions – a step which some Labour MPs regarded as a betrayal of principle. Alongside the NHS went a comprehensive social insurance scheme under which the entire adult population paid regular compulsory contributions and in return received, as appropriate, cash benefits for sickness, unemployment, maternity, widowhood and so on. Separate legislation established family allowances – a small weekly sum paid to mothers with more than one child. Taken together, these measures constituted the Welfare State, but it was inaugurated in the 'age of austerity'. In the early post-war years, the rationing of essential commodities – including bread – was more severe than it had been during the war. Cripps, the zealous Christian Socialist who became Chancellor of the Exchequer in 1947 when Dalton inadvertently leaked part of his budget, urged the nation to work out its own salvation and preached the virtues of hardwork(109).

Some Labour MPs saw no reason for the party to be satisfied with these achievements. They urged that there was no alternative for Socialists but to Keep Left. They wanted more planning, more controls and more nationalization, but the government was not enthusiastic. There was, indeed, only one further substantial measure of nationalization under consideration and its future was uncertain. The Iron and Steel Bill, introduced into the Commons in late

1948, led to a protracted constitutional wrangle involving the House of Lords. It was passed a year later, but would not come into effect until after a General Election. Such parliamentary manoeuvring indicated that the Conservatives now felt strong enough to challenge the government. Attlee and some of his senior colleagues decided in December 1949 to hold the next election in February 1950. A draft manifesto, *Labour Believes in Britain*, had been debated at the party conference in the summer when the 'consolidationists' confronted those who wished to press on to further Socialist advance. Morrison, who presented the manifesto to the delegates, was anxious not to forfeit the middle-class votes the party had gained in 1945. 'We do not want to be a narrow party', he declared, 'we want to be the party of all the useful people, the Party of the Nation.'[1] The manifesto stressed the need to build on what had already been accomplished and indicated that sections of the food industry, meat wholesaling and cold storage, sugar, cement and part of the chemical industry, were ripe for nationalization. Tate and Lyle, the sugar company, countered the threat of extinction by launching 'Mr Cube' into the world.

Despite its achievements, the government seemed at this juncture to be losing impetus. The strain of continuous office since 1940 (in the case of the leading figures) was all too visible. Both Cripps and Bevin were sick and ageing men and one weary minister committed suicide. Bevin, with his trade union past, was able to secure substantial backing for the government from the movement. Tewson, Citrine's successor as General Secretary of the TUC was 'moderate', as was Arthur Deakin of the TGWU in 1947, for example, Morrison praised in Cabinet the 'sense of responsibility' shown by leaders, though the 'rank and file' needed to be 'educated' in the matter of wages policy. Labour's reversion to contracting out helped the party's finances, but also increased union strength at party conferences. Aided by this good relationship with the TUC leadership, Attlee could be congratulated on the quiet skill with which he held together the 'industrial' and 'political' wings of the party, the government and the national executive of the party and, not least, his colleagues with their diverse class and educational backgrounds. It was the future that was the problem. The sybaritic Bevan was brilliant, but his celebrated description of the Conservatives in July 1948 as 'lower than vermin' was thought to indicate that he was erratic. Gaitskell and Wilson, clever and ambitious university men, might eventually prove more generally acceptable(110).

The 1950 Election produced another victory for Labour[D]. The electors turned out in very high numbers and, amazingly, the proportion of the popular vote corresponded unusually closely with the seats gained by the Conservatives and Labour. It scarcely needs to be said that this was not true for the Liberals. Although it fielded many candidates, hopes that the party might pick up votes from discontented Labour supporters who could not bring themselves to vote Conservative were disappointed. The future now looked bleak for the Liberals, though that was scarcely a new development. There was a gentle irony to be found in the fact that Labour lost ground in the most democratic election yet to be fought. The 1948 Representation of the People Act abolished university seats and thereby the dual vote possessed by university graduates. Other plural voting was similarly ended and constituency boundaries were extensively revised [C]. In analysing the result, the party's experts concluded that it had lost ground in particular among women voters and inhabitants of dormitory suburbs and private housing estates. In the months before the election, Wilson, President of the Board of Trade, had done his best to abolish controls, but his bonfire was by no means complete and Conservative spokesmen successfully hammered home the point that government by Whitehall purchase and planning was expensive [D].

Despite the Communist party's poor showing, the Labour Left claimed that the party had been insufficiently Socialist. The Right and Centre drew another conclusion – that it would have to 'modernize'. By the end of 1951, however, the government was out of office, having lost another election. Its final months on its small majority of six (over all opposition parties) had been characterized by squabbles over the shape of the NHS, the scale of rearmament and the German question and, on an acrimonious personal level, on who should succeed Attlee when he decided to step down. It was a rather miserable conclusion to Shawcross's surmise that the party would be in power 'for a very long time to come'. The novelty of Labour's achievement should not be exaggerated. Its leadership's mental world had been moulded by a particular experience and interpretation of the 1930s, tempered a little by the war. Perhaps inevitably, they set about planning to avoid the '1930s' – when that decade of the world's history was not going to return anyway. Obsessed by a vision of a Socialist future, and dominated by memories of the past, Labour tended to bypass the present.

At the age of seventy-seven, and in less than complete health, it was also inevitable that Churchill, too, should have felt the pull of the past, though it was a rather different kind of past from Labour's. To the dismay of some younger Conservatives he seemed anxious to surround himself with old cronies. The refurbishing of the party during its years of opposition, both intellectually and organizationally, had been carried out by others. Lord Woolton did give the party structure a thorough overhaul, though its extent and significance may be overestimated. Organizational restructuring in the wake of defeat is a normal and cathartic activity because it persuades the faithful that the reason for defeat can be identified and rectified. For their part, the Young Conservatives, with an increasing number of branches, were keen to show that Socialism was not inevitably the wave of the future. Butler became chairman of the committee responsible for party policy statements and made use of the young and able minds of Powell and Macleod. They were busy producing papers in the Conservative Research Department. These were the years of *One Nation*, a pamphlet they inspired. Macleod wrote:

> Socialism would give the same benefits to everyone, whether or not the help is needed, and indeed whether or not the country's resources are adequate. We believe that we must first help those in need. Socialists believe that the State should provide an average standard. We believe that it should provide a minimum standard, above which people should be free to rise as far as their industry, their thrift, their ability or their genius may take them.[2]

The objective of Conservative social policy should not be equality, but 'to see that men had an equal chance to make themselves unequal'. Powell, Macleod, Heath and Maudling still had to work their passage, but they showed that one side did not have a monopoly of intellectual ability and that there was new talent beneath the Churchillian crust(112).

When they came into office it was not easy for the Conservatives to put Macleod's dictum into practice. In his early years as Chancellor of the Exchequer, Butler found that 'setting the people free' could not be done at a stroke. By 1954, however, production and consumption reached new heights and, unbelievably, there was no price explosion. It was in this exuberant mood that the government ended food rationing in 1954. By the mid-1950s, it did begin to appear as though a new phase in British history was being reached. Some twenty-five years of depression and austerity in peace and war seemed to be coming to an end. 'Full employment', which Labour achieved after the war seemed to be ensured. Between 1950 and 1954, some 1,140,000 houses were built and Macmillan, the Housing Minister, laid the foundations of a property-owning democracy. Before the war, Macmillan had represented the north-eastern industrial constituency of Stockton and had been author of *The Middle Way*. Its title indicated his approach to Conservative policy and his prominence and effectiveness as a minister seemed further proof that the party offered a haven for 'moderation'. Impeccably educated and connected, he too carried a conscience about the 1930s. There thus appeared to be a degree of inter-party consensus about the basis of this burgeoning prosperity. When they came into office, the Conservatives did not reverse the fundamental measures of nationalization introduced by Labour, with the exception of the always controversial Iron and Steel Act, and Road Transport. There seemed to be a judicious mixture of planning and State control, freedom and private industry. Despite Labour abuse, only limited charging was introduced into the NHS(113).

Although the industrial scene was never completely tranquil, there was no major conflict between organized labour and the government. Churchill, Butler, and Monckton (the Minister of Labour) went out of their way to be conciliatory, especially where wages were concerned. The TUC welcomed their readiness to consult and were correspondingly approachable. The great fear of the leadership was that unless they did co-operate with the government and employers, unemployment would return. By the mid-1950s, however, a new generation of trade union leaders, and the workers they represented, were coming to accept 'full employment' as a basic fact of life. Their task was to press for higher wages and better conditions, without being unduly concerned about the general state of the economy.

It was in these promising but uncertain circumstances that a new Prime Minister took over in 1955, when Churchill at last stood down. The young Queen Elizabeth II had succeeded her father in 1952 and there was glib talk in the press of the dawning of a new Elizabethan age. If such an era was imminent, Eden, so long the obvious successor, seemed an admirable new Elizabethan knight, with his charm, intelligence and quick temper. He speedily called a new election in May 1955. The Conservatives both increased their majority and their share of the vote. The two-party system was dominant – the Liberals did not perform as disastrously as they had done in 1951, but were insignificant in the Commons. Communists and Nationalists from Wales or Scotland made no headway. After this defeat, under a new leader, Labour would have to sort out its soul if it were ever to regain the initiative. The new Prime Minister confidently took control of the kingdom he had waited so long to inherit. (B, D)

---

1. See also B. Donoughue and G. W. Jones, *Herbert Morrison* (1973), pp. 455–61
2. N. Fisher, *I. Macleod* (1973), pp. 78–9

CHAPTER 23

Depression and recovery

In the mid-1950s, it at last seemed that Britain was on the verge of a new economic era. Butler, the Conservative Chancellor of the Exchequer, suggested that Britain should aim to double its standard of living in the next twenty-five years. *The Economist*, also in June 1954, reported that the economic miracle had happened: full employment without inflation. The contrast with the position in the early 1930s seemed complete. Then, unemployment as a proportion of the labour force had averaged 12 per cent (in the years 1931–32) and the world economy seemed on the point of collapse. In the mid-1950s, unemployment seemed to be settling at about 2 per cent and world trade was apparently expanding. Of course, the Second World War requires more than a footnote in the middle, but it makes more sense to look both backwards and forwards from it rather than to think in terms of 'between the wars' or of a 'post-war' era. The war in 1939 did not shatter a flourishing and stable economic order; some argue that it was itself the ultimate expression of economic dislocation. The task in 1945 was to create an international system which would promote prosperity without encouraging autarky. In any case, 1945 is now so remote that 'post-war' has little explanatory value.

Within such a quarter-century there are distinct phases, though the dates are not easy to determine. Different years can suggest different conclusions. For example, if the real national income of the United States and Britain is indexed in 1929 at 100, by 1932 the British index had only dropped to 99 while the American was down to 63; by 1937 the British index was at 118 and the American at 96. However, if 1932 is chosen as the base, then the American recovery from 63 to 96 was steeper than the British recovery from 99 to 118(195). Again, the relatively poor performance of Britain after 1925 helps to explain the relative mildness of the depression in Britain in the late 1920s. Cross-national and cross-cultural comparisons are inevitable, but they can be misleading. The percentage unemployed in Germany was higher in the years 1931–33 than in Britain, but it fell thereafter more rapidly and to considerably lower percentages in the period up to 1939. Is it helpful to compare Britain and Germany either in these years or in the decade after 1945? Can relative growth-rates be measured on the same scale as one which records the presence of concentration camps? For these reasons, it is tempting to consider economic performance not in relation to some specific comparator or universal average but to the historic levels achieved by Britain over two centuries. In this light, Saul has suggested that the upsurge of the first two-thirds of the nineteenth century was exceptional and 2 per cent was Britain's 'natural' growth-rate, determined by historical and natural conditions.[1] That is, perhaps, a comforting conclusion, but there is no guarantee that the historical and natural conditions perpetuate the same balance of advantage and disadvantage through time. Concentration on economic performance alone ignores the fact that planning for war may sometimes dictate priorities. Invisible income came to have an even greater significance in the 1930s when the balance on current account was frequently in deficit; it was also a time when the security of overseas investment was much in doubt. The British economy was at the mercy of world developments in a fashion that became ever more conspicuous.

Departure from the Gold Standard in 1931 did not produce the crisis that some had predicted. After a brief period with the bank rate at 6 per cent, the value of the pound stabilized at $3.40 early in 1932. The United States, Germany, France and some other European countries remained on gold, and for a time British goods had a competitive advantage. The Treasury (not the Bank of England) established an Exchange Equalization Account in 1932 whose purpose was to keep the pound's fluctuations under some control by judicious buying and selling of foreign exchange. It reached a low of $3.17 and a high of $4.95, drifting down from near the latter figure as war approached. Its value was fixed at $4.03 for the duration of the conflict. Some economists thought that this kind of 'pegging' still indicated a yearning for an unobtainable fixed parity. While the pound's loss of value helped exports (enabling Britain's share in world exports to pass 10 per cent again in 1933), the United States left gold in that year and France and other countries devalued, so the edge was only temporary. Indeed, some economists blame the depreciation of sterling for the collapse of respect for an international monetary standard and the ensuing network of currency restrictions(188,191).

The other major change of the 1930s was the frank abandonment of Free Trade. In 1930, over 80 per cent of all imports entered Britain free of duty, but the National government introduced the Abnormal Importations and Horticultural Products Acts, and between 1932 and 1934 a tariff policy evolved. In 1932, a general tariff of 10 per cent *ad valorem* was introduced – though there were exemptions for wheat, meat and bacon, British-caught fish, raw cotton and raw wool. All colonial imports were permanently exempted, as were those from the Dominions pending discussions scheduled for Ottawa in 1932. That conference eventually only agreed to a system of quotas by which Britain would ensure entry for empire products at the expense of 'foreign' importers(197). In return, the Dominions agreed to raise their tariffs against 'foreign' countries to a higher level than those on British goods. Hopes of a vast expansion of intra-Commonwealth trade were disappointed, though between 1931 and 1936 the Dominion share of United Kingdom imports rose from 28.7 per cent to 39.2 per cent, largely at the expense of imports from Europe. There was a less significant shift in United Kingdom exports. The 10 per cent *ad valorem* duty on manufactured goods was raised a little later to 20 per cent, and there were even higher tariffs on certain specific items. In 1935, for example, the steel tariff was raised to 50 per cent as part of a struggle with European steelmakers. Most industrial countries in the world were now engaged in a kind of bartering. The 1933 World Economic Conference in London failed to find a different international framework. Even so, Ashworth observes that the temporary cessation of international investment left untouched the intricate network of indebtedness on which world production and trade depended. Most channels remained at least partially open(196). British Treasury controls actually prevented overseas investment, though empire borrowers could receive favourable treatment. The ratio of the United Kingdom's foreign trade to national income dropped below 20 per cent(189).

The abandonment of the Gold Standard and of Free Trade did not necessarily entail the end of *laissez-faire*. Nevertheless, there was more government intervention, though in the 1930s it would be premature to speak of a 'mixed' let alone a 'managed' economy. Keynes, who was no friend of *laissez-faire*, argued in his *General Theory* (1936) that a general deficiency of demand could explain unemployment. Natural forces were crude and inefficient, and official financial policy could do the trick. In addition to low interest rates and easy credit, government expenditure (relative to revenue) could be raised, or taxation lowered, as appropriate. Low interest rates did in fact prevail, though they were not seen as part of a Keynesian economic programme. For their part, Hayek and Robbins ensured that the economic argument was not all one way, stating that market forces, if imperfect, were more likely to promote necessary change and growth than deliberate planning. The arguments were complex and perhaps the manifest divisions among economists continued to weaken their public standing. Certainly, Chamberlain and his Treasury advisers remained committed to the idea of a balanced budget – something the 'expansionists' thought old-fashioned(204).

As for industry, economic historians have been chipping away at the image of the 1930s though, beyond agreement that all was not doom and disaster, there is no consensus. Different indices of production produce different rates of growth, but there was growth, particulary in the mid-1930s, with a downswing in 1937 and a further upturn by 1939. Even the staple industries showed signs of improvement or at least of stabilization. Steel production, which had fallen to just over 5 million tons in 1932, rose to 7 million in 1933 and 13 million in 1937. Tariff protection undoubtedly helped, and indeed had only been granted on condition that there would be 'rationalization'. New plants at Corby, Scunthorpe and Ebbw Vale got off to a good start. It was another question, however, whether their location was ideal(193).

Shipbuilding just managed to survive. The United Kingdom share of world shipping output, which had averaged 51 per cent in the years 1926–29 fell to 34 per cent in 1937–38; British output fell quite sharply. The National Shipbuilders Security did reduce capacity by 1 million tons – a programme which has been described as 'ruthless', though within that figure were yards like Beardmores at Dalmuir and Palmers at Jarrow which had, in effect, ceased to function. The fall in British output was unevenly distributed, but even in areas where production held up there was some loss of confidence. Protection became an integral aspect of survival – the 1934 North Atlantic Shipping Act enabled the construction on the Clyde of the *Queen Mary* to resume. The following year, a 'scrap and build' scheme also provided work. Just before the war, naval demands revived, though companies which had only survived earlier by shedding labour did have difficulty in reconstituting their workforce. Arguably, the British industry failed to grasp that, in the future, success might hinge upon managing integrated shipyards. The United Kingdom did not gain the lead in building diesel-engined vessels (over half of world tonnage used oil in 1939) which she had enjoyed with reciprocating steam-engines; once again, her pre-eminence in the latter may explain her failure to exploit the new.[2]

The tonnage of coal exported fell from 76 million tons in 1929 to 46 million in 1938 – despite the barter arrangements (involving coal) negotiated with such countries as Argentina and Denmark. The new producers and other protected producers made the international coal market extremely competitive. British labour costs, as a proportion of total costs, were considerably higher than elsewhere. The 1930 Coal Mines Act set up a cartel scheme to regulate output, sales and prices. A Coal Mines Reorganization Commission was meant to encourage mergers and, in theory, could compel them. In fact, although there was much talk about the economies of large-scale production, Buxton has noted no general correlation between the size and efficiency of mines(193).

In cottons, the industry was mildly assisted by tariffs, but its exports continued to decline while those of Japan rose. Under the 1936 Cotton Spinning Industry Act, a Spindles Board was set up to reduce capacity and, partly through its work, there were only 37 million spindles in 1939 (a reduction of 21 million in a decade). Woollens, less dependent on exports, and gaining more from protection, fared better. Thus, over these industries, there was a degree of State intervention, though not on a common pattern or with the same conclusions. Industrial reorganization schemes still left Britain with an inappropriate pattern of capacity in too many spheres for comfort.

Much emphasis has been placed on the 'new' industries in the 'surge forward' during the 1930s(199). They certainly boosted investment during the slump when it was not forthcoming elsewhere. On the other hand, Buxton argues that during the crucial recovery years of 1932–34 they only accounted for 7 per cent of total employment and some 3 per cent of total net investment in any single year. So, their contribution should be treated with caution, though not discounted(193). The production of synthetic organic–chemical materials (helped by protection) grew steadily – celluloid and Bakelite, for example. Perspex, polystyrene and polythene were being developed, but their major impact was still to come. The market for photographic chemicals, films and cameras grew steadily. Rayon production increased threefold in the decade ending in 1939. Courtaulds, who had pioneered the viscose process, dominated the British market, but British Celanese, who developed an alternative process, grew steadily. But Britain lost its early lead, and by the late 1930s its output was only a third of the German and Japanese industries, and half that of the American and Italian. After its relatively slow start, the British motor industry accelerated. Annual production of cars and commercial vehicles rose above half a million in the years just before the war. Producing mainly for the home and imperial markets, it outgrew its European rivals. Mergers reduced the number of manufacturers, but a wide range of makes and models was still on offer. Prices were reduced in the 1930s and a mass market opened up. Hesitating between a baby and a Baby Austin, some married couples opted for the latter. Morris and Austin led in the British market, followed by two American-owned companies, Ford and Vauxhall (General Motors). Ford's Dagenham plant (1931) was the most striking industrial project in the British car world. Increased vehicle production naturally benefited cognate fields – body-building, machine tools, brakes and hydraulics, tyres and glass, to name only some. The motor-cycle and pedal-cycle industries also expanded, as did aircraft manufacture (firms like Rolls-Royce, Bristol and Armstrong-Siddely also had motor-car interests), but it was not yet a major employer. Public subsidies were used to promote the growth of air traffic. British Airways (1935), the result of an amalgamation of smaller companies, merged with Imperial Airways in 1939 to form the nationalized British Overseas Airways Corporation. Internal services improved, but there was no direct flight between London and Glasgow until 1939.

The most striking boom perhaps lies in the provision of electricity and the industries which fed upon it. The Central Electricity Board had been set up in 1926, empowered to construct, own and operate a national grid on behalf of the State. Baldwin had set up a board 'managed by practical men closely in touch with the industry', that is to say it was composed of Ayrshire Scots. The Board and its engineers energetically established the framework of the grid and reformed the basis of power generation. The task was to build a new range of large power-stations and bring order among the mass of small stations. By late 1935, over 4,000 miles of transmission lines were in operation, and the original grid completed. The growth both in domestic and industrial consumption was spectacular. The under 3 million consumers in 1929 had more than trebled a decade later; two out of three houses were then wired for electricity. While, in 1929, Britain was surpassed by the United States, Canada, Germany, France and Italy in output of electricity per capita, in the 1930s she caught up France, overtook Germany and Italy, and was not very far behind the United States. Capital investment and construction continued through the worst years of the depression and unit costs dropped appreciably. Ironically, this success stems in considerable measure from the slow beginning, reversing what is often held to be the pattern. Britain reaped the benefits of being a latecomer while others had carried the burden of research and development.

The corollary of supply improvement was the expansion of electrical, engineering, electrical machinery, wires and cables and kindred activities. The 'Big Three' in these areas were Associated Electrical Industries (AEI), General Electric (GEC), and English Electric, covering a wide range of products from power stations to light bulbs. The big firms were also moving into domestic appliances and radio, hitherto the province of small and specialized companies. In these areas, British industry made up lost ground and there remained ample room for expansion in the domestic durables market. On the eve of war, though 77 per cent of householders with electricity had electric irons, only 27 per cent had vacuum cleaners and a mere 2 per cent refrigerators and only 1 per cent had washing machines.

Elsewhere, the 'retailing revolution' continued. Marks and Spencer, for example, expanded its store network and sales turnover at a very fast rate during the 1930s. Other multiples, like Woolworths or Sainsburys were established in most important towns. Clearly, there was sectoral enterprise and expansion but, partly because of protection, restrictive practices flourished and in some fields competition virtually disappeared. As much effort was devoted to operating restrictive schemes as to cutting costs. Such a business mentality was to have adverse consequences after 1945.

When war broke out in 1939, no one believed that it could be run on the basis of private enterprise. The economy had to be 'managed', and in the event, central control was to prove more complex than it had been in 1914–18. As far as industry was concerned, practice varied widely, ranging from the direct provision of government factories to general guidance, with many steps in between. The resulting lack of standardization in many products has often been criticized – the Americans could assemble sixty aircraft a week per factory and the British only ten(105). On the other hand, the pragmatic approach has been commended as a realistic recognition of the time and uncertainty involved in setting up new management systems(209). Using 'manpower budgets', the Treasury dictated the pattern of investment. Outside economists were drafted into the Civil Service, many of them forming the 'economic section' of the Cabinet Office. Keynes himself had a roving brief within the Treasury and, convinced that voluntary savings would not be sufficient to draw off purchasing power which could not be spent on consumer goods, was to an extent successful in devising schemes for compulsory saving. Rates of direct and indirect taxation were roughly doubled. PAYE was introduced in 1943, and after 1945 levels of taxation were never to drop to their pre-1939 levels.

There was general satisfaction in 1945 at what had been achieved during the war in the economic field. Even economists who objected, in theory, to planning patriotically offered their services and enjoyed the work. In June 1944, a White Paper stated that the government 'accepted as one of their primary aims and responsibilities the maintenance of a high and stable level of employment after the war'. To describe this statement as Treasury conversion to fiscal means of avoiding cyclical employment is going too far, but it is an indication of the political climate that it was assumed that the White Paper would be 'honoured' by whatever party formed the new government(71,105). For this and other reasons, it has been assumed that the war permanently altered the relations between the State and industry, establishing a tradition of close co-operation between organized industry and the central administration, with every section of trade and industry being assigned to one or other of the economic departments(201). We ought to beware, however, of a word like 'permanent'. In any case, the efficiency of the wartime management of the economy has been a matter of assertion rather than investigation – though the relevant criteria are difficult to establish. Whatever the answer, it left behind among the population the view that the State could manage the economy; wartime propaganda had cultivated this impression and it seemed faintly unpatriotic to question it. It was in this mood that the Labour government launched itself on post-war problems.

It needed such optimism because, once again, war had entailed a substantial loss of overseas capital; large debts had been incurred, and it would take time for the economy to be readapted. In such circumstances, as has been observed, the State was setting out to attain far-reaching targets simultaneously: full employment, price stability, a positive balance of payments, security for sterling, a 'fairer' distribution of income, increased public services and economic growth(202). Initially, debts and deficits loomed large. The United Kingdom had borrowed and had sold capital assets roughly equivalent to the total British foreign investment in 1939. That was from the non-dollar world. The sum raised from the dollar world was almost twice as much(186). Lend-Lease had enabled Britain to survive, but one authority suggests that the absolute dollar cost of the war to Britain would have financed sixteen years of British imports from the United States at the 1938 level and prices(190). The abrupt ending of Lend-Lease in August 1945 compelled the United Kingdom to seek the orthodox loan which she had avoided during the war. It was estimated that exports would have to reach the level of 175 per cent of pre-war exports within five years in order to repay the sterling debt, rebuild the gold and dollar reserve, and meet other commitments. The loan would be needed to cover the adverse balance anticipated in the meantime. Keynes and the other negotiators found the mood in Washington more frosty than they had expected, but Britain did receive a substantial loan which was supplemented by Canada. Although the terms could be thought reasonable (interest was at 2 per cent and repayment was not to start until 1951) some opinion found Britain's indebtedness a poor reward after her long struggle. Most controversial was the quid pro quo, by which Britain had to ratify the Bretton Woods agreement at once and thereby, among other things, agree to make sterling fully convertible within a year of the loan coming into operation.

Financial and political considerations had mingled in the final years of the war. In London and Washington, it was agreed that the restoration of world trade was a priority and that new institutions might be needed to this end. The Lend-Lease agreement stated that both countries looked to the elimination of all forms of discrimination in international commerce and the reduction of tariffs and trade barriers. An international gathering at Bretton Woods in 1944 approved proposals which had been discussed for years. There was to be an International Monetary Fund to facilitate multilateral international payments; members would contribute a quota to a currency pool on which they could draw to correct temporary problems. A return to gold was ruled out, though each member had to pay a portion of its quota in gold. By mid-1949, there were nearly fifty members and it undoubtedly assisted in creating exchange stability without hampering internal development or international trade. There was also to be an International Bank for Reconstruction and Development – though it proved more difficult to fund and its progress was slower. Although an International Trade Organization proved unacceptable, the General Agreement on Tariffs and Trade (GATT) emerged from a meeting at Geneva in 1947. It involved bilateral tariff reductions and a general agreement not to increase existing preferences or create new ones except in special circumstances. Liberalization proceeded and the world economy – in which the dollar reigned supreme – revived.

Initially, in such a context, it did look as though British exporters might rise to the stiff challenge confronting them. The aggregate deficit might be kept within the confines of the North American loans. By mid-1947, however, the loan was being drawn on too rapidly. Nevertheless, Britain honoured the pledge to restore convertibility – for a month. As the dollar deficit shot up, it was clear in August 1947 that the experiment could not be sustained. The 'suppressed' inflation seemed in danger of becoming visible. This financial crisis occurred within the developing Cold War context and fortunately Marshall Aid was to come to the rescue. In the short term, however, government morale was sapped and the confident talk in its *Economic Survey* about manpower targets, sector outputs and economic budgets looked threatened(107). Running the economy at full employment led to upward pressure on wages and prices. Perhaps Britain had over-full employment? In these circumstances, the need to increase exports became a constant theme – Marshall Aid only offered a breathing space. Exports were indeed doing remarkably well, but the reserves remained relatively small. In 1949, the combination of a mild recession in the United States and the first relaxation of domestic controls led to speculation on a sterling devaluation. Eventually, after considerable Cabinet argument, the pound was devalued from \$4.03 to \$2.40 – a fall of 30 per cent. As always, the move was controversial. Convertibility was not restored. In the immediate aftermath, the balance of payments looked healthy and it proved possible to suspend Marshall Aid payments. But the terms of trade moved against Britain and the Korean War introduced unanticipated demands. Managing the economy by aiming at an overall budgetary surplus was clearly not proving an easy task.

Butler, the Chancellor of the Exchequer after the Conservative victory in 1951, declared that in his first budget he was using 'the whole machinery of economic forecasting'. Perhaps nothing much had changed. However, the Conservatives did begin to use the bank-rate in a way which had not been done since 1932. The idea of allowing the pound to float freely, without support from the foreign exchange reserves, was considered in 1952, but then abandoned. Critics feared that the Bank of England would have had to raise interest rates still further to support the pound and thus reproduce the situation of the late 1920s. Some believed that even to consider the plan showed an unhealthy concern on the part of the nationalized Bank of England with the status of sterling. By the mid-1950s, the Conservatives could claim that wartime controls had disappeared and, in this sense, a new era of freedom was beginning. Some commentators noted, however, that beneath the party rhetoric about 'planning' and 'freedom' the changes of policy between governments were minor rather than major. The phrase 'Butskellism' was used to indicate the central economic ground supposedly held by Butler and Gaitskell.

Nationalization between 1946 and 1949 had brought coal, steel, airlines, long-distance road transport, the railways, electricity and gas into public ownership. For some of these industries, this represented a sharp break in control, but for others it was merely a further stage in the extension of government regulation. Only road haulage and steel (after a fashion) were denationalized by the incoming Tories. The rationale behind nationalization had been largely political. There was very little discussion of the extent to which certain industries were to be regarded as 'social services' or 'profit-making organizations'. There was, indeed, talk of an integrated transport policy, but such talk is never to be taken seriously.

Coal was the major inherited problem. During the war, coal exports had virtually ceased and productivity dropped. The Ministry of Fuel and Power commissioned studies with a view to increasing efficiency. The National Coal Board's 1950 plan envisaged a production of 250 million tons by 1965, to be achieved by substantial re-equipment and the closure of uneconomic pits. However, although coal was in high demand immediately after the war, the 227 million tons achieved in 1952 was the high point from which production declined. The energy source of the future seemed to be oil and, ironically, it was the shortage of coal which accelerated its widespread use. Crude petroleum imports rose to 27 million tons in 1955. Imports of refined petroleum products dropped from over 12 million tons to under 9 million – this, and a large rise in refined exports during this period, reflected the major expansion in United Kingdom oil-refining capacity. The refineries were owned by major oil companies, but the nuclear programme, also embarked upon after 1945, remained under the direct control of the Atomic Energy Research Establishment (followed by the United Kingdom Atomic Energy Authority). Calder Hall, a dual purpose station designed both to generate electricity and produce plutonium, was started in 1953. The 1955 White Paper, *A Programme for Nuclear Power*, envisaged a major programme of investment and a further dozen stations. Here, surely, was a field in which Britain did have an early lead. The surge of oil imports, mainly from the Middle East, did not cause undue concern since, despite the Iranian crisis of 1951, supply looked assured. It seemed only logical to take advantage of a relatively cheap energy source. That Britain might have access to her own oil supply never crossed anyone's mind(200).

In manufacturing generally, the years after 1945 resembled those after 1919. British manufacturers did well in the late 1940s when competition was weak, but then failed to maintain the momentum. In cottons, for example, the early post-war years showed large increases in output and big exports, but production fell away sharply in the early 1950s, leaving substantial excess capacity once more. In steel, however, the prospects looked more promising. Production steadily rose and in 1952 it was planned to raise capacity to over 20 million tons by the mid-1950s. This figure, however, was still below national needs and forced Britain to spend foreign exchange on imports of sheet steel and other similar products. In the late 1940s, shipbuilding contributed to this demand for steel on a major scale. The United Kingdom built 38 per cent of the world total in 1949–51, but by 1956 she had fallen behind Japan and Germany and was building less than 14 per cent. The motor industry, on the other hand, still appeared to be flourishing. In 1945, there were 1½ million cars in Britain (a drop on the pre-war figure), but by 1955 that figure had risen to 6 million. Petrol rationing ended in 1950. The two leading British manufacturers, Morris and Austin, joined to form the British Motor Corporation (BMC) in 1952. The difficulty lay not in disposing of cars but in making enough to meet the demand. Prices fell, more or less in line with improvements in manufacturing technique. The formation of BMC was only one of several mergers which reduced the number of manufacturers. Once again, however, by the mid-1950s, other countries were making more and perhaps better cars; the period of effortless superiority was passing(210).

In general, therefore, British industry stood in an ambivalent condition. The post-war record was not unsuccessful and expectations were quite high. During the years of the Labour government over 14 million man-days were lost through strikes – a relatively modest figure. In the six years after the First World War (if that is thought a valid comparison) more than ten times that number were lost. Even so, the productivity of British industry was a matter of constant if not strident concern. The Industrial Organization and Development Act, 1947, gave the government power to set up Development Councils in particular industries. In the same year a Committee on Industrial Productivity was established, designed to suggest which scientific research would prove most beneficial to industrial productivity. It is difficult to determine what benefit, if any, these bodies were. Labour set up the Monopolies and Restrictive Practices Commission in 1948, but was in some ideological uncertainty about the merits of competition. After all, it was itself engaged in setting up the biggest monopolies of all. The general importance attached to 'full employment' meant that a blind eye was frequently turned to evidence of overmanning. Similarly, fear of unemployment was a partial explanation for restrictive practices within industry and demarcation disputes between trade unions concerned about long-term security and traditional wage differentials. There was a growing awareness (and some apprehension) of automation in industry. 'If full employment continues to be general', a report from the Department of Scientific and Industrial Research stated in 1956, 'it will be fairly easy to introduce automation because displaced workers can soon obtain other work, though not always with their old firms or in their old occupations(194).' There was resistance to change none the less, probably on a greater scale than was the case with Britain's competitors. The contrary point, that full employment might be jeopardized unless there was a rapid diffusion of automatic processes received less emphasis and less acceptance.

---

1. Saul has had subsequent doubts about his own proposition: *Industrialization and deindustrialization? The interaction of the German and British economies before the First World War* (1980), p. 30
2. A. E. Musson, *The growth of British industry* (1978), p. 311

CHAPTER 24

A kingdom united

NORTHERN IRELAND

The relationships between the component parts of the United Kingdom were more stable during this period than they had been in the past or were to be in the future. Principally, of course, this was because of the apparent settlement of the Irish question. The Northern Ireland government steadily established itself, moving out to its splendid new building at Stormont in 1931. The Unionist party remained dominant in a ratio of around 4 : 1 – helped by the ending of elections by proportional representation in 1929. Any social or economic issues were minimized and politics remained centred on the issue of the border. Nationalists, troubled by internal divisions, refused the title of Loyal Opposition. They made no serious attempt to safeguard the minority's position within the system, arguing that such action would recognize its legitimacy. Unionists, in turn, saw no reason to be conciliatory to avowed enemies of the State(137).

Unemployment in Northern Ireland increased by some two and a half times in the decade up to 1938. At its highest, three out of ten had no job. Each side attempted to look after its 'own', and the Protestants were able to do so more effectively. 'Many in the audience employ Catholics', a future Prime Minister of Northern Ireland told a meeting in 1933, 'but I have not one about my place. Catholics are out to destroy Ulster with all their might and power.'(144) Sectarian riots recurred, the most serious resulting in deaths and many injuries in Belfast during the summer of 1935. However, although there was some comment in the British press, the Speaker at Westminster had ruled that parliamentary questions could not be asked on matters which had been transferred to the Stormont Parliament. The constitutional relationship was in fact a little more complicated, but it never became a major issue. There were no major administrative difficulties either, but there were financial problems. Over a decade of experience confirmed that Northern Ireland could not hope to be self-sufficient and provide services at the same level as those in the rest of the United Kingdom. In 1938, the then United Kingdom Chancellor of the Exchequer accepted the principle that in the event of a Northern Ireland budget deficit, not caused by higher social expenditure or lower taxation, the United Kingdom government would supply the funds to maintain the same services and standards as in Britain(142). Conversely, the IRA decided to strike in England to bring home the fact that it would never accept the arrangement in Ulster as permanent. The most serious incidents took place just before the war, notably a bomb attack in Coventry, when five people were killed and some seventy injured.

Northern Ireland showed its usefulness during the Second World War, particularly since the United Kingdom government had given up its rights to use certain ports in the Irish Free State in 1938. Londonderry became a major base for Atlantic operations. The industry of Belfast boomed, its geographical position suddenly becoming an advantage rather than a handicap. Harland and Wolff's became a general arsenal, building bombers and flying boats, repairing naval vessels and freighters but, above all, producing about one-tenth of the whole of the United Kingdom's wartime shipping output. There was a ready market across the Irish Sea for Ulster agricultural products. Although conscription was not applied, for fear of political complications, there was a large voluntary enlistment. Several hundred people were detained under the Special Powers Act, though that figure had dropped by the end of the war. Naturally, the Northern Ireland government was anxious to stress the active role of he province. Large numbers of American servicemen came to Ulster and no opportunity was lost to contrast its role with the neutrality of the Irish Free State. Belfast was afraid that a deal might be negotiated over its head whereby Dublin would be persuaded into the war by an agreement to reopen the border issue.

It was against this wartime background that when the Irish Free State became the Republic of Ireland in 1949 and left the British Commonwealth, the Labour government was prepared to make a specific declaration that Northern Ireland would in no event cease to be part of the United Kingdom 'without the consent of the Parliament of Northern Ireland'. So fortified, Lord Brookeborough, who had been Prime Minister since 1943, consolidated his Unionist administration. There was some discontent among Labour MPs at Westminster, particularly from those with an Irish Catholic background, about aspects of the housing, education and employment situation in the province, but these matters were not discussed at Westminster. No one questioned, either, that the Northern Ireland government had a perfect right not to follow Labour in Britain in equating the local government and parliamentary franchise – even if it was unwise of it not to do so. Occasional exception was taken to the use by Stormont of the Civil Authorities (Special Powers Act) to detain and intern without trial, but 'there were no prosecutions at all in seven of the eleven years 1945 to 1956'(142). The rest of the United Kingdom tended to assume that no news from Northern Ireland was good news. The small number of non-Unionist MPs elected to Westminster made little impact, frequently not taking their seats. The IRA began a fresh series of raids in 1954 and in December 1956 made a formal declaration of war, but the massive statue of Sir Edward Carson outside the Stormont Parliament buildings seemed to symbolize the solidity of the system it set out to destroy(138).

SCOTLAND

At a large gathering in Stirling in June 1930, a Scottish Covenant was launched. Those who signed it declared their belief in 'the urgent need and necessity of self-government for Scotland', but twenty years later there had been little progress towards such a goal. In the early 1930s, there was a great deal of feuding between different groups more or less dedicated to this end before the Scottish National party (SNP) emerged in April 1934. It was, however, still confused in its objectives. As the war approached, the anticipated increase in membership failed to materialize. In 1939, some wished to resist what they termed the propaganda effort to march Scotland to war, but to little purpose. A few SNP supporters spent some time in prison in protest against conscription. By 1942, the party had split between those prepared to co-operate with other political bodies to gain some kind of Home Rule and those, who were in the ascendancy, who desired full independence and would not co-operate with others in the meantime. The SNP did not observe the wartime electoral truce and in April 1945 gained its first parliamentary seat in a by-election at Motherwell. The seat was lost at the General Election and the party's other candidates did badly. Its failure led to other disputes and decline. McCormick, who had long dabbled in the intricacies of Home Rule politics, advocated another Covenant. In the late 1940s, a Scottish Parliament within the United Kingdom seemed popular – over 2 million Scots signed the Covenant. However, neither Labour nor the Unionists were swept off their feet by this result. In the 1950 and 1951 General Elections, the issue did not come to the fore, but a number of instances of 'direct action' about this time caught the press headlines. The most daring was the removal of the Stone of Scone from Westminster Abbey by a group of Scottish patriots. The SNP seemed in the doldrums and the Covenant Association faded away almost as rapidly as it had risen. A splinter group expressed its despair in a pamphlet *The English: are they human?* which came to a substantially negative conclusion(130).

This rather confused picture seemed to suggest that there was a continuing degree of dissatisfaction in Scotland with the administrative and political structure, but no real agreement on how it should be replaced or improved. The SNP had not been able to focus this discontent in such a way that it turned into support for independence. No Scottish Home Rule Bill was even introduced during this period. There were some administrative changes. The 1937 Gilmour Committee had successfully recommended that the Scottish Office should be brought together under one roof and St Andrew's House began its operations in 1939. The four departments of the Scottish Office – Home, Health, Education and Agriculture – came directly under the Scottish Secretary. There was some support in the Labour party in Scotland for some form of Home Rule, but neither in government nor in opposition did it take the matter up. However, Thomas Johnston, a Labour man who became Churchill's Scottish Secretary in February 1941, kept specific Scottish claims before the government and was able to push through a hydroelectric scheme for the Scottish Highlands. The Conservatives after 1951 added a Minister of State to the Scottish Office, but otherwise the political status quo remained.

WALES

In September 1936, three Welshmen, Saunders Lewis, D. J. Williams and the

Rev. Lewis Valentine set fire to some buildings on land in the Lleyn peninsula which was to be set apart as an RAF bombing school. Lewis, a prominent writer, declared at his trial that he had acted on behalf of the nation, its language, its literature, its separate traditions and immemorial ways of Christian life.[1] The trial had been transferred to the Old Bailey and the three were sentenced to nine months in prison. It was a dramatic demonstration of alienation from the British State(145). Land steeped in the traditions of the Celtic saints took precedence over the defence preparations of a British government. The Blaid, of which Saunders Lewis was still the president had, in 1932, made little progress. It remained committed to restoring a sense of Welsh nationhood of which the language was an integral part. The party claimed a membership of some 2,000 by 1939, but the outbreak of war caused problems in its ranks. Lewis denounced the war as a foreign affair into which Wales was dragged by English imperialism – a view which was a little too simple for some party members. Nevertheless, despite allegations of Fascist sympathy, the party persisted in its viewpoint. There was criticism of the fact that North Wales was designated a reception area for English evacuees. Saunders Lewis did reasonably well in 1943 when the parliamentary seat of the University of Wales was contested at a by-election, but his supporters had hoped for victory. In 1945, he warned of the dangers confronting Wales from English post-war reconstruction, but the party's candidates made little impact in the 1945 General Election(135).

Lewis notwithstanding, it appeared that only a small percentage, even of Welsh-speakers, were ready to support Plaid Cymru's aims. The proportion of Welsh-speakers showed a further decline in the 1931 census and it seemed a little ambitious to talk of doing away with the English language in Wales. The Socialist view in South Wales seemed to be that Wales should share fully in the reforms being introduced by the Labour government. Aneurin Bevan argued that there was no solution for the Welsh coal industry which did not apply throughout Britain. Even so, by 1950, spurred on by the Scottish Covenant, moves were afoot to collect signatures for a 'Parliament for Wales'. By 1956, when the rather protracted campaign was wound up, some 250,000 signatures had been collected. Enthusiasm varied between different parts of Wales, being greatest in Welsh-speaking rural areas. Only a sixth of Welsh MPs gave the campaign much support. The Labour government had set up an advisory nominated body, the Council for Wales and Monmouthshire, in 1949, but opinion was strongly against any further developments. It was the Conservatives who carried out their pledge to assign a special responsibility for Wales to a member of the Cabinet. The first such Minister for Welsh Affairs (1951) was the then Home Secretary. In 1955, a revolt of farmers in South-west Wales led to the formation of the Farmers' Union of Wales which claimed to represent the needs of small farmers and of Wales better than the National Farmers Union (NFU) had done. This step was one of a number of indications that, while rejecting self-government, there was a feeling that Welsh interests within the United Kingdom ought to be more adequately defended. And in 1956 Wales at last had a capital city – Cardiff. 'Welsh' Wales had claimed that Cardiff was not really Welsh, but in the end there seemed something ludicrous about small towns like

Caernarfon or Aberystwyth competing with Edinburgh, Belfast or London.

The English manifested no separatist tendencies. The reformation of the constitutional structure of the United Kingdom held no interest. The kingdom seemed united and, if not altogether at peace with itself, at least there was little hint that it might be on the verge of dissolution.

---

1. A. R. Jones and G. Thomas, *Presenting Saunders Lewis* (Cardiff, 1973), p. 122

CHAPTER 25

Town and country (planning)

In the early months of the Second World War, many schoolchildren were 'evacuated' from big cities to 'reception areas' where they would be less vulnerable. Children from Liverpool came to North Wales, and what most struck them, apart from linguistic and religious differences, was the countryside. They had to come to terms with sheep and cattle, and accommodate themselves to the alien rhythms of rural life. Teachers took such pupils out of doors for classes to give them an experience of 'nature' at first hand. For their part, while the children often enjoyed their new experiences they were not sorry to return to their urban ways.

This experience can be generalized. In the 1930s, coaches, motor cars and motor cycles took increasing numbers of town-dwellers along country roads which had never been designed to receive them, and the necessary adaptation took time. Hikers and ramblers spread through fields and forests like the rash of wild flowers they so often swooped to cull. The 1938 Holidays with Pay Act stimulated holiday-making and about a third of the population took a holiday away from home. This was normally a week at the seaside, but the traditional landlady faced competition from Billy Butlin, who opened his first holiday camp at Skegness in 1937. The idea caught on immediately. Bank holidays apart, the exodus was still confined to July and August when visitors packed the resorts. On August Bank Holiday in 1937, for example, Blackpool received over 500,000 visitors who arrived in 50,000 motor vehicles and 700 trains, 425 of which were 'specials'.[1] This pattern resumed after 1945, despite the fact that the major resorts badly needed an overhaul. In 1948, some 625,000 people went to the Isle of Man. By 1949, it has been calculated that some 30 million people went for holidays around the coasts of Britain(249). The majority were still conveyed by rail to their destinations and, once they had arrived, the visitors either stayed on the beach or enjoyed the local entertainments. It was only in the mid-1950s that rail lost this predominance and the private car began to dictate the pattern of holiday-making. There was an increasing demand for more sophisticated leisure facilities. The country was at the mercy of urban requirements in a way it had never been before.

Unobtrusively, individuals and pressure groups had been preparing themselves for this invasion. The activities of bodies like the CPRE merged with the growing academic, official and parliamentary concern about land use to produce a spate of enquiries and recommendations during the Second World War. Despite measures like the 1935 Restriction of Ribbon Development Act, agricultural land continued to be taken over for other purposes at a high rate. Over 60,000 acres a year were used for building throughout the 1930s and a further

20,000 for sporting and military purposes and as woodlands. Military requirements naturally increased during the war, approaching 100,000 acres a year, only a third of which eventually found its way back to agriculture. These figures related to England and Wales, Scottish data not being available before 1951–52. Loss of farming land continued immediately after the war on a substantial scale. Concern about such a prospect had prompted a demand for accurate information and Sir Dudley Stamp directed the first Land Utilisation Survey in 1931–33. It purported to account for every acre in Great Britain, though there were formidable classification difficulties and official statistics produced a somewhat different answer. The Uthwatt Report (1942) tackled the problem of the development value of land and the Scott Report (1942) considered the use of land in rural areas. The latter, which contained paragraphs on recreation and conservation, advocated the creation of National Parks and Nature Reserves. The Forestry Commission already had a number of Forest Parks, but the idea behind the National Park scheme was to open up large areas, mainly upland and sparsely populated, for public enjoyment, while protecting that sort of countryside and maintaining farming. It was not easy to reconcile these aspirations, and the political relationship between the commissioners and the local authorities also proved contentious. Nevertheless, the 1949 National Parks and Access to the Countryside Act established a principle in relation to such areas as Dartmoor, Snowdonia, the Peak District, the Lake District and the North York Moors. In the same year, the Nature Conservancy, charged with the responsibility for providing scientific advice on the conservation and control of flora and fauna, and managing Nature Reserves, was given a royal charter(163).

Laudable though these developments were, resources were not available to provide more ambitious schemes. The location of industry and the redevelopment of towns proved more pressing concerns. During the 1930s, a fresh spate of investigations took place into social conditions in the towns – in Bristol and on Merseyside and Tyneside, for example. There was a *New Survey of London Life and Labour* (1934) and Rowntree published *Poverty and Progress* (1941), a further study of York taken in 1935. The authors of the London survey concluded that the percentage of the population below the poverty line was only about one-third of that found by Charles Booth in East and South-east London forty years earlier. Nevertheless, they still found cause for concern. Rowntree, without being complacent, also had a story of improvement to tell. But almost half the children of working-class parents spent their first five years in poverty and almost a third lived below the poverty line for a decade or more. The biggest improvement was in housing, thanks both to council and private building. In many areas, the trend of the 1930s in the housing 'mix' reversed that of the previous decade. In Birmingham, for example, whereas between 1924 and 1931 32,829 municipal and 14,869 private houses were built, from 1932 to 1938, 38,070 private houses were built and 13,484 municipal(164). Everything depended upon the local socio-economic climate. In Glasgow, for example, there was a virtual stop to building for home ownership, though in Edinburgh the private bungalow made a quite extensive appearance. Some of the worst housing areas, however, lay outside the cities(154). In the small and largely mining communities of South Wales or North-east England there was a cycle of unemployment and deprivation leading to chronic depression and loss of morale. John Newsom issued a 'Challenge to the comfortable' in *Out of the pit* (1936). Writing as Director of the Community Service Council for County Durham, he painted a picture of a society losing faith in itself. 'The Durham pitman has always been noted for his independence', one of their number noted, 'but that's going now, and in some ways it's the greatest tragedy of all.'[2] Newsom argued that the economic health of the nation could only be considered as a whole. Edward VIII was shocked by the poverty he saw in Dowlais in November 1936, observing, 'Something must be done.'(135).

In 1934, the first modest attempt was made to deal with this distress. Four 'Special Areas' were designated – South Wales, North-east England, West Cumberland and Central Scotland. Unpaid commissioners were appointed to disburse limited amounts of public money to local authorities and other public bodies. It would be grandiloquent to describe such steps as a regional policy, but it was a mild recognition by central government that the prosperity of the United Kingdom ought to be more uniform. Within a few years, more money was available, supplemented by donations from private sources. Following the 1937 Special Areas Amendment Act, the commissioners could give special reliefs to firms setting up in these areas. Workers could also obtain grants to help in migrating to places where there was work. But was this the answer? The Barlow Commission was set up in the same year to consider the distribution of the industrial population. In its report (1940), there was general agreement on a 'National Industrial Board' which would research into, advise upon and regulate the location of industry. The drift of the industrial population to London and the Home Counties demanded 'immediate action'. In fact, of course, while the Commission was investigating, the country moved to war. The report noted that the vulnerability of the South-east to German attack had forced employers to consider dispersal. There was some hope that Bristol, Cardiff, Birmingham, Manchester, Liverpool and Glasgow might attract some industry 'especially if they became Regional capitals (and if these Regional capitals become important governmental, administrative and financial centres) . . .'. If this trend was encouraging, the problem might well return after the war when the stimulus it gave to the heavy industrial regions came to an end.

The 1945 Distribution of Industry Act established new 'Development Areas', placing responsibility for future policy and executive action on the Board of Trade. It could build factories, reclaim sites and, on certain conditions, make loans. The most important innovation, however, was the 1947 Town and Country Planning Act, establishing a ministry of that name. Its predecessor, the 1932 Act, had been thought in effective. The new measure took planning powers from the districts and gave them to county and county borough councils – a drastic reduction in the number of bodies involved. Each planning authority had to produce a development plan which had to be updated from time to time. Any material change of use had to accord with the plan. The Board of Trade now had authority to issue 'industrial development certificates' for all new factory building, or substantial modification to existing factories. The Development Areas did benefit, with something like half of the new industrial building in the late 1940s coming their way. This, combined with a strong initial post-war demand for coal, markedly reduced the disparity in their unemployment rates as compared with the non-assisted areas. Since all seemed to be going well, the policy was then relaxed. The Conservatives, in particular, yielded to the wishes of industrialists to set up in the Midlands, London and the South-east where, they argued, most of the population lived and the biggest economies of scale for consumer-orientated industries could be found. By the mid-1950s, 'regional policy' was faltering badly.

There were, however, other vigorous developments which owed their origin to the wartime reports. The 1946 New Towns Act sprang directly from a committee chaired by Lord Reith. New towns were to be entrusted to development corporations appointed and financed by the Minister of Town and Country Planning or the Scottish Secretary. They could acquire sites to develop complete new towns – providing houses, factories, commercial buildings and all necessary public services. The original intention was to begin 20 new towns, though in fact between 1947 and 1950, 14 were started – 12 in England, 2 in Scotland and 1 in Wales. Cumbernauld in Scotland became the fifteenth in 1956. Learning from the experience of Welwyn Garden City (which was taken over), these new towns were designed to be self-sufficient communities of modest size which could relieve pressure upon London and Glasgow, while Corby, Cwmbran, Glenrothes, Newton Aycliffe and Peterlee were all designed to diversify their region's industrial base(154,165).

There was scarcely anything about these new communities that was not controversial but, on the whole, they thrived. In addition, the 1952 Town Development Act, and its Scottish counterpart, opened the way for agreements between big cities and small towns or country areas to receive population and industry from congested areas. There were, however, considerable financial problems in such arrangements. Dramatic progress was difficult but, in the case of Glasgow, was badly needed. It has been noted that Glasgow's congestion in 1956 was unparalleled in the United Kingdom. There were 700,000 people living in the centre of the city at an average density of over 360 people per acre. Some 12,000 people were huddled together in one area of 7 acres. About 40 per cent of all houses were of one or two rooms, compared with only 5 per cent in London and 2.5 per cent on Merseyside and 30 per cent of Glasgow's families shared toilets, compared with 2.6 per cent in London and 1.1 per cent on Merseyside. Destruction and dispersal seemed to provide the answer.

The new towns generated a great deal of interest and enthusiasm but they could not, in themselves, solve the problems of London or the other major cities in the United Kingdom. Indeed, there was some feeling, apparently given justification by the first selection of towns, that the scheme had no application for the major provincial centres. Some of them, of course, had to rebuild their city centres anyway because of wartime destruction. However, there was one statement made in 1955 by the then Minister of Housing and Local Government, Duncan Sandys, that brought to at least temporary conclusion a discussion that had been going on for twenty years. A White Paper gave official blessing to the 'green belt' and defined its purpose. It could be used to check the growth of a built-up area, prevent the merging of two neighbouring towns, or preserve the special character of an existing town. The green belt, on which, except in extraordinary circumstances, no new building was to be allowed, was of particular relevance to the London area, but it applied generally. The trouble with London remained that it continued to grow. The first planning projections were based on false assumptions; the 1943 County of London Plan and the 1944 Greater London Plan both assumed that the task was not to cope with an expanding population but to redistribute the existing population out of the older inner areas to new and existing towns beyond the green belt. But, despite the wishes of successive governments, the attraction of London remained overwhelming. The notion of 'strong countervailing regional centres' canvassed widely before and during the war, virtually disappeared. London seemed the centre of virtually everything – it became, for example, the hub of the national air network which linked most of the major centres of population. This concentration was widely regretted, but no one seemed to know how to prevent it.

Agriculture sat awkwardly between the continuing growth of the towns and the aspirations of conservationists. In the late 1930s, advocates of a subsidy to assist the depressed industries looked enviously upon the government's attitude to agriculture. It had, indeed, undergone a dramatic change with the ending of Free Trade, though the maintenance of imperial preference meant that there was still a major place for imperial food products. Even so, the British Sugar Corporation was established on a permanent basis to stimulate sugar production and operate the subsidy. More generally, the 1931 Agricultural Marketing Acts made the marketing scheme agreed by a majority of producers of a given commodity compulsory for all. Marketing Boards came into operation for a number of products – the most familiar to the public was the Milk Marketing Board. Information services for farmers were expanded and the 1937 Agriculture Act established a national veterinary service. Further assistance was provided with land drainage. The remarkable researches of Sir George Stapledon at Aberystwyth into grass strains, clover and the system of 'ley' farming, transformed some Welsh hill areas into worthwhile pasture. The cumulative result of these various developments was that although less than one-third of the food consumed in Britain in 1939 was grown there, farming was in better heart than had seemed possible a decade earlier. Cattle, sheep and poultry were all at considerably higher levels than they had been in 1914, though they were heavily dependent upon overseas feeding-stuffs – which would largely have to be sacrificed in the war. Once more, a new programme of ploughing had to be started, and home-grown crops encouraged. It became vital to 'lend a hand on the land' and 'dig for victory' and the results were impressive. There was a new enthusiasm about agriculture and a lasting appreciation of its importance – which did not prevent 'real' farmers from allowing the newly ploughed land in traditional pastoral area in northern England to revert to pasture at the first opportunity.

After the war, the structure of State support for farming was not dismantled. The 1947 Agriculture Act declared that farming was to be a 'permanent' part of the national economy. Farmers received public money to cover some of the cost of capital investment on farms and were given guaranteed prices for their products. A National Agricultural Advisory Service was set up in 1946, concerning itself not simply with husbandry but also with financial management and other business matters. Farms became cleaner and neater, machinery became more complex and labour-saving. The benefits were not all confined to fertile areas. Hill-farmers in Scotland and Wales received subsidies for hill sheep and cattle which could not have been contemplated twenty years earlier. They particularly benefited from the extensive investment in the electricity supply industry following nationalization. A. G. Street, in a 1950 postscript to *Farmer's Glory* thought that 'the present prosperity of British farming is mainly due to one man, who is now dead. His name is Adolf Hitler. . . .'[3] Street believed that it was the fear of famine during the 1940s which taught the British nation that when real danger came the land was their only permanent asset. When world production picked up after the war, and the memory of Hitler began to fade, that commitment began to weaken, but by the mid-1950s it was still strong. Indeed, though it never became a party political matter, certain MPs from urban constituencies attacked the 'feather-bedding' of farmers.

Forestry also benefited from this concern to safeguard natural resources. During the war, the Forestry Commission fixed an ambitious target of 5 million acres of productive woodland, to be achieved in fifty years. A survey of woodland was carried out and further afforestation and replanting schemes commenced. State forestry had substantially larger targets than the private sector. By the early 1950s, however, the Commission was already having difficulty in obtaining the land it needed, facing competition and conflict with farmers and the water authorities. The National Parks created a further complication. Environmentalists complained about the impact on the landscape of too many conifers. But was it the Forestry Commission's business to be concerned with amenity provision? The emergence of these and other related questions showed that in the case of forestry, and more generally, 'planning the environment' in a way which reconciled town and country and the requirements of different, but equally meritorious users was a more difficult task than had perhaps been assumed when the apparatus of planning was established.

---

1. L. C. B. Seaman, *Life in Britain between the wars* (1970), p. 165
2. J. Newsom, *Out of the pit* (1936), p. 41
3. A. G. Street, *Farmer's glory* (1950), Penguin edn., p. 224

CHAPTER 26

Education and sport

Another war produced another spurt of interest in education. Books poured from the presses, despite limitations on paper. 'England', wrote Sir Richard Livingstone in 1943, 'has probably never been so interested in education as to-day.' People perceived the obvious and increasing importance of knowledge to life and realized that 'our democracy is very ill-educated'. He even argued that a great victory in 1918 had been thrown away 'with a rapidity and completeness perhaps unexampled in history and . . . this has partly been due to political ignorance'.[1] Education needed to be extended if equality of opportunity was to be more than a phrase. The content of education, however, was as important as its organization. Livingstone, president of an Oxford college, believed that it had become 'a mass of unco-ordinated subjects, a chaos instead of a cosmos'.[2] The spiritual element in education was weak, where it had not perished, with disastrous consequences for civilization. The theme of another of Livingstone's best-selling books was that nothing could be done until that element was restored. Other writers on education saw its failure partly in the fact that it did not take sufficient account of scientific progress – 'Lack of knowledge of the potentialities of science is frustrating the goodwill which our education in values should develop.'[3] For their part, politicians stressed that in what would be a hard post-war world the national future rested 'upon the efficiency of our education service'. There was nothing, it seemed, that education could not do and for which it was not vital. It was against this background that the 1944 Education Act was passed – by a House of Commons 56 per cent of whose members had been at public schools, 21 per cent at State secondary schools and 22 per cent at elementary schools only.

The 1930s had been a decade of discussion, but little new legislation. A 1931 Report on the primary school for the Board of Education suggested that for pre-adolescent children the curriculum should be considered in terms of 'activity and experience' rather than of 'knowledge to be acquired'. Some parents found the amount of 'activity' that developed rather disturbing. At the secondary level, the 'Hadow reorganization' was carried out by local authorities with their usual lack of uniformity. By 1938, nearly two-thirds of all elementary schools had been reorganized and in that year the Spens Committee reported to the Board of Education on the evolving pattern of secondary education. It recommended the expansion of technical high schools (which it considered to offer something more than vocational education) and suggested that the grammar schools should reckon to absorb about 15 per cent of the relevant age group. Relying on psychological evidence, it was 'evident that different children from the age of eleven, if justice was to be done to their varying capacities, require types of education varying in certain important respects'. It considered the possibility of establishing what it called 'multilateral' schools, but favoured separate schools largely on grounds of size, of doubts about the viability of sixth forms and of the difficulty in finding head teachers who would be capable of inspiring both sides of a multilateral school. Selection at eleven was quite feasible, it thought, though there should be a further review at the age of thirteen. The establishment of parity between all types of secondary school was 'a fundamental requirement'(226).

The Spens Report had to be put on one side with the outbreak of war, but early in 1941 the Board of Education drew up a Green Book on education after the war which, though supposedly confidential, became the basis for public discussion. R. A. Butler, who became President of the Board of Education in July, was anxious to gather a wide variety of opinions. The religious issue, which had led to so much difficulty in the past, needed particularly careful handling. Though their facilities fell below what could be offered in council schools, about half of the schools in England were still church schools. Far fewer church schools had been reorganized along Hadow lines and these disparities required some attention. The Green Book was followed in July 1943 by a White Paper on educational reconstruction which formed the basis of the subsequent bill. Extensive consultations meant that in its final form the 1944 Education Act had the general support of all the interests concerned. The dual system of local authority and church schools survived, but was modified. Church schools were split into 'aided' and 'controlled' – a division which corresponded to the Roman Catholic and the Anglican approaches. In the former, the governors retained the right to give denominational religious instruction if they could provide half the cost of alteration or rebuilding in their schools. They would be paid grants covering the other half and also be paid the cost of salaries of the staff whom they would still appoint. Where the governors of a school could not contribute 50 per cent, local authorities nominated a majority of governors in the 'controlled' schools and accepted responsibility for their maintenance. Religious instruction would be according to an 'agreed syllabus', with some provision for specific denominational instruction. That agreed syllabus, which had still to be worked out, would also form the basis for religious instruction in the local authority schools at primary and secondary level(221).

The Minister of Education (his new title) was empowered to 'promote the education of the people in England and Wales . . . and to secure the effective execution by local authorities, under his control and direction, of the national policy for providing a varied and comprehensive educational service in every area'. Power to raise an education rate and borrow money was placed in the hands of the 146 county and county borough councils as the 'Local Education Authorities' (LEAs). This meant, with certain exceptions, that the large number of urban district councils were squeezed out of their educational role. Small authorities with a 'progressive' outlook argued that they would be swamped, but other commentators wondered whether they would be large enough. Few grasped the size of the responsibility which was going to fall on these LEAs within the next decade. The Act raised the school-leaving age to fifteen and a motion that it should be raised to sixteen was quite narrowly lost. It was left to the minister to raise the age to sixteen when he was 'satisfied that it has become practicable'. It was evident that neither buildings nor teachers were available for the immediate implementation of such a policy. Schooling itself was not compulsory, but it was the duty of the parent to cause the child 'to receive efficient full-time education suitable to his age, ability, and aptitude, either by regular attendance at school or otherwise'. The LEAs were given extended duties and powers in the provision of school medical services, milk and meals.

The Act further declared that the statutory system of public education was to be 'organized in three progressive stages to be known as primary education, secondary education, and further education'. The Norwood Report (1943) had reinforced the conception of three 'types of education', the secondary grammar, technical and modern. Each type should have, as far as possible, 'parity of amenities', but added 'parity of esteem in our view cannot be conferred by administrative decree nor by equality of cost per pupil; it can only be won by the school itself.' It took the view that, however carefully devised and sympathetically carried out, differentiation at eleven-plus could not be regarded as final and the curricula of all schools until the age of thirteen should be so designed as to permit the efficient transfer between types of school. It was on this basis that the expansion of the post-war decade took place. Labour ministers supported this differentiation as eagerly as the educationalists, but at the county level there were doubts among Labour supporters about the fairness of the system. Anglesey, in Wales, became the first LEA to establish a completely 'comprehensive' system of secondary education – it did so by 1953 – but it was most unusual in this regard(222).

The 'direct grant' and the public schools both survived. The 1944 Act abolished fee-paying in maintained schools and an attempt was made to abolish them in direct grant schools but it failed. After the war, there were 232 such schools, containing nearly 18 per cent of the total grammar-school populations, although only 4 per cent of the proposed secondary sector. Some 25 per cent of their pupils had free places, and in some of the best-known schools the figure was nearer the maximum of 50 per cent. The other pupils paid fees, but they could be reduced in the light of parental income. The total number of such schools began to fall, though the number of pupils remained the same, and such schools as Bristol Grammar, Manchester Grammar and King Edward's, Birmingham, maintained high reputations for academic excellence.

The Fleming Committee (1944) had been set up to consider some means whereby the association between the public schools and the general educational system could be extended. Though convinced that educational choice should not depend on financial considerations, neither of its alternative recommendations found much acceptance. The proposal which was most discussed was that public schools should reserve at least 25 per cent of their places for children from primary schools. The LEAs should pay their fees and recover the money from parents on an income-related scale and from the ministry. Selection of such pupils proved a major difficulty and LEAs were not prepared to pay the much higher costs of boarding-school education. Notable products of public schools, like

R. H. Tawney, were not slow to find public schools incompatible with the kind of society they envisaged. However, the Labour party as a whole did not take up a specific policy towards the public schools. Some members hoped that financial pressures would lead to their demise and, in some cases, this happened. An independent school had to be registered with the Department of Education under the 1944 Act, though this provision was not implemented for some years. Schools like Gordonstoun and Millfield, founded in the mid-1930s, consolidated their positions. The former had the good fortune to educate the duke of Edinburgh and the latter was merely bent on becoming 'the most efficient teaching organization in the world'(223).

Yet another report in 1944, presided over by another lawyer, Sir Arnold McNair, produced its findings on increasing the number and quality of teachers necessary to staff the expanded educational service. While no scales were stated, it recommended that salaries should be substantially increased. The ban on married teachers was condemned. The Burnham Committee ought to be composed of a single committee for teachers in primary and secondary schools. Several proposals were canvassed for linking the training of teachers to the work of universities and, after the war, 'Institutes of Education' were established. The number of students who successfully completed initial training courses rose from some 6,000 in 1939 to some 14,000 in 1956. Although three years had been suggested as the minimum period of training for non-graduate teachers by McNair, this proposal was shelved. An Emergency Training Scheme was put into operation to channel ex-service people quickly into schools. No less than 15 per cent of teachers in primary and secondary schools had been so trained by the time the scheme ended in 1951 – with dubious effects(224).

The universities, also, were expanding, Just before the war there were some 50,000 university students in Britain and by the mid-1950s that figure had risen to 82,000 and represented about 3½ per cent of their age group. Universities became more expensive to run and much more heavily dependent upon public funds – a measure of that dependence was the fact that collectively nearly 75 per cent of their income came from that source in 1955/56. The UGC, in a report on university development from 1935 to 1947 wrote that the rapid expansion of staff and buildings imposed upon the universities 'a task which is unparalleled in their earlier development'. Large sums had to be earmarked for building new laboratories, halls of residence and libraries. Provision was made for the award of a limited number of State scholarships to universities, and LEAs had the power to make further awards. The Norwood Committee had also concerned itself with school examinations. It recommended that the School Certificate and the Higher School Certificate be phased out. In their place it suggested what became the General Certificate of Education, with Ordinary, Advanced and Scholarship levels in 1951. It was claimed that the new system would lead to the elimination of cramming and premature specialization. The expansion of student numbers was not met by the rapid creation of new universities – with one exception. Rather, all existing universities grew in size and the university colleges of Nottingham, Hull, Southampton, Exeter and Leicester all became full universities between 1948 and 1957. The exception was Keele, initially known as the University College of North Staffordshire, which began life, on a wholly residential basis, in 1949. Under the guidance of the former Master of Balliol, A. D. Lindsay, who pioneered a degree course extending over four years, Keele excited a great deal of interest. Academically and socially, though no longer numerically, Oxford and Cambridge remained preponderant. Concomitant with this expansion, the size and terms of reference of the UGC were amended. In 1952 it was explicitly stated that the committee was to assist in the planning of university development 'in order to ensure that they are fully adequate to national needs'.

About half of the total university population in the 1930s continued to study arts subjects (within which are included the expanding 'social sciences') and over 40 per cent were studying them in the mid-1950s. In such a context, there was continuing concern about higher education in technology. The Percy Committee (1945) reported serious shortcomings both in its quality and quantity. It suggested that a select number of technical colleges should be designated colleges of technology, still to be under the control of LEAs. Regional advisory councils would eliminate wasteful duplication and competition. However, little came of these proposals and the idea of a technological university, canvassed in the early 1950s, was also rejected. The 1956 White Paper on technical education went over this familiar ground, but stressed the need for urgent action because 'the romance of science is catching on . . .'. The following year, the colleges of advanced technology were set up as the apex of the system of technical education. It was not clear how such institutions stood in relation to the universities. The Barlow Committee, which in 1946 had tried to estimate the country's scientific manpower needs, reported that there was 'clearly an ample reserve of intelligence in the country to allow both a doubling of university numbers and at the same time a raising of standards . . .', but the scientists on the committee attached 'the greatest importance to the atmosphere of an association of men and women which takes all knowledge as its province and in which all branches of learning flourish in harmony'(222).

This moving picture of a community of scholars contrasted with the *Crisis in the University* (1949) discovered by Sir Walter Moberley, a chairman of the UGC. He wrote that despite the façade of development and hopefulness, British universities had little inner self-confidence because they lacked an agreed sense of direction and purpose. They shared rather than transcended the spiritual confusion of the age. 'Bruce Truscott' in his *Red Brick University* (1943) had no doubt that a large number of idle professors were ruining the traditions of their calling. He felt that if an arts faculty had half its week free for research it would not be used for that purpose 'but there would be a tremendous improvement in the standard of the Arts staffs' front gardens!'[4] Kingsley Amis's *Lucky Jim* (1954) presented a less didactic impression of provincial university life. Readers of the novel were privileged to hear 'History speaking'.

The educational changes made throughout the rest of the United Kingdom during this period followed a broadly similar pattern. Separate Education (Scotland) Acts were passed in 1945 and 1946. Since, in Scotland, denominational schools had been taken into the local authority system, though leaving certain powers to the Roman Catholic Church, the English dual system did not apply. Local authorities also retained the right to charge fees in any of their schools. Responsibility for educational administration remained with the Scottish Secretary and not with the Minister of Education. A limited number of schools in Scotland were 'grant aided', a system comparable to the direct grant, although such schools were not in return required to reserve any fixed proportion of their places for children from local authority schools. The English debate about the structure of secondary education did not precisely apply in Scotland; many small-town academies were virtually comprehensive in practice. In 1951, the Scottish Leaving Certificate also ceased to be a group certificate and candidates were allowed to take any number or combination of subjects, though this was only an interim solution. It had still to be decided whether the 'O' and 'A' level system in England and Wales should be copied. The debate involved not only educational issues but also national and cultural susceptibilities. Similar questions hung over the universities of Scotland with their tradition of broadly based initial years of study. After 1945, they all expanded, though no new university was established. A variety of 'central institutions' also flourished, though under the direct control of the Scottish Education Department, whereas their counterparts in England were run by local authorities. A major institution like the Royal College of Science and Technology in Glasgow steadily expanded, raising in the process questions about its ultimate future. The immediate pressure, in all sectors, was to provide accommodation and resources – in the last half of 1953 Glasgow was opening a new school every month – and more far-reaching questions might be tackled when, if ever, such accommodation had been provided(218, 220, 225).

The ripples of the Butler Act also reached Belfast. Since the 1923 Education Act (Northern Ireland), its educational system had moved away from previous Irish precedent and come closer to the English model – with certain exceptions. The Northern Ireland government had provided that aid should be distributed to schools in proportion to the degree of control they accepted from local authorities. It tried to prevent local authorities from giving any kind of religious instruction, while allowing ministers and clergy to give denominational instruction to their members. Lord Londonderry, the Minister of Education, stressed that the State was thus 'non-sectarian, but not secular . . .' and his main concern was to safeguard education from denominational pressures which produced 'division when union is so essential to the well-being of this province'. The Catholic bishops declared their total opposition and Protestants were scarcely less hostile. Only when an amendment in 1925 removed the ban on religious instruction did the transfer of Protestant schools into the local authority system accelerate. A further Act of 1930 empowered the system to provide bible instruction if a school failed to provide it, though it was to be neither catechetical nor compulsory. The Catholic bishops would not transfer their schools on such a basis, but claimed the same grants as those paid to transferred schools. The government agreed to pay 50 per cent, but would go no higher.[5]

The 1944 Education White Paper (NI) envisaged a tripartite secondary school system, with different names but fulfilling the same function as those in England

and Wales. In the subsequent 1947 legislation, fees were not abolished and ministers and clergy retained their 'right of access' to schools. Critical shortages, both of teachers and accommodation, meant that the principles underlying the legislation across the Irish Sea were put into practice more slowly in Northern Ireland. After several postponements, the school-leaving age was not raised to fifteen until 1957. In 1949, a committee on the examination system suggested that papers for the Senior Certificate should be set at 'O' and 'A' levels, corresponding to the changes proposed in England, though when the change was made in 1952, the group certificate principle was initially retained. These alterations did, for a time, give rise to problems of interchangeability and acceptance between different parts of the United Kingdom, but not on a very serious scale. Although divergencies of structure and ethos existed between the four parts of the kingdom, it seemed to be moving in the direction of a common system(220).

SPORT

In 1953, the English football team lost its proud record of never having been beaten in England by a foreign national team, when Hungary won a famous encounter 6–3. That this was no fluke was proved by the 7–1 defeat England sustained in Budapest the following year. In 1908, England had won 7–0 in Budapest. It seemed to be an indication that even on the football field England had to endure a loss of status. The home Football Associations and clubs in the Football League had to reconsider the basis of their game and throw off the insular assumptions of superiority.

Before the war, arising out of the political complications of the 1920s, United Kingdom football had been cut off from some international developments. No home team competed in the World Cup in 1930 (the first World Cup) and the same was true in 1934 and 1938. Even so, isolation from the world game was not complete. Between 1929 and 1939 England played twenty-three matches on the Continent and entertained France, Spain, Germany, Austria, Italy, Hungary, Norway and Czechoslovakia at home. There were also some club tours in Europe, but the results were much closer than they had been before 1930. British coaches were at work across the Channel and the retiring FA secretary noted in 1934 that there was no longer any question of stopping counting after British teams had scored ten goals(247). Most domestic British excitement continued to focus on the clashes between England and Scotland. This match became an all-ticket affair for the first time in 1937 – with 150,000 being sold. Football, it seemed, could not escape political complications. The Foreign Office could see no reason why the English team should not give the Nazi salute before the kick-off in the match against Germany in 1938. It was important for the virility of democracy that the team should give a good account of itself. Such concern coexisted uneasily with a previous Home Secretary's attempt to discourage the idea 'that a sporting fixture in this country has any political considerations'(248).

During the Second World War, the initial ban on organized football was soon lifted, but many difficulties remained in practice. It was now thought, in contrast to the First World War, that football matches provided a demonstration of the country's capacity to carry on as usual. Football certainly flourished in the armed services, though the standard of the game at club level – apart from such happy exceptions as Aldershot – inevitably declined. With the return of peace, there was a great surge of excited interest. Attendances in the post-war seasons reached levels not attained before or since. Some 60,000 people regularly crowded on to the bleak, open terraces at St James's Park, Newcastle, to watch the skill of Jackie Milburn. Football matches of this order were great (overwhelmingly male) communal rites. In the years of austerity there were few competing counter-attractions. There was little in the shops to lead men to succumb to a domestic tug in that direction. In the peak season of 1948/49, there were more than 41 million attendances. An international flavour had early been provided by the visit of Moscow Dynamo who beat Arsenal, the dominant English side of the 1930s, in a match characterized by the inability of the players to distinguish each other in the fog. After these heroes of the Soviet Union departed, spectators settled down to the routine excitements of cup and league. The English side did appoint a team manager, but he had to accept the priority of club commitments. England and Scotland did play in the 1950 World Cup for the first time – but England were defeated by the USA team captained by a free-transfer Scottish player from the Welsh club Wrexham. It was not an auspicious début. The 1954 World Cup was televised in Europe and gave the still-limited number of British viewers a glimpse of different football fare. At a time when attendances were beginning to slump, enterprising managers, like Cullis of Wolverhampton Wanderers, believed that matches against foreign clubs would revive interest; his club's match against the Hungarian club Honved in December 1954, marked a turning-point. At long last, English and Scottish clubs seemed on the verge of becoming part of footballing Europe.

In 1932, when the seventeen-year old Stanley Matthews played his first senior game for Stoke City it would not have entered his head that he would, in course of time, become the first professional footballer to receive a knighthood. In the 1930s, footballers were indubitably working class; a grammar-school boy such as the English international Jack Pickering was indeed a rarity. They compared their wages with their friends and neighbours and were not dissatisfied, but they did not expect large financial rewards and were restricted by tight contracts and a minimum wage. If they enjoyed local fame and glory (if of a transient kind) they rarely departed from their social and economic origins; pulling pints behind a local bar was the destiny that frequently beckoned when boots were hung up. However, money was being made in football, and the ancillary 'pools' business became a major industry, bringing yet more glory to Liverpool. With the exception of wartime, amateurs disappeared from the international game (the last one captained Scotland in 1937). After 1945, however, amateur clubs enjoyed a revival – a team like Pegasus could excite almost as much interest as a professional club. In public parks and private grounds the enthusiasm for the game almost exceeded the supply of referees and groundsmen. Nevertheless, by the mid-1950s football was ceasing to attract so many players and spectators. As other leisure pursuits developed, it remained to be seen whether it could hold its own in more affluent conditions.

Rugby Union still prided itself on its wholly amateur character. Indeed, the home countries desisted from playing France from 1932 until, as it turned out, after the Second World War, because of suspicions that illicit payments were being made in France. In England, the game retained its predominantly public-school character (though not all public schools played it). It seemed entirely appropriate that a Russian prince, Alexander Obolensky, should have been one of England's stars in the mid-1930s. The temporary break with France made rugby even more a game of the British Commonwealth. Regular tours were made to New Zealand, Australia and South Africa, and the teams from these countries were received. Rugby suffered far more disruption from the war than football and it took a little time for the game to be reorganized. Matches with France were resumed and the honours in the early post-war period went to Ireland and Wales. Scottish rugby was in the doldrums, suffering seventeen consecutive defeats after the 1951 season. Rugby in Wales flourished and a club side like Cardiff could attract as many as 40,000 spectators. There was never that degree of support for English clubs. At the international level, however, the game lacked sparkle, leading to suggestions that the rules might be changed in order to provide more of a spectacle.

Rugby League went through a flourishing period in the 1930s. The game spread to France and in 1934/35 it was possible to establish a three-way championship between England, Wales and France. Economic conditions in South Wales tempted Welsh Rugby Union players to 'go north' – Rugby League never succeeded in Wales itself. In some Welsh valleys, the 'poacher' from the north of England was almost as unwelcome as Winston Churchill. Australians, New Zealanders and also the occasional Scot or South African also signed. This tendency continued when full-scale competition resumed after 1945. By 1949, there were so many overseas players in England that an 'Other Nationalities' team competed in the international championship, winning it in 1952/53 and 1954/55. By this time, however, the Commonwealth domination was coming to an end as restrictions were placed on the signing of overseas players. In addition, overseas players increasingly found that they could make a better living in their own countries. In this sense, the composition of Rugby League sides provides a good indicator of status and wealth within the British Isles and Commonwealth.

In 1932, it was cricket that engendered more controversy between England and Australia than anything that had led to the Statute of Westminster the previous year. During 1930, when four-day tests had been introduced to England, the Australians won the series, largely because of Bradman's magnificent performances. Jardine, who captained the MCC tour to Australia in 1932/33, hit upon 'body-line' bowling. Larwood and Voce were to deliver fast and rising balls on or outside the leg-stump to a packed leg-side field. They did so with conspicuous success. The Australian Board of Control protested to London about 'unsportsmanlike behaviour' and the tour was in jeopardy as feelings mounted on both sides. The tour did continue, but in 1935 the MCC yielded to Australian pressure and attempted to outlaw 'intimidating' bowling. Australia won the next two Test series, on largely perfect wickets. Bat certainly seemed to have the upper hand over ball.

Perhaps English cricket in this decade reflected the different social experiences of the country. Cardus paints a grim picture of the 'Roses' matches between Lancashire and Yorkshire during the depression when a flamboyant gesture, like hitting a four before lunch, was frowned upon. Leonard Hutton emerged in this gritty world. In Somerset and Gloucester, however, buccolic boundaries were struck by Wellard and Gimblett, Hammond and Barnett. The return of cricket after 1945 excited great enthusiasm. There seemed nothing wrong with the game or with the crowds. In 1947, the Middlesex pair of Compton and Edrich both exceeded the previous record number of runs in a season, with Compton also making the record number of eighteen centuries. The Australian visit in 1948 attracted huge crowds and the undreamed-of happened – Glamorgan won the county championship. The Australian team completed its programme without losing any matches and showed all-round superiority. The lack of steaks in post-war England may account for the absence of English fast bowlers. In 1950, the batting distinction of Worrell, Weekes and Walcott, and the spin bowling of Valentine and Ramadhin gave the West Indies their first Test victory (and the series) in England. Was this another loss of status? Such fears were apparently banished when England regained the Ashes in 1953, beating Australia at home. It was deemed wise, however, to send the strongest possible side to the West Indies the following winter, but it could only draw. That was not a happy tour – perhaps the first indication of impending social, financial and political pressures. Captaining England against India in 1952, Hutton became the first professional to lead England. His approach did not please everybody whether it was the flowing public schoolboy Peter May, the graceful direct-grant schoolboy Graveney or 'fiery' Fred Trueman, the new fast bowler (who had managed to find a few steaks). At home, a certain malaise settled over the county championship. When Warwickshire won the title under a professional captain in 1951 there were those who thought that the abolition of the distinction between 'gentlemen' and 'players' (which had enjoyed a long post-war innings) was overdue. There was a certain deathly hush over the fact that cricket might be ceasing to be a white-flannelled epitome of the social structure and turning into a game played for profit.

All sports were increasingly afflicted by this question. Until the 1920s, lawn tennis had been an amateur sport and its popularity was then very high. Tennis was a more agreeable mixed social occasion than cricket. There was something inherently elegant about women playing tennis which not even the feats of Mollie Hide, captain of the England's women's cricket team from 1937 to 1954 could alter. Wimbledon gained prestige socially from royal patronage and the duke of York (the later George VI) was of sufficiently high standard to appear in the men's doubles – perhaps trying to emulate his elder brother who had once played rugby against a Japanese side on an official visit to that country in 1923. By the 1930s, however, the best players were turning professional. Fred Perry reigned supreme, capturing the Wimbledon title three times in succession (1934–

36) and the major foreign titles before he turned professional. It was the old difficulty. Standards of play were rising to such an extent that, unless endowed with substantial private means, it was impossible for 'amateurs', in any traditional sense, to remain at the top. The outbreak of the war postponed the issue, and even in the mid-1950s, the pretence was maintained that professionals were a different species from the amateur who only received expenses. The Olympic Games were not yet seriously afflicted. They came to a rather austere London in 1948. British athletes did not distinguish themselves, though it was not until the next games that Britain had to rely on a horse, Foxhunter, for its sole medal. British athletes had more success in the British Empire Games, first held in Canada in 1930 and staged for the first time after the war in New Zealand in 1950. There was one major triumph on the track. A four-minute mile had long been a goal of runners and the barrier was broken by Roger Bannister in May 1954.

In the mid-1950s, therefore, all major sports stood at a difficult point. Did they all need star performers to attract spectators if, and the phrase is used advisedly, they were to stay in business? It was apparent that the sporting public was more mobile and adventurous than ever before. Anglers departed to the river bank at week-ends and badminton, bowls, golf and skating all had their enthusiasts. Television was about to make a major impact. Stirling Moss drew increasing crowds to revived Grand Prix motor-racing. Few cared to guess what the social pattern of sport would be in another twenty years.

---

1. Sir R. Livingstone, *Education for a world adrift* (Cambridge, 1943), p. ix
2. Sir R. Livingstone, *The future in education* (Cambridge, 1941), p. 126
3. S. R. Humby and E. J. F. James, *Science in education* (Cambridge, 1942), p. 141
4. B. Truscott, *Red brick university* (1951), Pelican edn., p. 352
5. N. Atkinson, *Irish education* (Dublin, 1969)

CHAPTER 27

Cultures and creeds

'Of all the Great Powers', the Prince of Wales declared in 1935, 'this country is the last in the field in setting up a proper organization to spread a proper knowledge and appreciation of its language, literature, art, science and education. . . .' Thus, in the same year the British Council was born. The Foreign Office hoped to 'use our cultural work as a very definite political instrument. This work should go hand in hand with our foreign policy. . . .'[1] Although its budget was limited, there was clearly a demand for the Council's services. Lecturers were sent across the globe: there were British art exhibitions in Johannesburg, Paris, Vienna and the New York World Fair; concert tours were arranged in Europe and even the Fleet Street Choir ventured across the Channel in 1938; British books were advertised and distributed abroad. What were these achievements about which the world should learn?

LITERATURE

'For this immediate future', wrote T. S. Eliot in January 1939, 'perhaps for a long way ahead, the continuity of culture may have to be maintained by a very small number of people indeed. . . .' Those who were concerned with that small part of literature which was really creative, though seldom popular, should keep to their task. Eliot became more and more convinced that 'culture is the one thing that we cannot deliberately aim at'. It was the product of a variety of activities, each pursued for its own sake.[2] From a different standpoint, F. R. Leavis wrote in the 1930s on mass civilization and minority culture. He founded a new journal, *Scrutiny* (1932–53), which purported to establish new standards of acceptability in criticism.

Whatever the critics wrote, literature continued in its wide variety. Eliot himself continued to write poetry, reaching its high point in the wartime *Four Quartets*. Down to 1954 he also wrote verse-plays, the most successful being *Murder in the Cathedral* (1935). De la Mare and Masefield continued to write extensively until the early 1950s. Robert Graves showed his versatility over a wide field. Edith Sitwell specialized in English women and English eccentrics. These were all established writers from the 1920s and earlier. A new generation made their mark in the 1930s, with such diverse talents as Roy Campbell, Cecil Day Lewis, Louis MacNeice and Stephen Spender. The master was W. H. Auden who characterized the 1930s as the 'low, dishonest decade' – a reflection delivered from the security of New York in 1939. These writers all showed a high degree of political commitment – usually to the Left. After the war, this commitment crumbled. New talents, like Dylan Thomas, came to the fore. He shone briefly and brightly. The London literary scene was not very congenial to men who liked the protection of a Celtic mist. W. R. Rodgers, Edwin Muir, G. S. Fraser, Norman MacCaig, Vernon Watkins and Alun Lewis were indeed not English, though they wrote for a British readership.

Such diverse novelists as Somerset Maugham, P. G. Wodehouse and Virginia Woolf, of established reputation, continued to write in the 1930s and, in the case of the two former, on into the 1950s. Compton Mackenzie wrote at length on love, but found more profit in whisky – galore. Dorothy Sayers turned from detective stories in the 1930s to radio plays, Dante and Christian apologetics. Popular with the reading public in the 1930s, if not with the critics, were Stephen McKenna, Frank Swinnerton and E. M. Delafield. Most novelists did not persist with the lines of exploration opened by either Joyce or Woolf. J. B. Priestley's solid novels were well received and he turned with equal success to writing for the stage. The books by Charles Morgan brought him a European reputation, if not a British one. Evelyn Waugh and Graham Greene, widely, if misleadingly paired as Catholic novelists, reached new heights of fame and achievement. It was not until after the war that L. P. Hartley's novels were acclaimed. C. P. Snow and Anthony Powell began sequences of novels which explored the higher reaches of English society. In Wales, Scotland and Northern Ireland, Jack Jones, Lewis Grassic Gibbon and Patrick Greer respectively analysed the rather different conditions of their societies. A. J. Cronin, in similar style, reached a much wider readership. Perhaps characteristic of this period is the diversity of form employed by many of these writers – essays, short stories, novels, poetry and plays. There were some who simply considered themselves playwrights. O'Casey continued to write throughout this period, but perhaps nothing so good as his earliest plays. James Bridie revived the Scottish theatre. After the war, Christopher Fry had a certain success with his verse-dramas and Terence Rattigan far more with his plays. Noel Coward remained in a class of his own.

The English, George Orwell wrote in 1941, lacked artistic ability and were outside 'the European culture'. The one art in which they had shown plenty of talent was literature, but this was the only art which could not cross frontiers. 'Literature', he concluded, 'especially poetry, and lyric poetry most of all, is a kind of family joke, with little or no value outside its own family group.'[3] Naturally, the war did accentuate British detachment, but Orwell's own post-war writings showed that Britain might not be immune from certain European political developments. Poets and writers who had once enthused about the prospect of a popular culture under the aegis of a Socialist state now trembled before the prospect that they might become literary bureaucrats in a British Ministry of Culture.

MUSIC

A Child of Our Time was the title of an oratorio by Michael Tippett first performed in London in 1944. It had been suggested by an incident in Paris in 1938 when a young Polish Jew shot a German diplomat – an act which in turn led to a pogrom against the Jews in Germany. Making skilful use of Negro spirituals, it emphasized the universality of human suffering and exploitation. The composer, too, was a child of his time. Tippett refused both military and 'alternative' service and was sentenced to prison for three months in 1943. Benjamin Britten and Peter Pears were also pacifists, but were given exemption on condition that they gave song recitals across the country. In August 1945, Britten toured the concentration camps of Germany with Yehudi Menuhin – an experience which led to his defiant setting of Donne's sonnet, 'Death be not proud'. The world of British music had moved on from the rather smug preciousness of the 1920s.

The mood had in fact begun to change in the 1930s. Constant Lambert gave up trying to compose large-scale works. Vaughan Williams did sense a more sinister atmosphere – his Fourth Symphony, with its passages of violence and bitterness, upset the impression that he was an elegiac, pastoral spirit. His choral work, *Dona Nobis Pacem*, speaks for itself. Walton's First Symphony (1935), even if the product of a personal crisis, could be taken to register a wider unease, as could Bliss's sinister march for the film *Things to Come*. The 'Crown Imperial' celebrated in Walton's expansive 1937 *Coronation March* sat less securely than might appear.

British music had come of age. When the newly formed BBC Symphony Orchestra went on its first Continental tours in 1935/36 it could include works by Bax, Elgar, Vaughan Williams and Walton without fear of derision. The role of the BBC in music-making was increasingly important. It had saved the Promenade Concerts from extinction in 1927 – Sir Henry Wood was delighted to be free from 'the everlasting box-office problem'. The formation of the London Philharmonic, under Beecham, in 1932 and the reconstruction of the London Symphony Orchestra a few years earlier were indications of the increasing importance of music in the life of the capital. The Hallé Orchestra flourished in Manchester under the Ulsterman, Sir Hamilton Harty. The BBC also had a military band and a choral society, not to mention an organ. In 1935, the BBC formed orchestras in Scotland and Wales. It was Sir Henry Wood who felt that broadcasting made attainable his 'life-long ambition of truly democratizing the message of music. . . .'(250).

For the moment, however, the gap between 'serious' music and popular taste remained wide. The BBC Dance Orchestra (1928) preceded the Symphony Orchestra by two years and it flourished under the direction of Jack Payne and then, after 1932, of Henry Hall. Other well-known bands were those of Jack Hylton, Ambrose and Geraldo. American influences on this British musical scene were strong but not all-conquering. The talent of Noel Coward and Ivor Novello ensured success for British musical revues. The BBC took determined steps to prevent its musical output becoming an endless stream of American gramophone records. Al Bowlly, who was British, was as good a 'crooner' as Bing Crosby. Music from the Café Colette, broadcast between 1933 and 1937 was 'designed to present Continental dance music as an alternative to American Jazz'. The musical plays chosen for the Silver Jubilee productions in 1935 were all British. The continuing authenticity of British musical culture was demonstrated by the fact that British singers did not get as close to the microphone as their American counterparts. When American artists did perform in Britain the electric circuits were altered to permit their customary intimacy with the microphone. Europe tried to beat off the American challenge. Damsels in dirndls dominated *The White Horse Inn* and Richard Tauber was the distinctly Teutonic heart's delight of millions. Musically, at least, it appeared that the country was moving in the direction of 'mass culture'. Gramophone records hastened the process. While the north of England liked its own shows, orchestras and bands, the music actually played was British/American. It seemed that only in the sphere of jokes did it maintain a fierce autonomy.

One (untrue) joke is that the Second World War was started by Vera Lynn's agent.[4] However, she did become the most successful singer of the war, offering the universal hope that 'We'll Meet Again'. She sang for Princess Elizabeth on the occasion of her sixteenth birthday. The 'White Cliffs of Dover' was the patriotic offering, but 'Yours' went down just as well with the troops. The pre-war dance-band fraternity re-emerged in the RAF as the Squadronnaires. The Entertainments National Service Association (ENSA), under Basil Dean, masterminded concerts of all kinds. It had competition from the Council for Education in Music and the Arts, formed in 1940. Classical music found new audiences in the provinces and among the troops. When the BBC Symphony Orchestra played at Aldershot, it broke the record for takings previously held by Gracie Fields. Dame Myra Hess gave celebrated lunch-time concerts in the National Gallery. Established composers played their part by writing film music. Vaughan Williams took off with *The Coastal Command* and Walton lauded the Spitfire in *The First of the Few*. Alan Bush, composer of an *Ode to the Red Army*, who had not been in favour with the authorities before June 1941, now broadcast Soviet Russian songs with the help of a suitable 'Labour Chorus'. Bliss, for a while Director of Music with the BBC was aware of the danger that zeal to gain the maximum audience for music could easily degenerate into wooing the lowest common denominator of that audience. The jazz band was suitable 'for artificial excitement and aphrodisiac purposes', but not for spreading 'eternal truths'.[5] Bliss thought it was no more possible to popularize great music than to popularize Christianity. He suspected that songs with titles like 'Russian Rose' would prove ephemeral.

In 1932, the *Daily Express*, ever with its finger on the pulse, opposed any subsidy for opera at Covent Garden on the grounds that it was 'a form of art which is not characteristic of the British people'. Dent, Clive Carey, Lilian Baylis and others were doing their best to prove the *Express* wrong, but it was in the decade after 1945 that both public and composers found great excitement and interest in opera. It was the genius of Britten and the success of his opera *Peter Grimes* which gave impetus to this development. Among his later works were *Albert Herring* and *The Turn of the Screw*. Walton's *Troilus and Cressida* came in 1954. It could no longer be said that opera was not 'characteristic' of the British people, though it still remained true that opportunities to see opera outside London were extremely limited. The Edinburgh International Festival (1947) quickly established a very high reputation, but the city did not have its own opera-house. Britten set up his own festival at Aldeburgh in 1948. The Cheltenham Festival encouraged the performance of contemporary British music. The BBC's Third Programme (1946) provided a regular outlet for 'serious' music. Such developments naturally increased the openings for British singers. Peter Pears became most closely associated with the work of Britten. Kathleen Ferrier's mellow contralto voice speedily took her from obscurity to the front rank in what was to prove a tragically short career.

There was little sign, however, that the vigorous musical life of the post-war decade had become 'popular' in the fashion some had anticipated during the war. The social contours of British musical life were still clearly defined. Popular music remained in the grooves which had proved so acceptable during the war. American influence, dating back to the days of the Glenn Miller orchestra and the US Army Air Force band, remained strong. Bing Crosby maintained his groaning momentum. The new phenomenon was Frank Sinatra, and his occasional visits to Britain inspired scenes of devotion which were then unprecedented. Native singers felt compelled to try to imitate American intonation and dress so that 'mid-Atlantic' became increasingly acceptable. Winifred Attwell, who played boogie-woogie on her honky-tonk piano became the most popular pianist of the early 1950s. In this period, British singers finally abandoned the notion that they could sing without a microphone. *London Laughs* was Vera Lynn's successful show which ran for two years from February 1952, but the domination of Broadway and the latest American musicals was imminent. However, her song 'Auf Wiedersehn, Sweetheart', despite its risky employment of German, was the first British record to top the charts simultaneously in Britain and the United States. Among the younger generation, however, the styles and stars of the war years were coming to seem old-fashioned. Fortunately, a young lorry-driver from Memphis, Tennessee – Elvis Presley – came to their rescue.

PAINTING

In his 1955 Reith Lectures, *The Englishness of English Art*, Pevsner did not believe that English contributors would figure prominently in any future display of twentieth-century painting. In his view, English painting was simply a reflection of Continental movements, without any original English angle. He advanced a social interpretation for this condition – England disliked violence and believed in evolution, but the leaders in art were, in a sense, violent. They were breaking up without reassembling.[6] Whether or not we accept this judgement, in the 1930s British artists were in fact in quite close touch with Continental developments. Some European painters (like Mondrian or Kokoschka) settled in this country. In the years just before the war there were substantial exhibitions in London of Continental surrealist, impressionist, cubist and expressionist painters. In 1938, Picasso's *Guernica*, with a large number of preparatory studies, went on tour in England.

The merits of these various artistic movements were, as usual, vigorously contested. Ben Nicholson became fascinated by abstract-geometrical arrangements. Paul Nash complained of the 'lack of structural purpose' in English art, but then a more romantic vein reasserted itself in his own work. Graham Sutherland came rapidly to the fore in the 1930s. Stanley Spencer's eccentric innocence was losing its force. Augustus John successfully turned to portraiture – that of Dylan Thomas (1936) being conspicuously successful. Believing that art ought to be directed to a wider public, William Coldstream thought that a new kind of 'realism' would succeed. There is no evidence that it did. An idiosyncratic realist was L. S. Lowry, who held his first London exhibition in 1939 when he was fifty-one. Recognition only came after 1945. The 'artistic public' went to summer exhibitions at the Royal Academy, where very conservative standards prevailed in the hanging policy. And not only in the hanging policy – top hats and tails were required dress for 'private view' days. This practice died only in 1940. The war itself offered ample material for artists. John Piper's paintings and watercolours of bomb devastation were widely praised. For a time, artists were drawn to themes of suffering and transfiguration. In these years, a group of painters with strong literary connections emerged – Robert MacBryde, Robert Colquhoun, Lucian Freud, Michael Ayrton and Francis Bacon(240). Bacon's 1945 London exhibition helped to make him one of the few internationally acclaimed British artists of the century. There was also praise in the field of sculpture for the work of Henry Moore and Barbara Hepworth. Pevsner accepted in 1955 that Moore had given his country a position in European sculpture 'such as she had never had before'.[7] But the general public remained indifferent, if not hostile, to 'modern art'. Nevertheless, the increasing, if indirect, role of the State through the Arts Council (itself a feature of the post-war world), both in providing patronage and circulating exhibitions, did create a slightly better climate of appreciation.

FILMS

By the 1930s, the weekly visit to the cinema had become a well-established social routine for millions, but the cultural status of the film remained uncertain. Financially, the industry moved from crisis to crisis to crisis before, during and after the war. Critics and producers agonized about what made a 'good British film'. One answer was given by an unexpected Hungarian, Alexander Korda who, after varied foreign experience, formed London Film Productions in 1932. *The Private Life of Henry VIII* made his fame and paved the way for his fortune. He was also responsible for *Catherine the Great* and *Things to Come*, but the much-heralded *I, Claudius* failed to materialize. *Lady Hamilton* (1941) went down particularly well with the Prime Minister and before the year was out Korda had become Sir Alexander. After the war he was also successful in obtaining government backing where others failed. The other big name in British film-making was equally unlikely – J. Arthur Rank, a millionaire from flour-milling and a Methodist. He banged the gong of British film-making with some vigour –

on the screen a rather more athletic figure performed the trick. Both Rank and Korda had their successes, but financial problems eventually became too great for both of them. It was another Hungarian, Gabriel Pascale, who made a great impact as producer and director of films made from Shaw's plays, but *Caesar and Cleopatra* (1945) proved a financial disaster and Pascale departed for the United States. An Italian exile, Del Giudice, produced Olivier's wartime *Henry V* and had earlier persuaded Noel Coward to co-direct and star in *In Which We Serve. Blithe Spirit* also came his way, but Del Giudice himself proved financially insubstantial and disappeared, it was believed, to an Italian monastery. British films seemed to depend on enigmatic aliens(243).

The war had revived a flagging industry. Those cinemas which had been closed in 1939 in order to provide space for the storage of coffins (a big demand being anticipated) were later allowed to show films. Exhibitors could show American films like *Citizen Kane, How Green was my Valley* and *Dr Jekyll and Mr Hyde* to eager British audiences. Contemplation of Gielgud as Disraeli in *The Prime Minister* provided uplift for some. *The Forty-Ninth Parallel* (1941) and *One of our Aircraft is Missing* (1942) were both film fictions with an obvious war message. Similarly, Leslie Howard starred as Mitchell, the designer of the Spitfire in *The First of the Few* (1942). A film of Greenwood's novel *Love on the Dole* had appeared in 1940, but by 1943 more people seemed to want *I Live in Grosvenor Square*. Herbert Wilcox went on to make other films with desirable addresses in their titles. James Mason and Stewart Granger gained the kind of popularity in *The Man in Grey* which could only lead to their transference across the Atlantic. Margaret Lockwood emerged as *The Wicked Lady* (1945), but was not to go unchallenged in this capacity. Anthony Asquith offered Victorian melodrama and 'war' films like *We Dive at Dawn* (1943).

After the war, Michael Balcon's Ealing Studios at last produced a series of comedies which everybody agreed were 'very English'. *Hue and Cry* (1946), *Passport to Pimlico* (1948) and *Whisky Galore* (1949) represented a welcome change from star-studded Hollywood or the seriousness of war. Alec Guinness excelled himself by playing eight parts in *Kind Hearts and Coronets* (1949). Some critics regretted that to understand these films 'a good working knowledge of the English language and the English people' was required. By the mid-1950s, however, harsh critics felt that the Ealing material, unlike that worn in *The Man in the White Suit* (1952), was beginning to wear thin. Finance compelled Balcon to sell Ealing Studios to the BBC in 1955 – a distinctive phase in English film-making came to an end.

Balcon was not the only man to be in financial difficulties. Seemingly endless negotiations took place after the war, all designed to put the British film industry 'on a proper footing', but each solution proved only temporary. Between 1946 and 1951, cinema audiences fell by 5 million and the decline was accelerating. By 1955, the challenge presented by television was inescapable as the little set began to invade working-class homes in increasing numbers. Cinemas could not survive merely as a haven for courting couples and they began to close on a large scale. Fewer films were made and a vicious circle set in. Americans seemed convinced that Cinemascope was the answer – wide screens and stereoscopic sound.

The Robe (1953) proclaimed that redemption, not least of the cinema, was still possible.

It was the so-called 'documentary' movement, however, which provided the most conspicuous British achievement in film-making. *Drifters* (1929), describing the work of the Scottish herring fleet, launched John Grierson, a gritty Scotsman, on his somewhat stormy career. 'The basic force behind it', he later wrote, 'was social and not aesthetic. It was the desire to make a drama from the ordinary to set against the prevailing drama of the extraordinary.' He joined the Empire Marketing Board and built up a famous film unit – which was transferred to the GPO in 1932. The most famous production was *Night Mail* (1936), designed to explain the postal service between London and Scotland. Auden wrote the words and Britten the music. Basil Wright and Edgar Anstey were also active in making documentary films. During the war such productions – this time by the Crown Film Unit – celebrated the delights of orange juice, cod-liver oil and oatmeal porridge. The techniques could also be seen in the films which various ministries commissioned in order to document the war – such as *Desert Victory* (1943) or *Western Approaches* (1944). After 1945, the passage of time inevitably diluted the sense of a 'documentary movement', but release from the pressures of the box-office did enable dedicated and talented men to contribute a distinctive British genre to the history of the film.

SCIENCE

In 1928, working in St Mary's Hospital, Paddington, Fleming discovered the drug penicillin. The way was open for a transformation in the methods of treatment of many diseases and the chances of recovery. It was not until the war, however, that Florey and Chain, working at Oxford, were able to develop new techniques of production to enable the drug to be widely available. Other antibiotics then began to be developed at a rapid rate for specialized purposes. Fleming, Florey and Chain all received the Nobel Prize for Physiology and Medicine in 1945 as did Krebs for his work in biochemistry (1953). Just after the war the Nobel Prize for Physics almost became a British monopoly, being awarded to Appleton (1947), Blackett (1948), Powell (1950) and Cockcroft (1951). This was a tribute to the major wartime work in the nuclear field. Robinson was the only British scientist to gain the award for chemistry (1947).

THE FESTIVAL OF BRITAIN

The year 1951 would be 100 years on from the 1851 Exhibition. What better idea could there be than to mount a festival to show the world the range and splendour of British achievements and demonstrate that the country was back on its feet again? It took place on London's South Bank, with the Festival Hall being a lasting legacy of this cultural feast. Due allowance was made for all tastes by a fun-fair a little further along the river. A festival ship, the *Campania*, toured the country with an exhibition on board to bring enlightenment to benighted sea-ports. The festival came in for a good deal of mockery, but in the end was judged to be a success. 'London's own' Morrison was the government minister initially in charge of proceedings. Even when he became Foreign Secretary, he itched to answer questions on this great cultural spectacular. The Foreign Office primly took the view that Battersea did not come within its province and concen-trated on the cultural task of persuading the Foreign Secretary that the word 'Euphrates' really did have three syllables.

CREEDS

What deeper values undergirded this splendid civilization? Lectures on *Our Culture: Its Christian roots and the present crisis*, delivered in London in 1944 amid flying bombs, suggested that the plight of civilization was due to the separation 'of our culture from its religious roots'.[8] 'It is for a world containing freedom, hope and purpose', wrote another popular wartime writer, 'that we believe God is fighting in all the smoke and horror of war. We did not discover it in peace-time; we have the opportunity to discover it now.'[9] On 18 June 1940 the new Prime Minister made his own weighty contribution to the discussion. 'The Battle of Britain', he declared, 'is about to begin. Upon this battle depends the survival of Christian civilization.'[10] Was the prefix 'Christian' anything more than rhetor-ic? Certainly, the cardinal archbishop of Westminster broadcast to the forces in August 1940 stating that he hoped 'every one of you Christian knights of the British cause' would wear a little cross. Christian civilization, at this unique mo-ment in history depended upon 'England' with its suet puddings and red pillar-boxes. He knew the troops would never be happy away from these delights for any length of time.[11]

That there was some all-pervading spiritual crisis had been common ground even before war broke out, though diagnosis in detail varied. Events in Europe demonstrated that there was nothing inevitable about the survival of liberal democratic ideas. On the contrary, 'totalitarianism' seemed everywhere in the ascendancy. The rulers of the Soviet Union and Germany had lost the meaning of liberty, justice, mercy and truth in the sense in which civilized Christian men had used them. While some thought this merely a matter of 'ideology', Sir Richard Livingstone, from his Oxford educational standpoint, saw it as a major transformation in the world's history: 'suddenly and somehow the whole bottom has fallen out of our civilization . . .'. There could be many explanations for the change – the emergence of the gullible mass mind, the alleged uniformity of in-dustrial life and urban conditions – but, though Britain had so far escaped the 'contagion' of Continental barbarism, he noted with dismay the intelligence and zeal devoted to football pools. He concluded that many inhabitants of the United Kingdom had no philosophy of life at all.[12] They were ripe for Hitler or Mussolini to come and do their work. Bishop Bell of Chichester, whose speeches in the House of Lords were controversial, thought a Fascist or Communist state unlikely. Even so, he detected the extension of the dominion of the State in a much more subtle way – 'through a paternal democratic regime with its apparatus of social services'. A special kind of 'Anglo-Saxon' totalitarianism might emerge(233).

Such a prospect might be prevented by an increased public awareness of the way in which the British balance between liberty and order, tradition and change, had been reached. The historian Butterfield urged his countrymen in 1944 to remember their good fortune in being able to draw strength 'from the continuity of our history'.[13] Englishmen had acquired a characteristic mode of behaviour in their public life. They normally resisted the wildest aberrations and the 'solid body' among them stole for the whole nation what they could appropriate in the traditions of monarchy, aristocracy, bourgeoisie and Church. His implication was obvious. Writing before the war, T. S. Eliot contended that 'we have today a culture which is mainly negative, but which, so far as it is positive, is still Christian'. That position could not last, and there was a clear choice 'between the formation of a new Christian culture, and the acceptance of a pagan one'. Britain was in danger of finding itself with nothing to stand for 'except a dislike of everything maintained by Germany and/or Russia'.[14] The Church of Scotland joined this debate with a weighty report on *God's Will for Church and Nation* (1946). It was, another Christian writer argued, 'an issue of vital importance for mankind whether the aims of society are directed by pagan conceptions of life, or are in accord with the Christian view that men have been created in the image of God'. But there was no virtue in clinging to Christian faith 'merely in the hope of thereby retaining our ideals of Liberty, Mercy, Justice and Truth'. The social benefits of Christianity could only be secured 'if we are convinced of its truth'.[15]

There lay the problem. Intellectuals from Bertrand Russell to Julian Huxley did not believe that it was true and set about establishing the autonomy of ethics. 'Morals without Religion' became a common theme. There was, however, no single 'alternative' to Christianity, but rather a set of principles and values which each man evolved for himself. Part of the objection to Christianity was its universalizing pretension. Rationalist ideas, however, still tended to operate within certain British unspoken assumptions. The various existentialist philosophies which flourished in post-war Europe reflected an experience of social breakdown and utter intellectual chaos which the British had been spared. George Orwell recognized that there were differences of outlook and opinion within Britain on major issues, but 'somehow these differences fade away the moment that any two Britons are confronted by a European'. The public discussion of the principles of civilization was indeed rather un-British and did not long survive the return of peace. People went back to the more prosaic tasks of everyday life, which they at least thought they could manage.

Church leaders welcomed this discussion, and contributed to it, but with a sense of unease about what it implied for the churches as institutions. The question of its established position bothered the Church of England, but there was no unanimity about what should be done. Most churchmen continued to defend it as the official expression of what they believed was the nation's Christianity. A 1935 Report on Church/State relations was not taken further by the Church. The continuing political importance of the establishment was demonstrated the following year during the abdication crisis. It was Anglican teaching about divorce which, in a sense, caused the problem. Supporters of Edward VIII disliked Archbishop Lang's censorious role. In general, however, apart from the special position of the monarch in relation to the Church of England, it was accepted that the legal enactment of the Christian view of marriage was no longer possible. It was a reluctant recognition – Lang abstained when A. P. Herbert's more permissive divorce bill reached the Lords in 1937 – but it was a recognition none the less. Likewise, acceptance of artificial birth-control was accompanied by a wish that unrestricted advertisement and purchase of contraceptives should be prevented.

Temple moved from York to succeed Lang at Canterbury in 1942. He was a prolific writer on many subjects. His *Christianity and Social Order* (1942), published as a Penguin Special, quickly became a best seller. With an authority on the *Socialist Sixth of the World* (1939) already installed as dean of Canterbury, the Church of England seemed poised for a bout of social radicalism. Temple was dubbed the 'people's archbishop', but died unexpectedly in 1944. His successor, Fisher, was of a different temperament and disposition. A much better headmaster than Temple had been, he had a formidable capacity for work. Eschewing the prophetic touch, he concentrated on husbanding the Church's material resources in the difficult years of reconstruction that lay ahead. There was also much profitable work to be done in the field of canon law. Fisher liked a tidy ship and he believed the bark of Christ was sailing in quite promising waters. Another report on Church/State relations (1952) came and went without being implemented. Disestablishment might mean the loss of the special opportunities the Church of England had for presenting the Christian message to the nation. And Fisher sensed 'a fairly widespread beginning of a return' to the Christian religion. Part of his evidence for this was supplied by the remarkable nightly attendances (over three months) at the Harringay arena in 1954 to hear the American (Baptist) evangelist Billy Graham. Relays across England were also well patronized. North of the border, Tom Allan had a similar message to 'Tell Scotland'. And, despite jibes from the Left, the 1953 Coronation – televised for the first time – seemed to be popularly accepted as a necessary aspect of the legitimization of authority(232,233).

Such occasions stressed the centrality of the Church of England in what was a British occasion. Anglican 'triumphialism' was very manifest, but a more ecumenical temper was emerging. The British Council of Churches was formed in 1942 (with many other councils at local level subsequently emerging) to provide a regular basis for discussion and collaboration among all the main non-Roman Catholic churches. In a post-war sermon at Cambridge, Fisher looked to more intimate relations with the Free Churches. Many of their leaders welcomed this possibility, though not disguising the differences of doctrine and practice that remained. Among many younger Free Church ministers there was a renewed stress upon church order and a tendency to look askance at Victorian and Edwardian developments in the history of their denominations. They stressed what they called the 'catholicity of Protestantism'. The Roman Catholic Church itself held aloof from any of these developments. It was not just another church in the British scene. Such limited appeals for co-operation among Christians 'in the face of a semi-pagan world' came from laymen (in this instance the editor of the *Catholic Herald*) and not from the episcopate(229). Despite its increasing numbers, the Roman Catholic Church seemed almost to relish the 'marginal' position which it occupied in cultural and political life. That all the denominations were 'marginal' was not something one would easily have concluded from the mood of relative confidence which prevailed among their leaders in the mid-1950s(236).

---

1. A. J. S. White, *The British Council, 1934–1959* (1965), Appendix B
2. *The Criterion*, January 1939 (its last number)
3. G. Orwell, *The lion and the unicorn*, (1941), p. 29
4. V. Lynn, *Vocal refrain* (1975), p. 76
5. A. Bliss, *As I remember* (1970), pp. 149–51
6. N. Pevsner, *The Englishness of English art* (1956), p. 181
7. Pevsner, op. cit., pp. 181–2
8. C. W. Dugmore, ed., *Our culture: Its Christian roots and the present crisis* (1944), p. 35
9. J. Hadham, *Good God* (1940), p. 96
10. See J. Baillie, *What is Christian civilization?* (Oxford, 1945)
11. Cardinal Hinsley, *The Bond of Peace* (1941), pp. 105–6
12. Livingstone, *Future in education*, p. 109
13. H. Butterfield, *The Englishman and his history* (Cambridge, 1944), v–vii and p. 139
14. T. S. Eliot, *The idea of a Christian society* (1939), pp. 13–19
15. H. G. Wood, *Christianity and civilization* (Cambridge, 1942), p. 16

PART FOUR

1956–1975

1956   White paper on the economic implications of full employment (Mar): Last British troops leave Suez (June) – Nasser seizes Suez Canal (July): Restrictive Trade Practices Act and Court (Aug): British outline plan for EFTA (Oct): Ultimatum to Egypt (Oct) – fighting at Suez ends (Nov): UK gains stand-by credits following the post-Suez balance of payments crisis (Dec).

   Osborne, *Look back in anger*: Sillitoe, *Saturday Night and Sunday Morning*: Calder Hall nuclear power station comes into operation – the first in Britain (May): Third-class rail travel abolished.

1957   Macmillan succeeds Eden as PM (Jan): Macmillan–Eisenhower conference at Bermuda (Mar): Treaty of Rome signed by the Six establishing the EEC (Mar): Ghana becomes independent (Mar): Royal Commission on local gvt. in Greater London appointed (July): Council on Prices, Productivity and Incomes set up (Aug): Wolfenden Report on homosexual offences published: Malaya becomes independent (Aug).

   Royal Ballet formed: Consumers' Association founded.

1958   Thorneycroft, Powell and Birch resign from gvt. over failure to cut gvt. expenditure (Jan): Liberals win Torrington by-election (Mar): State of emergency declared in Aden colony (May): Life peerages created (July): 'Racial' rioting in Nottingham and Notting Hill, London (Aug): Campaign for Nuclear Disarmament launched (Feb): Clean air Act comes into force (June).

   Gatwick airport opened (Jun): Jodrell Bank radio telescope comes into operation (Oct): Election of Pope Paul XXIII: Empire Day becomes Commonwealth Day (Dec): Report on conversations between the Church of England and the Methodist Church: Parking meters grace London streets.

1959   First EEC tariff reductions come into effect: Plowden Report on the control of public expenditure (July): Radcliffe Report on the monetary system (Aug): Formation of CENTO (Aug): General Election (Oct) – Cons. majority: EFTA formed (Nov).

   The Manchester Guardian becomes *The Guardian*: Basic travel allowance for British tourists ends: First section of M1 motorway opened: Pope convenes Second Vatican Council

1960   Macmillan makes 'wind of change' speech in Cape Town (Feb). Deaths at Sharpeville in S. Africa (Mar): Cyprus becomes independent republic (Aug): Monckton Report on the federation of the Rhodesias and Nyasaland (Oct): OECD formed by inclusion of the United States and Canada into OEEC (Dec): Nigeria becomes independent (Oct).

   Pinter, *The Caretaker*: Last steam rail locomotive named (Mar): Blue Streak missile abandoned (Apr): *News Chronicle* and the *Star* cease publication: archbishop of Canterbury visits the Pope.

1961   UK and Iceland settle a fishing dispute (Feb): British troops assist preservation of Kuwait (June): Establishment of National Economic Development Council (July): S. Africa decides to leave the Commonwealth (Mar): UK applies to join the EEC (July): Large CND demonstration in Trafalgar Square (Sept): Commonwealth Immigration Bill proposed (Nov): Tanganyika becomes independent (Dec).

   New Testament of New English Bible published (Mar): Betting shops opened (May): Crick and Brenner claim to determine structure of DNA and thus break the genetic code.

1962   Liberals win Orpington by-election (Mar): National Incomes Commission established (July): Commonwealth Immigration Act (July): Macmillan 'purge' of his

Cabinet (July): British–French agreement to develop Concorde supersonic airliner (Nov): Macmillan and Kennedy meet at Nassau – Polaris to be made available to the UK in place of Skybolt (Dec).

Royal College of Physicians Report on smoking and health: Pilkington Report on broadcasting (June): Coventry cathedral consecrated (May):

1963 De Gaulle vetoes British entry into the EEC (Jan): Gaitskell dies and Wilson succeeds as Labour Leader (Jan/Feb): O'Neill succeeds Lord Brookeborough as PM of N. Ireland (Mar): Polaris sales agreement with the United States (Apr): 'Kennedy round' negotiations for tariff cuts (May): Peerage Act – permits disclaimers (July): Test-ban treaty (Aug): Central African Federation dissolved (Dec): Douglas-Home succeeds Macmillan (Oct).

Beeching Report on reshaping British Railways: Buchanan Report on traffic in towns: Newsom Report recommends raising the school-leaving age to 16: Robbins Report on higher education: J. A. T. Robinson, *Honest to God*.

1964 Smith becomes PM of S. Rhodesia (Apr): Resale Prices Act (July): First Commonwealth Secretary-General appointed (Aug): General Election – small Labour majority (Oct): Gvt imposes 15 per cent import surcharge – 10 per cent in Apr 1965 and abolished in Nov 1966: Ministry of Technology set up (Oct): TSR-2 makes maiden flight (Sept): White Paper on monopolies, mergers and restrictive practices.

Paul Report on the deployment and payment of the clergy: *Daily Herald* ceases publication: Gvt grants licences to drill for oil and gas in the N. Sea.

1965 Merger of Foreign and Commonwealth Service as the Diplomatic Service (Jan): Regional economic councils set up (Feb): Death of Churchill – State funeral (Jan): Prices and Incomes Board established (Mar): After resignation of Douglas-Home, Heath defeats Maudling for Conservative leadership (July): Monopolies and Mergers Act (Aug): BP strikes oil in the N. Sea (Sept): Unilateral declaration of independence in Rhodesia (Nov): Rent Act (Dec): National Economic Plan (Dec): Ministry of Education circular requests local authorities to submit plans for comprehensive schools: Greater London Council formed. Abolition of the death penalty: 70 mph speed limit introduced on roads.

1966 Industrial Reorganization Corporation set up (Jan): Commonwealth Conference on Rhodesia at Lagos (Jan): General Election – Labour majority increases (Mar): Seamen's strike (May–July): Decimalization to be introduced in 1971 (July): Plaid Cymru wins Carmarthen by-election (July): Prices and Incomes Act (Aug): Sterling crisis (Jul).

England win World Cup in football (July): Severn road bridge opened (Sept): Hovercraft service begins.

1967 First landing of N. Sea gas (Mar): Gvt. announces intention to apply to join the EEC (May): First Parliamentary Commissioner appointed (May): Defence cuts – decision to withdraw from East of Suez by mid–1970s: Scottish National party wins Hamilton by-election (Nov): Withdrawal from Aden (Nov): Sterling devalued, £1 = $2.40 (Nov): de Gaulle's second veto on EEC membership (Nov).

Colour TV begins on BBC 2 (July): *Queen Elizabeth II* launched at Clydebank (Sept): Vietnam War demonstrations in London (Oct).

1968 Two-tier gold system inaugurated (Mar): Nuclear non-proliferation treaty (July): Race Relations Act: Fulton Report on the Civil Service: EEC common external tariff comes into effect (July): Clashes in Londonderry – beginning of N. Ireland troubles (Oct): Student unrest at various universities.

Theatres Act abolishes censorship (Sept).

1969   White paper *In Place of Strife* proposes a Commission on Industrial Relations and other items, including a 28-day 'conciliation pause' for strikes (Jan): General Election in N. Ireland (Feb): Gvt publishes Industrial Relations Bill (Apr): Voting age reduced from 21 to 18 (Apr): Chichester-Clark replaces O'Neill as PM of N. Ireland (Apr/May): Redcliffe-Maud Commission on local gvt. in England and Wales reports (May): Gvt. drops Industrial Relations Bill and agrees to TUC proposals for dealing with unconstitutional and inter-union strikes (June): Family Reform Act reduces age of majority to 18 (July): Serious rioting in Belfast and Londonderry, British army called in (Aug): Dvlpt. of Tourism Act sets up British Tourist Authority with boards in England, Scotland and Wales (Aug): Wheatley Commission reports on local gvt in Scotland (Sept): SAYE scheme starts (Oct): Hunt Committee on N. Ireland recommends that the police should be relieved of military duties. Ministry of Community Relations set up (Oct).

Church of England rejects scheme for unity with the Methodist Church – which had accepted it (July): Post Office Corporation set up: Colour comes to BBC1 and ITV (Nov): Isle of Wight pop festival.

1970   Currency restrictions on foreign travel by UK residents lifted (Jan): Local authorities in England and Wales required to set up social services committees and appoint directors of social services (May): Rhodesia proclaims itself a republic (Mar): S. African cricket tour of England cancelled (May): Equal Pay Act designed to prevent discrimination between men and women regarding terms and conditions of employment – to operate from Dec 1975 (May): General Election – Conservative victory (June): New gvt. no longer requires local authorities to submit their proposals for comprehensive schooling: Dept of Environment unifies ministries concerned with housing and local government, public building and works, and the transport (Nov): Industrial Relations Bill published (Dec).

1971   Commonwealth heads of government meet in Singapore (Jan): Receiver appointed for Rolls-Royce (Feb): Faulkner succeeds Chichester-Clark as PM of N. Ireland (Feb/Mar): Prices and Incomes Board disbanded (Mar): Upper Clyde Shipbuilders shop stewards take over the yards in protest against the company's liquidation (July): Industrial Relations Act comes into operation (Aug): N. Ireland gvt introduces internment under Special Powers Act – camp established at Long Kesh (Aug/Sept): Immigration Act gives certain people described as 'patrial' the 'right of abode' in the UK (Oct): Commons votes in favour of joining EEC (Oct).

Divorce Reform Act comes into effect: Union of Congregational and Presbyterian churches in England and Wales agreed: Dissolution of Industrial Reorganization Commission (May): First Open University broadcast (Jan).

1972   'Bloody Sunday' – 13 people killed by British army in Londonderry (Jan): N. Ireland Parliament prorogued (Mar): Wilberforce Court of Inquiry ends 6-week miners' strike with 22 per cent pay increase recommendation (Feb): Treaty of accession to EEC and to Euratom (Jan): Operation 'Motorman' ends 'no-go' areas in N. Ireland (July).

School-leaving age raised from 15 to 16 (Sept): White Paper, *A Programme for Inflation* – 90-day standstill.

1973   Britain joins the EEC (Jan): Immigration Act comes into force (Jan): N. Ireland poll reaffirms wish of large majority to remain part of the UK (Mar): VAT introduced (Apr): Fair Trading Act (July): Middle East War and fourfold price increase (Oct): 'Stage Three' anti-inflation proposals (Oct): Kilbrandon Commission on the Constitution recommends a scheme of devolved gvts. (Oct): 'Three-day Week' planned to start in Jan 1974 (Dec) – miners start overtime ban.

1974　New N. Ireland 'Executive' takes office: General Election – Labour victory (Feb): State of Emergency ends and miners return to work (Mar): Ulster Workers' council strike in N. Ireland, resignation of Chief Executive, fall of executive, Assembly prorogued (May): Pay Board abolished and all statutory wage controls end (July): Trade Union and Labour Relations Act replaces the 1971 Industrial Relations Act: Gvt sets out plans for a wealth tax (Aug): General Election – Labour victory (Oct): Prevention of Terrorism (Temporary Provisions) Act proscribes the IRA and gives wide powers to the police – follows bombings and deaths in Birmingham (Nov).

1975　Abandonment of the Channel Tunnel announced (Jan): Thatcher replaces Heath as Conservative leader (Feb): Gvt accepts recommendation that it should take over British Leyland (Apr): Parliament endorses 'renegotiation' of terms of British membership of the EEC (Apr): Referendum on British membership of the EEC (June): First landing of N. Sea oil (June): White Paper, *The Attack on Inflation*: 'Final Act' of Helsinki Conference on security and co-operation in Europe (Aug): National Enterprise Board set up (Nov): Employment Protection Act sets up Advisory, Conciliation and Arbitration Service and amends law relating to rights of workers (Nov): Education Bill compelling comprehensive system published (Dec): Simonstown naval base agreement with S. Africa ends.

CHAPTER 28

Britain and the European Economic Community

In June 1975, the British people were asked in a referendum whether they wished the United Kingdom to stay in the European Economic Community (EEC). Nearly two-thirds of the electorate voted, with 67.2 per cent in favour and 32.8 per cent against. It appeared at long last as though a great question had been settled, and in a manner which was then unique in British practice. Never before had the voters been directly asked to express an opinion on a specific question of this kind. The referendum was vigorously contested and, notwithstanding the Labour government's endorsement of continued membership, prominent Labour speakers like Anthony Wedgwood Benn and Peter Shore, and some Conservatives, made their opposition very plain. The arguments were concerned both with the economic consequences of membership and with the broad political implications. For some, the Community would bring to an end Britain's proud history as a nation-state. For others, it represented the beginning of an exciting partnership. All agreed that the decision was momentous and in one sense they were right. It was time to end twenty years of vacillation and uncertainty with a clear answer and the response was indeed decisive(28).

In another sense, however, 1975 was less of a turning-point than either side supposed. Despite the verdict, the Labour governments after 1975 did not display conspicuous enthusiasm for the Community, partly because of their hostility to the idea of monetary union and their dislike of possible direct elections to the European Parliament. As Prime Minister, Callaghan reiterated Labour's opposition to federalism and strongly asserted the rights of national governments and parliaments. In taking such a position, however, the British were often only more blunt than other members, despite the obloquy they incurred. There were times in the later 1970s when the Community did appear little more than a cockpit in which all the governments concerned were simply fighting to satisfy their own interests. That had always been so but, in adverse world circumstances, the impetus towards greater political or economic unity seemed to be flagging. Some aspects of Community policy which both political parties sought to modify (like the Common Agricultural Policy) stemmed from the fact that Britain had in the end joined an organization which she had played no part in shaping. Whether it could be made more congenial to Britain without destroying its own cohesion was an open question(29).

At its foundation, twenty years earlier, the British had tried to obstruct the creation of the Common Market either by laughing at its prospect or by more Machiavellian means. Early in 1956, Macmillan, then Chancellor of the Exchequer, reputedly referred at an OEEC meeting to some 'archaeological excavations' at Messina. He had learnt of their existence, but hoped that he would not hear more about them. It was at Messina that negotiations had taken place about establishing both a Common Market and a European Organization for Atomic Energy (Euratom). In Venice during May 1956 the Foreign Ministers of the Six accepted the Spaak Report (which had been commissioned at Messina) as the basis for a treaty. In the months that followed, the French staked out for themselves a strong position but, after hard bargaining, both the Common Market and Euratom were accepted in treaties signed at Rome in March 1957. After a transitional period, there would be free movement of people, services and capital within the countries concerned – France, Federal Germany, Italy, Belgium, The Netherlands and Luxembourg. A special Social Fund would assist them in dealing with the difficulties which would inevitably occur in this process. The Treaty of Rome had an underlying supranational philosophy, but final authority rested with a Council of Ministers representing the existing governments in the Community. While its decisions were initially to be unanimous, there was an expectation that majority voting would be introduced later.

Nearly all these features were unacceptable in London. In the Commons on 26 November 1956, Macmillan claimed to be speaking for the whole House in declaring that he could never agree 'to our entering arrangements which, as a matter of principle, would prevent our treating the great range of imports from the Commonwealth at least as favourably as those from the European countries'. This objection, even if there were no other, would prevent Britain taking part in a European Common Market by joining a customs union with a common external tariff. Britain pressed instead for a European free trade area which could consist of the Six (as one unit if they wished), Britain and such other countries as might wish to join. However, it was not until October 1957 that the OEEC set up a committee to consider this problem, after the Treaty of Rome had been ratified by the major countries concerned. The discussions of this committee continued throughout most of 1958, but Franco-British suspicion prevented any progress. The great crisis in France over Algeria, which brought de Gaulle to power, was not conducive to any French concessions. The first 10 per cent reduction in the internal tariff of the Community took place on 1 January 1959 without any agreement being reached with Britain or the other European countries concerned. De Gaulle was no more enthusiastic about supranationalism than were the British but, since the market was working, he maintained a structure which was proving congenial to French commercial and economic interests. It could serve as an ideal accompaniment to that Franco-German reconciliation he was to establish with Adenauer(25).

For their part, the British immediately set about encouraging the formation of a European Free Trade Association (EFTA) in which she would be joined by Austria, Denmark, Sweden, Switzerland and Portugal. The Stockholm agreement, signed in January 1960 (to come into effect a few months later) aimed to establish a free trade area among its members within a decade. EFTA was a rather curious grouping which was created in a hurry, principally with the hope of keeping together a negotiating bloc for a further round of talks, at some stage, with the EEC. Meanwhile, Europe was very much at sixes and sevens(27).

The Treaty of Rome stated that any European state could apply to become a member of the Community, and in July 1961 Macmillan told the Commons that the government now wished to join, provided that Britain's interests, those of the Commonwealth and those of EFTA could all be safeguarded. The application was formally submitted the following month and negotiations began in October, with Heath leading the British delegation. In his opening statement, he claimed that that the British people had been through a searching debate and were now anxious to become 'full, whole-hearted and active members of the European Community'. He believed that 'faced with the threats which we can all see, Europe must unite or perish. The United Kingdom, being part of Europe, must not stand aside.'[1] He praised the economic achievements of the member states and indicated Britain's willingness to accept the existing EEC tariff as the basis of the tariff of the enlarged Community. He conceded that there were difficulties about the Commonwealth and agriculture, but they could be overcome. A statement by the National Executive Committee (NEC) of the Labour party in September 1962 was considerably less enthusiastic. Britain's position, it argued, was 'not the same as that of the other countries of the Community. While our histories have certainly overlapped, they have also diverged.... Our connections and interests, both political and economic, lie as much outside Europe as within it.' Membership of the Common Market would decisively change Britain's world position for, unlike the Six, 'Britain is the centre and founder member of a much larger and still more important group, the Commonwealth'.[2] At Brighton in the following month, Gaitskell, leader of the Labour party, raised the spectre of European federation at the climax of an emotional speech to his party conference. Britain, he declared, would become like the states of the United States or Australia in a new Europe. It meant 'the end of Britain as an independent nation state. It may be a good or a bad thing but we must recognize that this is so....' There was little doubt that Gaitskell thought it a bad thing.[3]

Against this emotional background, the negotiations for British membership dragged on throughout 1962 with both Heath and the French attempting to be uncompromising. The British view was that a successful conclusion was in sight. Then President de Gaulle brought the negotiations to an end by remarks he made at a press conference in Paris on 14 January 1963. He declared that Britain still cherished ties with the United States and with the Commonwealth and, whatever the government might now say, the British people as a whole were not 'European' in outlook. These, of course, were general charges, and not untrue, but the veto arose more from French concern that the entry of Britain (and Denmark) would upset the position France wished to play in the Community. The other member states expressed more dismay at the failure of the talks than they probably felt. De Gaulle, who found the Nassau agreement of December 1962 – which provided for the purchase of American Polaris nuclear missiles by Britain – particularly distasteful and an illustration of his basic thesis, consolidated his relationship with Federal Germany in an agreement signed with Adenauer in January 1963, other plans for more general political co-operation among the members of the EEC having failed. On the British side, the collapse of the talks was a particular disappointment to Macmillan. His own administration seemed to be losing its way and the Prime Minister had come to see British membership of the Community as an essential part of his strategy for reviving the country and restoring his government's fortunes(30).

The failure of the talks was rather a relief to the Opposition among whom the issue of membership was a source of open division. Harold Wilson, who became the party's leader after Gaitskell's death in January 1963, had appeared to be opposed to entry, but was fortunate in that the issue of membership could not be an immediate possibility in 1964 when the election was fought. Only the Liberals campaigned unambiguously for membership. However, in April 1966, the Queen's speech at the opening of Parliament (coming just after Labour's election victory) revealed that the government intended to negotiate entry subject to the usual safeguards. Two years in office had led Wilson to reverse his former indifference, if not hostility. Perhaps, after all, the market of over 250 million people was vital to the well-being of the British economy and his earlier rhetoric about not being 'dictated to by foreigners' faded away. The Commonwealth factor seemed less inhibiting, not only because of its general evolution, but because some of its leading members were already beginning to assume that at some stage the United Kingdom would join the EEC and were planning accordingly. In 1965, too, there had been a major crisis in the functioning of the EEC. De Gaulle had gone to the brink of breaking up the Community by leaving an 'empty chair' in order to preserve what he regarded as the proper rights of the national governments and in protest against the Commission's growing influence. His eventual success apparently meant that the EEC was to remain, at least in the immediate future, an economic community and therefore, on the right terms, one safe for Britain to join. But, of course, it was also precisely this assertion of the vital importance of the national governments – the French blocked the gradual progress towards majority voting envisaged in the Treaty of Rome – which made the French objections to British membership so formidable, if they were still maintained.

Wilson and his Foreign Secretary, Brown, toured the capitals of western Europe in the winter of 1966 and spring of 1967 trying to persuade other political leaders of the reality of Labour's conversion to the EEC and drumming up support, particularly from Federal Germany, for the application. They were sanguine about their chances, but de Gaulle remained obdurate. By the end of 1967, another veto had been delivered. Invited to choose between France and Britain, the other members of the Community had no doubt where their interests lay. On this occasion, the French President laid stress on Britain's financial and economic difficulties. She would be a liability in the EEC rather than an asset until she pursued financial policies which recognized the gravity of her condition. The other members had sufficient doubts themselves on this score not to wish to precipitate a crisis. It was the case that the economic performance of the Six, taken as a whole, was more impressive, on almost all counts, than was the British and no one wanted to jeopardize it. This second setback depressed some (though not all) members of the government and a considerable section of the British people. By the mid-1960s, there was evidence from opinion polls that enthusiasm for the Community in Britain was mounting, only to fall back with the failure of the applications to join. Disappointment brought with it some bitterness, particularly towards France and de Gaulle personally. The continued exclusion had the unfortunate effect of reinforcing the notion that entry in itself would rejuvenate British industry and that there was nothing much that could be done until it eventually happened. It was believed that de Gaulle could not go on for ever, but while he did remain in power London found it convenient to regard him as a wicked old man whose personal whim was blocking progress. If convenient, such an outlook contained a large measure of self-deception. De Gaulle's analysis of Britain's predicament, if it contained a personal element, had more truth than it was customary to concede. The extent to which Britain, by her policies and attitudes, was excluding herself from the EEC was not a question which Wilson was inclined to tackle. Substantial elements in the parliamentary party and the trade union movement continued to feel that if changes were required they should come from the side of the EEC.

After his election victory in 1970, there was little doubt that the new Prime Minister, Heath, would seek to achieve the success which had eluded his immediate predecessors in Downing Street. His own convictions on British entry were deep and well established and had survived his experience of negotiating with the French for the Macmillan government. The resignation of de Gaulle seemed a good omen, but in the late 1960s the mood of the British people had become more sceptical. A White Paper published by the Labour government before it left office painted a forecast of fairly heavy costs which would fall upon Britain if she joined and, although such estimates were necessarily speculative, the picture was not very comforting. Nevertheless, Heath's negotiator, Rippon, pressed ahead and Heath himself established a better relationship with President Pompidou than had been possible with his predecessor. As a result, Britain's entry into the EEC, along with Ireland and Denmark, was fixed for 1 January 1973. A transitional period of over four years was envisaged, during which time the EEC's external tariff would apply to British industrial imports from third countries. Britain accepted the Common Agricultural Policy with a transitional period of six years. Transitional arrangements were also made to cushion the impact of membership for those Commonwealth countries which had formerly relied on the United Kingdom as their major market for certain products. A complicated formula was thought to settle the matter of Britain's contribution to the Community budget.

At a meeting in Paris in October 1972, the heads of government of the new Nine were sufficiently euphoric at what had been achieved to draw up an ambitious programme which envisaged economic and monetary union by 1980 and wide-ranging regional, environmental and energy policies for the Community; progress in many of these schemes has been conspicuously lacking. In the same year as Britain entered the Community the dramatic rise in oil prices occurred. It was hardly a favourable moment to begin a period of transition. It proved extremely difficult to say how much of the continuing rise in prices experienced in Britain was due to Community membership. Whatever the answer, in 1974, the incoming Labour government felt obliged to threaten to withdraw from the

Community unless the terms of entry accepted by its predecessor were renegotiated in its favour. The language used by Callaghan, the Foreign Secretary, was found offensive in Europe, nevertheless there was sufficient renegotiation, in form if not in substance, for the government to be able to declare itself satisfied with the terms and to recommend the British people to remain in the Community. It seemed that the 'British question' had been settled, but by then the mood in Europe and in the world as a whole was changing. The short sharp shock which it was believed would have a salutary affect on the underlying weaknesses of the British economy seemed only to make them more glaring. The optimistic forecasts of the early 1970s did not seem to be coming true. Britain's place was certainly in Europe, but on what terms and with what ultimate objective, still remained subject to alarming and unpredictable fluctuations.

Over a period of a quarter of a century, critics of potential or actual membership of the EEC had fastened on a number of arguments. They suggested that it represented an exclusive concentration upon what had in the past been only an aspect of Britain's position in the world. They noted that even an enlarged Community to a membership of nine would not be co-extensive with Europe. On the Left, it was particularly suggested that the EEC was a way of perpetuating the division of Europe when it would have liked to establish closer contacts with eastern Europe. They continued to stress the importance of the Commonwealth as a link between North and South, rich and poor states, and between peoples of different colour and creed. If they felt European in some general sense they either did not know (or did not admire if they did know) much about political and social organization on the mainland. They felt that the British economy could not be jolted into a Continental framework which, over centuries, it had not been a part of. The Left presented the Community as a den of capitalism which would prevent a Labour government from taking complete control of the economy and moving irreversibly in a Socialist direction. A theoretical internationalism marched together with an unwavering insularity. Some or all of these arguments were used across the party divide, though they came to be anchored most firmly in the Labour party.

Supporters argued that a strong western Europe was desirable in the kind of world that was emerging in the 1960s and 1970s and Britain's place was in such a collection of states. If it was a narrowing of the British perspective, Britain was no longer a Great Power able to pick and choose in an independent fashion. The Commonwealth was still a useful organization, but its very nature precluded it from becoming the basis of British foreign policy. They doubted whether Britain could play any significant individual role as a mediator between East and West in Europe. Some British politicians did try. In 1960, Macmillan had the brief glory of bringing together Khrushchev, Eisenhower and de Gaulle for the Paris summit. The effort proved fruitless since Khrushchev speedily returned home because of the U2 'spy-plane' incident. Thereafter, as a crisis like the Cuban Missile Crisis of 1962 showed, Moscow and Washington dealt with each other direct. Britain did not have the kind of historical connection with eastern Europe which enabled de Gaulle to make spectacular tours of Poland or Romania. Nor, it must be said, did Britain have a de Gaulle. Yet, as the Russian suppression of

'Socialism with a human face' in Czechoslovakia in 1968 demonstrated, there was nothing any one European state or even combination of states could do to restrain the Russians within what they regarded as their sphere of interest. It was an experience that showed that, despite the Labour party's claim in 1962 that Britain had to retain 'full freedom of action in foreign policy' such freedom was not available. Supporters of membership sometimes confessed that they did not know the precise form European integration would take or at what pace it would develop. It would entail political, social and cultural changes in the United Kingdom, but they were excited rather than apprehensive at the prospect. The economic impact might be severe in some sectors, but in others there were great opportunities. Everything would depend upon the skill and resilience of the British people – about which much was said.

---

1. U. W. Kitzinger, *The European common market and community* (1967). pp. 151–2
2. Kitzinger, op. cit., p. 169
3. P. Williams, *Hugh Gaitskell* (1979), pp. 729–36

CHAPTER 29

Britain in the Commonwealth of Nations

In 1956, important areas in Africa, Asia and the West Indies were still ruled, ultimately, from London; twenty years later, that direct control only existed over such incongruous islands as Hong Kong, St Helena, the Falkland Islands and a few other peculiar territories. Few empires in history have disappeared so swiftly, so completely and with so little armed conflict. It is still not clear why it happened. The transition to independence in the Indian subcontinent in 1947–48 could be plausibly presented as the culmination of a policy extending over decades – even if that was not the full story. Against such a background, it became fashionable to present the granting of independence elsewhere in Asia, Africa and the West Indies as but a further phase in a process controlled and even initiated by London. It was simply a matter of going through the routines, now well established, of modifying a constitution here or there, hauling down a flag in some suitable royal presence, and departing in peace. 'If the British Empire and its Commonwealth should last for a thousand years', Churchill had declared in 1940, 'men would still say that this was their finest hour.'[1] There now seemed no question of a thousand-year British Reich. Instead, the emphasis was upon evolution to independence as a natural process; something Britain had been apparently working towards all the time.

It was evident, however, that such 'preparation' as had existed in India found no real parallel in Africa, or at least the transitional stages followed each other so rapidly that they left no room for intermediate consolidation of experience. Colonial officials found themselves trapped between trying to create what they regarded as the basis for 'good government' and the accelerating rate of political and social change. In the 1960s, ideals and intentions envisaged within a longer time span had to be abandoned. In any case, by the end of the decade, it had become evident that the constitutions and structures set up at the time of independence had often not lasted. British politicians and officials became somewhat cynical about what they were doing. Wise commentators began to observe that the 'Westminster model' was not suitable for African conditions and it had been a mistake to suppose that it could ever work in a situation where the opposition to a government had a tribal or religious base. The emergence of military rulers in some African countries was thought to be 'natural' and not undesirable; though whether the brutality of an Idi Amin in Uganda was also 'natural' was more contentious. Whatever the truth of these points, the subsequent history of former colonies cast doubts on decolonization as an orderly process in which block by block of the imperial edifice was removed on instructions from London according to a grand design.

A contrary model stressed the degree to which successive governments were pushed and prodded into rapid decolonization by forces they could not resist. Externally, these pressures came from various quarters. Each successive grant of independence made it more difficult to sustain a case for delay elsewhere. West African states gave themselves a mission to speed up the end of colonial rule throughout the continent. The other European countries – with the initial exception of Portugal – were abandoning, or being forced to abandon, their imperial role, thus creating the impression that a global 'movement of history' was taking place from which Britain could not stand apart. Voices in the United Nations increasingly joined in the onslaught on European imperialism and demanded a complete timetable for independence. British governments refused such requests, but could not ignore the feeling behind them. Anti-colonial feeling in the United States was also still a factor, although as Washington itself adopted a quasi-imperial role in South-east Asia in particular, that perspective change somewhat. The message seemed to be that any delay in handing over power to local 'nationalists' would only benefit 'world Communism'. Finally, the Soviet Union itself offered London vocal advice, secure in the knowledge that its own empire stood firm.

Although the situation varied from territory to territory, it was also argued that internal opposition was growing on such a scale that speedy withdrawal would be the only way to avoid military confrontation. Throughout the period of British rule in Africa, it had rested very little on military force. Once 'power' had been used to consolidate control, it was replaced by 'authority'. Now, when 'authority' was ceasing to be accepted, 'power' to shore it up did not exist. Other European states which did try to maintain their authority by military means – like the French in North Africa, for example – were not succeeding. If it was the case that British rule was no longer acceptable in a country of the size and population of Nigeria, it was inconceivable that it could be held down by force. The appearance of mass political parties (like the Convention People's Party in the Gold Coast), and the occasional riot, produced a West African version of the earlier Indian pattern – detention of political leader, subsequent release of political leader and elevation to ministerial responsibility, handover of power to political leader. The most conspicuous example was Kwame Nkrumah in the Gold Coast who led his country to independence in 1957 under the name Ghana. Within a few years Nigeria (1961), Sierra Leone (1962) and even Gambia (1965) followed suit. This rapid pattern of change was not without benefit for all concerned. The imperial power looked far-sighted and magnanimous and the indigenous leader experienced just enough martyrdom to enhance his domestic reputation. It was particularly convenient in these few years to assume that what the 'leaders' led were 'nations'. Subsequent developments made it obvious that nation-building, in a European sense, had only just begun(41).

The transition to independence in West Africa was made relatively straightforward by the economic prosperity of most of the territories involved. No communities of White settlers complicated the process. The handover of power in East and Central Africa proved much more difficult. By 1956, the Mau Mau rebellion among the Kikuyu people of Kenya was under control, but the position both of the Whites and Asians had to be taken into account in the subsequent constitutional changes. The notion of an East African Federation had to be abandoned and in the early 1960s Tanganyika (Tanzania), Kenya and Uganda all emerged as separate independent states. It was indeed a bad time for federations. British politicians and officials believed that such unions could offer considerable economic and other advantages, but they proved politically unacceptable. A Federation of the West Indies was tried in the late 1950s, but had to be abandoned. The biggest islands, Jamaica and Trinidad, became independent a few years later, followed subsequently by the smaller islands not previously thought 'viable'. The federal formula was tried also in Central Africa, without ultimate success. Two of its units, Northern Rhodesia and Nyasaland became independent as Zambia and Malawi respectively. In November 1965, the Prime Minister of Southern Rhodesia, Ian Smith, assumed 'sovereign independence' for his country – Whites had enjoyed internal self-government since 1923. Rhodesia was to prove the most intractable of all the problems Britain experienced during the period of decolonization. It lingered on for a further fifteen years and, from time to time, had important repercussions on British domestic politics. Rhodesia apart, there was satisfaction in official circles that British rule in Africa had been brought to an end in a relatively orderly fashion.

Decolonization continued outside Africa. Malaya (1960), Guyana (1966) and Fiji (1971) were among the territories to become independent. In the latter two instances, there were times when the position of the Indian communities seemed likely to cause serious difficulties, but in the end things went more smoothly than had been feared. There were also problems in establishing 'Malaysia' and the initial attempt to include Singapore had to be abandoned. This new federation, established in 1963, survived a 'confrontation' with Indonesia over the next few years. In the Mediterranean, there were endless difficulties in the cases of Cyprus and Malta. In the former, after years of guerrilla activity in support of union with Greece, a cease-fire came into effect in March 1959 and the island became an independent republic in August 1960. There was a state of emergency in Malta in 1958 followed by internal self-government in 1961 and independence in 1964. In Aden, there was violence before the People's Democratic Republic of Yemen was set up in 1967. There was nothing very glorious about these final years of British rule in the Mediterranean. Only Gibraltar remained in British hands, though the Spanish government considered it a colonial anachronism.

A Commonwealth of a kind survived these rapid changes. The tensions brought about by the 1956 Suez Crisis dissolved surprisingly quickly. The addition of such states as Malaysia and Ghana, Guyana and Cyprus meant that observers were quickly to stress the uniqueness of the Commonwealth as a 'multiracial association'. Its members kept complete independence, but still wished to retain what was valuable in their connection with Britain and with each other. The English language facilitated these continuing contacts. It was not clear, however, whether the Commonwealth stood for anything more than a rather obscure kind of sentiment. Some believed that the position of South Africa constituted a 'test case' for the Commonwealth. Under successive Nationalist governments after 1948 the system of apartheid had been steadily consolidated. Party spokesmen in Britain all condemned it, though whether this apparent unity was popularly endorsed is more doubtful. In January 1960, Macmillan delivered a speech before the South African Parliament in which he spoke of the 'wind of change' which was blowing through the continent. A few months later, anti-pass law demonstrations at Sharpeville in the Transvaal led to the death of sixty-nine Africans. World-wide condemnation of the South African police followed. There were moves to expel South Africa from the Commonwealth, but they came to nothing. However, the following year, when South Africa became a republic and therefore had to make a formal application to remain in the Commonwealth, criticism became so intense that the South African Prime Minister decided to withdraw the application. There had been suggestions that other states would leave if South Africa remained and thus the Commonwealth would break up. The South African withdrawal was the first time a member of long standing had departed. Some commentators suggested that the incident showed that the Commonwealth did in fact stand for certain basic principles and would now advance from strength to strength. Others believed that there were shortcomings in the internal policies of other Commonwealth states and that the cardinal principles of the Commonwealth – non-interference in the internal affairs of member states – had been destroyed.

The Rhodesian issue then moved to the forefront of Commonwealth discussions. After Salisbury's unilateral declaration of independance (UDI) there were demands from African states that Britain should use force to restore legal government. Wilson ruled out such a step and appeared to place his faith in the imposition of economic sanctions. A special Commonwealth Conference was held in Lagos, Nigeria in January 1966 – the first time it had been held outside the United Kingdom. The Prime Minister drew on his rich fund of economic knowledge to declare that sanctions would be effective 'in a matter of weeks, not months'. By September, when another conference was held in London, that forecast was evidently wide of the mark. Britain was bitterly criticized for failing to take more effective action. After a further abortive round of talks between Wilson and Smith, the British government asked the United Nations to impose selective mandatory sanctions against Rhodesia. Six principles were established as the basis on which a return to legality might be granted, the most significant being that there should be unimpeded progress towards majority rule. These principles remained the centre of discussions between London and Salisbury under Labour. Sir Alec Douglas-Home, the Conservative Foreign Secretary, seemed to make some progress when he visited Rhodesia in 1971, but the agreement failed to meet the principle that the proposals should be acceptable to the people of Rhodesia as a whole – the British government sent out a commission to test opinion. Notwithstanding this failure, Heath made it clear to the 1973 Commonwealth Conference in Ottawa that Rhodesia was a British responsibility. It was the United Kingdom which would take whatever steps it deemed necessary – though the Commonwealth would be consulted. African countries were not very happy with this stance and made their feelings plain. There was, however, less talk than there had once been that Rhodesia would destroy the Commonwealth. By sticking to their line, British ministers made it clear that the demise of the Commonwealth would be a matter of great regret, but not one on which Britain could any longer be blackmailed. There was a limit beyond which even 'toothless bulldogs' could not be pushed. Realism returned in the mid-1970s and eventually contributed to the atmosphere in which the Rhodesian question was settled.

The other Commonwealth countries had come to understand that their independence also entailed the independence of the United Kingdom. At the Commonwealth Conference held in Singapore in 1971, the British Prime Minister had insisted on his country's right to sell arms to South Africa in accordance with the agreement which then pertained for the joint defence of the sea routes round the Cape. He stuck to this policy in the face of bitter opposition. Whatever the merits of the particular issue, it was a demonstration that British policy would not be decided by Commonwealth views. It was the other aspect of the fact that the Commonwealth had ceased to be a British organization. By the 1970s, its meetings would normally take place outside the United Kingdom. Their organization no longer rested with Whitehall. A separate Commonwealth Secretariat was formed in 1965 with a Canadian as its first Secretary-General (to be followed by a Guyanese). While some writers talked about 'strains in Commonwealth unity', it was evident that there neither was nor could be 'Commonwealth unity' in any sense which might have applied as late as 1956. The Commonwealth now contained a great variety of regimes and alignments. The Queen remained its Head, but such symbolism was not of great significance. Membership of the Commonwealth did not prevent member states going to war with each other, as India and Pakistan did over Kashmir. A further Indo-Pakistani War in 1971 resulted in the emergence of Bangladesh which joined the Commonwealth, though Pakistan itself left. The Nigerian Civil War (1967–70) diminished the impact of African criticism of British policy towards Rhodesia.

It is not surprising that in these circumstances scepticism about the value of the Commonwealth increased. It was a factor in the decision of successive British governments to seek membership of the EEC. Important organizations still fostered Commonwealth contacts in the educational, economic and sporting fields, but the idea that Commonwealth countries were not 'foreign' was steadily abandoned, though some sentimental ties survived with Australia, New Zealand and Canada. In 1965, the United Kingdom ceased to have a Foreign Office and a Commonwealth Office. Some had hoped that a complete break with the past might be made by establishing a single Ministry of External Affairs, but the title of Foreign and Commonwealth Office was retained for the amalgamated service. Other problems remained unresolved, most notably in the area of nationality and citizenship legislation. Successive governments were reluctant to unscramble the complex inheritance of the imperial past and provide definitions of citizenship which more accurately corresponded to Britain's position in the world. This task was, of course, enormously complicated by the emotions aroused by continuing immigration from the Commonwealth.

It is difficult to generalize more widely about the significance of the demise of the Empire/Commonwealth. In 1962, Dean Acheson caused a great stir by declaring that Britain had lost an empire but had not yet found a role. Despite the ensuing furore, the remark was a commonplace, confirmed by the strivings of policy-makers over the next decade. Whether the nation as a whole was psychologically disorientated is more doubtful. The Movement for Colonial Freedom had attempted to accelerate the speed of decolonization and the League of Empire Loyalists to prevent it; the great mass of people probably accepted what was happening without undue apprehension or excitement. Enthusiasm for the Commonwealth could still be found in both major parties, and decolonization had not seriously disrupted either of them. Macleod as Colonial Secretary (1959–61), was sometimes thought too clever by half by some members of his own party, but there was no question of the Conservatives actually changing course. The Labour party appeared to be more enthusiastic about the new Commonwealth that had emerged than were the Conservatives, but such enthusiasm may not have gone very deep among its supporters(46).

By the 1970s, historians began to attempt some initial assessment of the British Empire. Few saw the final stages of its history as an unexpected cataclysm. They stressed the limitations which hedged around imperial rule even when it appeared unchallengeable. Since 1870, one historian argued, Britain had been in unbroken decline relative to other nations in all significant aspects. The empire had been acquired in an attempt to stave off that decline, but its subsequent loss was only confirmation that this relative decline could not be reversed. In so far as Britain 'possessed' an empire, it was 'very rarely a source of strength to Britain, despite the imperialists' efforts to make it so'(32). It was little more than a temporary shield against the consequences of this decline, though almost everyone thought otherwise during its glory. Other historians continued to think that the empire was much more important and that the post-1945 abandonment of formal control masked a reality of continuing economic exploitation. On the other hand, there were those who stressed the burden which, at least latterly, the Empire/Commonwealth had become. Such economic advantages as there were, were balanced by the 'feather-bedding' effect which a largely captive market had on British industry, protecting it disastrously from the innovative thrust which exposure to global markets provided. Whatever the balance of advantage and disadvantage, however, no one could doubt that the sun had at length set on the British Empire(50).

---

1. W. S. Churchill, *Into Battle* (1941), p. 234

CHAPTER 30

Retreat from world power

In the summer of 1956 the United Kingdom still seemed not simply a European power or the hub of the Commonwealth but a world power in a more general sense. British forces were still deployed across the globe. However, it was the military aspects of the Suez Crisis which caused as much of a shock as the political. Unsuitable men, unsuitable ships and unsuitable aircraft were hastily brought together – some 45,000 men, 100 ships and 300 aircraft. Quite what the expedition was designed to do was never very clear, but it was apparent that it did not succeed. It was the British, not the Egyptians, who were using Second World War rifles. Of course, military factors were not the only, or even the chief, factors which led Eden to agree to a cease-fire, but lengthy discussion of Britain's defence options and world role inevitably followed this débâcle. It was commonly accepted that the armed forces were inadequate, but it was also politically difficult to devote additional resources to improve them. A 'realignment of roles' seemed the obvious answer(75).

In the aftermath of Suez, the favourite target for spending cuts lay outside Europe. It was evident that the United States would not underwrite any British attempt to act independently overseas. It also seemed likely that the pressures of local nationalism would make even limited operations difficult and costly, even if a politically plausible case could be made for them, and that was increasingly hard. Nevertheless, there was no abrupt and complete withdrawal from east of Suez after 1956. Governments of both parties could still discern a role in the Persian Gulf or the Straits of Malacca. From time to time, there were outbursts of discontent from politicians in both parties at their colleagues' failure to read the anti-British graffiti on the walls of the world. Perhaps it was Enoch Powell's linguistic talents in this respect that led him to write in February 1957: 'The Tory Party must be cured of the British Empire, of the pitiful yearning to cling to relics of a bygone system.'[1] November 1964, however, saw the incoming Labour Prime Minister proudly declaring 'we are a world power and a world influence or we are nothing'. In February 1966, Mayhew, the Navy Minister, resigned from the Cabinet when it would not sanction a new aircraft-carrier while it asserted that the armed forces should be capable of operating east of Suez. In his view, a world role and the existing defence budget were incompatible.

Defence commentators, however, denied that the undoubted difficulties in a reorientation were sufficient reason not to attempt them. Scarcely a year passed without political changes taking place which in turn required the termination or revision of general defence agreements or permission to use specific bases – in Iraq, Libya or Sri Lanka for example. Even so, British governments were not so frightened by 1956 that they refrained from any military action overseas. In 1958

British troops landed in Jordan to protect the State, supposedly against Egypt – though this would probably not have happened if the Americans were not doing the same in the Lebanon. In 1961 they were sent to defend Kuwait from supposed Iraqi designs. A few years later they played a most important role in helping Malaysia in the 'confrontation' with Indonesia. There were also brief excursions to East Africa to maintain governments threatened by refractory soldiery. There was one rather disturbing aspect of all of these operations – they were successful limited measures. The same could not be said about the fighting in Aden until independence in 1967. It was, however, the devaluation of the pound in that year (itself precipitated by the Six Day Arab–Israeli War in June) that forced a further reconsideration of defence plans. The government announced in January 1968 that 'sacred cows' would not be spared and defence would have to suffer cuts. Except for Hong Kong, British forces would be withdrawn from the Persian Gulf and the Far East by the end of 1971. The next Defence White Paper in February 1969 explicitly stated that political and economic realities reinforced the defence arguments for concentrating Britain's military role on Europe(72).

Even so, also in 1969, the energetic Leader of the Opposition told the puzzled rulers of the Gulf states that Britain might, after all, stay on to assist them. But, as one who accompanied him on this trip noted, the obstacle to a continuing British presence in the region 'did not lie with the rulers or their people, or with the Shah. Nor, at this period, was it the result of lack of money. We had simply lost the will to continue the effort, and Mr Heath was unable to revive it.'(121) When the Conservatives returned after 1970, withdrawal was not reversed. Television viewers watched unconcernedly in subsequent years as the last ships of the Royal Navy sailed out of Valletta harbour or some other scene of former glory. There was nothing anyone could do now. Some few British bases did remain in far-flung parts of the world, but they did not fit into a coherent strategy. It was reassuring, nevertheless, to see companies of the Parachute Regiment, ably assisted by such men as could be spared from the Metropolitan police force, flying the Atlantic to deal with a constitutional crisis between the small West Indian island of Anguilla and its smaller neighbours. There were still some problems which the British could tackle effectively. Inevitably, this reduced military capacity meant that, when the Vietnam War was at its height, British governments resisted the notion that British forces might participate. By the same token, their advice on how the war might be brought to an end (which was freely given) carried little weight.

This protracted and messy disengagement from the world outside Europe did not necessarily mean that the United Kingdom was ceasing to be a Great Power in a military sense. Britain's nuclear weapons still preserved a foothold in the land of the Great Powers. Governments after 1956 reaffirmed that they were vital for Britain's security – but they were also very expensive. The paradox was that a good part of the emotional support for an independent deterrent rested on a lingering uncertainty about whether the United States would act in a crisis involving Europe at the same time as it was becoming clear that American cooperation would be necessary if Britain were to retain an 'independent' force.

The 1957 Defence White Paper issued by Duncan Sandys placed great stress upon nuclear weapons. The first British hydrogen bomb tests were successfully completed in the same year. Assiduous diplomacy had gone a long way to restoring co-operation with the Americans after the strains brought about by Suez. The Americans responded by taking a less strict view of their McMahon Act and allowed some information on nuclear matters to be passed to Britain. The nuclear deterrent did not immediately occasion great controversy. Politicians and the public were pleased that it seemed to permit the reduction of conventional forces and, in particular, the army. Conscription (still widely thought of as un-British) could then be brought to an end. It had been introduced by Labour in 1947. Initially for eighteen months, but later reduced to a year, National Service aroused conflicting feelings. Quite apart from its military value, it was defended and advocated as an improving form of social discipline for eighteen-year olds – but by the later 1950s such sentiments were coming to sound old-fashioned(76).

It soon became apparent, however, that there were problems in a nuclear strategy. Great faith was placed in the British Blue Streak missile but, by 1960, it had to be sadly admitted that it was technically inadequate and was cancelled. It had already cost a great deal of money to develop and featured awkwardly in a programme designed to reduce defence expenditure. It seemed that more flair was shown in finding names for rockets than in actually making them go. The British had no alternative but to rely on the American Skybolt missile to supplement the force of V-bombers. Unfortunately, two years later, the Americans cancelled Skybolt. It was against this background that Kennedy and Macmillan met in December 1962 at Nassau. The British now wished to have access to the American Polaris missiles. They would be fired from nuclear submarines which the British would build, though even here they depended to an extent on American expertise. While it was agreed to assign the submarines to NATO, in certain exceptional circumstances Britain could withdraw them; in this sense it was right to talk of an 'independent' force. The great advantage for Britain was that Polaris was relatively cheap and would last for at least a decade. This change of emphasis meant that in the early 1960s the navy became the most expensive of the services. The British nuclear shield had apparently been firmly buckled on, even though it became increasingly difficult to envisage circumstances in which it would be used without American approval.

Few people could grasp the full complexities of nuclear weaponry and strategy, but it did all seem very frightening. The implications of nuclear warfare did, nevertheless, seem clear enough to those who founded the Campaign for Nuclear Disarmament (CND) in 1958. All those who supported the campaign and marched from the Aldermaston research station to London at Eastertime had no doubt that nuclear weapons constituted a menace to the survival of the British Isles and of mankind. Eminent figures like Bertrand Russell, A. J. P. Taylor, J. B. Priestley and Canon John Collins lent their support. The strategy seemed to be to gain the backing of the Labour party for unilateral disarmament. In 1960–61 this precipitated a major internal crisis for the party. By the middle of the decade, however, the impetus of the movement was lost and various splinter groups flirted with violence in pursuit of their objectives. Despite all the controversy, Labour's long-serving Defence Secretary (1964–70) Healey, did not carry out any substantial shift in nuclear policy. A decade after the formation of CND it seemed as if a generation had stopped worrying and come to live with the bomb. Even so, both the expense and morality of retaining nuclear weapons caused grave disquiet, though efforts to devise systems of arms control met with scant success.

One significant change was that doctrines of 'massive retaliation' were going out of fashion. There was more talk of a 'flexible response' and this required the maintenance of well-equipped, if relatively small, conventional forces, particularly for service in Europe. This change of emphasis brought difficulties because the nuclear orientation Britain had chosen to adopt was firmly American. For de Gaulle, the Nassau agreement was evidence that Britain was not European. Over the years before this agreement, Britain had not co-operated with the other European powers on questions of nuclear strategy and had not shared information. There was disquiet in Federal Germany about proposed reductions in the British Army of the Rhine and haggling, which threatened to become annual, over the German contribution to British military costs. Although the idea of Franco-British nuclear co-operation was sometimes mooted, no significant body of opinion in Britain favoured it. Britain did in fact honour her commitment to maintain troops in West Germany and Berlin, but the size of these forces did cause concern, especially when relations between East and West deteriorated. Anxiety grew when it became evident in the early 1970s that British troops were likely to be required on duty in Northern Ireland for an indefinite period.

Occasionally, there were mutterings even within Britain about the need to bring back conscription and end this insular peculiarity, but this never obtained sufficient support. The armed forces, too, rather prided themselves in being (as their advertisements stressed) 'the professionals' with a high degree of skill. For all three services, the Second World War was coming to seem a distant conflict as technological change thrust relentlessly onwards; even the aircraft-carrier had become obsolete. It became questionable whether the British economy could sustain the research and development costs of new aircraft, and the export of military equipment came to assume increasing importance. It not only helped the balance of payments but maintained a sufficiently large manufacturing base for Britain's own requirements. Within the NATO alliance, the need for standardization of equipment was frequently endorsed but often ignored, as member countries struggled to ensure the prosperity of their own industries. If co-ordination remained difficult at this level, changes took place inside Britain which at long last established an integrated defence service. In the early 1960s, one of the last Conservative decisions was to make the War Office, the Admiralty and the Air Ministry simply departments in a new Ministry of Defence. The Secretary of State would be assisted by ministers of State who headed these departments. The Defence Council was restructured in consequence. In the later 1960s, Healey eroded the significance of service boundaries even further by appointing, under the Secretary of State, two ministers with responsibilities for equipment and administration respectively – whether for land, sea, or air. Despite these improvements, if a conventional war broke out in Europe, and remained conventional, Britain's armed forces, which would be in action at once, were still small and substantial reserves were not available. The Territorial Army was downgraded and even lost its name. Britain could make a contribution if the war did become nuclear – with what consequence it would be hard to say. Everything would depend upon the precise circumstances of conflict.

By the middle 1970s, Britain's resources and commitments were arguably better matched than at any time since the Second World War – but only as part of an alliance and, as such, subject to all its tensions. And it was in the field of defence that Britain tended to stay close to the United States at a time when her political and economic relations with western Europe were becoming more intimate. It was frequently stated that the 'special relationship' with the United States was either not what it had been or was dead, but the senior generation of politicians could not quite believe it even so. The avuncular Macmillan passed on advice to the boyish Kennedy, though whether it was of much consequence is another matter. Since American policy generally favoured British membership of the EEC, the failure to achieve it caused problems. In the last resort, Cabinets of both parties were aware of the fact that Britain was a kind of American dependency – something occasionally found irksome but on the whole generally accepted. By the middle 1970s, however, when the United States appeared to falter in the wake of Vietnam, Watergate and economic problems, it again became urgent to reappraise the defence policies of the Western alliance. History had ensured that Britain could understand the perceptions both of the Americans and the West Europeans. History also made it difficult for Britain to decide where her own interests lay in the matters that divided them. The only alternative for Britain in the world seemed to be a policy of neutrality which would entail withdrawal from NATO and nuclear disarmament, whatever the consequences of such a step might be. In the mid-1970s such a course had some support inside the Labour party, but not very much. Few now supposed that the United Nations could in itself offer an alternative basis for Britain's role in the world. Governments of both parties had given general support to the activities of that organization, though they were not above expressing criticism of the way it conducted its affairs. Such support, however, was accompanied by an acute appreciation that it had become a rather different body in ethos and aspiration from when it had been shaped during the Second World War. Britain's continuing permanent seat on the Security Council seemed increasingly anomalous as the decades passed, but there was no disposition to seek a change. And if, in strict terms, it was hard to justify, there was still a residual sense in which, despite the retreat from world power, history had left with the British, for good or ill, a range of global contacts, connections and experience which still made the United Kingdom just a little more than an offshore island.

---

1. Cited in J. Ramsden, *The making of Conservative party policy* (1980), p. 213

CHAPTER 31

A United Kingdom in doubt

By the middle 1970s, it was a commonplace to observe that the United Kingdom was not united. A spate of books and articles appeared which predicted, with enthusiasm or regret, the end of 'British' history. Some observers found it paradoxical that the United Kingdom should be disintegrating at the very point when it was struggling to find a place in a Europe which was believed to be uniting. Others saw nothing strange in such a coincidence. For them, the United Kingdom had outlived its usefulness. 'Macro' decisions should be taken on a European Community basis while 'micro' decisions should be taken at a lower level than that of the United Kingdom. Therefore, far from being the fulcrum on which all else turned, the Westminster Parliament was a redundant intermediary; direct access to Brussels from Cardiff or Edinburgh was thought to be the order of the day. It was also thought that this growing regionalism or nationalism which, at the least, appeared to be forcing a change in the constitutional structure of the United Kingdom, coincided with the end of the British Empire. The chronological coincidence could not be accidental. It suggested that the United Kingdom only made sense (if repugnant sense) in an age of imperialism. Since Britain no longer ruled the waves, there really was little need for Britain to exist at all. It was seriously suggested that Scots, who had played such a part in the Empire, could now find adequate outlet for their talents only in the creation of an independent Scotland. Strenuous efforts were made in certain quarters to avoid being considered 'British' or to think in terms of 'Britain' – culturally, politically or economically. It was even argued that unless constitutional change took place there would be violence(142).

The readiness with which some of these arguments were accepted in England was itself an aspect of that English ignorance which fuelled some of the discontent. It was only with difficulty that Englishmen were weaned away from the tendency to equate Britain with England. The very teaching of history, from school to university, perpetuated this fallacy. Otherwise excellent histories which purported to be about *Social Conditions in Britain Between the Wars* or about *Public Opinion and the Making of British Foreign Policy* contained no reference to conditions or opinion in Scotland.[1] It is only half-way through a volume on *The British Experience, 1945–75* that its author stumbles across evidence of dissent in what he calls 'the Celtic fringes'. He himself, however, continues to talk about 'England' having been a world power and it is not surprising to see the Northern Ireland problem discussed in a section called 'The English in Ireland' and to read its final sentence 'The British, convinced that their presence was at least preventing the killing from getting even worse, clung on, but the long and mostly unhappy story of the English in Ireland was clearly nearing its end.'[2] If that was how it appeared from London, it might not do so from Glasgow. Yet, as the title of another book demonstrates, *Englishmen and Irish Troubles*, exactness is not to be looked for. Lloyd George, who features prominently as Prime Minister, was not English.

What was lacking, in public life generally, was an awareness of the true complexity of the British experience; that it embraced a variety of interests and cultures which were interwoven, but still identifiable. Hence the simple assumption in government circles in London, confronted by evidence of discontent in Scotland and Wales, that the 'solution' lay in giving 'the Scots' or 'the Welsh' what it was believed 'they' wanted – separate assemblies. Somehow, in the process, an undefined 'unity' of the United Kingdom was to be strengthened. Yet in reacting to 'realities' outside England, they were given a hardness and homogeneity which they lacked. When, in March 1979, the people in Scotland and Wales were (as a concession) allowed to vote on proposals which were supposed to be responding to a deep swell in public opinion, massive endorsement was lacking. Amidst general confusion, it was at least evident that in political terms, not to mention any other, 'Welshness' and 'Scottishness' were ambiguous notions. To try, in however incomplete a form, to separate the Welsh or Scottish nation from the British nation only divided the Welsh and Scottish nations. The United Kingdom remained united, but it was not uniform. The tensions generated by its diversity would not disappear, but a strong desire to maintain political unity endured(148).

NORTHERN IRELAND

Writing in 1955, a historian with a keen interest in Ireland could nevertheless conclude that after the legislation of the early 1920s the Irish Question 'simply disappeared as a major factor in British politics' and its resurrection was not then anticipated(146). The verdict of an expatriate Ulsterman on *Ulster under Home Rule* was 'a feeling of surprise that it has worked so well'[3] despite the hostility of a large minority and recurrent outbreaks of violence. That also represented the prevailing impression in Britain. The best hope of softening intercommunal tensions lay in an improvement of the economic situation and in a renunciation of the Irish Republic's jurisdictional claims over the North. As Unionist fears diminished, so would such discriminatory practices as were believed to exist in the fields of housing and employment. Meanwhile, sporadic IRA violence continued. The campaign which was launched in December 1956 claimed that 'resistance to British rule in occupied Ireland has now entered a decisive state . . .' (146). It lasted, on and off, until February 1962, solidifying the Unionist party and not endangering the structure of government. An Ulster civil servant, looking back on this period, feels that the record of the Home Affairs ministry was remarkable: IRA activity was contained, prevented from spreading to Belfast and Protestant para-military retaliation was avoided.[4] However, the Hall Report on the Northern Ireland economy (1962) did not see an encouraging future; Ulstermen should look for jobs outside Northern Ireland as much as inside it.

In 1963, Captain Terence O'Neill became Prime Minister of Northern Ireland. From the outset, he was determined to give Unionism a fresh face and make it attractive to middle-class Catholics. He had a famous meeting with the then Prime Minister of the Irish Republic in 1965 and the two men seemed to have established a co-operative relationship without compromising on the constitutional issue. However, suspicion on this score soon developed. For a time, O'Neill succeeded in creating more optimism about economic prospects. The Wilson Plan (1965) stressed the need for 'an environment more favourable to the sustained expansion of output and employment'. The author's detailed plans for growth centres could be fitted into the Belfast Regional Survey and Plan which had been commissioned a few years earlier from Sir Robert Matthew. New towns were designated at Craigavon (a 'rural city'), Antrim and Ballymena. The strategy was 'simultaneously to demagnetize the centre, and re-invigorate the many attractive small towns in the region'. Only if Belfast were curbed could it begin to flourish again, although the problems of its industrial infrastructure could not easily be overcome. In this context, there were complaints that 'west of the Bann' was being neglected. A Londonderry Area Plan was published in 1968 which advocated a substantial programme of urban renewal. Civil servants denied partiality as between different parts of the province. One commented that 'departments probably gave more than a fifth of their thinking to the western parts as there was usually much less local initiative there' – about a fifth of the population lived in the West.[5] However true, such a remark epitomizes Ulster attitudes. Drive and initiative were an aspect of the Protestant spirit.

What took place in Londonderry in the autumn of 1968 was not an amicable discussion of the development plan but a dramatic confrontation between 'civil rights' marchers and the police – the march having been banned by the Home Affairs Minister, William Craig. The Civil Rights Association had been formed the previous year and developed a style of protest influenced by contemporaneous American movements. Ostensibly non-sectarian, it in fact expressed the resentments of the minority. It was infiltrated by republican elements and therefore, in the eyes of some not unsympathetic Protestants, was tainted. Not the least of the ironies was that many of the Ulster-born civil rights leaders benefited from a British system of higher education which they might not have obtained in the Republic. Names like Bernadette Devlin, Michael Farrell and Eamon McCann became notable figures in a matter of months – and not only in Ulster. The violent clashes in Northern Ireland appeared on television screens across the water and south of the border. O'Neill felt obliged to dismiss Craig, but the marches continued in 1969, as did attempts to disrupt them. The Prime Minister's position weakened, and was shattered by the result of the 1969 General Election. His patrician liberalism had almost succeeded in alienating every group and his confidence that he could carry a substantial 'Liberal Unionist' vote was misplaced. The coming men appeared to be Civil Rights figures like John Hume and Austin Currie on one side and Ian Paisley, founder of his own Free Presbyterian Church, on the other.

The civil disturbances in Londonderry in August 1969 – again widely seen on television – were followed by others in Belfast. Charges of brutality and provocation filled the air and were subsequently investigated. As the situation deteriorated, Callaghan, the British Home Secretary, in consultation with Chichester-Clark, the new Prime Minister, ordered in British troops and their protection was at first welcomed by the Catholic community. The troops were there 'on a temporary basis in accordance with the United Kingdom's ultimate responsibility'. London stressed the 'equal rights and protection under the law' of all United Kingdom citizens. At the same time, various other changes were made. Universal adult suffrage in local government elections had just been conceded and the most controversial decision was the reorganization of the Royal Ulster Constabulary. The auxiliary 'B' Specials were disbanded and replaced by the Ulster Defence Regiment which was linked to the British Army. A Ministry of Community Relations was to be established and a new system devised to try to avoid discrimination in housing(144).

It was, however, one thing to pass the 1970 Prevention of Incitement to Hatred Act (NI) and another to restore civil order. In December 1969, the IRA split into two groups, the 'officials' who were willing to participate in the protest movement and the 'provisionals' who were committed to a military campaign. The latter became increasingly active and, in trying to deal with them, the British Army found its good name in the Catholic community increasingly jeopardized, though it was not until February 1971 that the first British soldier was killed. Protestant opinion in turn put pressure on Chichester-Clark to maintain a policy of strict law enforcement. Protestant para-military groups blossomed. In August 1970, the new Conservative Home Secretary, Maudling, warned that if the recent changes were reversed Northern Ireland's devolved government would be in jeopardy. In the same month, the Social Democratic and Labour Party (SDLP) was formed. Led by Gerry Fitt, it proclaimed a dislike of violence, but felt that the recent changes represented only a beginning. Always in danger of losing support to the IRA, Fitt led his group out of the Stormont Parliament in July 1971, having failed to bring about an enquiry into a shooting incident involving British soldiers. By this time, there was yet another Prime Minister (the only one to be educated in the province), Brian Faulkner, a forceful and energetic man, well aware of the pitfalls, but with more shrewdness than either of his predecessors. Still violence and destruction of property continued, and in August 1971 internment was introduced. It was clumsily executed. It also failed to stop the violence and substantially alienated the Catholic community. The ending of Stormont – a clear republican objective by this juncture – was clearly in prospect. 'Bloody Sunday', when British troops killed thirteen people in Londonderry on 30 January 1972 during an 'illegal' demonstration that got out of hand, brought matters to a head. The death of these 'unarmed civilians/vicious rioters' meant the end of Stormont. The London government felt that a radical new departure was required. Ironically, it was a Conservative government, the party with the closest links with the Ulster Unionists, which prorogued Stormont on 24 March 1972 and announced the introduction of 'direct rule' from Westminster. Supposedly a temporary step, few expected that the devolved Parliament would return, at least in its old form. There was great bitterness among Unionists, though already the old Unionist party was fragmenting. Republicans rejoiced that the first step had been taken towards the dismantling of the 'Protestant State'.

Under the new arrangements, Whitelaw became the first Secretary of State for Northern Ireland, dividing his time between Westminster and the province. His immediate task was to stop the violence from developing into full civil war. By the summer, the 'no-go' areas of Belfast and Londonderry had been brought back under control. The street parades of the Ulster Defence Association were an indication of the Protestant majority's anxieties. In March 1973, the British government issued a White Paper on Northern Ireland which was subsequently embodied in the Northern Ireland Constitution Act. The border poll of the same month again showed a substantial majority in favour of remaining within the United Kingdom. Under the government's plans, elections were held, with a system of proportional representation, for a new Assembly. A 'power-sharing' Executive, composed of Faulkner's supporters, the SDLP and the small new Alliance party, took up office (though with limited powers) at the beginning of 1974, but their majority was precarious. 'Loyalists', now organized in various parties, disliked the new arrangement intensely, being particularly critical of the revived Council of Ireland agreed to as part of the package by Heath, Faulkner and the Irish Prime Minister at Sunningdale in December 1973. Opponents of 'power-sharing' won eleven out of the twelve Northern Ireland seats at Westminster in the February 1974 General Election. A new body, the Ulster Workers' Council, organized a General Strike in May which brought the province to a halt. The executive collapsed. Direct rule returned, but the new Labour government still sought a formula to permit the restoration of some form of devolved government. The next move was to form a Constitutional Convention, but the United Ulster Unionist coalition dominated this body and its proposals were not acceptable in London. The Convention was abandoned and there did not seem room for a new 'initiative'.

By the autumn of 1974, about 1,100 people had been killed since August 1969 and that number continued to rise – the security forces carrying an increasingly heavy burden of casualties. The scale and type of violence fluctuated from month to month and year to year, but it did not end. Direct rule settled into a routine and it began to seem as if it offered the best solution when local agreement was not possible. Through the Secretary of State and his assistants, the Westminster government could attempt to be fair to both communities. At the same time, with increased parliamentary representation from Northern Ireland at Westminster, the clear wish of the majority to remain 'British' would be safeguarded. However, by definition, such an integration would not recognize the 'Irish dimension' of the North, let alone an aspiration to Irish unity. For its part, the IRA could only hope that the continuing level of casualties sustained by the British Army in Ulster and terrorist activity in Britain, would lead the rest of the United Kingdom to abandon Ulster. From time to time, such a desire did surface, though it did not prevail.

Behind the rhetoric and slaughter lay the question of identity. The Protestant

Ulsterman was not English, but that did not preclude him from being British. Ulster flags were waved when Stormont was dying, but even if the Ulster identity is called 'a kind of embryonic nationalism' it was still one which sought a wider context, not least for economic reasons. In these respects, the imposition of direct rule caused problems. Even before that decision, there was resentment at the fact that the British government sent a Foreign Office official to maintain a watching brief on its behalf. Later, the advent of more officials from London brought more men whose ignorance of Ulster geography and society was not remedied by hotel residence and official cars. Paradoxes abounded. One of the foremost advocates of 'integration' within the United Kingdom was the MP for South Down after October 1974, the Welsh-speaking Englishman from Birmingham, Enoch Powell. Sean McStiofain, one-time IRA Chief of Staff, turns out to be John Stevenson, born and bred in England of mixed English and Irish parentage. In the 1970s there were some 1 million Irish-born residents in Britain, three-quarters of whom came from the Republic. Inevitably, their position became somewhat uncomfortable when the IRA bombing campaign reached England. To add to the paradoxes, Irish immigration into Britain in the 1960s came most heavily from Connacht, the 'most Irish' province of Ireland. Complexities of this kind made it likely that if there could ever be a solution to the north of Ireland/Northern Ireland question it could only be one which arose from greater understanding between the United Kingdom and the Republic in a European context. On the one hand, the work of Irish historians began to make apparent that the dominant post-independence ideology in the Republic failed to do justice to the cultural pluralism of the island. On the other hand, political developments within Britain made its cultural pluralism more evident. Events in Northern Ireland itself since 1969 seemed to suggest that there could be no return to the past, but that no way forward could be internally generated.

WALES

In 1966, after many years in which he and his party had lost parliamentary elections, Gwynfor Evans, President of Plaid Cymru, won a by-election at Carmarthen. Great play was made in Wales in the mid-1960s with the shortcomings of the Labour government. It was, allegedly, inconceivable that the Conservatives could do better since they were 'un-Welsh'. Plaid Cymru presented itself as the heir to a Welsh radical tradition which had been Liberal and Labour. Elements in the party busily tried to move it out of the orbit of the Welsh intelligentsia – lecturers, ministers and writers – into the world of pit closures and industrial transformation in South Wales. Further by-elections showed a considerable increase in votes. Even so, the prime concern of the Plaid remained with 'cultural politics'. 'We Welsh', Evans wrote in a volume which claimed to be concerned with *Celtic Nationalism* 'are not just being denied self-expression as a nation today. . . . We are fighting in the last ditch for our very identity.'[6] It was frequently stated that the end of the Welsh language would mean the end of the Welsh nation. In 1962, the writer Saunders Lewis delivered a much-discussed radio lecture on 'The Fate of the Language' which inspired the formation of the Welsh Language Society in the same year. It embarked on a campaign of 'sit-ins' and other forms of protest designed to increase the use and improve the status of the Welsh language. The Hughes–Parry Report (1965) was followed by the Welsh Language Act, 1967, which gave it equal legal validity with English. Nevertheless, the campaign continued, finding fresh inspiration in Welsh pop-songs some of which found a target in the newly invested Prince of Wales (1969). The language had powerful supporters in education and broadcasting, but despite these varied activities the 1971 census disclosed that only 21 per cent of the Welsh population could speak Welsh.

Yet, while there was much goodwill among non-Welsh-speakers, there was also resentment at increasing attempts to make the learning of Welsh compulsory. The tension could be explosive. It was only in 1968 that Plaid Cymru accepted a policy of bilingualism for Wales, and bilingualism was a concept which could be variously interpreted. A Welsh-speaking historian noted that there were other factors besides languages which made up a sense of Welsh identity. Evans himself had to concede that 'common membership of the Welsh community rather than language or descent is the test of nationality in Wales', but it was not clear how that 'common membership' was achieved. Nevertheless, such a statement represented a further attempt to broaden the party's appeal beyond 'Welsh Wales'. From 1970 onwards, Plaid Cymru fought every parliamentary seat in Wales. Its highest poll was in 1970 – though it gained no seats. In both elections of 1974 it lost votes but gained seats, reaching a maximum of three in October 1974 – all in areas where a majority could speak Welsh. The tone of its campaign in February 1974 can be seen from its manifesto title – *Rich Welsh or Poor British*. A good deal of the richness of Wales seemed to be based on undiscovered oil in the 'Celtic Sea'(135,149).

No one could doubt that in the mid-1970s Wales was a more than usually volatile country. Advocates of devolution believed that they were at the helm – the formation of a Wales TUC (1973) being yet one more sign. It was only partially in response to the apparent growth of Plaid Cymru that such eminent 'Welsh' Labour MPs as Callaghan and Foot came to espouse the cause. It was not long before the bubble was to be pricked. Despite the lack of attention accorded them, it was in fact the Conservative party in Wales which was making steady progress, adding a further enigmatic element to the place of Wales as a nation within the United Kingdom(145).

SCOTLAND

In November 1967, the Scottish National party won the normally safe Labour seat of Hamilton at a by-election and its rapid growth then ensued. Observers believed that the class alignment of the Labour Conservative division was being eroded and 'Scottish consciousness' was replacing it. They also agreed that SNP voters did not really want independence or separatism (though some clearly did) but a party which would 'speak for Scotland'. The continuing economic failures of the United Kingdom as a whole persuaded many Scotsmen, at least for a time (as it had done some Welshmen), that they could do better on their own. The discovery of oil in the North Sea seemed to strengthen the argument. Its advantages for Scotland and for the United Kingdom might differ. The SNP put the point explicitly with the slogan 'England Expects . . . Scotland's Oil'. While the Liberals, long committed to a Scottish Assembly and with a prominent Scot, Grimond, as leader of the United Kingdom party, had made progress in Scotland in the mid-1960s, it was now the SNP which took the votes of those who were dissatisfied with the Labour and Conservative parties. However, once again, it proved easier to criticize the existing political system than devise an acceptable alternative. From 1968, when Heath told the Scottish Conservatives at their Perth conference that he favoured a Scottish Assembly, and set up a committee to consider the practicalities, to the 1978 Scotland Act and beyond, a succession of proposals have flowed from all quarters without commanding the degree of acceptance necessary for their implementation.

In the early 1970s, while the Kilbrandon Commission was investigating the Constitution, attitudes in Scotland continued to fluctuate, making it difficult to form a balanced judgement. When its report was published in October 1973, most of its members favoured the establishment of legislative assemblies for Scotland and Wales, with corresponding executives. A dissenting memorandum argued that devolution should also extend to England – suggesting five regional divisions. The divided mind of the Commission made it easy for the Conservatives to leave the matter in abeyance. Labour would probably have done the same had it not been for further SNP advances in the 1974 elections, rising to eleven seats and 800,000 votes in October.

Over the next two years, before the Scotland and Wales Bill was put before the House of Commons, discussion centred on the complex financial and legal issues. Although what was envisaged for Scotland was more far-reaching than for Wales, a single bill was proposed – though in July 1977 the government gave way and announced that two separate measures would be introduced. They, in turn, were debated in the spring of 1978 and a 'consultative' referendum was conceded. There was also a new clause (moved by an expatriate Scot) that 40 per cent of the electorate (in Scotland and Wales) should vote in favour before the measures were implemented. The Scottish result (the referendum was held on 1 March 1979) produced a small majority in favour among those voting, but failed to clear the hurdle. The views of commentators that the United Kingdom was entering a new phase in its history had to be sharply revised. In the subsequent General Election of 1979 both the SNP and Plaid Cymru lost ground and plans for devolution were put away. In the Scottish case, if either of the major United Kingdom parties had produced 'limited devolution' proposals before the spectacular expansion of the SNP they might have been generally accepted in Scotland. Paradoxically, it was the growth of the SNP which both prodded a divided Labour government (and party in Scotland) into action and frightened a sufficient proportion of the Scottish electorate to vote against the Scotland Bill because it would be the first step to separation(130).

If the path of devolution were to be trodden again, its only chance of success might be if it were to be approached from the standpoint of the United Kingdom as a whole. The membership of the Kilbrandon Commission was geographically biased and the Labour government's recognition of the 'English dimension' quite inadequate. The implications of devolution were most acutely perceived in the north-east and north-west of England. It was strange that English electors were not thought worthy of a vote (not necessarily a deciding one) on proposals which, if implemented, would have affected the entire United Kingdom. There was some resentment that Scotland and Wales would both have their own assemblies and retain their unique 'regional' representation in the Cabinet. Such influence hardly seemed fair to those parts of England with economic and social difficulties as serious as those in Scotland and Wales. This reaction was regional rather than 'English national', but if the proposals had succeeded, an English feeling might have emerged, with unpredictable consequences(142).

IDENTITY AND IMMIGRATION

If questions of identity did not emerge in England, to any degree, because of the 'devolution debate', they did emerge on the issue of immigration. Coloured communities in Britain before the Second World War had been small and largely confined to ports like Liverpool or Cardiff. There had been occasional disturbances in these cities, but the numbers involved meant that the impact remained local. The immigration into Britain that took place after 1945 coincided with a period of full employment, when less attractive jobs could not be filled. Some 4,000 West Indians had worked in factories and for the RAF during the war and it seemed natural to stay in Britain and to encourage others to come. Even so, in 1951 there were only some 15,000 persons born in the West Indies living in England and Wales. Asian immigration also had wartime origins. Men frequently jumped ship in Britain. There were also some 1,000 Indian doctors practising in Britain in 1949. The total coloured population of England and Wales in 1951 amounted to 74,500 – 1.70 per 1,000. A decade later, the figures had altered to 336,600 and 7.30 per 1,000, much the largest proportion of that increase having come from the West Indies. Immigrant distribution in Britain was determined by the factors governing their migration. They tended to move into areas where indigenous low-paid workers were moving out. Where unemployment was high – on Merseyside or Tyneside for example – there was, relatively speaking, little coloured immigration. The areas of greatest concentration were Greater London, the West Midlands and West Yorkshire, though Asians and West Indians tended to have considerably different settlement and employment patterns. And, of course, within these conurbations, the density varied very widely from area to area. By 1966, the coloured immigrant population of England and Wales had reached 595,100 or 12.6 per 1,000, and both total and proportion continued to rise in the ensuing decade.

The early phases of this population movement had not caused much public comment or concern. By 1956, however, the then Conservative Parliamentary Under-Secretary at the Home Office considered that the numbers now constituted a 'headache'. She painted a picture of the newcomers arriving by air and at once beginning to draw National Assistance (151). Bilateral talks took place with the Indian and Pakistani governments, without much effect. These were delicate years in the history of the Commonwealth, and Conservative ministers did not want to jeopardize its survival. Labour tended to oppose any notion of control and to concern itself with the evidence of discrimination. The Notting Hill, London, race riots of 1958 and the continuing higher level of immigration meant that, sooner or later, some control would be introduced. Fear of such a step only increased the level of immigration. The 'bilateral solution' was tried once more, but by 1961 the Conservative government felt obliged to act. The 1962 Commonwealth Immigration Act introduced an entry system based on employment vouchers. Ministers suggested that the measure represented 'control rather than a stop' and the Labour party was still apparently committed to its total repeal.

The 1964 General Election disclosed that in the West Midlands and other areas commitment to end immigration brought votes. Wilson, the new Prime Minister, denounced one MP as 'a kind of parliamentary leper' on these grounds, but the 1962 Act was not repealed. Further agreements with Commonwealth governments were sought and Labour prepared legislation on discrimination and incitement to racial hatred in the form of the Race Relations Act. If conciliation failed to settle cases of alleged racial discrimination, prosecutions would follow. In August 1964 a White Paper on immigration policy showed how Labour had changed its mind. It proposed a substantial reduction in the annual number of employment vouchers, abolished entry for unskilled workers and proposed 'strict tests of eligibility' in the case of dependants. The Home Office's power to repatriate was extended. The White Paper caused a furore. Although its reception led to it being withdrawn, it was an indication of a changing mood among many Labour supporters. Fundamental divisions of principle did not now seem to separate the parties. Further evidence of this was provided by the Kenya Asian crisis at the end of 1967 when many Asians who retained British passports at the time of Kenyan independence found themselves denied entry into the United Kingdom. In defending the measure that was rushed through to prevent their admission, government spokesmen pleaded the changed circumstances within Britain.

The 1968 Race Relations Act, on the other hand, extended the powers and functions of the Board set up under the first Act. In April of that year, Enoch Powell (then a Conservative MP) declared, with widespread support, that the nation was mad to permit the entry of an annual flow of some 50,000 dependants, the material for the future growth of the immigrant-descended population. By the end of the year he was arguing that the repatriation of a substantial proportion of Commonwealth immigrants was not beyond the country's resources and abilities. Both the tone and content of Powell's speeches led to his dismissal from the Opposition Shadow Cabinet, but he gained, for a time, a substantial public following. He forecast 'rivers of blood' in the future, but his critics accused him of indulging in self-fulfilling prophecy. The debate ranged far and wide into the 1970s, fluctuating in ferocity, but never completely dying away. From time to time, there were disturbing clashes, particularly in London, exploited for their own purposes by other political groups. It still remained to be seen how race relations would evolve, but the size of the immigrant population was an aspect of British life in the mid-1970s which few had anticipated twenty years earlier. In previous decades, Jewish and other nationalities from Europe had been 'assimilated' without benefit of government agency or specific legislation. In the middle 1960s, however, the then Labour Home Secretary, Jenkins, talked not about assimilation which he called 'a flattening process', but about integration which he defined as 'equal opportunity, accompanied by cultural diversity in an atmosphere of mutual tolerance'. Such an aspiration, however, had to be worked out at a time when the cultural and political identity of the indigenous communities of the United Kingdom and their economic prospects looked more uncertain than they had been for many years.

---

1. J. Stevenson, *Social conditions in Britain between the wars* (1977); D. P. Waley, *Public opinion and the making of British foreign policy* (1975)
2. P. Calvocoressi, *The British experience 1945–75* (1978), p. 196
3. T. Wilson in the volume he edited, *Ulster under Home Rule* (1955), p. 210
4. J. Oliver, *Working at Stormont* (Dublin, 1978), p. 92
5. Oliver, op. cit., p. 182
6. O. D. Edwards, ed., *Celtic nationalism* (1968), p. 259

CHAPTER 32

The two-party system in difficulties

The Suez Crisis momentarily shattered the image of self-confident party unity displayed in 1955 when the Conservatives had won the election. Two junior ministers, not in the Cabinet, resigned in disapproval of government policy and some thirty Conservative MPs may have shared their views – though they were matched by an equal number who felt that, having gone in, it was wrong to bow before outside pressure and withdraw. There was, however, no one of sufficient standing from either group to challenge the Cabinet. Nevertheless, the strains in the party were considerable. The government was helped by the difficulties in the Labour party. In December 1955, Gaitskell, rather than Morrison or Bevan, became the new leader. His victory had partly been one for a new generation, but it also heralded a new style and approach, different from the traditional Right represented by Morrison or the traditional Left by Bevan. Associated with Gaitskell were a number of 'revisionists', Crosland, Jay, Jenkins and others, who sought a new definition of Socialism. The 'Bevanites' were still active, suspicious that this revisionism was in fact a deviation from the path of true Socialism. The Suez Crisis therefore presented Gaitskell with his chance to stamp his authority on the party and make an impact on the nation at large. Until the launching of the expedition itself, there had been a remarkable degree of accord between government and Opposition. By early November, however, that had collapsed. Labour speakers, both in the Commons and in public meetings, attacked the government with an emotional ferocity rare in post-war politics. In a broadcast on 6 November Gaitskell called upon Conservatives to reject their government's policy. By this time, press, platform, public house and pulpit registered a deep split in the nation. Formally, the division was on party lines, but many more working-class Labour voters favoured a strong line and middle-class Conservative voters doubted its wisdom than the party leaderships acknowledged (at least publicly). Opinion seemed about equally divided on the government's use of force.

A fortnight after the Suez cease-fire, Eden departed to the West Indies to recover his health. Returning on 14 December, he declared that he had no intention of resigning as Prime Minister, but in January 1957 he tendered his resignation to the Queen. It was a sad end to what might have been a great career. It was clear, however, that if the country and the ruling party were to recover from the traumatic experiences of the previous few months a new leader was needed. The Conservative party had no machinery for choosing a successor, though the choice obviously rested between Butler and Macmillan. The Queen chose Macmillan. It was not easy to assess the new Prime Minister – intelligent, urbane, of proven executive capacity, Etonian, Christian, patrician, 'Edwardian', radical, shy, sensitive, yet a superb showman. He had supported the Suez expedition but, as Chancellor of the Exchequer, was equally keen to withdraw when he saw the financial consequences – hence the 'first in, first out' jibe. The task of restoring confidence would be difficult. He decided that the country's morale could not stand excessive genuflection before foreign critics, declaring in his first broadcast to the nation that Britain was still a great country, and asking people not to feel bashful in saying so. He tried to restore harmony in the Conservative party by finding room for both Left and Right, for Boyle and Amery, in his government. Initially, some commentators thought of Macmillan as rather a stopgap, but he was to remain consecutively in office for longer than any other Prime Minister since Asquith. The 'Macmillan years' had begun.

A feature of the by-elections in some constituencies over the next few years was the strong performance of the Liberals, whose prospects of recovery had long been written off. Early in 1958, a grandson of Asquith won a West-country seat from the Conservatives. The Liberals did not do uniformly well, but they began to make some impact on the commuter in the South-east and North-west and stake out ground for the future. It certainly seemed that, while considerable dissatisfaction with the government remained, there was no feeling that Labour would necessarily do better. In part, this was because Labour was still feeling its way towards policy agreement, although the personal feuds were moderating. Gaitskell and Bevan achieved a reconciliation and the latter acted controversially as shadow Foreign Secretary until his death in 1960. Labour now talked about increasing government investment in industry rather than embarking on a further programme of direct nationalization. Yet, despite further promises to expand the social services, the Labour leaders had an uneasy feeling that they had failed to harness those voters who had felt strongly against Suez but had previously voted Conservative. Within a period of three years, much of the passion that crisis had excited had disappeared. Somehow or other, the Conservatives seemed to have established themselves as the natural party of government once again. The Prime Minister did appear to have restored Britain's international relationships and, though there had been public disagreement amongst his colleagues on financial and monetary policy, the economy seemed relatively prosperous. All that was needed was a small drop in income tax for the public to express its confidence in 'SuperMac'.

The Conservatives gained their third victory in a row in October 1959 with a substantial majority over the Opposition parties (D). The Labour vote actually fell and books and articles began to appear with such titles as *Must Labour Lose?* Sociological changes, the *embourgeoisement* which accompanied greater affluence, were thought to make the future bleak for a Labour party with such a clear working-class base. At the 1959 Labour conference, the Left as usual argued that failure had been due to the fact that Labour had not been Socialist enough. There were millions of voters who would apparently respond to a reiteration of basic principles. Gaitskell, however, argued that the reason for Labour's failure lay in significant changes in the economic and social background of politics. Labour was too doctrinaire rather than the reverse. On the issue of nationalization, for example, the electorate clearly took an empirical rather than a dogmatic view. Some publicly owned industries appeared to be successful, others did not; a blanket endorsement of the principle had a limited appeal. He proposed to adjust clause four of the party's constitution so that it became clear that common ownership was a means, not an end in itself. Labour should register formally that it had come to accept a mixed economy for the foreseeable future. The Left, with some support elsewhere, accused Gaitskell of betraying Socialism and the proposal was defeated. Once again, although Bevan was no longer the idol of the fundamentalists, the Labour party seemed to be made of two elements co-existing very uneasily together. Many commentators argued that the party leader made a tactical mistake in trying to force the issue directly, but he felt that if the party was ever to regain power it had to have a coherent sense of its objectives. He could only take comfort in the fact that the NEC agreed that there should be a new statement of principles. (114,115)

In 1960, however, the party was again in disarray, this time over the issue of nuclear disarmament. Unilateralism was approved at the party conference against the wishes of the leader and a majority of the parliamentary party. Gaitskell pledged himself to 'fight and fight and fight again' on the issue, but it raised again the structural problems of the party.[1] Where did authority rest? Whose opinion was final? The Campaign for Democratic Socialism successfully organized anti-unilateralist opinion so that after the Blackpool conference in October 1961 the party in the country, in Parliament and the leader were again in accord; but the fundamental constitutional issue had only been postponed and ideological rifts remained conspicuous. Sufficient union support had this time been mobilized, but there were signs that the comfortable post-war relationship between the party leadership and Right-wing trade union leaders was coming to an end. It was the TGWU leader, Cousins, an ardent unilateralist, who was one of Gaitskell's strongest opponents. In 1958, state trumpeters from the Blues and Royals had celebrated the opening of the TUC's Congress House in Bloomsbury, but a new generation of leaders were not satisfied with the status their presence seemed to symbolize.

The turmoil inside the Labour party helps to explain why, in 1962, it was the Liberals who made the running and stole the headlines. They captured Orpington, a hitherto safe Conservative seat in the London suburbs, in a by-election and polled well in others across the country. Grimond, the party's articulate Etonian leader and MP for the most northerly constituency in the United Kingdom, came into public prominence, offering a radical but non-Socialist programme. He hoped to appeal both to the professional middle-class 'Orpington man' and to regions of the country which had always been about to share in a national boom when it petered out.

Further evidence of Liberal advance led Macmillan to take the dramatic course of summarily sacking a third of his Cabinet, including Selwyn Lloyd, whose only crime had been to echo his master's voice. The years since 1959 had not gone well, particularly on the economic front. In 1961, the Chancellor of the Exchequer, Lloyd, raised taxes in his spring budget and, in July, raised the bank rate to 7 per cent and, even more dramatically, announced a short wage freeze. He tried to soften the blow by establishing the National Economic Development

Council (NEDC), composed of ministers, businessmen, trade-unionists and some independent representatives, charged with carrying out a 'joint examination of the economic prospects of the country'. The freeze was to end in March 1962 and at that point negotiators were to be led on by a 'guiding light' – wages to be limited to a 2 per cent increase in line with the anticipated growth of productivity. In May, the NEDC members adopted an annual rate of growth of 4 per cent as the target for the next five years. What was now developing, under Conservative management, was a kind of voluntary collectivism and no one knew where it would lead. Younger men like Boyle, Maudling and Joseph were promoted in the July reshuffle but, far from restoring confidence, such drastic steps seemed to show an elderly Prime Minister losing his nerve. Macmillan himself stayed on, though for a time nothing seemed to go right for him. The notion of a steady 4 per cent growth-rate evaporated. His handling of the Profumo affair – when his War Secretary was having an affair with a 'model' who has also obliging a naval attaché at the Soviet Embassy – seemed a far cry from the masterful Macmillan of earlier years. 'Eleven years of Conservative rule', *The Times* opined, 'have brought the nation psychologically and spiritually to a low ebb.' In October 1963, sudden illness forced Macmillan to resign. The 'customary processes of consultation' produced as his successor neither Butler nor Hogg (as Lord Hailsham had hastily become) but the 14th earl of Home, Foreign Secretary since 1960. Home, who renounced his peerage to become Sir Alec Douglas-Home, had difficulty in forming his government but when, despite his disappointment, Butler agreed to serve under him, the crisis was resolved. Even so, two of the ablest politicians of the younger generation, Macleod and Powell, declined office in protest against the way the new leader had 'evolved'.

By the autumn of 1964, Labour urged the electors to look on the long period of Conservative government as 'thirteen wasted years'. In his heyday, Macmillan told the people that they had never had it so good. Both parties could point to facets of national life to support their contentions. The General Election gave Labour a majority of only four seats over Conservatives and Liberals combined. Douglas-Home did far better than many had supposed likely. Nevertheless, the Conservative era was over and, in defeat, it came to seem remarkable that it had lasted so long. The party's leadership during this period had remained remarkably patrician. Sampson's *Anatomy of Britain* (1962) seemed to show how important it was to be related to the duke of Devonshire. Even during a period of rapid change (perhaps because of it), the Conservatives could successfully still appeal to tradition and epitomize continuity. Business and the middle classes (apart from latter-day flirtations with the Liberals) supported them strongly, but their electoral success depended on their ability to attract working-class votes – it was estimated that about one-third of manual workers voted for the party. 'Discovery' of this fact produced a rash of studies designed to explain this outrageous deviancy. The unsurprising conclusion was that many persisted in voting according to their impression of the leaders or what they considered best for the 'nation as a whole' rather than the working-class loyalty which deviant middle-class sociologists assumed should have guided them. Some were alleged to vote Tory because of continuing 'deference' while others were 'secular'. Even Conservatives assumed that this former group would be a waning asset and that their support would be drawn from 'aspiring' workers(116).

Douglas-Home was widely regarded as a 'gift' by Labour. A competent Foreign Secretary, he had been cut off from the rough and tumble of parliamentary elections since 1951, when he had inherited his former title. His opponents made merry at the absurdity of a Scottish aristocrat leading Britain at this juncture – and Douglas-Home accepted the attacks with amiability. The General Election, however, turned out not to be between an Etonian and a Wykehamist, for Gaitskell had suddenly died in 1963. After a contest with Brown, Wilson succeeded to the leadership, presenting an image of professional efficiency to contrast with aristocratic amateurishness. He set about establishing his mark on the country and party with great energy. His theme was the need to modernize Britain. Science would come to the aid of Socialism and Socialism to the aid of science; Sir Alec would go back to his grouse moors. Such an aura of technological modernity pushed disputes about nationalization conveniently into the background. If he would have liked a more decisive success, Wilson had at least avoided failure. If Labour had been defeated four times in a row that 'radical realignment' for which Grimond hankered might well have occurred [D].

Given his small majority between 1964 and 1966, however, it was vital for Wilson to give an impression of vigour so that, if thwarted in Parliament, he could appeal for a fresh mandate. The Cabinet considered a further devaluation, but the Prime Minister (an economist) ruled it out, believing that it would be seen as a sign of failure. The government lost no time, however, in stressing the gravity of the balance of payments position so that the Tories could be blamed for it. After all that Wilson had said about the stupidity of 'stop–go', Labour could not resort to established deflationary methods. Instead, it introduced a system of export rebates and a temporary import surcharge. It was an article of faith that the smack of firm government would be heard during the first 100 days. Callaghan, the Chancellor, was committed to raising old-age pensions and abolishing National Health prescription charges. The promise of a tax on capital gains and a corporation tax was thought likely to help Brown, the new Secretary of State for Economic Affairs in his dealings with the trade unions.

Above all, the government was determined to seek 'growth'. Brown tried to gain trade union assent to some kind of 'incomes policy' while his new department prepared an ambitious 'National Plan'. He persuaded both sides of industry to sign a portentous 'Declaration of Intent' in which they both stated their agreement that wages and prices should voluntarily be tied to productivity. It was the vaguest of commitments, but was received with some rapture. The TUC General Secretary (the only one to possess a first class honours degree) was Woodcock. In office since 1959, he was anxious to give the government support and spoke in favour of the plan at a special meeting of trade union executives. It was notable that the September 1965 TUC only backed the policy by 5.3 million to 3.3 million. The country as a whole seemed bewildered by the economic situation and voters at by-elections did strange things. They prevented the Foreign Secretary, Patrick Gordon Walker, from finding a seat to replace the one he had lost in the General Election and Scottish electors returned a young Liberal,

David Steel. The government proudly unveiled the National Board for Prices and Incomes (1965) and there was talk of a 'norm' for wage increases of some 3 per cent. The TUC reluctantly agreed to this target, feeling that unless it made a gesture, even a Labour government would limit free bargaining or the right to strike. There was something about a 'special relationship' with a Labour government(118).

Sir Alec stepped down as Conservative leader in July 1965. This time, there was an open contest for the succession – between Heath, Maudling and Powell. The latter polled poorly and Heath defeated Maudling in a close fight. It appeared that the party had accepted a tough, energetic and well-informed leader, if a somewhat wooden one. Unperturbed, Brown continued on an endless round of discussions in the autumn designed to produce 'early warning' of price increases and wage claims which, in turn, would be vetted by the National Board for Prices and Incomes (NBPI). There was an idea of a 25 per cent increase in output by 1970. Wilson and Brown kept up an appearance of believing that it was still possible. 'You *know* Labour government works' was their message to the electorate in the wake of a small surplus on current account in the final quarter of 1965. Heath struggled manfully to put his own themes across. Typically, he had prepared them with great care, but his presentation failed to catch fire. He talked about tax reform, trade union reform, selectivity in the social services and stressed, all the time, the danger of inflation. The 1966 Election campaign was dull, perhaps because the outcome – which gave Labour its highest share of the vote since 1951 – was so predictable. Labour's clear majority meant that there was no longer a parliamentary alibi for failure [D].

Once again, political and economic questions seemed virtually inseparable. Much faith was placed in a selective employment tax designed to reverse the trend towards service industries. Wilson embarked on a series of speeches to trade union audiences, attacking the defensive work-sharing practices bred in the years of depression. His immediate problem was a dock strike which lasted for six weeks. The possibility of making the 'early warning' of wage and price increases mandatory produced division in the Cabinet. Even more divisive was the issue of devaluation which rumbled on for months. A total freeze on incomes was decreed in July 1966 to be followed, after six months, by a period of severe restraint. These policies, though accepted for a couple of years, in turn brought a period of severe tension between the government and some elements in the trade unions. The TUC only supported the freeze by a margin of 4.5 to 4.2 million. It was an indication of the growing influence of the Left – in particular Scanlon of the Amalgamated Engineering Union (AEU) and Jones of the TGWU. The freeze worked, but by the end of 1967 the TUC had registered its opposition to intervention in collective bargaining(118).

In 1965 Wilson set up a Royal Commission under Lord Donovan to consider the reform of industrial relations and it reported in 1968. Most of its members saw no need to enclose industrial relations within a clear legal framework. However, it recommended that all unions should be registered and only such unions would have the right to strike. The Commission found that 95 per cent of strikes were 'unofficial'. The Cabinet did not react immediately, but in 1969 the

293

Employment Secretary, Barbara Castle produced a White Paper, *In Place of Strife*. It rejected the Donovan Plan for restricting unofficial strikes, but proposed a 'cooling-off' period of twenty-eight days where procedures had not been followed. The Employment Secretary would also have power to call a ballot of all workers involved in official strikes. The plan aroused opposition within the parliamentary party from trade-union-sponsored MPs and others. Callaghan, then party treasurer, voted against such legislation as a member of the party NEC, but he was a member of the Cabinet. Although Wilson declared that such a bill was 'essential to the continuation of this government in office' he had to back down. Instead, in June 1969, the TUC General Council (which was, of course, in no position to deliver) gave a 'solemn and binding undertaking' that member unions would observe its own guidelines on regulating unofficial strikes. The dual nature of the Labour party was again disclosed. The leadership, not least for financial reasons, could not afford to alienate the trade unions, but unless it could appear to be independent of them it might well alienate the electorate. Wilson, to his amazement, lost the General Election of 1970 [D].

In the previous few years, while Labour struggled, confidence had not been unambiguously transferred to the Conservatives(111). If the opinion polls (an obsessive feature of these years) showed that the Conservatives were more popular than the government, Heath had failed to make a strong impact. Quite apart from his personal qualities, the party was not of one mind on a number of important domestic issues. The failure of Boyle, the party's education spokesman, to stand firm in defence of grammar schools allegedly upset many Conservative voters. The Liberals were very active but they, too, had their leadership problems. In January 1967, Grimond, upset by the party's failure to make a decisive electoral breakthrough made way for the flamboyant Thorpe. The 'protest' vote in Scotland and Wales seemed to be going to nationalists rather than the Liberals. The Conservatives could not decide how far they should themselves seek to become a party of 'modernization' with a classless (that is to say professional middle-class) image. It was, after all, difficult to think of any reason for showing social deference to Heath or some of his closest associates, although Sir Alec still lent enchantment to the view. The stress on continuity lived uneasily with the urge to change. As Ramsden points out, the 1970 Conservative government was not very 'traditional', containing fewer members whose fathers had been politicians than its Labour predecessor.[2]

Domestically, the Heath government seemed very well prepared, indeed in late 1968 one of his aides suggested calling in historians to prepare an account of how the party was getting ready not merely for an election but for the 'real business of government'. The Prime Minister was determined to tackle the trade union reform which had been shirked by Labour. To some commentators it seemed a foolhardy enterprise to attempt, in the Industrial Relations Act, 1971, to bring that complex field within a comprehensive legal framework. Supporters argued that such a framework existed in other countries. Unlike Labour, the Conservatives had little difficulty in getting the legislation on to the statute-book. The difficulty lay in enforcing it in the face of determined opposition from most trade unions. Trade union leaders objected to the new legal rights given to the individual workers in relation to trade union membership. Stated bluntly, there was a clear confrontation between 'individualist' and 'collectivist' conceptions of the appropriate relationships between persons and groups in society. The National Industrial Relations Court, set up to deal with offences under the legislation, was the particular target of union hostility. The September 1971 the TUC carried an AEUW motion instructing all unions not to register under the Act – against the wishes of the General Secretary and General Council. Since there were certain benefits to be gained from registration a number of unions were dismayed at this decision. The sections of the Act extending protection from unfair dismissal and information about the terms of employment were not sufficient palliatives. In July 1972, the Official Solicitor (not a hitherto prominent figure) acted to secure the release of five dockers from prison following the involvement of the National Industrial Relations Court in the container dispute. The number of days lost through industrial disputes spiralled upwards in an atmosphere of increasing bitterness and accelerating inflation. Price controls and pay restraint formed the centre of discussions between the government, employers and trade unions, without agreement.

In November 1972, the Cabinet announced a freeze for three months on pay, price, rent and dividend increases. In January 1973 it announced in a White Paper that 'Stage Two' of controls would operate from April. There would be controls on the range of price and pay increases, with statutory backing. Then there would be 'Stage Three', coming into effect in November which would aim to restrict pay increases to around 7 per cent, though there were to be 'special cases'.

Was such a programme politically feasible? Everything seemed to hinge on the attitude adopted by the miners. In the spring of 1972, their strike had brought them a settlement which was three times the offer originally made by the National Coal Board. In November 1973, the government announced emergency measures to conserve electricity and the following month it stated that in the new year it would introduce a three-day working week for most workers, with the same objective. However, the contemporaneous oil crisis also strengthened the bargaining position of the miners. Everything seemed set for a major battle. Government supporters feared that if the miners were successful then the chances of restraint elsewhere and the maintenance of anything like an 'incomes policy' were remote. A strike was called for early February when talks, in which the TUC was involved, broke down.

Possibly reluctantly, the Prime Minister came round to the view, which some colleagues (notably the Chancellor of the Exchequer) had been pressing earlier, that only a General Election could hope to give the government the necessary authority to deal with the crisis. At the same time (perhaps unwisely) an investigation into the miners' case was put in hand, whose findings the government would accept. The Prime Minister attempted to explain, apparently, that the defence of democracy hinged upon Stage Three. In the event, the strategy of the 'mandate' failed, though only narrowly. Slightly different timing might have brought success, and unfortunate comments from unexpected quarters did not help.

The fragmented result – with substantial percentages of the vote going to both the Liberals and the Nationalists – showed a nation deeply divided, without much confidence in either of the major parties. The power of trade unions caused alarm, but so did the prospect of severe restrictions on them. Labour was able to form a government, but it clearly could not claim the support of a majority of the nation. The 'wasted votes' cast in February 1974 raised doubts about whether such an electoral system could continue to be tolerated and added another element of unrest.

When the second election was held in October 1974 Labour only marginally improved its position in the Commons and began uneasily to govern, aware that only a few by-election defeats could jeopardize its slim majority. Political stability now seemed in doubt. Labour talked of a 'Social Contract' with the trade unions, and in the months that followed received advice from the TUC on a vast array of subjects ranging from wage policy to Vietnam; such submissions had to be taken seriously. The Conservatives were demoralized and Heath paid the price of failure. In February 1975 they elected Margaret Thatcher as party leader. The Liberals were frustrated that their electoral advance had in the end brought them so few seats and such little influence. The United Kingdom itself, as is discussed elsewhere, seemed in danger. Class, regional and industrial conflicts fused to produce a sense of anxiety about the ability of Britain's parliamentary institutions to cope. It was an inauspicious moment at which to join the EEC.

THE PROBLEM OF GOVERNMENT

Beneath the ebb and flow of party fortune, the years since the mid-1950s had seen increasing concern about the structure and functioning of British government as a whole. The powers of the House of Lords, for example, had been much discussed, even if they remained unchanged in the end. In 1967 Labour sought both to reduce them and to eliminate the hereditary basis of the Chamber. This intention gained point when the peers defeated the Rhodesia Sanctions Order in 1968. The Prime Minister dissolved an existing all-party committee on reform of the Lords and pressed ahead with a bill to phase out all hereditary peers and replace them with life peers nominated by party leaders in such a way that the government of the day would have a working majority. Their power to delay legislation would be exiguous. However, critics who disliked the patronage thereby placed at the disposal of the party leaders combined with those committed to the total abolition of the Second Chamber to cause the proposed legislation to be abandoned. The only significant change, therefore, flowed from the 1958 Life Peerages Act. Life peerages were awarded both to politicians and men and women of distinction in other walks of life.

The Commons, too, seemed impervious to the attempts by reformers to change its way of working. A common theme in the 1960s and beyond was the powerlessness of Parliament. The executive was held to be in a position of 'near total power'. Members of Parliament responded diligently to the crack of the Whip; all that was required was their vote in the lobby. If an issue arose which might produce cross-voting, governments magically made it one of confidence. No political party would permit its own members to assume an independent stance in Parliament. And, if a member did take a stand against his government's policy he could find himself in trouble with his constituency association. Nigel Nicolson, a critic of Suez, lost the nomination of his constituency association in Bournemouth. In the 1970s, this was more likely to be the experience of Labour MPs. Here was a variant on the question of whether an MP was a representative or a delegate. In its new form, however, attention was focused on the representative character of constituency associations. Was there not something to be said for a 'primary'? Who should select the selectors? Whatever the outcome of this particular issue, there was a certain irony in the fact that those who had talked of the powerlessness of Parliament complained about precisely the opposite situation which developed in the later 1970s.

There were also periodic attempts to introduce a Bill of Rights, proportional representation or alter the Official Secrets Act. Advocates of a Bill of Rights were concerned about the possible erosion of civic rights as the power and influence of government spread. The absence of a written constitution was now thought to be dangerous for the liberty of the subject. A kind of alternative was the appointment in 1967 of the first Parliamentary Commissioner for Administration (the Ombudsman), who was to investigate complaints passed to him by MPs about the actions of any government department. Discussion of proportional representation took place with renewed vigour in the 1970s. It was noted that in a European context the British electoral system was odd. The Liberals, not surprisingly, believed that votes and seats should correspond much more closely, but neither major party was prepared to change a system which, it was argued, produced a clear-cut government, whatever its theoretical defects. It also proved easier to favour 'open government' than agree on the precise scope of secrecy. Lord Franks's Report (1972) argued that democratic government did require a measure of secrecy, though he advocated the repeal of the Official Secrets Act and its replacement by one concerning official information. Effective legislation in this area proved elusive. However, the widespread discussion of these matters reflected a feeling that the British way of government was not inherently superior to any other.

A similar unease prompted the Fulton Enquiry into the Civil Service which reported in 1968. Its report noted the massive increase in public expenditure which, in turn, required public control. It noted the 'complex intermingling of the public and private sectors' and the fact that the Civil Service had to handle social, scientific, economic and technical problems in an international setting. It believed that the Service had failed to keep up with its changing tasks, deploring the cult of the 'generalist', the 'all-rounder'. It attacked the system of 'classes', the lack of scientists, engineers and other specialists in positions of high authority and felt, in general, that there was not enough 'awareness of how the world outside Whitehall works, how government policies will affect it, and the new ideas and methods which are developing in the universities, in business and in other walks of life'. In response, the government set up a Civil Service department to assist in implementing the changes which flowed from its acceptance of the report's major conclusions. Great emphasis was now placed upon 'management' and a Civil Service college played its part in this new programme. Big changes did take place, though some were still not convinced of the justice of the criticisms. On the other hand, some members of the Fulton committee felt that Whitehall effectively smothered their suggestions (119, 120).

At another level, few governments could resist tampering with the departmental structure of central government. Each such reorganization led to doubt as to whether the result really was an improvement. Characteristic of the period after 1956 was the emergence of 'giant' departments of State. In 1956, there were twenty-six departments, but by 1972 the figure had been reduced to seventeen. Defence and foreign affairs are considered elsewhere (Chs. 28–30), but the significant mergers were the creation of a Department of Trade and Industry, a Department of Health and Social Security and a Department of the Environment. Each had multiple but linked responsibilities. One other such amalgam, the Department of Economic Affairs had a short life that was neither sweet nor merry. Each new administration felt under an obligation to make sure that the structures suited its needs, but by the middle 1970s the impulse to change seemed to be exhausted. Perhaps more important, if less publicly controversial, was the extensive discussion between the Treasury and the spending departments on appropriate methods of determining allocations between departments. In addition, a White Paper in 1970 set out a programme for a Central Policy Review Staff which would, among other things, produce a 'strategic' definition of objectives' – something which often got lost in the day-to-day business of other departments.

Throughout this period, and particularly in the 1960s, it was plausibly suggested that the office of the Prime Minister (whoever held it) had grown in status and power. Cabinet government, Crossman in particular contended, had in practice given way to Prime Ministerial government. This might more accurately be described as partial Cabinet government – the Prime Minister operating with a close group of colleagues in the presentation and handling of business. As such, however, it was not without precedent and it would also be a mistake to suppose that power continually aggregated to the Prime Minister by some automatic process. Prime ministers retained the right to 'hire and fire', but there were limits to the frequency with which this could be done if their own position was not to be weakened. It was true, however, that the steady access of Prime Ministers to the television screen did make them better known to the nation at large than had been the case in the pre-television era, but even this could be a not unmixed blessing.

Particularly in the years that conclude our period, the issue of trade union power in relation to government power moved steadily to the fore. To it was linked the question of elections, authority and decision–making within trade unions themselves. What was the relationship between the 'policy' of a given union and the views of the membership? In 1956, for example, members of the Communist party occupied all the key positions at national level in the electricians' union. There were some 700 Communists in a total union membership of 200,000. In this instance, the issue of ballot-rigging went through the courts and the TUC was compelled to intervene. Other Communists could be elected perfectly legally under union rules, though in elections in which perhaps only 10 per cent of the membership, for one reason or another, voted. This position led to increased calls for the use of postal ballots in union elections. Only the AEUW moved comprehensively in this direction, with significant changes in the level of voting and its political complexion. Communists might also be entrenched in key positions as shop stewards – in the motor industry, for example. Some of the best-known names in the British trade union movement in the early 1970s (and television made them more well known than any of their predecessors) had been members of the Communist party – Hugh Scanlon, Lawrence Daly, Frank Chapple, Clive Jenkins and Tom Jackson. Such a list, of course, at once makes it apparent that some moved further away from it than others. Likewise, there is no necessary correspondence between personal life style, 'industrial' militancy and general political outlook. Such things have an intrinsic interest in particular cases, but the underlying issue of the political position of trade unions remained unresolved in the crisis of 1974–75.

1. Williams, *Gaitskell*, pp. 622f
2. C. Cook and J. Ramsden, eds., *Trends in British politics since 1945* (1978)

CHAPTER 33

The sick economy

The condition of the British economy in the twenty years after 1955 was a source of much interest, amazement and concern. Its performance baffled economists, industrialists and politicians alike, though they did not often admit it. The 'English sickness' broadened, on examination, into the 'British disease'. Essays and articles on 'the nature and causes of the nation's lagging wealth' showed an impressive growth-rate. It was unusual not to find economists describing and (normally) remedying Britain's economic problem. Some of them disinterred the judgements of their colleagues and concluded that their assessments bore little relation to what actually happened. In an essay on 'A Plague of Economists' a distinguished economic historian urged them to descend from the realms of macro-economic theory and immerse themselves in the problems of particular industries alongside genuine managers and scientists.[1] Some feared that they had been doing that already.

It seemed that the more detailed the diagnoses the more uncertain the conclusions. Distinguished economists from both sides of the Atlantic met in 1970, for example, to consider central topics – fiscal and monetary policy, investment, demand management – and could only conclude that the causes of the crises were obscure and the remedy uncertain. Sir Alec Cairncross, after a lifetime in academic economics and as adviser to governments, suggested that social and political values had as much to do with growth as economic variables(206). Explanations poured out from press and pulpit. From the Highlands of Scotland came the suggestion that the full impact of the neglect of the Sabbath had not been properly evaluated; certainly, it was true that those university departments investigating social and political values did tend to concentrate on what they thought were more important matters. Metrication, the left-hand drive, too much defence expenditure, too much overseas investment, too little overseas investment, too high wages, too low wages, bad industrial relations, trade unions, public schools, too little research and development, too much futile and non-market-oriented research and development, poor managerial talent – the catalogue could continue – were all adduced by luminaries at one time or another.

Historians surfaced occasionally to observe that if there was indeed a crisis, many of its supposed features had been present for a long time; an observation which may, or may not, be helpful. The paradox was that though the economy seemed almost 'out of control', a great many people seemed to find their lives more rounded, more varied and less full of drudgery than they could remember. If professors of history were less well paid than their German counterparts and, in real terms, less advantaged than their predecessors before 1939, there were at least more of them and a greater chance of becoming one than formerly.

Perhaps such complacency was the ultimate expression of the malaise.

Increases in retail prices, at a modest rate – 1, 2, 3 or at most 4 per cent – had occurred every year since the mid-1950s. That level had generally been accepted as quite tolerable. Wage rises, almost without exception, were higher and unemployment never reached 3 per cent. From 1968 on, however, retail prices steadily mounted and, with brief exceptions in 1972/73 came to a climax in 1975 when they were 24.2 per cent higher than they had been in 1974. Wage increases reached double figures in 1970, soaring to 29.4 per cent in 1974 and 25.4 per cent in 1975. The unemployment rate for the period 1970–75 averaged 3 per cent. Taking 1970 as a base of 100, consumer prices were 60 in 1955 and 184 in 1975, and still rising sharply. Thus, although some degree of inflation had always been present throughout these twenty years, it was only in the late 1960s that it moved inexorably to the forefront of discussion. The year 1975 was bleak for the United Kingdom economy. Business and financial confidence at the beginning of the year had sunk very low. The *Financial Times* share index fell below 160, compared with 530 in May 1972. The industrial countries of the world were in their worst recession of the post-war period and United Kingdom exports fell 5 per cent by volume between the second half of 1974 and the second half of 1975. Over the same period, gross domestic product declined by over 3 per cent and manufacturing production by 7 per cent. It seemed that the country was now actually in absolute decline – the culmination of a period when it had ceased to grow as fast as its international competitors(207).

Inflation was not confined to Britain. Until 1968, United Kingdom rates of inflation were not significantly higher than those of the Organization for Economic Co-operation and Development (OECD) taken as a whole, though they were worse than those of some key countries. Thereafter, while rates everywhere began to accelerate, Britain took the unenviable lead. Clearly, the international economy was in trouble, and no treatment of British economic problems simply in terms of endogenous factors can be adequate. The Bretton Woods system became unstable and finally collapsed. In the mid 1950s, the dollar was still supreme as the central currency of the international system. Gold was maintained at $35 per ounce, but throughout the 1960s and early 1970s the United States ran large balance of payments deficits. The ratio of dollars held outside the United States to its gold reserves rose dramatically. The market price of gold rose above the official level and, in August 1971, following massive speculation, the convertibility of the dollar was suspended. The world's major currencies floated briefly before fresh attempts were made to fix parities within certain bands – though this system broke down in turn(208). New currency groupings and agreements were then attempted, centring around the German mark and the US dollar, but in circumstances of great volatility. Critics thought the international machinery was being patched up when what was needed was thorough reconstruction; but that was easier said than done. Not all was lost. In 1969, an enlarged International Monetary Fund implemented a decision to establish a system of special drawing rights which could be issued to members in relation to their quota payments. Initially, they were backed by gold, but then came to be related to a weighted average of the world's major currencies. Great hopes were placed in these rights as an international paper reserve asset, but it would clearly take some time for confidence to return, particularly in the wake of the 1973 oil crisis. During the Israeli–Egyptian War in October the Arab oil-producing countries imposed both a restriction of supplies and a rise in price on oil supplies for the West. A period of uncertainty about future supplies ensued before they were re- sumed at the end of the year – at a price some four times higher than they had been a few months earlier. Massive problems of economic and political readjust- ment followed these events. It is difficult to measure the impact of the 'oil factor' precisely in relation to the general dislocation of these years, but some commen- tators saw the price rise as bringing to an end an era of unprecedented growth and prosperity(196).

While these developments certainly exacerbated Britain's difficulties, they cannot be said to have caused them. In the mid-1950s Britain achieved a surplus on current account in her balance of payments and indeed, in 1956 and 1958 there was a surplus on visible trade for the first time in the twentieth century. Even so, the United Kingdom's share in world manufacturing exports declined from 20.4 per cent in 1954 to 17.9 per cent in 1959 – but that was largely ex- plained as the inevitable process of 'catching up' after the war by Germany and Japan. Yet, the proportion continued to decline – to 11.9 per cent in 1967 and 8.8 per cent in 1975 – while the volume of world trade in manufactures between 1959 and 1973 grew at rates of 7–10 per cent and Britain, alone of major indus- trial countries, showed a substantial drop of export share(207). Ample statistical accounts confirm the picture, and a detailed comparison between the United King- dom and West German manufacturing industry from 1954 to 1972 makes the point vividly. At the first date, the two countries had roughly similar levels of output and capital per person employed, and this was also probably true of the manufacturing sectors. The West German share of world trade in manufactures in 1955 was 19.2 per cent (a few points behind the United Kingdom), while in 1973 it had risen to 22.4 per cent (the United Kingdom percentage having fallen by about a third). The relative deterioration occurred most sharply from the late 1960s.[2]

The early 1960s saw increasing alarm about the balance of payments as the domestic booms – in 1958–60 and 1963–64 – sucked in not only materials but manufactures and semi-manufactures on a scale that could not be maintained. Bouts of stagnation alternated with phases of expansion, producing the famous 'stop–go' pattern. Governments usually claimed that a process of continuous acceleration was round the corner, but it never appeared. Higher productivity, harder work, fewer strikes would produce faster growth and a solution to the problem of the balance of payments but so, it seemed, would a nil rate of growth or a low rate. The view grew that the pound was overvalued and that some flex- ibility in the exchange rate was desirable. On the other hand, the 'defence' of the pound was as much a matter of politics as economics. Although nearly twen- ty years had passed since the previous devaluation, there were anxieties that accelerating intervals between devaluations would lead to disaster. The interna- tional role of sterling (sometimes considered an advantage and sometimes a drain) might be jeopardized. There was also a fear that it would open the way to increased inflation. Theoretical arguments could be advanced in either direction. In the end, in November 1967, the government had no option, after a couple of months of pressure on sterling, but to devalue by one-seventh. The Prime Minister claimed that the 'pound in your pocket' retained its value.

Some commentators saw devaluation as a refusal to tackle underlying inflation, though various deflationary measures were brought in concurrently. Domestic expenditure had to be held down so that additional output could be exported. Higher taxation was the answer. It was thought important that this devaluation should appear 'once-for-all'. Initially, in 1968, the balance of payments actually worsened but then the deflationary measures, together with an import deposit scheme (which lasted for a couple of years), brought about a steady improvement. In the two years after devaluation, exports grew four times as fast as they had done over the previous four years, though there was disappointment that imports grew at a nearly comparable rate. The current account surplus in 1971 was an unprecedented £1,058 million. Such an improvement cannot altogether be attributed to the devaluation – it coincided with a further liberalization of world trade in the 'Kennedy round' of tariff reductions. Nevertheless, there was a good deal of satisfaction; something seemed to have worked(207).

But, from 1971 to 1974, the balance on current account deteriorated extremely swiftly. Demand soared in the early 1970s and imports of manufactured goods poured in – with the Japanese making substantial advances in a wide variety of electrical goods and cars. There was a 25 per cent deterioration in Britain's terms of trade. The domestic British boom coincided with one in Japan and the United States. Then came the oil price-rise and the initial impact of EEC membership. Sterling again came under pressure and in June 1972 the government abandoned the attempt to keep it at a fixed parity; henceforward, the market would determine the equilibrium exchange rate. Some argued that if this step had been taken earlier, successive governments throughout the 1960s would have avoided many of their difficulties. A steady fall in its value was at once apparent and by the end of 1975 the pound had lost 30 per cent of its value at the end of 1971. Although what went down could come up, that did not seem very likely when the scale of British deficits and loans was considered. It was not easy to avoid a cataclysmic note. Elements of panic and anxiety were everywhere apparent. There was, for example, a serious crisis in the secondary banking system. The Bank of England was forced to give substantial support for fear that general confidence would be further undermined. It was not difficult to believe, at this juncture, that there was a fundamental crisis of capitalism. Things could not go on as they were. The record of British industry and its relationship to government was subjected to intense scrutiny in an attempt to discover what had gone wrong. What course would be taken in the future could not be determined, but it was unlikely to be guided by the ideas which had been dominant for the previous quarter of a century.

One simple approach, which 'surfaced' during the 1960s, was to suggest that over several hundred years what had, literally, fuelled British industrial development was coal. When, how and why the 'industrial revolution' (if there was one) had started became a matter of considerable historical debate. Whatever other factors were relevant, it was the availability of coal as a domestic energy source, and then as an export, which had made Britain's greatness possible. That age had finally come to an end in the mid-1950s. In 1956, the National Coal Board declared that their task was 'to raise the output of coal as high as they can to meet the country's increasing need for energy' but, three years later, stated that there was no need to plan to meet a continuous increase in demand. Targets were scaled down; the number of pits was more than halved between the mid-1950s and the mid-1960s and the labour force fell by nearly a half; mechanization and reorganization led to rapid improvements in output per man. It seemed that a fitter but slimmer industry was being established in circumstances of extreme social and political delicacy.[3]

However, by the middle 1970s, with the rise in the cost of oil and the discovery of large coal reserves in England (which could be efficiently exploited) it was again possible to plan for expansion. Not only that, but there seemed good opportunities for expanding exports of deep coal-mining equipment to Asia and North and South America(211). A major reason for the decline in the demand for coal had been that both domestic and industrial consumers had been switching, over the previous couple of decades, to electricity, gas and oil. The 1956 Clean Air Act, for example, heralded the disappearance of coal from many urban hearths. Decline would have been even swifter without a degree of protection extended to the industry. Coal imports were banned between 1959 and 1970 and the 1967 Coal Industry Act compelled the electricity industry to burn 6 million tons of coal per annum – more than it would have done on purely commercial grounds. However, what proportion of the energy market coal would in fact gain in the future depended on a host of uncertain variables – the rate of inflation, mining productivity, world oil prices and the pricing policies followed by governments in the nationalized industries.

Until 1965, when the first commercial strike of gas was made in the North Sea, the gas industry had not excited much interest or attention, supplying well under 10 per cent of energy needs. This discovery transformed the position and over the next decade the industry flourished, on the whole displaying great technical ability in setting up a new network of supplies to consumers. The British Gas Corporation took over from the Gas Council in 1972 and in 1974 it was supplying some 20 per cent of United Kingdom energy use. The industry had become, in effect, a wholesale organization, buying gas from the exploring companies and selling it to a variety of consumers; carbonization plants virtually disappeared. Although the total number of consumers did not rise substantially, the quantity of gas sold rose very swiftly. The industry was aware, however, that the North Sea reserves would be likely to be depleted some time in the 1990s and gas would again have to be manufactured from other sources. Much effort was being extended to preparing appropriate methods of production against that day. But if natural gas was a 'transitional' fuel, it nevertheless produced an unexpected boost to the economy.

Even more dramatic was the discovery of North Sea oil. While the 1973–74 oil price-rise created serious problems, as has been seen, the fact that, more or less contemporaneously, the size of the North Sea oil reserves became apparent, made Britain's position better. Heavy investment would be required to exploit the discovery, and a certain euphoria was evident before it was realized that there were many technical difficulties. Production costs were very high, but the more the world price of oil rose, the less serious they became. There was the prospect of Britain becoming self-sufficient in oil in the not-too-distant future. Very substantial benefits to the balance of payments and government revenue were in prospect. The full significance of oil proved difficult to grasp, but there was no doubt that the prospects for the British economy were changing just at the point when gloom was widespread. Even so, there were complex decisions to be made about the rate of extraction and pricing. Developments in nuclear fusion, solar, wave and even wind power, in the decades ahead, might equally unpredictably upset the energy scene.

The nuclear supply industry had experienced far more difficulties throughout the period than had been anticipated in the heady days of the early 1950s. The capital costs of power-stations were enormous, and many technical problems were encountered, both in construction and maintenance. The advantages of different types of station were endlessly, but somewhat inconclusively, discussed. Thus, although nuclear energy played a part in electricity generation, it did not expand as rapidly as had been anticipated in the early 1950s. The tragedy was that, unlike the United States, Canada, France or Federal Germany, Britain did not succeed in developing an indigenous reactor technology which was acceptable both for home and export markets. Much of this failure stemmed from problems in the organization of the industry(211).

Demand for electricity itself grew by just under 10 per cent per annum in the decade after the mid-1950s, slackened to around 5 per cent in the mid-1960s, and then the rate of increase fell back even further. Iron and steel, engineering and chemicals were electricity's chief industrial users. The domestic demand stemmed from the increased use of electricity for cooking, water and space heating. The 'cleanliness' of electricity was its strongest selling point. On the supply side, the major problem was the variation in the level of demand as between the seasons of the year and the times of the day; supplying the peak demand was very expensive. Pump-storage schemes might alleviate this problem. In general, however, the industry proved difficult to manage – its appetite for capital was rapacious and demand proved erratic. It suffered, as did all energy industries, from great uncertainties in pricing policy in the nationalized sector. It was not clear, for example, whether gas and electricity were to complement or compete against each other. Sometimes political considerations led to coal being given a privileged position, sometimes purely economic criteria were used. On occasion, the energy suppliers were expected to hold down their prices for the benefit of the industries they supplied or the domestic consumer; at other times they were expected to operate within their own financial targets. Fluctuations of policy could occur within the lifetime of a government as well as between administrations. In the 1970s, in particular, the industrial/political power of coal-miners and power-workers, the anti-nuclear lobby and, finally, the growing awareness of the finiteness of fossil fuels complicated the position further. Conservation became increasingly important. If policies could still seem to conflict, the United Kingdom did look as though it would have a greater range of energy supplies within its control than many other industrialized states. That could prove to be as much of an advantage as coal had been during an earlier phase of industrialization.

If coal was to stage an unexpected late revival (though output per man-shift in certain sectors of the coalfield was low by international standards), the same could not be said of the other staples, all of which went through recurrent crises. The older textile industries were in continuous decline. In 1958, the United Kingdom recorded its first adverse balance of overseas trade in cotton since the emergence of the mill industry. The 1959 Cotton Industry Act provided compensation for the scrapping of obsolete plants and assisted in the introduction of new machinery. The labour force fell and productivity rose as a retreat was made in the 1960s to higher grounds of specialization. How long such positions could be held was a matter of opinion. Quota agreements could help, but it was difficult to see how cotton could survive as a major industry.

Output in the British steel industry doubled between 1950 and 1966, and average furnace capacity (a fair measure of technical efficiency) increased threefold; but in the same period world production almost quadrupled. The average British furnace was still much smaller than that of its main rivals in Europe and Japan, and the British share of world output steadily dropped. The 1967 Iron and Steel Act nationalized the industry once again. New confident noises were made – without any justification. The management structure of the new Board was inadequate, overmanning was rampant and production targets were constantly having to be revised. Although in 1973, Britain was fifth in world steel output, that only amounted to 3.8 per cent of the total and that figure looked in jeopardy. The accelerated decline after 1967 can be attributed to nationalization – or at least seen as the climax of decades in which the future of the industry had been at the mercy of party politics. It can be said that in the small private sector which was allowed to survive, a number of firms did prosper in the manufacture of 'special steels'. In 1974, the British Steel Corporation (BSC), at last emerging with some sense of its own *raison d'être*, suggested a radical reshaping of the industry. Integrated units would enable the necessary volumes of scale to be achieved. Political pressures, however, were to result in the survival of works like Consett and Shotton which the BSC wished to close. Even one plant where there was major investment, Ravenscraig near Motherwell, was nearly 50 miles from the huge dock at Hunterston on the Firth of Clyde where its ore was to be landed. No industry trudged on more firmly with the past on its back than the steel industry. Its management looked in imminent danger of losing its nerve and its markets.

Shipbuilding was no healthier. Japanese competition in the 1960s could not be matched, either in technical achievement or cost. The 1966 Geddes Report told the predictable story of obsolete equipment, poor location and demarcation disputes. Further financial support was forthcoming and another round of 'rationalizing' was attempted. These problems were most acute on the Clyde. The Fairfield yard went bankrupt in 1966 and was rescued with government support.

A further reorganization produced Upper Clyde Shipbuilders, but in 1971 that, too, faced financial disaster. After a political battle it was saved, temporarily, but it was scarcely possible to believe that there was a long-term future for the structure that was devised. There was no comfort in the news that the *Queen Mary*, whose subsidized construction had sustained employment on the Clyde at an earlier period, was no longer the pride of the seas. Air travel destroyed the passenger ship.

By 1975, after a long saga of disappointment, the British car industry, in the shape of British Leyland, joined the queue on the insolvency bench. The 1960s saw the turn-round from a situation in which the British motor industry had been very profitable to one in which all the manufacturers were in difficulties. In 1960, Leyland was a small and prosperous truck company. Over the next few years it expanded, taking in Standard-Triumph, Associated Commercial Vehicles and, in 1967, Rover. Meanwhile, BMC had acquired Jaguar, but was clearly in trouble, showing a substantial drop in its market share. BMC and Leyland merged in 1968 to form British Leyland, but a host of management, engineering and marketing problems remained. Whether it was sensible to attempt such an integrated enterprise was to remain doubtful. A car like the Mini could become world famous, but still yield an inadequate return. In 1975, Lord Ryder produced his report outlining a new strategy for the company which would require substantial public funding.

In February 1971, it was announced that Rolls-Royce was bankrupt, though three years earlier there had been rejoicing, in public at least, at the contract to supply the RB211 engine for the Lockheed TriStar aircraft – which had caused the trouble. It had always been a risky arrangement, though arguably one worth making, but in the effort to win the contract the profit-margin had been too fine. In the upshot, the car and diesel engine division was transferred to a new company, and Rolls-Royce (1971) Ltd, owned by the government, tried to pick up the expensive pieces. The British aircraft and aerospace industry did achieve considerable successes, though there were also some notable failures. It was frequently criticized for failing to spend enough on research and development, but the difficulty, in this very expensive industry, was to make accurate assessments of 'product viability' in the market. Of this there could be no more conspicuous example than the supersonic airliner, Concorde Its development was only financially possible in collaboration with France, but opinion seemed equally divided on whether it was a disastrous diversion of valuable resources or a significant technological development; perhaps it was both.

It was, of course, the industrial crises and disasters that dominated the headlines and, particularly in chemicals and petrochemicals, there were substantial successes for firms like ICI. The electronics industry did not lead the world, but it was not as far behind as some had feared. Nevertheless, in area after area, Britain was being too frequently eclipsed to erase the general impression of crisis. It was in this context that the Wilson government's 1975 Industry Act established the National Enterprise Board, with £1,000 million at its disposal, to be spent over the four financial years up to 1980 in roughly equal amounts. Needless to say, its purpose was to improve industrial efficiency and, consequently, international competitiveness. Firms short of funds could be assisted, shares of private companies could be bought on the open market and the Board would also look after existing government shareholdings in private companies. The formation of the Board, and its precise functions, had been a matter of considerable political controversy, and the role it would adopt in practice was a matter of some speculation. It could be merely a holding company or it could behave as a kind of public merchant bank. It might even have a social role, injecting funds into enterprises with little commercial prospect in deprived regions. There was mention of industrial democracy – whatever that phrase precisely meant. For some, the Board offered the only way to reverse Britain's slide and was the culmination (if still inadequate) of the efforts made by government in relation to industry, from the 1961 NEDC onwards.

The alternative seemed to be to contemplate a more thorough distancing of government from industry and reliance on the market than had been practised for decades. The attempt by the Conservative government to follow such a course in the early 1970s had not been followed through. Despite talk of 'lame ducks', it had been the government which had come to the rescue, both in shipbuilding and in engineering. It was argued that there was no substitute for the reality of market performance. The assumption that there was a safety-net always available had accelerated the cycle of decline; such a net would not always be available. Government-sponsored bodies like the Industrial Reorganization Corporation had helped to perpetrate the management structure with which British Leyland was saddled. Supposed impartial enquiries into particular industries, whether by Geddes or Ryder, in practice always took too optimistic a view of the prospects of revival. The large investment which they recommended was never considered in relation to alternative outlets for investment with possibly greater chance of growth. Intervention to preserve jobs for their own sake only postponed the hard decisions that had to be taken. At the level of economic theory, Keynesianism came under increasing competition with the revival of interest in monetary theories. There was, it was suggested, a clear correlation, over time, between the growth of the money supply and inflation. If the cancer of inflation was ever to be controlled it could only be done through the money supply, whatever the temporary consequences might be. Either path could not be considered simply in economic terms and contained complications and complexities which advocates could only guess at; either, or neither, might be successful(212).

Success might also hinge upon developments in three other areas – all of which were the subject of much public debate and discussion – namely the structure of taxation, labour productivity and strikes, and the scale of public sector employment (and the revenue the government required to fund it). As inflation accelerated, these three issues were seen to be increasingly interrelated, though opinions varied on which element was primary.

It was frequently suggested that the levels of income tax – the government's biggest single revenue-raiser – were such as to inhibit industry and effort. But there was no easy way of determining the truth or falsity of the general proposition. Viewpoints on this matter tended to reflect party political attitudes. The Conservatives moved towards lower direct taxation – on expenditure rather than income. Labour continued to approach taxation not simply in terms of raising revenue but also as an instrument for promoting its concepts of social justice. There was frequent talk of introducing a wealth tax, but no specific measure was brought in. It was a popular proposal with many Labour supporters, but in government it was stated that the technical problems were formidable. In opposition, in the late 1960s, Conservative backroom boys toyed with the notion of a wealth tax – it seemed to chime in with a shifting of tax benefits from owners to earners by making possible more extensive cuts in direct taxation. The idea eventually made no progress for the simplest of reasons – the party would not have accepted it. Controversy continued because fundamental (if untestable) propositions were involved. On specific matters, there were also difficulties because of heavy reliance on taxation of motoring, smoking and alcoholic drink – all addictions which governments, wearing different hats, were attempting to discourage. Petrol, drink and tobacco usually formed a higher share of low-income budgets than of middle- or high-income budgets, and in an inflationary period some of these pressures were reflected in industrial relations and strikes. One other fundamental change was the introduction of value added tax in 1973 to replace purchase tax on 'luxuries' and the selective employment tax in service industries. The incentive for this change came largely from a desire to conform to this accepted system throughout the EEC. Since the major items of expenditure in low-income budgets were often zero-rated, the general impact on the cost of living was small.

The number of days lost in strikes rose steeply in the later 1960s – though this trend should not be thought a specifically British phenomenon. More and more unions decided to strike and the process fed on itself. In 1958, a strike by London busmen had been a failure, but throughout the later 1960s and early 1970s (with the exception of the postal strike in 1971) they were normally almost completely successful. Nationalized industries, where the government had to pay the bill, seemed to be as much, if not more vulnerable than industry in the private sector. 'Productivity' deals were often worked out with a regularity that became somewhat cynical. Claims for 'parity' were urged with the same vigour as claims for the maintenance of vital 'differentials'. Paradoxes littered the scene. The Left-dominated Associated Society of Locomotive Engineers and Firemen (ASLEF) executive fought and struck long and successfully to increase traindrivers' pay in relation to other railwaymen and to resist the takeover by the National Union of Railwaymen (NUR). In this jungle, groups of workers went on strike for the first time, and it soon became clear who were the lords – basically those in energy-related sectors like the miners, power-workers and oil-tanker drivers. The power of the miners in the early 1970s contrasted sharply with their weakness in 1926 and the comparison had a particular satisfaction in an industry where son followed father to an extent that was becoming unusual. Ironically, it was the mechanization of the industry which made the difference. Capital-intensive industries were usually anxious to settle speedily and could 'afford' to because wage costs were a smaller proportion of total costs. Such awards were then used as the basis of a 'fair' comparison in labour-intensive industries. The 'knock-on' effect of these developments threatened to destroy the competitive position of the United Kingdom, but no solution to it had been found in 1975.

The final conspicuous aspect was the expansion of public sector employment. Definition of who is and who is not a 'civil servant' is notoriously difficult and makes comparisons between different decades very imperfect. Even so, under both Conservative and Labour governments, public sector employment – in education, health and welfare services in particular – grew at a significantly faster rate than in employment generally. In the period 1965–73, for example, the administrative staff in National Health Service hospitals more than doubled, while the number of beds occupied daily dropped by one-ninth. It was not the public experience in this and other public services that increased manning levels were accompanied by increased efficiency and excellence of service. The same phenomenon was evident within local government. There seemed to be no slump when private industry slumped. The country could neither afford (nor perhaps control) this plausible bureaucratic Leviathan – so some argued. Some went even further and suggested that the manifest strains in British life stemmed from 'overload'. Governments were attempting to do too much. The public sector borrowing requirement was too high with adverse consequences for productive industry. Such assessments were equally vigorously contested and it was suggested that the Civil Service frustrated governments which could usefully do more. It was a matter of orientation, not of size. In the outcome of this argument might lie the future both of British industry and society.

----

1. M. Postan, *Fact and relevance* (Cambridge, 1971)
2. M. Panic, ed., *The U.K. and West German manufacturing industry, 1954–72* (1976)
3. G. L. Reid and K. Allen, *Nationalized industries* (1970)

CHAPTER 34

Town and country: the end

'There was nothing big in Liverpool', wrote one of its most famous citizens of the 1960s, '. . . it was going poor, a very poor city, and tough. But people have a sense of humour because they are in so much pain. . . .'(246) In due course, John Lennon left Liverpool, the Beatles, Britain and, sadly, the world behind, but in 1970 his comments reflected a mood which characterized many English northern cities. Liverpool itself was more congested and with more slums than anywhere else in England. In 1961, its population was 747,490 in 27,810 acres, compared with Manchester's 661,041 in 27,255 acres, Birmingham's 1,105,651 in 51,147 acres, Leeds's 510,597 in 40,615 acres and Sheffield's 493,954 in 39,586 acres. The Liverpool conurbation, with just over a million population had, at that juncture, some 80,000 slum or obsolescent buildings in urgent need of replacement. Redevelopment could not take place within the confines of the city because of lack of space and the need to preserve precious green belt. Part of the answer lay in a new town. When the site for Skelmersdale was designated in 1961, it was the first new town in England for eleven years. A population of 50,000 was envisaged, with provision for growth to 80,000. A few years later, Runcorn, south of the Mersey, was also designated a new town which would receive population dispersed from Liverpool. There were also ambitious plans for the expansion of Warrington. By the end of the 1960s it was hoped that the basis had been laid for both the rehousing and industrial regeneration of the English North-west(165).

By the mid-1970s, while improvement in urban conditions was undeniable, some of the optimism had faded. While dispersal did solve some problems, it created others. Within Liverpool itself, 'urban renewal' had to take place in a harsher economic climate than had been anticipated. The docks, which Lennon had seen as defining the character of the city, were in serious trouble. Liverpool and other northern ports, traditionally associated with long-distance trade in heavy goods, lost ground as that business declined, relatively if not absolutely. Southern and eastern ports like Southampton, Dover, Felixstowe and Harwich were in a better position to handle the growing European trade. That in turn became a factor in the location of new industry(168). Modernization and closure seemed to be the only answer, but could not be achieved easily in the context of high unemployment. Improved communications by road were obviously necessary and, in due course, the motorway network arrived. Until the building of the M62, it could be said that Liverpool's songs went around the world, but its heavy lorries could scarcely cross the Pennines.

Glasgow suffered for similar reasons and its problems were graver than those even of Merseyside. Between 1955 and 1972, no less than 268,000 dwellings were demolished in a massive clearance scheme. Even so, in 1971, the number of Glaswegians living in overcrowded houses had risen in a decade from 187,890 to 226,902. This overcrowding often occurred in relatively new housing estates. Some began to wonder whether it had been wise to pull down so many buildings when their handsome refurbishment might have preserved communities. In matters of health and housing, taken in the round, the city's record was worse than anywhere else in the United Kingdom. The scale of the problems to be tackled was at once daunting and challenging, often beyond the capacity of the Glasgow City Council or the Strathclyde Regional Council of which Glasgow became a part. The Scottish Office took over direct responsibility for rejuvenation, sponsoring the Glasgow Eastern Areas Renewal Programme with a budget exceeding anything that had been allocated previously for such a project. The Scottish Development Agency (1975) had the task of trying to create a satisfactory economic base, for the urban decay was intimately connected with industrial decline in a cycle which was becoming increasingly vicious. There was no blinking the fact that oil, particularly in the North-east, was shifting the focus of prosperity in Scotland. During this period, Glasgow was changing dramatically. Its population fell from just over 1 million in 1961 to under 900,000 a decade later, and continued to fall. Some families simply left the city of their own accord, but the steady departure of others was part of a planned programme. The majority went to new towns like Cumbernauld, Livingston and Irvine, but there were also overspill agreements with neighbouring burghs. But attracting the young, the skilled and the energetic into 'growth areas' only solved some difficulties to exacerbate others. There was, in any case, by the mid-1970s an increasing revulsion against a planning philosophy which seemed to regard demolition, down to the uprooting of every innocent tree, as the solution to every problem. The destruction of city centres (either by planners or non-planners) became a matter of concern throughout the British Isles and was not confined to certain actions in Glasgow. Although there were some successes (Sheffield being one example) the general record was dismal. Conservation, it slowly became clear, was not a concept only to be applied to the countryside. The very fact that Glasgow had not very successfully adjusted from the days of its commercial glory meant that some of the relics of its great days survived in greater profusion than in other, more successful, cities. Its Victorian architecture, art galleries, museums and opera-house might blend with its excellent communications to make it once more a major European city(154,167).

It was the seemingly inexorable growth of road traffic which played havoc with the post-war urban development plans. The British car population rose from 4,650,000 in 1958 to 11,078,000 in 1968 and was still rising steadily. By the 1970s, some three-quarters of total travel was by car. Peak figures for passengers travelling by bus and train were attained in most parts of the country in the early 1950s. The constant rise in car ownership put pressure on roads which had never been designed for such numbers. Congestion became characteristic of most towns, at any rate at the peak hours. Sir Colin Buchanan produced his well-known Report, Traffic in Towns, in 1963. Planners in nearly every city wrestled with their inner ring roads or their outer ring roads. They experimented with one-way systems, pedestrian precincts and two-level highways. They constructed concrete palaces in strategic situations to house the cars that had successfully insinuated themselves into city centres. 'Planning blight' became a dismal reality for thousands as they waited for the building of a road – which sometimes never came.

Only in the mid-1970s did it appear that the fuel to power this seemingly endless flow of cars might become very expensive and in due time cease altogether. In part against this day, major capital expenditure was authorized to create or modernize underground services on Merseyside, Tyneside and Glasgow. Having defeated the suburban train, at least outside South-east England, the bus was now in grave jeopardy, and in the early part of the period it almost seemed as if the notion of a public transport system was redundant. Despite a modernization programme which had been authorized in 1955, by the early 1960s the nationalized railway industry was in grave financial difficulty. Costs had risen, far outstripping charges, and traffic both of passengers and goods was falling. Lord Beeching, as he became, was given the task of reshaping the railways. His 1963 Report stressed that if the deficit was to be curtailed by the end of the decade, manpower and route mileage would have to be drastically pruned. A revitalized system would concentrate on inter-city passenger services and long-distance freight. Consequently, branch lines were closed on an extensive scale – areas whose road communications were already poor received another blow. Their closure also added to road traffic pressures in suburban regions. But despite the economies made, receipts from freight had been overestimated and it took some time for the inter-city network to become efficient. By the mid-1970s, however, a new era in rail transport was believed to be dawning, with more attractive marketing and the introduction of high-speed trains on some of the most important passenger routes. Sceptics remained to be convinced – for even the streamlined 'freightliner' system found it difficult to complete with the flexibility of road transport which could use the motorways.

The motorway programme was not without its technical complications, but the first stretch was opened in 1959. Expenditure on road improvement and construction reached steadily higher figures through the 1960s and over 1,000 miles had been built by the mid-1970s. Once the initial euphoria had passed, and without denying their benefits, some opinion became increasingly critical of the damage motorways caused to the environment and the land they used up. It was apparent, in any case, that the level of public expenditure on roads could not be maintained. During this period, however, there were a number of major bridges and tunnels built – over and under the Clyde, over the Firth of Forth, the Severn and the Tamar, for example – the benefit of which few denied. The airports of the major provincial cities all had to expand (and in some cases find new sites) to cope with both increased business and larger aircraft. While some direct international flights developed both to Europe and North America from airports like Manchester, the pressure remained on London's airports, leading to a protracted and unsuccessful search for a third airport site to supplement Heathrow and Gatwick. Once again, the benefits had to be weighed against environmental considerations.

The thrust behind these developments came from the realization that the ability to move goods speedily might be a key factor in the country's commercial success. For that reason, the actual routes of the motorways and the order in which they were constructed had some political importance. In particular, peripheral regions such as South-west England or North-west Wales realized that access to motorways, if not motorways themselves, critically affected their capacity to attract new industry. Inevitably, however, they were first constructed between the major centres where most benefit could be most speedily reaped – a situation which reinforced their existing advantages. Motorways, widely advocated as a means of reducing the commercial significance of distance, could not do so universally. The persistent problem of regional variations in Britain moved steadily, if somewhat forlornly, to the centre of politics.

By the later 1950s, the assumptions that had been made earlier in the decade that the regional problem could look after itself were proving false. The regional unemployment statistics once more reflected the regional concentration of those staple industries whose difficulties have already been discussed. The 1958 Distribution of Industry (Industrial Finance) Act hastily extended the number of development areas including, for the first time, non-urban areas like the north-west of Wales and the Western Isles of Scotland. The 1960 and 1963 Local Employment Acts attempted to promote industrial growth in specific areas where unemployment was deep-seated and services and amenities were inadequate. The problem, however, was that while the unemployment was real, the area concerned was not necessarily a natural 'growth point'. In the early 1960s the planning of growth was a growth area. The 1961 Toothill Report on the Scottish economy drew renewed attention to the loss of jobs in basic industries which were not being replaced on a sufficient scale. The 1963 Central Scotland Plan talked about improving the infrastructure to attract new industry(134). A White Paper on the north-east of England (1963) envisaged a 'growth zone' between Tyneside and Teesside, and a government minister, Lord Hailsham, was given special responsibility for this area.

The Labour government after 1964 increased this regional planning. 'Regional development' became the responsibility of the Board of Trade and then of the newly established Department of Economic Affairs. Until the end of the 1960s, new plans regularly appeared with promising titles like: 'A Region with a Future: A Draft Strategy for the South West' (1967). Mere plans then became strategic plans – for the North-west or the South-east. Ten economic planning councils were set up, one each in Scotland and Wales and eight in England. These were advisory and their task was not to frame policies agreed by the regions for consideration by central government but to use the experience of their members to produce some suggestions for further consideration by all levels of government and private bodies(169). Geographers wrote at this time that 'a structure exists, the techniques of analysis are available and a growing number of professional planners and other specialists are aware of the needs and also of the means by which these needs can be satisfied'(168).

Such confidence was misplaced. The regional plans looked impressive, but planning had to take place within a national framework and involved decisions about the allocation of resources between regions. Such a nettle was very difficult to grasp, particularly since every region considered that it needed special treatment. 'Grey' areas were already complaining that too much attention was being given to 'black spots'. After the Hunt Committee reported on the intermediate areas (1969) the government designated the Yorkshire coalfields, North-east Lancashire, the Nottingham/Derby coalfield, North Humberside, Plymouth, part of South-east Wales as areas to receive qualified development assistance, though not on the scale given to the development areas. Immediately, other areas considered that their needs had been overlooked, and additions and alterations were made in 1971, 1972 and 1974. Keeping pace with the development map became a major occupation. The Hunt Committee sadly recognized that 'the supply of mobile industry available to stimulate economic growth is, taken as a whole, insufficient at present to meet the needs of the development areas and overspill towns, let alone areas of slow growth. We recognize that remedial measures for areas of slow growth may hold back progress elsewhere.' There was the rub.

It was also becoming evident that the population estimates on which new towns and cities were to be based had gone badly wrong. A new town like Telford, for example, experienced considerable difficulties. Planners and writers began to ask themselves whether it was worth creating more new and 'expanding' towns at all. They might only make a 'marginal contribution to the relief of housing need' and probably never offer a solution to the hard-core problems in the conurbations.[1] The post-war generation of planners and politicians had been too optimistic. While a town like Swindon, with its good communications by road and rail successfully changed its economic base away from almost total dependence on rail workshops for employment, this could not happen everywhere. Firms were not rushing to remote areas and thereby possibly jeopardizing their commercial futures, despite the special concessions dangled in front of them. In 1970–71, for example, the Location of Offices Bureau reported that 77 per cent of firms who wished to move out of London only wanted to move to the suburbs or to not more than 20 miles from the centre(170). At best, the development regions received branches rather than the headquarters of major enterprises. It has been noted that as late as 1939 most companies in the west of Scotland were controlled by Scottish interests, generally resident. By 1960, however, over 60 per cent of firms in manufacturing employing over 250 people were controlled by non-Scottish interests. A once-vigorous and self-sustaining region had been reduced to the status of a 'branch-factory economy'.[2]

By the later 1970s, scepticism about over a decade of regional planning was surfacing. A new Conservative government decided to revert to an earlier phase of policy by reducing the total number of areas receiving assistance and by concentrating the reliefs available to firms. Writers even began to wonder whether the conventional indictment of nineteenth-century building was so justified when they surveyed post-war planned towns. 'Even the much-maligned speculative housing of the Victorians', one critic wrote, 'when painted, cleaned, fitted with bathrooms and central heating and manageably compact kitchens, provides as satisfactory a domestic environment as anything our architects and builders and town planners can construct for us afresh.' He very much doubted whether he would live to see any creation of the Department of the Environment listed for preservation.[3] The belief that even the best architects and planners blighted all they touched may be going a little far, but it expresses a mood far different from the confidence of the early 1950s. The planner, once thought the embodiment of disinterested wisdom, was becoming an ogre and the demand for 'public participation' was raised – though appropriate mechanisms were not easy to determine.

Even the green belt has come in for some subsequent stricture on the grounds that it raised house prices and rents to a level higher than they would otherwise be. On the whole, however, despite all its complications, the protection of the countryside was welcomed. By the early 1970s, large areas of Britain had been 'designated' so as to preserve the rural landscape. Besides the National Parks and Forest Parks there were some twenty-five Areas of Outstanding Natural Beauty – like the Chilterns, the Surrey Hills and the Kent Downs. There were also Areas of High Landscape Value. There were tight restrictions on development in these areas. Both the Nature Conservancy and the National Trust extended their work and influence. The latter embarked on 'Enterprise Neptune' to protect as much of the unspoiled coastline of Britain as possible.

The amenity represented by the countryside became increasingly popular, which in turn brought fresh problems. Some 35 million holidays a year were taken by the British during the 1960s, of which 5 million were spent abroad – a figure which does not include innumerable short trips and week-ends. Foreign tourists rose from nearly 2 million in 1960 to over 10 million in 1976 – the United States providing the largest single supply. The 1969 Development of Tourism Act set up the British Tourish Authority and separate boards for England, Scotland, Wales and Northern Ireland. The scenic and other attractions of the United Kingdom were vigorously promoted. There were even suggestions that the whole country might become a kind of extended museum with its post-industrial inhabitants being photographed against the exotic background of cotton mill or coal-mine. For the moment, however, the foreign visitor, at least initially, went to London, Oxford and Stratford. The British urban holidaymaker went to South-west England, Wales or Scotland and tourism had major economic importance, particularly for remote rural regions.

A vast change took place in the style of holidaying, with a massive switch to self-catering. The motor car and the motorway brought problems of overcrowding never previously experienced in areas like the Lake District. The problem with tourism in the holiday areas was its necessarily seasonal nature, though its development could mean that marginal farming could be combined with 'farm holidays' to provide a reasonable income. The needs of the tourist could be the incentive to improve the infrastructure for local residents and thus in turn enable an area to escape total dependence upon tourism. But there was the other danger that too much 'improvement' might destroy the 'character' of an area that attracted tourists in the first place. In some areas, there was resentment at the consequences for the local social and cultural structure of an influx of visitors and there was a good deal of ill-defined talk about 'ways of life' being threatened.[4] If 'alien' pressures were resisted by rural communities in England, Scotland or Wales their cultural identity which was being preserved might turn out to be not much more than a culture of relative poverty. This problem particularly arose in the case of 'second homes'. The number of these had increased only slowly – some 1 per cent of British households possessed them in 1967 – and the volume of holiday use was far below that of other western European countries. Nevertheless, some villages near enough to big cities for easy access were in danger of becoming 'week-end villages'. In some areas, too, there were intrepid 'settlers' pursuing the good life and seeking self-sufficiency. Such a tendency could be seen in a rather different form elsewhere. In the mid-1960s, about a third of the agricultural land to the south-east of London was farmed by part-time farmers. Some of these were 'real' farmers, who often had other sources of income, others were 'hobby' farmers motivated by status or tax considerations or by a love of farming, but whose major income was derived from other pursuits(170).

In 'real' farming, there was a steep decline in the number of non-family hired farm workers, and the farmer and his family now provided the greater part of the agricultural labour force in England and Wales. In the early 1970s, some 60 per cent of farms were owner-occupied. The 'industrialization' of farming continued at a rapid rate, with high productivity fostered by the scientific advances being mediated to the farmer by various advisory agencies. Awkward survivals of a previous age, like hedges and spinneys, had to be eradicated in the interests of the machine. Large-scale management was all the rage. Improved new strains, more fertilizers and other forms of chemical control produced substantially heavier yields across the board. The average yield of wheat rose by 10 cwt per acre to reach 32 cwt in the twenty years to 1969 and the yield of potatoes rose by rather under a half over the same period. Factory farming became widespread in egg, chicken, pork and bacon production, with notable economics of scale, whatever else might be said. By the mid-1970s, the younger generation, in particular, pressed an 'ecological' standpoint and talked about the exhaustion of the soil and the 'inhumanity' of factory farming(172).

From another standpoint, the new farming methods placed an increasing premium upon capital and stimulated fresh efforts to persuade farmers to operate on a 'group' system for foodstuffs, machinery and marketing. This trend became well established, encouraged both by the NFU and the 1967 Agriculture Act, but it was not without its technical and financial complications. In general, however, there was a good deal of satisfaction about the state of British farming so that there was even some smugness in the industry when Britain joined the EEC and had to operate the Common Agricultural Policy. Accession necessitated a major change in the basis on which British farming had operated since the war, but one which could benefit the existing prosperous sectors. More problematic was the future of 'hill farming', a sector which had only survived through the support it had received from central government. Even before Britain joined the EEC, energetic efforts were made to promote amalgamations and encourage 'integrated' farming, especially in collaboration with forestry. The British government argued that it was socially desirable that farming in the upland areas of the United Kingdom should not die out. In the end, Community support was forthcoming under the Regional Development Fund, though awkward problems remained.

Efforts continued to stimulate and diversify enterprise in the remoter areas. The Highlands and Islands Development Board (1965) in Scotland had quite extensive powers. Some of its ideas – bulb development, for example – proved less than satisfactory. There was also the grim news that whereas in 1900 the bag from the grouse moors on the six sporting estates of the Strath of Kildonan amounted to 5,200 brace, the annual average between 1959 and 1969 was only 1,813.[5] Such a problem was not of concern in mid-Wales; what mattered there was the loss of population. The task was to match the area's agriculture with tourism and also expand Newtown. Rural Development Boards all confirmed that it had become pointless to ask whether a particular area, people or community was 'rural' or 'urban'; it was now 'relatively' rural or urban. Once again, however, it was easier to talk of planning developments than actually to bring about development. In 1970 the Rural Development Board for Wales was abolished, its drive for amalgamations being successful only in creating combinations against its own plans.

In local government, the continued official distinction between urban and rural areas was clearly inadequate, leading to increasingly contentious and futile disputes between counties, county boroughs and rural and urban districts – sometimes requiring ministerial intervention to solve. Commentators found it unsatisfactory that more and more people lived in the area of one local authority and worked in that of another. Attempts to tackle the problem before the mid-1950s made little progress. Between 1958 and 1974, however, both the national framework of English local government and its inner workings experienced major change. That was the view of Lord Redcliffe-Maud whose Commission's activity had, of course, laid the groundwork for the changes(174). Critics were less satisfied with what had been done. The reformed system, in their view, remained similar to the old because, although the number of authorities was greatly reduced, the old two-tier principle remained. Central control was undiminished and popular representation was reduced. Local government reform allegedly had fallen between the two stools of efficiency and democracy. It was often thought that local government would have to be reviewed in the light of the 'devolution' which was frequently believed to be imminent(142,150).

Whether satisfactory or not, local government reform had certainly been a major administrative operation. The 1963 London Government Act embodied in modified form the report of the Herbert Commission (1957–60). The Greater London Council came into being in 1965, covering 620 square miles and including a population of nearly 8 million people. There were thirty-two new London boroughs. The London and Middlesex County Councils disappeared, as did the County Boroughs of Croydon and East and West Ham. The boundaries of the counties adjoining were also substantially altered. The Local Government Commission, set up under the 1958 Local Government Act to consider boundaries, was replaced in 1966 by the Redcliffe-Maud Commission, whose brief was wider. It had to suggest ways of revivifying local democracy, as well as make boundary recommendations. Its 1969 Report favoured 58 all-purpose authorities in England outside 4 conurbations. London having been settled, the Commission favoured metropolitan and metropolitan district councils for Birmingham, Manchester and Liverpool. The government agreed that the old system of counties, county boroughs, municipal boroughs, and urban and rural districts should disappear, but it rejected the proposed unitary system. Instead, the 1972 Local Government Act established a two-tier system of counties and districts – 39 counties and 296 districts. Most of the names, if not the boundaries, of the old counties were retained, though there were 4 newcomers – Avon, Cleveland, Cumbria and Humberside. This represented a very considerable reduction in the number of councils and councillors. In addition, there were 6 metropolitan counties, each containing metropolitan districts – Greater Manchester, Merseyside, South Yorkshire, Tyne and Wear, West Midlands and West Yorkshire. In Wales, there were 8 counties and 37 districts, the total number of local authorities being reduced from 181 to 45. A separate Commission, chaired by Lord Wheatley, had been at work in Scotland and it likewise recommended simplifying Scottish local government. The 1973 Local Government (Scotland) Act provided for 9 regional and 53 district councils, except for the 3 island areas of Orkney, Shetland and the Western Isles, which became 'most-purpose' authorities. Geographical factors also determined that the planning powers of the Scottish regions were not identical, though the division of powers between the regions and the districts was clearer than the comparable division in England and Wales. The Scottish regions contained much greater variations of size and population than the English counties.

Besides these important structural changes, there were detailed investigations into management. Ombudsmen were appointed to act on behalf of the public in alleged instances of maladministration. Instances of corruption in local government led to a further Commission whose task was to try to establish the appropriate rules and principles for those engaged in council work. Whether the major upheaval in local government really benefited the public it is perhaps too early to say. Certainly, in the early years, officials seemed obsessed with structures and the service to the public suffered. Important matters were, at the same time, taken out of the hands of local authorities altogether. A 'unified' health service became the responsibility of area health authorities. Sewage disposal became the responsibility of the nine English regional water authorities and the single Welsh authority. The regions retained responsibility for sewerage in Scotland. It is perhaps significant that the word 'reorganization' came to replace 'reform' to describe all these changes. Experience of some of them may well have played a part in defeating the proposals for devolution. A sceptical public no longer believed in miracles brought about by administrative change. Nevertheless, the Redcliffe-Maud Commission had to its credit that it officially declared that, 'Town and country have always been, and must be, interdependent.' It was worth waiting until 1969 to hear this authoritative conclusion.

1. M. Harloe, *Swindon: a town in transition* (1975), pp. 283–4
2. A. Slaven, *The development of the West of Scotland, 1750–1960* (1975), p. 228
3. D. J. Olsen, *The growth of Victorian London* (1976), pp. 327, 331
4. J. Ashton and W. H. Long, *The remoter rural areas of Britain* (Edinburgh, 1972)
5. J. Bryden and G. Houston, *Agrarian change in the Scottish Highlands* (1976), p. 49

CHAPTER 35

All for education – and sport for all

'All the barriers to opportunity must come down', declared the Conservative Education Minister in 1957, 'whether this is done by providing financial help sufficient to enable students to stay on at school or go to technical college or university, or by ensuring a way forward for those whose talents develop late.' The post-war decade had seen educational administrators and teachers wrestling with the task of implementing the Butler Act, but educational spending had not yet reached a plateau. The government felt able to announce that the long-proposed three-year course of teacher training would begin in September 1960. Teachers welcomed this step on the grounds that 'better qualified teachers must inevitably produced better opportunities for the nation's children'. Report after report advocated increased spending on education in all sectors(222).

'Between 1938 and 1955', stated the 1956 White Paper on technical education, 'the number of university students in science and technology has doubled. ... But this is nothing like enough.' It went on to make invidious comparisons with the United States, the Soviet Union and Western Europe. The 1959 Crowther Report argued that most British children between the ages of fifteen and eighteen were not being educated. Teenage problems were only being hidden by letting boys and girls leave school at an age when they were not sufficiently mature to be exposed to industry and commerce – the kind of comment that could only have come from very mature adults. It was not only at the top but 'almost to the bottom of the pyramid' that the scientific revolution needed to reach. It suggested that secondary education for all up to the age of sixteen should come into operation between 1966 and 1968. In the longer term, it hoped that by 1980 half of the nation's children would remain in full-time education until they were eighteen. It later wrestled with the problem of 'specialization', describing the English system as 'singular' but admitting that a 'broad curriculum' had its drawbacks. The perfect sixth-form curriculum was one which would develop the literacy of science specialists and the numeracy of arts specialists, but it did not say how this could be done. The 1960 Albemarle Report offered the illuminating suggestion that adolescents were 'the litmus paper of a society' and thought that Britain could no longer make do with a Youth Service which was so plainly ill-equipped to meet the needs of the day. The 1963 Newsom Report on the education of pupils between thirteen and sixteen of average or below-average ability advocated, among other things, an extension of an element of compulsion into what were often broadening but hitherto voluntary activities. The strictly educational problems of less able pupils were not different in 'slum schools' from other schools, but such schools did require a specially favourable staffing ratio. An inter-departmental working party (a touchingly modest notion) might be needed 'to plan the strategy of a grand assault' on the wider social problems, but that was no reason to postpone the opening of the campaign. 'Today's average boys and girls', it concluded rather quaintly, 'are better at their books than their predecessors half a generation ago.' The sociologists, themselves an expanding race, brought an increasing complexity, if not profundity, to these enquiries. The 1967 Plowden Report carried the social emphasis in education a stage further. 'Positive discrimination' and 'educational priority areas' were the new phrases. Although admitting that probably two-thirds of parents preferred their children to be taught in classes streamed by ability, it nevertheless argued against the practice. Streaming involved selecting, it impressively revealed, and selecting involved social selecting, or could do. In addition, selectors could make mistakes and (a clinching argument) the practice was 'almost unknown on the continent of Europe'. The views of parents were no match for such formidable argumentation (222, 226).

Lord Robbins and his committee, working from 1961 to 1963, produced the most bulky of all these enquiries. Their field was the pattern of higher education in Great Britain. The authority of this report was buttressed by six volumes of appendices – an early sign of inflation. Robbins discovered the existence of 'large reservoirs of untapped ability in the population, especially among girls'. It was axiomatic that 'courses of higher education should be available for all those who are qualified by ability and attainment to pursue them and who wish to do so.' Expansion of numbers would not be at the expense of achievement or quality. There were 216,000 full-time students in higher education in 1962/63 and the figure should rise to 390,000 in 1973/74 and 560,000 in 1980/81. Such a programme would entail major institutional changes – the colleges of advanced technology should be given university status and the colleges of education should come within the orbit of the universities. Government machinery would also have to be adapted and the report favoured one ministry for schools and one for higher education and science.

Even though the Conservative government rejected this last proposal, the general expansion of higher education was started and carried on by Labour after 1964. In the early 1960s, new universities were set up at a rapid rate – Sussex, Kent, Essex, East Anglia, York, Warwick and Lancaster. Some of them had actual lakes for the reservoirs of talent to admire. A great deal of publicity attended their launching and for all those involved, down to the humblest assistant lecturer, there was a unique excitement to be gained from the planning of new courses and structures from scratch. It was far from certain, however, that the experimentation Robbins had in mind found its richest fruition in the rash of 'confrontations', 'sit-ins', 'occupations' and strikes which the taxpayer observed on his television screen in 1968. Used to the unhistorical notion that universities were places of quiet study and deep reflection, it was odd to find the London School of Economics in turmoil. Eventually, the crisis passed, but not without a lasting effect on the constitutions and operations of many universities.

Expansion continued apace, with the older civic universities anxious to show that their substantial library and other amenities were not to be despised in favour of cathedral cities and holiday resorts. Colleges of advanced technology, while retaining their own emphasis, did become fully-fledged universities. In 1966, the Labour government outlined its plan for a 'binary' system of higher education. In the years that followed, some twenty-one polytechnics were designated, all under the control of the LEAs. A Council for National Academic Awards was set up in 1964 to validate their courses and standards. The creation of polytechnics would enable the target figures to be reached more easily and more cheaply. From the outset, however, their real function and their relation to the universities was somewhat mysterious. Some commentators regretted that a unitary system of higher education had not been created. Some thought polytechnics did have a distinct vocation and even attempted to say what it was. The universities did not quite know what they should do or say about them and did and said very little. Except in a very limited number of subjects, there was little staff mobility between the two systems. Universities, in any case, ever more dependent upon public funds (even if they were gracefully channelled through the UGC), were not in a position to talk about their 'independence'. Those who felt that he who paid for a 'piper-in-residence' would sooner or later call the tune, established the independent University College of Buckingham without public money. A further innovation was the Open University, which received its charter in 1969. It operated by a mixture of correspondence assignments and specially made radio and television programmes, backed up by short residential courses and tutorials. It was at once apparent that it did meet the needs of many adults who had missed the orthodox route to university; whether it attracted the social groups the Labour government had in mind in setting it up was another matter. One final change which flowed from Robbins was the closer association of the colleges of education with the universities through the award of the B.Ed. degree, initiated in 1968.

Expansion was not confined to England, for the Robbins Committee concerned itself with Britain. In Scotland, the technological institutions of Glasgow and Edinburgh emerged as the universities of Strathclyde and Heriot-Watt respectively. Dundee finally separated from St Andrews. One new university, Stirling, was set up in 1966 – the last in Britain. Practically the only novelty left for Stirling to attempt was to copy the semester system operated in North America. Like Strathclyde, however, it did offer a BA honours degree. The older Scottish universities maintained their MAs, while agonizing about the relationship between ordinary and honours degrees, and the merits of specialization and a broad curriculum. Certain books revived faith in Scotland's 'democratic intellect' but, with an irony not uncommon in these matters, other opinion in Scotland was becoming impressed by the merits of English degree courses just at the time when there was some disenchantment with them in England itself. Similarly with the pattern of Scottish school examinations, consisting of 'ordinary' and 'higher' grades. In Wales, no new constituent college was added to the federal University, though the existing ones all expanded and the Institute of Science and Technology in Cardiff was incorporated into it. One polytechnic was started. In Northern Ireland, under devolved government, the Robbins Committee had no remit to investigate, but the same mood prevailed. A New University of Ulster was set up at Coleraine after much controversy about its siting. Both it and the Queen's University of Belfast had a rather complex relationship with the UGC. A thrusting polytechnic was also created in Belfast.

By any standards, the expansion of higher education was a remarkable achievement. One major cause of this accelerated growth was the belief that shortcomings in the educational system explained the national economic malaise. The graduate/age cohort ratio might well be the clue which unlocked the secret of economic success. But by the mid-1970s doubts were expressed about future expansion. The questions were chiefly financial because costs rose steeply but, more fundamentally, after nearly twenty years, there was little sign that increased higher education on the scale that had been provided had solved the country's economic problems. Of course, it could be argued that these problems would have been even worse if it had not taken place and the universities themselves had not offered a magic formula. Phrases about 'reservoirs of talent' came to have a rather tired sound and those who had predicted, with the novelist Amis, that 'more meant worse' felt themselves vindicated. The universities had to begin to consider their roles in a context in which they were no longer universally popular.

At the secondary level, the most striking development of the 1960s was the programme of comprehensive reorganization. At the beginning of the decade, about one in twelve pupils were in non-selective schools, but the Labour party was moving strongly in favour of the comprehensive principle. In 1965, the new government announced plans for the ending of the eleven-plus examination and 'separatism' in secondary education. Circular 10/65 requested local authorities to suggest six ways in which it could be done and a great deal of argument ensued. By the end of the 1960s, further pressure had been applied and the majority of local authorities had complied with the circular. The Conservatives withdrew it in 1970, but by then some 35 per cent of the secondary age-group were in comprehensive schools and the proportion continued to rise (216). Many Conservatives now accepted the comprehensive principle, but that did not end the argument. There was, in fact, no such thing as a 'comprehensive school', but rather various types, some purpose-built, others more or less satisfactorily adapted. Privilege and inequality were allegedly undermined by the comprehensive principle, but even those who supported it feared that standards would be undermined too. Alongside the general reorganization went other changes in school design and in the syllabus. The emphasis in teaching was upon discovery rather than the inculcation of established verities. 'Guides' and 'projects' became the order of the day. The percentage of seventeen-year olds at school slowly but steadily rose though, as always, there was considerable regional variation in its incidence. The ethos of sixth forms began to change in these circumstances and, although sixth-form colleges had their advocates, they were not universally supported.

In 1965, the Certificate of Secondary Education (CSE) was introduced for those candidates who had a reasonably high level of competence below GCE 'O' level. Its novel feature was that the teachers would have a major role in operating the examinations and shaping the form of the three 'modes'. Some of them wanted to extend this involvement to 'O' level. It can be judged that examinations became a matter of great concern in England and Wales. The Schools

Council, established in 1964, with representatives from higher education, teachers, inspectors and the LEAs talked about a new relationship between the actual work of schools and the examinations. Examinations, it was said, could all too easily 'stand in the way' of necessary innovation. 'Curriculum development' gathered momentum. Initiatives stemming from the Schools Council led to a proposal to introduce a common system of examining at sixteen-plus by 1975. Later, 'N' and 'F' levels were proposed as a way of eliminating the 'tyranny' of 'A' level.

In schools themselves, projectors protruded into classrooms (if such they could still be called) and were accompanied by record-players, tape recorders and television sets. Languages were learnt, or at least spoken, in what were called language 'laboratories' – a curious usage. Collectively, such pieces of equipment became known as 'learning resources', though teachers were not yet generally known as 'resource managers'. However, Crosland, the first Secretary of State for Education and Science, did on one occasion invite teachers to think of themselves increasingly as if they were surgeons in an operating theatre, able to summon resources, human and mechanical, at will. He did not extend the comparison to pay. Exciting, innovative and expensive though all this was, it did not go unchallenged. Critical *Black Papers* were produced – not all of which were written by men of the Right. The language 'laboratories' installed in thousands in the 1960s were wearing out a decade later, but their mass installation had in no discernible way improved the level of attainment in foreign languages. By the mid-1970s, a new mood was detectable in the discussion of secondary education. Although the battle for and against comprehensive education still rumbled on, attention increasingly focused on the factors that made some comprehensive schools conspicuously more successful, on all counts, than others. Finance would prevent further large-scale reorganization, but standards might still be raised. Grammar and clarity of expression, thought fussy in the 1960s, became a matter of public concern. So did 'basic numeracy', even in an age of calculators. To some extent, attitudes on these questions reflected party divisions. Party views were more explicit when it came to ancillary aspects of education like the provision of school meals and milk. Briefly emerging in 1970, they re-emerged at the end of the decade.

Some advocates of comprehension argued that they could not yield their best results while other kinds of school survived and could 'cream off' gifted children. Maintained grammar schools still survived in the 1960s on a considerable scale and the direct-grant schools flourished. It was the success of pupils from these schools which kept up a challenge to the public schools. However, the Labour party became increasingly critical of the direct-grant system and the 1974 Labour government abolished it. Such well-known schools as Bristol Grammar School and Manchester Grammar School were among the majority which opted for independence. About the public schools, however, Labour did nothing. In 1968, Sir John Newsom had chaired an enquiry into the public schools with the objective of securing a socially mixed entry. It reported at some length but to no avail. Divided between those who wished to end, those who wished to mend and those who wished to ignore the public schools, Labour took no action. The Conservative government took no notice of the Public Schools Commission. However, by the mid-1970s the notion that the public schools would wither away because of financial pressures seemed wrong. On the contrary, the independent sector expanded and more parents seemed prepared to make financial sacrifices to obtain the education they wanted for their children. It was also argued that without a thriving independent sector there was no way in which the success or failure of the State system could be monitored. But there was no sign that arguments about independent schools were coming to an end.

There were interesting developments in secondary education outside England. In Wales, both the school and examination system remained on the same pattern as England, but responsibility for primary and secondary education (though not the university sector) was transferred in 1970 from the Department of Education and Science (DES) to the Welsh Office in Cardiff. The place of the Welsh language in schools differentiated the educational debate from that of the rest of the United Kingdom. The 1968 Gittins Report, which was supposed to be considering primary education and the transition to secondary education in Wales, deliberated lengthily on the language issue, and suggested that 'each child should be given sufficient opportunity to become reasonably bilingual by the end of its primary stage', but opposed compulsion which 'loses the moral issue if it is applied and is likely to be ineffective'. By the mid-1970s, certain local authorities did not seem to agree with that latter point. Comprehensive education was, on the whole, accepted earlier in Wales and with less controversy than in England. One feature was the establishment of some Welsh-medium comprehensive schools, a few in largely English-speaking areas. By the end of the period, analysis of examination results seemed to suggest that the tradition of devotion to education in Wales no longer corresponded to the reality.

After considerable discussion, schoolchildren in Northern Ireland took 'O' and 'A' levels. The examinations (under devolution) were organized by the Education Ministry, though a high proportion of candidates actually took the examinations organized by London University and the Associated Board in England. The eleven-plus examination system remained. Educational arguments centred on the funding and basis of denominational education. After direct rule, there were suggestions under Labour that the comprehensive principle should extend to the province so that in this respect, too, Northern Ireland would be like the rest of the United Kingdom, but no action was taken.

The Scottish educational system remained different in certain respects. The comprehensive battle had been fought in Scotland with the same vigour as in England, with substantially the same result — though the old system was somewhat different from the English and in the smaller towns and country areas could be said to have a comprehensive element. However, both the age of transfer to secondary education (twelve) and the sequence and nature of subsequent examinations remained different. These 'O' and 'H' grades remained the responsibility of the Scottish Education Department, not university boards as in England and Wales. Nothing comparable to the CSE was introduced in Scotland, though a Certificate of Sixth Year Studies was brought in for those pupils who wished to stay on for a further year after taking their 'H' grades.

Thus, some diversity has remained in the educational provision within the United Kingdom but, even during a period of developing national or regional pressure, it has not intensified. There is, perhaps, a central perversity in that higher education in the United Kingdom comes within the purview, ultimately, of the Secretary of State for Education and Science and his department, but it is only in England that he has responsibility for primary and secondary education. Even devolution would not have changed this position. This inconsistency, from whichever side it was approached, seemed to some a pleasing aspect of the puzzling mixture of unity and diversity which had come to characterize the United Kingdom (220).

SPORT

In 1966, three years after the centenary of the Football Association, England won the World Cup for the first time. It was a fitting climax to a tournament which, being played in England, excited enormous public interest. Some 400 million people across the world are believed to have watched the game on television. Here, apparently, was a worthy event, fully justifying a special postage stamp – though the Post Office was in process of introducing a new policy which guaranteed any event or anniversary a postal celebration. It was as well to celebrate since there was a feeling that the virtues of English play would not be sufficient for future success abroad. By 1978, England could not even qualify for the finals of the World Cup. Scotland did qualify, but performed ignominiously.

In the later 1960s, the ethos and spirit of the game changed substantially. A High Court ruling established that players could no longer be held by their clubs against their wishes. The principle of freedom of movement, together with the abolition of the maximum wage, created a quite different financial climate for the players. The clubs in turn required additional money, to be found in increased charges at the turnstiles and by a host of ancillary activities. Transfer fees steadily mounted, with only a small number of clubs able to afford the biggest sums. Contrary to some expectations, this did not lead to a sharp drop in the number of professional clubs. Transfer money worked its way down to the small clubs – if they were lucky. It did mean, however, that the money which television rights could bring became vital since, on the whole, attendances continued to drop. Nevertheless, television was regarded with suspicion, as it was felt that it might eventually ruin the game. Too many previous spectators would stay at home and watch the game in the comfort of their sitting-room stadium, especially if it could be screened at the time of the actual match. Live coverage, therefore, was prevented except in rare instances. Steadily, however, the television camera became more intrusive, contributing further to the fame and fortune of the stars. The television authorities made the strange assumption that verbal and footballing skill invariably coincided. It was true, however, that some holders of university degrees moved on to higher things in the First Division.

In the early days of this commercial liberation, the Welshman, John Charles, and the Scotsman, Denis Law, both left England to play in Italian football – the beginning of a trend which was to see many British footballers playing in Continental leagues and in the United States. It was not until the later 1970s that English clubs signed European or South American players. Helped again by television coverage, both English and Scottish clubs began to play a full part in the plethora of European football competitions which developed during the 1960s. Glasgow Celtic became the first British club to win the European Cup (1967), to be followed later by Manchester United, Liverpool and Nottingham Forest. These additional competitions added to the stress of the game for both players and managers. In general, the latter could only rely on a short tenure if they did not achieve success. Matt Busby, of Manchester United, demonstrated such great staying power that he became the first club manager to be knighted (1968). Ramsey, manager of the England side, had been knighted after the 1966 World Cup victory. The international dimension of the game meant that even the FA or Scottish Cup Final lost some of their glory.

By the 1970s, petulance and violence on the field, though it had never been absent, seemed to be getting worse. The behaviour of 'fans', both in the ground and in the 'no man's land' which surrounded it, caused disquiet and anger. This problem was passed to psychologists and sociologists, some of whom saw soccer hooliganism as a secularized form of ritual or a substitute for the real fighting which previous generations had enjoyed. Thanks to 'Match of the Day' and 'The Big Match' on television, it was difficult to avoid some exposure to football. Historians, on occasion, dedicated books to their favourite teams, though they may have blushed when one particular Prime Minister in the 1960s discussed all the problems of the world with the aid of footballing metaphors. Anxiety grew that entire Cabinets might need to be 'kitted out' in the increasingly exotic and expensive equipment now needed in order to kick a ball.

Rugby Union still resisted any suggestion that players should become professionals, but it was not immune from the pressures of finance and commerce. The home international matches were televised 'live' and rugby's star players became more widely known than ever before in the history of the game. Its popularity increased, particularly in State schools, and the distinction between players of rugby and players of football became less of a social one. From time to time the rules were modified, with the result that play became more 'open' and attractive. The home competition continued as before. After a brief period of English ascendancy in the late 1950s, Wales dominated throughout the 1960s and 1970s, combining the individual brilliance of players like Edwards, John and Bennett with a fine team spirit. Wales was the first home country to appoint a national coach and to inaugurate regular squad training. The 1969–70 tour by the South African side took place in an atmosphere of political controversy and demonstrations which were without precedent. The game's administrators found themselves increasingly caught up in political discussions. There were also visits to Britain by Japanese, Romanian, Fijian and Argentinian sides – an indication that the game's popularity was spreading outside its Commonwealth heartland. Perhaps unfortunately, increased competition bred increased competition. In 1972, the English Rugby Union established a club knock-out cup and a similar scheme followed in Scotland. The demands on the time of the players increased to such a point that they were scarcely compatible with normal employment. Some leading players retired early because of these pressures. They also disliked the physical violence which became more noticeable in the 1970s. If rugby had once been a rough game played by gentlemen, it showed signs of becoming a rough game played by hooligans.

Compared with the first post-war decade, Rugby League was not in a flourishing condition, though it did offer copy for novelists. It remained confined to northern England. Fewer Rugby Union players were enticed into the game because, in changing economic circumstances, it could not offer very attractive financial rewards. For the same reason, Australian players tended to stay at home, and the balance of talent swung to the southern hemisphere. It was argued that new defensive tactics reduced the game's excitement. The aggregate attendance at Rugby League games in the 1972–73 season was about a third of what it had been in 1952–53. Television provided a much-needed source of financial support, but southern viewers never stirred from their seats to give the game a more certain future.

By the mid-1950s, it was becoming apparent that the intense interest in cricket, which had characterized the post-war decade, was fading. The county sides were experiencing financial difficulties and relied on their share of Test match receipts for viability. In the 1960s, however, a number of steps were taken to change the image and organization of the game. In 1963, the long-standing distinction between amateurs and professionals was abolished. Five years later, when counties were allowed to engage an overseas player on immediate registration, some of the best-known cricketers in the world arrived – perhaps the most dazzling being Garfield Sobers who played for Nottinghamshire. Such talent revived public interest, though there were some who feared that the move would ultimately injure the progress of young English players. Experiments were made with limited-over cricket and the Gillette Cup, inaugurated in 1963, proved so successful that it was followed by others – with different sponsors. Excitement and the prospect of a result brought back the crowds, on Sundays at least. A reduced programme of county matches continued – for the smaller number of people who thought that they embodied the real cricket. Yorkshire won the championship seven times in the decade leading up to 1968 – a triumph for a side which insisted on relying on its own natives. Interest in Test matches remained high, though not on the former scale. Australia held the Ashes after 1958–59 until 1970–71 when Illingworth's side regained them. The encounter with Australia remained the 'needle' series, but tours by the West Indies, India and Pakistan were increasingly frequent features of the English summer. In the 1970s, however, financial pressures became more serious and at the end of the decade an Australian entrepreneur seemed likely to make dramatic changes in both the organization and style of the game.

The battle over professionalism raged in lawn tennis in the 1960s, though it had been apparent before then that it would have to be faced. The vast, worldwide expansion of the game had removed it from the time when it had been almost an incidental background to strawberries and cream on a middle-class English lawn. The British LTA was prepared to move faster to reach a settlement with the promoters of professional tennis than was the world body. It announced the abandonment of all distinctions between amateurs and professionals in late 1967. The first 'Open' Wimbledon took place in 1969 – with Ann Haydon (Jones) winning the women's title. The major competitions were dominated by the Australians and Americans, though British players like Roger Taylor, Mike Sangster and Virginia Wade occasionally broke the monopoly of success. British women did better in the Wightman Cup matches against the United States than they did between 1931 and 1958 when they failed to win at all. The Davis cup was so dominated by the United States and Australia that other countries pressed for a 'zoning' arrangement which would open up the competition. Britain performed respectably after it was introduced in 1972.

The Olympic Games, though not untroubled by political and economic problems, did continue to expand in size and range. There were no gold medals for Britain either in 1956 or 1960, but in 1964, in Tokyo, Lynn Davies won the men's and Mary Rand the women's long jump. In 1968, David Hemery won the 400 metres hurdles and in 1972 Mary Peters won the women's pentathlon. Such individual achievements (and there were others) were backed up by solid performances in many track and field events in European and Commonwealth Games. That was also true of swimming and diving. On the whole, however, the British public had given up expecting a substantial British presence among the medals at the major athletic encounters. It was argued that failure to identify talent at a sufficiently early age, and inadequate training facilities, explained such results. While this may be so, remedial steps raised questions about the purpose of sport and its place in society to which there was no unanimous answer.

In the late 1950s, direct central government grants for sport came to under £500,000, the largest single amount being directed through the Central Council for Physical Recreation. In the early 1960s, there were spasmodic appeals for greater public funding, but Baroness Burton of Coventry found she was sprinting ahead of the field. Just before the 1964 Election, however, the Shadow Chancellor of the Exchequer declared that Labour would set up a Sports Council with a much bigger budget. It came into existence in 1965, with an advisory function chaired by the 'Minister for Sport' – the first occupant being Dennis Howell, a former football referee. The Conservatives decided in 1972 to establish an independent council on the model of the Arts Council, the first chairman being Roger Bannister, the former runner. It now had the power to make its own grants (working through regional councils) for the improvement of sporting facilities. 'Sport for all' was its objective, but there remained many millions who resisted the plan. They preferred to rest their feet watching ice-skating or show-jumping on television to taking up jogging or playing squash. The 'stars' in all spectator sports were reaching rewards in status and income which they had never before achieved. Public interest in sport was also, in one sense, at a high level, but in recreational terms, participation in the major games was declining and was not altogether being replaced.

The notion of 'Sport for all' received powerful support from medical circles. 'Health for all' was another laudable objective. The Health Education Council was set up in 1968, receiving most of its funds from the Department of Health and Social Security. Fresh importance was attached to preventive medicine, particularly as further reports stressed the damage to health caused by smoking. Government took limited steps to restrict cigarette advertising and to draw attention to the dangers involved in smoking cigarettes. Cumulatively these warnings had some effect, though mostly on those social groups whose health was better anyway. Likewise, there was increasing concern about excessive consumption of alcohol, often previously thought of as an aspect of poverty but now frequently considered an aspect of affluence. Doctors were now more worried by the obesity than the emaciated character of their patients. Emphasis on exercise received further stimulus as the cost of treatment in the NHS mounted. At the time of its inception in 1948 there was a 'pool of untreated ill-health' which could be dealt with within the existing medical technology. It seemed reasonable to suppose that there would, in time, be a steadily reducing need for treatment. However, the medical art did not remain in the state at which it existed in 1948. Since the middle 1950s there have been major strides in pharmacology, biochemistry, medicine and surgery – brain surgery, transplants, artificial hips, 'antidepressant' drugs, to name but a few developments. Bevan had declared in 1948 that the new service, for rich and poor alike, would be available solely in accordance with 'medical need'. Thirty years on, however, the Office of Health Economics was concluding that shortages were inherent in any system of medical care which was more or less 'free at the point of access' and which at the same time permitted unlimited scientific innovation and improvement in the quality and scope of care. 'Rationing' – other than by price outside the NHS (a subject of political controversy between Labour and the Conservatives) – had great dangers. Its administration would also be very difficult. So, it might be necessary to help the public believe that 'good health' was primarily their responsibility and they should not expect too much from high-technology medicine.[1] Hence the Health Education Council's campaign to 'Look After Yourself'.[2] If the message was a little muffled by the time it reached the pubs and terraces, education and sport might yet produce a healthy society.

———————————————

1. Office of Health Economics, *Scarce resources in health care* (1979), p. 17
2. I. Sutherland, ed., *Health education* (1979)

CHAPTER 36

Cultures, creeds and values

The culture of contemporary Britain proved difficult to discern and define, despite the devoted efforts of sociologists and literary men, some of whom were established in 'centres' for just such a purpose. In the opaque conclusion to his *Culture and Society, 1780–1950* (1958) Raymond Williams saw as the fundamental difficulty 'the compatibility of increasing specialization with a genuinely common culture'.[1] It was apparently only soluble 'in a context of material community and by the full democratic process'. Hoggart in *The Uses of Literacy* (1957) looked at 'the assumptions, attitudes and morals of working-class people in northern England' and the way in which they might be influenced by magazines, films and other mass media. The great majority of people, he concluded, were merging into one class – 'we are becoming culturally classless'. He feared, for example, that the world of club singing was being replaced by that of 'typical radio dance-music and crooning, television cabaret and commercial-radio variety'. A 'faceless' culture was emerging and it was 'to be regretted'.[2]

Culture in its more restricted sense was also in a puzzling condition. There were those who hoped that the proliferating universities and polytechnics could integrate the bewildering range of knowledge and artistic achievement. Needless to say, a *Crisis in the Humanities* (1964) was again detected. Philosophers, theologians, historians, sociologists, economists and classical scholars brooded more on the limitations than on the strengths of their disciplines. They regretted specialization, but were not very forthcoming about the alternatives to it. A new vice-chancellor at a new university talked of the need to create 'a solid basis of general culture', but had to confess that 'however imaginatively a university may try to supplement the education of victims of specialization, its efforts can only be palliatives. As cures they are about as effective as parking an ambulance at the foot of a cliff.'[3] If such pessimism accompanied the beginning of university expansion, nothing that happened over the next decade invalidated his judgement. Elaborate changes of nomenclature in the organization of study did not really produce changes in intellectual attitudes. Some educational casualties, however, appeared to be permanent. A knowledge of a classical language could no longer be assumed to be part of the equipment of the student of literature or history. Sociology, on the other hand, underwent a period of rapid expansion since, to many students, it appeared to possess the key to an understanding of the world they lived in. Its popularity subsequently waned when it revealed less than had been supposed. In the late 1960s, sociology students in particular wanted to change the world, but when that later appeared either not desirable or not possible the discipline lost its zest.

Despite difficulties in the 'management of knowledge' the British intelligentsia, its ranks swollen, was generally optimistic. In the 1960s, American contacts and influences were strong. This interchange was not unconnected with the power of the purse – there was periodic alarm about a 'brain-drain' across the Atlantic. When it came to 'changing places' (David Lodge's novel of that title recounts such an experience) it was normally to an American place. This North Atlantic connection to some extent replaced the weight of European influence caused by the influx of pre-war and wartime European refugee scholars. Only in the 1970s did academic exchange with other European countries begin to mount, again partly for political and economic reasons. During this period, the assumption, peculiar to England and Wales (though not to Scotland) that a three-year honours degree (perhaps 'topped off' by an MA 'course') offered the ideal university education, survived unscathed, but added another awkward dimension to the EEC.

In 1959, C. P. Snow, novelist and scientist, and a man who had at least walked the corridors of power, delivered lectures at Cambridge on *The Two Cultures*. His theme was the division in British society and culture between the scientist and non-scientist. It was the most serious intellectual divide of the age. He held that scientific culture was a whole because, although a physicist and biologist might not understand each other's work in detail there were common attitudes, standards and patterns, approaches and assumptions which united them. Snow contended that some, perhaps the majority, of the cleverest people in the modern world had no more understanding of modern physics than their neolithic ancestors. The thesis was not new and might be criticized in detail, but its description of the cultural divide was substantially accurate. The poverty of the treatment of British science in this volume is further testimony to its validity. But in this field British achievement in almost all areas was outstanding. Nobel prizes came to this country with considerable regularity, particularly for chemistry. Laureates between 1955 and 1975 included Sir Cyril Hinshelwood, Lord Todd, Dorothy Hodgkin, Sir Peter Medawar and Sir Alan Hodgkin. Perhaps the discovery which attracted most attention outside the world of science was the unravelling of the structure of the DNA molecule by Crick and Watson for which they received the Nobel award for physiology and medicine in 1962. How deeply the significance of their work penetrated the popular consciousness can only be guessed. It was often remarked, however, that British achievement lay mainly in 'pure' science and other countries made the running in its application.

CREEDS AND CHURCHES

If a common culture proved elusive, a common creed proved even more difficult to discern. It became a commonplace to describe the United Kingdom as a 'post-Christian' society, though it was less clear when the transition was made and what precisely it signified. Certainly, it was now *The Idea of a Secular Society* that critics began to explore. Sociologists, historians and theologians debated the term 'secularization' with great zeal and far from complete unanimity. Did it mean a society in which most people had either ceased to believe in God, could not decide whether He existed, or did not think the question important? It was not very clear how satisfactory answers to these queries could be found. Opinion polls did show that God appeared to be losing ground – a notion dear to the heart of some radical theologians who argued that Christianity could only survive if belief in God was jettisoned(229,234). Investigations of popular knowledge of the Bible and the main Christian doctrines showed that religious education in schools had made little impact.

A brief moment of confidence among Christians about church attendance in the mid 1950s disappeared. Decline, both in attendance and membership, became the pattern. But it was also pointed out that increased mobility and the advent of television adversely affected all communal social activities. A Christian context for the rites of passage – birth, marriage and death – still seemed in substantial demand. Some Christian commentators drew no comfort from what they termed vestigial 'folk religion' of this kind. They welcomed the 'secularization' of society, for it meant that the churches could again become the leaven in the lump and cease to be identified as the lump itself. They became impatient with the institutional constraints of organized religion and disparaged the 'plant' which the churches had inherited and now had to maintain so expensively in an age of inflation. Such priests and laymen hoped that Liverpool and Coventry cathedrals would be the last such buildings erected by the Church of England.

Others did not despair of the churches but believed that Christianity could only prosper if they came together in unity. Despite much prayer and conference the visible progress was slight. The two established churches – the Church of England and the Church of Scotland engaged in conversations, but in 1957 the Kirk declined to take bishops into its system in the manner proposed. The *Scottish Daily Express*, not often renowned for its theological insight, detected another English takeover. Conversations between the Church of England and the Methodists in the mid-1960s produced a two-stage scheme for unity which was acceptable to most Methodists, but failed to gain a sufficient majority in the Convocations of the Church of England in 1969 and in its Synod in 1972. This rejection was a great disappointment to the then archbishop of Canterbury, Michael Ramsey. A plea that there should be unity among the non-Roman Catholic churches made at an influential conference at Nottingham in 1964 (with a target of 1980) fell well short of fulfilment. The only merger that was achieved was between Congregational churches and the Presbyterian Church of England in 1972 to form the United Reformed Church.

Despite these disappointments for those who believed strongly in 'ecumenism' the individual relationships between different ecclesiastical families were frequently transformed. After the Second Vatican Council in 1966 the Catholic Church in the United Kingdom for the first time allowed itself to be drawn into these encounters, though it still stopped short of membership of the British Council of Churches. When a Roman Catholic archbishop addressed the General Assembly of the Church of Scotland for the first time in 1975 he was warmly greeted – and other comparable encounters could be mentioned. But it was also clear that there were serious differences of opinion, outlook and practice within as much as between the major churches. Anglicans, notwithstanding the increased evidence of 'democracy' both at parochial level and nationally – with the establishment of a rather elaborate system of Synodical government in 1969 – were still divided in their attitude to the State. More immediately, the Church of England, through its Liturgical Commission from 1965 onwards, began a major revision of Anglican worship which was to culminate in a new Prayer Book in 1980. The linguistic changes angered a good many distinguished non-believers. Some believers were not very happy either. The same tension also affected Roman Catholics with the post-conciliar introduction of the vernacular. Questions concerning authority, structure and discipline were more publicly discussed within that Church than ever before. It was not a development which the existing episcopate found easy to handle. Conservative elements in the churches, whether 'Evangelical' or 'Latin Mass', found many of these developments in belief and practice unacceptable and welcomed the return of Billy Graham on another campaign or the papal opposition to birth control in the encyclical *Humanae Vitae* (1967)(234).

By the mid-1970s it became increasingly clear that unity, if it could be achieved, could not mean uniformity, either of church structure or of detailed articles of belief. It was already obvious that denominational and theological divisions did not invariably correspond. What was uncertain was how far plurality of belief could be reconciled institutionally. It was an issue which, for a time, centred around the best-selling book by an Anglican scholar and bishop, J. A. T. Robinson, *Honest to God* (1963). Ideas which had been debated for decades in a German context were brought before an English audience which appeared to find them novel. It was another example of the time-lag in the transmission of ideas from mainland Europe – a delay which affected the Roman Catholic Church to no lesser degree.

In part, at least, the churches were suffering from what sociologists called the privatization of values which was taking place in society at large. Any restrictions on individual behaviour, especially in the sexual sphere, imposed either by status or convention was now felt to require justification. Doing what comes naturally seemed much the best thing to do. If it seemed natural to different people to do different things, so be it. On the whole, in their professional capacity, philosophers did not feel obliged to offer any general guidance in the realm of morals; that was not their business any more. Linguistic analysis was at its height and Oxford philosophy was held by Oxford men to be the centre of the philosophical world – though the new pilgrims came from the United States and not from Europe. Concern for traditional metaphysical and ethical questions might perhaps survive in Scotland, but from such a location it posed no threat to the swinging sixties.

Christianity, therefore, was the active religion of a minority and, as such, was full of confused life rather than moribund. However, in this period, the growth of immigrant communities meant that it was no longer the only world religion with a significant body of adherents in Britain. Mosques and temples sprang up in places where their existence would have seemed inconceivable even twenty years earlier. Although there was a rather fashionable youthful interest in what purported to be the spirituality of the East and some more fundamental attempts at a 'dialogue', most Moslems and Hindus were drawn from the immigrant communities. It also remained to be seen how loyal they would remain to their religious inheritance with the passage of time. This new religious pluralism led some (and some Christians most vocally) to criticize the continuing official recognition of the intertwining of Christianity and British national identity. It was indeed impossible to state with any confidence what the creed of the British' might be.

MUSIC

Music in Britain flourished as never before and there were some who correlated its rise with the decline of organized religion. London became the musical 'capital' of the Western world. Its orchestras maintained the highest standards and a wide repertoire. Under the auspices of the BBC, the Proms provided a feast of music-making with performances of medieval and contemporary works alongside standard classical favourites. Opera and concert-going steadily increased. Music in schools was one of the few areas of education where the improvement was unambiguous. It became fashionable again to play an instrument – and by no means just the piano. Many counties had their school orchestras from which some of the most talented graduated to the National Youth Orchestra. Young musicians could assess their skills at innumerable competitions, some of which were sponsored by the broadcasting authorities. Television took over from radio in giving encouragement to symphony orchestras, pop groups, opera and ballet. New musical festivals spread rapidly and older ones consolidated their positions. The Three Choirs Festival maintained the choral tradition; the Bath Festival owed much to the inspiration of Yehudi Menuhin; the Llandaff and St Asaph Festivals enriched the musical life of South and North Wales; Edinburgh reigned supreme in Scotland; the Aldeburgh festival retained the strong impress of Britten's work. These musical occasions, particularly in Scotland and Wales, gave opportunities for local composers to get their work performed, but they also brought some of the best orchestras, string quartets and soloists to the regions. Distinguished playing of their baroque organs by a visiting British Prime Minister finally convinced the Germans that Britain was no longer a land without music.

More British composers were at work than ever before. University music departments encouraged close contacts between composers, performers and musicologists. Even so, regular performances of belligerently *avant-garde* works were difficult to achieve. The death of Vaughan Williams in 1958, though he had been musically active to the end, virtually brought to a close the 'English national school'. His works were still performed after his death, though the same could not be said of some of his disciples. Walton's works remained popular, though there were few additions to their number. Britten, by contrast, was prolific over a wide range, showing a particular sensitivity to the voices of children. The work

335

which immediately made the most impact was his *War Requiem* (1962) and his last opera was *Death in Venice* (1973). At the time of his death in 1976 no English composer had a higher international reputation. Tippett remained the most idiosyncratic of established composers, insisting on providing the libretti for his operas *The Knot Garden* (1970) and *King Priam* (1962). English and Welsh singers proved themselves well able to meet the demands of composers. The Welsh National Opera and Scottish Opera gained a reputation beyond the British Isles. Among the younger generation of composers fame and fortune have fluctuated. By the 1960s, the influences of Vienna, often mediated through European composers who had found their way to Britain in the 1930s, had a great appeal. As a result, it is impossible to speak of an 'English school'. Malcolm Williamson, Richard Rodney Bennett and Malcolm Arnold wrote excellent music which also had a wide appeal, but it was not easy to occupy this musical middle ground(241).

In the popular music world American influences remained paramount in the late 1950s. Crosby and Sinatra revived their appeal and were joined by Johnnie Ray, Connie Francis and Johnny Mathis, among others. Their records sold widely and it was American songs which were frequently sung by their British imitators. The Dave Brubeck quartet of 'modern jazz' gained a following in Britain. The teenage rock revolution set off by Bill Haley and the Comets in 1955 quickly spread across the Atlantic. Elvis Presley also received adoration. Rock and roll, country and western, folk rock – all seemed assimilable. Add to this musicals like *My Fair Lady* (1956) and *West Side Story* (1957) and American domination seemed complete. The Beatles changed this picture. The 1960s belonged to them. '*She Loves You*', released in 1963 by the established quartet of Lennon, McCartney, Harrison and Starr had an advance sale of half a million copies. 'Yeah', 'Yeah' (said in swift succession) became their hallmark. They topped the bill at the Palladium and appeared before the Queen Mother. 'Beatlemania' greatly interested press and television and, of course, the sociologists. In 1963 2½ million Beatle records were sold – a record in British pop music. The Beatles reached the United States in person in February 1964, with equally dramatic success. '*Can't Buy me Love*' (1964) had an advance sale of 3 million. *A Hard Day's Night* showed that their talents could be transferred to the screen. *Sergeant Pepper's Lonely Hearts Club Band* was an ambitious and successful song-cycle. By the late 1960s, however, the Beatles began to go their separate ways and the partnership was formally dissolved in January 1975. The group had carried British pop music to heights, both commercial and artistic, never before achieved(246).

The record industry boomed. The LP disc had arrived in 1950 and soon carried all before it, necessitating wholesale rerecording – a pattern repeated on a smaller scale after 1958–59 with the advent of the stereo process. Production of LP and EP records in the United Kingdom soared from nearly 27 million in 1957 to over 100 million in 1964 and continued to rise. But cassettes loomed on the horizon.

Where the Beatles led, others were not far behind. The Rolling Stones, cultivating a barbaric image which seemed to become reality, first toured the United

States in 1964 and were back again in the two following years. Millions came to see Mick Jagger stick out his tongue in the middle of a song. Controversy – whether about drugs, sex or violence – attended them every day of their lives. Herman's Hermits, in comparison, seemed harmless and their 'bubble gum rock' sold millions of records too. The Dave Clark Five aimed higher, and usually succeeded. The Who had to wait until 1967 before their exhibitionist wrecking act – smashing of guitar and kicking of drum – entranced the faithful at the Monterey Pop Festival. Led Zeppelin were the last group in the 1960s to capture the United States for British music – poignantly describing their art as the folk music of the technological culture. It required a huge amplifying system, not to mention laser beams and smoke machines. The first rock star of the 1970s was Elton John, a specialist in 'gear' rather than technology. He was even invited to tour the Soviet Union. Tommy Steele, Cliff Richard and Frankie Vaughan were other stars who contrived a singular longevity at the top because they could adapt and diversify.

This eruption of British popular music upon the world came as a surprise – not least to many of those involved. It was a British success at a time when success was elusive. Musical, commercial and political authorities did not quite know where they were. The Beatles were – briefly – MBEs and received scholarly attention from music critics. But, despite this interaction, on the whole, the musical worlds of Britain remained far apart and even André Previn, American, composer, performer and conductor of the London Symphony Orchestra looked as though he had acquired a good deal of moss when set beside the Rolling Stones.

PAINTING

By the mid-1950s, with the easing of travel restrictions and an increasing volume of exhibitions, the world of British painting and sculpture again became open to international influences. The attraction of living and working on mainland Europe again asserted itself but with the 1956 exhibition at the Tate Gallery of 'Modern Art in the United States' a new generation of painters tackled America much as its predecessor had tackled Europe. 'Pop art' emerged, described by Hamilton in 1957 as popular (designed for mass audience), transient (short-term solution), expendable (easily forgotten) as well as being witty, sexy, glamorous, big business and much else besides. The world of the comic strip and advertising was never far away and artefacts became an obsession. The *Elvis Presley Wall* (1962) by Peter Blake 'put it all together'(242).

The 'Kitchen Sink' school, purporting to bring a new stress on social realism, was also active in the late 1950s – John Bratby being its most celebrated exponent. But the painting 'star' of the 1960s was David Hockney. Despite his youth (b. 1937), few critics doubted that he was a very considerable painter and his etching was superb. Quite apart from his technical brilliance, he had a refreshing indifference to the fashionable and questioned whether art in fact 'progressed'. He wrote in 1970 that he had stopped bothering about modern art(239). Such openness struck an answering chord in the interested but uncommitted public which was impatient with the dogma of competing artistic schools. There was still room for the differing approaches of a John Piper, a Francis Bacon or a Graham Sutherland. Critics were generally impressed by the number and variety of serious painters at work and argued that British painting had regained much lost ground. There was a refreshing self-confidence in the spheres of drawing and design. The world of painting seemed briefly to share the exuberance of the world of fashion, of Mary Quant, of the mini-skirt and of Carnaby Street. Painters were more often ex-directory rather than starving in garrets. Although American influences were strong, certainly stronger than European, it could not be said to stifle native talent or indeed to destroy a pronounced British cultural chauvinism in the sphere of art.

FILMS

A number of British films in the mid-1950s showed that the industry could still make excellent films despite gloom about its financial future. There were three forms – classic, comic and the war, epitomized by *Richard III* (1955), *Genevieve* (1955) and *The Dam Busters* (1955) or *The Bridge on the River Kwai* (1957). However, at this juncture a 'new wave' appeared, though at a time when the constant closure of cinemas suggested the impending death of the industry. Films gained, in the eyes of critics, immeasurably in status if not in popularity; that is to say they became another minority culture. The National Film Theatre had been established on the South Bank in London in 1952, and a decade or so later a rather precarious regional network of film theatres was supported by universities and local authorities. Film-making reflected the social criticism and commentary apparent also in novels and the theatre in the age of the 'angry young men'. Quite independently, the products of the revived film industry in Europe reached Britain – from Poland, France, Sweden and Italy in particular. 'Commitment' became virtually compulsory and it became difficult to escape 'real life' on the screen. The north of England, where everyone was blunt, brash and brutal, starred in films directed by Tony Richardson and Lindsay Anderson in the early 1960s. John Schlesinger, having made his obligatory début with a trip to the North in *A Kind of Loving* (1962) moved on to *Far from the Madding Crowd* (1967) and *Midnight Cowboy* (1969). Joseph Losey, an expatriate American, directed several films which showed a rather different attitude to war from that which had predominated in the post-war decade, but his version of *The Go-Between* (1971) showed his capacity to handle very 'English' situations. Bryan Forbes moved between social commentary in *The L-Shaped Room* (1962) to rather nostalgic relief of *The Railway Children* (1971). Such names and titles can only give a limited indication of the range of British film-making. Despite the fears of the mid-1950s, the British industry experienced a revival, with its best products receiving international acclaim. The 'committed' tone of many productions certainly contrasted with the Ealing comedies, and its impression of life in the United Kingdom was as partial in its own way as they were(243).

LITERATURE AND THE MEDIA

There was a wide range of literary talent in the United Kingdom, but little agreement about the nature of the novel and the function of the novelist. What was a 'well-made' novel? If it existed, could it be quickly destroyed? The novel of traditional realism, it was commonly argued, was 'outmoded and unavailable for truly serious expression', but it struggled on bravely. The English tradition kept getting in the way of those, like Christine Brooke-Rose and John Berger, who looked for style and idiom to current writing in French. The latter's Marxism and philosophical preoccupations placed him in a 'Continental' category where, besides David Caute, there were not many fellow-travellers. One feature of many of the writers of the late 1950s was their resolute insularity. The problem with Portugal, one of Amis's characters explained, was that it was located abroad and the people were foreigners, 'so we can't understand each other or get to know each other as chaps from the same nation can.'[4]

Other writers did not like it here quite so much. The 'angry young men', as the press described them, saw pain, poverty and squalor amidst the affluence of a decaying imperial society. Tory, post-Suez Britain seemed a long way away from the hopes of 1945. Braine's *Room at the Top* (1957). Sillitoe's *Saturday Night and Sunday Morning* (1958), Waterhouse's *Billy Liar* (1957) and Storey's *This Sporting Life* (1960) – which were all filmed – inhabited a different world from the Sitwells and Ivy Compton-Burnett. The new tone was most apparent in the theatre with the opening of the Royal Court in London in 1956. Its third production, Osborne's *Look Back in Anger* caught the contemporary mood and *The Entertainer* was equally successful. Wesker wrote a rash of plays such as *Chips with Everything* (1962) which audiences at the time seemed to find stimulating. Pinter's *The Caretaker* (1960) showed a more discriminating and less timebound talent. Tynan, critic and man of the moment, was not alone in believing that a new theatrical era had dawned. The Theatre of the Absurd mingled with the Theatre of Commitment. Happenings were happening. Continental influences were flooding in – Ionesco, Beckett, Brecht and Genet. In the hands of a Peter Brook plays were transmogrified beyond the dreams of the humble writers. In 1968, the Lord Chamberlain ceased to function as a dramatic censor – *Hair* was one of the first things to be let down(244).

Some of these writers have come and gone; some have altered their style and changed their themes; some have certainly adopted different political views. The 'angries' were neither as ubiquitous nor as united as it was tempting to believe at the time. Greene continued to write throughout the period and arguably remained the master of them all. Wilson, who turned late to writing, showed himself a masterful explorer of Anglo-Saxon attitudes. Golding had a rather different set of preoccupations. Also 'eccentric' in their concerns were Durrell and Lowry. Murdoch and Spark wrote a dazzlingly prolific stream of novels from the mid-1950s onwards. There were, later, the historical fictions of J. G. Farrell or Paul Scott, or the works of Fowles, Drabble, Lessing, Burgess or Le Carré. Such a list is still not exhaustive, but enough have been mentioned to make it clear that they cannot be fitted into a single category or made to belong to a single tradition. The same point, *mutatis mutandis*, can be made about poetry and drama. To be summoned by Betjeman, Larkin, Hughes, Porter or Mitchell is to be presented with a varied feast. Poetry in Wales, in both languages, has continued to flourish, with R. S. Thomas attracting most attention outside the Principality. A remarkable group of poets emerged in Northern Ireland, notably Heaney. And there are English poets, like Gunn and Davie at work in the United States – a reminder, too, of the importance of American influences on British writers, 'By and large' one critic elegantly puts it, 'Europe has been a dead loss.'[5] It is noteworthy, however, that Fowles, Spark, Lessing and Burgess (as Bradbury comments) have their main audiences outside Britain (and in some cases their homes too) and 'only slowly have their reputations been seriously accepted here, and this often by a grudging process'.[6]

Most people did not read even the best-known of these names. Historical romances and detective stories remained the staple popular literary form, but many millions never read any books at all – and indeed it became apparent that hundreds of thousands had survived compulsory schooling and could scarcely read at all. The basic purveyor of popular culture was the popular press where competition and costs were fierce. In the 1960s the *Daily Mirror* led with a circulation of just under 5 million on average, followed by the *Daily Express* with around 4 million and the *Daily Mail* around 2 million. Rupert Murdoch's *Sun* launched in 1969 – he had purchased the *News of the World* earlier in the year – rapidly reached a circulation of 3 million and put pressure on its rivals. The drift towards a tabloid format seemed inexorable and pin-up girls parted company with their bikinis. The casualties were in the middle ground. The *News Chronicle* could not survive with a circulation of just over a million and came to an end in 1960. The TUC gave up political control of the *Daily Herald* in 1960 and it staggered on until 1964 when it turned, unsuccessfully, into the pre-Murdoch *Sun*. The 'quality' press – the *Daily Telegraph, Guardian* and *The Times* – all increased their circulations in the squeeze of the 1960s but had financial problems. The Thomson Organization acquired 85 per cent of *The Times* in 1966 and set up Times Newspapers Ltd to publish both *The Times* and *The Sunday Times*. Colour supplements both fuelled and depended upon consumer spending and in themselves created a new 'week-end culture'. The *Sunday Telegraph* appeared in 1961 designed, in the words of its editor, to fill the gap between the popular and quality press. The *Sunday Citizen* closed its doors in 1967. There would be more casualties in the future(245).

Disciples of the Canadian theorist Marshall McLuhan believed that television viewing, by altering people's sensory equipment, would erode, if not eliminate, the printed word. Certainly, television was thought to have reached virtually every home by the mid-1970s, though its impact on the press had not proved as great as some had supposed. The major development in 1954 was the decision to set up the Independent Television (later Broadcasting) Authority which enfranchised companies to produce television programmes on a regional basis and kept an eye on 'standards'. In subsequent years some of the companies lost their franchise. Their dependence on advertising caused some to believe that trivialization could only result. Others were pleased that the BBC would not retain a monopoly. Fears that competition would force the BBC to lower the quality of its programmes were in part allayed by Parliament's decision in 1964 to award it another channel. From the beginning of 1968 colour was available on all channels and within a decade black and white came to seem old-fashioned. A series of programmes on '*Civilisation*' by Kenneth Clark in 1969 reached a far wider audience than would a consideration of this theme by any other means – the book of the series became an increasingly familiar publishing enterprise. On the other hand, there were those who feared the impact of television, particularly upon the reading habits of the young. It possibly encouraged violence by its ready portrayal of it on the screen; it simplified and distorted; its domestic convenience undermined the viability and vitality of valuable local societies. The weekly programme of the early 1960s, '*That Was the Week that Was*' set new standards of 'outrageous' comment. Public men thought that David Frost and his friends were going rather far, but could the 12 million people who watched it be wrong? Perhaps, after all, this 'savage satire' showed the resilience and openness of Britain.[7]

Through this era of television expansion with all the cultural, social and political problems it posed, radio struggled on with a reduced but contented audience. A series of sweeping changes took place in its structure and organization in an attempt to accommodate both different cultural levels and regional opinion. Devolution succeeded where it failed elsewhere, though programme content sometimes raised eyebrows for those who remembered those of Lord Reith. The first group of BBC local radio stations were launched in 1969 and independent local radio began in London, Manchester, Birmingham and Glasgow in 1973–74. Radio now brought the listener not only that 'metropolitan culture' on which Lord Reith had set such store but also news of local rain clouds, traffic jams, strikes, power failures and what is on at the zoo. The culture of contemporary Britain had become comprehensive.

---

1. R. Williams, *Culture and society*, (1961), Pelican, edn., p. 319
2. R. Hoggart, *The uses of literacy* (1958) Pelican cdn., pp. 284–5
3. Cited in J. H. Plumb ed., *Crisis in the humanities* (1964), p. 164
4. K. Amis, *I like it here*, discussed in J. Gindin, *Postwar British fiction* (1962), p. 48
5. P. Swinden in C. B. Cox and A. E. Dyson, *The twentieth-century mind*, III (1972), p. 403
6. M. Bradbury and D. Palmer eds., *The contemporary English novel* (1979), p. 15
7. A. Briggs, *Governing the BBC* (1979), pp. 217–21

PART FIVE

1976–1992

FRAMEWORK OF EVENTS 1976–1992

1976   Wilson announces resignation as PM (March): Callaghan elected leader of the Labour Party and PM (April): Thorpe resigns as Liberal leader over the 'Scott' affair (May): Steel elected new Liberal leader (July): IMF crisis (Sept–Dec): Inflation at 17 per cent (Dec).

1977   Roy Jenkins leaves government to become President of the EEC Commission: 'Lib-Lab Pact' sustains government in office (March): Silver Jubilee of Queen Elizabeth II (June).

1978   'Lib-Lab Pact' ends but Callaghan announces that there will be no autumn election (Sept): 'Winter of Discontent' begins (Dec): Labour Party conference rejects proposed 5 per cent wage rise limit (Oct): Commons rejects sanctions against employers breaching the 5 per cent pay policy.

1979   Establishment of the European Monetary System (Jan): Devolution referenda in Scotland and Wales fail (March): Gvt defeated on 'no confidence' vote (March): General Election – Conservative victory (May): First direct elections to the European Parliament (June): Thatcher proposes cuts in Britain's EEC contributions (Nov): Dublin EEC summit ends in deadlock (Dec).

1980   Steel strike begins (Jan) – called off (April): Riots in St Paul's area of Bristol (April): Inflation at 21.8 per cent (April): Labour Party conference requires re-selection of MPs (Sept): Callaghan retires as Labour leader and is replaced, after a contest with Healey, by Foot (Oct): Unemployment passes two million mark (Oct).

1981   Labour Party special conference establishes electoral college and 'Gang of Four' leave the party (Jan): First Cabinet changes (Jan): Social Democratic Party launched (March): Bobby Sands begins hunger strike (Mar) and dies (May): Brixton Riots (April): Livingstone becomes GLC chairman (May): Toxteth Riots (July): Second Cabinet reshuffle (Sept): Shirley Williams (SDP) wins Crosby by-election (Nov): Arthur Scargill elected President of the National Union of Mineworkers (Dec).

1982   Roy Jenkins (SDP) wins Hillhead (Glasgow) by-election (Mar): Argentinian invasion of the Falkland Islands and Carrington resigns as Foreign Secretary, replaced by Pym (April): Surrender of Port Stanley to British (June): Roy Jenkins leader of the SDP (July): Rail strike fails (July): Majority of miners vote against strike action (Nov).

1983   Franks Committee exonerates gvt over the Falklands invasion (Jan): General Election – Conservative victory (May): Foot and Jenkins resign as party leaders (June): Cabinet reshuffle (June): Inflation (3.7 per cent) hits 15-year low (June): Unemployment falls – first time since 1979: Kinnock elected Labour leader (Oct): Cruise missiles arrive at Greenham Common (Nov).

1984   Trade Unions banned at GCHQ (Jan): Coal strike commences (March): Anglo-Chinese Accord on future of Hong Kong (Aug): Cabinet reshuffle (Sept): IRA bombs Conservatives at Brighton (Oct): British Telecom privatized (Nov).

1985   Ponting acquitted of breaching Official Secrets Act (Feb): Coal strike ends (March): Abolition of GLC and metropolitan authorities receives royal assent (July): Handsworth, Brixton, Tottenham Riots (Sept–Oct): Cabinet reshuffle (Sept): Anglo-Irish Agreement signed (Nov).

1986   The 'Westland Affair' leads to resignation of Heseltine and Brittan (Jan–Feb): GLC abolished (April): Liverpool 'Militants' expelled from Labour Party (Oct): Privatization of British Gas (Dec).

1987   British Airways privatized (Feb): Rolls-Royce privatized (May): British Airports privatized (July): General Election – Conservative victory: Cabinet reshuffle (June): Unemployment falls to 2.65 million (Nov), the lowest for five years.

1988   House of Commons votes in favour of six-month experiment to admit television (Feb): Ferry strike by National Union of Seamen (May): Law Lords reject gvt claim for a permanent ban on publication of *Spycatcher* but condemn its author, Wright (Oct): Pan Am Boeing 747 crashes at Lockerbie – worst ever British air disaster (Dec).

1989   Gvt White Paper *Working for Patients* outlines sweeping NHS reforms (Jan): *Satanic Verses* publication causes rupture in British relations with Iran following death threat against author Salman Rushdie (Feb): USSR President Gorbachev visits London (Apr): Hillsborough football disaster (Apr): Major succeeds Howe as Foreign Secretary (who becomes Deputy PM and Leader of the House of Commons) (July): Britain dissents from sanctions against S. Africa proposed at meeting of Commonwealth Heads of Government in Kuala Lumpur (Oct): Thatcher defeats Meyer in first ballot for leadership of the Conservative Party held since 1975 (Dec).

1990   Britain and Argentina resume diplomatic relations (Feb): Anti-poll tax demonstrations and riots in Nottingham, London and elsewhere (Mar): Steel tubes for Iraq detained on Teesside (Apr): Social Democratic Party wound up (June): Britain and Iran resume diplomatic relations (Sept): Howe resigns as Foreign Secretary – Conservative leadership ballot – Major elected on second ballot – Thatcher resigns (Nov): Electricity privatization (Dec).

1991   Operation 'Desert Storm' for liberation of Kuwait begins (Jan): Kuwait re-entered (Feb): Major declares Britain to be 'at the very heart of Europe' in Bonn (Mar): Gvt launches 'Citizen's Charter (July): 'Options for Change' defence review (July): EC and EFTA agree to form European Economic Area (Oct): Collapse of Maxwell publishing empire (Dec): EC agrees Maastricht Treaty (Dec).

1992   Conservatives win General Election (Apr): Fighting begins in Sarajevo (Apr): Queen addresses European Parliament at Strasbourg for first time (May): Smith succeeds Kinnock as Labour leader (July): Britain suspends membership of the ERM (Sept): British troops leave for Bosnia (Oct): Extensive pit closures ordered (Oct): Queen to pay tax (Nov): Russo-British Treaty of Friendship (Nov): Church of England Synod votes to support ordination of women (Nov): Separation of Prince and Princess of Wales (Dec).

CHAPTER 37

Labour decline and the emergence of Thatcher, 1974–1983

The pattern of government in Britain over the previous quarter of a century seemed to confirm that it was essentially a two-party affair(251). Power shifted between competing elites at election time. Ex-ministers had a reasonable chance of returning to office after a modest spell in Opposition. While power did not invariably alternate between the two major parties after each election, a 'swing of the pendulum' was to be expected. It was indeed the case that Labour administrations after 1964 had replaced the Conservative governments that had dominated the 1950s. Then, after 1970, the Conservatives regained power, only to be followed by Labour in 1974. In 1979, however, a period of as yet unbroken Conservative ascendancy began.

The General Elections of February and October 1974, which gave Labour its new lease of office, were often taken at the time to show that in contemporary Britain only a party which had the confidence, or at least the support, of the trade unions could successfully govern. In fact, the votes accorded the two major parties in February – the lowest share for Labour since 1931 and for the Conservatives for some fifty years – indicated considerable public dissatisfaction with both major parties. Labour gained more seats than the Conservatives with 1 per cent less of the vote. The Liberal share of the vote rose by more than 10 per cent, though that only yielded three more seats in the Commons. Nevertheless, for the first time since 1929, a government had to be formed which could not function without support from beyond the governing party. Indeed, Heath only resigned as Prime Minister when it became clear that he could not secure the Liberal support which he needed in order to continue in office. The expectation then became that Wilson would go to the country at the earliest convenient opportunity in the hope that he would obtain a clear working majority and thus resume 'normal business'. The Liberals, disappointed by their poor reward in seats, did not know which way to turn. In September 1974, public opinion polls pointed to a comfortable Labour victory. In the event, however, there was no landslide. Labour had an overall majority of only three seats(256). The incoming administration could not survive by-election defeats or voting indiscipline in its own ranks. It was by no means clear that Labour would avoid either fate since a sense of political, social and economic crisis remained pervasive throughout the country. It is with the political aspects of that feeling that this chapter is concerned(252).

The precarious position of the government was seen by many as further confirmation that Britain was becoming 'ungovernable'. Many voters (and perhaps, even more, the 28 per cent of the electorate which did not vote at all in October) doubted the ability of any government to handle Britain's complex problems effectively. Even the Liberals sounded less optimistic than usual and their share of the vote dropped slightly. Although defeated in February, Heath and the Conservatives had come near to persuading the country that the very authority of government itself was under threat. It was not difficult to argue that Labour in office would be beholden to the power of trade unions and their leaders. Much of the appeal of Liberalism rested in its claim that the time was ripe to forge a new and different national consensus. In October 1974, Heath too talked about the need for a 'government of national unity' – an admission that something more was needed than even the Conservatives could provide(253).

Labour found these assertions spurious. It would be the party which provided the political framework for late-twentieth-century Britain. Its manifesto, *Britain Will Win* (although the title appeared to acknowledge that there was room for doubt), aimed to regain the momentum towards a Socialist Britain which had faded in the late 1940s. There remained, however, some obscurity about how 'victory' would be achieved(254). Between 1970 and 1974, Labour had been in policy turmoil. Capitalizing on opposition to the Industrial Relations Act and the Housing Finance Act, an increasingly powerful combination of groups and individuals steered the party leftwards. Howls of rage against 'the system' were uttered by Tony Benn – formerly known to the public as Anthony Wedgwood Benn. At the 1973 party conference, Denis Healey promised that 'the rich' would be provoked to 'howls of anguish' by the tax changes which Labour would introduce. Socialist intellectuals had nothing less than the complete corporate transformation of British industry in mind. Multinational firms were to be a particular target. The National Enterprise Board would become the major shareholder in banks, insurance, building societies and finance houses. It would have the same role in the construction industry, road haulage and shipbuilding. The Left wanted to go further still but, for the time being at least, Wilson successfully resisted proposals to take 25 major companies directly into public ownership.

In addition, the 'Social Contract', drawn up by a committee from the unions, the Parliamentary Labour Party (PLP) and the National Executive Committee (NEC) offered the prospect of union co-operation on wages in return for government action on prices and the provision of a 'social wage'. This 'Social Contract' might also provide a structure by means of which lasting shifts in the distribution of wealth could be accomplished. These changes of policy reflected the fact that the Left could now normally produce a majority on the NEC. Yet that ascendancy could not be complete unless the PLP came to the same mind. To assist in this process, various 'entryist' groups and individuals put pressure, at constituency level, on MPs they found uncongenial. The Campaign for Labour Party Democracy, launched in the summer of 1973 had three objectives: to place control over the election manifesto in the hands of the NEC alone, to compel MPs to face reselection by their constituency parties each parliamentary session, and to take away from the PLP the exclusive prerogative of electing the party leader.

It was against this background that Wilson again took office. He appeared as confident and as combative as ever. He was widely believed to be a superb tactician. If anyone could steer a survival course for Labour, it was Wilson. From the outset, however, acute division was evident between the advocates of the policies fashioned in Opposition, articulated by Benn and others, and the more pragmatic course charted by the Prime Minister, whether that reflected his own inclination or was dictated by force of circumstances. Certainly, there were alarming developments which appeared to constrain the Cabinet. The effects of the oil price rise were still being felt. Wage increases running comfortably into double figures were being regularly recorded. The miners felt that their part in bringing about the end of the Heath government merited further handsome increases. It was a situation which even began to tax the industrial wisdom of Michael Foot, newly installed at the Department of Employment. Advocates of revolutionary change felt confident that cataclysm could only benefit Labour. The Prime Minister, however, knew that a high inflation rate – around 25 per cent in the summer of 1975 – could lead the international financial community to feel that the British economy was out of control. Any such perception would have unfortunate consequences.

Yet Wilson knew very well that he had a hard struggle to keep the party and the Cabinet in harmony. 'Employment Protection' (the preservation of jobs) was almost Labour's *raison d'être*, but it now appeared to be taking second place behind the struggle to control inflation. The much-vaunted 'Social Contract' delivered little. Healey, now Chancellor of the Exchequer, tried to persuade both the unions and the party that wage inflation was in fact a major cause of unemployment(270). Crosland, the Environment Secretary, told local authorities, including those bent on high social spending and municipal socialism, that the party was over. These admonitions had some effect in so far as it was the TUC itself which initiated a policy, in the spring of 1975 – which was accepted by conference in September – of voluntary wage restraint based upon an identical flat-rate rise for all. It was a time when such trade union leaders as Jack Jones and Hugh Scanlon were household names. In the somewhat fevered atmosphere, there were suspicions that Communists and ex-Communists in the trade union movement were seeking to destabilize the country as a prelude to revolution. It was even possible for some to believe, in a mysterious manner, that the Prime Minister himself would not have regretted such an outcome. A more reliable indication of Wilson's attitude, however, can be seen in the speed with which he moved Benn from the Industry to the Energy Department in the summer after the national referendum endorsed British membership of the EEC (which Benn opposed). The question of industrial policy had proved particularly divisive. To the Left, the lack of a comprehensive strategy was a betrayal of all that it had thought it had achieved over the previous few years. On the other hand, the collection of failing or failed enterprises, backed by Benn as Industry Minister, were derided by his critics as 'Benn's follies'.

The sense that the British state was in jeopardy was never far away, during these months, from the minds either of its most committed defenders or its most ardent detractors. Somehow or other, Wilson weaved his way between the contending factions and contrived to keep the show on the road. It came to be assumed that he would continue to do so in perpetuity(254).

In March 1976, however, to general amazement, he announced his own resignation – an action which gave rise to a never-ending speculation. The reasons advanced by commentators included the suspicion that his supposed 'treason' was about to be unmasked – MI5 itself contained extraordinary individuals who appeared to believe that the Prime Minister was not above suspicion. In fact, 'the second time around', his zest for the job was waning. In the end, even the pleasure to be derived from manipulating Labour's discordant factions seems to have palled. The galaxy of business tycoons elevated to the peerage as a result of Wilson's final suggestions for honours could suggest a certain indifference on his part to the sensibilities of those battling for true Socialism. It was an odd end to the career of a man who, a decade earlier, had seemed on the point of ensuring Labour an unchallengeable political supremacy.

Wilson was succeeded by an older man – James Callaghan. His wealth of experience – Chancellor of the Exchequer, Home Secretary, Foreign Secretary – no doubt compensated to some extent for the fact that, unlike the rivals he defeated, he had not been educated at the University of Oxford, indeed he had not been educated at any university(268). He gave the appearance of down-to-earth geniality and solid common sense. It was evident that he listened to what people had to say. Yet, even from the outset, the odds were against him. Optimism about the economy at the beginning of 1976 soon gave way to despondency. Another Healey budget was required. Public expenditure was to be cut. If the international bankers were not satisfied with this package, a loan from the International Monetary Fund looked the only option. The government was being forced by circumstances to rethink assumptions about the merits of public expenditure which had become axiomatic in Labour circles. Crosland, the Foreign Secretary, wrote in his commonplace book that he detected the breeding of an 'illiterate and reactionary attitude to public expenditure' which he called 'horrible'. At the autumn party conference, the Prime Minister committed himself boldly to the proposition that it was impossible now for the country to spend its way out of recession. Perhaps it always had been.

In the remaining months of the year, confronted by a fall in the pound, bank rate at 15 per cent, and pressure on the currency reserves, the Cabinet wrestled in meeting after meeting – twenty-six in all – with the terms on which an IMF loan might be accepted. Mindful of 1931, when the Labour government had split, the Prime Minister was determined to keep the Cabinet united around whatever in the end was decided. Opinion and argument largely followed a Left/Right division. However, although he did not have a Bennite 'alternative strategy', Crosland remained obdurate for a long time in questioning the proposed cuts. In the end, a package of cuts was agreed in return for the large loan from the IMF. It was also agreed that part of British Petroleum should be privatized – though that word was not used. It was undoubtedly a substantial political achievement on the part of Callaghan, but it was far from clear whether the arrangement was merely an unpalatable 'one-off' to tide Britain over until, as was thought likely, the steady expansion of North Sea oil production brought with it greater prosperity. In the short term, however, it was humiliating to have to accept that Britain could not 'pay its way' in the world. In addition, it was not only the Labour Left which was demoralized by the apparent abandonment of its distinctive aspirations at the behest, once more, of the international banking community.

Even if the economy did recover in the late 1970s, it was doubtful whether Labour would be in a position to reap the benefits. The government's slim overall majority had disappeared as Callaghan came into office. He depended for survival on a small miscellany of Plaid Cymru, Scottish Labour and Irish Nationalists MPs – not a combination which could be relied upon to offer unwavering support. In addition, not all Labour backbenchers could be relied on. Sensing that the end was near, Conservatives primed a vote of no confidence. The government was saved from disaster, however, by the willingness of the Liberal Party, under its new leader, David Steel, to enter into a pact in the spring of 1977 to last for one year. The attractiveness of Liberal ideas had been tarnished by the extraordinary personal behaviour of its erstwhile leader, Jeremy Thorpe. An election in the bizarre circumstances obtaining was not in the Liberal interest. So weak was Steel's hand that he could not even insist on arrangements which might bring about proportional representation. The details of the much-trumpeted 'Pact' were somewhat exiguous. It was, in fact, the Ulster Unionists who were able to exploit the government's precarious parliamentary situation to best advantage when they were able to extract extra seats at Westminster in the continuing absence of a devolved government in Northern Ireland. For the time being, Callaghan was safe.

By 1978, it was even possible to glimpse the prospect of a Labour victory after all. Opinion polls and by-elections pointed to a Labour recovery, despite the fact that unemployment remained at a post-war high, some one and a half millions. The Liberals were still not eager to bring the government down at the first available opportunity. Inflation was in single figures, oil revenues were rising and sterling was strong. Suddenly, the prophets of Britain's doom were being confounded. For some, the recovery was an indication that the IMF prescription which the government had been forced to accept was in fact the right medicine and should in future be voluntarily embraced. For others, recovery was happening despite what the government had done. Either way, there was anxious discussion through the summer of 1978 concerning the timing of an election.

When the Prime Minister came to address the TUC conference in the autumn, his audience expected an election announcement but were left, in Callaghan's own words, 'waiting at the church'. Perhaps the polls did not offer a secure enough vision. An elderly Prime Minister who knows that if he gets the date wrong he will not have another chance is likely to be more than usually cautious. In the event, it may be judged to have been a miscalculation which meant not only that Callaghan was not returned to power but – at the time of writing – also that he has yet to have a successor as a Labour Prime Minister.

What intervened was the so-called 'Winter of Discontent' of 1978–79. At its heart lay the problem of engineering a return to something more akin to 'free collective bargaining' after a period of formal pay restraint. In the summer of 1978, Callaghan announced a norm of 5 per cent for increases over the ensuing twelve months. It was not a figure of which leading members of the Cabinet were proud – subsequently. Although the Labour Party conference rejected this norm in October, Callaghan and Healey declared that they would stick by it. The atmosphere soured as swiftly as it had improved. The star of Tony Benn waxed. Younger firebrands like Skinner and Kinnock came on to the NEC. Even more serious, the relationship between Callaghan and the unions, so sedulously cultivated, fell apart. It was in vain that the Prime Minister pointed to statistics which suggested that unemployment had peaked. Low-paid workers had had enough. The frustrations of a decade could no longer be contained. The avuncular Callaghan of the summer lost his touch. Ford workers made nonsense of the 5 per cent norm in the wage settlement they won. Firemen and lorry drivers were among other groups of workers now bent on strike action in pursuit of their pay-claims, brushing aside any suggestions that the Labour government had a right to their loyalty. Christmas and New Year offered little secular encouragement.

It was on this gloomy scene of rubbish piled in the streets and pickets turning away ambulances from hospitals that a sun-tanned Prime Minister returned from conferring with President Carter in Guadeloupe to declare that other people in the world would not share the view that there was mounting chaos in Britain. It was a remark which did not chime in congenially with the perceptions of increasingly dispirited sections of the population. They believed they were witnessing the unacceptable face of union power. After further strikes, chiefly by public sector workers, in February and March, the TUC offered some amendment of life in the shape of guidelines concerning the closed shop and picketing. The prospect of bringing inflation down to 5 per cent over a three-year period was also unconvincingly offered. In February 1974 Heath had unsuccessfully sought to persuade the country that the issue before it was simple: who governs? Given a second chance, a new Conservative leader might ride to power determined to confront rather than to conciliate the unions.

On 28 March 1979 the government lost by one a vote of confidence in the Commons on its handling of the industrial crisis. In this defeat, Liberals, Scottish Nationalists and Ulster Unionists voted with the Conservatives, though their antagonism towards the government stemmed as much from its handling of issues concerning the governance of the United Kingdom (see pp. 284–5). The Callaghan government had survived longer than many had predicted, but now it became the first administration to be voted out of office in the Commons since the first Labour government in October 1924. On 4 May, after a campaign which Callaghan appeared not to believe he could win, he conceded victory to Margaret Thatcher(256). The first woman Prime Minister in British history was determined that she would leave her distinctive mark in other respects too(264, 265).

THATCHER

The defeats suffered by the Conservative Party in 1974 had not left it in a happy condition. Heath would not bow out gracefully, but the identity of who might stand against him was not clear. The personality of a challenger would of course be important, but at issue was the meaning of Conservatism in the late twentieth century. The party's capacity to adapt was legendary. A feeling grew that it was time for another shift if it was to survive and prosper. Margaret Thatcher's successful challenge for the leadership in 1975 did not, however, seem ideologically clear-cut at the time. What attracted comment was naturally her sex, her modest social background, her energy, and her determination. Some observers even thought it worthwhile to mention that she was the first Prime Minister with a science degree (chemistry). She was an outsider, but of course a Conservative outsider. In electing her, the MPs were taking a more than usually large gamble. She had no large personal following and was conspicuously 'on trial', at least until she won a general election. She had no fully articulated doctrine to offer, but she did have instincts that mattered profoundly. 'Thatcher the milk snatcher' had behind her not only that controversial period as Education Minister under Heath but also a substantial range of shadow posts. Foreign and defence policy apart, she was well-versed in public business and impressed by her capacity to master a vast range of subjects(258).

The word master is used advisedly. The world in which she operated remained a man's world and she could not afford to be found wanting in those capacities which men set such store by. Clearly, however, she was not a man and could, on occasion, display a charm which an earlier age might have been willing to call feminine. She was proud of the role of women in public life but was not a strident feminist. The fact that she had got where she had showed that there was no insuperable barrier to advancement, at least not if you were fortunate enough to marry a wealthy man who accepted the primacy of his wife's activities. These personal aspects were the focus of much attention as the press, the media and politicians generally tried to come to terms with this new phenomenon.

She was so conspicuously not an old-style Tory grandee that no one quite knew what to make of her. Her background and career, in which 'Self-Help' had been emphasised, would not make it easy for her to adopt grand patrician gestures of social concern or to identify with the feckless and improvident. She was to find endlessly quoted against her by bishops and others a remark that there was no such thing as society. Critics took it to reveal her naked indifference to that sense of mutual responsibility which moral philosophy and Christian teaching enjoined. Her starting point, however, seems to have been different. Individuals were responsible for their own conduct and destinies. 'Society' should not be made to shoulder responsibilities and to take the blame for what people failed to do for themselves. It was the 'dependency culture' which sapped moral behaviour.

Although intellectuals were pretty confident that she did not have an original mind, there was distressing evidence that she would insist on speaking it regularly. It was entirely understandable, they condescendingly thought, that a former chemist should relish the company of businessmen. When she believed in things, observers discovered, she believed in them passionately. If you agreed, you joined in the struggle and became 'one of us'. If you did not agree, you were necessarily an enemy. She did not seek consensus. By her own admission, she was a 'conviction politician'. It was the 'can do' ethos of the United States which attracted her. She preferred men who did things to men who thought about doing things. She was intelligent but not an intellectual(259).

The full import of these qualities and capacities was not apparent in 1975 and her conduct as Opposition leader subsequently was sufficiently circumspect for it to remain so in 1979. It was also the case, during these years, that she was still surrounded by men who had not voted for her in the leadership election and still could not quite accept the outcome. Heath's unwillingness to go through the motions of goodwill, however, helped to consolidate her position. During the 1979 General Election campaign Callaghan tried in vain to warn the country against a woman who would tear everything up by the roots. 'If you must have a Conservative Prime Minister' a *Sunday Mirror* cartoon ran, 'I'm your man'. The strident vision of the new Labour Left was now matched by the strident vision of the Conservative Right. Callaghan and Heath were both yesterday's men. It was indeed easy and, up to a point, convincing to see matters in this light. There was a pervasive sense in the country that 'we cannot go on as we are', even if there was little agreement on where 'we' should go instead(261).

It is here that the limitations of political vocabulary make themselves evident. Thatcher's self-conscious 'radicalism' was nonetheless presented by her as authentically 'Conservative'. She felt little attachment to the great institutions of England which more socially secure members of her party thought it the duty of a Conservative party to conserve. The restrictive practices and lingering exclusiveness attached to them held no attraction for her. Yet, although no historian, she felt that the country should not and could not escape from the weight of its great past. At moments she thought appropriate, she turned in public to words by 'Winston', perhaps in an awareness too that his relationship with the Conservative Party was scarcely straightforward. Her nationalism, English rather than British in its formation – with consequences for the United Kingdom to be subsequently considered on pp. 397–98 – was more blatant and more populist. 'Populist' was a word used by commentators who were distressed that her nationalism contributed to rather than detracted from her popularity.

The renewed emphasis upon individual liberty and personal responsibility made it possible for her Conservative detractors to regard her as a latter-day nineteenth-century Liberal. Her suspicion of government intervention and established bureaucracy, it was said, would have fallen from the lips of many earlier Manchester cotton magnates. She wanted to set the clock back. True Conservatives, it was said, had a much better understanding of the beneficent role the State could properly play. Indeed, in her references to 'Victorian values' which she admired, Thatcher appeared to give substance to such contentions. Yet, as she herself was to find, the paradox in the attempt to 'roll back the State' was that it seemed on occasion to require 'the State' to act powerfully in order ultimately to divest itself of power. Thus there was not only a tension between individualism and nationalism, there was also one between 'strong government' and liberty.

Critics were more impressed by the way in which intermediate institutions and associations were being crippled or by-passed as authority (and power?) was centralized. They did not believe that the government's ultimate purpose was to 'empower' the individual. Supporters of the policy, for whom it was indeed the essence of the enterprise, came reluctantly to see how difficult it was to attain in practice. Only a very determined lady would try. Finally, it did not take long for the ambiguity of individualism to become apparent. Thatcher held to a notion of concerned individualism. Pounds in pockets gave the individual the opportunity to make his or her choices. It was proper and desirable that some of them should be used to give a renewed impulse to voluntary bodies which had languished too long when the view had prevailed that the State should be the all-purpose provider. High taxation not only caused enterprise to atrophy, it placed too many resources in the hands of administrators who stood at too great a remove from the 'customers' whose money they were in fact deploying.

Yet the model was often at variance with the reality. Individualism appeared as much to issue in self-centred hedonism as in concerned citizenship. One word which lost popularity was greed. It has been suggested that 'Mrs Thatcher had an immoral majority, not a moral one, at her back'(260). Families and churches, to name only two groupings within which the individual had traditionally been exhorted, disciplined and sustained, seemed in disarray. Elections, however, are not won by moral minorities, even supposing they exist. Conventional wisdom had come to believe that the 'feel good' factor was what mattered. Class loyalties and communal identities formed or supported by a common pattern of work continued to be buffeted and to disintegrate. The precise voting implications of these social changes continued to be a matter of debate among political scientists, but there could be little doubt that the social stereotypes which had underpinned party allegiance remained under severe stress. In this situation, the pursuit of votes corresponded ever more closely to a market place. To establish itself with a parliamentary majority sufficient to govern, Thatcher's radicalism only needed to be the most compact minority in that diverse collection of minorities which had come to comprise the United Kingdom electorate by the end of the 1970s and thereafter. Whether that compact minority was moral or immoral is another matter.

GAINING POWER: 1979–1983

The task before her generation, the Prime Minister declared a few months after taking office, was to demand an end to decline. As an aspiration, it had little novelty; what was new was the imperious term 'demand'. As has frequently been observed, however, voters would not find it easy to determine how this should be done on the strength of specific commitments in the 1979 manifesto. But there was no mistaking a different tone. Even the defeated Callaghan, who had served in the Royal Navy, conceded that a sea change, a shift in opinion such as perhaps occurred at thirty-year intervals, was taking place. Sixty committees of the Centre for Policy Studies, founded by Sir Keith Joseph in 1974, were busy working out the precise implications of this shift. Joseph himself had undergone one such sea change. Pending illumination from the Centre and other quarters, it was evident that the initial emphasis of the administration was on what it would not do rather than on what it would.

The Cabinet shared a view that some re-orientation was necessary but grandees, intelligent and less intelligent, did so with restrained enthusiasm. Among their number were Soames, Whitelaw, Pym and Gilmour. The Prime Minister had not placed any of them in the economic departments where the new Chancellor, Howe, assimilated new economic doctrine rapidly. Only six weeks into office, his first Budget reduced the top marginal rate of tax on earned income from 83 to 60 per cent and on basic rate from 33 to 30 per cent. It was argued that high levels of direct taxation reduced the incentive to work and save. On the other hand, VAT (then at split levels) was increased to a standard rate of 15 per cent. Exchange controls were totally scrapped. There was a toughness and determination to root out inflation, or so it was believed, which constantly surprised. Already, the Cabinet would seem to be divided between 'wets' (as sceptics were termed) and 'Thatcherites', though perhaps part of the wetness of the former was their inability to combine effectively against the latter.

Public expenditure formed the battleground. At times, it might be more accurately described as a playground for economists. They argued back and forth about the consequences of monetary restraint with all the precision of their science. The conquest of inflation might in time be achieved but it was still alarmingly high at 21.9 per cent in May 1980 – although that turned out to be its peak. Unemployment was growing. The Medium-Term Financial Strategy, unveiled by the Treasury in March 1980, set out an ambitious money supply policy to extend over four years. It was apparently no longer the business of government to try to secure 'full employment'. Military metaphors were liberally deployed as the Prime Minister dug in. She let it be known that she was not for turning. It appeared that government itself could almost be reduced to mastery of complex economic theories which go under the name of 'monetarism'. Politicians claimed to understand them. Men came not to praise Keynes now but to bury him. Money supply could be controlled with beneficial consequences for inflation. In order to do so, however, it had to be measured. That proved to be a task which was far from straightforward.

The 1981 budget, which raised taxes steeply on petrol, tobacco and wines and spirits, caused anguish among the 'wets' in the Cabinet – though it is possible to argue that this resort to fiscal means indicated a certain underlying scepticism on Mrs Thatcher's part about monetarism as a panacea. Nevertheless, the Prime Minister reproved her critics for their lack of guts. No less than 364 economists wrote to *The Times* in the belief that the government's path was leading to disaster. A large number of their colleagues believed they were wrong. Opinion polls registered plummeting support for the Prime Minister. The decline in output and manufacturing industry was rapid – it is sometimes suggested that the United Kingdom industrial base shrank between 1979 and 1982 by 17 per cent. Of course, this shrinkage did not begin in 1979. Critics were prepared to concede that in honouring the public sector pay increases determined by the Clegg Commission set up under Callaghan, the government had contributed to an inflationary pressure against its better judgement. However, they continued to believe that the stewardship of the economy in the initial years of the government was disastrous. Somewhat inured to disaster, the public was largely bemused by the arcane arguments concerning money supply. It was more alarming that rioting took place on a serious scale in London and Liverpool in districts where conditions generally were poor and unemployment high. The social fabric of the country looked to be at risk. It was perhaps no bad thing that a sharp shock had been administered to the economy, so long as it was short. But was there really light at the end of the Mersey Tunnel?

These early years continue to be a source of debate. By the later 1980s, Mrs Thatcher believed that she had proved the distinguished economists wrong. Recovery began in the spring and summer of 1981. Inflation was in single figures by the spring of 1982 and the government could claim that all the pain had been worthwhile. As usual, much of the argument about the scale of depression and the pace of recovery revolves around the years of comparison which are chosen. In any event, the Prime Minister's policy had more than an economic significance. The rhetoric of determination was designed to establish that her government would govern – at a time when it was fashionable to believe that Britain was ungovernable. Better to give the illusion of authority, even when making mistakes, than to give real substance to such a fashionable interpretation. After her own political downfall, however, her contemporary Cabinet critics publicly reiterated their view that these early years were disastrous. At the time, it was clear that the overall strategy being attempted by the Prime Minister was a very high risk. If, by some means, she could not pull the government round in advance of the next General Election her first period as Prime Minister would be her last.

In fact, the Prime Minister's position was not as parlous as it appeared. She felt strong enough by September 1981 to remove Gilmour, Carlisle and Soames from their offices and to send Prior to Belfast as Northern Ireland Secretary(266, 267). Those who thus suffered exile or demotion believed that the Prime Minister's objective was to create a Cabinet more in tune with her thinking than the one with which she had been forced by circumstances to begin. Perhaps their only mistake in making such an accusation was to suppose that Thatcher thereby showed herself to be an exceptional Prime Minister. It could not be denied, moreover, that the government had begun successfully, from its perspective, to tackle the question of trade union power. It was, of course, aided in this regard by continuing public memories of 1978–79. In addition, 'Pussyfoot Prior' had moved circumspectly as Employment Minister, seeking to find a solution which many trade unionists themselves would be willing to accept. Government money was to be provided when union elections or strike calls were conducted by secret ballot. Picketing was restricted to a striker's place of work. Legal immunity for secondary action was to be restricted. Tebbit, who followed Prior, so narrowed the definition of a trade dispute that 'political' strikes lost their immunity. It would have been possible to go further, but enough had been done to convince government supporters that it had succeeded where other administrations, Labour and Conservative, had failed(258). Even so, the achievement was in a sense symbolic. Whether it would contribute as much as was claimed to the recreation of an enterprise economy would depend upon the broader industrial issues confronting the country which are discussed on pp. 67–71.

The impact of the Falklands War of 1982 apart, considered subsequently on pp. 388–89, the other factor which enabled the Prime Minister to sail her task force through stormy domestic waters and face 1983 with the amazing prospect of victory, was the impact which her earlier triumph had had on her opponents. In the aftermath of the 1979 defeat, Labour gave every sign of tearing itself apart. Tony Benn emerged charismatically as the champion of the 'Hard Left' and, for a time, it looked as though his march to power might not be long. The traditional centre-right of the party was bemused and dispirited. Callaghan hung on as leader, trying vainly to maintain some semblance of unity. His old opponents were released from any need to suggest that the previous Labour government had been a success. Instead, they sought to create checks and conditions which would prevent any future Labour government from 'betraying' its supporters again. It was much more important to do that than to make the party sufficiently attractive to ensure that there would ever be such a government. When Callaghan resigned in November 1980, the leadership went not to Healey but to Michael Foot, a rebel of rather earlier vintage than those currently wanting to keep left. In January 1981, at a special conference, Labour adopted a new electoral college to select a leader in which 40 per cent of the votes went to the trade unions and kindred bodies and 30 per cent each to the constituency parties and the PLP.

Such a step, and the confirmation of unacceptable policies which it presaged, proved too much for Owen, Rodgers and Williams, articulate Labour ex-ministers of the centre-right. Back in November 1979, Roy Jenkins had drawn on his new European experience as President of the Commission in Brussels to argue in the BBC Dimbleby Lecture that the United Kingdom needed a new kind of centre party. Now, this 'gang of four' launched the Social Democratic Party and hoped for substantial defections from Labour(263). They had some success in this respect – nearly 30 MPs – but not as much as they hoped for. David Steel, as leader of the Liberal Party, was under the impression that he led an effective third force, but, amidst not inconsiderable mutual suspicion, an informal working relationship developed with the new party. The fact that in September 1981 Healey only defeated Benn by a small majority in the contest for the deputy leadership of the Labour Party was alarming to many Labour 'moderates'. In the event, however, from this point on, Benn's star began to wane.

It was in this atmosphere that the SDP achieved stunning by-election successes. Shirley Williams overturned a massive Tory majority at Crosby outside Liverpool in November. Jenkins won Glasgow Hillhead from the Tories in March 1982. Opinion polls around this time suggested that the Conservatives, Labour and the Liberals/SDP had roughly equal support. However, the 'third force' did not move on inexorably and indeed the formation of a formal 'Alliance' in early 1983 showed, in its negotiation, how difficult co-operation actually was, even when co-operation was the essence of the 'new politics' which both parties preached. In February 1983 the loss of Bermondsey by Labour to the Liberals was taken as a sign that the Alliance might actually replace Labour – as the second party.

Although Alliance hopes sometimes ran higher, and Jenkins stood waiting as Prime Minister-designate (probably), the lasting beneficiaries of the turbulence among other parties could only be the Conservatives.

So it proved. The Alliance vote increased by more than 11 per cent as compared with the Liberal vote in 1979 and constituted the largest third-party share at a General Election in half a century – but the mould had not been broken. Its success was achieved largely at the expense of Labour which only narrowly held on to its second place as regards votes cast (27.6 to 25.4 per cent) – its lowest share since 1918. It did not seem that the electorate was impressed by Labour's manifesto commitment to a non-nuclear defence policy and withdrawal from the European Community, not to mention further nationalization and central planning. The studiously dishevelled leadership of Michael Foot proved the disaster that it had always threatened to be. The bottom line, however, was that the Labour Party had survived. The Conservatives lost 1.5 per cent of their vote but were now substantially the largest party in terms of the vote, though at 42.4 they fell short of a voting majority of the country. They probably gained around a half of the trade union and 'working class' vote. In terms of seats, their majority over allcomers was more than comfortable and over Labour alone it was impregnable. It was from such a base that a lasting Conservative ascendancy might be built(256).

CHAPTER 38

The Conservative ascendancy

The election result in 1983 was above all a triumph for the Prime Minister. She was in a very different position from 1979 when she formed her new Cabinet. For better or worse, her courage had sustained her administration through the difficult years. No one now hinted that she was a liability. It had never been her view that her agenda for changing Britain could be completed in one term of office. Now she had her real chance. Yet the security of a large majority could be illusory. It had been a national sense of insecurity to which she had responded successfully in the years after 1979. That almost apocalyptic mood had now passed. It was also the case that the very extent of her personal success made her vulnerable to personal attack to an unusual degree. If, 'this day, the battle, and all things depend upon the king' as Henry V found at Agincourt, then it was best for her enemies to erect an obnoxious stereotype which, as with all human beings, was not without some foundation in fact.

Perhaps it was because the Prime Minister was thus singled out as exceptional that it seemed, for a time, that the government as a whole had also lost its sense of urgency and was beginning to seem like an ordinary government. True, a new team had to play itself in: Pym, who had publicly ventured the view that it would not be helpful if the government gained a large majority, was no longer found necessary as Foreign Secretary; Howe replaced him; Lawson became Chancellor of the Exchequer. Even so, it looked as though some kind of drama, bigger than the Trade and Industry Secretary's begetting of a child by his secretary, was necessary to galvanize the government. The miners' strike provided it.

Coal had come to loom so large in the political mythology of both of the major parties that rational discussion of the fate of the industry, viewed simply in economic terms, was impossible at this time. More than that, its future tapped sociological and psychological seams which remained below the surface of public debate. Whatever improvements had been made in health and welfare, coalmining was a dirty business. The pollutant effects of coalburning became unpalatable as environmental consciousness developed. Yet the symbolic power of coal, as the substance which had made the industrial world possible, remained enormous. Around coal clustered close communities where, without it, there might not be communities at all. Kent apart, mining took place far away from Whitehall and Westminster. It was male, macho and sometimes mysteriously attractive, at a safe distance, to middle-class intellectuals otherwise adamantly in favour of sexual equality in employment. Yet, although the actual costs of

360

British coal were often covered in a thick dust of obscurity, the scale of the industry was, to say the least, questionable.

Miners, however, had suffered from governments and they had made governments suffer in a recurrent cycle which seemed, from the outside, an enduring aspect of British public life. Heath had been the latest Conservative Prime Minister who perhaps in retrospect saw the wisdom of Macmillan's dictum that the miners ranked with the Brigade of Guards and the Roman Catholic Church as bodies with whom it was not wise for a politician to tangle. Perhaps because she knew less about the Brigade of Guards and the Roman Catholic Church than Macmillan, Mrs Thatcher was not afraid of the miners.

Neither was she precipitate. In 1980–81, when the steelworkers and civil servants had struck, the government had elaborately made clear that it would not produce more money over beer and sandwiches. In the case of the miners, however, when the then chairman of the NCB (National Coal Board) announced the intention to close a substantial number of pits, the government withdrew its initial support in face of NUM objections presented by Joe Gormley the NUM leader. The uneconomic pits were subsidized and a kind of peace reigned. The fact was that at this juncture neither the coal stocks nor the necessary reserves of public support were high enough for the government to risk a show down. Steps were taken to repair the former deficiency and the election had remedied the latter. In addition, the 1981 urban riots had resulted in improved machinery to co-ordinate police forces.

Scargill, organizer of the 1972 flying pickets, succeeded Gormley as leader of the miners in 1982 and perhaps believed that the government would buckle before a second challenge. It would be an exaggeration to say that the Cabinet courted a confrontation; it would be wrong to believe that it wished to avoid one at any cost. The Prime Minister had even taken the precaution of installing Walker, the most durable 'wet' in the Cabinet, as Energy Secretary. The voices of Scottish miners would undoubtedly be heard in any dispute, Thatcher reciprocated by bringing in the elderly Ian MacGregor, whose Scottish accent had been attenuated by long years in America, to chair the NCB. Scargill had made previous unsuccessful attempts to gain the 55 per cent vote for strike action which NUM rules required. In April 1984 the NUM leadership declared a national strike against pit closures and in favour of a large wage increase – without holding a national ballot (in only one of the nine areas where local ballots were held was there a majority for a strike, and that an insufficient one). Scargill's failure to ballot has been held to have been his crucial mistake – but if he had done so he might not have had a strike at all. What he wanted was a revolutionary strike in which power workers, railwaymen, lorry drivers and other sections of the union movement would come together to paralyze the country and bring down the government. Such co-operation as he did get, however, was quite insufficient to achieve his ends.

A year-long struggle then began. It was not a gentlemanly affair. The 'Battle of Orgreave' outside Rotherham, ironically on the anniversary of Waterloo, saw a violent confrontation between massed strikers and massed police, an event which in turn produced recriminations and counter-accusations. Viewers could see these extraordinary encounters on television. In the long run, however, a government victory was likely, though there were a number of occasions when clumsy action threatened that outcome and made a compromise or even defeat a possibility. The government chose not to make use of the courts as the NCB would have been entitled to do under the 1980 and 1982 trade union legislation. The drift back to work was apparent in the New Year. It proved to be a mild winter. A confident Energy Secretary declared that even if the strike continued into 1985 there would be no power cuts. By April, it was over(273).

Scargill claimed that the strike had changed the course of British history. So it had, but not in the direction he desired. The NUM split and the coal industry was about to undergo a drastic reshaping and contraction which would eradicate mining from areas of Britain with which it had been virtually synonymous. Occasionally, as in 1992, a further phase in this process could still open old wounds and lead to the ritual replay of speeches and demonstrations. However, the 1985 victory, brutal though it was, at length meant a public acceptance that coal was no longer king. It also marked the end of a decade in which the 'union question' had dominated. The government could proceed, at a.pace of its own choosing, to refine and tighten still further the legal framework within which unions had to work. Organized labour was not insignificant, but it was not an estate of the realm. In the new climate, individual unions lost and competed for members, and, in some cases, merged. The General Secretary of the TUC became of little more political significance than the Archbishop of Canterbury. Although she pretended not to be directly involved in the coal strike, there was little doubt that victory over the 'enemy within' was the Prime Minister's. If any further evidence of her courage and determination were required, her brave reaction to the IRA attempt on her life at the Conservative conference at Brighton in October 1984 provided it.

It is arguable, however, as had happened before, that once a great crisis had been transcended, the qualities in Mrs Thatcher which had been seen as admirable at such points, came to seem irritating or even unacceptable in calmer times. Of course, the Prime Minister's increasing involvement in European and world issues, discussed in chapters 40 and 41, meant that there was never a time of quiet, but in domestic affairs after the summer of 1985, somewhat coded criticisms were made by some ministers about the way the government conducted its business. What was happening tp the hallowed doctrine of collective responsibility and those marvellous occasions when the whole Cabinet ruminated over policy? Commentators have indeed detected 'dictatorial' tendencies at the heart of this government. Yet, while it would be futile to deny Thatcher's imperiousness, there is never a standard model Cabinet. A contrast, say, with the Callaghan Cabinet's collective consideration of the IMF loan, is not the full story. In his remaining period, Callaghan seemed subsequently distinctly interested in extending the power of Downing Street(271, 272).

It was true, however, that while Thatcher herself grew ever more established, ambitious and able ministers wished to spread their wings with less supervision. In January 1986, Heseltine, the Defence Secretary, stormed out of a full Cabinet and resigned. Helicopters caused this drama. Should a European or an American package rescue the British firm of Westland which manufactured them? In the play that followed, press secretaries and Cabinet ministers struggled against each other. What did the Prime Minister know about 'leaks' apparently designed to discredit Heseltine? Well-directed questions from the Leader of the Opposition might have destroyed her, but Kinnock's crucial speech was a failure. She survived, but the Trade Secretary, Brittan, sacrificed himself in the process. Although equilibrium was regained, the government as a whole was still in the doldrums. The customary confirmation of this fact was provided by an Alliance by-election victory. There were allegations that the government was excessively concerned about Official Secrecy as civil servants who leaked embarrassing information were prosecuted. It was easy to suggest that the government was dictatorial, repressive and frightened. There was a case for arguing that the work of GCHQ, the government security centre at Cheltenham, should not be jeopardized by industrial action, but a complete ban on free trade unionism there seemed excessive.

The sense of governmental malaise and public unease, at least in certain quarters, can perhaps have several explanations. The Thatcher experiment was ceasing to be new. A situation was beginning to develop in which personal alignments and policy manoeuvring within the governing party came to seem more significant than the routine confrontation between 'the government' and 'the Opposition'. For what was 'the Opposition'? In October 1983, under its new machinery, the Labour Party had elected Neil Kinnock as its leader. He was a Welsh son-figure to Michael Foot, of impeccable left-wing unilateralist convictions but, significantly, he had not supported Benn in the earlier contest for the deputy leadership against Healey. In choosing him at the age of 41, the party was consciously moving down an entire generation with an eye to the future. This inevitably means that, whatever his gifts as a speaker, he lacked ministerial experience and to that extent the party further removed itself, in the eyes of voters, from being a governing party. His vigour, youthfulness and freshness, however, brought back some hope in its ranks. He felt strongly that the 1983 campaign had been a shambles. If nothing else, he would ensure that, in organizational and publicity terms, the party presented itself well.

But what to present? Son of a miner and with mining in his Welsh constituency, the 1984–85 strike scuppered any chance of getting Labour to rethink its policies and image fundamentally. Everything in Kinnock's upbringing suggested support for the miners, but there was the indubitable fact that no ballot had been held. As party leader, too, he had to distance himself from violence, but in so doing opened himself to the charge that he was lukewarm in the cause. The longer the strike went on, the more it became clear that there was a gulf between Scargill and himself. Naturally, after the strike failed, there was party recrimination which, mingled with the controversy over Militant – the left-wing faction which had come to dominate the local politics of Liverpool – produced a sour mood. Kinnock wrestled with some of his own cherished convictions as he increasingly saw the need for policy changes as well as further reorganization. Even so, Unilateralism remained in Labour's manifesto when it came to the June 1987 General Election, together with a wealth tax and a commitment to the 'social ownership' of British Gas and British Telecom. There was some prospect of Labour recovery from the debacle of 1983, but scarcely of victory.

The Alliance won a by-election at Brecon and Radnor in July 1985 but its euphoria had disappeared. Following the 1983 General Election, David Owen replaced Jenkins as leader of the SDP, but talk of a merger with the Liberals was put off. Personal rivalries and policy suspicions made a combined operation hard to amount. Defence was the most difficult area, as became evident in 1986. Owen was firmly committed to the British nuclear deterrent and was appalled by the hostility towards it displayed at the Liberal Assembly in September. The polls recorded that this disagreement was doing grave damage to the Alliance and early in 1987 a compromise was cobbled together on defence. The following month, February, the SDP captured Greenwich from Labour and it looked as though the bandwagon was beginning to roll again. A joint Alliance manifesto was produced and Steel and Owen agreed to fight the election campaign as joint leaders. Perhaps the occupancy of 10 Downing Street could be left until after the result was known(269).

Once again, therefore, there seemed little prospect that the Conservatives would be replaced as the largest party in such circumstances. So it proved. Labour clawed its way back from its disastrous 1983 showing to gain some 30 per cent of the vote and 21 extra seats (compared with the dissolution). It reasserted itself over the Alliance which lost five seats held at the dissolution and saw its share of the vote drop by nearly 3 per cent. The Conservative share of the vote, at 42.2 per cent, showed only a loss of 0.2 per cent over 1983 and the party clearly remained the largest minority in the country. In parliamentary terms that ascendancy was even more marked, with a majority of 102 over all-comers. Mrs Thatcher became the first Prime Minister to win three successive General Elections since Lord Liverpool in 1826(256).

It seemed more than ever clear that, short of an electoral pact or some other working arrangement between the Opposition parties, the Conservatives would continue in government into the indefinite future. That they were a minority in the country as a whole was undoubtedly true, but any other party represented an even smaller minority. As events were shortly to prove, a merger even between the Liberals and the Social Democrats was fraught with difficulty. Labour and the Liberals were adamant that profound and deep differences divided them. In any case, any putative coalition, with or without changes in the electoral system, could well leave the smallest minority of all in a position to determine national policy. In this situation, if there were to be any altering of course in the future it would be because of a shift of opinion within the governing party, not because of its replacement by another. It was a fact that the Prime Minister was to discover before very long.

CONSERVING POWER – WITH AND AFTER THATCHER: 1987–92

There were signs, as the new government began work, that the Prime Minister had not fully grasped that pride can come before a fall. In the immediate aftermath of the election there seemed every reason for satisfaction. It was not only that grumbling Conservatives on the left of the party were floundering, she had also asserted her own personal supremacy over others not normally placed in this category, of whom Tebbit was the chief. The 1987 victory could not be put down to any adventitious factor like the Falklands War. It could be seen as confirmation that 'Thatcherism' would not be a transient phenomenon. The Prime Minister herself could go 'on and on'. In fact, she went on until November 1990 when the Conservative parliamentary party deposed her as leader. The dissatisfaction which her attitude towards the European Community had caused in some sections of the party will be noted subsequently (see pp. 383–84) but in itself that would not have been a sufficient reason for her defeat. She could indeed still claim that she gained more votes in the leadership contest than anybody else – but that was not the point. The rules required the victor to defeat his or her nearest rival by a margin of 15 per cent of those entitled to vote. A better-run campaign might just have achieved this objective. As it was, the Prime Minister did not go to the second ballot. If she had done so, she would probably have lost to her primary opponent, Heseltine. In the end, however, the victor was neither Heseltine nor Hurd but Major, the Chancellor of the Exchequer, a man who at this point certainly could not be described as 'anti-Thatcher'.

What had gone wrong? At one level, no major explanation is required. A machinery for annual election existed and it was used. The leader of the party had no proprietary rights over the leadership, even if she had relatively recently won a General Election. As in 1975, so in 1990, what was uppermost in the minds of Conservative MPs was the next General Election. There seemed good grounds for supposing that the continuance of Thatcher in office would produce a Conservative defeat. Only a different leader could reverse the tide of unpopularity which seemed to be flowing so strongly. Two major elements in that unpopularity can be identified.

The first is the Community Charge or 'poll tax' as it became popularly known. For many years, the existing property tax, the rates, had been found to be an unfair and unsatisfactory way of raising finance for local government. The trouble with its replacement was that it came rapidly to be perceived as even more unfair and, from an administrative standpoint, unsatisfactory. Its defenders pointed out that the poll tax involved extra expenditures on rebates and argued that the opposition of those who had never paid rates but who now had to pay an individual community charge would swiftly dissipate. In fact, the volume of protest and non-payment grew, though the Prime Minister was no more inclined to listen to critics at this point than she had been to criticisms from within her own party when the scheme was originally formulated. It appeared to be one further example of the Prime Minister's tendency to storm ahead no matter what reasoned criticism emerged.

This issue occupied the headlines, but perhaps more weakening to the Prime Minister's overall reputation was the re-emergence of inflation – a giant theoretically slain by Thatcherite methods. In 1989–90, however, it was rising once again – something which fundamentally undermined the view that a decade of

Conservative government had brought about a sea change where inflation was concerned. Of course, the Prime Minister was able to place the blame on Lawson, her Chancellor of the Exchequer, with whom she had clearly fallen out but, even if he could be blamed, no one could ever say that she had not interested herself in the economic and financial policies of her administrations. The buck had to stay, ultimately, in 10 Downing Street.

It was, therefore, a combination of domestic and 'European' factors which led to Thatcher's downfall. Accusations of 'betrayal', 'desertion' and 'treachery' were not lacking from those who felt that the party as a whole had let down someone to whom its recent success had largely been due. What was more problematic, however, was whether the new Prime Minister genuinely carried on the torch of Thatcherism. Certainly he owed his success in the ballot to the support of those who knew that Heseltine would not. His own background, which did not include a university education, clearly suggested that he was not a wealthy Tory who agonized over inequality. His commitment to privatization was firm and there was an urgent note in his desire to improve the country's education. In public, however, he appeared less abrasive than his predecessor. The Community Charge would be replaced and there seemed to be a more relaxed approach to European issues. Even if he wished to change tack in important respects, however, his primary problem was the maintenance of party unity ahead of the next General Election. Few Tories doubted that the recession which had followed the period of inflation would make it difficult to achieve victory. Recovery would not come in time to persuade those voters who had suffered economically to trust the Tories again. In addition, 'Thatcher loyalists', disgusted by her overthrow, might be lukewarm in support of the new regime. They might use the opportunity of defeat to suggest that all would have been well if she had remained as leader.

Against the predictions of the polls and of many commentators, however, Major contrived to win the 1992 election. It was widely believed that this was in no small measure due to the impression which Major himself had made, particularly in the latter stages of the campaign. It was a dispiriting outcome for Kinnock, the Labour leader who had revived his party's spirits and appeared to believe that victory was in his grasp. Failure led to his resignation. The Conservative ascendancy had been saved after all. Yet, within a year, the plummeting personal stature of the Prime Minister, the protracted delay in the economic recovery and the virulence of the party's debates over Europe suggested that the Conservatives had still to find an ideological equilibrium 'after Thatcher' which would, with certainty, carry that ascendancy into a fifth successive term of office.

CHAPTER 39

A question of culture?

ENTERPRISE AND INDUSTRY

'English history in the eighties', declared an American historian in a book published in 1981 'may turn less on traditional political struggles than on a cultural contest between the two faces of the middle class'(274). He had been reflecting on the deep cleavage which he perceived in English life between a middle class which was fundamentally hostile to the world of business and commerce, and one which revelled in enterprise and innovation. He developed his thesis in an attractive manner, though many scholars thought his contrast overstated. It could also be questioned whether the cleavage, supposing it really did exist, was so uniquely an English (or British) phenomenon that it could go a long way towards explaining why Britain apparently found it so difficult to flourish in the current competitive international environment(275). Nevertheless, when scholars had had their critical say, a residual feeling remained that Professor Wiener had hit upon something which needed to be taken out of an academic environment and addressed as a matter of urgent public importance. Here was a shaft of illumination which suggested that some remedy could be found, though not easily. If the British decline with which all politicians still wrestled in the late 1970s was a matter of culture, then that culture might be reshaped. The revival of enterprise might be a more fundamental and more important task than anything else which might remedy the 'British disease'.

There were, of course, many difficulties both of analysis and prescription(276). To speak about the revival of enterprise was to presuppose that there had been a Golden Age when it had been universal only subsequently to fade and wither. It was just such an assumption which some historians questioned. Commercial and industrial enthusiasm, some asserted, had always been a minority taste. Other scholars were to develop the notion that a particular form of 'gentlemanly capitalism' had evolved in England from at least 1688 and its resonance and influence was by no means over(277). Gentlemen may have distanced themselves from manufacturing and provincial urban life but they were certainly directly involved in land, finance and associated businesses, or derived income from them. Their interests and their often high-minded conceptions had shaped the British Empire. They needed to keep industry and industrialists content (viewing that world from the City, Whitehall and Westminster) but that world was never allowed to take control of the commanding heights of British policy. The British Empire was now dead but its cultural/commercial legacy lingered on powerfully. As usual, the fact that historians were addressing such issues was itself a reflection of current concerns. The debate was further fuelled by a devastating analysis of the British domestic performance during the Second World War by Corelli Barnett(280). In 1945, he suggested, Britain came out of the war with an obsolescent economy. Instead of devoting every effort to remedying the weaknesses that were transparent, he argued, the Labour government loaded on to the economy the vast and potentially limitless cost of the Welfare State. In part it did so because of the highminded perceptions of that powerful section of the middle class which never understood the imperatives of industry. The consequences, he thought, were very evident at the time he was writing.

Imprecise though it was, the word 'enterprise' began to be encountered with great frequency. The National Enterprise Board had been the dream of Labour's Left before the party came back to power in 1974, but Wilson had only permitted it an emasculated existence. Benn had envisaged it as the great engine of national regeneration through public ownership. Instead, its preoccupation was with the rescue, if possible by means of workers' co-operatives, of further casualties in the industrial world. One of the most dismal was the once dominant Norton Villiers Triumph motorbike firm in the Midlands. The achievements of the workers' co-operatives did not inspire confidence. Everybody, it seemed, was in favour of enterprise but political opinion was increasingly bifurcating on how it might best be cultivated(299).

After several decades in which, more or less, the boundaries of the private and public sectors seemed to have settled into an accepted pattern, the virtues of the mixed economy were now being challenged from both Left and Right. On the one hand came the complaint that the Attlee government had not extended public ownership sufficiently widely, particularly into growing industries(278). It was impossible to be satisfied with the status quo – and it would also be necessary to consider afresh how public ownership could be made transparently democratic(281). Major companies expressed increasing alarm that the free enterprise system, as they called it, would be squeezed out of existence. In turn, Conservative writers began to re-open the whole question of public ownership. Of course, events sometimes cut across ideological predispositions. When British Leyland was on the brink of bankruptcy, the Labour government took a majority share and injected massive public funds. However, Callaghan brought in a South African, Michael Edwardes, who set about the reorganization of the company in a vigorous manner, making no secret of the fact that he ultimately wanted to see it returned to the private sector. In short, there was a mood of change on this central matter of enterprise. The path it took would be determined by the outcome of the 1979 election.

In Opposition, the Conservatives had not formulated a comprehensive strategy, but there were general assertions that the preponderance of state ownership should be reduced and the basis of ownership widened. The 1979 manifesto merely promised the return to the private sector of Labour's latter-day nationalization of aerospace and shipbuilding. Naturally, the National Enterprise Board's shareholdings in the private sector would not survive. There was no suggestion of a wholesale disposal of public utilities. The initial disposals in 1981/82 – Amersham International, British Aerospace, Britoil, and Cable and Wireless – seemed primarily designed to hold down the public sector borrowing requirement. The receipts in the financial years 1979/80–1982/83 were all under £500 million in each year. In that final year, however, the momentum of change began to accelerate. Statements were increasingly made to the effect that a special case would have to be made for any industry to be kept in the state sector. Privatization as a concerted programme can really be said to have taken off after the 1983 election with the partial sale of British Telecom in the following year. The method of disposal was also important – the objective being to widen share ownership throughout the population as well as to gain revenue. A steady stream followed during the life of the second Thatcher government, including British Gas (1986), British Airways (1987), Rolls Royce (1987), British Airports Authority (1987) and British Steel (1988). In addition, there were further sales of government holdings in existing private companies. By 1987/88 privatization receipts were ten times higher than in 1982/83.

The merits of 'public' as against 'private' ownership, or vice versa, can be, and have been, discussed extensively at a philosophical level. To an extent, however, it was replaced in these years by at least an attempt to evaluate the shift pragmatically. Of course, the disposal outlined above was by no means as straightforward as it sounds. Arguments advanced for the change included (naturally) greater efficiency – to be achieved by giving managers greater freedom and employees a direct stake in the companies for which they worked; greater responsiveness to the customer and consumer which would flow from the market; greater discipline – to be exerted by shareholders who wanted a return on their investment and, ultimately, the threat of a takeover. Government spokesmen detected the appearance of these benefits at an early stage and the success of the experiment was deemed to be self-evident before it had bedded down.

It has often been observed, however, that the objectives outlined above are not necessarily invariably compatible – though neither are they necessarily incompatible! All depends upon the regulatory framework within which the privatized companies have to work, and their relations with the regulators (Oftel, Ofwat etc.). From the outset, it was recognized that there might in the end be little benefit in transforming a public monopoly into a private monopoly but it was not easy to find a solution. Short of breaking up the major organizations into smaller, competing units it would take a very long time and prove extremely complicated. Or so it was held. A little space for competition could be found – for example, Mercury against British Telecom – but, in the eyes of some Conservative critics, not enough. In each individual case there were complex specific issues to be addressed and particular solutions were found. It is not possible, therefore, to speak of privatization as though it was merely the simple application of a formula. In the next phase, the winter of 1987–88, saw a lively debate on the future structure of electricity generation. Eventually, the Central Electricity Generating Board (which became National Power) did not remain an integrated generating and transmission system in private hands. It faced competition from a new company (Power-Gen), from the two separate Scottish suppliers and from supply brought in from France. A galaxy of distribution companies completed the picture. In the end, nuclear generation was treated as a special case. In this and in certain other instances, critics were able to say that the government trusted the market so long as it provided the solutions it wanted to see. The water authorities were sold off separately but environmental and regulatory matters were placed in the hands of a new National Rivers Authority which remained a public body. Further disposals of British Telecom could be envisaged without undue difficulty. Further down the line, though awaiting the attention of the fourth successive Conservative government, was some kind of privatization of British Rail, perhaps the most intractable of all issues. There might also, in the end, be the disposal of an attenuated British Coal (as the erstwhile NCB became).

The cumulative effect of this process during the years of Conservative government has been to transfer, so far, around two-thirds of previously state-owned industries to the private sector. By any standards, it has been a major change of emphasis. Initially, in 1983, Labour reacted with total hostility to what was being proposed. A couple of years later even the former Conservative Prime Minister, Macmillan spoke disparagingly of the disposal of family silver. By the 1987 election, and even more by 1992, Labour's hostility had been substantially muted, to the dismay of some of its supporters. Instead, various rather unclear modifications were talked of. In practice, it looked as though privatization had come to stay. It was an achievement which came to have unexpected relevance as Communism collapsed in Eastern Europe. Naturally, Conservatives took the view that other countries were copying the British example. To an extent, indeed, they were but it may also be said that privatization, and indeed the whole thrust of Conservatism since 1975 has been but a local example of a trend evident in the United States and other parts of the industrialized world. It is premature, however, to speak of unambiguous success. All that can be said is that the scene has been transformed. In quarters not confined to Labour there has remained a yearning for some overarching perspective – a national energy plan, for example. Surely there was somebody or some body superior to the market? Such aspirations resurfaced in 1992 when the consequences for the British coal industry became apparent of the freedom of the electricity generators largely to make their own arrangements and contracts.

This programme must be seen in the wider 'enterprise' context. Much attention was devoted to the 'supply side' and to loosening what were perceived as debilitating rigidities in the labour market. Tax cuts took high priority, with the top rate coming down to 40 per cent and basic rate, eventually to 25 per cent, though with 20 per cent as the ultimate goal. There were corresponding reductions in corporation, capital transfer and capital gains taxes. 'Deregulation' was another objective – the abolition of price, dividend, pay and foreign exchange controls. The latter opened the way for what was to prove a major period of foreign investment. Although the share of outward investment flows to the EC rose, the United States was the most attractive area for acquisitions. Legal and institutional barriers on mainland Europe were seen as a deterrent, though the situation changed again in the late 1980s with the imminent advent of the EC Single Market. Even if higher commercial returns could be obtained abroad, however, could not investment in the social and physical infrastructure in Britain itself in turn have increased the possibility of higher domestic returns? Opinions were divided, as they always have been, about the benefits and disadvantages of overseas activity. It was, however, a very vigorous period for the City – in the case of some firms, where there was more than a whiff of impropriety, rather too vigorous. In turn the City itself was hit by 'Big Bang' in October 1986 when the Stock Exchange's fixed commission structure was abolished with the objective of making dealing much more competitive and making London better equipped in the world securities arena made possible by technology. The expansion in the financial sector was marked in these years and it was a favourite area for the 'yuppy' (young upwardly mobile person). By the early 1990s, however, the 'yuppy' was having a hard time.

In regions of the country where yuppies were not numerous, a small number of Enterprise Zones were set up where businesses were exempt from impositions which would normally have applied. Increased competition was seen as the only way in which the customer/consumer could benefit, in price, product and service, whether that was in the purchase of spectacles or the choice of bus or airline, to give only a few examples. It was time also to encourage the creation of small businesses through tax incentives and advice centres where the necessary skills and information could be acquired. From the perspective of Lord Young, a businessman brought into politics at the Department of Employment, after running the Manpower Services Commission, the whole country was beginning to hum with enterprise in a way he had not experienced in the post-war period(279). Here was the 'Thatcher miracle' which was indeed producing the necessary culture change(282).

It is premature to pronounce on the permanence or the depth of the 'enterprise revolution'. Even supposing that the case for a culture change has been made, cultures cannot normally be changed fundamentally in a decade. Sociologists and political scientists used poll evidence to suggest that the values and attitudes of large swathes of the population remained impervious or hostile to the liberation which was being imposed on them. They (and the Prime Minister's Conservative critics) reminded their readers that some 60 per cent of United Kingdom voters, throughout this decade of supposed transformation, had never supported what they sometimes dismissed as 'enterprise froth'. The political demise of Mrs Thatcher, though not of Conservative government, has now begun to produce a more nuanced and less partisan assessment. In the circumstances of severe economic depression, once again, and the return of unemployment levels approaching three millions, together with the collapse of many small businesses so enterprisingly begun in the 1980s, the exaggerated estimates of national renewal have been generally abandoned. Small shareholders by no means all hung on to their purchases or, even if they did so, studied their company annual reports with avid attention. Even so, it could be said that Britain had become more 'businessminded' than would have been thought likely in 1975.

EDUCATION

That there was some profound but tantalizing relationship between a country's economic performance and its educational system had not, as we have seen, escaped previous generations(283). It fell to Callaghan in 1976, in a speech at Ruskin College, Oxford, once again to suggest that education was in need of attention. He thereby inaugurated what was referred to in the press and on television as 'the great debate'. It has continued, sometimes with great intensity, ever since. The Prime Minister suspected that the educational world was too enclosed. Teachers and parents, schools, communities and business should all be in greater contact with each other. The curriculum and its delivery should be reconsidered. These propositions were not vastly contentious, but it was another matter to devise structures and systems which achieved these objectives. It was helpful for the Conservatives that the issue had been broached by a Labour Prime Minister since they could observe that their solutions, while contentious, were addressing a genuine problem. The educational crisis was not an invention of the government. But how far should (or could) government centrally produce a solution? Even to suggest solutions brought the possibility of collisions with vested interests, from local education authorities and teaching unions to universities who were certain that they knew their business better than Whitehall. All these bodies resented what were considered to be the imperialist aspirations of the Department of Education and Science. There was a powerful resistance, not confined to one party, to what were thought to be dangerously totalitarian tendencies. Education in a free society required pluralism and variety not 'state education'. It was sometimes argued, though without overwhelming evidence, that mainland European states with a strong centralist tradition were looking with increasing admiration at the loose English structures. Besides, the people who knew about education were teachers. Leave it to the professionals. But were they not part of the problem? The mode of their professional formation made them ignorant of or hostile to (or both) the 'real' needs of the country and their pupils. And so the debate continued, often at no very high level.

It was clear that there was little prospect of a consensus on which to base a legislative programme and the Conservative governments did not try very hard to find one. If there had been a body in England which was not a trade union, which could have represented the 'professional' voice of teachers, the situation might have been different. There was no such body. Hence the apparently inextricable entanglement of wider issues of change with the bitter disputes about pay and conditions of service for teachers which characterized the mid-1980s. Teachers complained of low morale and resented the note of contempt which crept into the comments of Conservative politicians. The decline in the school population raised many questions about 'plant' which local authorities were reluctant to face, for very understandable reasons. Pupil-teacher ratios were arguably as good if not better than they had ever been, but perceptions and facts were somewhat at variance with each other.

The government looked increasingly vigorously for ways in which it could by-pass an 'educational establishment' which it regarded as intransigently archaic. Two methods suggested themselves: to launch initiatives outside conventional frameworks and, by means of parents and possibly business, to focus resources on particular schools and institutions which could thereby escape the 'beneficent' but indubitably bureaucratic services of local authorities. In the former category come the Manpower Services Commission which through the TVEI (Technical and Vocational Education Initiative) required work experience of all pupils of 14+. This reflected the view, strongly held in some quarters, that 'education' and 'training' belonged together. A programme specifically designed to promote enterprise culture came from the Department of Trade and Industry. In the latter came moves to broaden the composition of school governing bodies and to make it possible for parents both to find out more about levels of achievement and to choose schools.

The thrust of these and other developments was clear and had naturally required particular legislation. However, it was not until the third Thatcher government that a major statement appeared – the 1988 Education Reform Act. The result has been a series of far-reaching changes in the requirements placed upon the maintained system in England and Wales. Their final consequences, however, if indeed such a concept is useful in a situation which has throughout been characterized by fluidity and impermanence, remains unclear. A national curriculum has indeed been formulated and it is now the required basis of instruction but the content of each subject, at its various stages, has been extremely difficult to formulate. Likewise, there has been continuing debate about what should be regarded as 'core' subjects and how much flexibility should remain with the teacher. In addition, the stipulation that there should be national assessments at the ages of seven, eleven and fourteen (with the results at the latter two ages made public) has proved very hard to implement in the face of objections from teachers and their unions. The form of the assessment proposed has proved cumbersome and timeconsuming – a somewhat ironic outcome since the path that led to them was in part a consequence of objections from teachers to more simple and 'primitive' tests. The extent to which 'league tables' of school results will appear remains unclear. It might be said that the entire argument, over twenty years, points to the difficulty, perhaps the impossibility, of devising a system which simultaneously evaluates the performance both of teachers and of pupils. It also illustrates the difficulty the Conservatives have found in combining parental choice, and elements of a free market in education, with the continued maintenance of an adequate, indeed improving, national educational system. The longer-term impact of the changes may be to create or reinforce a three-tier system: the private sector (the traditional 'public' schools with which may now be lumped the small number of City Technology Colleges); the 'prosperous' public sector (including those schools which have decided, as is now possible, to 'opt out' and receive their grant directly from the renamed Department for Education centrally, and schools which continue to be funded through local education authorities but which are also able to achieve significant voluntary funding); the 'poor' public sector (including many schools in socially deprived areas where 'underachievement' continues from generation to generation). The result may be to improve standards significantly but only differentially; the 'under-class' will remain.

Higher education also received government attention and received a series of shocks which it was unusual to find described as congenial. Perceived financial and organizational imperatives on the part of government mingled uneasily with questions of autonomy and a subdued but intense concern with what a university should be. The universities thought they had succeeded in brushing aside awkward questions addressed to them before leaving office by the Labour Education Secretary, Shirley Williams, when her first Conservative successor offered 'level funding'. Given the overall situation in 1979–81 it was not an offer which would last. The University Grants Committee had to administer cuts in 1981 and did so differentially. Student enrolments were reduced to protect the 'unit of resource' per student in the system. That good idea had the effect of sending students into polytechnics and colleges, then still under the control of local education authorities but which could apparently manage on less favourable financial terms. By stages, initially through a National Advisory Board, the polytechnics and colleges moved towards institutional autonomy, something generally welcomed by their directors but not pleasing to local authorities. Universities coped by parting with some good, and some not so good, staff under a premature retirement compensation scheme and almost simultaneously were funded to make some 'new blood' appointments. The viability of some institutions was in doubt. One, University College, Cardiff, had to be rescued from bankruptcy. The Jarratt inquiry found that significant improvements could be made in university management, though some academics found the notion inconceivable. Awkward questions were asked about funding as between teaching and research. The UGC, itself in a terminal condition, began a series of subject reviews: the talk was all of 'rationalization'. Perhaps, too, there might be a rationalization of the 'binary system'. Joseph, the Education Secretary, as was his wont, agonized but did not deliver. A Green Paper in 1985 fell on unreceptive ears. University managements did not know whether they were to expect a large increase in students; they themselves did not know whether they wanted a large increase in students – if the unit of resource went down as a consequence. The Treasury would surely insist that it did. The Education Reform Act, unsurprisingly, had messages for higher education. From April 1989, the UGC and the NAB were replaced, respectively, by the UFC (Universities Funding Council) and the PCFC (Polytechnics and Colleges Funding Council). At least half of their membership was drawn, by nomination, from outside higher education and the language of 'grants' came to seem somewhat antiquated. Academic tenure, seen as a defence of 'academic freedom' in some quarters but as a recipe for immobilism in others, was abolished in universities. Organizational change continued, so that by 1993 the old 'binary line' had come to an end and as a consequence there followed the general adoption of the name 'university'. Higher and Further Education now came under the Funding Council system but at the same time it ceased to operate on a United Kingdom basis with the establishment of separate bodies for England, Scotland and Wales.

One important consequence of this step was that now at all levels education ceased to be a United Kingdom matter. The Education Secretary now only spoke for England and the responsibilities he exercised in England were now paralleled by the respective territorial departments elsewhere in the United Kingdom. It is worth adding, in parenthesis, that at the school level the 'national' curriculum was not 'British national'. Although changes did take place in the Scottish school system, Scotland stood apart from the debate that raged south of the border. And the curriculum in Wales showed differences from that introduced in England, most notably but not exclusively in the enhanced status accorded to the Welsh language.

The organizational changes which have been sketched were accompanied by a dramatic change of attitude concerning student numbers, which began to accelerate. The proportion of eighteen and nineteen year olds going to higher education rose from roughly one in eight in 1979 to one in four in 1992. A 1991 White Paper envisaged a proportion of one in three by the end of the century. In turn, this gave rise to unresolved problems concerning fees, grants and loans. Alongside this expansion went a continuing concern for transparency in funding. Scholarly publication and research became subject to peer-group review at regular interviews. It was not clear that the writing of a widely used textbook was something a scholar should be doing. 'Education and Science' were in part unscrambled and it was clear that investment in all 'science' for its own sake was no longer an automatic commitment but that it too would be subjected to a more rigorous attempt to discern its importance for industry and enterprise. The objective was to identify and to give financial support to achievement – it remains to be seen how far, either in intention or in consequence, a rank order of universities emerges. Complex moves were also made to try to monitor teaching and procedures so that recipients of student charters would have little cause to complain.

The course followed by four Conservative administrations could not be said to have followed a clearly delineated path which could have been discerned by any intelligent observer in 1979. The key to their approach, however, lay in their assumption, across the board, that nothing less than a comprehensive assault would release the shackled or submerged spirit of enterprise and give the 'sick man of Europe' lasting life. It was not a medicine which all in the academic and educational world thought either appropriate or necessary. That enterprising institution, the University of Oxford, gave its verdict in 1985 when it decided that it would not give an honorary degree to the foremost figure in contemporary British public life – its graduate, Margaret Thatcher, the Prime Minister. It may be a little early to discern whether Prime Minister or University more correctly interpreted the needs of the times.

CHAPTER 40

Britain in the European Community

TOWARDS CLOSER UNION?

The writing of the first edition of this book was completed in 1981. Any historian who writes about the recent past is well aware of the difficulties of perspective and periodization. In 1981, however, a case could be made for what was then the final part of a book which did not attempt to go beyond 1975. It was in the summer of that year that two out of three British voters registered their desire to remain within the European Economic Community (see p. 259). This vote appeared to bring to an end decades of uncertainty about the relationship between Britain and that Community. It was surely now clear that for the foreseeable future Britain would be a member. In that sense, British history was coming to an end, if that history was seen as self-contained and distinct from 'Europe'. The Community to which Britain was now apparently committed was not, however, a static entity. It was itself in evolution, though its ultimate shape and structure were far from clear. Its development was not steady and constant, but moved in fits and starts. There was, however, a momentum towards ever closer union, whatever that precisely entailed. It was a momentum which left British governments and a substantial section, perhaps a majority, of the British people, distinctly uneasy(284).

In this context, the significance of the 1975 vote is arguable. The electorate probably did not think very deeply about what the ultimate direction of the Community might be. It was not carried away with a positive vision of a new European future, rather it feared the upheaval which might follow a failure to ratify British membership. The referendum itself was an extraordinary affair for it confirmed in a very public way the extent to which the issue of 'Europe' divided, to greater or lesser extent, all the major political parties. Even to have a referendum at all on such an issue involving the United Kingdom electorate was itself extraordinary. It reflected the particular tensions within the Labour Party rather than any fundamental conversion on the part of parliamentarians to the view that such matters should be put to such a test. And, although there appeared to be a finality about the referendum outcome, there remained deep divisions within the British political class, and within the country at large, about what the British place in 'Europe' should be(287).

It remained the case, in the media and in popular parlance, for example, that 'Europe' was one thing and 'Britain' was another. The notion that Europe was itself a complex of national identities was little understood. It was probably not widely believed that it was possible both to be 'British' and 'European'. The entire country, in so far as it shared a sense of the past, knew from schooldays that 'British history' was quite distinct from 'European history'. Different textbooks and even different teachers had confirmed the point over many years.

Nevertheless, whatever problems of identity were still unresolved, 'Europe' has been an increasingly significant factor in most important facets of British life in the twenty years since entry into what was then still habitually only referred to as 'the Common Market' or the European *Economic* Community on a scale without precedent(288). The extent to which government departments, business and professional organizations, and educational bodies have become enmeshed in the initiatives and activities of the Community has varied in depth but few have been totally immune. It is for this reason that we have characterized these decades as a twilight period. The transnational relationships inherent, in the defence sphere, in membership since 1949 of NATO, have now extended, as a result of the Community, over many other spheres.

In governmental terms, the simple division between 'domestic' departments on the one hand and the Foreign and Commonwealth Office on the other, no longer suffices. The Ministry of Agriculture, Fisheries and Food is one conspicuous example of a department with a large European dimension to its work. The Home Office has necessarily become involved in issues arising from the free movement of labour within member states, Co-ordination of policies and practices has become imperative across Whitehall. British ministers have increasingly had to forge close working relationships with their counterparts across the Community if they are even to be able to carry out their domestic duties effectively. We might speak, on occasion, of a 'departmental' foreign policy which may be at variance with the Foreign and Commonwealth Office view of foreign policy. That office, in turn, has had to blend traditional conceptions of British interests, and its own high belief in its capacity, with the requirement to move in the direction of trying to co-ordinate foreign policy within the Community. The co-ordination of trade, economic and defence policy has always been a formidable task even within a national framework. The complex relationships which have steadily built up across the Community have added to this difficulty(272).

It has increasingly produced a situation, for example, in which pressure groups and lobbies – on issues ranging from environmental protection to women's rights – have formed close working relationships with comparable bodies in other Community countries. Although such combinations have not been easy, and have often still encountered strong national interests (for example, in the fishing industry), nonetheless lobbying 'Brussels' has become a fact of life. Pressure groups, together with commercial organizations and trade unions have set up, or shared, facilities and offices in Brussels in order to make their views heard at the appropriate level. British ministers, often against their inclination and sometimes beyond their capacity, have had to come to terms with different ways of transacting business, different legal frameworks and different political cultures if they were to succeed even as 'British' ministers. They have had to reckon with the existence of a Commission in Brussels whose members are required, on taking office, to forswear their national allegiances in their handling of their responsibilities.

The respective boundaries or competences between the sphere of the Commission on the one hand and national governments (through the Council of Ministers) on the other has been an endemic difficulty, sometimes producing a tension which goes beyond being creative. British governments have appealed successively to the Commission to take action against restrictive practices engaged in by fellow Community members as they have in turn been at the receiving end of Commission criticism. The Commission can take a particular issue to the Court of Justice of the European Communities and can impose sanctions on companies found to be violating competition law. The British government has itself been compelled by the European Court, on the initiative of the Commission, to comply with a Council directive. As a consequence, no major aspect of industrial policy or company activity can ignore the regulatory and legislative framework established by the Community.

'Intrusion', is not confined to scrutinizing corporate commercial behaviour. European Community law, as interpreted by the European Court, takes precedence over domestic law. In consequence, various cases brought by British subjects have placed British governments in difficulty, on such matters as equal pay and retirement, for example. It is a novel experience in Britain for laws passed by parliament to be found defective. The pronouncements by the Court on 'constitutionality' did not appear strange to countries with written constitutions. In Britain, they highlighted the extent to which deeply entrenched notions of parliamentary supremacy were being circumvented.

On occasion, too, this was most dramatically illustrated by the rulings of the Commission and Court of Human Rights based in Strasbourg. Britain signed the European Convention on Human Rights but the convention has not been 'domesticated'. British cases have been taken to Strasbourg and the Court has ruled against existing British practice on issues ranging from caning in schools to the rights of prisoners. As a result, British governments have felt obliged – they cannot be compelled – to make substantial modifications in the light of the judgements. Another example of the necessity to adjust domestic British practice concerns the age of retirement where a different age for men and women was found to be unacceptable.

The context of British history has therefore shifted significantly, but it has done so obscurely. The public rituals of British life seem, at certain levels, to continue as if 'Europe' did not exist. British history is no longer 'purely' insular but neither is it unreservedly 'continental' and 'European'. The tensions inherent in this condition can be seen in the behaviour of political parties and their leaders throughout these years. In turn, this behaviour was also influenced by wider international considerations.

The predominant emphasis of the Labour government in its final years of office was on 'value for money' in a context of continuing domestic economic crisis. The focus of debate and argument was on support for agriculture and the British contribution to the Community budget. The deep divisions among Cabinet ministers could not be disguised. Callaghan, as Prime Minister after April 1976, had to cope with such leading figures as Benn, Shore and Foot whose hostility to the Community in no way abated, but he was not an enthusiast himself. In

1977 Roy Jenkins left the Cabinet and became the first British President of the Commission. The British presidency of the Council of Ministers in the first half of 1977 caused irritation in Bonn and Paris. Callaghan, whose disposition was basically 'Atlanticist', sought to prevent a widening of the cleavage on economic issues between Paris and Bonn, on the one hand, and Washington on the other. A public letter at this time to the Secretary of the Labour Party concerning the Community, however, seemed narrow in its focus on British interests, almost to the exclusion of any wider reflection.

From the Prime Minister's perspective, however, there was nothing to be gained from 'Euro-froth'. Whatever the rhetoric, all European states sought to defend their own interests. It began to appear that the formula which had been agreed to correct the imbalance of British contributions (relative to British wealth) was not going to work in the way the British had hoped. Another renegotiation would be called for. In addition, for Labour Party internal reasons and because of a continuing suspicion of 'regional' arrangements, Callaghan refused to take sterling into the European Monetary System (EMS) which developed from a speech made by Jenkins, as President of the Commission, in October 1977. The idea was that the EMS would create a zone of monetary stability in Europe. By means of a mechanism involving support from the relevant central banks, it was hoped to minimize exchange rate fluctuations among Community members. In the background lay the 1970 Werner Report which suggested a common European currency. The EMS, which came into existence in March 1979, would be a necessary step in that direction – or so its advocates hoped. The Prime Minister, according to his memoirs, also feared the deflationary consequences of entering the system at too high a rate. Whatever the force of these anxieties, the political reality in 1978–79 was that once again, the initiative rested with France and Germany. If Britain did eventually join the exchange rate mechanism, it would once again be as a reluctant latecomer.

Another indication of prevailing attitudes was the extreme reluctance to contemplate direct elections to the European Parliament. The European Council in September 1976 had agreed to advance from the existing indirectly elected Assembly, consisting solely of members of national parliaments, to one whose membership would be decided directly by national electorates. British obstruction and prevarication, however, meant that the elections throughout the Community had to be put back from the planned beginning in 1978. Eventually, however, direct elections for 'Euro-constituencies' were first held in the United Kingdom in June 1979. The notion of a European Parliament affronted some denizens of Westminster. They thought that a body which divided itself between Strasbourg and Luxembourg (not to mention Brussels) could not be serious. There was a reluctance to use the word parliament to describe it. On the other hand, even worse, if it did become serious and gain fresh power and authority, it could contribute further to the erosion of Westminster's influence. A mixture of contempt and anxiety prevented any effective consideration of how British members of the European Parliament should function in relation to the House of Commons. It was another example of a disinclination to consider the deeper implications of Britain's place in the evolving Europe.

The Conservative victory under Mrs Thatcher in 1979 did not produce a significant change of atmosphere. In Opposition, the Conservatives had exploited Labour's manifest divisions on Europe, but the new leader equally obviously did not share Heath's profound commitment to European integration. In fact, there was a broad continuity between Labour's stance and the style adopted by Mrs Thatcher. She was abrasive and determined in her defence of 'our money'. Her conduct at the Dublin Council in December 1979 gave her European colleagues an initial taste of an approach which was to become familiar as the years passed. The Prime Minister's personal convictions were undoubtedly evident but they also chimed in with a broad public sentiment which seemed to take the view that Europe consisted simply of wine lakes and butter mountains.

There was, however, a particularly serious issue posed by the Common Agricultural Policy of the Community. Its founding members were loath to tamper with something which was a 'success', not least in the eyes of their powerful agricultural sectors. Arguably, the policy could never have been implemented in the way it was had Britain been a founding member of the Community. From the Brussels perspective, whatever its imperfections, it was a Community achievement. As things stood, Britain's imbalance in net contributions to the budget largely stemmed from its relatively low level of receipts from the Community's agricultural funds. Mrs Thatcher, therefore, hammered away at this issue. Only at the June 1984 European Council meeting held at Fontainebleau, did she become a 'good European' and accept a settlement of the budgetary dispute. The Prime Minister had not achieved the radical overhaul of the Common Agricultural Policy she had desired, but there seemed some prospect of adjustment here and there. It is arguable that the rigidity of her protracted battle proved counter-productive in so far as it led other Community leaders to stiffen their own resolve not to make Britain 'a special case'. Perhaps what persuaded Mrs Thatcher to settle in June 1984 was the possibility, hinted at by President Mitterrand, that the Community might embark on new steps towards integration – if need be, without Britain.

Mrs Thatcher's strident tone on European issues had clearly not harmed her with the bulk of the British electorate, or so her election victory in June 1983 seemed to confirm. Her attitude also reflected the fact that after 1979 Labour swung emphatically against continued membership of the Community – one of the major reasons which led 'pro-Marketeers' to leave the party and form the Social Democratic Party (see pp. 358–59). No Conservative leader could afford to appear 'soft' on Europe. It was in such an electoral context that Mrs Thatcher maintained after Fontainebleau her resolute opposition to joining the EMS. In these circumstances, the British understanding of the European momentum scarcely deepened. While the Community itself was in the doldrums that perhaps did not matter. If it lurched forward again, the British might be required to demonstrate more than a capacity for nagging suspicion about whatever was happening. Yet British obduracy should not be exaggerated or thought to be unique. Political elites across Europe were struggling to cope simultaneously with the need to address both a domestic constituency and a transnational one. In British politics it was not easy to be both a 'good Briton'

and a 'good European', yet it was becoming an inescapable necessity, whatever
the rhetoric.

Public polemic was one thing; it was also necessary to have a European policy
as the Community began to emerge from the complex interlocking issues of
enlargement, the CAP and the budget which had taken so much time and
effort through 1983–84. Mrs Thatcher was now a veteran of these sessions and
her new Foreign Secretary, Sir Geoffrey Howe, seemed content to play the
supporting role which she required of him. Yet her hand was not an easy
one. She frequently found herself on the same wavelength as the Americans.
The United States seemed much more the model for a vigorous capitalism than
anything she encountered in continental Europe. The Falklands crisis of 1982
(see pp. 388–89) apparently showed that the 'special relationship' was still alive
after all. She had not been impressed by the reaction of the Community to the
British case.

Yet European leaders were in the process of reassessing their relationship with
the United States. The Second World War had ended some forty years earlier. It
was unrealistic to suppose that the interests of the United States and of Western
Europe were set in the mould which obtained then. Particularly in France, there
was concern that the countries of the Community were being outstripped by the
United States and Japan in key spheres of technology. It was not clear, also,
whether American conventional forces would remain in Europe on the scale to
which European states had become accustomed. There was much speculation
about the need to rethink transatlantic relationships now that 'Europe' had 'come
of age'. Spain and Portugal were due to join the Community in January 1986.

In such a reappraisal, the British were liable to find themselves torn in different
directions. The concept of 'fortress Europe' – that is to say of a Community which
was in an economic and military sense self-sufficient – sometimes attributed to
European leaders, held little attraction, at least not to Mrs Thatcher in the mid-
1980s. Britain had no wish for the politics and economics of Europe to develop
to a condition which produced a confrontation with the United States. On the
other hand, it would be disastrous for Britain not to be involved in the various
Community projects designed to enhance European technology. There would
inevitably be circumstances in which British governments might have to choose
between an American and a European orientation. The choices to be made might
cause conflicts which would go to the very heart of government(285).

It was in these circumstances that the idea of a concerted attempt to remove
non-tariff barriers to trade within the Community appealed to the British
government. It had long been the British view that such barriers in financial
services and transport were particularly damaging to British prospects. It was
one of the hitherto rare occasions when a British government did not drag its
feet. The negotiations for the Single European Act were concluded ahead of
the Luxembourg European Council of December 1985. The intention was that
the internal market would come into operation at the beginning of 1993. This
enterprise chimed in with a belief in the virtues of deregulation which was not
confined to Mrs Thatcher (see pp. 370–71). It could scarcely be doubted that if
the internal market functioned in the way that was anticipated it would be yet

another area of British life which would be subjected to challenges and changes. Mrs Thatcher, however, seemed prepared to accept them with equanimity and gave no scope to doubters in her own party. At long last, here was a European endeavour which received wholehearted support from a British government.

The appearance of unanimity, however, was deceptive. Whereas for Mrs Thatcher the single market was an end in itself, for other European leaders it was a step which required other steps. For the French, in particular, it was to be complemented by a wide-ranging programme of collaborative technological research. It was also argued, particularly by European parties of the Left, that there was a need for a 'social dimension'. Europe was more than a glorious market. Workers needed a reinforcement of their rights. It would be necessary to ensure that there was a 'level playing field' in the new market. The Luxembourg Council had accepted the need to extend majority voting within the Community and to give to the Commission fresh powers of initiative. Taken together, these objectives pointed to the achievement of economic and monetary union. Only such a course could give Europe the cohesion and strength it needed to deal on equal terms with the United States or with Japan.

The British government did not share this enthusiasm. It suspected that such a programme would render Community products uncompetitive by increasing the welfare costs which employers would have to absorb, and hence raise the unit costs of production. There was also concern that other European countries would agitate for a ban on the free entry of goods from outside the Community when the internal market began to function after 1992. It was also apprehensive that a trade war with the United States could develop. Washington would expect the removal of non-tariff barriers to apply not only within the Community but also to the rest of the world. The 'Uruguay Round' of GATT negotiations, which began in 1986, might founder on just such issues. It was obvious that Britain would be more willing to reach a settlement with the United States than would France.

These ideas were in the air when Mrs Thatcher won her third election victory in June 1987. It seemed, for a time, that her renewed mandate would allow her to sabotage or at least delay their implementation. Her most celebrated attack on the attempt to expand the 1992 project was delivered in Bruges in September 1988. She conjured up the prospect of an 'identikit European personality' – which the British people would surely not want. She rejected the notion that working together more closely required power to be centralized in Brussels. She could not believe that the British people, having successfully rolled back the frontiers of the state in Britain (as she saw it), would want them reimposed at a European level, with a European super-state exercising a new dominance from Brussels. The tone of the speech was frequently described as 'Gaullist', but she also declared that Britain did not dream of some cosy isolated existence on the fringes of the European Community. Britain's destiny was in Europe as part of the Community but its future did not lie only in Europe. Mrs Thatcher, with her carefully balanced antitheses, was saying what most of her predecessors would have said. She simply said it in more shrill tones.

Although one particular group of admirers formed themselves into a 'Bruges Group' to fight federalism, the domestic political context was shifting. In the 1983

General Election, Labour had promised to take Britain out of the Community within the lifetime of a Labour government. Kinnock, the new Labour leader, concluded that this promise had not proved attractive to the British people. It was time to shift away from this stance. The attitude of the British Labour Party had long been a puzzle to European Socialists. Kinnock developed European contacts energetically. He began to persuade his party to move away from its negative attitude and, instead, to be critically constructive in its approach towards the evolution of a Community which Britain could not leave. This change did not go unchallenged but over the course of the decade from 1979 the party as a whole altered its ground dramatically. Of course, it placed stress upon the 'social dimension' as an essential element in the building of the new Europe but it now contrived to appear to be in the main stream of European thinking. Some erstwhile Labour opponents of the Community eagerly saw the light. A visit from Jacques Delors, the French Socialist who was President of the Commission, to the TUC conference at Bournemouth in 1988 was rapturously received as he outlined the 'Social Europe' of the future. Delors was not popular with Mrs Thatcher. The episode was another example of the interpenetration of 'British' and 'European' politics.

The fruit of this change of front was gathered in the elections to the European Parliament held in June 1989. Neither previous election had excited much interest. Only a third of the electorate had bothered to vote. On both occasions, the British electorate seemed to take the view that it was not the business of the European Parliament to have a particular view on Europe. Voters used the occasion to register their attitude towards the British government of the day. The position in June 1989 was not that different. Only 37 per cent of the electorate voted – the lowest percentage in the Community – and Labour wanted the electorate to pronounce on ten years of Mrs Thatcher. Even so, despite the fact that Labour's campaign was co-ordinated by Bryan Gould, who found it difficult to disguise his hostility to the Community, the Labour gains were held to confirm that Britain had chosen a European future. Conservative propaganda, which held out the dire prospect of Britain living 'on a diet of Brussels' unless Conservative Euro-MPs were returned, seemed to have misjudged the mood of the country.

In addition, in that same summer, the Prime Minister was in difficulties with several of her senior Cabinet colleagues. She had retained her hostility to membership of the exchange rate mechanism (ERM) of the EMS but Labour, in the person of John Smith, the shadow chancellor, urged Britain to join. The argument was that it would be an invaluable counter-inflationary discipline because it would stabilize the exchange rate of sterling within certain bands. The fateful British habit of relying on a depreciating currency to pass on increased costs would be conquered. It was also a necessary step towards economic and monetary union, which Labour now also supported. A willingness to join the ERM became the conviction of all sensible people. Since the Foreign Secretary, Howe, and the Chancellor of the Exchequer, Lawson, were also sensible people, they at length had the unusual success of persuading the Prime Minister to commit Britain to join, albeit after certain 'conditions' were allegedly met. Howe's reward was demotion from the Foreign Office. She made little effort to retain Lawson as

383

Chancellor when he resigned in protest against her reappointment of an economic adviser who was a known opponent of the ERM. Even so, early in October 1990, Britain did join the ERM, to general rejoicing among those who claimed to understand the indubitable benefits it would bring. When market pressure forced the British government to withdraw from the ERM in September 1992, enthusiasm for its benefits dwindled. It was alleged that membership had severely inhibited the economic recovery which was so badly needed. The government, having tried desperately to keep sterling in the mechanism, put a brave face on what had happened. Labour, in turn, could not make much of the government's difficulty because it had been an even keener advocate of membership. Wise men concluded that the mechanism was basically something which could work. It was just that Britain had gone in at the wrong rate in 1990.

The government concerned, however, was the government of John Major, not of Margaret Thatcher. Exasperation with her attitude towards the Community had boiled over inside the Conservative Party. There was a point at which the Prime Minister's style became a matter of substance. The mood Mrs Thatcher had struck would make it more difficult for Britain to retain a position of influence in the vital debate on Europe's future. So declared Sir Geoffrey Howe in his resignation speech of November 1990. The following day, Michael Heseltine, in announcing his intention to stand against Mrs Thatcher in the Tory leadership election, identified Mrs Thatcher's handling of European issues as the main reason for his challenge. That challenge failed but Mrs Thatcher was compelled to resign. As has been seen, there were other factors in this outcome but it can be said that it was 'Europe' which brought about her downfall. It was a matter for speculation where precisely the new Prime Minister stood on 'Europe'. For some, it was a matter of great relief that he declared in Bonn in March 1991 that he wanted Britain to be where Britain belonged – 'At the very heart of Europe, working with our partners in building the future'.

From one standpoint, therefore, it is not surprising that the Maastricht agreement, concluded on 11 December 1991, produced a national debate during the protracted process of ratification which echoed many of the arguments deployed at the time of the referendum in 1975. The Maastricht Treaty, more argued over than read in detail, was the culmination of one of those surges towards closer union which have characterized the evolution of the Community. Strictly speaking, it was not a treaty at all but a series of amendments and adjustments to what was already in the founding Treaty of Rome. Needless to say, Britain was not in the van. The momentum came from Bonn and Paris, with strong support from the Dutch and Belgian governments. The new British Prime Minister, John Major, was well aware of the opposition within his own party to any new arrangements, either political or economic, which could be considered 'federal' (although that was undoubtedly what was in the minds of the leading mainland governments) and had to be as much concerned for what he could persuade his own party to accept as with what might be in the best interests of Europe as a whole – at a time, in any event, when so much was happening in Central and Eastern Europe which perhaps invalidated some of the assumptions which lay behind the plans.

It is worth recalling, however, that John Major, who was to put his signature to the Maastricht agreement, was not even an MP in 1975. His expressed desire that Britain should be at the heart of Europe was indeed the voice of a new political generation, though that generation did not speak with a single voice on Europe. Even so, from Hurd, the Foreign Secretary, downwards, it continued to be asserted that Britain was divided from the other members of the Community by its different history. The debates surrounding the content of the history syllabus to be taught in schools in England and Wales, which raged in parliament and the press in the late 1980s, revealed strong support for the emphasis government wished to place upon British history as a discrete entity, to be treated separately from 'European history'. Even the Working Party set up to consider the curriculum, in justifying in 1989 the teaching of European history, could only talk about the fact that 'links' between Britain and her immediate European neighbours were currently 'growing closer'. It did not dare suggest that schoolchildren in the 1990s should be helped to address the history of the Community of which they were a part. Of course, each member state has its particular history, but whereas for 'Continentals' European history includes the history of Great Britain, in Britain European history largely continues to mean 'Continental' history(286).

It is against such a background that the 'opt-outs' negotiated by Britain alone of EC members at Maastricht must be seen. The refusal of the British government to implement the 'Social Chapter', which attempted to establish uniform provisions on a whole range of social and industrial issues, reflected the particular social philosophy of the government. However, the British refusal to agree to move to Stage Three of the proposed timetable for economic and monetary union without a separate decision to do so by its government and parliament reflected a more general disquiet. The British did not want to see themselves 'irrevocably' committed to a single currency and a European Central Bank by 1 January 1999 without having an opportunity to pass judgement on the stages towards that goal. No other Community government insisted on these 'opt-out' rights, assuming that their parliaments or populations would ratify the entire package. The failure of the Danish people to do so, by a small majority, and the narrow approval extended by the French people in a referendum indicated that the pace and direction of European integration gave rise to more than insular anxieties.

In turn, different sections of British opinion chose to stress, approvingly or disapprovingly, according to taste, the fact that a new article in the Maastricht agreement enshrined the principle of 'subsidiarity' – the notion that any action by the Community should only be taken if its objectives could not be sufficiently achieved by the member states individually. There was also dismay in some quarters that economic and monetary union still formed the clear objective of the Maastricht scheme. For some, Maastricht was one further step in the inexorable process of European unification, with Britain as a leading player in that process. For others, Maastricht was a futile fossil – a relic of policies which had lost their relevance in a world which had changed dramatically since the notion of European union had been first canvassed. The conditions which were decreed to make Economic and Political Union possible – convergence of exchange rates, public debt ratios and inflation – would not in fact be achieved. British MPs who declined to support the government in ratifying Maastricht were sometimes also heard to say that it would not work. It remains to be seen whether the agreement is a 'marginal comment on the flow of Europe's history' or whether it will provide the blueprint for Europe in the twentieth century.[1] In the summer of 1993, the virtual collapse of the ERM as a result of pressure on the franc seemed to suggest that at the very least the timetable for monetary union would need adjustment.

When the British parliament came to consider the Maastricht agreement at very great length in 1992–93, it was only too apparent that the Conservative Party was bitterly divided on its merits. An unsuccessful campaign was mounted to achieve another referendum on the lines of 1975. Great passion and bitterness was displayed and it was only with great difficulty in the summer of 1993 that parliamentary consent was achieved. From the perspective of Delors, the 'British problem' in Europe remained, both psychologically and politically.

Yet nothing stands still. The Maastricht agreement was the climax to developments which had been initiated in the mid-1980s – before the dramatic events of 1989–90 which witnessed the collapse of Communism in Eastern Europe and the reunification of Germany. By 1993, it did appear that the British obsessions and concerns, expressed over nearly twenty years, no longer appeared quite so idiosyncratic and perverse. In other states, notably in Germany, national needs and perspectives, for very understandable reasons, were voiced with less reservation than formerly. In a situation of currency volatility, of doubts about the feasibility of 'convergence' within the timetable envisaged, of desire for 'enlargement', of anxiety about GATT, to mention only a few matters, it may well be that the Community in the year 2000 will have a form and substance which will have moved both beyond what successive British ministers have feared and beyond what 'Brussels' has desired – to take a shape which it is as yet impossible to predict.

---

1. A. S. Milward, *The European rescue of the nation-state* (1992), p. 444

CHAPTER 41

Britain in the world

In the decades after 1945, as the Empire dissolved, there was much anguished discussion, at least in some quarters, of the extent to which Britain remained a 'world power'. 'We are a world power and a world influence', Harold Wilson had declared in his Mansion House speech of November 1964, 'or we are nothing'. A decade later, however, such declarations sounded somewhat hollow. That British Prime Ministers felt obliged to describe matters in such stark terms was itself symptomatic of an inability or an unwillingness to contemplate a more modest but still significant future as an upper-middle-rank European power. This state of mind helps to explain Britain's difficulties in the Community which we have just considered.

In the later 1970s, however, if there was indeed a stark choice between being a 'world power' and being 'nothing', there were grounds for supposing that Britain was on the verge of being 'nothing'. Gloomy British diplomats across the globe sensed that they were no longer being given the attention they were used to when they presented their country's case in foreign capitals. The 'valedictory despatch' of Sir Nicholas Henderson, British Ambassador in Paris, in March 1979, argued that the economic weaknesses of the 1970s had undermined British standing in the world. In turn, the foreign policy that had been attempted had itself contributed to that decline.

Much turns, of course, on the meaning of the term 'world power'. The fact remained that the United Kingdom retained its status as a Permanent Member of the United Nations Security Council and as a nuclear power. It also retained a close relationship with one of the 'Superpowers', the United States, yet at the same time, through the Commonwealth, it had access to a network of relationships with the Third World. These were, of course, inheritances from the past, but were these assets wasting assets – if indeed they were assets at all? It was the case that Britain had a world position, but did it have the *power* to sustain that position in a meaningful manner? The decisions made earlier in the decade meant that Britain was no longer burdened to anything like the same degree with fixed and expensive military bases across the globe. By the same token, it was likely to prove extremely difficult to maintain adequate forces for every conceivable 'out of area' operation where British interests of some kind were involved(289).

The fate of rebellious Rhodesia was a case in point (see pp. 268–70). The administrations of Heath, Wilson and Callaghan had all tried a mixture of coercion and negotiation to end the illegal white minority government led by Ian Smith. However, they had not succeeded in achieving an arrangement which was acceptable to the black majority of the rebellious territory and, hence, to 'world opinion' as expressed through the United Nations. In 1979, however, the ingredients for a settlement were there. The 'internal solution', devised in Rhodesia, of a government headed by Bishop Abel Muzorewa had not proved acceptable internationally. On the other hand, the Rhodesian forces were still effective and it would take a long time for the various black guerrilla groups to defeat them. South Africa appeared to want a settlement.

Between August and November 1979, at Lancaster House in London where the future of the country was being considered, pressure was exerted on the white minority with the result that Rhodesia became independent (as Zimbabwe) the following year. The good offices of various outside figures from the Commonwealth played a significant part in achieving this outcome. That the Conservatives achieved this settlement occasioned some surprise, since commentators supposed that the new administration would not have been prepared to move so far and so quickly. It demonstrated, however, a determination to resolve an issue which had been causing difficulties for Britain within the Commonwealth and the United Nations for years. Washington would be satisfied. Something might happen which might make goodwill in those quarters important. Few supposed that a battle in the South Atlantic would prove that occasion.

Except among philatelists and admirers of sheep, the Falkland Islands, with their less than two thousand people, had not been featured prominently in British public consciousness. Located some 300 miles from the Straits of Magellan, the islands had been repossessed by Britain in 1833 which had governed them thereafter. The Argentine claim was based on earlier occupation and proximity. Successive British governments were embarrassed rather than elated when they considered the future of the Falkland Islands. Although the inhabitants were indubitably of British stock, they were a long way away. It was wisdom that their future prosperity required good relations with 'neighbouring' Argentina. Unfortunately, successive governments in Buenos Aires claimed the islands. It was especially unfortunate that the military junta in power saw an opportunity for fame and glory. A successful campaign would perhaps take the mind of the population off its domestic ills.

Needless to say, for years, various ingenious formulae to 'solve' the problem had existed. The one pursued initially involved transferring sovereignty to Argentina but in return for a long-term lease of the islands to Britain. It met its nemesis in the Commons in December 1980 at the hands of both Tory and Opposition MPs. Nothing much then happened for some months. However, the future of the islands then became caught up in a Defence Review. The government was supposedly pledged, in line with NATO thinking, to increase defence expenditure by 3 per cent in real terms. Pym, the Defence Secretary, had been removed at the beginning of the year because he had not stood up effectively to the military lobby – or so it was said. It is, of course, common for governments to seek better defence and cheaper defence simultaneously. Nott, Pym's successor, tried to square the circle by planning to reduce British capacity outside the NATO area. In June 1981 it was announced that one casualty of this ordering of priorities would be *HMS Endurance*, a survey ship which operated in the South Atlantic. It had its limitations as deterrent against possible aggression but the Foreign Office saw in its continued presence on station a symbol of continuing British commitment. The Foreign Office lost the argument. Understandably perhaps, the fate of the Falklands did not move to the top of the government's agenda. It did not even do so, however, in March 1982, when there were indications of impending Argentinian unilateral action. On 1 April the invasion took place. What should the British reaction be?(290).

The mood of the Commons on 3 April was indignant and bellicose. It was incredible that a British territory should have been invaded. There was a substantial cross-party consensus – with few exceptions – that something had to be done and done quickly. The tone of the Prime Minister was restrained by comparison with other voices. She knew that something was already being done to prepare a naval task force but she also knew that the risks were large. As things stood, the government was open to the accusation of negligence and incompetence. Carrington's resignation as Foreign Secretary was accepted, that of Nott, the Defence Secretary was refused. Only a successful outcome, however, could guarantee the survival of the Prime Minister. Pym, Carrington's successor appeared still to think that a solution could be found without war. That was not the Prime Minister's view. There are few grounds for supposing that she was wrong.

After three weeks of fighting, beginning on 21 May, British forces achieved a complete victory. The sinking of the Argentine cruiser, the *General Belgrano*, at the beginning of the month, was to prove a source of continuing argument for many years. Critics claimed that it represented an attempt to scupper negotiations which might yet have succeeded. Whether or not this was the case, and the picture is not yet complete, it demonstrated the single-mindedness with which the government approached the entire affair. The efficiency of the operation and the modest level of British casualties enabled the government to present it to the world as a triumph.

It was indeed an outcome which mysteriously lifted the spirits of the nation – though there were dissenters who were appalled by the whole affair or who, like the Archbishop of Canterbury, resisted the triumphalism which accompanied the success. In itself, it was an event so singular in character that it did nothing to change the fundamental factors which determined Britain's position in the world, but it did have a strong if temporary influence on national morale. The British could do something successfully. Such an achievement swept into obscurity questions which supposed realists reasonably wished to ask about the long-term costs and benefits of the Falkland Islands. A point had been made to the world – even if it greatly complicated the overall assessment of Britain's defence needs.

No care was taken to emphasize the extent to which the co-operation of the United States had proved of great assistance in the whole affair. Nonetheless, the success of British diplomacy in Washington and New York was highly significant. Above all, the personal rapport between the Prime Minister and President Reagan brought back all the old language about the 'special relationship'. Given the apparently deteriorating international situation as evidenced by the Soviet invasion of Afghanistan (1979), the Iran-Iraq war (1980), the Israeli invasion of Lebanon (1982), some comfort could be drawn in Washington from the notion of Britain under Mrs Thatcher as the most reliable ally of the United States.

This intimacy, in turn, complicated Britain's relationships in Europe. It was conspicuous that the British government had no reservations about the deployment of Cruise and Pershing missiles, in response to the Soviet deployment of SS20s. Some other European governments wobbled, partly because their public opinions seemed more hostile than the British. There was some disquiet in Britain too – symbolized by the women who took up residence on Greenham Common as a gesture of protest against the siting of the missiles and by the revived appeal of the Campaign for Nuclear Disarmament. The Defence Secretary, Michael Heseltine, appointed in January 1983, attempted with a certain success to defend the merits of the government's policy. The robust line taken by the Prime Minister left no room for doubt about the alignment of Britain in a Cold War that seemed to be getting colder. Her handling of the Falklands affair enhanced her own confidence in conducting foreign policy and produced a situation, by no means without precedent, in which the Prime Minister seemed to be in personal charge of foreign policy and to have taken the organizational steps necessary to perform effectively in this role.

Yet, the fact that in October 1983 the American administration sent troops into the Caribbean island of Grenada to overthrow a Marxist regime without consulting the British government was a reminder, if one were needed, that despite the rapport between Thatcher and Reagan, and their general identity of outlook, particularly concerning the Soviet Union, it was the United States which was the superpower. Grenada was a small member of the Commonwealth – a fact which created the expectation in London that the British government should have been consulted even though, of course, Grenada did not 'belong' to Britain. Perhaps the Americans could be forgiven for failing to understand that Queen Elizabeth II mysteriously remained head of state in this independent island. The Queen and the President subsequently made their peace with the aid of horses. When the two met, their common and conspicuous devotion to these animals helped them to remove hard feelings. Mrs Thatcher's anger subsided in due course without equine assistance.

The Conservative election victory of 1983 led to the replacement of Pym by Sir Geoffrey Howe as Foreign Secretary. It may have been Howe's influence that led to a more nuanced approach to the Soviet Union and the countries of Eastern Europe, though still within the same basic framework. In February 1984 Mrs Thatcher achieved a considerable personal success on a visit to Hungary. Even more significant was her favourable impression of Mikhail Gorbachev when he visited London on an extended stay in December 1984 before becoming Soviet leader. It was her perception on this and subsequent occasions that he was a man with whom it would be possible to do business. A strong ideological dislike of Communism, it seemed, could be combined with a pragmatic approach to particular countries and individuals. In the years that followed, the strength of Mrs Thatcher's personality made a big impact in Eastern Europe – greater, indeed, than any other British Prime Minister had made in that area. Her standing, however, was also strengthened by the extent to which it was perceived that her views carried weight with President Reagan. In the mid-1980s, she achieved, for a time, that status of 'go-between' in East–West relations to which Churchill had aspired thirty years earlier.

Even so, it should not be supposed that the Prime Minister 'controlled' Washington's foreign policy. There were periodic reminders of Britain's subordinate status. The American administration launched its Strategic Defence Initiative ('Star Wars') without prior discussion in 1983. Considerable scepticism existed in Whitehall about this programme, voiced in public by Sir Geoffrey Howe at intervals over the next two years. While not criticizing the Americans in public, the Prime Minister succeeded in getting agreement that any shift from research to actual deployment would have to be negotiated. She also thought she had ensured contracts for Britain for SDI research.

A more dramatic incident was the American bombing of Libya in April 1986. Allegedly it was because F111s flying from land bases would be more accurate than carrier-based aircraft that the British government was asked to allow such an operation. Given American support over the Falklands, the Prime Minister felt she could not refuse – though no other European government would agree. The raid caused considerable public controversy and the government some embarrassment – not least because it appeared to identify Britain as a client of the United States. President Gaddafi survived the attack though its deterrent value was perhaps greater over the longer term than critics were willing to concede at the time. Whether or not that was the case, the British government did not want to be placed in the same invidious position again. The raids were not repeated on subsequent occasions.

The importance of British policy was again demonstrated in the autumn of 1986. In October, at Reykjavik in Iceland, Reagan and Gorbachev discussed wide-ranging proposals for the reduction of nuclear weapons during the course of one of the more bizarre 'summits' in recent history. At one point, indeed, it looked as though 'the elimination of all nuclear weapons' was a serious possibility. In the event, the exchanges came to nothing since Gorbachev wanted a drastic curtailment of the SDI programme as the basis for an agreement. Reagan saw in the SDI initiative a system which would make it safe to agree to drastic reduction of nuclear weapons. From a European perspective, this extraordinary discussion had threatened to remove, without consultation, the nuclear deterrent on which the defence of Western Europe rested. If the Americans were going to continue on this track, Western Europe would be exposed to the superior conventional forces and arms of the Warsaw Pact countries. The limitations of the 'independent' British nuclear weapon would become very evident.

Since the importance of the nuclear deterrent was a key element in the Prime Minister's defence thinking and the issue which separated her most clearly from the Labour Opposition, the Prime Minister visited Washington at the end of 1986 determined to put matters back on what she considered to be an even keel. On this occasion, too, Mrs Thatcher was in the rare position of being able to speak not only for British Conservatives but also for most of the European members of NATO. In the outcome, it was officially asserted that nothing had changed in basic NATO strategy. As for reduction in weaponry, it would be limited, if at all, to an intermediate-range missile deal and a 50 per cent cut in strategic weapons. Mrs Thatcher received what was to her of crucial importance, namely an assurance of the availability of Trident missiles with which to modernize the British deterrent. It would be an exaggeration to describe the outcome as a 'triumph' for Britain alone and testimony to London's substantial influence. Mrs Thatcher's success was as much the result of deep disquiet in United States defence circles in the fall-out from Reykjavik as of the inherent strength of argument. It is unlikely, however, that any other European leader could have been as effective at this time. Britain remained the junior partner but could not be ignored on such a major issue.

The resolution of the Rhodesian crisis at the beginning of the first Thatcher government did not mean that the controversies within the Commonwealth which it had occasioned came to an end. The most conspicuous source of debate and dispute concerned the future of South Africa. South Africa itself was of course not now a member of the Commonwealth but the apartheid system there was anathema not only to African member states but to the Commonwealth as a whole – at least to judge from the frequent declarations of governments on the subject. Demands for the imposition of mandatory sanctions, led by African member states, became more strident. The British government was not impressed. The more pressure mounted, the less the British government was impressed. The Prime Minister mounted a crusade to expose hypocrisy in her critics. It was not too difficult to do so. Commonwealth Heads of Government Meetings had condemned racialism repeatedly – but racialism, of one kind or another, was not confined to South Africa. It was also not hard to detect that there were many Commonwealth governments whose systems of government and public conduct departed from the glorious example which Britain itself so manifestly provided. In turn, however, the spotlight could be turned on Britain itself. Did not the supposed concern for the sufferings which sanctions would impose on the black population in particular cloak British concern for its substantial economic interest in South Africa? And so it continued.

The Commonwealth conference held in Nassau in the Bahamas in October 1985 was a conspicuous example of the tensions the South African question engendered. The British Prime Minister was virtually alone in her adamant opposition to the tough regime of economic sanctions demanded by many speakers – a fact which lent strength to her conviction that she was right. In the end, she consented to some modest sanctions but with an ill-grace and no confidence in their utility. It was better, she believed, to persuade the Afrikaners rather than attempt to coerce them – a tactic she tried with President Botha. An 'Eminent Persons Group' was assembled and sent off to southern Africa as an indication of the Commonwealth's concern.

It was not only the specific question of South Africa, however, where the Commonwealth aroused the barely concealed scorn of the Prime Minister. She seems to have felt that its high-minded discussions of issues such as the relationship between the Northern and Southern hemispheres led nowhere. The reasons for this disdain are not straightforward. Some have supposed that opposition to Commonwealth demands was a polite way of pandering to racialist sentiment in Britain. That is easier to surmise than to prove. It may also reflect a complex sense of irritation and dismay at what the Commonwealth had turned out to be. In the early post-war decades, too much optimism about its importance had been expressed. It was being replaced by a sense that the whole thing was an elaborate farce.

Whatever interpretation is placed on the Prime Minister's personal emotions and motives, it would be misleading to suppose that her reactions set her apart from the majority of the British people. Indeed, it would have been difficult for any Prime Minister to have identified the Commonwealth as the key to understanding Britain's place in the world. It was not only the military regimes which had come to predominate in African member countries or the recurring instability in the Indian sub-continent which promoted indifference or disdain. There was a steadily growing realization that the comfortable intimacy associated with the language of 'Old Dominions' was almost a thing of the past. Post-1945 immigration into Australia, for example, had produced a society there which found it increasingly difficult to relate to the surviving symbols of Australia's 'Britishness'. It appeared likely that, by the time it achieved its centenary, 2001, Australia would have declared itself a republic. Linguistic and ethnic tensions in Canada, likewise, led successive federal administrations to pursue 'multiculturalism' in an attempt to defuse them. In the process, it was important not to give too much emphasis to the British element in Canada's past. It became questionable in the 1980s, indeed, whether Canada as such would survive. Nevertheless, in the educational, sporting and other fields there remained a multitude of Commonwealth links and organizations. And, in the person of the Head of the Commonwealth, it was very conspicuous that whatever might be the attitude taken by her government in the United Kingdom, there was one lady in London for whom the significance of the Commonwealth had not diminished – Queen Elizabeth II.

The future of the Commonwealth as a whole might be dubious but there still remained specific lingering issues from the imperial past which still had to engage a British government in the 1980s and beyond. The most conspicuous of these was the future of Hong Kong – a centre of commerce and manufacture which had enjoyed brilliant success from the 1950s onwards. Its future had to be considered since British leases on over 90 per cent of the territory would expire in 1997 and return to China. It would be idle to suppose that the remaining 10 per cent was viable. This legal position hardly constituted a strong basis for reaching an agreement with the Government of the People's Republic of China which would give some security for the capitalist system on which the colony's prosperity was based and also for whatever 'democratic' aspects of its government existed. In a century of British rule, democracy had not been very conspicuous, but in the short time that was left there was scope for development.

In the event, as a result of the agreement concluded in 1984, 'two systems' were to exist within one country for half a century after 1997. This outcome was received somewhat euphorically but it remained to be seen how far it would hold, even until 1997. One could only speculate about the future beyond that date. A new form of nationality – British National (Overseas) was on offer for those who did not wish to register as Chinese, though it did not convey a right to settle in the United Kingdom. For the time being, however, Sino-British relations seemed good and the settlement was generally held to be a satisfactory one, even though substantially conducted by the Foreign and Commonwealth Office without too much Prime Ministerial assistance. Her visits to China, however, further encouraged the idea that, despite everything, Britain still had some kind of special role. It was one which diplomats as much as politicians were reluctant to let go.

That there still remained some disconcerting substance in this notion appeared to be shown by events in the late 1980s and early 1990s. In South Africa, President de Klerk's speech of February 1990, announcing the unbanning of black political parties and his intention to end apartheid, brought about a major change in the politics of southern Africa. The British government took some credit for this development since it was claimed that British pressure on the South African government had more effect than boycotts and the attempts to impose sanctions. Whatever the truth of the claim – and it is difficult to prove one way or the other – Britain remained in a position, as Douglas Hurd, the Foreign Secretary put it, to act as 'a sympathetic, friendly observer'. However, it was not the intention of the British to stick their noses into discussion uninvited. All sides realized just how difficult it would probably prove to translate de Klerk's speech into a constitutional settlement which would prove generally acceptable. At this time, Britain remained overall South Africa's most important economic partner and her historical and cultural links with a country in which the English language was clearly becoming dominant were of great importance. No other European country had such a strong link. The virtual 'normalization' of dealings with South Africa and the near coincidence of Mrs Thatcher's departure from office removed at a stroke the issue which had threatened sensible discussion within the Commonwealth.

In addition, the role of Britain in the Gulf War of January 1991 stood out in comparison with that of her European Community partners. The Iraqi invasion of Kuwait in August 1990 was of course the invasion of a state which Britain had protected until 1961. It hardly needs saying that the British connection with the Gulf area went deeper and had lasted longer than that of any other European state. Unlike the years immediately after Kuwaiti independence, however, Britain was in no position to reverse the Iraqi invasion. However, unlike the reaction in most other West European states, it was clear from an early stage that Britain was prepared to contemplate war. In consequence, over the months that followed, Washington found it far easier to co-ordinate military plans and diplomatic strategies with Britain than it did with any other ally. It became evident just how difficult it was to formulate a common approach in the European Community. Of course, the military power of the United States, and the support of some Arab countries for the deployment of that power was vital to the success of the enterprise. Nevertheless, the professionalism of the British Army both in planning and in operations was of no small significance in the success of the campaign. Some commentators contrasted the 'civilian society' which they detected in continental Europe with British society which was apparently willing to contemplate the war with a certain equanimity. In diplomatic terms, there was a need to pick up the pieces in Europe and start, once again, on the long and elusive road to a common foreign policy. And, at each moment when sensible journalists pronounced that the 'special relationship' no longer existed, something seemed to happen to show that it did.

Above all, however, the most dramatic event of these years was the complete collapse of Communism in Eastern Europe and, with it, the coming together of the two German states. It was only this last development which caused alarm in some quarters as old apprehensions about the power of a single Germany at the centre of Europe resurfaced. The post-Cold War future might require a total reconsideration of British foreign policy. Looking at events in 1989–90, however, even Mrs Thatcher's warmest admirers may find it difficult to credit her with the sequence of events which collectively signified the end of that Cold War which had dominated the international scene since 1945. On the other hand, the warmth of her personal reception in Eastern European countries, together with her relationship with Gorbachev, suggest that there was a part which British foreign policy had effectively played in the final stages of the process.

There were grounds, therefore, for supposing, after ten years as Prime Minister, that Thatcher had raised the standing of Britain in world politics(288). The vigour, simplicity and clarity of her convictions could be thought to have triumphed. She had put to flight the pessimism and pusillanimity of those who yearned that Britain should become an insignificant medium-sized European power released from the debilitating grandeur still epitomized in continuing permanent membership of the Security Council of the United Nations. It was that world role, however, which Major, the new Prime Minister was determined to uphold, as he declared during the 1992 General Election campaign. As so often in the post-1945 world, the rhetoric of British aspiration and the reality of British power remained uneasily matched.

CHAPTER 42

Unity and division

REGIONS AND NATIONS

Such unity as the period from 1975 to the early 1990s possesses derives, politically, from the impact made by Margaret Thatcher. Unity was indeed one of the themes she stressed. Both domestically and externally she believed she pursued the 'national interest' without reservation and could point to her three successive victories as evidence that she had identified it correctly. She upheld the unity of the state in the face of those who sought to undermine it. Yet, throughout these years, there was a paradox, if not a contradiction. It has already been noted that her governments never had the support of a majority of voters, though the Conservatives could validly claim that they enlisted consistently more support than any other party. Whereas in the 1950s, Conservative and Labour had the support of more than 90 per cent of those who voted, by the 1970s their combined support was only more than 70 per cent(293).

That difference is largely accounted for by the rise of the Liberal/Liberal Democrat vote and of the emergence of Plaid Cymru and the Scottish National Party as fixtures in the political landscape in Wales and Scotland. In the 1970s and thereafter, too, the Unionists in Northern Ireland, both Official and Democratic, were conspicuously unwilling to accept the firm alignment with the Conservative Party which had formerly been largely axiomatic. The representation of all shades of opinion from Northern Ireland at Westminster stood therefore at a tangent from the main thrust of British politics, though the increase in seats for the province also increased their importance at certain critical parliamentary junctures when a government majority was in jeopardy. Most recently, for example, that turned out to be the case in the final debate in the Commons on thes Maastricht Treaty in 1993(295).

Viewed from this perspective, it is not so much the unity of the United Kingdom which stands out as its increasing division. That division was masked by the fact that the two main parties continued to hold more than 90 per cent of the seats at Westminster between them. Of course, the disparity between the parliamentary picture and the preference of those who voted (not to mention that quarter (roughly) of the electorate which did not vote, for whatever reason) did not escape attention. Naturally, it was the Liberal Party which constantly stressed the inequity, even the corruption, of the existing system. From that perspective, the electoral system, with its insistence on 'first past the post' obscured the plurality of the country and gave an appearance of unity which was spurious. One in four voters had no means of making any impact on the political process commensurate with the total that represented. The country was in fact a patchwork of minorities and, it was claimed, British democracy would be stronger if that fact were recognized. Some carried the argument a stage further to suggest that professional politicians, as most had become, were out of touch with opinion in the country. The mistakes and misjudgements made by all governments reflected the poverty of experience (outside Westminster) on the part of ministers.

The issue of the governance of the United Kingdom outside England did not again come to the forefront of discussion, as far as Scotland and Wales were concerned, in the way it had done at the beginning of the period. The failure of the referendums held in 1979 in Scotland and Wales was held by the incoming Conservative government to be conclusive proof that the devolution issue was dead (see pp. 284–5). Unlike Heath, who had flirted with the idea, Thatcher had no patience with it. She had no intention of reviving the debate by introducing any legislation of her own. Her successor, in the 1992 General Election, campaigned vigorously in favour of the kind of unity in which he believed. That he should have felt a need to do so with such passion was an indication that in fact, in the intervening years, the issue had not disappeared. The Conservative ascendancy was an English ascendancy. The Conservatives had made progress in Wales in 1979 and 1983 but had not sustained their advance thereafter. They were not the majority party in Wales and did not appear likely to become such. Labour remained the majority party in Wales, though Plaid Cymru seemed to be consolidating its hold on the peripheral western constituencies which contained a majority of Welsh speakers. Labour also remained the largest party in Scotland, though the SNP, whose fortunes fluctuated, became solidly entrenched in certain areas in Scotland. Indeed, in both countries, when Liberal representation is included, a four-party system operated as compared to England where, to all intents and purposes, a three-party system operated.

It is scarcely surprising, therefore, that a sense of alienation from the United Kingdom, as it existed, was widespread. There was a feeling of disunity, not unity. Previous parts of this book have made it clear that non-Conservative governments were imposed on England by the seats at Westminster gained outside England. That had sometimes rankled with English Conservatives but it had not threatened to be a permanent phenomenon. From the late 1970s onwards, it looked as though English Conservative preponderance was such that no swing of the pendulum could be envisaged and return at Westminster a government with which the majority of voters in Scotland and Wales felt comfortable.

Mrs Thatcher and her successor were both, in their different ways, very English and their rapport with other parts of the kingdom was uncomfortable. In the case of Thatcher, it could appear that she was either indifferent or uncomprehending in her handling of Scottish issues and perspectives. Since she did not need a majority in Scotland to govern the United Kingdom, why should she worry about its particular problems? The Conservatives in Scotland felt beleaguered. It was baffling that they could not share in the popularity of their counterparts south of the border. They were divided, in response, between a strong defence of the benefits of the status quo for Scotland and a willingness to swim a little way with the devolutionary tide. In some quarters it seemed plausible to describe the Secretary of State for Scotland, a Scottish Conservative MP, as an embattled colonial governor facing a sullen population with barely enough supporters to man the Scottish Office.

That same feeling existed in some quarters in Wales. Whatever their personal qualities, three Conservative Secretaries of State for Wales were Englishmen representing English constituencies. For some, of course, national considerations of this kind were petty and irrelevant. It was conceded, for example, that Walker's term of office in Wales was an energetic one in which he brought his considerable political experience to bear for the benefit of the principality(292).

However that may be, the sense of alienation in Scotland was not assuaged, although opinion polls which had suggested a majority in 1992 in favour of Scottish independence proved to be wrong and the Conservatives modestly made up a little ground. Even so, unity still looked a little precarious, particularly since all of the non-Conservative parties, in varying degrees, favoured devolution or independence. That fact was not the force it might be because, for other reasons, they found it impossible to concentrate on this issue to the exclusion of all others. In particular, the Labour Party in Scotland and Wales could not escape from the dilemma that the creation of separate parliaments would almost certainly entail some reduction in representation at Westminster and thus make a Labour government even more difficult to achieve than was already the case. Yet, in the eyes of the English electorate, Labour had come to have something of a non-English image. After Wilson resigned in 1976, no Labour leader represented an English constituency and latterly no Labour leader has been English.

Disunity remained the defining characteristic of Northern Ireland. The resolution of its communal problems remained intractable throughout the period and they were of a different order from those in Scotland and Wales which have just been alluded to. Violence, although it fluctuated in intensity and remained to a degree localized, was nevertheless endemic. Politics continued to revolve around interlocking religious, cultural and social perceptions of identity. There could be no acceptable complete union with the Irish Republic. There could be no complete assimilation into the norms (in all their diversity) prevailing in Great Britain. There could be no union in the province itself. Successive British Secretaries of State for Northern Ireland (who were English or Welsh) shuttled between Belfast and London with great regularity, sometimes carrying with them new proposals to find a 'solution' on which all parties could agree, gathered round a table. The British Army maintained its operations, alienating first one side and then the other either by the ferocity or the feebleness of its conduct. The 'armed struggle' of the IRA continued both in the province and in Britain. Bombs in London and elsewhere caused very considerable damage and some loss of life(294).

The Northern Ireland question aroused mixed emotions and reactions in Britain. Over twenty years, the endless reporting of bombs and assassination in the province had left a considerable section of the British population in a condition of indifference, from which only some particular incident occasionally jolted it. The best way to deal with Northern Ireland was to forget about it. On the other hand, bombs in the City of London evoked the spirit of defiance. Prime Ministers declared that the IRA would never succeed in bringing about a change in the status quo by use of such tactics. On the Left there were calls for 'troops out' and on the Right some unreserved commitment to 'no surrender'. The majority of British people did not know what to think and just hoped that one day the violence would all come to an end. Politicians could not rest content with such fatalism.

It seemed in the early 1980s that a new mood of understanding was dawning between Dublin and London, whatever might be happening in Belfast itself. Inter-governmental conferences began talking a new language which seemed to suggest that the totality of relationships between both parts of Ireland and Britain should be looked at afresh. In 1985 came what the London press insisted on referring to as the Anglo-Irish agreement, in blissful ignorance of the past and present importance of Scotland in the Irish conflict. It was 'bounced' on the Unionists and caused intense anger and fear because, from their perspective, the limited and legitimated interest of the Republic's government in the North, in particular in the affairs of the Catholic/Nationalist minority, was seen as, if not an abhorred 'joint rule' at least as a strong step in that direction. Thatcher, who knew very well what Irish terrorism was like, argued that the recognition that there were indeed two proper traditions in Northern Ireland was a necessary step towards their reconciliation. The constitutional position remained unchanged. Great hopes were placed in the agreement but, at least as far as the abatement of terrorism was concerned, it did not bring about the hopes placed in it. Its existence both made possible further inter-party talks and their success impossible. Parliamentary exigencies, that is to say the support of the Ulster Unionists in the Commons, seemed latterly to make the British government more sympathetic to their view. The end of the Irish question – or perhaps it was the British question – was not in sight.

These long established historical issues were by no means the only examples of division. Commentators placed increasing emphasis on a North/South split within England itself. Of course, this too was not without its history. Only in simplistic presentations was the division between a depressed North and a prosperous South absolute, but, when every allowance had been made for exceptions and variations, it did appear that there was some substance in the broad categorization. However, when the detailed pattern of regional development had been compiled, there was no unanimity about its significance.

For some writers, not well-disposed towards the government, the 'shake-out' was a deliberate calculation. The base of Conservative support was in the South of England and the dynamic nature of some areas there was a plot to secure Conservative hegemony over Britain in the way made possible by the electoral system. For others, the dynamism of the South-east of England or of East Anglia was itself in large measure a product of circumstances which not even a Thatcher government could direct. That part of England which was closest to the European mainland was sucked into its prosperity. It was fortunate for the country as a whole that this was the case.

It was, however, true that on the whole the 'shake-out' hit the North hardest. It is arguable that the steel and other industries which went through rationalization and de-manning emerged as more efficient and competitive enterprises but the loss of employment in many industrial areas grievously affected their vitality and self-esteem. An atmosphere of decline in turn made it more difficult to bring in alternative employment.

The outcome was again a sense of alienation from the base of political power. It was rare to find a Cabinet minister, even one of northern origins, who represented a northern constituency in parliament. Correspondingly, it was rare to find a Labour shadow spokesperson who was attuned to vibrant towns in the South. The bulk of new jobs created in the years after 1983 were southern and the bulk of old jobs lost before 1983 were northern. A city like Liverpool seemed to be sunk in a decline which seemed irreversible – though Glasgow, by contrast, seemed to be lifting itself into a more prosperous period.

Once again, it must be emphasized that the contrast can be overstressed in particular instances, but the conviction that there was a great divide, itself a political fact of some importance, was by no means purely propaganda. The imbalances of skills, the problems of housing and transport, which were all part of this phenomenon in turn made it difficult to think of any single economic policy which was appropriate not only for the United Kingdom as a whole but for England as a whole. Action to deal with 'overheating' as it manifested itself in the South-east was scarcely appropriate in other areas where it was nowhere to be seen. Population movement, however, was not all one way, though it did serve to show the dominance of the South-east. Householders there who realized the value of their houses could acquire more substantial properties at far less cost away from London, with the result that more peripheral regions in both England and Wales received an unanticipated influx of 'newcomers'. To some extent, however, at the very end of our period, the imbalance began to shift. In the depression of that period parts of the South suffered severely and the housing market collapsed. Relatively speaking, a 'leaner' North of England and South Wales proved more resilient. For at least a decade, however, it was divergence rather than convergence which was most characteristic(291).

SOCIETY UNDER STRESS

Linked to these regional and national divisions were other divisions which seemed to some commentators to be as defining of the Thatcher years as the 'enterprise culture'. Indeed, perhaps the two were inextricably linked. Those very incentives and deregulation initiatives of which the government was so proud served to deepen divisions of wealth, health and welfare. These in turn were related to poor skills, poor opportunities and the breakdown of family life in the form of accelerating divorce (from which the royal family was conspicuously not exempt) and illegitimacy rates. There was much argument about the extent to which family disintegration was a cause or a consequence of many of these conditions. What could not be disputed were the facts which showed a dramatic change. In 1963 there were a mere 23,000 divorces in England and Wales. Thirty years later it was a normal assumption that one in three marriages would end in divorce. The 1971 Divorce Law Reform Act had of course made divorce easier. It might also be argued that the 'real' as opposed to the 'legal' breakdown had not changed so dramatically. Although there was an increasing acceptance of various kinds of relationship which stopped short of marriage, the incidence of re-marriage suggested that the institution itself was not as dead as some commentators supposed(296). The one-parent family, however, was now an established and commonplace phenomenon. The legalization of abortion, subject to certain constraints, which had been enacted in 1968, resulted in a normal pattern of more than 100,000 terminations per annum and remained a topic of passionate debate.

Alongside these developments went an apparently inexorable rise in recorded crime and the seeming inability of the police, despite increased resources, to contain it. In turn, perhaps as a result of the pressure they were under, cases of police misconduct and corruption contributed to a sense of malaise. The greatest source of concern was the rise in crimes against the person, and vandalism. Even when every allowance had been made for the difficulties in interpreting statistics – was there more crime or more recorded crime? – the picture was disturbing and, for many, frightening. In a single year, 1986–87 crimes against the person increased by 12 per cent. Other indicators of social stress were not lacking. Although figures are again difficult to be dogmatic about, the number of alcoholics was apparently steadily rising – perhaps three-quarters of a million in Britain. Although fashions in drug-taking appear to have fluctuated, experimentation among the young was thought to be widespread. Heavy drugs in turn produced in some quarters a drug culture. It was widely supposed that a considerable portion of the increase in crime could be explained, at least in urban areas, by the need to finance to drug habit. Against these trends, it was possible to note a very considerable shift away from smoking – at least among men. A considerable change in public attitudes to drinking and driving was also detectable.

Some inner city areas and peripheral housing estates, in these circumstances, teetered on the edge of communal breakdown and violence. Occasionally rioting did occur. There was always a danger, in some areas, that this would take the form of racial conflict. Homeless people begging and sleeping in the street became a new phenomenon in its extent. Violence against the elderly and the sexual exploitation of the young frequently hit the headlines in a popular press itself without parallel in Europe for its uninhibited sensationalism.

Pessimistic observers detected a complete collapse of social values but were by no means unanimous in their diagnosis of the causes and certainly by no means confident in the remedies they advanced. Were the consequences of a long slow drift away from religious belief and practice at length making themselves evident in a fashion that secular liberal humanists had dismissed as impossible? It was certainly the case that all of the mainline churches, latterly including Roman Catholics, struggled against the tide of opinion and behaviour. There were notable exceptions, but most clergy in all churches found it difficult to come to terms with what had become a missionary situation(300).

Where could the cycle of improvement begin? Was a divide between 'haves' and 'have nots' an unpalatable aspect of a sophisticated technological society which could not recapture a more primitive sense of 'community' even if it wanted to? It was easy to lay the blame for these disconcerting phenomena on 'Thatcherism'. However, just as it was claimed that its supposed hallmarks had not in fact been accepted by the majority of the population, so it is unrealistic to suppose that it could have in itself have spawned so much that was disagreeable, even threatening, in the Britain of the early 1990s. It was incontestable, however, that the range of problems which now came within the sphere of the 'Welfare State' showed no sign of diminution. In turn, its future functions and financing, scarcely ever moved off the political agenda. The National Health Service survived but in an atmosphere of constant inter-party argument about resources and funding. How could one find a way to produce a more effective service, given that no government could ever hope to meet all the demands which might be placed upon it? In establishing NHS Trusts and fund-holding by GPs, in the final years of our period, the government claimed that it could create a system which would be more cost-effective and also serve the interests of patients. It was a claim widely contested by the medical profession. Thus even the maintenance of national health and social harmony was itself a cause of national disunity and debate(297, 298).

The distinguished French historian, Elie Halévy, in writing on Britain in the 1890s spoke of the country as being 'en pleine décadence'. 'Decadence' was indeed something much discussed a century ago. Somehow or other, however, the country had come through. It might do so again. The causes (and consequences) of the rise and fall of Great Powers do not indeed admit of any easy generalizations.

COMPENDIUM OF INFORMATION

A: THE POPULATION OF THE UNITED KINGDOM, 1871–1991
(000s)

	UK	England	* %	Wales	* %	Scotland	* %	Ireland All	N.	* %
1871	31,398	21,203	67.5	1,421	4.5	3,362	10.7	5412	(1,359)	17.2
1881	34,884	24,398	69.9	1,577	4.5	3,735	10.7	5174	(1,304)	14.8
1891	37,732	27,227	72.2	1,776	4.7	4,025	10.7	4,704	(1,236)	12.5
1901	41,459	30,514	73.6	2,015	4.9	4,472	10.8	4458	(1,237)	10.8
1911	45,222	33,630	74.4	2,442	5.4	4,760	10.5	4390	(1,251)	9.7
1921	47,123	35,357	75.0	2,656	5.6	4,882	10.4	4228	(1,256)	9.0
1931	46,038	37,324	81.1	2,593	5.6	4,842	10.5		1,279	2.8
1951	50,225	41,160	82.0	2,599	5.2	5,096	10.1		1,370	2.7
1961	52,709	43,462	82.5	2,644	5.0	5,178	9.8		1,425	2.7
1971	55,515	46,026	82.9	2,724	4.9	5,229	9.4		1,536	2.8
1981	55,818	46,363	83.06	2,792	5.0	5,131	9.19		1,532	2.74
1991	54,487	46,161	84.71	2,798	5.13	4,957	9.09		1,570	2.88

* % indicates percentage of United Kingdom population.

Notes: Southern Irish population is included in the United Kingdom total for the last time in 1921. The pre-1931 figure for N. Ireland, placed within brackets, approximates to the area of the subsequent 'province'. The first independent census in N. Ireland was taken in 1926 and the second in 1937; these figures have been entered in 1921 and 1931 respectively.

B: HOLDERS OF THE PRINCIPAL OFFICES OF STATE, 1868–1992

Government	Prime Minister	Foreign Secretary	Chancellor of Exchequer	Home Secretary
1868 (Lib)	Gladstone 59	*Clarendon*	Lowe	Bruce
		Granville 1870	Gladstone 1873	Lowe 1873
1874 (Cons)	Disraeli 70	*Derby*	Northcote	Cross
		Salisbury 1878		
1880 (Lib)	Gladstone 70	*Granville*	Gladstone	Harcourt
			Childers 1882	
1885 (Cons)	*Salisbury* 55	*Salisbury*	Hicks Beach	Cross
1886 (Lib Feb)	Gladstone 76	*Rosebery*	Harcourt	Childers
1886 (Cons Aug)	*Salisbury* 56	*Iddesleigh*	Churchill	Matthews
		Salisbury	Goschen	
1892 (Lib)	Gladstone 82	*Rosebery*	Harcourt	Asquith
1894 (Lib)	*Rosebery* 46	*Kimberley*	Harcourt	Asquith
1895 (Cons)	*Salisbury* 65	*Salisbury*	Hicks Beach	Ridley
		Lansdowne 1900		Ritchie 1900
1902 (Cons)	*Balfour* 54	*Lansdowne*	Ritchie	Akers-Douglas
			A. Chamberlain 1903	
1905 (Lib)	Campbell-Bannerman 69	Grey	Asquith	H. Gladstone
1908 (Lib)	Asquith 55	Grey	Lloyd George	H. Gladstone
				Churchill 1910 McKenna 1911
1915 (Coalition)	Asquith 62	Grey	McKenna	Simon
				Samuel 1916

Government	Prime Minister	Foreign Secretary	Chancellor of Exchequer	Home Secretary
1916 (Coalition)	Lloyd George 53	Balfour	Bonar Law	Cave
1918 (Coalition)	Lloyd George 56	*Curzon*	A. Chamberlain	Shortt
			Horne 1921	
1922 (Cons)	Bonar Law 64	*Curzon*	Baldwin	Bridgeman
1923 (Cons)	Baldwin 55	*Curzon*	Baldwin	Bridgeman
			N. Chamberlain 1923	
1924 (Lab Jan)	MacDonald 57	MacDonald	Snowden	Henderson
1924 (Cons Nov)	Baldwin 57	A. Chamberlain	Churchill	Joynson-Hicks
1929 (Lab)	MacDonald 62	Henderson	Snowden	Clynes
1931 (Nat Aug)	MacDonald 64	*Reading*	Snowden	Samuel
1931 (Nat Nov)	MacDonald 65	Simon	N. Chamberlain	Samuel
				Gilmour 1932
1935 (Nat)	Baldwin 67	Hoare	N. Chamberlain	Simon
		Eden 1935		
1937 (Nat)	Chamberlain 68	Eden	Simon	Hoare
		Halifax 1938		
1940* (Coalition)	Churchill 65	*Halifax* Eden 1940	Wood Anderson 1943	Morrison
1945 (Caretaker)	Churchill 70	Eden	Anderson	Somervell
1945 (Lab July)	Attlee 62	Bevin	Dalton	Ede
			Cripps 1947	
1950 (Lab Feb)	Attlee 67	Bevin	Cripps	Ede
		Morrison 1951	Gaitskell 1950	

Government	Prime Minister	Foreign Secretary	Chancellor of Exchequer	Home Secretary
1951 (Cons)	Churchill 76	Eden	Butler	Maxwell-Fyffe
				Lloyd George 1954
1955 (Cons)	Eden 57	Macmillan	Butler	Lloyd George
		Lloyd 1955	Macmillan 1955	
1957 (Cons)	Macmillan 62	Lloyd	Thorneycroft	Butler
		Home 1960	Heathcoat Amory 1958	Brooke 1962
			Lloyd 1960	
			Maudling 1962	
1963 (Cons)	Douglas-Home (formerly *Home*) 60	Butler	Maudling	Brooke
1964 (Lab)	Wilson 48	Gordon Walker	Callaghan	Soskice
		Stewart 1965		Jenkins 1965
1966 (Lab)				
		Brown 1966	Jenkins 1967	Callaghan 1967
		Stewart 1968		
1970 (Cons)	Heath 53	Douglas-Home	Macleod Barber 1970	Maudling Carr 1972
1974 (Lab)	Wilson 57	Callaghan	Healey	Jenkins
1974(Oct) (Lab)	Wilson 58	Callaghan	Healey	Jenkins
1976	Callaghan 64	Crosland	Healey	
1979 (Cons)	Thatcher 53	*Carrington*	Howe	Whitelaw
		Pym 1982		
1983 (Cons)	Thatcher	Howe	Lawson	Brittan
				Hurd 1985

Government	Prime Minister	Foreign Secretary	Chancellor of Exchequer	Home Secretary
1987 (Cons)	Thatcher	Howe	Lawson	
		Major 1989	Major 1989	
		Hurd 1989		Waddington 1989
	Major 1991 48			
1992 (Cons)	Major	Hurd	Lamont	Clarke
			Clarke 1993	Howard 1993

* Morrison was not a member of the war cabinet until 1942

Note: Italics denote peers of the realm.
Figures under Prime Ministers indicate their ages when appointed.

C: ELECTORAL REFORM

1. The reforms of 1867–1868

(a) Changes in the distribution of seats in England and Wales
 (i) Three double-member borough and 1 single-member borough disfranchised for corruption.
 (ii) Boroughs with a population of less than 10,000; 3 lost both members, 35 lost 1 of their 2 members and 4 lost their single member.
 (iii) Two new double-member and 9 new single-member borough constituencies created.
 (iv) Birmingham, Leeds, Liverpool and Manchester increased from double- to triple-member constituencies. Merthyr Tydfil and Salford become double-member constituencies.
 (v) Ten counties elect 2 additional members each: Lancashire elects 3 additional members; Yorkshire (West Riding) elects 2 additional members.
 (vi) University of London to elect 1 member.

(b) Main qualifications for the franchise in England and Wales
 (i) In *county* seats – those with lands of a clear yearly value of at least £5, owned or on lease of 60 years or more; those occupiers of lands to a rateable value of £12 per annum who have paid the relevant poor rates; otherwise as established in 1832.
 (ii) In *borough* seats – adult male owners and occupiers of dwelling house, if resident for at least 12 months; lodgers occupying lodgings worth at least £10 per annum, if so occupied for at least 12 months; in county or borough seats with 3 members, no elector could vote for more than 2 candidates; in the 4-seat constituency of the City of London no elector could vote for more than 3 candidates.

(c) Size of the electorate in England and Wales
The electorate reached nearly 2 million – a proportion of 1 in 3 of the adult male population.

(d) Scotland
An 1868 Act made substantially the same provision for Scotland, though the property qualification for county occupiers was fixed at £14 rather than £12. The Scottish electorate in 1869 has been estimated at over 230,000, giving much the same proportion of the adult male electorate as in England and Wales.

Glasgow and Dundee gained additional members (1 each): Aberdeenshire, Ayrshire and Lanarkshire were each divided into 2 divisions returning 1 member each: Peebles and Selkirk shires were joined and had only 1 member: there were 2 new Scottish university constituencies each returning 1 member.

(e) Ireland
Electoral law in Ireland remained on a different basis from that in Britain. It produced an electorate estimated at over 220,000 in 1869 – representing 1 in 6 of the adult male population.

2. The reforms of 1884–1885

(a) The Representation of the People Act, 1884
This eliminated the anomalies in the basis of representation between different parts of the United Kingdom. It established a uniform householder and lodger franchise for every borough and county, based on that for English boroughs in 1867. It also provided for an occupation franchise for those with lands or tenements worth £10 a year. Different structures of population and ownership meant that the differences between England,

Wales, Scotland and Ireland in electoral terms still existed though they were not as great as formerly.

(b) Size of electorate

	1883	1886	
England and Wales	2,618,453	4,380,333	2 in 3 in 1886
Scotland	310,441	550,831	3 in 5 in 1886
Ireland	224,018	737,965	1 in 2 in 1886

Source: H. J. Hanham, *The Reformed Electoral System in Great Britain, 1832–1914* (1968).

(c) Major redistributions under the 1885 Act

England and Wales: 132 seats lost and 138 new seats created.

Disfranchised: 13 boroughs returning 2 members merged in the counties: 66 boroughs returning 1 member merged in the counties: 36 boroughs returning 2 members deprived of 1 member and 2 boroughs returning 2 members lost them both.
Enfranchised: London (including Croydon) to return 62 members (+40): additional members allocated to provincial boroughs, new provincial boroughs and additional members to counties (+66).

Scotland: 2 seats lost and 12 new seats created.

Disfranchised: 2 boroughs returning 1 member each merged in counties.
Enfranchised: 7 new seats allocated to counties and 7 to Aberdeen, Edinburgh and Glasgow.

Ireland: 25 seats lost and 25 new seats created.

Disfranchised: 22 boroughs returning 1 member each, 3 boroughs returning 2 members each deprived of 1 member.
Enfranchised: 21 seats allocated to counties and 4 seats to Belfast and Dublin.

The redistribution worked to the advantage of Ireland, Scotland and Wales in so far as they had smaller MP/electorate ratios than obtained in England.
Source: C. Cook and B. Keith, *British Historical Facts, 1830–1900* (1975) pp. 114–17 (adjusted).

3. Representation of the People Act (1918)

This Act abolished the property qualification for voting and enfranchised women aged 30 and over. The residence qualification was reduced to 6 months. Certain changes were also made in electoral administration – elections were to be held on the same day, candidates were required to pay a deposit of £150 to be forfeited on failure to poll more than one-eighth of the total votes cast (though they were no longer required to pay the charges of the returning officer).

There was also a redistribution of seats, with more emphasis placed than hitherto on equality of size. The membership of the House of Commons rose to 707, though it fell within a few years with the creation of the Irish Free State. The creation of a devolved Parliament in Northern Ireland resulted in a smaller number of MPs being returned to Westminster than would have been justified on population grounds.

4. The Equal Franchise Act (1928)

This enfranchised women at 21 on the same basis as men. The measure was passed by 387 votes to 10 – an indication of changed attitudes compared with the period before 1914. It added 5¼ million women to the register; they then comprised over 52 per cent of the total electorate. When allowance has been made for plural voting arising from business or university qualifications, the electorate as a proportion of the adult population rose from 27 per cent in 1900 (58 per cent of the male population) to 90 per cent in 1929 and 97 per cent in 1939.

5. Representation of the People Act, 1948

This Act abolished all plural voting and university seats. It also brought into operation the first recommendations of the Boundary Commission which had been set up under the Redistribution of Seats Act, 1944. This Commission was originally charged with making recommendations every 3 to 7 years but, although the intention was to neutralize the drawing of appropriate boundaries, the Commission was to experience difficulty with the Labour government in 1969. By then, in any case, it was only required to make proposals every 5 to 10 years. Major changes in electoral boundaries took place before the 1950, 1955 and 1974 (Feb) General Elections.

6. Representation of the People Act (1969).

This Act reduced the voting age to 18.
Sources: D. Butler and A. Sloman, *British Political Facts, 1900–1979* (1980); F. W. S. Craig, *British Electoral Facts, 1885–1975* (1976).

The House of Lords

The 1911 Parliament Act stipulated that:
  (i) Bills certified by the Speaker of the House of Commons to be money bills were to receive the royal assent one month after being sent to the House of Lords – even without its consent.
 (ii) Any other public bill (except one for extending the life of a Parliament) passed by the House of Commons in three successive sessions and rejected by the House of Lords was to receive the royal assent, provided that 2 years had elapsed between the second reading in the first session and the third reading in the third session of the House of Commons.
The 1949 Parliament Act reduced the delaying powers of the House to two sessions and one year.
At various points after 1918 (the Bryce Report of that year was one instance) attempts were made to devise means of joint consultation between the Lords and Commons or to introduce an elected element into the composition of the Lords, perhaps on a regional basis. In 1967, the Labour government announced its intention to reform the Lords, but two years later a plan was abandoned. There have, however, been three significant constitutional changes:
  (i) beginning in 1946, 'regular attenders' could be reimbursed their travelling expenses.
 (ii) the Life Peerages Act, 1958, provided for the creation of life peers and peeresses. The introduction of this category raised the membership of the Lords to over 1,000 in the early 1970s.
(iii) Peerage Act, 1963, allowed peers to disclaim their titles, permitted all Scottish peers to attend, and admitted all female holders of hereditary titles.

The Monarchy

VICTORIA	June 1837–Jan 1901
EDWARD VII	Jan 1901–May 1910
GEORGE V	May 1910–Jan 1936
EDWARD VIII	Jan–Dec 1936 abdicated
GEORGE VI	Dec 1936–Feb 1952
ELIZABETH II	Feb 1952

D: UNITED KINGDOM GENERAL ELECTIONS: 1874–1992

Part 1: Great Britain and Ireland, 1874–1918

This chart does not distinguish between Conservatives and Liberal Unionists, and treats Irish Nationalists as a single entity. The figure on the top line indicates the number of seats won and that on the bottom line the percentage of the poll (in whole numbers). Presenting information in this easily assimilable fashion involves some distortion – for example, no account is taken of the considerable number of unopposed returns. In particular, most Irish Nationalists (IN) were unopposed.

	UK				England			Wales			Scotland			Ireland		
	C	L	La	IN	C	L	La	C	L	La	C	L	La	C	L	N
1874	352	242		58	*288*	171		11	19		20	40		33	12	58
(Con)	45	49		6	50	50		42	58		33	67		26	31	44
1880	238	354		60	203	*256*		2	*28*		9	*53*		26	17	60
(Lib)	46	50		4	50	50		37	63		33	67		28	23	49
1885	250	334		86	214	*237*		4	*29*		8	*51*		16	0	85
(Lib)	44	47		7	48	51		39	58		34	53		25	7	68
1886	393	191		85	*333*	122		8	26		27	43		17	0	84
(Con)	51	45		4	53	47		46	54		46	54		50	1	49
1892	314	271		81	261	190		3	*31*		20	*50*		21	0	80
(Lib)	47	45		7	51	48		37	63		44	54		21	1	78
1895	411	177		82	*343*	112		9	25		31	39		19	1	81
(Con)	49	46		4	52	45		42	57		47	52		26	7	67
1900	402	183	2	82	*332*	121	1	6	27	1	*36*	34		19	1	81
(Con)	50	45	1	3	52	46	1	38	59	4	49	50		32	2	57
1906	156	399	29	83	122	*306*	26	0	*32*	1	10	*58*	2	15	3	82
(Lib)	43	49	5	1	44	49	5	34	60	4	38	56	2	47	20	24
1910 (Jan)	272	274	40	82	233	188	33	2	*27*	5	19	59	2	19	1	81
(Lib)	47	44	7	2	49	43	7	32	52	15	40	54	5	33	10	54
1910 (Dec)																
(Lib)	272	271	42	84	234	186	34	3	*26*	5	9	*58*	3	17	1	83

	C	L	La													
1918 (Coal)	335*	133*	10*													
	23	28	63													
	3	12	22												SF	
														23	72	6

* Coalition supporters gained 478 seats and took 47 per cent of the poll.

Note: Italic figures indicate where the party with the largest number of United Kingdom seats and/or the governing party also had a 'local' majority in England, Wales or Scotland.

Part 2: Great Britain, 1922–1955

	UK			England			Wales			Scotland		
	C	La	L	C	La	L	C	La	L	C	La	L
1922	344	142	62	307	95	44	6	18	2	13	29	15
(Con)	39	30	19	42	29	20	21	41	8	25	32	22
			Nat L			Nat L			Nat L				Nat L
		53			33			8					12
		10			8			26					8
1923	258	191	158	221	138	123	4	19	11	14	34	22
(Lab)	38	31	30	40	30	30	21	42	35	32	36	28
1924	412	151	40	347	109	19	9	16	10	36	26	8
(Con)	47	33	18	48	33	18	28	41	31	41	41	17
1929	260	287	59	221	226	35	1	25	9	20	36	13
(Lab)	38	37	24	39	37	24	22	44	34	36	42	18
1931 (Nat)												
*1935	432	154	20	351	116	11	9	18	6	42	20	3
(Nat)	54	38	7	53	39	6	28	45	18	49	37	7
1945	216	393	12	166	331	5	4	25	6	27	37	0
(Lab)	39	48	9	40	49	9	23	59	15	41	48	5
1950	298	315	9	253	251	2	4	27	5	31	37	2
(Lab)	44	46	9	44	46	9	27	58	13	45	46	7
1951	321	295	6	271	233	2	6	27	3	35	35	1
(Con)	48	49	3	49	49	2	33	61	7	50	48	3
1955	344	277	6	292	216	2	6	27	3	36	34	1
(Con)	50	46	3	51	47	3	30	58	7	51	47	2

* The parties supporting the National government received 554 seats and gained 67 per cent of the vote. The Liberal MPs were divided 35/33 between Liberal National and Liberal. Labour with 52 MPs and 33 per cent of the vote formed the Opposition.

Note: One Communist MP was elected in 1924 and 1935 and two in 1945, but not since. From 1955 onwards no MP has been returned unopposed.
Throughout this period N. Ireland almost invariably returned 10 Unionists and 2 anti-Unionists.

Part 3: Great Britain, 1959–1992

This table illustrates the growth of national parties in Wales and Scotland. In 1970 and 1974(2) the SNP gained 1, 2 and 3 per cent respectively of the UK vote. Plaid Cymru never gained 1 per cent. Until 1970 the Ulster Unionists retained their traditional relationship with the Conservative party and their MPs are recorded in the UK. Conservative total in that year for the last time. Thereafter, because of the fragmentation of Ulster political parties, they have been left out of the UK totals.

	UK			England			Wales				Scotland			
	C	La	L	C	La	L	C	La	L	PC	C	La	L	SNP
1959	365	258	6	315	193	3	7	27	2	0	31	38	1	0
(Con)	49	44	6	50	44	6	33	57	5	5	47	47	4	1
1964	304	317	9	262	246	3	6	28	2	0	24	43	4	0
(Lab)	43	44	11	44	44	12	29	58	7	5	41	49	8	2
1966	253	364	12	219	286	6	3	32	1	0	20	46	5	0
(Lab)	42	48	9	43	48	9	28	61	6	4	38	50	7	5
1970	330	288	6	292	217	2	7	27	1	0	23	44	3	1
(Con)	46	43	8	48	43	8	28	52	7	12	38	45	6	11
1974	297	301	14	268	237	9	8	24	2	2	21	40	3	7
(Lab)	38	37	19	40	38	21	26	47	16	11	33	37	8	23
1974	277	319	13	253	255	8	8	23	2	3	16	41	3	11
(Lab)	36	39	18	39	40	20	24	50	16	11	25	36	8	31
1979	339	269	1	306	203	7	11	22	1	2	22	44	3	3
(Con)	44	37	14	47	37	15	32	49	11	8	31	42	9	17
1983	397	209	23	362	148	13	14	20	2	2	21	41	8	2
(Con)	42	28	25	46	27	26	31	38	23	8	28	35	25	12
1987	376	229	22	358	155	10	8	24	3	3	10	50	9	3
(Con)	42	31	23	46	30	24	30	45	11	7	24	42	19	14
1992	336	271	20	319	195	10	6	27	1	4	11	49	9	3
(Con)	42	34	18	46	34	19	29	48	12	9	26	40	13	22

E: INFORMATION ON WARS AND THE ARMED SERVICES

These figures should be treated with care and only as a preliminary to further investigation. Few books or even official statements give the same figures for enlistment or casualties, reflecting in part the difficulty of determining how far, for example, war wounds were a cause of death and how long, in this respect 'war' lasts into 'peace'. It is not easy, either, to make straightforward comparisons between the major wars or even to define who a 'British soldier' is. Likewise, the concept of 'mobilization' for war involves a rather wider category of people. What follows gives an idea of the 'order of magnitude'; it does not offer precision. Figures are in millions.

1. The South African War, 1899–1902

About 0.45 troops were deployed, of whom about 0.02 were killed or died of disease and about the same number were wounded.

2. The First World War, 1914–1918

By the end of the war 5.7 had been mobilized, of whom 0.6 were killed or died of wounds and 1.6 were wounded (in varying degrees of gravity). The army, which stood at 0.5 million on the eve of war rose to 1.6 by the end of the year, 2.6 by December 1915, 3.3 by December 1916, and 3.7 by December 1917, at which figure, approximately, it remained until the end of the war. The army bore the brunt of the deaths in a proportion of about 25 to 1 to the losses suffered by the navy. Air force deaths were small in total number, but high in proportion to the size of the service.

3. The Second World War, 1939–1945

By the end of the war 6.5 had been mobilized, of whom 0.3 were killed or died of wounds and approximately the same number were wounded. It is thus clear that total deaths or injuries were significantly lower than in the First World War. On the other hand, the nature of the conflict is reflected in the fact that naval deaths were twice what they had been and about a third of the losses suffered by the army. Merchant navy losses were also significantly higher. The RAF suffered just under half the total of army losses – and among bomber crews in particular the chances of being killed were very high. Civilian deaths from air raids and rocket attacks at some 0.06 were roughly 60 times greater than in the First World War.

Sources: C. Cook and J. Stevenson, *Longman Atlas of Modern British History* (1978); C. Cook and J. Paxton, *Commonwealth Political Facts* (1979).

4. Wars and Counter-Insurgency after 1945

British forces were engaged in operations in Malaya against Communist (largely Chinese) insurgents from 1949 to 1955. They were engaged in Kenya in the middle 1950s after the outbreak of the Mau Mau rebellion in 1952. In 1955 open warfare also broke out in Cyprus between British forces and the Greek underground organization, EOKA, which advocated union with Greece. Forces were, in addition, sent to British Guiana (Guyana). Neither the total number of troops deployed in these operations nor the casualties sustained were large in comparison with the Second World War but the 'guerilla' nature of the warfare and the fact that young national servicemen were often involved combined to magnify their impact. In general terms, however, these operations were 'successful' in the short term at least, in comparison with counter-insurgency strategies pursued by other European powers and by the United States in Vietnam. They were also successful in comparison with activity during the final period of British rule in Aden and with the short and aborted British military activity in Egypt during the 1956 Suez crisis.

The Korean War (1950–1953) was the only sustained 'conventional' war in which British forces were engaged – under UN auspices. Second World War collaboration lingered on in the form of the 1st Commonwealth Division. The achievements of the 'Glorious Gloucesters' were widely celebrated. British casualties amounted to 686 killed and 2,498 wounded. In the much shorter Falkland Islands campaign of 1982, 255 British servicemen and civilians were killed.

The ending of the Cold War, coupled with the wish of government to reduce defence expenditure produced wide-ranging reviews which sought to reduce force levels in all of the services to a significant extent. The Gulf War and UN operations in the former Yugoslavia combined to show, however, that British forces demonstrated a high degree of 'professionalism' despite contraction in size. In an uncertain world, it proved difficult for politicians to decide the role and scope of the British armed services.

Size of armed forces

	Army	Navy	RAF
1946	2,950,000	492,000	760,000
1958	443,000	121,500	187,000
1974	177,000	81,000	103,000
1991	147,000	65,500	83,000

F: INDUSTRIAL AND EMPLOYMENT INFORMATION

1. Size of labour force (millions):
1901	16.3 (M–11.5, F–4.7)
1931	21.0 (M–14.7, F–6.2)
1951	24.6 (M–15.6, F–9.6)
1970	24.7 (M–15.9, F–8.7)

   The number of married women at work as a percentage of all married women reached 40 per cent in 1971, having increased by some 10 per cent in each of the three previous decades.

2. Density of union membership as a percentage of the labour force:
1901	12
1933	22
1956	44
1975	51

3. Total trade union membership in millions:
1906	1.9
1931	4.8
1956	9.7
1975	11.9

   (between 1906 and 1931 the peak membership was 8.3 in 1921 before it fell away in the later 1920s). In recent decades union membership has been densest in coal-mining, the railways, road and sea transport and weakest in agriculture and forestry, and the construction and distribution industries. Membership of white-collar unions has increased by over 100 per cent 1948–74 for men and women. Membership of manual unions has slightly declined for men but risen by over 50 per cent for women over the same period.

4. The years in which the number of working days lost rose above 10 million (in most other years the figure was below 5 million):
1908	(10.7)	1923	(10.6)
1911	(10.1)	1926	(162.2)
1912	(40.8)	1970	(10.9)
1919	(34.9)	1971	(13.5)
1920	(26.5)	1972	(23.9)
1921	(85.8)	1974	(14.7)
1922	(19.8)		

5. Employment in specific industries (in millions)

	1871	1901	1931	1951	1971
Agriculture	1.8	1.5	1.3	1.1	0.4
Mining	0.6	0.9	1.2	0.9	0.4
Manufactures	3.9	5.5	7.2	8.8	8.1
Construction	0.8	1.3	1.1	1.4	1.3

G: RELIGION AND CHURCH ALLEGIANCE IN THE UNITED KINGDOM

All these figures should be treated with extreme caution and offer only general guidance. Inter-denominational comparisons are very difficult to make when different notions of what constitutes 'membership' or 'adherence' abound. Some churches maintained careful membership records while others did not; some figures reflect the number of communicants (say at Easter) in a given year – a higher figure than the numbers committed to active church life, but probably lower than the number of those who might still, at least in certain circumstances, identify themselves as Christians of a certain persuasion.

	England (000s)				
	1871	*1901*	*1931*	*1951*	*1971*
Roman Catholic*	1,354	1,600	2,206	2,837	4,010
Church of England	1,384	1,945	2,288	· 1,900	
Presbyterian	38	78	84	68	59‡
Methodist			769	681	571
WMC†	319	412			
MNC†	22	32			
BC†	18	28			
PMC†	148	188			
UMFC†	61	72			
Baptists	150	243	254	205	173
Congregational	190	258	286	207	151‡

* Roman Catholic figures are for England and Wales.
† WMC = Wesleyan Methodist Church; MNC = Methodist New Connexion; BC = Bible Christians; PMC = Primitive Methodist Church; UMFC = United Methodist Free Church.
‡ Presbyterians and Congregationalists united to form the United Reformed Church in 1972.

There were an estimated 1.5 million Easter and 1.6 million Christmas communicants in the Church of England in 1990.

Wales (000s)				
	1871	*1901*	*1931*	*1951*	*1971*
Roman* Catholics	1,354	1,600	2,206	2,837	4,010
Anglicans*	86	144	185	185	123
Calvinistic Methodists	93	160	185	157	108
Wesleyan Methodists	26	44	53	46	33
Baptists	70	109	124	105	
Independents/ Cong.	90	149	161	143	105

* Roman Catholic figures are for England and Wales.
* After disestablishment in 1920 the Anglican church took the style The Church in Wales.

Scotland (000s)					
	1871	*1901*	*1931*	*1951*	*1971*	*1991*
Roman Catholic	326	450	605	748	818	798
Episcopal	56	116	118	103	85	
Presbyterian: C of Scotland				1,273	1,154	
C of S*	400	500	650			770
FC of S*	253	350	} 538			
UPC*	163	200	}			
Methodist	5	8	11	13	11	
Baptist	7	17	22	19	16	
Cong.	23	30	38	35	25	

* C of S = Church of Scotland; FC of S = Free Church of Scotland; UPC = United Presbyterian Church.

	Ireland (000s)	
	1871	*1901*
Roman Catholic	4,150	3,308
Church of Ireland	667	581
Presbyterian	497	443
Methodist	43	62

	Northern Ireland (000s)						
	1926	*%**	*1951*	*%**	*1971*	*%**	*1981*
Roman Catholic	420	33	471	34	477	31	414
Presbyterian	393	31	410	30	405	26	339
Church of Ireland	338	27	353	25	334	22	281
Methodist	49	3	66	4	71	4	58

* Uniquely, the census in Northern Ireland elicits information on church allegiance.
The figure in the percentage column therefore represents the proportion of the total population not of the 'religious population'. It should be noted that in 1971 over 9 per cent of the total population refused to state their religion – though this is not necessarily to be taken as an indication that such people had no religion. The total numbers recorded above are higher than those emanating from church sources – whether of 'adherents', 'members' or 'communicants', but not very much higher – the correlation between denominational profession and active membership being closer in Northern Ireland than in Great Britain.

	United Kingdom (000s)		
	1975	*1982*	*1991*
Roman Catholic		4,280,180	
Presbyterian	1,650		1,290
Methodist	610		483
Baptists	270		242

Information on United Kingdom church adherence has been derived from R. Currie, A. Gilbert and L. Horsley, *Churches and Churchgoers: Patterns of Church Growth in the British Isles since 1700* (Oxford, 1977), and from W. E. Vaughan and A. J. Fitzpatrick, *Irish Historical Statistics* (Dublin, 1979).

Church leadership

The leadership of the various churches has differed in its nature and purpose, reflecting in part diverging attitudes to authority and the respective spheres of the clergy and laity.

Within the Church of England, the archbishops of Canterbury were:

1868	A. C. Tait	1942	W. Temple
1883	E. W. Benson	1945	G. Fisher
1896	F. Temple	1961	A. Ramsey
1903	R. Davidson	1974	D. Coggan
1928	C. Lang	1980	R. Runcie
		1991	G. Carey

After the disestablishment of the Church of England in Wales, the archbishop of Wales in the Church in Wales was chosen from among the bishops of that church and not tied to a particular see. Likewise with the primus of the Episcopal Church in Scotland. The archbishop of Armagh, the primate of the Church of Ireland was chosen from among the church's bishops – an arrangement which survived the political partition of the island.

The Roman Catholic Church in the United Kingdom was organized in three hierarchies – England and Wales, Scotland and Ireland (again in this latter instance surviving political partition):

Westminster		*St. Andrews and Edinburgh*		*Armagh*	
1875	H. E. Manning	1878	J. M. Strain	1870	D. McGettigan
1892	H. Vaughan	1885	W. Smith	1887	M. Logue
1903	F. Bourne	1892	A. MacDonald	1924	P. O'Donnell
1935	A. Hinsley	1900	J. Smith	1928	J. MacRory
1956	W. Godfrey	1951	G. Gray	1946	J. D'Alton
1963	J. Heenan	1985	K. O'Brien	1963	W. Conway
1976	B. Hume			1977	T. O'Fiach
				1990	C. Daly

Among the non-episcopal churches in England, Ireland, Scotland and Wales, leadership was normally exercised on a rotating basis for a year at a time by the moderator of the General Assembly (of the Presbyterian churches), of the president of Conference (among Methodists) and of the president of the Union (among Baptists and Congregationalists).

In the latter instances, the president might not be an ordained minister.

Non-Christian religious communities

Before post-Second World War immigration, the only significant community was Jewish as shown in table below:

Estimated Community figures (in 000s)

	1901	1931	1951	1975	1990	1992
Jewish	160	300	450	410		350
Buddhist				21	30	
Moslem				400	900	
Sikh				115	175	
Hindu				100	140	

H: THE CHANGING FACE OF BRITISH SOCIETY

The Family

1.   Total live births (England/Wales)   Total outside marriage

1975	603,445	54,891
1986	661,018	141,345
1991	698,885	211,237

Health

2. Age distribution in Great Britain in 1991:

Under 15	Over 65
11.041 million	5,945 million

3. Causes of death. Tuberculosis was the largest single cause of death in England and Wales at the beginning of the century, but by 1975 it had been virtually eliminated. Deaths from cancer and heart disease showed a fourfold increase of the same period.

4. Government expenditure on the national Health Service rose from £6,896 million in 1977/8 to £20,598 million a decade later. As a proportion of GNP it fluctuated between 5 per cent and just over 6 per cent. The pressure on the service derived from three principal sources: increasingly expensive equipment and drugs, increased wage and salary costs, and the changing age structure. In these circumstances, the question of 'free' and 'universal' provision came onto the agenda, as did 'management' and 'bureaucracy'.

5. The number of legal abortions in England and Wales rose from some 22,000 in 1968 to over 115,000 in 1975.

6. The proportion of consumer expenditure in the United Kingdom on alcoholic drink fell by about one-third between the beginning of the century and 1975. The amount of wine consumed (million gallons) rose from 37 to 80 over the decade ending in 1976.

The ethnic mix

7. The 1991 Census was the first to elicit information on ethnic origin. The figures were as follows: 840,000 Indians; 499,000 Black Caribbeans; 475,000 Pakistanis; 207,000 Black Africans; 160,000 Bangladeshis; 158,000 Chinese.

Homes and property

8. In England and Wales in 1986, 65 per cent of householders owned their own homes. The Housing Acts of 1980 and 1985, amongst other things, encouraged the 'right to buy'. In consequence more than 1 million council, housing association, and new town homes, were purchased by their occupiers.

9. In 1979, the percentage of the population owning shares was around 4.5 per cent: a decade later, the figure had risen to around 20 per cent. The majority of shareholders were likely to have shares in only one company. Around half probably had share assets worth less than £1000.

The Great Outdoors

10. Membership of the Camping Club of Great Britain and Ireland rose from 14,000 in 1950 to 175,000 in 1976, of the Ramblers Association from 9,000 to 30,000, of the British Horse Society from 4,000 to 22,000 and of the Royal Yacht Association from 1,000 to 49,000. Most dramatic of all was the expansion of National Trust membership from 26,000 (1950) to 607,000 (1975) to 2,177,000 (1992).

Youth and leisure

11. The Scouts and the Girl Guides were the largest uniformed youth organizations, averaging a membership of some half a million in the quarter-century to 1975. Membership of the Boys' Brigade and the National Association of Youth Clubs was running at about a third (each) of the membership of the Scouts.

12. There were 102 million cinema admissions in 1992, from a low point of 54 million in 1984.

Communications

13. Railway (standard gauge route miles) (000s): 1870,13; 1900, 18; 1930, 20; 1960, 18; 1976, 11; 1991, 10.

14. The number of passenger trains running between London and Cardiff per diem doubled between 1951 and 1978 and the running time was reduced from 3 hours to $1\frac{3}{4}$ hours. The journey by rail between London and Glasgow was reduced from $8\frac{1}{2}$ hours to 5 hours over the same period.

15. Motor cars: 1905, 15,000; 1930, 1.7 million; 1975, 15 million; 1989, 21 million.

16. No. of telephones: 1900, 3,000; 1930, 1.9 million; 1950, 5.1 million; 1978, 23.2 million; 1989, 24.5 million.

17. Holidays abroad (000s):

	1981	1990
European Community	8,474	14,083
United States	717	1,248

I: ECONOMIC INFORMATION

1. National income (1992) = 456,387 (£ million)

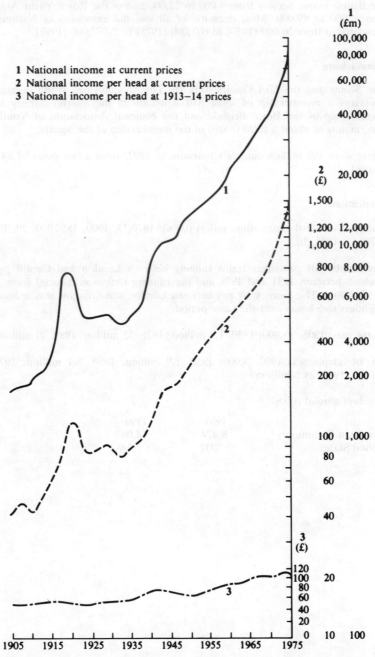

1 National income at current prices
2 National income per head at current prices
3 National income per head at 1913–14 prices

From T. O. Lloyd, *Empire, Welfare State, Europe: English History 1906–1992*.
(Oxford, 1993)

2. Government expenditure (central and local) 1900–1967

(a) Government expenditure by function (% of GNP)

	1900	1920	1928	1938	1955	1967
Administration	0.8	1.2	1.1	1.1	1.1	1.2
National Debt	1.0	5.4	6.7	4.0	4.2	5.5
Law and Order	0.5	0.5	0.7	0.7	0.7	1.6
Military and defence	6.9	8.6	2.8	8.9	9.6	7.0
Social services	2.6	6.8	9.6	11.3	18.0	24.9
All services	14.4	26.2	24.2	30.0	36.6	55.2

Adapted from Lloyd, *op cit.*

(b) (i) Government expenditure per head (£) at 1900 prices. Index 1900 = 100

1900	1920	1928	1938	1955
6.8	12.9	12.2	17.9	25.7
100	189	179	262	377

(ii) GNP per head (£) at 1900 prices

47.2	49.6	50.2	59.6	68.8
100	105	106	126	146

Adapted from A. T. Peacock and J. Wiseman, *The Growth of Public Expenditure in the United Kingdom* (Princeton, 1961) p. 42.

3. Prices 1890–1975

(a) Indexes of prices 1890–1955

	Goods and services	Government expenditure	GNP
1890	98	98	98
1895	91	91	90
1900	100	100	100
1905	101	100	100
1910	105	103	104
1913	109	107	108
1920	278	282	–
1925	204	204	204
1930	191	190	191
1935	174	174	174
1938	185	186	187
1946	303	307	312
1950	370	380	385
1955	455	469	479

Adapted from Peacock and Wiseman, *op. cit.,* pp. 155–6.

(b) Cost of living 1906–1975

(This series can only be a general indication, since over the period it covers, what constitutes 'living' has fluctuated as much as prices.)

1906	94	1955	422
1910	96	1960	474
1914	99	1965	564
1920	250	1970	705
1925	190	1974	1,047
1930	178	1975	1,482
1935	162	1980	2,495
1939	177	1985	3,396
1940	202	1990	4,499
1945	255	1991	4,848
1950	345		

Source: Adapted from Lloyd, *op. cit.,* Table 1

(c) Index of comparative inflation 1950–1975

	W. Germany	Japan	UK	US	Total OECD
1950	64.3	38.1	47.3	61.9	–
1955	70.7	51.5	60.3	69.0	64.0
1960	77.4	56.7	67.9	76.3	72.0
1965	88.7	76.7	79.9	81.2	81.6
1970	100.0	100.0	100.0	100.0	100.0
1974	127.1	152.7	148.4	127.0	134.9
1975	134.7	171.2	184.4	138.6	150.3

Source: Adapted from F. Hirsch and J. H. Goldthorpe, *The Political Economy of Inflation* (1978), p. 10.

4. Trade 1900–1975

(a) Volume of trade 1910–1975

	1910	1925	1930	1950	1975	1992
Total imports (£ million)	678.3	1,320.0	919.5	2,602.9	24,037.0	120,453.0
Total exports and re-exports (£ million)	522.0	927.4	523.3	2,255.0	19,761.0	107,047.0

(b) Direction of trade (imports col. 1 and exports col. 2)

	1910	1925	1930	1950
British Empire/ Commonwealth (less Canada)	21.3/26.2	27.2/30.6	31.8/41.8	36.0/41.5
W. Europe	33.9/35.5	27.5/31.0	24.3/27.6	24.2/26.4
E. Europe	0.5/ 0.5	1.4/ 1.4	2.8/ 2.6	1.5/ 1.1
Russia	6.4/ 4.1	2.5/ 2.4	3.2/ 4.2	1.3/ 0.6
Middle East	3.2/ 1.8	3.2/ 2.1	2.8/ 3.3	4.3/ 5.1
Far East	2.2/ 4.7	2.7/ 4.9	2.6/ 2.3	1.5/ 1.4
N. and C. America	22.4/17.8	25.8/13.7	21.4/10.8	17.3/12.4
S. America	8.8/ 9.2	8.2/ 6.7	7.2/ 6.0	7.3/ 5.8
Other	1.3/ 0.2	1.5/ 7.2	3.9/ 8.6	6.6/ 5.7

(c) Direction of trade 1975 (imports col. 1 and exports col. 2)

	1975	1990
EEC	36.1/32.1	52.2/53.0
Other W. European	14.6/16.5	12.5/ 8.7
N. American	13.3/11.7	13.3/14.4
Other developed	7.4/ 9.6	6.6/ 4.5
OPEC	13.8/11.5	2.4/ 5.4
Communist	3.0/ 3.4	1.4/ 1.4
Rest	11.1/14.8	11.0/11.7

(d) Balance of payments 1900–1975

Only a sample is provided. Different years and different intervals would create a different impression, but these years broadly correspond with those employed elsewhere.

	Imports	Domestic exports	Re-exports	Net overseas investment earning	Net invisible trade	Overall balance on current account
1900	523.1	291.2	63.2	103.6	109.1	37.9
1910	678.3	430.4	103.8	170.0	146.7	167.3
1920	1,932.6	1,334.5	222.8	200.0	395.0	252.0
1930	1,044.0	570.8	86.8	220.0	194.0	25.0
1937	1,027.8	521.4	75.1	210.0	176.0	−144.0
1950	2,608.2	2,171.3	84.8	237.0	357.0	221.0
1965	5,071	4,848		435	215	−110.0
1975	21,972	18,768		949	1,695	−1,673.0
1992	120,453	107,047		5,777	4,786	−8,620.0

The tables in this section draw upon the Annual Abstract of Statistics and the work of Lloyd, *op. cit.*

5. Industry

(a) Output of individual industries, 1907–1973 (£ million)

	1907 Gross output	Net output	1935 Gross output	Net output	1973 Gross output	Net output
Food, drink, and tobacco	283	87	665	203	11,975	3,493
Chemicals and allied industries	90	27	206	89	7,673	2,693
Metal manufacture	147	45	245	88	5,601	1,823
Engineering and allied industries	–	–	710	357	22,721	10,572
Textiles, leather, and clothing	458	187	656	249	6,143	2,631
Other manufactures	–	–	413	237	10,884	5,591
Mining and quarrying	134	115	167	136	1,439	1,022
Construction	–	–	295	150	12,531	5,337
Gas, electricity, and water	51	32	181	128	3,836	2,043

Source: Annual Abstract of Statistics.

The Standard Industrial Classification was revised in 1980, complicating comparison with the above table. The Gross Output was as follows (£ million):

	1984	1992
Coal extraction etc.	1,662	3,550
Chemical industry	23,764	33,553
Food, drink, tobacco	44,205	60,237
Motor vehicles	12,641	21,053
Textiles	6,140	7,283

(b) Output per man-hour in manufacturing 1961–1974.

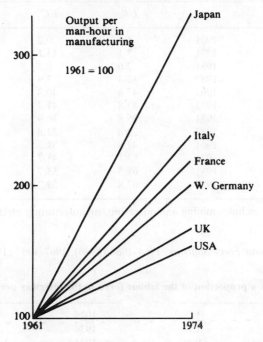

From R. Bacon and W. Eltis, *Britain's Economic Problem* (1976) p. 2.

(c) Size of plant in terms of employment

Number employed in plant	Percentage total employment			
	1935	*1951*	*1963*	*1973*
11–99	25.6	21.9	17.3	15.6
100–499	39.0	33.8	31.7	26.4
500–999	13.9	13.6	14.6	14.4
1,000–1,499	6.3	7.2	8.2	7.3
1,500+	15.2	23.6	28.6	36.3

From J. F. Wright, *Britain in the Age of Economic Management* (Oxford, 1979) p. 40.

(d) Composition of total employment, by sector 1961–87, UK, EC and OECD (per cent)

		UK	EC	OECD
Agriculture	1961	4.6	20.2	20.8
	1971	3.1	13.1	13.3
	1981	2.6	9.3	9.7
	1987	2.4	7.9	8.4
Industry	1961	47.6	40.3	35.5
	1971	43.8	41.3	36.4
	1981	35.8	36.9	33.1
	1987	29.8	32.8	30.1
Services	1961	47.8	39.5	43.7
	1971	53.1	45.7	50.3
	1981	61.5	53.7	57.2
	1987	67.8	59.2	61.6

Note: Industry here includes mining and quarrying, manufacturing, electricity, gas, water and construction.

Source: OECD Labour Force Statistics, 1964–1984 (1986), 1967–1987 (1989).

6. Unemployment as a proportion of the labour force in the interwar period

1913	1.2	1929	5.9
1920	1.8	1930	9.3
1921	9.6	1931	12.6
1922	8.1	1932	13.1
1923	6.6	1933	11.7
1924	5.8	1934	9.9
1925	6.4	1935	9.2
1926	7.1	1936	7.9
1927	5.5	1937	6.7
1928	6.1	1938	8.1

Adapted from A. J. Harrison, *The Framework of Economic Activity* (1967) p. 52.

Unemployment in Great Britain

1975 (monthly average in 000s)	902
1982 (Jan)	2,334
1990 (Jan)	1,520
1992 (Jan)	2,503

MAPS

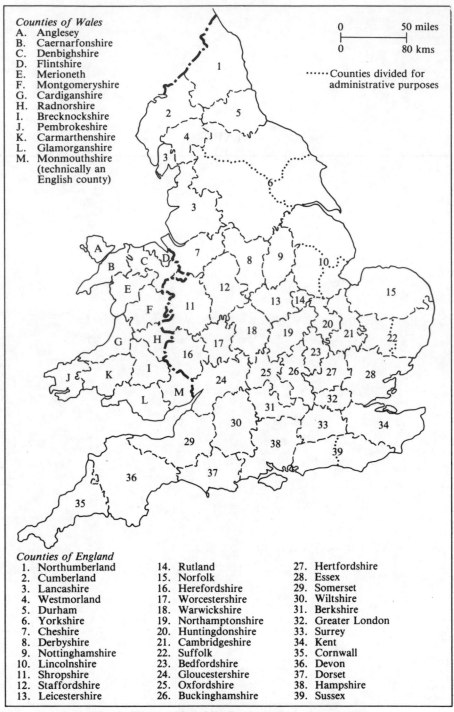

Counties of Wales
A. Anglesey
B. Caernarfonshire
C. Denbighshire
D. Flintshire
E. Merioneth
F. Montgomeryshire
G. Cardiganshire
H. Radnorshire
I. Brecknockshire
J. Pembrokeshire
K. Carmarthenshire
L. Glamorganshire
M. Monmouthshire
(technically an
English county)

0 ────────── 50 miles
0 ────────── 80 kms

·······Counties divided for
administrative purposes

Counties of England
 1. Northumberland
 2. Cumberland
 3. Lancashire
 4. Westmorland
 5. Durham
 6. Yorkshire
 7. Cheshire
 8. Derbyshire
 9. Nottinghamshire
10. Lincolnshire
11. Shropshire
12. Staffordshire
13. Leicestershire
14. Rutland
15. Norfolk
16. Herefordshire
17. Worcestershire
18. Warwickshire
19. Northamptonshire
20. Huntingdonshire
21. Cambridgeshire
22. Suffolk
23. Bedfordshire
24. Gloucestershire
25. Oxfordshire
26. Buckinghamshire
27. Hertfordshire
28. Essex
29. Somerset
30. Wiltshire
31. Berkshire
32. Greater London
33. Surrey
34. Kent
35. Cornwall
36. Devon
37. Dorset
38. Hampshire
39. Sussex

Map 1. The counties of England and Wales before 1975

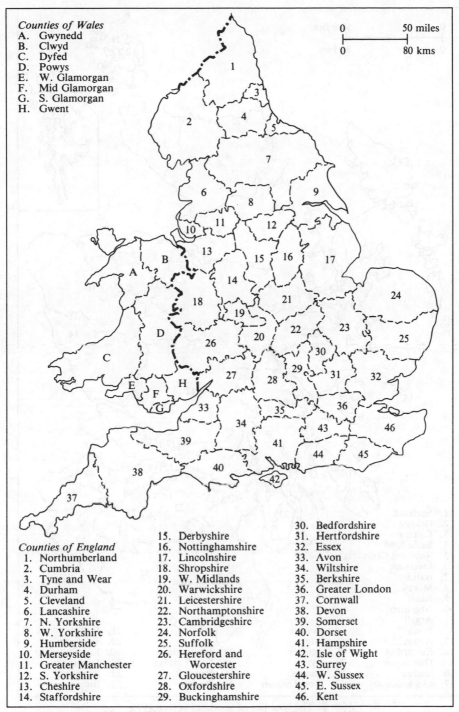

Counties of Wales
A. Gwynedd
B. Clwyd
C. Dyfed
D. Powys
E. W. Glamorgan
F. Mid Glamorgan
G. S. Glamorgan
H. Gwent

| 0 | | 50 miles |
| 0 | | 80 kms |

Counties of England
1. Northumberland
2. Cumbria
3. Tyne and Wear
4. Durham
5. Cleveland
6. Lancashire
7. N. Yorkshire
8. W. Yorkshire
9. Humberside
10. Merseyside
11. Greater Manchester
12. S. Yorkshire
13. Cheshire
14. Staffordshire
15. Derbyshire
16. Nottinghamshire
17. Lincolnshire
18. Shropshire
19. W. Midlands
20. Warwickshire
21. Leicestershire
22. Northamptonshire
23. Cambridgeshire
24. Norfolk
25. Suffolk
26. Hereford and
    Worcester
27. Gloucestershire
28. Oxfordshire
29. Buckinghamshire
30. Bedfordshire
31. Hertfordshire
32. Essex
33. Avon
34. Wiltshire
35. Berkshire
36. Greater London
37. Cornwall
38. Devon
39. Somerset
40. Dorset
41. Hampshire
42. Isle of Wight
43. Surrey
44. W. Sussex
45. E. Sussex
46. Kent

Map 2. The counties of England and Wales in 1975

435

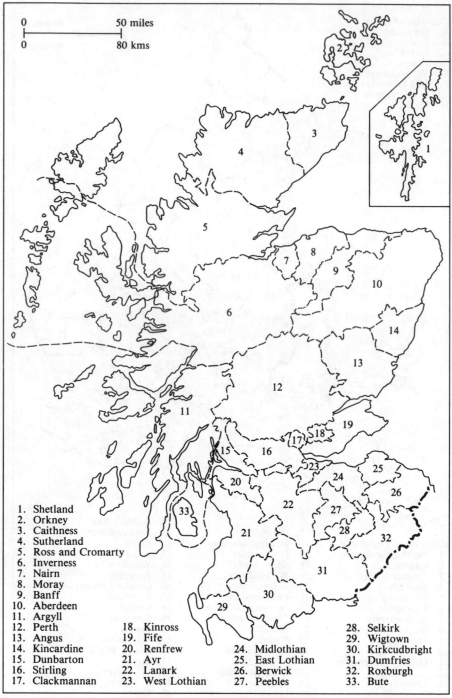

0   50 miles
0   80 kms

1. Shetland
2. Orkney
3. Caithness
4. Sutherland
5. Ross and Cromarty
6. Inverness
7. Nairn
8. Moray
9. Banff
10. Aberdeen
11. Argyll
12. Perth
13. Angus
14. Kincardine
15. Dunbarton
16. Stirling
17. Clackmannan
18. Kinross
19. Fife
20. Renfrew
21. Ayr
22. Lanark
23. West Lothian
24. Midlothian
25. East Lothian
26. Berwick
27. Peebles
28. Selkirk
29. Wigtown
30. Kirkcudbright
31. Dumfries
32. Roxburgh
33. Bute

Map 3. The counties of Scotland before 1975

Map 4. The regions of Scotland in 1975

0   50 miles

0   80 kms

DONEGAL

LONDON-
DERRY

ANTRIM

TYRONE

DOWN

FERMANAGH

LEITRIM

MONAGHAN

ARMAGH

LOUTH

SLIGO

CAVAN

M A Y O

ROSCOMMON

LONGFORD

MEATH

WESTMEATH

G A L W A Y

O F F A L Y

KILDARE

DUBLIN

C L A R E

LAUIGHIS

WICKLOW

KILKENNY

CARLOW

LIMERICK

TIPPERARY

WEXFORD

KERRY

WATERFORD

C O R K

—·— Boundary between the United Kingdom
and the Republic of Ireland

Map 5. The counties of Ireland, 1870–1975

GREENLAND
(left EEC 1973)

Map 6. The growth of the European Economic Community, 1992 (national boundaries pre-1989)

CANADA

NEWFOUNDLAND

GIBRALTAR

MA

TRINIDAD,
BARBADOS,
ANTIGUA etc.

SUI

NIGE

BR. HONDURAS

GAMBIA

JAMAICA

SIERRA
LEONE

BR. GUIANA

GOLD COAST

·ASCEN

ST HELENA·

·TONGA,
COOK

S.W. AFRICA

Self-governing dominions

Protectorates, colonies, direct control

(M) Mandates
* Not exhaustive

ᴐᴘ FALKLAND IS.

Map 7. The British Empire in 1919

0   2000 miles

0   3200 kms

RUS

PALESTINE (M)

TRANSJORDAN (M)

IRAQ (M)

BURMA

EGYPT

ADEN

HONG KONG

INDIA

NORTH BORNEO

SARAWAK, BRUNEI

SOMALILAND

CEYLON

NEW GUINEA (M)

NDA

MALAYA

KENYA

SINGAPORE

TANGANYIKA (M)

PAPUA

FIJI

NYASALAND

N – S. RHODESIA

AUSTRALIA

GILBERT IS.

ELLICE IS.

BECHUANALAND

AFRICA

NEW ZEALAND

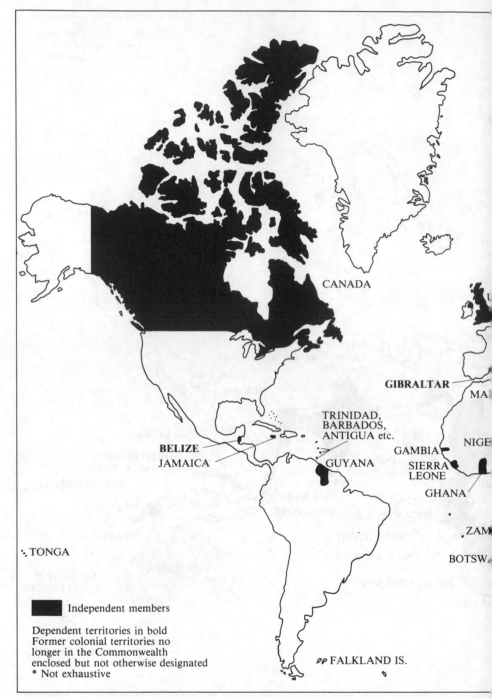

CANADA

GIBRALTAR

MA

TRINIDAD,
BARBADOS,
ANTIGUA etc.

BELIZE

JAMAICA

GUYANA

NIGE

GAMBIA

SIERRA
LEONE

GHANA

ZAM

TONGA

BOTSW

Independent members

Dependent territories in bold
Former colonial territories no
longer in the Commonwealth
enclosed but not otherwise designated
* Not exhaustive

FALKLAND IS.

Map 8. The Commonwealth in 1975*

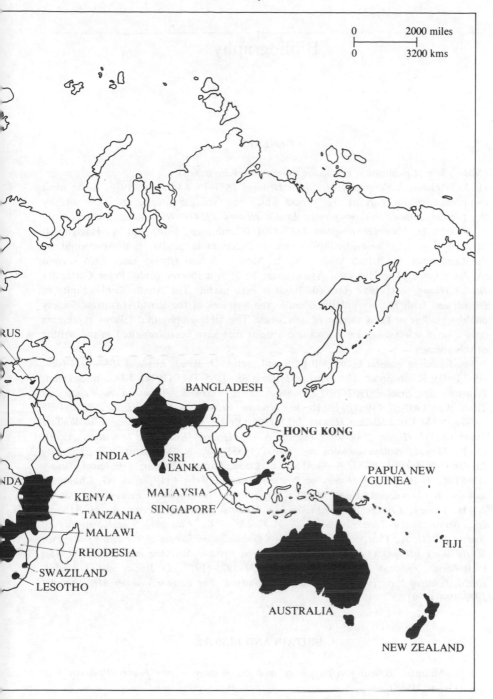

0   2000 miles

0   3200 kms

RUS

BANGLADESH

HONG KONG

INDIA

SRI
LANKA

PAPUA NEW
GUINEA

MALAYSIA

KENYA

SINGAPORE

NDA

TANZANIA

MALAWI

FIJI

RHODESIA

SWAZILAND

AUSTRALIA

LESOTHO

NEW ZEALAND

Bibliography

GENERAL

(*Note*: place of publication is London unless otherwise stated)

H. J. Hanham, *Bibliography of British History, 1851–1914* (Oxford, 1976) is the most comprehensive for part of the period which this volume covers. Its successor, by the present author, *Bibliography of British History 1914–1989*, is nearing completion. J. L. Altholz, *Victorian England 1837–1901* (Cambridge, 1970) and A. Havighurst, *Modern England* (Cambridge, 1976) are two admirable guides, both sponsored by the Conference on British Studies. C. L. Mowat, *British History since 1926* revised by Peter Lowe (The Historical Association, 1977) is a shorter guide. Peter Catterall's *British History 1945–1987* (Oxford, 1990) is very useful. The Annual Bibliography of British and Irish History published under the auspices of the Royal Historical Society enables readers to keep abreast of new work. The bibliography that follows represents only a small selection of the books and articles that have been consulted in the writing of this volume.

The following general books will be found useful: D. Read, *England 1868–1914* (rev. edn. 1993); R. Shannon, *The Crisis of Imperialism 1865–1915* (1974); L. C. B. Seaman, *Post-Victorian Britain, 1902–1951* (1966); A. J. B. Marwick, *Britain in the Century of Total War 1900–67* (1968); E. Royle, *Modern Britain: A Social History 1750–1985* (1987); N. McCord, *British History 1815–1906* (1991); T. O. Lloyd, *Empire to Welfare State: English History 1906–1985* (1986); A. Havighurst, *Britain in Transition* (1979); C. L. Mowat, *Britain between the Wars* (1955); W. N. Medlicott, *Contemporary England, 1914–1974* (1976); A. Sked and C. Cook, *Post-war Britain: A Political History* (1988); C. J. Bartlett, *A History of Postwar Britain, 1945–74* (1977); A. G. Champion and A. R. Townsend, *Contemporary Britain: A Geographical Perspective* (1990); A. H. Halsey, *Change in British Society* (Oxford, 3rd edn. 1986); A. H. Halsey, ed., *British Social Trends since 1900: A Guide to the Changing Social Structure of Britain* (1988); A. Thorpe, *The Longman Companion to Britain in the Era of the Two World Wars 1914–45* (1994); T. Noble, *Modern Britain: Structure and Change* (1975); F. Bédarida, *A Social History of England, 1851–1975* (1979); D. Butler and G. Butler, *British Political Facts 1900–1985* (1986); C. Johnson, *The Economy under Mrs Thatcher 1979–1990* (1991).

1. BRITAIN AND EUROPE

1 R. Millman, *British foreign policy and the coming of the Franco-Prussian War* (Oxford, 1968)
2 K. Bourne, *The foreign policy of Victorian England 1830–1902* (Oxford, 1970)
3 R. T. Shannon, *Gladstone and the Bulgarian agitation, 1876* (1963)
4 R. Jones, *The nineteenth-century Foreign Office* (1971)

5 W. N. Medlicott, *Bismarck, Gladstone and the concert of Europe* (1956)

6 C. J. Lowe, *Salisbury and the Mediterranean, 1886–1896* (1965)

7 K. Bourne, *Britain and the balance of power in North America, 1815–1908* (1967)

8 A. J. P. Taylor, *The troublemakers: Dissent over foreign policy, 1792–1939* (1957)

9 C. J. Lowe and M. L. Dockrill, *The mirage of power: British foreign policy 1902–1922* (1972)

10 F. H. Hinsley, ed., *British foreign policy under Sir Edward Grey* (Cambridge, 1977)

11 K. G. Robbins, *Sir Edward Grey* (1971)

12 Z. S. Steiner, *Britain and the origins of the First World War* (1977)

13 P. M. Kennedy, *The rise of the Anglo-German antagonism 1860–1914* (1980)

14 P. M. Kennedy, *The realities behind diplomacy* (1981)

15 D. Dilks, ed., *Retreat from power,* I *1906–1939* and II *After 1939* (1981)

16 V. H. Rothwell, *British war aims and peace diplomacy, 1914–1918* (Oxford, 1971)

17 K. J. Calder, *Britain and the origins of the new diplomacy* (Cambridge, 1976)

18 D. Carlton, *MacDonald versus Henderson: the foreign policy of the second Labour government* (1970)

19 W. R. Rock, *British appeasement in the 1930s* (1977)

20 F. Hardie, *The Abyssinian crisis* (1974)

21 J. T. Emmerson, *The Rhineland crisis* (1977)

22 K. G. Robbins, *Munich 1938* (1968)

23 E. L. Woodward, *British foreign policy in the Second World War* (1962)

24 K. Kaiser and R. Morgan, eds., *Britain and West Germany* (1971)

25 R. Vaughan, *Post-war integration in Europe* (1976)

26 F. S. Northedge, *Descent from power: British foreign policy, 1945–73* (1974)

27 M. Camps, *Britain and the European Community, 1955–1963* (1964)

28 U. Kitzinger, *Diplomacy and persuasion: how Britain joined the Common Market* (1973)

29 S. Z. Young, *Terms of entry: British negotiations with the European Community 1970–72* (1973)

30 R. Jowell and G. Hoinville, eds., *Britain into Europe: Public opinion and the EEC 1961–75* (1976)

Additional recommended books (Second Edition)

M. Chamberlain, *'Pax Britannica'?: British foreign policy 1789–1914* (1988)

M. L. Dockrill and J. D. Goold, *Peace without promise: Britain and the peace conferences 1918–1922* (1986)

G. Schmidt, *The politics and economics of appeasement: British foreign policy in the 1930s* (1986)

K. Robbins, *Appeasement* (1988)

J. Charmley, *Chamberlain and the lost peace* (1989)

R. A. C. Parker, *Chamberlain and appeasement: British policy and the coming of the Second World War* (1993)

A. S. Milward, *The reconstruction of Western Europe, 1945–51* (1984)

A. S. Milward, *The European rescue of the nation-state* (1992)

J. W. Young, *Britain, France and the unity of Europe, 1945–51* (1984)

S. George, *Britain and European integration since 1945* (1991)

D. Reynolds, *Britannia Overruled* (1991)

2. BRITAIN AND THE EMPIRE

31 R. E. Robinson and J. Gallagher, *Africa and the Victorians* (1961)
32 B. Porter, *The lion's share: A short history of British imperialism, 1850–1970* (1975)
33 D. A. Low, *Lion rampant* (1973)
34 D. R. Gillard, *The struggle for Asia* (1977)
35 A. Seal, *The emergence of Indian nationalism* (Cambridge, 1968)
36 C. C. Eldridge, *England's mission: The imperial idea in the age of Gladstone and Disraeli, 1868–1880* (1973)
37 R. Hyam, *Britain's imperial century, 1815–1914* (1976)
38 E. Monroe, *Britain's moment in the Middle East* (1963)
39 W. D. McIntyre, *Commonwealth of Nations: Origins and impact 1869–1971* (Oxford, 1978)
40 J. M. Brown, *Gandhi and civil disobedience* (Cambridge, 1977)
41 H. S. Wilson, *The imperial experience in sub-Saharan Africa since 1870* (1977)
42 P. S. Gupta, *Imperialism and the British labour movement, 1914–1964* (Cambridge, 1975)
43 C. Thorne, *Allies of a kind: The United States, Britain and the war against Japan, 1941–1945* (Oxford, 1979)
44 W. R. Louis, *Imperialism at bay: The United States and the decolonization of the British Empire, 1941–1945* (Oxford, 1978)
45 L. Epstein, *British politics in the Suez crisis* (1964)
46 D. J. Goldsworthy, *Colonial issues in British politics, 1945–61* (Oxford, 1971)
47 H. V. Hodson, *The Great Divide: Britain, India, Pakistan* (1970)
48 N. Mansergh, *The Commonwealth experience* (1969)
49 W. P. Kirkman, *Unscrambling an empire* (1966)
50 G. Woodcock, *Who killed the British Empire?* (1975)

Additional recommended books (Second Edition)

P. Kennedy, *The rise and fall of the great powers* (1988)
D. K. Fieldhouse, *Economics and empire 1830–1914* (1984)
B. Semmel, *Liberalism and naval strategy: ideology, interest and sea power during the Pax Britannica* (1986)
B. Porter, *Britain, Europe and the world: delusions of grandeur, 1850–1986* (1987)
J. Darwin, *Britain and decolonisation: the retreat from empire in the post-war world* (1988)
R. F. Holland, *European decolonization 1918–1981: an introductory survey* (1985)

3. WARS AND WORLD POLITICS

51 W. S. Hamer, *The British army: Civil–military relations, 1885–1905* (1970)
52 J. Luvaas, *The education of an army: British military thought, 1815–1940* (1965)
53 G. Harries-Jenkins, *The army in Victorian society* (1977)
54 B. J. Bond, ed., *Victorian military campaigns* (1967)
55 P. M. Kennedy, *The rise and fall of British naval mastery* (1976)

56 S. R. Williamson, *The politics of grand strategy: Britain and France prepare for war, 1904–1914* (Cambridge, Mass., 1969)
57 E. Spiers, *The army and society 1815–1914* (1980)
58 T. Pakenham, *The Boer war* (1979)
59 R. Graves, *Good-bye to all that* (1929)
60 P. Fussell, *The Great War and modern memory* (1975)
61 E. L. Woodward, *Great Britain and the war of 1914–1918* (1967)
62 K. G. Robbins, *The abolition of war: The British peace movement, 1914–1918* (Cardiff, 1976)
63 B. J. Bond, *British military policy between the two world wars* (Oxford, 1980)
64 H. M. Hyde, *British air policy between the wars, 1918–1939* (1976)
65 S. W. Roskill, *Naval policy between the wars* (1968 and 1976)
66 M. Ceadel, *Pacifism in Britain, 1914–1945* (Oxford, 1980)
67 R. Shay, *British rearmament in the thirties: Politics and profits* (Princeton, 1977)
68 M. E. Howard, *The continental commitment: The dilemma of British defence policy in the era of two world wars* (1972)
69 C. Barnett, *Britain and her army, 1509–1970* (1970)
70 M. M. Gowing, *Britain and atomic energy, 1939–1945* (1964)
71 H. Pelling, *Britain and the second world war* (1970)
72 P. Darby, *British defence policy east of Suez, 1947–1968* (1973)
73 R. N. Rosencrance, *Defence of the realm: British strategy in the nuclear epoch* (New York, 1968)
74 A. J. Pierre, *Nuclear politics: The British experience with an independent strategic force 1939–1970* (1970)
75 C. J. Bartlett, *The long retreat: A short history of British defence policy 1945–70* (1972)
76 I. W. F. Beckett and J. Gooch, *Politicians and defence* (Manchester, 1981)

Additional recommended books (Second Edition)

D. Weigall, *Britain and the world 1815–1986: a dictionary of international relations* (1987)
I. F. W. Beckett and K. Simpson, eds., *A nation in arms: a social study of the British Army in the First World War* (1985)
J. M. Winter, *The Great War and the British people* (1985)
J. M. Bourne, *Britain and the Great War 1914–1918* (1989)
J. Baylis, *Anglo-American defence relations 1939–1980: the special relationship* (1991)
K. Kyle, *Suez* (1991)

4. PARTY POLITICS

77 H. J. Hanham, *Elections and party management: Politics in the time of Disraeli and Gladstone* (1959)
78 H. J. Hanham, ed., *The nineteenth-century constitution, 1815–1914* (Cambridge, 1969)
79 C. O'Leary, *The elimination of corrupt practices in British elections, 1868–1911* (Oxford, 1962)

80 D. Hamer, *The politics of electoral pressure* (Hassocks, 1977)
81 D. Hamer, *Liberal politics in the age of Gladstone and Rosebery* (Oxford, 1972)
82 K. G. Robbins, *John Bright* (1979)
83 R. Blake, *The Conservative party from Peel to Churchill* (1970)
84 P. Smith, *Disraelian Conservatism and social reform* (1967)
85 H. A. Clegg, A. Fox and A. F. Thompson, *A history of British trade unions since 1889*, Vol. 1. *1889–1910* (Oxford, 1964)
86 J. Ramsden, *A history of the Conservative party: The age of Balfour and Baldwin* (1978)
87 J. Harris, *Unemployment and politics: A study in English social policy 1886–1914* (Oxford, 1972)
88 P. F. Clarke, *Lancashire and the New Liberalism* (Cambridge, 1971)
89 P. F. Clarke, *Liberals and Social Democrats* (Cambridge, 1978)
90 M. Freeden, *The New Liberalism* (Oxford, 1978)
91 N. Blewett, *The peers, the parties and the people: The general elections of 1910* (1972)
92 B. K. Murray, *The people's budget, 1909/10* (Oxford, 1980)
93 M. Pugh, *Women's suffrage in Britain, 1867–1928* (1980)
94 R. McKibbin, *The evolution of the Labour party, 1910–1924* (Oxford, 1974)
95 K. O. Morgan, *Consensus and disunity: The Lloyd George coalition government, 1918–1922* (Oxford, 1979)
96 G. Phillips, *The General Strike* (1976)
97 M. Bentley, *The Liberal mind, 1914–1929* (Cambridge, 1977)
98 J. Lovell, *British trade unions, 1875–1933* (1977)
99 R. M. Martin, *TUC: Growth of a pressure group* (Oxford, 1980)
100 R. Currie, *Industrial politics* (Oxford, 1979)
101 R. Skidelsky, *Politicians and the slump* (1967)
102 B. Pimlott, *Labour and the Left in the 1930s* (Cambridge, 1977)
103 T. Stannage, *Baldwin thwarts the Opposition* (1980)
104 A. Calder, *The people's war: Britain, 1939–1945* (1969)
105 J. M. Lee, *The Churchill coalition, 1940–1945* (1980)
106 P. Addison, *The road to 1945* (1975)
107 R. Eatwell, *The 1945–1951 Labour governments* (1979)
108 D. N. Chester, *The nationalization of British industry, 1945–51* (1975)
109 D. Fraser, *The evolution of the Welfare State* (1973)
110 M. Harrison, *Trade unions and the Labour party since 1945* (1960)
111 D. Coates, *The Labour party and the struggle for Socialism* (1975)
112 J. D. Hoffman, *The Conservative party in opposition, 1945–1951* (1964)
113 Lord Butler, ed., *The Conservatives* (1977)
114 S. Haseler, *The Gaitskellites* (1969)
115 J. Goldthorpe et al., *The affluent worker: Political attitudes and behaviour* (Cambridge, 1968)
116 B. Hindness, *The decline of working class politics* (1977)
117 R. H. S. Crossman, *The diaries of a Cabinet minister* (3 vols., 1975–1977)
118 K. Middlemas, *Politics in an industrial society: The experience of the British system since 1911* (1979)
119 R. A. Chapman, *The Higher Civil Service in Britain* (1970)
120 P. Kellner and Lord Crowther-Hunt, *The civil servants: An inquiry into Britain's ruling class* (1980)
121 D. Hurd, *An end to promises* (1979)

Additional recommended books (Second Edition)

M. Pugh, *The making of modern British politics, 1867–1939* (1982)

P. Clarke, *A question of leadership: Gladstone to Thatcher* (1991)

M. Bentley, *The climax of Liberal politics: British Liberalism in theory and practice 1868–1918* (1987)

H. C. G. Matthew, *Gladstone 1809–74* (1986)

B. Coleman, *Conservatism and the Conservative party in nineteenth-century Britain* (1988)

M. Pugh, *The Tories and the people* (1985)

P. Hollis, *Ladies elect: women in local government* (1988)

G. R. Searle, *Corruption in British politics, 1895–1930* (1987)

D. Tanner, *Political change and the Labour party 1900–1918* (1990)

J. Turner, *British politics and the Great War* (1992)

S. Ball, *Baldwin and the Conservative party* (1988)

K. Robbins, *Churchill* (1992)

P. Addison, *Churchill on the Home Front* (1992)

R. Blake and W. R. Louis, eds., *Churchill* (1993)

J. Charmley, *Churchill: the end of glory* (1993)

T. Burridge, *Clement Attlee* (1985)

P. Hennessy, *Never again: Britain 1945–51* (1992)

K. O. Morgan, *Labour in power, 1945–51* (1984)

H. Pelling, *The Labour governments, 1945–51* (1984)

A. Seldon, *Churchill's Indian summer, 1951–55* (1981)

B. Pimlott, *Harold Wilson* (1992)

P. Ziegler, *Harold Wilson* (1993)

C. Ponting, *Breach of promise: Labour in power, 1964–70* (1989)

5. THE NATURE OF THE UNITED KINGDOM

122 J. P. D. Dunbabin, *Rural discontent in nineteenth-century Britain* (1974)

123 L. P. Curtis, *Anglo-Saxons and Celts: A study in anti-Irish prejudice in Victorian England* (Bridgeport, Conn., 1968)

124 F. S. L. Lyons, *Ireland since the famine* (1973)

125 F. S. L. Lyons, *Parnell* (1977)

126 F. S. L. Lyons, *Culture and anarchy in Ireland, 1890–1939* (Oxford, 1979)

127 H. J. Hanham, *Scottish nationalism* (1969)

128 C. Harvie, *Scotland and nationalism* (1977)

129 J. G. Kellas, *Modern Scotland* (1980)

130 J. Brand, *The national movement in Scotland* (1978)

131 P. M. H. Bell, *Disestablishment in Ireland and Wales* (1969)

132 K. O. Morgan, *Wales in British politics, 1868–1922* (Cardiff, 3rd edn, 1980)

133 L. M. Cullen, *An economic history of Ireland since 1660* (1972)

134 B. Lenman, *An economic history of modern Scotland, 1660–1976* (1977)

135 K. O. Morgan, *Rebirth of a nation: Wales, 1880–1980* (Oxford, 1981)

136 P. Buckland, *Irish Unionism* (Dublin, 1972–73)

137 P. Buckland, *Factory of grievances* (Dublin, 1979)

138 P. Buckland, *History of Northern Ireland* (Dublin, 1981)

139 B. Thomas, ed., *The Welsh Economy* (Cardiff, 1962)

140 P. Jalland, *The Liberals and Ireland* (Brighton, 1980)

141 D. Smith, ed., *A people and a proletariat: Essays on the history of Wales, 1780–1980* (1980)
142 V. Bogdanor, *Devolution* (Oxford, 1979)
143 M. Hechter, *Internal colonialism: The Celtic fringe in British national development* (1975)
144 R. Rose, *Governing without consensus* (1972)
145 A. B. Philip, *The Welsh question: Nationalism in Welsh politics, 1945–1970* (1975)
146 J. Magee, *Northern Ireland: Crisis and conflict* (1974)
147 J. C. Beckett, *The Anglo-Irish tradition* (1976)
148 A. H. Birch, *Political integration and disintegration in the British Isles* (1977)
149 G. Williams, *Religion, language and nationality in Wales* (Cardiff, 1979)
150 M. Minogue, *Documents on contemporary British government* (2 vols., Cambridge, 1977)
151 E. J. B. Rose, *Colour and citizenship* (1969)

Additional recommended books (Second Edition)

K. Robbins, *Nineteenth-century Britain: integration and diversity* (1988)
G. H. Jenkins, and J. B. Smith, eds, *Politics and society in Wales 1840–1922* (Cardiff, 1988)
G. A. Williams, *When was Wales? A history of the Welsh* (1985)
R. Colls and P. Dodd, eds., *Englishness: politics and culture 1880–1920* (1986)
P. Payton, *The making of modern Cornwall* (1992)
G. Elton, *The English* (1992)
M. Lynch, *Scotland: a new history* (1991)
T. Gallagher, *Glasgow: the uneasy peace* (1987)
R. F. Foster, *Modern Ireland: 1600–1972* (1988)
J. J. Lee, *Ireland 1912–1985, politics and society* (1989)
K. T. Hoppen, *Ireland since 1800: conflict and conformity* (1989)
S. V. Ward, *The geography of interwar Britain: the state and uneven development* (1988)
F. M. L. Thompson, ed., *The Cambridge social history of modern Britain 1750–1950: vol. 1: regions and communities* (Cambridge, 1990)

6. TOWN AND COUNTRY

152 J. Saville, *Rural depopulation in England and Wales, 1851–1951* (1957)
153 H. J. Dyos and M. Wolff, eds, *The Victorian city: Images and realities* (1973)
154 I. H. Adams, *The making of urban Scotland* (1978)
155 B. I. Coleman, ed., *The idea of the city in nineteenth-century Britain* (1973)
156 R. Williams, *The country and the city* (1973)
157 G. S. Jones, *Outcast London: A study in the relationship between classes in Victorian society* (Oxford, 1971)
158 G. E. Mingay, ed., *The Victorian countryside* (2 vols, 1981)
159 F. M. L. Thompson, *English landed society in the nineteenth century* (1963)
160 C. S. Orwin and E. H. Whetham, *History of British agriculture, 1846–1914* (1964)
161 R. A. Butlin, *The development of the Irish town* (1977)
162 P. J. Perry, ed., *British agriculture, 1875–1914* (1973)
163 R. H. Best and J. T. Coppock, *The changing use of land in Britain* (1962)

164 T. W. Freeman, *The conurbations of Great Britain* (Manchester, 1959)
165 F. J. Osborn and A. Whittick, *The new towns* (1969 edn)
166 M. W. Beresford, *Leeds and its region* (Leeds, 1967)
167 S. G. Checkland, *The Upas tree: Glasgow 1875–1975* (Glasgow, 1976)
168 H. D. Clout, ed., *Regional development in Western Europe* (1975)
169 J. B. Cullingworth, *Town and country planning in Britain* (1976)
170 J. H. Johnson, ed., *Suburban growth* (1974)
171 G. E. Jones, *Rural life* (1973)
172 V. Bonham-Carter, *The survival of the English countryside* (1971)
173 J. Lees-Milne, ed., *The National Trust* (1945)
174 Lord Redcliffe-Maud and B. Wood, *English local government reformed* (1974)

Additional recommended books (Second Edition)

F. M. L. Thompson, ed., *The Cambridge social history of modern Britain 1750–1950: vol. 2: people and their environment* (Cambridge, 1990)
J. Brown, *Agriculture in England: a survey of farming 1870–1947* (Manchester, 1987)
D. Cannadine, ed., *Patricians, power and politics in nineteenth-century towns* (1982)
R. J. Morris, ed., *Class, power and social structure in British nineteenth-century towns* (1986)

7. THE ECONOMY

175 S. B. Saul, *The myth of the Great Depression, 1873–1896* (1969)
176 K. Warren, *The British iron and steel industry since 1840* (1970)
177 P. L. Payne, *British entrepreneurship in the nineteenth century* (1974)
178 B. Supple, ed., *Essays in British business history* (Oxford, 1977)
179 P. Deane and W. A. Cole, *British economic growth, 1688–1959* (Cambridge, 1969)
180 W. H. B. Court, *British economic history, 1870–1914* (Cambridge, 1965)
181 C. H. Wilson, 'Economy and society in late Victorian England', *Econ. H.R.* 1965.
182 W. J. Reader, *Professional men* (1966)
183 P. L. Cottrell, *British overseas investment in the nineteenth century* (1975)
184 D. N. McCloskey, ed., *Essays on a mature economy* (1971)
185 D. H. Aldcroft, ed., *The development of British industry and foreign competition, 1875–1914* (1968)
186 S. Pollard, *The development of the British economy, 1914–1967* (1969)
187 R. S. Sayers, *A history of economic change in England, 1880–1939* (1967)
188 W. A. Lewis, *Economic survey, 1919–1939* (1949)
189 A. J. Harrison, *The framework of economic activity: The international economy and the rise of the state in the twentieth century* (1967)
190 A. S. Milward, *The economic effects of the world wars on Britain* (1970)
191 S. Pollard, ed., *The gold standard and employment policies between the wars* (1977)
192 S. Glynn and J. Oxborrow, *Inter-war Britain: A social and economic history* (1976)
193 N. K. Buxton and D. H. Aldcroft, eds, *British industry between the wars* (1979)
194 R. W. Breach and R. M. Hartwell, *British economy and society, 1870–1970* (Oxford, 1972)
195 G. M. Holmes, *Britain and America: A comparative economic history* (Newton Abbot, 1976)

196 W. Ashworth, *A short history of the international economy since 1850* (1975)
197 I. Drummond, *British economic policy and the empire, 1919–1939* (1972)
198 E. J. Hobsbawm, *Industry and empire* (1968)
199 H. W. Richardson, *Economic recovery in Britain, 1932–39* (1967)
200 J. H. Dunning and C. J. Thomas, *British industry: Change and development in the twentieth century* (1961)
201 J. W. Grove, *Government and industry in Britain* (1962)
202 G. A. Phillips and R. T. Maddock, *The growth of the British economy, 1918–1968* (1973)
203 A. J. Youngson, *Britain's economic growth, 1920–1966* (1968)
204 B. W. E. Alford, *Depression and recovery? British economic growth, 1918–1939* (1972)
205 R. Bacon and W. Eltis, *Britain's economic problem* (1976)
206 A. Cairncross, ed., *Britain's economic prospects reconsidered* (1971)
207 A. R. Prest and D. J. Coppock, eds, *The U.K. economy: A manual of applied economics* (1976)
208 D. Morris, ed., *The economic system in the U.K.* (1979 edn)
209 J. F. Wright, *Britain in the age of economic management* (Oxford, 1979)
210 G. Turner, *Business in Britain* (1971)
211 K. Pavitt, ed., *Technical innovation and British economic performance* (1980)
212 F. Hirsch and J. H. Goldthorpe, *The political economy of inflation* (1978)
213 M. W. Kirby, *The decline of British economic power* (1981)

Additional recommended books (Second Edition)

M. Dintenfass, *The decline of industrial Britain 1870–1980* (1992)
W. P. Kennedy, *Traditional structure, capital markets and the origins of British economic decline* (Cambridge, 1987)
S. Pollard, *Britain's prime and Britain's decline: the British economy 1870–1914* (1988)
T. R. Gourvish and A. O'Day, eds., *Later Victorian Britain* (1988)
A. Cairncross, *Years of recovery: British economic policy 1945–51* (1985)

8. EDUCATION, RELIGION, CULTURE AND SPORT

214 H. C. Dent, *1870–1970: A century of growth in English education* (1970)
215 G. A. N. Lowndes, *The silent social revolution: An account of the expansion of public education in England and Wales, 1895–1965* (1969)
216 J. Lawson and H. Silver, *A social history of education in England* (1977)
217 G. Davie, *The democratic intellect* (Edinburgh, 1964)
218 J. Scotland, *The history of Scottish education* (1969)
219 M. Sanderson, ed., *The universities in the nineteenth century* (1975)
220 R. Bell and N. Grant, *Patterns of education in the British Isles* (1977)
221 J. Murphy, *Church, state and schools in Britain, 1890–1970* (1971)
222 J. S. Maclure, *Education documents: England and Wales, 1816 to the present day* (1973)
223 B. Gardner, *The public schools* (1973)
224 P. H. J. H. Gosden, *The education of a profession* (Oxford, 1972)
225 G. S. Osborne, *Scottish and English schools* (1966)

226 D. Rubenstein and B. Simon, *The evolution of the comprehensive school, 1926–1966* (1969)
227 W. O. Chadwick, *The Victorian Church* (vol. 2, 1970)
228 D. M. Thompson, *Nonconformity in the nineteenth century* (1972)
229 A. D. Gilbert, *The making of post-Christian Britain* (1980)
230 A. D. Gilbert, *Religion and society in industrial England* (1976)
231 S. Koss, *Nonconformity in modern British politics* (1975)
232 R. Lloyd, *The Church of England, 1900–1965* (1965)
233 E. R. Norman, *Church and society in England, 1770–1970* (Oxford, 1976)
234 D. Perman, *Change and the Churches* (1977)
235 D. Jenkins, *The British: Their identity and their religion* (1975)
236 D. Martin, *A sociology of English religion* (1967)
237 B. Wilson, *Religion in a secular society* (1966)
238 D. Farr, *English art, 1870–1940* (Oxford, 1978)
239 J. Rothenstein, *Modern English painters* (1974)
240 R. Shone, *The century of change: British painting since 1900* (Oxford, 1977)
241 F. Routh, *Contemporary British music: The twenty-five years from 1945 to 1970* (1972)
242 D. Piper, ed., *The genius of British painting* (1975)
243 E. Betts, *The film business: A history of the British cinema, 1896–1972* (1973)
244 J. R. Taylor, *Anger and after: A guide to the new British drama* (1969)
245 A. Smith, ed., *The British press since the war* (1974)
246 W. Mellers, *Twilight of the Gods: The Beatles in retrospect* (1973)
247 J. Arlott, ed., *The Oxford companion to sports and games* (1975)
248 J. Walvin, *The people's game* (1975)
249 J. Walvin, *Leisure and society* (1978)
250 A. Briggs, *History of broadcasting* (1979)

Additional recommended books (Second Edition)

J. A. Mangan, ed., *'Benefits bestowed'? Education and British imperialism* (Manchester, 1988)

F. M. L. Thompson, ed., *The Cambridge social history of modern Britain 1750–1950: vol. 3: social agencies and institutions* (Cambridge, 1990)

T. Mason, ed., *Sport in Britain: a social history* (Cambridge, 1989)

G. Parsons, *Religion in Victorian Britain*, 4 vols (Manchester, 1988)

E. M. Sigsworth, ed., *In search of Victorian values: aspects of nineteenth-century thought and values* (Manchester, 1988)

J. Wolff and J. Seed, eds., *The culture of capital: art, power and the nineteenth-century middle class* (Manchester, 1988)

1975–1992: RECOMMENDED BOOKS

251 K. O. Morgan, *The people's peace: British history, 1945–1989* (Oxford, 1990)
252 M. Pearce and G. Stewart, *British political history 1867 1990: democracy and decline* (1992)
253 T. Gourvish and A. O'Day, eds., *Britain since 1945* (1991)
254 D. Dutton, *British politics since 1945: the rise and fall of consensus* (Oxford, 1991)

255 G. Williams and J. Ramsden, *Ruling Britannia: a political history of Britain 1688–1988* (1990)

256 D. Butler, *British general elections since 1945* (Oxford, 1989)

257 P. Riddell, *The Thatcher decade: how Britain has changed during the 1980s* (Oxford, 1989)

258 P. Jenkins, *Mrs Thatcher's revolution* (1987)

259 D. Kavanagh and A. Seldon, *The Thatcher effect: a decade of change* (Oxford, 1989)

260 P. Hennessy and A. Seldon, *Ruling performance: British governments from Attlee to Thatcher* (Oxford, 1987)

261 D. Kavanagh, *Thatcherism and British politics: the end of consensus?* (Oxford, 1987)

262 B. Lenman, *The eclipse of parliament: appearance and reality since 1914* (1992)

263 G. L. and A. L. Williams, *The rise and fall of the Social Democratic party* (1988)

264 M. Thatcher, *The Downing Street Years* (1993)

265 H. Young, *One of us: a biography of Margaret Thatcher* (1989)

266 J. Prior, *A balance of power* (1986)

267 I. Gilmour, *Dancing with dogma: Britain under Thatcherism* (1992)

268 J. Callaghan, *Time and chance* (1987)

269 R. Jenkins, *A life at the centre* (1991)

270 D. Healey, *Time of my life* (1989)

271 P. Hennessy, *Cabinet* (Oxford, 1986)

272 P. Hennessy, *Whitehall* (Oxford, 1989)

273 M. Adeney and J. Lloyd, *The miners' strike: loss without limit* (1985)

274 M. Wiener, *English culture and the decline of the industrial spirit, 1850–1981* (Cambridge, 1981)

275 B. Collins and K. Robbins, eds., *British culture and the decline of the industrial spirit* (1990)

276 W. D. Rubinstein, *Capitalism, culture and decline in Britain 1750–1990* (1993)

277 P. J. Cain and A. G. Hopkins, *British imperialism: innovation and expansion 1688–1914* (Vol. 1): *British imperialism: crisis and deconstruction 1914–1990* (Vol. 2) (1993)

278 W. Ashworth, *The state in business: 1945 to the mid 1980s* (1991)

279 Lord Young, *The enterprise years* (1990)

280 C. Barnett, *Audit of war: the illusion and reality of Britain as a great nation* (1986)

281 A. Gamble, *Britain in decline: economic policy, political strategy and the British state* (1986)

282 A. Walters, *Britain's economic renaissance* (1986)

283 D. H. Aldcroft, *Education, training and economic performance: 1944 to 1990* (1992)

284 G. Radice, *Offshore: Britain and the European idea* (1992)

285 M. Franklin, *Britain's future in Europe* (1990)

286 K. Robbins, *History, religion and identity in modern Britain* (1993)

287 M. Hewstone, *Understanding attitudes towards the European Community* (Cambridge, 1986)

288 P. Byrd, ed., *British foreign policy under Thatcher* (Deddington, 1985)

289 M. Dockrill, *British defence since 1945* (Oxford, 1988)

290 L. Freedman, *Britain and the Falklands War* (Oxford, 1988)

291 R. Hudson and A. M. Williams, *Divided Britain* (1989)

292 P. Jenkins, *A history of Modern Wales* (1992)

293 R. J. Johnson, C. J. Pattie and J. G. Allsopp, *A nation dividing?: the electoral map of Great Britain 1979–87* (1988)
294 G. Boyce, *The Irish question and British politics 1868–1986* (1988)
295 W. L. Miller, *The end of British politics? Scots and English political behaviour in the seventies* (Oxford, 1981)
296 A. J. B. Marwick, *British society since 1945* (1990)
297 M. Hill, *The Welfare State in Britain: a political history since 1945* (1993)
298 R. Lowe, *The Welfare State in Britain since 1945* (1993)
299 K. Middlemas, *Power, competition and the state: vol. 3: the end of the postwar era: Britain since 1974* (1991)
300 A. Hastings, *A history of English Christianity 1920–1990* (1991)

Index